Anna Kris Wolff

THE UNCONSCIOUS TODAY

MAX SCHUR, M. D.

THE UNCONSCIOUS TODAY

Essays in Honor of Max Schur

Edited by

MARK KANZER, M. D.

INTERNATIONAL UNIVERSITIES PRESS, INC.
New York New York

Library of Congress Catalog Card Number: 74-143377

ISBN 0-8236-6680-8

Manufactured in the United States of America

CONTENTS

PART III

Psychoanalytic Theory

PART IV

Clinical Contributions

PART VI

Applied Psychoanalysis

Editor's Preface

Max Schur unobtrusively entered Freudian history when, as a medical student in Vienna in 1915, he was already sufficiently drawn to psychoanalysis to attend the original introductory lectures. Among his fellow classmates were Anna Freud, Helene Deutsch, and Otto Fenichel, all destined, like himself, to participate in the future development of their specialty.

For nearly two decades, he pursued a successful career as a general practitioner in Vienna. During this period, he wrote some 50 papers on medical problems, showing the same devotion to the scientific aspects of his specialty as he was to do later when he transferred his interests more completely to psychoanalysis. At the same time, he undertook a personal analysis and, in 1932, was accepted as a member of the Vienna Psychoanalytic Society.

On the recommendation of Marie Bonaparte, he had already (1928) become Freud's personal physician. In Jones' words (1957), Schur was a "perfect choice for a doctor. He established excellent relations with his patient, and his considerateness, his untiring patience and his resourcefulness were unsurpassable. He and Anna made an ideal pair of guardians to watch over the suffering man. . . . Their watchful care . . . prolonged Freud's life by years" (p. 145).

Schur continued his ministrations during his patient's last difficult days when both had found refuge in England. There he carried on his activities in both specialties until settling with his family in the United States after Freud's death. His practice then became more and more exclusively devoted to psychoanalysis, especially after becoming a member of the New York Psychoanalytic Society. His important contributions to the analytic literature steadily increased in importance. His broad grasp of issues, his scholarship and critical acumen, made familiar both in his writings and as an eagerly sought participant at panels and society meetings, launched him on an editorial career which included three terms on the editorial board of the *Journal of the American Psychoanalytic Association*, editor of an anniversary volume dedicated to Bonaparte (*Drives, Affects, Behavior*, Vol. 2, 1965), and co-editor of a volume to honor the seventieth birthday of Heinz Hartmann (*Psychoanalysis—A General Psychology*, 1966). Three Freud Lectures addressed to as many different psychoanalytic societies afforded him an opportunity to present studies on Freud that had long been under way and included hitherto unpublished documents, as well as his own unique perspectives on the thinking and personality of the founder of psychoanalysis. These have been incorporated in a recent book, *Freud: Living and Dying* (1971).

In 1953, he began a distinguished teaching career at the Division of Psychoanalytic Education at the State University of New York, Downstate Medical Center, where he attained professional status in the Department of Psychiatry, served as a training and supervisory analyst, and became chairman of the committee on research—a position he also held at the New York Psychoanalytic Society. In 1955, Schur joined in the founding of the Psychoanalytic Association of New York and was its president in 1967 when his seventieth birthday occurred. As part of a celebration, the officers and Board of Directors undertook to present him with the present volume in the belief that a contribution to psychoanalytic knowledge would constitute the most acceptable of all tributes to a man who, at 70, continued to pursue knowledge with the avidity of a student, and who himself had made such varied and outstanding contributions. Before this work could be completed, Max Schur died. It was then amended so that its core should consist of a unified presentation of Schur's own works, which we hope belong to the future, as well as to the past history of psychoanalysis.

We wish to thank the many friends who served in various capacities to bring this enterprise to fruition. Dr. Helen Schur (Mrs. Max Schur) is, of course, far more than a valuable contributor to our work—we think of her in so many ways as inseparable from her husband. Henry Rosner undertook and carried out with an enthusiasm worthy of Schur, himself, an integrative review of Schur's works, a task which also became an opportunity to present, from scattered notes, several virtually new and important papers on psychoanalysis. Many members of the Association served not only as readers of the articles submitted but as commentators whose opinions were of the greatest value to the editors: Drs. Renato Almansi, Joseph T. Coltrera, Edwin I. Corbin, Alan J. Eisnitz, Jan Frank, Mervin H. Hurwitz, Merl M. Jackel, Paul Kay, Judith S. Kestenberg, Jerome M. Levine, Roy Lilleskov, Shelley Orgel, Gilbert J. Rose, and Leonard Shengold. Gratitude is also due to Dr. Helen Schur for her many gracious acts of assistance. We also wish to acknowledge our debt to Dr. Harry Slochower for placing at our disposal his commentaries in the fields of literature and mythology. Mrs. Natalie Altman and Mrs. Irene Azarian added substantively to the value of this work and to the lightening of editorial tasks.

The Seventieth Birthday—A Letter to Max Schur

Anna Freud, LL.D., Sc.D.

Dr. Schur, Friends and Colleagues,

I regret that I am not with you tonight to share in this celebration. But, as you will see from what follows, I join you in spirit and with many thoughts.

I assume that I have been selected as one of the speakers—or rather as writer—for this occasion, not only because of my close and friendly association with Max Schur over many years, but also as one of the few in our group who can speak to a 70th birthday from personal experience. Having passed the mark myself in the not too distant past, I know how it feels, and I am able and ready to let him, as a newcomer, share in my experiences.

I have to warn him, though, that not all I have to say will make pleasant hearing. When my father reached the figure of 80, and later my mother that of 90, people used to say to me: "What wonderful age!" But, is old age in reality so wonderful? Is this not rather a myth, parallel to the "happiness of childhood," which is rare enough, or to the "innocence of childhood" which, as we know, does not exist at all? Are not these rather exaggerated congratulations and felicitations of one's friends their way of denying the awe and fear of their own oncoming old age, or of hiding their contentment that this is still remote?

I concede, for purposes of reassurance, that 70 is far from 80, and further still from an almost legendary 90. But still—! It would be dishonest to promise the entrant into the new decade that all will be smooth going; that there will be no illness; no gradual decrease in the spirit of adventure; that he will not, perhaps, find his daily work more of a strain; traveling more uncomfortable; his longing for holidays increasing; that his friends will not observe him surreptitiously for signs of bodily or—worse still—mental decline and that he himself will not watch his body and mind with the same suspicion.

There will also be compensations, of course. People who throughout their younger years have suffered from shyness, or inhibitions, or lack of self-confidence find that, to their surprise, after 70 they begin to like themselves better, to be more content with themselves and tolerant toward the way they are, sometimes in addition to, and sometimes instead of, becoming from year to year more amenable and more tolerant toward the ways of others. Disharmonies and quarrels seem to matter less after 70; sometimes even disappointments and frustrations are survived more quickly.

Further—and this is not to be despised—after 70 it seems easier to find a seat in a crowded room or to be listened to with some respect—or even to have one's parcels or luggage carried by a younger person.

With such a mixture of good and bad experiences ahead, is it surprising that a 70th birthday is envisaged with mixed feelings? On the other hand, a 70th birthday (and, in fact, any other) is not a matter of choice. It happens, and it is lived through like other happenings.

To become personal. Every such anniversary is the occasion not only for looking into an uncertain future but also for reviewing a familiar past. In Max Schur's case, I have knowledge of some of the past events which he will remember. We have lived together through the many years of my father's final illness, he in the role of doctor, I in the role not only of daughter but of nurse. In the nurse-doctor relationship with him, I have met him at his best; quiet, competent, confidence inspiring, comfort-giving and unshaken. We formed a bond between us then, which will last for our lifetimes.

Since then his fate has been varied, high points and low points alternating, as it is in human life; emigration, change of work, hard study; professional success and authorship; bodily pain and illness;

distress and worry about those nearest to him. Friends are glad to share in the pleasurable moments; they stand helpless on the occasions for unhappiness and misery.

I remember an occasion, after one of my father's bigger operations, when his younger brother ceremoniously presented him with a gold piece inscribed like the medals with which Austrian soldiers were decorated for bravery in battle. This impressed me then and comes to my mind again today. I think if we as his friends celebrate Max Schur tonight ceremoniously, we should do so, not only because he is 70, but because he has known how to weather storms, and we could do it with the words inscribed on that medal:

"For Courageous Deportment in the Face of Enemy Forces."

Max Schur—Teacher

Samuel Lanes, M.D.

Max Schur's contributions and influence as a teacher are perhaps as significant as his contributions to the psychoanalytic literature. If the mark of a good teacher is his ability to inform in the broadest sense—to bring his subject alive, make it so meaningful to his students that it becomes part of their armamentarium—then Schur was a good teacher. His enthusiasm for his subject was contagious, encouraging students to further examination, questioning, and investigation.

In 1950, Schur joined the faculty of the recently organized Division of Psychoanalytic Education of the State University College of Medicine, Downstate. Although he had some reservations about university-affiliated Psychoanalytic Institutes, he was persuaded that a strong analytic faculty which chose its students and its own members could be viable and productive. Howard Potter, then Chairman of the Department of Psychiatry, expressed his desire to encourage research and a scientific approach to the practice of psychoanalytic medicine, suggesting that a course be created which would deal with attempts at experimental validation of psychoanalytic theory and practice. Schur now had the opportunity to realize two long-standing ambitions: he could teach psychoanalytic theory and practice, and he could foster student interest in research.

Schur's unique position in the history of psychoanalysis particularly qualified him to conduct reading seminars on the papers of Freud, Abraham, Ferenczi, and others. The young candidate was

---

Dr. Lanes is Senior Lecturer, Division of Psychoanalytic Education, Department of Psychiatry, State University of New York, Downstate Medical Center, Brooklyn, New York.

thus exposed to the excitement of being taught by someone who had rubbed shoulders with the early "greats," one who had been close to Freud himself. Although Schur never made capital of it, in the candidate's mind, the relationship affirmed the authority of his views on the evolution of analytic thinking.

It was in connection with his teaching of Chapter VII of *The Interpretation of Dreams* that the students spoke of Schur's "psychoanalytic exactitude," his insistence that "every line, line by line" be understood. The reading assignments were not long, merely a few pages a week, but every line was meant to be thoroughly digested. His was an effective teaching style, one which could only work with a teacher who was serious, searching, penetrating, eager to find all the meanings in so-called simple lines. When a group of recent graduates approached him many years ago to act as moderator in the study of the papers on ego psychology by Hartmann, Kris, and Loewenstein, his characteristic modest half-smile indicated his delight at having been sought out. I recall with some nostalgia the pleasure with which we anticipated working with Schur, a pleasure not unmixed with apprehension, knowing that we would be expected to search for meaning, not only on every line, but "between the lines."

Perhaps because his thinking was such a model of precision and clarity, he could at times grow impatient with the inept student struggling with formulations, definitions, or metapsychological concepts. Although a few were intimidated, hesitant about participating in discussions, most of the students responded to the challenge and were inspired to greater efforts. His criticisms, presented firmly and directly, were offset by his warmth and gentleness. When a member of our study group questioned the clinical usefulness of the concept of the undifferentiated ego-id, he dryly observed that a lack of understanding did not in any way nullify the concept, and then explained and illustrated by clinical example until what had been so difficult to grasp seemed embarrassingly obvious. He could be intolerant of divergent viewpoints, but it was impossible not to respect the closely reasoned arguments with which he defended his position.

Schur continued in his role as teacher. Even when President of the Psychoanalytic Association of New York, he was always available for consultation and guidance to the author writing his first paper.

Schur was a dedicated teacher not only in search of truth, but also dedicated to the concept that psychoanalysis is very much alive, that it can grow and change. He demonstrated that to be Freudian did not imply inflexibility. He encouraged us to question, to seek the new within the framework of the old. He subjected everything to a vigorous scrutiny, turning the light of his vast knowledge on all issues to be considered. I see him listening to a candidate's comments, head back, eyes closed, mind always alert and open. Then would begin the process of clarifying, reformulating, and testing with questions. Was it true or not? The Pleasure Principle? Well, what was pleasure? Was it an experience? Well, yes and no. . . What was the clinical evidence? To what conclusions does that statement lead? Schur stressed again and again, by example, the necessity for precision, for differentiating speculation and fact. Because his approach was rooted in the clinical, students in the process of studying theory learned technique as well.

It has been said that a teacher affects eternity, for he never knows where his influence ends. Max Schur's long-range influence on thinking about psychological functioning is assured.

Part I

Introduction

CHAPTER 1

Psychoanalytic Perspectives in Theory and Practice

Mark Kanzer, M.D.

The predominant lines of development in psychoanalysis during the post-Freudian period (since 1939) have continued the historical progression toward an analytic psychology that views the abnormal in relation to the normal, regards states of consciousness as aspects of, rather than divisions and goals of, psychic functioning, and approaches the diverse determinants of human behavior (biological, somatic, social) through their manifestations in mental events.

This program is by no means readily accomplished and must overcome the inertia resulting from earlier perspectives, hypotheses, and terms that were useful during one era of analytic formulations, but later required new integrative organization. Compare, for example, the contexts, ranging from chemistry to social behavior, within which "masculinity" and "femininity" have been described in the analytic literature. Systematic restatements are a necessary feature in the evolution of all sciences; the vicissitudes of mental phenomena are especially difficult to encompass in rigid forms. The subject matter, techniques, and concepts of psychoanalysis will assuredly continue to require reconsideration in the future as in the past, so that Freud's most characteristic scientific attitudes—constant open-minded self-appraisal and preparedness for revisions—must remain inherent forces in the analytic tradition.

Dr. Kanzer is Clinical Associate Professor, Division of Psychoanalytic Education, Department of Psychiatry, State University of New York, Downstate Medical Center, Brooklyn, New York.

Such works as Anna Freud's *The Ego and the Mechanisms of Defense* (1936), which introduced observations on the normal development of the child and the adolescent, and Heinz Hartmann's *Ego Psychology and the Problem of Adaptation* (1939), with its genetic viewpoint which surveyed the differentiation of ego functions against a broad biological background of nonconflictual as well as conflictual trends, appeared during Freud's last years and defined the tasks of the analyst for a generation. Anna Freud's (1965) *Normality and Pathology in Childhood*, the product of three decades of further scientific studies, may well be regarded as a summing up of the accomplishments of that generation and a blueprint for the next. A fund of accrued data, carefully correlated with theoretical terms and concepts, now gave more detailed meaning to analytic formulations and provided research tools for clinical work with patients as well as for expanding operations in the sphere of normal human behavior. Further research was especially facilitated by her concept of developmental lines of the personality, which elucidated not only defense mechanisms, but the adaptive functioning of the individual mind both intrapsychically and in environmental settings. The ability to predict and control developmental trends emerges, in consequence, as an exciting possibility for the future.

Schur's contributions are part of and influential within these general tendencies and can thus be presented within the framework of the issues that have dominated contemporary psychoanalysis. His works cover so wide a range of subjects that I have chosen to treat them according to their content, rather than chronologically.

The Body-Mind Problem. His predilections and experiences as a physician disposed Schur to make this indispensable foundation of psychoanalysis a subject of particular interest. An early paper on anorexia nervosa (Schur and Medvei, 1937) described for the medical profession the psychological factors in an endocrine disorder, while his first completely analytic article (on the Sulzberger-Garbe syndrome, 1950b) described for analysts the physical as well as mental aspects of a skin condition. In these papers he blended detail and theory and placed emphasis on each aspect of a medical approach—observation, pathogenesis, diagnosis, and therapy—in both physical and mental spheres. Not least important for him was the demonstration that "psychoanalysis was an eminently suitable methodological research tool for such investigations" (Rosner, Chapter 2, This Volume).

The interplay of constitution and environment, so inherent an assumption of Freud, Anna Freud, and Hartmann, Schur has carried over and effectively used in his idea of a "continuum which, taken in conjunction with the concept of a complementary series, is so essential for an understanding of all formulations of mental functioning" (Schur, 1966a, p. 40). The idea of a continuum implies that all psychological structures of the personality are represented and collaborate in a hierarchy of responses which, arising genetically in innate dispositions (*Anlagen*), seek to adapt to somatic as well as environmental pressures. The result is multidetermined patterning that requires multiple metapsychological viewpoints for its description. Schur concurs in the use of five modes of metapsychological formulation, proposed by Rapaport and Gill (1959), which add the genetic and adaptive to the traditional three—topographic (structural), dynamic, and economic—introduced by Freud.

The continuum concept was further supplemented and is also illustrated in its application to the body-mind problem by Schur's terms, "desomatization" and "resomatization" (1955), which won immediate and widespread acceptance and have already found their way into the official glossary of the American Psychoanalytic Association (Moore and Fine, 1967). The *Anlage*, the innate disposition with its primary apparatuses (the undifferentiated phase of Hartmann), is characterized by the dominance of the infant's somatic needs and responses. With maturation, the somatic component receives increasing representation within and increasing control through the psychological components of the response (desomatization); under both normal and pathological conditions, regressive tendencies once again bring to the fore the somatic components (resomatization).

Schur's continuum implies that maturation "is the result of interaction between innate, maturational, and experiential factors" and cannot be "simply based on the unfolding of an *Anlage*" (1966, pp. 70, 65), as some infer from the idea of a "ground plan" of development (von Uexkull, 1934). The somatization concept places the body-mind relationship within the perspectives of a full metapsychological description and provides a unified approach to phenomena that have been more loosely included under such overlapping and unsystematically chosen terms as conversion, psychosomatic disorders, organ neuroses, organ language, body ego, etc. Somatic functioning can now be placed in both clinical and theoretical formulations with respect to the primary and secondary processes and the stratification of symbols.

Clinically, the somatization concept calls attention to the regular occurrence and significance of bodily participation in all neuroses, as Schur himself has pointed out in specific studies to which we shall presently refer. More broadly still, the continuum concept has nosological implications: neuroses should be classified, not on the basis of symptoms, but of functions (as Valenstein [Chapter 6, This Volume], in particular among our contributors, brings out). Treatment requires a similar appraisal of personality functions and their pathology.

The Subject of Anxiety. Prominent in the development of ego psychology, first in its defensive and later in its structural and adaptive aspects, this affect provided a natural focus for both the derivation and further extension of Schur's views on the body-mind problem. "His work, rooted in the study of the ego and especially its adaptive function, flowered in his refinement of the anxiety response" (Rosner, Chapter 2, This Volume).

Freud's (1926) division of anxiety into separate id and ego components left a dichotomy between somatic and mental behavior which has tempted many analysts to propose more unitary theories. Schur applies the continuum and somatization concepts to this problem to depict a hierarchy of increasingly differentiated (or regressively dedifferentiated) ego-id biphasic evaluations of and responses to danger. These supplement a hierarchy of danger situation outlined by Freud as inducing anxiety.

Schur's solution makes it possible to define anxiety-reaction types in a series ranging from somatically predominant pain and tension, passively experienced by a helpless and archaic ego (in trauma), to gradients in which anticipation and mastery play greater parts and are registered through diminishing intensity ("taming") of feelings. That all metapsychological viewpoints can be applied to this scheme, Schur further demonstrates in his own studies, which extend from the sphere of animal psychology and infant development to the traditional analytic setting for the treatment of adult neuroses. In the course of these studies, his concept of anxiety broadens into a structural theory that includes all the affects.

Ethology. The animal psychologist and the child analyst have been moving toward a mutuality of interests and community of frameworks. The former supplants the monolithic notion of inborn instincts with detailed observations on interactions between mother, group, and young; the latter seeks to determine more specifically the phylogenetic elements in the timetable of the differentiating mental organization of infant and child.

"The conditioning of early life with respect to almost any physiological activity is much more lasting than anyone has anticipated," as Dubos (1969, p. 7) observed in summarizing recent findings in ethology. Diets established in early life are rigidly perpetuated even when better ones become available, and such predilections can be transmitted to the next generation. Crowded conditions leave residual endocrine as well as behavioral dispositions to aggressiveness. The continuum concept, and even Freud's ideas about inherited memories, find reverberation in Dubos' conclusion: "Evidently there is no sharp demarcation between the behavioral and metabolic condition, and for all I know, both are part of the same mechanism" (p. 7).

Schur's contributions to the establishment of an interdisciplinary approach include a synthesizing discussion of the multideterminants of separation anxiety. The latter is a key organizer of infantile differentiation from the parent and possesses maturational, adaptive, and pathogenic significance. He further draws upon Schneirla's (1959) work on the withdrawal and approach responses in biology to lend detail to Freud's postulates concerning the aggressive and life instincts and the mechanisms of their transmission into somatic and psychological responses. He proceeds from here to examine other affective trends and their vicissitudes as influenced by parental care during child rearing. The result is a systematic theory of affects in relation to both somatic sources and external object relationships—a systematization which promises to resolve long-standing problems in this sphere.

Affect Theory. Freud had been troubled and offered a succession of explanations about the concept of "unconscious" affects. At the root of the difficulty, as with anxiety, were separate approaches to the somatic and psychological aspects of the emotions. Schur's solution linked both from the start in an extension of the ego-id matrix so as to include the somatic and the mental elements of psychological activity. (Freud himself had postulated "id perceptions" of the somatic "interior" of the mental apparatus.) Cognition and memory lay the framework for an increasingly differentiated series of affects whose signal functions promote ego control over the inner and outer worlds and modify the affects themselves.

In the course of his presentation of a general affect theory, Schur examined and systematically replaced the metaphors which Freud tentatively introduced to describe the associated processes ("the ego is the seat of anxiety," "the ego produces signals of anxiety," etc.) and was able to include in a consistent arrangement the entire spectrum of affective variants (terror, fear, apprehension) from clinical, behavioral, and metapsychological viewpoints alike. Where older formulations could only suggest the "transformation" of the instincts into ego judgments of negation and affirmation, Schur traced in detail the successive steps from affect-dominated to ego-dominated responses to personality needs (see also Lichtenstein, Chapter 8, This Volume).

A study of the signal function in its hierarchic aspects, "Unconscious Affects and the Signal Response," one of Schur's unpublished papers, is included in this book in summary form (see Rosner, Chapter 2, This Volume). We also present a closely related discussion by Elizabeth R. Zetzel on "The Relationship of Defense to Affect and Trauma." Placing defense mechanisms in a context of signal controls over affects and viewing them in a maturational sequence, she stresses the importance of the experience and toleration of unpleasant affects, not only in relation to defenses, but as part of normal and superior mental functioning. Citing evidence from the lives and creating accomplishments of outstanding individuals (including Freud himself), she points out:

> There is much to indicate that those individuals who have previously experienced manifest sadness, or some subjective depression, prove to be more capable of accepting later life experience in a progressively adaptive manner. . . . This tolerance may be closely related to all that is involved in secondary autonomy of the ego and the emergence of conflict-free activity [Chapter 7, This Volume].

Symptom Formation. Proceeding from phylogenetic and developmental factors to the clinical sphere, Schur re-examined the traditional approach to symptom formation—instinctual demands, danger, defense, conflict, compromise formation, secondary gains—in a context of differentiating ego functions and a corresponding hierarchy of ego anxiety responses. This finds illustration in two clinical studies here published for the first time:

In "Metapsychological Aspects of Phobias in Adults" (Chapter 4, This Volume), symptoms are placed in their genetic and functional contexts, progressive and regressive, with the comment that "the ego of the phobic patient has lost, or more likely never acquired, the faculty of evaluating many instinctual demands on the level of reality-testing." Anticipatory aspects of the anxiety reaction lose their signal function (or have never properly acquired one), and the phobic individual responds to prospects of danger as though the crisis is already at hand. Schur examines in detail the disorders of function, object relationships, and intrasystemic organization, amplifying in such terms older formulations of regression, fixation, damming-up of energies, and the return of the repressed. Of great interest is his description of the phobic patient's libidinal pleasures which entrench his disorders: pregenital tensions assume the significance of genital excitement to fuse and libidinize anxiety. The patient "plays with danger": anticipation of danger becomes a signal for the anticipation of pleasure and a hidden motive for accelerating the processes of ego regression. Acting out is then precipitated, and realistic danger actually increases.

Schur further traces along this line of development the dispositions toward resomatization and the reaction types of other neuroses. Phobic symptoms occur in all neuroses; symptoms of other neuroses are to be found in the phobic patient. The functional analysis offers a more detailed approach to problems of therapy and raises questions as to nosologies based on symptoms. Schur applied similar considerations to a functional and nosological evaluation of "Psychiatric Sequelae of Massive Traumatization" in a presentation he never fully developed into a paper. He viewed the experiences of concentration camp inmates as a horrible but gigantic experiment in which the relationship between innate and acquired factors in symptom formation required the use of the continuum concept.

In "Correlation of Childhood with Adult Neurosis" (Chapter 5, This Volume), Schur assesses from structural and functional viewpoints the transition from a childhood phobia to an adult compulsive-obsessive neurosis. With normal maturation, somatic and motor responses in anxiety give way to intellectual controls. In obsessions, on the other hand, doubt—as an intellectual signal of anxiety—is reduced repressively to irrational thoughts that are incapable of protecting the individual from real danger.

The Id. The direction of Schur's investigations, with their exploration of the body-mind relationship and the successful application of a modern framework to a series of challenging problems, brought an invitation from the editors of the *Journal of the American Psychoanalytic Association* to prepare a monograph on the id as fourth in a series to present authoritative reviews and contemporary outlooks on special subjects in psychoanalysis.

The concept of the id, outlined in the structural approach to the mental apparatus (Freud, 1923a), had partly resolved old difficulties within the earlier prevailing topographic systems but left others and, in fact, added new ones. The concept was, in effect, a conglomerate of many indispensable postulates which had been incompletely defined, loosely connected among themselves, and had often involved contradictory assumptions—viz., the unconscious. Abrams (Chapter 10, This Volume) discusses for us the succession of concepts and frameworks within which this basic tenet of psychoanalysis has been placed: the instincts; the archaic heritage with its consignment of ancestral memories, primal fantasies, and innate symbols; repressed mental contents; the primary process; psychic reality; the pleasure principle; and the repetition compulsion.

Freud himself referred to the id as a "dark" and "obscure" area and showed a significant predilection for describing it in metaphorical terms. Modern stress on the ego had corrected many imbalances of a previous era, but at the same time had a tendency to introduce dissociations between the overlying structure and the id base which still remained the essential core of the mental apparatus, and the particular concern of the psychoanalyst.

In *The Id and the Regulatory Principles of Mental Functioning* (1966a), Schur reviewed and established continuity between the successive formulations of the id's components, subjecting them to the full range of metapsychological modes of description rather than permitting only one or two to attain disproportionate dominance. He replaced metaphors with systemic formulations and used the continuum as an integrative force in linking somatic and psychic processes which the id concept itself was especially designed to accomplish.

What emerged was a consistent set of assumptions, each grounded in Freud's own writings, but with new aspects which bore Schur's individual stamp. He came out firmly for a structured id that develops and plays an adaptive role in maturation. He recognized the wish as the fundamental unit of psychological functioning, relating it through the continuum to underlying and accompanying somatic "needs." Id wishes involve perceptions, memories, and intentions: consequently, they require structures and utilize, in common with the ego—with which, as Freud pointed out, they maintain close bonds—the apparatuses of both body and mind.

In the course of this systematization, Schur takes up fundamental problems associated with the pleasure and unpleasure principles, distinguishing between their experiential and metapsychological aspects and linking them respectively with biological dispositions to approach and withdraw. Schur, like many analysts, finds little to favor the idea of the death drive and prefers to separate clinical observations on the compulsion to repeat from the concept of a repetition compulsion, which he would place within a more broadly conceived view of adaptive tendencies inherent in maturation.

The editors of the *Journal of the American Psychoanalytic Association* correctly observe, in their introduction to the monograph, that it is a "scholarly, imaginative, and thought-provoking work . . . conceived by an analyst whose thinking, although adhering to the framework of Freud's fundamental contributions, takes bold steps forward in the elaboration of these contributions" (Schur, 1966a, p. 8). Loewald and Rosen discuss Schur's monograph in the present volume. The former, agreeing with many of Schur's points and proposing alternative and original solutions with respect to other problems presented by the id, offers the fascinating suggestion that it was Eros—not the death drive, as so often thought—that was the true innovation made by Freud's second instinct theory. Thus a progressive and creative force—not merely one that is reproductive and regressive—must enter into the analyst's theoretical considerations and clinical work. "To speak of such re-creative repetition as a 'compulsion' means speaking from a point of view which is outside the self, beyond the ego and the id and the superego, overreaching the pleasure and reality principles," Loewald (Chapter 3, This Volume) asserts.

Rosen (Chapter 3, This Volume) finds Schur's treatment of the pleasure and unpleasure principles "a particularly felicitous suggestion . . . [which] makes for a more coherent link between the concept id and its biological substrate. It also explains more concretely certain aspects of early psychic development where the strivings to re-establish perceptual identity with need-satisfying sources of stimulation go on side by side." The id, he reports, can now be integrated more readily into the structural operations of the rest of the personality. Rosen himself has pertinent and novel points to make concerning the process of differentiation by means of which the id and the ego, arising from the same innate apparatuses, achieve their separate organizations.

Schur's study of the id has been taken as our inspiration and unifying theme—though not as a limitation—in suggesting the title, *The Unconscious Today*. If our contributions justify the subtitle "Psychoanalytic Perspectives in Theory and Practice," they follow in the traditions of analysis and the inseparability of any partial realm of mental functioning from the total field of research.

Freud Commentaries. Schur will be remembered as an important chronicler and participant of Freudian history as well as for his many theoretical contributions. Three Freud lectures, given before different psychoanalytic societies, provided him with an opportunity to present new information about Freud himself, information gleaned through their close association as well as from hitherto unpublished documents.

"The Problem of Death in Freud's Writings and Life" (1964), a lecture delivered before the New York Psychoanalytic Society, tells us, for the first time, of his meeting with Freud and their close relationship thereafter until the moving events that marked the end. Illness and anticipation of death inevitably figured in this relationship. As Freud's own self-analysis revealed, the death of an infant brother, Julius, had already touched him deeply and instilled a lasting sense of guilt when he was only two years old. This early experience served as the prototype for a series of replacements for Julius, "revenants," that came to include Fliess during transference phases of the self-analysis. Schur scrutinizes this subject in his Freud lecture, "The Guilt of the Survivor." In 1969 this paper was awarded the Fifth Heinz Hartmann Annual Award "in recognition of [Schur's] unique researches on the life and inner struggles of Sigmund Freud." Further consideration of this subject was published posthumously under the title "The Background of Freud's Disturbance on the Acropolis" (Schur, 1969).

Freud's preoccupation with death was influenced by severe attacks of anginal pain in 1893-95, which, Schur thinks, may well have been organic. In accordance with Fliess' theory of periodicity, he came to fix a series of dates for his own death (successively at 42, 51, 62, and 81 years). The concept of the death drive was derived in large part from subjective factors, Schur believes, and he explores the background of many passages in Freud's writings that support this appraisal. While Freud, contemplating death, rejected the illusory comforts of religion, he was nevertheless courageous and found solace through work and recreation. He emphasized that Eros neutralizes the death drive and propels man forward as an individual and as a member of the human race. The reality principle appeared to him as a pillar of support against infantile anxieties. He was able to mobilize the creative imagination (as in the Moses preoccupation of the last years) and thus achieve new triumphs for the pleasure principle when confronted with inescapable woes. Schur tells us the title of the last book Freud read—*The Fatal Skin* by Balzac—and of the detached comment with which he laid down this Faustian narrative: "That was the proper book for me."

In "Some Additional 'Day Residues' of the Specimen Dream in Psychoanalysis" (1966b), Schur presented new biographical material which adds to our understanding of Freud's personality and works. This "specimen," the dream of Irma's injection, introduces *The Interpretation of Dreams.* Freud himself regarded it as the instrument through which he achieved insight into the meaning of dreams. The specimen dream deals with the examination of a girl's oral cavity and subsequent medical disputes over the proper diagnosis and treatment. What Schur reveals is that in the background was an operation Fliess performed on one of Freud's patients, a woman not mentioned in the analysis of the Irma dream. The operation was followed by a dangerous hemorrhage which resulted from negligently leaving a strip of gauze in the wound. The dream can now be better understood, especially as Schur delineates so masterfully the effect of Freud's transference relationship with Fliess on his interpretation of the Irma dream.

Two other studies in this volume add further dimensions to Freudian biography which supplement Schur's contributions. Zetzel notes Freud's capacity to experience depression and to surmount it by productivity in his work and growth in his personality. She cites the connection between the death of his father and the writing of the book on dreams (which he himself recognized), and analyzes in this connection the "dream of the burning child" which opens the important seventh chapter. She sees in the dead boy's approach of his surviving father a reverse of the sense of guilt experienced by Freud himself as surviving object of his dead father's reproaches. (The "revenant" aspect will especially strike us after reading Schur's lectures.)

Shengold, in a study of "Freud and Joseph," also pursues the theme of tragedy and death in relationships between father and son, as well as between brothers. By tracing the acknowledged Joseph-identification of Freud which existed for many years, we learn how he himself at last became a revenant as he identified with his dead father, Jacob Freud, and turned to his sons in England, the latter-day Egypt, for support during his final days. Shengold points to the displacement of oedipal rivalry from father to brother figures in both instances—the Biblical prototype and the latter-day replica.

The other contributors to this volume permit us to follow further the contemporary trends in psychoanalysis Schur so ably represented. A study on "Transference in Childhood" (Chapters 19 to 27, This Volume), organized among its members by the Psychoanalytic Association of New York and chaired by Neubauer, examined this key relationship of the patient to the analyst in the context of maturation during a succession of periods—prelatency, latency, and adolescence—when the real figures of the parents are still the paramount influences in the processes of personality formation. The older question—can a true transference develop under such conditions?—became part of a larger one: what part does the analyst, like the parent, play in mobilizing past reactive dispositions, and how does he, as a new object, promote the maturation of the child? (see also Anna Freud, 1965, pp. 38-39).

Schur's views on the repetition compulsion and the adaptive id find their counterparts in an associated topic: are transference phenomena themselves merely repetitions of repressed older experiences that have become walled off as id contents, or are they hierarchically ordered aspects of a differentiated ego-id, in which regressive as well as progressive trends are invoked to resolve the multiple tasks of growth and adjustment? Are not all these trends implicated in the transference and the transference neurosis, as well as in the therapeutic alliance and the normal manifestations of functioning in everyday life? Can transference or transference neurosis—or neurosis—be defined, except in relation to health? How reliable are the criteria by which we define illness and health, both within and outside the analytic setting, as we gauge disorder and aspire toward therapeutic goals? In considering these questions, we shall proceed beyond the study group to our other contributors and the broadening horizons of contemporary psychoanalysis.

The questions explored include: the phenomenology and interrelationships of transference and transference neurosis as determined by extensive reviews of the literature and personal observations; a reexamination of explanatory concepts such as regression, fixation, resistance, and the repetition of the past; and the formulation of a structural viewpoint with respect to transference, the role of the analyst, and the therapeutic process.

". . . transference should be explored in the context of the developmental progression," states Neubauer (Chapter 27, This Volume) in summarizing the studies of the group, "with particular reference to the concept of the continuous assimilation of the old into new forms of structural organization. . . . The child will perceive the analyst differently at different times, depending on the stage of the analysis, the developmental phase he has reached and the nature of his conflicts." Transference reflects the reality of the past, declares Abrams (Chapter 22, This Volume), and has its origins in "past states of adaptedness to earlier environmental conditions, including specific attitudes and behavioral modes of the parents." This makes it necessary, Jerome Silverman adds, for "the analyst to go beyond the relatively simple question of determining whether a relationship is 'real' or 'repeated,' " thrusting upon the analyst himself an inherently synthesizing role that may lie "outside the conventional psychoanalytic classification of therapeutic interventions" (Chapter 23, This Volume).

This latter admonition finds illustration in Neubauer's concept of "reverse transference." The analyst may become the first oedipal figure in the child's life, he asserts; only then may it be possible for oedipal attitudes to be transferred back on to the parents. Scharfman takes a similar position with a warning that an adolescent crush on the analyst should not be dismissed with transference interpretations. A new and important capacity for love may have been introduced through treatment—a view that places in a maturational and adaptive framework Freud's older recognition that transference love may well possess elements of the genuine feeling. Such considerations lend detail to the working through process and to Freud's reported pragmatic observation: "We may treat a neurotic any way we like, he always treats himself . . . with transferences" (A. Freud, 1965, p. 228).

The concepts of neurosis and health, diagnosis, interpretation, and therapeutic process all take on new dimensions in the structural framework. Lilleskov expresses a prevailing viewpoint when he remarks that "although transference neurosis has been a valuable concept both clinically and theoretically, its uncritical use in the past may have delayed our progress in understanding the full range of relationship processes in the analytic situation" (Chapter 21, This Volume).

Harley and Blum also take up problems of transference and transference neuroses in children. Harley, on the basis of new observations on her famous case of Anne, is able to demonstrate specific instances of the "repetition of the past" in the analytic setting. Blum correlates the transference neurosis with the therapeutic alliance and the progress of the analytic work. He also finds important points of difference from both transference and the original neurosis.

The lines of development of the normal personality serve increasingly as the background for defining other familiar analytic data and concepts. Neubauer and Martin A. Silverman present a study which seeks to outline a method for distinguishing and assessing a "progression-regression balance" as a prerequisite for determining a child's individual timetable of development and the significance within this scale of assumptions of "regression," "fixation," "infantile behavior," etc. Progression may, in long-range perspectives, assume pathological proportions, while regression may prove to be "normal." "The hallmark of psychological health," they conclude, "is not freedom from symptoms, but optimal progression toward mature drive- and ego organization" (Chapter 18, This Volume).

Kay (Chapter 20, This Volume) points out that "conflict, regressive and progressive, remains from the start a part of [the] dynamic parental bond." Interpretations are multidetermined and are directed and effective in relation to areas other than the resistance. The correct interpretation, as Lilleskov remarks, not only promotes insight, but cements a real relationship between the patient and the analyst.

The need to assess the long-range development of the personality as a background for the understanding of its disorders in a social setting, finds expression in another group of papers which includes contributions by Lichtenstein, Pollock, Helen Schur, Dickes, and Glenn. Lichtenstein re-examines the function of judgment, especially Freud's derivation of affirmation and negation, from the biological instincts of Eros and the death drive (Freud, 1925b). Schur, as we have noted, deals with the same problem by invoking a continuum of id-ego differentiation through interaction with the environment. Lichtenstein focuses especially on the sense of identity derived from an interplay of mutual "mirroring experiences" which relate the individual and the outer world, beginning with the infant-mother entity. The ability to negate, which Freud considered a precondition of thought and a basic characteristic of the ego—viz., the power to institute inhibition and delay—is an organizer of the greatest importance, inasmuch as the id, or unconscious, supposedly recognizes no contradiction among its unorganized strivings. Spitz (1957) stressed the identification with the aggressor in the acquisition of the inner "symbol of negation." Lichtenstein, however, following the path of the instincts among the budding self- and object images, relates the identification with the aggressor to the more fundamental mirror experiences that endow the individual with a sense of being confirmed or negated in his own existence through the satisfactions or frustrations encountered from external objects. He further distinguishes a special variant, the formation of the "malignant no," where the sense of self does not receive adequate confirmation from the mirroring objects in the outer world. Self-defeating patterns form, including the use of exaggerated sexual and aggressive behavior to coerce the required recognition. In addition to clinical material, Lichtenstein offers a fascinating sketch of the mutual mirroring of a "malignant no" in the relationship between the Marquis de Sade and the world of the French Revolution. He also makes some pertinent comments from the same standpoint on the alienated youth of today.

Another "line of development" with similar wide-ranging scrutiny is Pollock's exposition "On Time and Anniversaries." This follows the sense of time from earliest *Anlagen* in biological rhythms and a "physiological clock" through maturational sequences in which the ego system and the self become differentiated. Eventually, all three components of the personality contribute to the time sense, which is anchored to the memory of external events through institutional and individual observance of anniversaries. Cases and formulations, nonanalytic as well as analytic, are reviewed from the days of Anna O. and Elizabeth R. (Breuer and Freud, 1895). Pertinent too is an even wider continuity of human aspirations to escape the domination of time and death through a "vision of Paradise or the Garden of Eden" as lingering representations of the state of primary narcissism. "Fundamentally," Pollock concludes (Chapter 12, This Volume), "the anniversary response reflects the anxiety related to the sense of absolute helplessness which can result in a nothingness or destruction to the self.

Helen Schur's study, "Hallucinations in Children," approaches the symptomatology of this condition in relation to the associated functions of perception, cognition, and reality testing. Her emphasis is on the "how" as well as the "why" of the processes involved. She presents data gleaned from several hundred children seen in a psychiatric hospital, including three who could be analyzed in detail. Most of the children came from broken homes and from environments that offered little object constancy. Separation-individuation from unstable, even psychotic mothers was difficult to achieve. Under such circumstances, the attainment of reality testing was imperfect, and the pathway of regression readily followed. The menaces under which such children lived were revealed by frequent nightmares and inability to develop or utilize anxiety as a signal. The hallucinations seemed to be triggered by specific traumatic experiences and were not found to be indicative of a psychosis. Helen Schur suggests structural differences between visual and auditory hallucinations, the former appearing to be the more primitive.

Dickes undertakes a limited but intensive review of "Factors in the Development of Male Homosexuality," based essentially on a man with the unconscious conviction (substantiated also in other cases) that he possessed both male and female genitals. (This offers an intriguing supplement to the concept of bisexuality!) Dickes follows the significant trends in all phases of maturation, implicating particularly the preoedipal identification with a phallic mother and the environmental factors operative in the formation of a self image with symbiotic features that proved resistant to therapeutic change.

Glenn examines the mechanisms of "Regression and Displacement in the Development of the Body-Phallus Equation," especially in relation to the occurrence of this underlying fantasy in conjunction with the Isakower (1938) phenomenon. He traces several variants of the equation from personal observations. Glenn suggests that the self representations, displaced from the enlarged penis (and clitoris) to other extremities of the body, come to approximate the actual body image of infancy, and with it the fusion with the mother's breast which Lewin (1950) described in connection with the "oral triad." The mechanism of conversion is reviewed in this connection.

The nosological problem in establishing lines of development as a framework for the evaluation of personality disorders is discussed by several of our contributors. Lilleskov, in referring to the complexity of transference neuroses in children, maintains (Chapter 21, This Volume) that "one-word diagnoses" are inadequate and suggests the need for "paragraphs" which would delineate more meaningfully the intrinsic features of the condition. Valenstein undertakes a systematic study of "The Defense Mechanisms and Activities of the Ego," with recommendations for an approach to their classification. Valenstein examines the defenses from historical, clinical, behavioral, and metapsychological perspectives. He postulates a hierarchical order which ranges from id-dominated archaic processes and the early functioning of the mother as a "stimulus barrier," to the more complex, self-controlled, and reality-directed operations of later phases of maturation.

Defenses must be gauged, he emphasizes, not only in relation to pathology, but to normal living. Correlations customarily invoked between particular defenses and specific neuroses should be seen in the wider context of character style and adaptive function. Then "one has to ask of a classification of defensive activities of the ego, to what purpose? Is it primarily for a better psychoanalytical understanding of human development and the process of adaptation in a normative sense? Or is it for a more adequate assessment of intrapsychic conflict, its origin, course, and outcome, and the specificity of the neurosis which evolves from it? Or, finally, is it to enhance our diagnostic acumen and refine our psychoanalytic technique with a more thorough appreciation of its subtleties and therapeutic specificity?" (Chapter 6, This Volume). Thus, defenses too must be described from within a full metapsychological framework.

Therapeutic processes receive new scrutiny with the changing perspectives. Greenson, in a discourse on "The 'Real' Relationship between the Patient and the Psychoanalyst," challenges current emphasis on the transference relationship and its interpretation as the exclusively analytic contribution to the therapeutic process. The analyst as a real, new, and synthesizing force appears, in his concept of the working alliance, as a continuation into the sphere of adult analysis of formative influences that have operated in a similar capacity during early years. A real relationship, Greenson asserts, is a powerful factor in therapy, and he offers clinical examples. Some analysts use transference interpretations as a defense, fostering the patient's withdrawal from the world of reality. The operations of the real relationship must be understood and handled correctly: "Only those [patients] who have the capacity for forming a real relationship to the analyst are analyzable. . . . [T]he final resolution of the transference neurosis depends to a great extent on the transference neurosis being replaced by a real relationship" (Chapter 11, This Volume).

In applied analysis, the application of the structural concept has also produced invigorating trends. Rose traces the origin of creative impulses to the earliest experiences of bodily and mental reactions in relation to the mother. These, as he maintains in "Narcissistic Fusion States and Creativity," shape artistic form as an extension of a search for self-boundaries which alternate between emergence into new areas of growth and retreat to the old. He sees "the need to create [as] basic to the working of the mind. Growth is a form of self-creation. If we think of the creative impulse as the need to construct viable forms of reality for oneself, then it is clear that this need is as basic as growth" (Chapter 30, This Volume).

For the artist, his work "remains behind as the case of a mind reborn," while the mind itself—its problem solved—is free to continue its probings of new realities. Psychoanalysis, in its own growth processes toward a general psychology, is coming to recognize the creative processes of everyday life as within its own domain.

The "line of development" of man's most advanced creative activity—speech—is traced by Feldman from its origins in somatic activities to use in everyday language as illustrated by the metaphor "To 'lick' a problem." The tongue, as executive of the oral drive, is implicated in a series of mastery reactions which begin with the maintenance of unity with the mother through bodily and vocal contact and eventually differentiate into nonverbal and verbal attitudes which are seized upon in the popular vernacular to vividly characterize the "sucker," "asskisser," etc. Feldman follows the vicissitudes of these transformations in several languages ("tongues") and points to interrelations between actions, terms, and meanings in "spitting."

The origins of language are further illuminated by Niederland's surprising findings. The erroneous choice of the name "America" for the New World could not but challenge the interest of a psychoanalyst, accustomed to exploring the occurrence of "errors." If a "final analysis" could not be made in this instance, much of interest rewarded Niederland's research among ancient Portuguese, Spanish, and French archives. The personalities of Martin Waldseemueller, who made the error, and his poet-friend and roommate, Matthias Ringmann, both lifelong bachelors, suggest at least a latent homosexual bond between these men. Ringmann may well have shared in the "baptism" of the new land. To Waldseemueller, the name of America was a conscious feminine transposition of the masculine Amerigo. Through other threads, "America" was linked conceptually in the sixteenth century with the lost continent of Atlantis and with existing traditions about "islands of fortune" to the west. Still more deeply, Niederland suggests, the unconscious aspirations to establish contact once again with the bountiful mother of infancy, which lures explorers to find new lands beyond the sea and leads mapmakers to draw and name these lands, found resonance in the phonetic and onomatopoetic qualities of the word, America, itself. The sound patterns inevitably conjure up the primitive roots of mother, nurse (*amme*), and the symbolic sea (*meer*) in many languages. Thus, the "error," despite additional facts soon made available, found a ready-made anchorage in the imagination, and this may have contributed to the resistance to change thereafter.

The manifold lines of development discernible in the individual contributions to this volume, as well as in the summary of the works of Max Schur, thus reveal the ultimately unified patterns of a *Zeitgeist* permeating all contemporary work in psychoanalysis. The continuum between a work itself and the lines of development of the personality that creates it bears correspondingly distinctive features. We close this chapter, as Rosner (Chapter 2, This Volume) closes his, with a reflection on the inherent lesson:

> Max Schur's papers were written when he was past the age of 50, long after the period during which most men are capable of intensive creative effort and productivity. His papers testify to the validity of the analytic thesis, implicit in all his writing, that the human spirit is equal to extraordinary achievements when the ego, "that wonderful organ of adaptation," is free to express its full potential.

Part II

Psychoanalytic Contributions of Max Schur

CHAPTER 2

Psychoanalytic Papers of Max Schur

Henry Rosner, M.D.

This review of Schur's analytic ideas is meant to provide an overall survey of his many contributions to psychoanalysis and was facilitated by Schur's having made available to me numerous unpublished remarks from discussions at various scientific meetings. These, in addition to his published papers, make possible a comparison between his early views and his later formulations.[1]

That one who had practiced internal medicine for a quarter of a century should originally have been interested in the body-mind problem and that this interest should have led to a preoccupation with the problem of anxiety is understandable and should come as no surprise. During the last decade of his life, Schur's range of interests was so wide as to defy classification of his writings. I have divided them here for exegetic purposes only, fully recognizing the artificiality of separating papers which deal with somatization phenomena from those which have to do with anxiety, affects, object relations, and symptom formation. The final category under review presented no taxonomic problem: it deals with the subject of Sigmund Freud.

Dr. Rosner is Associate Clinical Professor, Division of Psychoanalytic Education, Department of Psychiatry, Downstate Medical Center, State University of New York, Brooklyn, New York.

[1]Two hitherto unpublished papers will be found in the present volume (Chapters 4 and 5). His monograph, *The Id and the Regulatory Principles of Mental Functioning*, is treated separately (Chapter 6, This Volume). For additional psychoanalytic contributions not discussed in this survey, see Supplementary References.'

EARLY ANALYTIC PAPERS

Hints of trends which were later to engage his attention appear in a 1937 paper written (with C. V. Medvei) while Schur was still an internist in Vienna. This, his first "analytic" paper, "On Pituitary Anterior Lobe Insufficiency" (see Kaufman and Heiman, 1964), dealt with anorexia nervosa and demonstrates that Schur already had a point of view, a beginning methodology for a genuine analytic exploration of the subject. Schur and his coauthor were able to show that psychological factors played an important role in what had been considered a physiopathological disease: anterior pituitary lobe insufficiency. They stressed the need for an examination of the total situation, including an evaluation of the cause of the illness, the trauma or conflict, as well as the adaptive processes available to the individual. Special attention is paid to the role of the *Anlage*—constitution in the biological sense—a term Schur later redefined as a psychoanalytic concept pertaining to the development and maturation of the ego. The authors endeavor to show that some of the so-called insufficiency diseases of the anterior pituitary are really cases of anorexia nervosa caused by neurotic conflicts. The fact that in many cases improvements followed the most bizarre therapeutic interventions suggested the presence of emotional factors. One woman who did not respond to treatment also had stomach trouble for which she had a resection. After losing contact with the authors for many years, she suddenly appeared, completely cured. She had, in the interim, abandoned orthodox medicine in favor of homeopathy where she was given vaginal massage. The authors conclude that a "trauma" or "conflict" can bring about a functional disturbance with signs and symptoms of anterior lobe insufficiency in patients who are of special makeup (genetic *Anlage*) and live in a certain milieu. They refer (Kaufman and Heiman, 1964) to the importance of the uniform approach for understanding the pathology of function.

> It shows us the functional connections of the whole organ systems which are in the service of the "vitality." It teaches us the importance of the instinct theory for the pathology of the dependence of certain drive tendencies. Thus it shows us the way which could turn out to be fruitful in the approach to all organ neuroses [p. 200].

Implicit in this paper is the idea that an analytic approach to these so-called incurable organic illnesses was warranted. The same concern for the interplay of physiological and psychological factors in human adaptation makes itself felt in almost all of Schur's scientific contributions. It is evident in his earliest analytic papers, based on studies conducted at Bellevue Hospital during the 1950's. At that time, he also sought to demonstrate that psychoanalysis was an eminently suitable methodological research tool for such investigation.

"Chronic Exudative, Discoid and Lichenoid Dermatitis (Sulzberger-Garbe's Syndrome: Case Analyses," 1950b) was Schur's first definitely psychoanalytic study. Of particular significance is that he chose as his theme a problem having to do with the body-mind relationship. In this paper, he hoped to show that an analytic approach "will teach us more than statistics based on generalizations" (p. 77). Here, for the first time, an incurable dermatological disease of unknown etiology was explained as the dermatological manifestation of a neurosis and treated successfully by psychoanalysis.

Whereas in 1937 he spoke of the need for a careful evaluation of the conflict or trauma, now his more profound understanding is reflected in his insistence that the anxiety response deserves special and scrupulous attention. The study of the adaptive processes is also stressed by his emphasis on the role that the defense of magical sacrifice *pars par toto* plays in these cases.

Schur's paper on the Sulzberger-Garbe Syndrome (1950b) shows how he evolved the methodology for his clinical studies and hints at his later theoretical formulations. He presented two case histories, the first, "one of the worst cases we had," of a 37-year-old married man who had been in and out of hospitals all his life. Following an incident which produced conflict having to do with money and his father-in-law, he developed a lesion on his penis, a symptom typical for the onset of this illness. The lesions soon spread to other parts of his body. Schur describes a profusion of symptoms, most of them traceable to the patient's having witnessed primal scenes "through all phases of his instinctual and ego development" (p. 73). Schur adds, "But his anxiety alone brings understanding into this maze of symptoms" (p. 74). After a year and a half of analysis, the patient's physical symptoms subsided. Then his father had a coronary attack. At first he took it well. But the sight of a catheter in his father's penis produced two dreams; in the first, he shaved his precious mustache, a symbol of masculinity. The second was a frank homosexual dream in which he sacrificed his male genitality. But this magical sacrifice was not enough; he still had anxiety. After a night of panic, the patient awoke with a lesion on his penis such as he had had at the start of the illness. "And so, under the spotlight of the analytic situation, we see a development equal in its validity to any clinical experiment" (p. 75).

In this clinical description, we observe what would soon become of special importance in Schur's thinking: the emphasis on a careful study of the danger situation and the ego's response to danger.

> When the conflict reaches unbearable intensity, only two ways are open: complete psychotic breakdown or the organic lesion. Corresponding to a very primitive super-ego, any upsurge of aggressive or sex-drives creates not yet guilt feelings, but deepest anxiety of retaliation from the outside, felt as castration fear. The symptoms, with all their self-destruction, are not just self-punishment, but correspond to the magic of sacrifice. The lesion on the penis is like thinness or homosexuality, a sacrifice of a *pars pro toto.* This mechanism of sacrifice applies also to other studies of various dermatological entities [p. 76].

The second case was of a Jewish man married to a Catholic woman. The patient began to gamble and lose money. Again, Schur paid special attention to the precipitating event. The patient bet his last $25 on the most holy of the Jewish Holy Days, the Day of Atonement. His horse was a 50 to 1 shot, barely won, and was then disqualified. After two weeks of rage and despair the patient developed a lesion on his penis, where, in his adolescence, he had had a painful swelling after masturbation. A doctor diagnosed scabies. The patient thought this meant venereal disease. He became even more anxious, and the generalized eruption followed. Analysis of the traumatic event revealed the following: (1) The $25: After the death of the patient's mother, the father remarried at 64. Indigent, he asked for money which the patient refused. Shortly thereafter, the father died. (2) Day of Atonement: The father had been a pious Jew who had encouraged his son's relationship with his present wife. Later, he disowned them. When their son developed pneumonia, the grandfather refused any help, and the boy died on the Day of Atonement. Schur describes how the uncovering of infantile material and connecting it with a traumatic scene and skin eruption brought about complete recovery. "In the film-script-like traumatic scene, were all the elements of the conflict. He failed in his final biggest gamble. The sequence was again: rage, humiliation, increasing hostility, unbearable increase of anxiety with the same outcome—the organic symptom. Again, the magic element of sacrifice" (p. 77). Although Schur stresses this defense in both cases, he is already describing the ego's regressive response to danger which he would later discuss more fully as resomatization responses.

ANXIETY PAPERS

Schur's early clinical studies convinced him that an intensive study of the anxiety reaction was necessary for a better understanding of his clinical data. His work, rooted in the study of the ego and especially its adaptive functions, flowered in his refinement of the theory of the anxiety response. It is in his papers on anxiety that we find the evolving of his metapsychological concept of the ego's biphasic function in the evaluation of danger and in the response to that evaluation. In "The Ego in Anxiety" (1953b), attempting to explain the different types of anxiety responses of his patients, he introduces the concepts of controlled and uncontrolled anxiety, resomatization, and secondary anxiety. Extending Freud's anxiety theories, he presents his own formulation of a unitary theory of anxiety, basing his thinking on the genetic principle and Freud's concept of the complementary series. Schur adds to Freud's hierarchy of danger situations a hierarchy of responses to danger. Anxiety, he believes, "is not only a reaction to danger, but also constitutes danger" (p. 95). The difference between controlled and uncontrolled anxiety depends on the nature of the ego regression.

The ego regression may be limited to the evaluation of danger. "The ego reacts to this evaluation, first, with . . . awareness of danger, . . . and secondly, it takes certain measures to avoid or eliminate the danger, e.g., it establishes defenses. . . . The ego strives to prevent a regressive type of reaction to a regressive evaluation of danger" (p. 79). The various signs of such a regressive reaction can be summarized as physiological regression (a term first coined by Michaels [1944]). In such a state, the ego responses are, to a certain extent, automatic reactions associated with discharge phenomena that were prevalent in infancy. Schur (1953b) wrote as follows:

> The failure of desomatization represents physiological regression. We can now establish another relation: on the one hand, coordinated motor action, desomatization, and secondary processes, on the other, random responses, involvement of basic vegetative processes and primary processes [p. 79]. The ego's restoration attempt uses secondary processes. . . . Danger thus becomes *potential* danger only. This stands in contrast to a situation of complete regression in which the attempt at restoration has been abandoned. Hence we may speak of controlled and uncontrolled anxiety. In such situations, we may expect reactions differing not only in quantity but also in quality, with the difference extending also to the somatic discharge phenomena. It is with such observations that my study started [p. 80].

Schur applies these concepts to clinical data:

> The first observation was of a patient with chronic, exudative, discoid and lichenoid dermatitis (Sulzberger-Garbe's Syndrome) for whom functions like shaving or taking a shower represented phobic situations. He tried to re-establish a precarious equilibrium by evading the phobic situation. Yet mere anticipation provoked anxiety, of the controlled variety. This was frequently accompanied by hives. Trained in thinking in terms of Cannon's theories about emergency reactions, I was at a loss for an explanation why urticaria, which is considered a condition connected in some way with histamine, and best relieved by adrenalin, should develop as a discharge phenomenon of anxiety. The same patient would, on the other hand, develop severe anxiety during analytic sessions due to homosexual fantasies in the transference situation. No sign of an attempt at restoration was to be detected in this situation. During such uncontrolled anxiety his discharge phenomena were quite different. He would shiver, cry, perspire, and complain about palpitation. Only after I learned to dissect the anxiety situation, could I understand that discharge phenomena in states of controlled anxi-

ety, in which the attempt at restoration has been incorporated, must differ from those in uncontrolled anxiety [p. 80].

Referring to earlier clinical studies on patients with vascular (1953a) and pulmonary disease (1950c), he continues (1953b):

> Another patient used to react in states of controlled anxiety with extrasystoles, in those of uncontrolled anxiety with paroxysmal tachycardia, reactions different not only in quantity, but also in quality. Still another patient, suffering from severe pulmonary emphysema, showed different types of respiratory distress in states of controlled and uncontrolled anxiety [p. 80].

Schur describes a special constellation of regressive responses. The primary response is one of somatization without any conscious awareness of anxiety or danger. Conscious anxiety is experienced only as "*secondary anxiety* to the primary somatized reaction" (p. 81). This secondary anxiety may result in even more severe but completely different types of somatization. He offers a clinical example to illustrate the complexities of such responses.

> During many months of his analysis, the above-mentioned patient, with pulmonary emphysema would wake up from sleep drenched with perspiration, and frequently also with his nose running ("vasomotor rhinitis"); very rarely was he aware of any preceding dream, nor was he consciously anxious. Yet he immediately checked whether he had perspired. If he felt wet, he developed anxiety, and with it somatization consisting in dyspnoea, so severe that he required oxygen. But what about the perspiration [pp. 81-82]?

The analysis revealed the genetic fear factors responsible. The patient had suffered from night sweats and fear of tuberculosis in his early twenties. Tuberculosis was also the threat his parents had used when he did not eat. Analysis disclosed that his perspiration and rhinitis were connected not only with masturbation, "but also with his infantile enuresis and with primal scene observations. The enuresis was both an anxiety reaction and a discharge of sexual excitation, in response to primal scene observations, and, later, to his fantasies"

(p. 82). Both the perspiration and the vasomotor rhinitis were "heirs of the enuresis" (p. 82). Schur considers them regressive anxiety reactions to incestual dreams. They were also sexual discharge phenomena. Later (1955) he calls such unconscious responses anxiety equivalents.

Schur suggests that "the regression to a preverbal, pre-ego stage explains the absence of a conscious anxiety experience in the primary reaction" (p. 82). Constitutional and accidental factors will determine the form that these reactions take, as well as "the points of fixation and regression, the predisposition to anxiety, the constellation of id and ego development, and the choice of the reacting organ system" (p. 82). He saw these factors as of great significance for the understanding of psychosomatic medicine. Regressive anxiety reactions may also produce a secondary anxiety with an even more profound disturbance of homeostasis than the original danger.

> It is not surprising that the ego would treat anxiety as danger or even as a traumatic situation—particularly if some somatization is outspoken. If this is correct, then defenses may be directed both against the source of the danger and against the resulting regressive anxiety reaction which has become a danger in its own right [p. 82].

Rapaport (1955) commented on the "exciting" implications of Schur's formulations for his theory of thought and especially the origin of anticipatory functions (pp. 314-315).

Schur (1953b) reviews Freud's formulations on anxiety and offers a definition which is an elaboration of Freud's concepts: "Anxiety is a response of the ego or of its matrix, to a traumatic situation or to danger, present or anticipated" (p. 93). He distinguishes between normal and neurotic anxiety:

> Neurotic anxiety comes about through a partial ego regression of various degrees. The regression may be limited to the evaluation of danger or it may involve the reaction. Except for outright panic in the traumatic situation—i.e., for uncontrolled anxiety—all other shades of anxiety represent an attempt of the ego to regain control (controlled anxiety). The somatic manifestations vary accordingly

> and differ not only in quantity, but also in quality. . . . Thus anxiety . . . has similarities to a symptom. If anxiety is libidinized, the approximation becomes striking [p. 93].

Schur's formulation differs from Freud's in that he substitutes for the concept of automatic anxiety originating in the id (e.g., in sexual frustration), the concept of the ego evaluating certain changes in the id as danger and reacting with anxiety. He stresses that in his thinking, anxiety is always an ego response and adds:

> Freud's difficulty to combine his clinical experience (that repression creates anxiety) with his new theory (that anxiety makes for repression) has also been clarified by this conception. Anxiety makes for repression, repression causes frustration, frustration may represent inner danger, and thus cause more anxiety. This closes the circle. Freud's concept of the 'economic justification' of this type of anxiety through changes in the id was replaced by the following formulation: Economic justification is inherent in any evaluation of danger and is proportionate to the degree of ego repression. . . . Regression can restore archaic situations and thus re-create economic conditions. . . . Thus no anxiety response occurs without 'economic justification' [pp. 93-94].

Schur also discusses the topic of *Angstbereitschaft* (preparedness for anxiety). If the self-perpetuation of anxiety is present in many areas of functioning, the ego responds with a state of constant preparedness. He considers this the explanation for "tension," i.e., the state of constant vigilance, of high cathexis of defenses which constitutes a precarious equilibrium. This state, too, can have its somatic manifestations.

Schur further explores the clinical implications of *Angstbereitschaft* in terms of an ego attitude. In many cases, in spite of good analytic work, the patient behaves in the same repetitious way. Freud designated as repetition compulsion the force behind this type of resistance. Schur, however, suggests:

> According to my formulation this repetitious response, for which repetition compulsion is an excellent descriptive term, originates in the primitive regressive part of the ego which developed, under the

> impact of the self-perpetuation of danger and anxiety, an automatic, reflex-like response pattern. This automatic primitive response, as an expression of ego regression is both the result of and the cause for the perpetuation of instinctual regression [p. 96].

Schur was later (1955, 1960b) to take up the subject of the repetition compulsion and to devote half of his monograph, *The Id and the Regulatory Principles of Mental Functioning* (1966a), to a fuller discussion of the problem.

"The Ego and Anxiety" offers tentative answers to two other questions which Schur repeatedly refers to in future writings. In reply to the first, "Why is it that instinctual demands so frequently represent danger to the ego?" Schur (1953b) makes two points: From the side of biology, pregenital satisfaction lacks direct discharge and is doomed to frustration (which can be a danger). And while oral gratification may be ego-syntonic, sexuality meets with the disapproval of the environment and also of the superego.

He also emphasizes the genetic link between sexuality and danger:

> We saw, in the discussion of hunger, that in the course of maturation the content of danger spreads to the condition under which it occurs, e.g., separation from the mother. The same applies to sexuality. Thus everything interfering with sexual satisfaction, in fact sexuality itself, its objects, any increase of sexual tension may become danger. We have to see castration fear . . . in this broader framework. . . . Castration enforces frustration, which is danger by itself. . . . Thus castration is genetically linked with hunger. Beyond castration which is outer danger looms frustration–i.e., inner danger [p. 83].

Important too is the fact that the maturing ego's awareness of inner danger is deficient, as is its capacity for anticipation. It still responds to inner danger with a regressive evaluation of the danger and with defenses which are primitive and show a limited capacity for neutralization and a regressive tendency toward somatization.

Schur's second question is: why is death so frequently the content of danger?

In Freud's view, all kinds of anxiety follow certain prototypes—even if the content of the danger changes. Schur suggests that the appraisal of death is derived from all previous traumatic situations. "What Freud called the core of the danger situation is the feeling of helplessness. This certainly applies to our attitude toward death. The fact that it is unfathomable as an experience, makes the helplessness supreme" (p. 97).

Schur realized that his first attempt to formulate a unitary theory of anxiety left many questions unanswered. For example, he repeatedly emphasized that ego regression could re-create a traumatic situation "with all its economic implications" (1958, p. 195): But he had not explained how such economic changes take place. He repaired this omission in "Comments on the Metapsychology of Somatization" (1955) (which I take up later). Schur also realized that although the id plays an important role in the anxiety response he had made no mention of it in his first paper. His next major contribution made good the deficiency. In "The Ego and the Id in Anxiety" (1958), after summarizing his previous formulations, he applies the genetic point of view to a study of the phylogenetic history of the anxiety situation, the releasing excitation, and the response to it, drawing on work of the ethologists, Lorenz (1937, 1950, 1952a), Tinbergen (1951, 1952), and Thorpe (1956), who had evolved a new theory of instincts and instinctive behavior. Responses of sign stimuli of danger are, according to them, innate, species specific and, especially in lower animals, not learned, but regulated by "instincts," expressed, for instance, by certain IRMs (innate releasing mechanisms). The ethologists assumed also "an innate drive" to avoid danger.

Ethologists, like most biologists who operate with the "instinct concept," are careful to emphasize that this hypothetical "drive" should not be confused with an "instinct of self-preservation." "Instinctive behavior" has survival value and therefore serves to preserve the species, but there is no proof of "intent" or "cognitive aspects" in such behavior.

Before attempting any correlation of the "instinctive avoidance and fright reaction" and the IRMs to the anxiety response, Schur, in large part following Hartmann (1939, 1948, 1950b), compares and contrasts the concepts "instinctual drives," id, and ego of psychoanalysis. He points out that the instinct concept of ethology comprises not only certain inherited, stereotyped patterns of coordinated behavior, but also an internal drive comprising a certain "action-specific energy" which, until released, accumulates in the form of a "specific action potential." The main emphasis of the instinct concept is on the "instinctive behavior patterns."

Schur states (1958) that the psychoanalytic concept of instinctual drives can be compared (but not equated) with the internal drive element of the ethological concept "instinct." He therefore uses, as did Hartmann, the term "instinctual drive" for the German *Trieb*, rather than "instinct" which is found throughout the *Standard Edition.* In his subsequent writings, Schur, in an effort to avoid confusion, continued to insist on this distinction. He also stresses the point that the "instinctual drives," defined by Freud (1915a) as "the *psychical representative[s]* of the stimuli originating from within the organism and reaching the mind" (pp. 121-122, Schur's italics) are "a psychological concept in contrast to need satisfaction and the hypothetical constancy principle, which are physiological, physical, and biological concepts" (p. 203). The difference between an "instinctual drive" and the "drive" element of an instinct "can only be understood in terms of psychic structure. . . . What I have in mind is Freud's description of the origin of a 'wish.' With the emergence of a wish begins psychic structure. . . . The 'wish' is the beginning of the cognitive anticipation in contrast to the purposeful directiveness and the survival value of the instincts" (1958, p. 203). Schur was to develop these concepts later (1966a).

Schur's study of what ethologists described as the instinctive roots of the anxiety response led him to these conclusions: He considered the assumption of an internal drive to avoid danger extremely hypothetical. (In later papers he uncategorically rejected this assumption.) He believed that Lorenz' "reaction-specific energy" utilized in the anxiety response was inseparable from the psychoanalytic concept of mental energy. And he thought the IRMs of animals have been replaced, in man, largely by learned responses.

Schur engages in what he, himself, described as a speculation. Following some formulations of Lorenz (1952b), Tinbergen (1952), and Ford and Beach (1951), who stressed the fact that fighting, courting, and mating are closely related in a large number of vertebrates, he considers the possibility that the link between sexuality and violence in man, and therefore also their link with danger, may be rooted in innate givens.

Schur sees innate, instinctual givens interlocking with a gradually evolving ego as playing a significant part in the problem of anxiety. He concedes that the development of the ego gives man the advantage of adapting to his environment, but adds (1958):

> However, beyond that: the simultaneous presence of instinctual givens and learned responses results in a strain on the faculty for evaluation of danger and of the response to it. The prevalence of learned responses permits variability and adaptiveness, but is also less stable and dependable. In addition, the prolonged immaturity and dependence of man accounts for what I have described as a complicated learning and unlearning process in relation to danger. What Freud calls the imperfection of the mental apparatus, by which he mainly meant the imperfection of the ego, is imperfection in a much stricter sense, namely in the genetic meaning of the word. Phylogenetically and ontogenetically it is the younger structure. Its development is in a much wider sense than implied by Freud in this context dependent on environmental influences. Its prime tool—reality testing—is late in coming. Secondary processes are limited in their effectiveness by the fact that perception of outer, but especially of inner, stimulation may also be under the sway of primary processes. Identification is a stimulus for maturation, but also potentially a great obstacle in the reality testing of danger. Finally, the imperfection of the ego to master the problem of danger and anxiety in the crucial area of sexuality is also explainable by both phylogenetic and ontogenetic causes.
>
> The phylogenetic link of mating and aggression links sex with danger. The innate instinctual patterns, represented by the id, are faced during the period of infantile sexuality by a weak ego. It is this innate phylogenetic pattern which probably adds to the fear-laden aspect of infantile sexuality. The latency period then represents a psychologically and biologically necessary adaptation rather than the indication of a cataclysmic evolution of the human race. This imperfection of the ego in dealing with the phylogenetically codetermined danger aspects of sexuality has found its precipitate in the development of society, culture, and of the super-ego [pp. 216-217].

Schur sums up by delineating some aspects of the anxiety response which could be seen as manifestations of the id, concluding with a modification of his 1953(b) definition of anxiety: "*Anxiety is a reaction to a traumatic situation, or to danger, present or anticipated. In this reaction, we have to distinguish between the affect anxiety, which is an ego reaction, and the discharge phenomena, which are also id manifestations"* (pp. 217-218).

ETHOLOGY

We have already seen how Schur addressed himself to the question of the relationship between psychic development, ego regression, and the vicissitudes of the anxiety response. His continuing interest in the problem is reflected in his contributions to discussions at various Panels of the American Psychoanalytic Association (Kaufman, 1958; Rubinfine, 1959; Ritvo, 1962; Schafer, 1965). His ideas on the relationship between early psychic structure formation and object relations are best viewed through his discussion (1960a) of Bowlby, who had presented his own formulations (1958, 1959, 1960) concerning the nature of the infant's earliest relationship to its mother, separation anxiety, and the affective responses of the infant and young child to object loss. When Schur discussed Bowlby's postulates, he was deeply involved with correlating the concepts of ethology and psychoanalysis (see Schur, 1960b, Ostow, 1960). The discussion of Bowlby's work, which I take up in some detail here, further reflects his interest in formulations which would provide a common ground between the two disciplines.

Schur is in full agreement with Bowlby on the importance of the infant's tie with the mother, and the severity of the reaction to any separation. Schur points out, however, that basic to Bowlby's ideas is the assumption that human infants start with a number of highly structuralized responses, some of which are active at birth, some maturing later.

Schur's basic disagreement with Bowlby is that Bowlby attributed to human behavior an instinct concept which neglects the factor of development and learning. Schur (1960a) thought Bowlby had endowed instincts with qualities of structure which analysts attributed to the ego only after a considerable period of development.

> The newborn is already equipped with a set of perceptive and executive apparatuses and with innate "discharge channels" all of

> which form the basis of what Hartmann calls primary ego autonomy. The five responses designated by Bowlby as IRS's are using such inborn apparatuses. The concept *Anlage* implies that eventually, under the motivational stimulation of the instinctual drives and in constant interaction with the environment, the human phenotype develops its individual, highly complex ego structures which enable the ego to become what Hartmann calls the organ of adaptation [p. 69].

For Schur, then, a concept that assumes the fully innate unlearned character of complex behavior patterns is in disagreement not only with analytic theory, but also with the concepts of most biophysiologists and ethologists.

> We can now summarize Bowlby's concepts as follows: the child develops the tie to the mother because it is *directed* by certain IRS's; it develops separation anxiety if these responses cannot be terminated. To this regulation by preformed IRS's is added "a process of learning of a simple kind." To summarize this theory in a form which may sound drastic but is not exaggerated: the infant eats because it has to suck; it develops a tie to the mother because it *has* to cling, follow and escape *to*; it develops separation anxiety if it cannot "terminate" these responses. All this is a determined and extremely systematic effort to show that the tail is wagging the dog and not vice versa [p. 76].

Schur, on the other hand, explains separation anxiety thus:

> The human infant is an altricial creature par excellence . . . utterly dependent on external help for any satisfaction of its needs which cannot be satisfied by automatic homeostatic regulations. Its structure formation is dependent on a steady stream of stimuli. . . . It learns to connect a "mother" figure with the source of all these "physiological" and psychological "nutriments." It enters the "symbiotic" phase . . . where self-awareness and body image start to develop—where, however, self and objects are not really differentiated. The capacity to tolerate delay depends on the development of . . . complex ego faculties. . . .
>
> With locomotion and increasing regard for the environment, the infant becomes aware of all kinds of external danger. . . . The child develops also the recognition of his own helplessness, which is the core of any traumatic situation . . . [and] is the expression of the

> weakness of his own rudimentary ego [and] can be overcome only through . . . the mother. It enters a phase in which it experiences various needs . . . and . . . restrictions. It becomes aware of its ambivalence [p. 77].

Schur contrasts his and Bowlby's views with regard to the disappearance of separation anxiety. For Bowlby it might have been owing to a "waxing and waning of the IRS's" when they are no longer biologically necessary. Bowlby concedes that "Here, learning and experience certainly play a considerable part also. *We* would say that ego development eventually guarantees an increased stability of what Mahler (1958) calls the separation-individuation phase" (p. 78).

Schur turns to Bowlby's concepts of grief and mourning in childhood. The latter claimed that the infant's reaction to actual separation from the mother, especially between the ages of six months and three years, has far greater significance than had been assumed. Bowlby preferred to call these reactions grief and mourning rather than depression.

Schur stresses that depression as well as anxiety both are affects which are ego responses. He extends the analogy between anxiety and depression to the assumption that, genetically, both affects have their precursors in pre-ego states.

> Both the affects, which are ego responses, and their precursors have their specific discharge phenomena. My concepts of "desomatization" and "resomatization" (1955) may also apply to depression, and might explain the economic consequences of various types of depression.
>
> While anxiety results in a mobilization of defenses, depression induces inhibition and eventually paralysis of ego functions. This process is paralleled by an inhibition of vital somatic functions. These considerations apply also to pre-ego states, where both the precursors of anxiety and of depression are truly "psychosomatic." The toleration of object loss and the ability to re-establish ego control, and thereby to limit the reaction to a "controlled" depression, are a measure of well-established ego autonomy. It is obvious that the budding ego of the infant has not yet reached this stage of development.
>
> I have pointed out . . . that the mother provides the necessary "nutriments" for structure formation. Her absence makes the child

> literally wilt away. This process has been vividly described by Spitz . . . (1945) and Engel and Reichsman (1956). Spitz (1956a) used the analogy to Selye's concept of the exhaustion phase of the stress reaction. We may speak even more appropriately of a deficiency syndrome, which is truly "psychosomatic." It might be pertinent here that on the one hand depressive illness results in hormonal inhibition, and that on the other hand, both avitaminosis and certain hormone deficiencies may stimulate depressive illness.
>
> Anna Freud mentions in her discussion the frequency of psychosomatic conditions in children after separation from their mother. I would assume that some somatic phenomena must be present in every case of bereavement.
>
> I have brought all this up to show that the concept "depression" is—if we use the metapsychological approach—broad enough to describe all responses of reaction to the accomplished loss of an object. The process of mourning could then be seen not as an especially severe type of depression, but rather as an attempt at restitution, which may or may not succeed [pp. 80-81].

Not only are these observations on problems of child rearing rare but important expressions of the application of Schur's views on this significant area, they also reflect the care with which he extrapolated from ethology. The same meticulousness is evident in his paper, "The Theory of the Parent-Infant Relationship" (1962), in which he examines object relations in the light of ethological studies. Here he concludes, "from purely theoretical considerations . . . that instinctual drives, which have to seek an object for their discharge, stimulate alloplastic action more directly than the 'avoidance and fright' response or than 'withdrawal' and therefore initiate other aspects of structure formation" (p. 244). His main assumption was that

> the development of object relations is a circular process depending on a well-balanced interplay between infant and mother (or a mother-surrogate). Specifically, there is more or less general agreement that on the one hand learning, or what we call 'structure formation' is greatly dependent on early object relationship, and that on the other hand the nature of this object relationship depends on the endowment, growth, maturation, and structure formation of the infant, as well as on the response of the environment, mainly the mother to the infant. There is . . . an increasing conviction that this circular process starts at birth . . . and may begin even *in utero* [p. 243].

Schur cites the formulation of the psychobiologist, Schneirla (1959), that "approach" and "withdrawal" are the two basic biological responses. These two basic responses, in the course of evolution, develop into such responses as "seeking" and "avoidance" resulting in changing

> an animal from a "biophysiological" to a "biopsychological" entity. This phylogenetic development is repeated in the ontogenesis of man. Schneirla [demonstrated] that stimuli of low intensity generally initiate approach responses, while stimuli of high intensity initiate withdrawal. Such stimuli can be chemical, thermal, olfactory, optic, acoustic, etc. The differentiation between low- and high-intensity stimuli is species-specific; it depends in man also on individual variations, present already at birth [p. 243].

Schur points out that "both the approach and the withdrawal responses require the presence of some executive apparatuses." In the human infant, there are present such vital "apparatuses for approach as rooting, sucking, and grasping" (p. 243), which will lead to gratification. Gratification will in turn lead to learning and structure formation.

Analytically (Freud, 1900), this was conceptualized "as the development of a 'wish' which presupposes the establishment of memory traces of gratification. The establishment of wishes represents the transition from a biophysiological to biopsychological entity; from 'approach' to 'seeking' . . . the transition from the functioning of 'primary autonomous apparatuses' to structure formation" (p. 243).

Schur contrasts the development of the approach response with that of the withdrawal response and its executive apparatuses. In sharp contrast to the former, its equipment for withdrawal is extremely limited. More important, it is

> inadequate for withdrawal from the most frequent and intense stimulation, which arises from the inside. The infant therefore reacts with *diffuse* (startle) reactions which invariably spill over into vegetative discharge (full somatization) . . . . Approach is well channeled, circumscribed, and brings gratification. Equipment for withdrawal is inadequate and cannot eliminate intensive (traumatic) stimulation. . . . Successful withdrawal has to wait for maturation

> of the visual apparatus and of motility [p. 244]. The spitting out of the breast . . . the turning of the head which makes the object disappear, are therefore not only, as Spitz has stated, important stepping stones for the separation of the 'I' and 'Not-I', and for the development of the concept NO, but more generally speaking for the development of the crucial biophysiological function of withdrawal, which also is the model of defense [p. 244]. This poor equipment for withdrawal may be also the biological counterpart for Freud's assumption of the absence of the concept NO in the 'unconscious' (as expressed by him in topographical terms [1925b]). The maturation of the equipment and the development of the faculty for withdrawal are important steps in the shift from helpless passivity to activity. When we look upon the classic reel or peek-a-boo games of the infant from this vantage point, we may speculate that the infant triumphantly practices not only its mastery to make the mother reappear, but also its own ability to withdraw. We may also perhaps detect in the infant's behavior two variants of pleasure: the delight at the reappearance of the mother and the peculiar tension-pleasure during her disappearance, a phenomenon which much later may return in the libidinization of anxiety, for instance in phobic patients [p. 244].
>
> My remarks may allow for the following conclusions: (i) the poor biological equipment for the function of withdrawal is an additional explanation why a certain amount of traumatization is unavoidable; (ii) the maturation of such equipment may give us a clue for the expected tolerance of delay and separation; (iii) both gratification and also pain-unpleasure exert an influence on structure formation [p. 244].

In a further attempt to bridge the psychological and biological, he suggests that these biogenetic considerations are complementary to Freud's ideas as they appear in his paper on Negation (1925b, p. 239).

AFFECT THEORY

Schur's ideas on affect and structure formation, subsequent to the publication of his anxiety papers, appear in two papers, one written in 1960, the other in 1967 (unpublished). In "Phylogenesis and Ontogenesis of Affect and Structure-Formation and the Phenomenon of Repetition Compulsion" (1960b), an expanded version of remarks made at the 21st Congress of the International Psychoanalytic Association, his interest was in the "background" of the human anxiety response:

> The character of the subjective experience of anxiety can probably be attributed partly to instinctive givens. It has been postulated . . . that in evolution paucity of I.R.M.'s is paralleled by increase of the elements of conation, emotions, and subjective experience. This development reaches its culmination in man, where anxiety becomes an ego response. The paucity of instinctive inhibitory mechanisms against intra-species destructiveness in man may perhaps also explain the species-specific quality of guilt feelings in man. *Anticipatory anxiety and guilt feelings became both the privilege and curse of humanity.*
>
> Ego development results in a "realistic" appraisal of danger, and with it the anxiety response becomes increasingly dependent on ego functioning. What, however, persists is the special quality of anxiety and the availability of resomatized responses, which in states of ego-regression resemble in their discharge character the species-specific instinctive responses of infants and differ from them mainly because the discharge apparatuses have in the meantime undergone maturation and adaptation [p. 281].

He then summarizes the phylogenetic and ontogenetic considerations of the concept of anxiety:

> The affect anxiety is evolutionally linked with the biological responses of "withdrawal" and "avoidance."
>
> These responses have achieved during evolution certain instinctive characteristics. They did not, however, reach the status of a "drive." "Withdrawal," "avoidance" and finally anxiety remain, therefore, *reactions* to certain perceptions.
>
> Perception and anticipation of danger are evolutionally linked with the perception of the intensity of stimuli and with instinctive I.R.M.'s and releasers.
>
> The evolutionary development of instinctual drives and ego and superego structures, and the "internalization" of the mental apparatus in man, result in the gradual development of "inner," instinctual danger. The ontogenetic development of the affect anxiety reflects this complex evolution of both danger and the response to its perception [p. 284].

Seven years later, with his "Unconscious Affects and the Signal Concept," presented at a Panel on the Theory of Affects (Löfgren, 1968), but never published in its entirety, Schur evinced his interest in the connection between the ego function of cognition and the affect, anxiety. He extends Freud's original formulation and suggests that the cognitive factor is an intrinsic part of all affective responses. Noting the "general dissatisfaction with the current status of the theory of affects," Schur poses these interrelated questions: "Can an affect be unconscious? Can we reformulate Freud's signal concept of anxiety? Can we apply this concept to affects other than anxiety?" Reviewing Freud's thinking on the subject, he contrasts Freud's

> pragmatic, clinical approach . . . exemplified, for instance, by his early use of the term "unconscious guilt," as a crucial factor in the development of obsessional rituals (1907) [with] his need for explanatory concepts, which, in turn, made use of different frames of reference. . . . Freud's objections to the possibility that affects can be unconscious were influenced by his assumptions about the close interrelationship of instinctual drives and affects—especially anxiety, his need to explain repression in terms [of] the economic point of view, [and] his attempts to understand affects within the framework of the "pleasure-unpleasure" principle.

Freud's predicament was that his clinical findings prompted the recognition of unconscious affects, especially guilt. But from the economic point of view, he had concluded that affects were discharge processes. Schur attempts to clarify the dilemma by examining Freud's various statements pertaining to the signal concept.

He quotes Freud (1926) to show where the problem of unconscious affects and signal anxiety converge: "If the ego, by making use of the signal of unpleasure, attains its object of completely suppressing the instinctual impulse, we learn nothing of how this has happened" (pp. 94-95). Schur adds, "The whole process remains unconscious. This is what we constantly encounter in the analytic situation; the patient may not be aware of the upsurge of an instinctual demand."

Freud's pragmatic approach—for example, "Anxiety is a reaction to danger"—enabled him to apply the genetic point of view to the developmental stratification of danger situations. Yet, Freud, says Schur, was also capable of teleological-anthropomorphic concepts such as "The ego is the seat of anxiety," "We are very apt to think of the ego as powerless against the id; but when it is opposed to an instinctual process in the id, it has only to give a *'signal of unpleasure'* in order to attain its object with the aid of that almost omnipotent institution, the pleasure principle" (1926, p. 92).

Schur objects to such anthropomorphic-teleological formulations. "We cannot say that the ego *'produces'* an affect any more than we can say that it produces a percept or a memory. Most important, however, is the comparison of this complex process with a thought process. *If the awareness is comparable to a thought process*, it can also remain unconscious. I presented this conclusion . . . in my paper, 'The Ego in Anxiety'. . ." (see Schur, 1953b, pp. 72-73). He points out that Freud, in his discussion of the signal concept (1933), clearly established the close link between a thought process and affect, and adds:

> It is equally clear that this link and also the whole signal concept is not restricted to anxiety, but is applicable to such affects, or rather to some shades of such affects, as guilt, anger, shame, hate, and perhaps others: for instance, to doubt, a state in which cognitive processes and "affective" responses are important. The logical conclusion of these formulations is also that such shades of all these affects can remain unconscious.

He believes that

> the cognitive factor . . . is an intrinsic factor of the total response. This assumption can be extended to other affects, implying that all affects consist . . . of a cognitive process and . . . of a response to this process, although the extent of the cognitive component varies with different affects. Here we should remind ourselves that the cognitive process and the response to it occur simultaneously and therefore are inseparable components of the affect. . . . all affects have their ontogenetic and evolutionary history. We encounter in evolution a progressive widening of the cognitive aspects in specific behavior problems, although no animal develops anticipation and judgment comparable to man. . . .

> It is not only the *cognitive* sector of *all* affects which has its history. That sector of an affect which is generally considered the main or the only one deserving of the name affect—if we equate this with feeling, or more precisely conscious feeling—also has its history, which is an integral part of our maturation and development.
>
> The link between certain cognitive elements and a certain quality of affect is partly based on innate givens and is therefore species-specific. Maturation and development, in constant interaction with the environment, account for the wide range of behavioral manifestations of affects which are essential for the uniqueness of our species and also guarantee the very special qualities of each individual. They also account for the variations of the somatic manifestations.

Schur does not want to give the impression that he is "disregarding or even discarding the importance of economic formulations for the psychoanalytic theory of affects," and therefore carefully delineates the limits of his objections:

> Freud's definition of affects as composite states including motor innervations and discharge processes; the transformation into a different quota of affect. . . . Freud's differentiation between "affects" and "ideas," based mainly on an economic formulation. . . . The close link between the theory of affects and the unpleasure-pleasure principles . . .

Noting that Freud had at first equated unpleasure with increase of tension, and pleasure with discharge of tension, Schur points out the dilemma:

> This *is* an economic formulation regardless of the fact that Freud himself and others after him, . . . [could not] explain pleasurable experiences as sexual foreplay and orgasm within the framework of this concept. . . .
>
> The unpleasure-pleasure principles retain their importance as regulatory of mental functioning. However, the inclusion of the cognitive factor as an intrinsic part of the affect frees us from the *necessity* to seek for the explanation in various fluctuations of tension and release of tension.

Schur's final objection to Freud's older conceptualizations pertained to the latter's inability "to reconcile his pragmatic approach and the clinical observations which had led him to describe affects as ego responses with his older economic formulations stating that affects are *mainly* discharge processes." The economic point of view was important for Schur

> in such explanatory concepts as the role of neutralization in the various manifestations of affects and the ability to limit certain affects to the signal level. The progressive desomatization of affects in maturation and resomatization in regression; controlled versus uncontrolled affects, for the relative preponderance of primary process on the cognitive factors of affects and for the propensity to respond with the various shades of affects to the inner perception of the "dammed-up state." Economic explanatory concepts . . . contribute to our understanding not only of quantitative differences, but also of qualitative differences of various shades of the same affect, as well as to the understanding of complex affective states and moods.

SYMPTOM FORMATION

Schur (1964b) believed that the formation of a symptom was for the most part

> an intermediary step in a long and complex process. The symptom can remain an isolated phenomenon, as seen so frequently in childhood phobias, which can even undergo a spontaneous "cure." In Freud's metaphor, the symptom can be "embedded" like a foreign body. It can be in some way integrated into the ego organization by its synthetic function. . . . Both in childhood and in adulthood the further development depends not only on the intensity of the struggle [against the impulse, and then the symptom], but also on how many ego functions lose their autonomy because they are drawn into the cauldron of the neurotic conflict, resulting in the vicious cycle of instinctual and ego regression. It is here that the ego's response in various situations (anticipated danger, present danger, traumatic situation) becomes crucial, not only for the perpetuation, but also for the deterioration of a neurosis [p. 148].

Using phobia as an example, he describes how "a stratification of dangers is accompanied by a stratification of anxiety responses. If the reaction in the phobic situation is regressive and results in re-somatization, another dimension is added to the phobic situation, which contributes to this stratification of danger" (p. 149). And he summarizes his formulation:

> The sequence of upsurge of an instinctual demand perceived by the ego as danger, signal anxiety, eventual emergence of a compromise, representing both the substitute gratification and the defense, describes the *formation* of a symptom. We meet, however, in neurotic illness a stratification of dangers and responses which determine its course and severity. In accordance with Freud's definition of a traumatic situation, any disruptive ego regression assumes increasingly the aspect of danger, becomes the source of anxiety and of further layers of defensive manoeuvres. In the original structure of the symptom, the conflict is mainly *inter*-systemic. With further stratification of danger, the conflict becomes also *intra*-systemic.

Schur left in somewhat rough form another paper he presented that same year (1964). The massive exposure of individuals to the conditions in concentration camps during the Second World War, and the mental disorders in survivors constituted an unintended experimental testing on a huge scale of the relationship between innate disposition and environmental pressures in inducing neuroses. "Psychiatric Sequelae of Massive Traumatization" examines such data as the late development of symptomatology after release, the persistence of anxiety after danger is removed, the development of guilt among victims, and the failure of mourning to achieve its normal functions. He finds evidence that neuroses can develop, in some instances, without apparent predisposing pathology, while in others, innate dispositions may well influence the form of the disorder (manic-depressive psychoses), but need not necessarily be held responsible for the actual illness. His conclusions, drawing on the continuum concept, are significant in relation to medicolegal as well as psychiatric problems.

BODY-MIND PROBLEM

A term that crops up repeatedly in Schur's writings is *Anlage* (or *Anlagen*). His preoccupation with the concept underlying the term is to be seen as early as 1950: "The first factor to be considered in the evaluation of the total condition of the patient is the 'genetic factor' which may manifest itself both in the somatic and in the psychic (mental) sphere" (1950a, p. 250). Fifteen years later he chaired a Panel on the Psychoanalytic Theory of Somatic Symptoms. His opening remarks (unpublished) explain his aversion to the term, psychosomatic, and again allude to the importance of the *Anlage.*

> I consider it a mark of progress that today's panel has been assigned the task of discussing the psychoanalytic theory of somatic symptoms instead of considering that unfortunate term, psychosomatic disorders, thus giving this subject a broader framework and at the same time blurring the frequently artificial delineations between conversions and "organic" changes, between abnormalities of function and of structure. . . . In our theoretical considerations, especially, we are more and more interested in the wider aspects of the mind-body problem, particularly with the psychological conditions under which somatization—or speaking in genetic terms with regard to adults—resomatization of responses can lead to abnormal functioning and structure. . . . There can be a linkage in predisposition between drive endowment and the *Anlage* for certain apparatuses of primary autonomy such as motility and coordination; between the predilection for certain defense mechanisms and certain somatic apparatuses serving as the somatic source for stimuli which, through mental representations, gain the status of component, instinctual drives.

In somatic terms, Schur thought, the pathological *Anlage* could involve not only each of the regulatory systems, the central and vegetative nervous systems, the endocrines, and the enzyme systems, but specifically, the "effecter organ" and any combination of these. He concludes that in "psychosomatic" disorders, "We must therefore consider not just *a* genetic factor, we are usually dealing with constellations of 'multiple *Anlagen*.' "

Schur's major contributions to the understanding of somatic symptoms were introduced in his paper, "Comments on the Metapsychology of Somatization" (1955). Here, in a skillful blending of the clinical and theoretical, he offers a metapsychological concept of somatization. This paper made it possible to speak more accurately of a psychoanalytic theory of somatic symptoms. The clinical feedback was immediate and profound, and it is safe to say that psychosomatic medicine has not since been the same.

Schur links psychosomatic disorders (as he then called them) to anxiety and regression. He discusses the consequence of this regression, the analogies and differences between the mechanisms leading to somatic disorders, conversion and schizophrenia, and, finally, the controversial concept of specificity of organ choice.

His hypothesis

> *assumes the interdependence of the ego's faculty to use secondary processes and to neutralize energy, and the desomatization of responses. It assumes, on the other hand, that resomatization of responses is tied up with prevalence of primary process thinking and the use of deneutralized energy . . . My hypothesis would assume that* [because the ego's response to anticipated danger has become thoughtlike] *the ego operates with secondary processes, uses thoroughly neutralized energy, and . . . these facts explain that somatic discharge phenomena are practically absent* [p. 124]. . . . *The ego function may deviate from the normal in the direction of the neurotic response by regressive evaluation of danger and by regressive reactions* [p. 125].

Schur uses as his chief clinical illustration a young woman with severe itching dermatosis whom he analyzed for four years. The woman was full of rage and expressed it freely. This did not accord with Alexander's (1950) specificity theory. Schur points out that Alexander's ideas are based on Cannon's (1920) theory that " 'great' emotions . . . resulted in a stimulation of the autonomic nervous system. . . . [and therefore] 'repressed hostility' must result in a 'damming up' of aggression and thereby in a 'chronic stimulation' of the sympathetic nervous system. 'Repressed hostility' then became a catchword to explain a host of somatic manifestations" (p. 130).

But Schur's patient, during the early part of her analysis, itched with any upsurge of aggression. Obviously, then, her rages were not having a cathartic effect. Later on, however, when although still angry she had more control, her aggressive outbursts were not accompanied by itching or eruptions. This leads Schur to conclude

> *that the emergence of somatic phenomena is linked to ego function. Ego regression, specifically, prevalence of primary process, may result in the failure of another essential function of the ego: the faculty to neutralize aggression. There seems to be a parallel between the prevalence of primary process thinking, the failure of neutralization, and the resomatization of reactions* [p. 133].

Schur examines the role of libidinal impulses in somatization. Because "the sexuality of these cases is predominantly 'pregenital,' . . . it is difficult to separate somatic manifestations of libido, aggression, and anxiety" (p. 135). He prefers to consider itching connected with libidinal drives their equivalent and not their concomitant. "More obvious is the connection between sexuality and the symptom of scratching" (p. 135), which may, in some dermatoses, have a clearly orgastic character. In many cases, it becomes the main or even the only means of sexual gratification, lending itself especially well to the discharge of sadomasochistic impulses. Scratching frequently assumes a compulsive character, and the battle against it takes over all the characteristics of the battle against masturbation.

Schur maintains that the first outbreak or individual relapses of the specific skin eruption come at the climax of an unbearable conflict, i.e., a situation in which ego control has disintegrated.

> It is in such deep states of regression that the patients do the greatest amount of damage. Such regressive states may precipitate prolonged relapses. It can easily be seen that itching and scratching can become dangerous obstacles when used in the service of resistance. The anticipation of such difficulties will direct the technique. Daily sessions are imperative. Id material has to be approached with utmost care. Secondary process thinking has to be encouraged first on the periphery and in areas less involved in conflict. Occasionally it becomes necessary to hospitalize the patient and continue the analysis during that period. The co-operation of an understanding dermatologist is essential [p. 137].

Schur points to a

> similarity between symptom formation in certain dermatoses, and hysterical conversion. In both, instinctual drives and defense find an expression in the somatic sphere which can be "translated" into words and "make sense" on a conscious level. However, this similarity is limited to the structure of the symptom "eruption" which constitutes but one aspect of the variegated pathology of such cases. They frequently often show obsessive, compulsive and phobic symptoms; . . . Libidinous regression goes much deeper, with prevalence of exhibitionistic and narcissistic tendencies. Differentiation between the self and the object is vague. The skin is being treated as both part of the self and as outer object [p. 146].

He also observes that patients with severe dermatoses, at the height of the eruptions, are reminiscent of schizophrenics. It is the "capacity of the former to restore secondary processes which probably represents a most significant difference" (p. 151).

With regard to the choice of symptom in psychosomatic disorders, Schur can find no "specificity of personality, of conflict, or of defense against one phase of sexuality, or of aggression and the defense against it" (p. 155). He does find, however, certain characteristics these patients had in common. They all had defective libido and ego development, tenuous object relations, and they all had suffered an unusual amount of early traumatization.

And he sums up with a diagram replete with intersecting arrows which he explains thus:

> We see . . . the innate factor which may be manifested in the somatic and mental sphere. The arrows indicate their mutual interdependence. The interaction of somatic genetic factors and the environment, under the influence of emotional factors . . . creates what . . . I have called the reactive state, indicating the readiness for reacting in the somatic sphere. Similarly, the term "emotional state" indicates the readiness to respond with neurosis, psychosis, or to supply the emotional background of "psychosomatic disorders." The arrows indicate the mutual interdependence of these variables [pp. 158-159].

At the previously mentioned Panel on Psychoanalytic Theory of Somatic Symptoms in 1965, Schur, as chairman, also set forth his ideas on conversion, symbolism, symptom formation, and other related subjects. These have not hitherto been published.

> The mental representation of an organ, of its function, or of any pre-existent somatic manifestation, can be utilized through condensation and displacement—so familiar to us from the dream work—for the conversion process. This process plays an important role in certain somatic responses which repeat a previous somatic symptom, regardless of whether or not the latter was originally precipitated by emotional factors. This mechanism is quite characteristic, for example, for phenomena of the allergic state. Take the hospital patient who had several times been admitted for a localized contact dermatitis developing upon exposure to a certain dye, which dye also produced, on testing, a severe local reaction. Avoidance of the allergenic substance and local treatment always resulted in speedy recovery. When this patient found himself in an insoluble conflict, he broke out in the same rash, generalized this time, which responded only to psychotherapy! Here the conflict had taken the place of the allergenic substance.
>
> This example is typical of many manifestations of the allergic state, including bronchial asthma. It is an important fact with regard to all such somatic responses that once the pathway to a certain response has been established, the *same* response *can* be precipitated by a great variety of conflicts and affects, the common factor always being a severe regression of various ego functions which can result in uncontrolled anxiety, aggression, guilt, depression, and so on. This mechanism also plays a great role both in the chronicity of somatic phenomena and in the development of secondary symbolization.
>
> Any symptom, with or without somatization, assumes an organizing function for a variety of responses. For example, the symptom as such assumes the role of a danger situation. This may result in a shift from object to narcissistic libido. The involved organ or organ system and every detail of the symptom are drawn into secondary symbolization.

In response to the question whether the analytic technique can provide a basis for making a distinction between primary and secondary symbolization, he says,

> In any chronic illness—for example, ulcerative colitis, atopic eczema or rheumatoid arthritis—which has an insidious onset, it is usu-

ally impossible to decide whether the initial symptom followed the line of conversion, especially in illnesses which go back to infancy. In such cases, the type of conflict or affect which precipitates a relapse after an asymptomatic interval does not permit us to draw any conclusions about the onset of the disease. If, however, the onset was acute, precipitated by a traumatic situation, then we can make deductions about that onset, although probably only if a relapse after remission occurs under the spotlight of the analytic situation, and repeats in all its intricacies, the structural, dynamic, and economic elements of the onset. This I was able to do, for example, in my cases of Sulzberger-Garbe's syndrome.

Too great an emphasis on "symbolism" goes hand in hand with an underevaluation of the intricacy of the interplay of all psychic elements in symptom formation, and with a tendency toward oversimplified formulas. I need only remind you of the obvious danger of relying too much on "symbols" in dream interpretation, and of the importance of a proper balance between what we call id and ego analysis.

On this occasion, Schur took issue with the Engel (1962, 1965)-Schmale (1964) concepts of hopelessness and helplessness, seeing in these reactions ego states of response to trauma along a hierarchy of organizations at different stages of development. Thus they possess phase-specific aspects and are not simple repetitions of infantile experiences.

FREUD LECTURES

In recognition of his contributions to psychoanalysis, Schur was invited by several societies of the American Psychoanalytic Association to deliver their Freud Anniversary Lectures: in 1964 by the New York Psychoanalytic Society, in 1966 by the Psychoanalytic Association of New York (1966a), and in 1968 by the Philadelphia Association of Psychoanalysis. These lectures, the first two of which are summarized here, treat different periods of Freud's life. The first, "The Problem of Death in Freud's Writings and Life" (1964a), includes a poignant description of Freud's final years.[2] Had Schur, as

[2] This lecture is to be published in expanded form, under the title, *Freud: Living and Dying.*

Freud's personal physician during that time, merely presented an anecdotal account of his experiences, this in itself would have been a significant contribution. In addition, however, on the basis of personal observation and Freud's writings and correspondence both published and unpublished, Schur offers his conception of Freud's attitude to death, firmly refuting the idea that Freud, though depressive, and throughout his life preoccupied with thoughts of death, was ever suicidal.

Schur reminds us that it is possible to learn about Freud's early contacts with death from *The Interpretation of Dreams* (1900) and the Fliess correspondence (1892-1899, 1887-1902); that the impart of his father's death had much to do with launching him on his self-analysis, through which he reconstructed the importance in his later life of the death of his younger brother.[3]

Schur believes that Freud's travel phobia and his "obsessional superstition" that he might die at certain ages–42, 51, 62, 81–"yielded to his self-analysis," that Freud disliked not so much the idea of dying as of aging and losing his creative powers; that once he recognized the illusion we all harbor about our own immortality, "*he subjected this illusion to analytic appraisal.*" "The Theme of the Three Caskets" (1913d) and "Totem and Taboo" (1913e) both contain discussions of the analytic aspects of death. Schur states that the First World War made death very real for Freud, but he draws attention to the enormous creative output during those years, in support of his belief that Freud was not driven to unmitigated pessimism. In a letter written to Ferenczi toward the end of the war, for example, Freud writes, "There is really nothing strange in a man of my years noticing the unavoidable gradual decay of his person. I hope you will soon be able to convince yourself that it doesn't mean I am in a bad mood. I work splendidly and I can hardly control my appetite."

Schur corrects past assumptions and adds new data. In the winter of 1919, Freud started on *Beyond the Pleasure Principle* (1920a). It had previously been assumed that this work was Freud's response to the death of his daughter. Schur quotes a letter from Freud to Eitingon in July, 1920: "The 'Beyond' is finally finished. *You* will certify that it had been half finished when Sophie was still alive and

[3] Cf. Chapter 29, This Volume.

flourishing." But Schur assumes that that essay, more than many of his others, had multiple determinants. Freud had already passed his "second" dateline for dying. It is Schur's contention that Freud's formulation of the death instinct in "Beyond" filled an important function in his inner struggle with the problem of death. Schur suggests:

> The strongest driving force in Freud, the scientist, was his wish to know. To uncover an instinctual drive—even if it be the death instinct—permitted him literally to live with it and to make it accessible to ego control. I would assume, therefore, that the formulation of the death instinct theory—paradoxical as this may seem—may not only have steeled Freud to the 16-year ordeal of his cancer, but have prepared him for his belief in the supremacy of the ego, the intellect, of Logos—the only force with which he could face Ananke. It prepared him for *The Future of an Illusion* [1927] and for the formulation of a "Wissenschaftliche Weltanschauung." His eventual statement: "where id was, there shall ego be" [1933, p. 80] can perhaps also be seen in this context. If my assumption is correct that Freud's formulation about the death instinct was partly determined by his own need to treat death scientifically in order to accept it without fear, we may understand why Freud's reasoning, through which he tried to prove this concept, did not reach his usual unfailing logic and power of conviction. Freud's conflict in dealing with the problem of death . . . may also have been responsible for his seeking immortality in the protozoa, in the germ-plasm, and to find in Eros *some* counterweight to the death instinct. This train of thought also led, however, to the widening of the libido concept, to the dual instinct theory, to a new and better understanding of ambivalence, and to the concept of fusion and defusion of instincts.

Schur describes the fateful year of 1923. He tells how, when Freud became aware of a lesion in his mouth, there began a "tragic chain of deceptions. . . . F. Deutsch diagnosed 'an advanced cancer' but spoke to Freud only of leukoplakia. . . . Deutsch concluded from [certain] remarks that Freud was thinking of suicide." Schur emphatically refutes this idea. He states, and supports from correspondence and his own experiences and conversation with Freud, that what the latter wanted "was to *prolong life* as far as possible," that he "asked only for the assurance that his *death* would not be prolonged." Schur supplies further support for this view from his own experience with Freud in the spring of 1938.

> Denial of death and mortal illness is an adaptive defense. While Freud did *not* want to use this defense, it was forced upon him. That he resented it—and was even ashamed of it—may be seen from a letter to Deutsch: "I could always adapt myself to any kind of reality, even endure an uncertainty due to a reality—but being left alone with my subjective insecurity, without the fulcrum or pillar of the *ananke*, the inexorable, unavoidable necessity, I had to fall prey to the miserable cowardice of a human being and had to become an unworthy spectacle for others.

Schur sees in this letter a confirmation of his interpretation of Freud's motivation for formulating the death-instinct concept as well as an indication that already then, he wanted to be told the complete truth about his condition.

A passage from a letter Freud (1887-1902) wrote to Fliess in 1899 is particularly relevant here: "The act of deceiving patients is certainly not very desirable. What has the individual come to, how slight must be the influence of the religion of science, if one no longer dare disclose that it is this man's or that man's turn to die. Shakespeare says: 'Thou owest Nature a death.' I hope that when my turn comes I shall find someone who will treat me with more respect and tell me when to be ready" (p. 276). To which Schur adds, "Reading these lines with the knowledge that fate permitted me to fulfill this wish more than 40 years later was one of my proudest moments."

Marie Bonaparte, one of Schur's patients, suggested to Freud in 1928, when he had been without a personal physician for five years, that he avail himself of Schur's services. Freud knew that Schur had attended his introductory lectures and that he was an internist with psychoanalytic training, but he nevertheless needed persuading. Schur assumes his hesitancy had to do with his, Schur's, youth—he was only 31 at the time—and that he had not quite finished his personal analysis. He describes their first meeting:

> I was admitted, for the first time, to the inner sanctum of his study. There was nothing patronizing in this meeting of the sage

> master with . . . a young doctor more than forty years his junior. . . . he put me immediately at ease by acknowledging his appreciation of the way I had handled the treatment of Marie Bonaparte, and [expressing] his readiness to establish a patient-doctor relationship based on mutual respect and confidence. But first he wanted a basic understanding to be reached on the conditions for such a relationship. He expressed the expectation that he would always be told the truth and nothing but the truth. My response must have reassured him that I meant to keep such a promise. He then added, looking searchingly at me: "Promise me one more thing; when the time has come, you won't let me suffer more than necessary." All this was said with the utmost simplicity, without a trace of pathos, but also with complete determination. We shook hands at this point.

Apart from his refusal to give up smoking, Freud proved a model patient. "Only an occasional tortured look, a helpless gesture indicated his suffering. He did not complain. We developed over the course of the years a nonverbal form of communication. . . ."

Schur vividly conveys the horror of the years that followed. What with one operation after another, agony with the prosthesis, and the increasingly menacing aspects of the political situation, he could be grateful for small respites: "During the first few months of 1933 Freud's health was not too bad. Even the prosthesis behaved occasionally." Once, Freud dropped the prosthesis and damaged it. "He felt embarrassed about this 'slip,' but I told him how often I had marvelled that it had not happened before!"

Freud's preoccupation with the "Moses Problem" in the mid-1930's was, for Schur, a sign of new upsurge of creativity and of his will to live. Nor would he accede to pleas from Schur and others that he leave Austria. When he did finally agree to leave, in 1938, Hitler had already invaded the country, and he had to wait for legal permission. Schur tells of those dreadful days.

> It is hard to describe our state of mind during that period when we were all outside the protection of common law. Friends and relatives were disappearing. The Gestapo had established its headquarters, making torture the method of interrogation. It was not until quite recently that Anna told me the following story and authorized me to report it. When things seemed hopeless, Anna asked

> Freud: "Wouldn't it be better if we all killed ourselves?" To which Freud replied: "Why? Because they would like us to?" This is not a man who would have considered suicide in 1923 when told he had cancer! There was still the wish in him to live; to establish a new center for psychoanalysis, to finish the *Moses*—and also, from sheer defiance!

Schur had decided to remain in England so long as Freud was alive. But in the spring of 1939 he was faced with a painful decision. Because his American visa could not be extended, he had to leave for the United States to take out his first citizenship papers. Although he trained a colleague to treat Freud, he knew Freud disapproved his going. "He was used to me and in a way dependent on me and probably felt somehow that I was deserting him—and more than than, that I had given up on him. . . . Freud had no confidence that in my absence he would be told the truth."

Schur left in April and returned to England in the first week of July to find his patient much worse. It was difficult to alleviate his suffering. Only after he was able to help Freud during a nocturnal attack of "cardiac asthma" did Freud "forgive" him for leaving. "The old relationship was now restored. I was greatly relieved, not only because of my own feelings, but mainly because I knew that this would be essential to him during the last, most trying chapter, which was about to start."

With the onset of the Second World War, Schur, "to be at hand in any eventuality," moved into Freud's home. He saw the detachment which had marked these last years grow more pronounced.

> The last book Freud read was Balzac's *The Fatal Skin*, . . . On finishing it, he remarked to me with apparent casualness: "That was the proper book for me." Until preparing for this lecture, I had not read the book. . . . This novel had been written in the spirit of . . . Goethe's *Faust*. Both Balzac's hero, Raphael, and Goethe's Faust make a pact with the devil. Raphael is given a magic but fatal skin of a wild ass. All his wishes will be fulfilled—but with every fulfilled wish the skin will shrink, and along with it his life. Raphael cannot master his wishes, and tries in vain to deny them. He cannot master the fear of death, and dies in hopeless panic. . . . Freud, . . . in contrast to Raphael, had overcome all his fears, as far

as this is humanly possible. But he was so desperately tired that he had only one wish left, one that can best be expressed in the words of one of Goethe's most beautiful poems:

You who come from Heaven
Allaying every pain and grief
Fill with doubly-measured calm
Him who doubly wretched is.
How tired I am of this struggle,
Why this senseless pain and joy?
Come, sweet Peace
Come, oh come to my breast.

Schur's second Anniversary lecture, "Some Additional 'Day Residues' of the Specimen Dream in Psychoanalysis" (1966a), takes us back to Freud's middle years, to the beginning of his analytic discoveries. The theme common to both lectures, the study of Freud's adaptive processes under severe stress, is in keeping with the main body of Schur's work. In this second lecture he examines the transference aspects of Freud's relationship with Fliess, with particular reference to the Irma dream.

A study of unpublished portions of the Fliess correspondence led Schur to the discovery of an unknown case of Freud's which, he believes, contributed to the formation of this dream. His aim is to show, by using only Freud's own words, how "transference phenomena manifested themselves in an episode preceding the Irma dream, influenced the content of that dream and Freud's associations to it, and probably also interfered to some extent with its interpretation" (1966a, p. 49).

For some time, Freud had been systematically analyzing dreams, his own, his patients', and those garnered for him by his friends and colleagues; but Schur thinks the Irma dream was the first to which Freud attempted "*a systematic application of free association to every single element of the manifest dream, after which he connected these associations until a meaningful trend emerged* (p. 48). . . . this systematic analysis alone enabled him to discover the mechanism of the 'dream work' " (p. 48).

The Irma dream occurred in July of 1895. In March of that year, Freud was treating another woman, Emma, for hysteria. Like Irma,

Emma had been examined by Fliess at Freud's request, to evaluate the possibility that "nasal origins" were responsible for her somatic symptoms. Fliess came to Vienna and recommended surgery. Schur notes the similarity between his subsequent operation on Emma (on the turbinate bone and one of the sinuses) with the content of the Irma dream.

From Freud's letters, it was possible to reconstruct the subsequent events. There was a stormy postoperative period. It was discovered that Fliess had left some iodoform gauze in the wound. Emma almost died when it was removed. Freud was present when the gauze was removed, felt sick when he saw her go into vascular collapse, and fled into the next room. He wrote to Fliess (the italics are Schur's):

> . . . I don't think I had been overwhelmed by the blood; affects were welling up in me at that moment. *So we had done her an injustice. She had not been abnormal at all, but a piece of iodoform gauze had gotten torn off when you removed the rest and stayed in for fourteen days*, interfering with the healing process, after which it had torn away and provoked the bleeding. The fact that this mishap should have happened to *you*, how you would react to it when you learned about it, what others would make of it, how wrong I had been to press you to operate in a foreign city where you couldn't handle the aftercare, how my intention of getting the best for the poor girl was insidiously thwarted, with the resultant danger of her life—all this came over me simultaneously. I have worked it off by now. I *was not sufficiently clear-headed to think of reproaching R. at that moment.* That occurred to me only ten minutes later; . . .

Schur points out that Freud was, throughout the entire episode, under the dominance of feelings rather than of logical thinking, a circumstance characteristic of transference.

He connects some of the links of the Emma episode and the Irma dream.

> Here was a patient being treated by Freud for hysteria, who *did* have an organic, largely "iatrogenic" illness; who had narrowly escaped death because a physician really had committed an error;

> whose pathology was located in the nasal cavity; whose case had confronted Freud with a number of emergencies requiring him urgently to call in several consultants, all of whom had been helpless and confused; Emma's lesion had a fetid odor (propylamyl); Freud had had to look repeatedly into her nose and mouth. The most pertinent link is to be found in Freud's attitude toward Fliess, reflected in his letters about the Emma affair, his associations about Fliess in connection with the manifest dream content and his final interpretation of the dream.
>
> [The letter] reads like a record of an analytic session. The explanation is obvious. Freud was by that time already in "analysis" at a stage where the "material" was pouring out in free associations. While Freud was in the main, his own analyst, he was manifesting at this stage in his relationship with Fliess what we would now call transference phenomena, and he could not yet afford to abandon his positive "transference" to Fliess [p. 68].

Only after he completed his self-analysis, following the death of his father in 1896, did Freud resolve his transference relationship with Fliess, a process that took several years. In 1895 Freud was quite unconscious of the transference elements of the relationship. And whereas he interpreted his Irma dream as a wish to exculpate himself from guilt with reference to Irma, Schur sees the additional element of Freud's wishing to exculpate Fliess (with reference to Emma) as well, "because only by keeping Fliess strong and 'steady' could he preserve both his ego ideal and his own security" (p. 73).

The Irma dream, in itself, is a milestone; Schur's additions give it still wider significance. Schur's interpretation of the Irma dream in no way invalidates Freud's; it merely adds to it.

Max Schur's theoretical concepts have profoundly augmented our understanding of the development, maturation, and functioning of the human mind. His contributions add further structure to psychoanalysis as a general psychology of human behavior. At a time when many of the basic psychoanalytic tenets were being challenged or undergoing reappraisal, he brought metapsychology out of the classroom and discussion hall into the analyst's office where it could be applied therapeutically.

I emerged from this study of Schur's work with a heightened appreciation of his skill as a clarifier, of his ability to hold Freud in the highest respect and affection without slavishly accepting all his ideas.

Schur disliked ambiguity, and the nature of his contributions reflected that dislike.

Max Schur's papers were written when he was past the age of 50, long after the period during which most men are capable of intensive creative effort and productivity. His papers testify to the validity of the analytic thesis, implicit in all his writing, that the human spirit is equal to extraordinary achievements when the ego, "that wonderful organ of adaptation," is free to express its full potential.

CHAPTER 3

The Id and the Regulatory Principles of Mental Functioning

Henry Rosner, M.D.,
Victor H. Rosen, M.D.,
and Hans Loewald, M.D.

EXEGESIS—HENRY ROSNER, M.D.

Schur's studies repeatedly brought him back to the origins of psychic structure and thus to the id. In his monograph, *The Id and the Regulatory Principles of Mental Functioning* (1966a), he shows that historically the concept, id, was still the least understood of the psychic structures and that there were many unanswered theoretical questions related to it. He postulates that the id has structure, and he describes his concept of that structure. His study of this most enigmatic and poorly-defined part of the psychic apparatus was motivated by his desire to try to resolve some of the ambiguities resulting from Freud's various statements, made both before and after he had formulated his structural theory.

Schur reviews what is known about the id, its relation to the primary process, the pleasure-unpleasure principle, and the instinctual

---

Dr. Rosner is Associate Clinical Professor, Division of Psychoanalytic Education, Department of Psychiatry, State University of New York, Downstate Medical Center, Brooklyn, New York.

Dr. Rosen is Clinical Professor of Psychiatry, Albert Einstein College of Medicine, New York City.

Dr. Loewald is Associate Clinical Professor of Psychiatry, Yale Medical School.

drives. In doing so, he implicitly, if not explicitly, opposes the views of those who may wish to eliminate or ignore some of Freud's early ideas as not relevant or necessary. Referring to Freud's (1915, pp. 121-122) definition, he stresses that "far-reaching conclusions can be drawn from one sentence which designated an instinctual drive as the psychic representative of somatic stimuli." "A mental representation," says Schur, ". . . is based on a memory trace. A memory trace in turn presupposes a perception of a stimulus which may originate from within or without the organism. Perception and memory are generally considered to be ego functions" (p. 38). Does the id have such functions? It is this ambiguity which characterizes the concept, id, and has to be clarified. Should the id be restricted to an energy concept, which would solve the problem, there would still remain the question of mental life before the ego. It is Schur's belief that reduction of the id to a pure energy concept, if pursued to its logical conclusion, would necessitate a complete reformulation of most analytic concepts. He prefers to examine the problem from the complete metapsychological points of view not merely the economic one.

In reviewing previous formulations concerning the id, he assumes that it has evolutional and developmental aspects, an assumption he had made in passing in earlier papers and discussions (1950a, 1960b; Markovitz, 1963). If this is so, he continues, the id must have its role in adaptation. It therefore must mediate in the adaptive function of the ego through the pressure of its instinctual demands. Schur concludes his review of Freud's developmental concepts noting

> that one set of *theoretical* formulations implies that the id is present at birth, is conservative, immutable, indestructible.
>
> The *pragmatic* formulations based on observations are quite different, however. . . . psychosexual development from the oral to the genital organizations is always described in terms of *development* of the instinctual drives. These . . . are also applied to the structure id [pp. 59-60].
>
> On the one hand, Freud assumed that the id . . . contained all that was inherited. On the other hand, he also described it as undergoing maturational (sexual phase) and developmental changes (addition of "the repressed") [pp. 61-62].

Schur was in agreement with this latter ontogenetic view of the id, and he utilized it to support his hypothesis of the id as an integrated structure. His main, original contribution in support of this point of view is expressed in his study of the genetic development of the concept, wish, which he calls the "functional unit of the id." "Ontogenetically, the progression from a *reflex* to a *wish*—mediated by a change in the infant's inner environment, the availability of an average expectable environment, and the presence of species-specific executive apparatuses—is the function of maturation and development" (p. 66).

On the basis of his belief that the emergence of the wish marked the beginning of the functioning of psychic structure, and stressing that there is a difference between the physiological concept, need, and the psychological concept, wish, Schur proposes that

> *this transition from the functioning on the level of a reflex apparatus to that of a wish represents the developmental model for the transition from "somatic needs" to instinctual drives as mental representations of stimuli arising within the soma, and for the development of the structure id from the undifferentiated phase.* This proposition, which is in line with Freud's definition of instinctual drives as mental representations, must assume that the development of the id makes use of certain—albeit primitive—perceptions and memory traces (pp. 68-69).

Now Schur offers his explanation of the original ambiguity regarding the concept id that he noted previously. How could it be that the id makes use of perception and memory which are considered to be ego functions?

> Some developmental considerations, both phylogenetic and ontogenetic, are in order here. We must always remind ourselves that the organism starts at birth with an *Anlage* and with certain apparatuses. Hartmann, who has taught us the importance of such innate apparatuses, traced their development mainly from the vantage point of ego development. *Nothing prevents us from assuming, however, that what we call the id also uses such innate apparatuses in its own development* [p. 69].

He quotes Fisher's research (1965) to show that this formulation has both been confirmed in recent research on sleep and dreaming and has "contributed to a possible explanation of the fact that the stage 1 of rapid eye movements is present at birth, at a time when, as Fisher says, it is inconceivable that dreaming is taking place because psychic structure has not yet developed."

His thesis focuses on the assumption that if "the id is subject to development and . . . utilizes some percepts and memory traces," then there must be an interaction between the *development* of the id and *development* of perception and memory. Such interaction has been studied mainly in relation to early ego development" (p. 70). He prefers to approach the problem from the point of view of the id. To this end, he lists certain characteristics of the infant's innate equipment and early development–the lability of its homeostatic equilibrium; its "low threshold of response to some kinds of perception of stimuli originating" from within; its much higher threshold against external stimuli; its tendency to progress in a cephalocaudal direction; and the self-propelling quality of each stage of maturation which results in "a spiraling effect in sensorimotor perception" (pp. 71-72).

> I postulate that all these factors, including the primary autonomous apparatuses, which are recognized to have such an important bearing on the early development of ego structures, also contribute to the development of the id out of the undifferentiated phase [p. 72].

Schur re-examines the development of the "wish" as follows:

> If the wish to establish a perceptual identity . . . is, so to speak, the functional prototype of the id, then it stands to reason to assume that the complexity of this experience of satisfaction will increase with the range of sensorimotor perception and the simultaneous development of neural trace affects [p. 72].

Examining the integral relationship between the id and primary process, Schur reviews how others have used the term, primary process and expresses concern with attempts to restrict it exclusively to an energy formulation. He stresses the need to distinguish between the functional manifestations of a structure or process, and hypothetical constructs which attempt to account for some of these manifestations. Schur prefers the formulation "thought organized according to the primary or secondary process" (Rapaport, 1951c) to "primary-process thinking."

In line with his previous work, Schur, applying the two concepts of a continuum and the complementary series, believes that both the id and the ego use thought processes organized according to the primary process.

> The mental functions organized according to the primary process range, therefore, from the most primitive elements that we attribute to the id, based chiefly on primitive perception and memory traces, to such relatively complex processes as fantasies also based on the memory traces of object and word representations [p. 114].

Were the primary process restricted to an energy formulation, "the next step would be to reduce the id to an energy concept." The id would then have neither content nor structure. According to Schur

> we could then speak about instinctual danger only in terms of quantities of energy. . . .
>
> We could no longer speak of an *inter*systemic conflict between the ego and the id—unless we phrased it as a conflict between the ego and "an energy" or between various types of energy. The next step would be to speak of defenses and dangers only in economic terms. If we followed this line of thinking to its logical conclusion, we would have to end up not only with a purely economical model but with a "physiological" one as well [p. 115].

Schur had earlier shown in his discussion of the development of the wish, the functional unit of the id, that the id does have maturational and developmental aspects. Now from the genetic point of view and the concept of a continuum, he concludes that the id is "structural" and has "content."

He closes this section of his monograph with some speculations regarding aggression and then turns to the regulatory principles, namely, the pleasure-unpleasure principle and the repetition compulsion, as commonly expounded. Freud linked the latter with the death drive and the Nirvana principle.

Schur approaches these postulates, with the puzzling aspects they have long presented, along original lines:

1. He distinguishes the pleasure and the unpleasure principles from each other, rather than assuming they constitute a coherent entity;

2. He further distinguishes between these principles and the complex affective experiences of pleasure and unpleasure with which they have often been associated in Freud's writings and in the analytic literature;

3. He undertakes a careful scrutiny of the "repetition compulsion" from the standpoint of its clinical and theoretical justification. He finds that the former could be more correctly designated as aspects of regressive ego functions rather than as an id manifestation. And he not only rejects Freud's link of the repetition compulsion with the death drive (as do most analysts), but also with the Nirvana principle as well.

In reviewing Freud's invocations of the pleasure-unpleasure principle, Schur points to the many different ways in which this concept was used. On further examination, he proposes, on the basis of evolutionary and ontogenetic considerations with respect to the "survival value" of these regulatory tendencies, to recognize the "unpleasure principle" as applying to the necessity to withdraw from excessive stimuli impinging on the mental apparatus from without ("outside" in the sense of both the organism and the mental apparatus). Such a necessity for protection against excessive stimulation is also the basis for Freud's invocation of a "protective barrier." The concept of a pleasure principle applies best to the need to re-create any situation of satisfaction (or, as in the case of the unpleasure principle, its memory trace) which is associated with the disappearance of drive tension. As memories become more complex, so do the conditions for the operation of these principles.

As a corollary to these views, Schur questions the assumed instinctual aspects of the unpleasure and pleasure principles. The former he sees as more primitive, but maintains, nevertheless, that

> *The need to withdraw from the source of pain and danger has not achieved in the course of evolution the degree of internalization which is the basis for an instinctual drive.* There is no motivational force to *seek* an object in order to withdraw from it. *We therefore cannot speak of an "instinctual drive" to withdraw from pain and danger.* (For the opposite view, see Brunswick, 1954.) There is only a propensity to respond to certain stimuli with withdrawal and certain species-specific discharge patterns. This response is the model for both the anxiety response and for defense . . . and it is regulated by the unpleasure principle. We usually assume that both the gratification of a wish . . . and the disappearance of pain-danger result in tension reduction. It seems justified to assume, however, that there are differences in the tension reduction in the two circumstances, both on the neurophysiological and the psychological (economic, structural, experiential) levels. . . . The development of many ego structures is required before the *need* to withdraw from danger (pain) develops into a *wish* to avoid danger. We can speculate, however, that the precursors of such wishes are autonomous and may also come under the influence of the pleasure and unpleasure principles [pp. 151-152].

The wishes to avoid danger and achieve satisfaction evolve into a continuum of complex id-ego responses which constitute the affects of unpleasure and pleasure.

Freud said that the clinical evidence of a repetition-compulsion had first put him on the track of the death-instinct. The constancy-Nirvana-pleasure and repetition-compulsion principles were then taken as proof of the death-instinct concept, which in turn is used as an explanation for these same principles—a classical example of circular reasoning.

It is difficult to escape the conclusion that Freud had already arrived at his death-instinct theory and was using the concepts of repetition-compulsion and of the "Beyond the Pleasure Principle" only to prove it.

As a clinical instance, Freud (1920a) stated that patients suffering from traumatic neurosis are not "occupied in their waking lives with memories of their accidents" (p. 13). Clinical observations, says Schur, do not confirm this statement.

> It is common experience that people who have had such accidents, unless they have suffered . . . complete amnesia, talk a great deal

> and think even more about them. They are concerned about every detail of the event, but mainly with one: Why did it happen? Could it have been prevented? . . . In severe psychosislike posttraumatic states observed during World War II, . . . the routine treatment was . . . to make the patient reconstruct the traumatic situation in a sodium pentothal interview, . . . rethinking, rediscussing and re-dreaming it [pp. 176-177].

A tendency to repress the memory of the trauma may be present. However, "*what the patient really wants is the undoing of the traumatic situation*, . . . using a mechanism so convincingly described by Freud (1909b) in his study of the Rat Man" (p. 177).

Returning to the post-traumatic dream, Schur sees a contradiction. Freud assumed on the one hand, that these dreams could not serve any wish fulfillment, while on the other hand he gave a teleological explanation for them. Freud was to repeat the same anthropomorphic formulation in *Inhibitions, Symptoms and Anxiety* (1926) when he said that the ego creates anxiety. He was aware, of course, "that a trauma can also represent a sexual assault, and that its repetition in dreams may represent the gratification of various id derivatives—passive, homosexual, masochistic and others" (p. 177).

In 1919 he added a paragraph to *The Interpretation of Dreams* (1900) which stated

> that "punishment-dreams indicate the possibility that the ego may have a greater share than was supposed in the construction of dreams" [p. 558]. The ego's wish in the post-traumatic dreams is the continuation of the wish of the waking state: the undoing of the traumatic event. *This cannot be attempted without the re-creation of the trauma. The anxiety in such dreams is the reaction to this re-enacted trauma.* The difference between Freud's interpretation and the one suggested by me is thus the following: Freud offers two interpretations . . .: (1) "These dreams are endeavoring to master the stimulus retrospectively, by developing the anxiety whose omission was the cause of the traumatic neurosis," and (2) they are *therefore* not under the dominance of the pleasure (unpleasure) principle, but are under the dominance of the repetition compulsion, which in turn expresses the instinct to restore an earlier—inorganic—state of things [1920, p. 36].
>
> According to my interpretation, the repetition of traumatic events in dreams represents—apart from the gratification of various id derivatives and superego "demands"—the ego's unconscious wish to *undo* the traumatic situation. This cannot be done without reliv-

> ing the latter in endless variation. The resulting anxiety is an ego response to danger, no different from the result of other anxiety-producing dreams, in which the wish represents a forbidden instinctual (sexual or aggressive) demand [pp. 177-178]...
>
> Once we have accepted the interpretation that posttraumatic dreams *can* be understood without recourse to the existence of a "daemonic force"—conceptualized in terms of the repetition compulsion ... it becomes easier to explain ... the other examples cited by Freud in support of his hypothesis [p. 182].

What is necessary is to apply the wish for undoing the past as a most important motivation for the repetition of painful affects and the re-enacting of traumatic events in the transference and fate neuroses. The analysis of such repetitive patterns can eventually replace the magical attempts of undoing a neurotic solution of a conflict.

BOOK REVIEW—VICTOR H. ROSEN, M.D.*

In selecting this work as the fourth in their monograph series, the Editors of the *Journal of the American Psychoanalytic Association* have demonstrated once again the high standards they are setting for contributions to this distinguished collection. Max Schur is at his best in this carefully wrought critique in which he functions as both renovator and innovator.

The formulation of the structural hypothesis served as a stimulus for investigating the more intricate details of both psychopathology and normal mental functioning. For a time the workshops of psychoanalysis were too busy employing the new tools to notice that some of them required more careful honing, while others needed redesigning to do the job for which they had been created.

Of Freud's basic concepts, few have gone unquestioned even by some of his most devoted followers. Most, however, have withstood the test of time with regard to both their internal theoretical consistency and their usefulness as guides to handling technical problems in treatment. The concept of the id has been perhaps the most consistently misused, misunderstood, and criticized of Freud's postulates. Some have contended that the theory lends itself to misuse and that the problem does not lie completely with those who misinterpret Freud's intentions.

---

*Reprinted from *International Journal of Psycho-Analysis*, 49:100-101, 1968.

The monograph is divided into two almost autonomous parts. In the first, Schur discusses the development of the concept of the id in Freud's work, the ambiguities inherent in its general formulation, as well as the ambiguities in the maturational, economic, and dynamic formulations derived from the primary hypothesis. The second part, "The Regulatory Principles of Mental Functioning," deals mainly with the pleasure and unpleasure principles, "beyond the pleasure principle," and repetition compulsion.

The chief ambiguity in the concept of the id arises from the attempt to conceptualize the id as unstructured chaos defined only by its energies and their modes of discharge, and, simultaneously, as a structure which implicitly contains primitive perceptions and memory traces for which a certain degree of structural organization is necessary. Schur unequivocally favors a structural interpretation of Freud's implicitly conflicting formulations. He says:

> *I propose that [the] transition from functioning on the level of a reflex apparatus to that of a wish, represents the developmental model for the transition from "somatic needs" to instinctual drives as mental representations of stimuli arising within the soma and for the development of the structure id from the undifferentiated phase.* . . . Hartmann, who has taught us the importance of . . . innate apparatuses, traced their development mainly from the vantage point of ego development. *Nothing prevents us from assuming . . . that what we call the id also uses . . . innate apparatuses in its development* [pp. 68-69].

This formulation, for which the author adduces biological, clinical, and theoretical evidence, clears the way for a re-examination of the pleasure-unpleasure principle and the repetition compulsion. The latter is the most unassimilated aspect of the concept of the id, i.e., that part which derives from Freud's ideas on the "death instinct."

I found the second part of the monograph especially edifying. Although some of Schur's exceptions to Freud's theoretical formulations are not new, the originality of their presentation is extremely helpful. For example, he makes a particularly felicitous suggestion in his discussion of the "pleasure-unpleasure principle." There are good grounds, both clinically and biologically, he asserts, for separating the "pleasure-principle" into two principles, a "pleasure principle" and an "unpleasure principle." Schur points out that "approach" and "withdrawal" responses are fundamental organismic reactions to different intensities and/or qualities of external stimuli. It is likely that as these two adaptive responses are internalized they become the bases for the regulation of the instinctual drives. This modification of the familiar formulation makes for a more coherent link between the concept id and its biological substrate. It also explains more consistently certain aspects of early psychic development where the strivings to re-establish perceptual identity with need-satisfying sources of stimulation, and to erect barriers against excessive stimulation, go on side by side. I should also remark in this connection that Schur makes an important distinction between pleasure and unpleasure as experiential phenomena, and the "pleasure principle" or "unpleasure principle" as regulatory processes.

Another example of brilliant exegesis and, to my mind, the major contribution of this monograph, is in Schur's discussion and reformulation of the "repetition compulsion." He asserts that there are no biological data which would support the postulate of a death instinct. The existence of those hereditary (or instinctual) behavior patterns which result in the extinction of a species can be explained more economically by the disparate rate of ecological and evolutionary change. A previously adaptive species-specific pattern becomes maladaptive with new conditions. Here, as in other aspects of the discussion, it is Schur's insistence on the methodological rule of parsimony that makes his argument so difficult to refute. He goes on to demonstrate that in Freud's development of his thesis on what lies "beyond the pleasure principle," the "repetition compulsion" and the "death instinct" are mutually interdependent propositions. Schur readily agrees to the clinical importance of the observations on the compulsion to repeat" and the usefulness of that concept for explaining certain regressive phenomena. He suggests, however, that all the repetitive psychological phenomena we deal with clinically can just as well be explained within the framework of the pleasure and unpleasure principles. To avoid the ambiguity of the term "repetition compulsion," Schur suggests replacing it with "compulsive (stereotyped) repetitiveness." This term, he feels, would contain all the familiar patterns of repetition in such conditions as the "fate" and "traumatic" neuroses, without the adverse implications of the unbiological "death instinct."

I do not think the author has confronted one methodological question as assiduously as he has others. Namely, the objection frequently raised by critics of the concept id, who assert that the term becomes redundant if one conceives all structure as part of a continuum. (Incidentally, the same problem exists for the concept of the superego.) I believe there is an answer to this objection, and that it is to be found in the discontinuities occurring in the attributes of some entities which are continuous with regard to other characteristics. Although the id and ego may arise from the same innate apparatuses, they may still become sharply separated systems by virtue of the manner in which their elements are organized. The Hegelian concept of nodal qualitative change emerging from quantitative increments may be applicable to this problem, but the subject is philosophically abstruse and requires more consideration than is available within the limits of a review.

I respect Schur for his ability to retain his demands for rigorous conceptual precision and consistency even from Freud, his esteemed friend and teacher, for whom he has so often expressed his admiration, affection, and intellectual indebtedness. By this work of pruning, reconciling, and elaborating, Schur has accomplished at least two important ends. He has clarified and sharpened the concept of the id so that it can be more readily integrated into the rest of the structural theory; and he has restored its links with modern biology in a manner which would, I am sure, have evoked Freud's appreciation.

DISCUSSION—HANS LOEWALD, M.D.

Schur's paper, wide-ranging, searching, closely reasoned, and dealing with some of the most abstract theoretical issues in psychoanalysis, requires concentrated attention and is not easy to discuss. I had the opportunity to read the manuscript of his forthcoming book, of which today's presentation is only one part, and an abbreviated part, because of time limitations. So much work and mature thought have gone into this study that it would be presumptuous to assume one could do justice to it in a brief discussion. What I will try to do is highlight and comment on some of the issues which have been of particular interest to me, as well as consider briefly aspects of some problems which he has not stressed, although I have good reason to think that he is well aware of them.

The work, of which this is the second section, is concerned with a reconsideration of the concept, id. The regulatory principles, pleasure-unpleasure principle and repetition compulsion, which Schur has chosen as subjects of today's paper, have particular relevance to the id and the instinctual drives, just as the reality principle has specific relevance to the ego. This is not to say that there is a one-to-one correlation between the pleasure-unpleasure principle or the repetition compulsion and the id, and between the reality principle and the ego. The regulatory principles, insofar as they are conceived as broad principles regulating mental functioning, mental life in its totality, would have to apply to all aspects or layers of it. Only the reality principle appears to be less inclusive, insofar as it is understood as a modification of the pleasure principle brought about by the exigencies of life, and insofar as the ego is seen as the agency shaped by these exigencies and specifically designed to deal with them.

One might speculate that it was Freud's idea of a *hierarchy* of principles which led him ultimately to postulate the repetition compulsion beyond and overriding the pleasure-unpleasure principle—as though he wished to enunciate three principles, the last two of which are modifications of the first, most comprehensive, and elementary principle: repetition compulsion; modifications imposed by the evolution from inanimate matter to biological and finally to mental life. The reality principle would apply to the highest forms of psychic life, but still be only a modification of the pleasure-unpleasure principle which, in its turn, would be but a modification of the repetition compulsion brought about by the development of life. In phenomena of human life which appear not to conform to the pleasure-unpleasure principle, one might then see evidence of deficient modification of the repetition compulsion; in behavior not conforming to the reality principle one might see evidence of deficient modification of the pleasure-unpleasure principle. I wish to make it clear that I am not committed to such a view, nor can it be said that Freud was. I mention it as a possible way of understanding Freud's hierarchy of regulatory principles.

Schur begins with an examination of the pleasure-unpleasure principle. Before doing so, he stresses an important distinction which he re-emphasizes a number of times in the course of his paper, the distinction between pleasure and unpleasure as used in the concept of a regulatory principle, and pleasure-unpleasure as affects or "experiences." It is in fact impossible to deal with the various aspects and implications of the pleasure-unpleasure principle, if these terms are understood as signifying solely the feeling of pleasure or unpleasure as conscious affective states. Confusion results, even in Freud's writings, when the applicability or nonapplicability of the principle is examined in terms of whether pleasure or unpleasure is felt. Further confusion may result when the question is raised whether it is the id or the ego that "experiences" the pleasure at issue, or whether it is the id or the ego whose wish is fulfilled or thwarted.

Freud in his earlier writings fequently used the term unpleasure principle, or the term pleasure-unpleasure principle. This is significant because of his basic theoretical assumption—from which he departed only in his last instinct-theory (life-death instincts)—by which stimulation and unpleasure are equated. To be more precise: stimulation, insofar as it implies accumulation of excitation in the system which is stimulated, the psychic system, leads to unpleasure, to a state of tension or unrest within the system which as soon as possible is reduced to zero or at least to a minimum. On the level of such a system as a psychic apparatus, stimulation, the accumulation of excitation, manifests itself as unpleasure; and any diminution of excitation manifests itself as pleasure. Unpleasure thus regulates the work of the apparatus, is the motive force of the apparatus. While it is true, therefore, that unpleasure and pleasure are not meant in this context as affects or feelings in the ordinary sense, I believe that, insofar as we are dealing with a *psychic* apparatus, unpleasure and pleasure are nevertheless to be understood as the psychic or mental representatives of accumulation and decrease of excitation, to be distinguished from the phenomena obtaining in purely biological systems (plants for instance, or lower animals).

What is involved here is the problem of whether and in what sense one can speak of unconscious affects, in other words, the uncertain status of affects in psychoanalytic theory. And it is not clear why the notion of unconscious affective states (which are not "experienced" as such) should give greater concern than the notion of unconscious thought processes or ideas (which also are not "experienced" as such). Thus pleasure-unpleasure, as used in the concept of the pleasure-unpleasure principle, to my understanding cannot be reduced to purely biological or purely economic terms, nor should they be taken as applying to conscious-preconscious affective states except secondarily. But the very term for the model situation for the development of a wish (Schur, 1966a; especially p. 68), namely the *experience* of satisfaction, indicates that something experiential, albeit unconscious, is denoted by these terms.

I believe it is justifiable to say that the repetition compulsion as a regulatory principle, tied as it is for Freud to the death instinct concept, does not go as far beyond the pleasure-unpleasure principle as one might think, except insofar as it enunciates the basic regulatory principle in more generally applicable terms, that is, in terms which apply to biological systems, and even to inanimate matter as well. It needs to be stressed at this point—and I fully agree here with Schur—that the concept "instinct" as used by Freud in the terms life and death instinct is a far cry from the concept "instinct" *Trieb* as used in the term instinctual drive prior to his last instinct theory. Instinct in his last formulation—Eros/Thanatos, life (or love) and death instinct—has connotations of primary polar forces universally applicable along the scale of cosmic evolution, connotations which were not implied in Freud's earlier instinct theories. Instinct, or instinctual drive, as used in the terms life and death instinct, is no longer a stimulus impinging on the psychic apparatus, which latter seeks to extinguish the results of a stimulation coming from outside the apparatus. In fact, what, in "Instincts and Their Vicissitudes" (Freud, 1915a), was defined as the task of the psychic apparatus in its dealings with instincts (as stimuli impinging on it), has now, in the formulation in "Beyond the Pleasure Principle" (Freud, 1920a), quoted by Schur (1966a, p. 161), become the definition of an instinct. And insofar as Freud, in the same sentence, calls an instinct "the expression of the inertia inherent in organic life," the constancy or inertia principle, the basis of the pleasure-unpleasure principle, is now called instinct.[1] It looks as though instinct now means regula-

[1] The relevant passages are as follows: "[T]he nervous system is an apparatus which has the function of getting rid of the stimuli that reach it, or of reducing them to the lowest possible level; or which, if it were feasible, would maintain itself in an altogether unstimulated condition" (Freud, 1915a, p. 120). "*It seems, then, that an instinct is an urge inherent in organic life to restore an earlier state of things* which the living entity has been obliged to abandon under the pressure of external disturbing forces; that is, it is a kind of organic elasticity or, to put it another way, the expression of the inertia inherent in organic life" (Freud, 1920a, p. 36).

tory principle. This, I believe, has implications for the whole conception of what a psychic apparatus is and does, and these implications have to do with the formulation of the structural theory—a theory conceptualizing the interplay of forces and the conflicts within an organization, constituting and structuring this organization, in contrast to a theory of an apparatus designed to reduce or eliminate forces or stimuli impinging on it from outside. It remained an insoluble problem for Freud to fit his life instinct into this new definition of instinct. While as a definition of instinct the formulation is new, it still contains his basic theoretical assumption, mentioned before. The inertia or constancy or unpleasure or Nirvana principle, of which the repetition compulsion is merely a broader, all-inclusive version with an emphasis on repeating or returning to an original state of things, fits in perfectly with the death instinct, insofar as the latter is "the expression of the inertia inherent in organic life." In this sense, the death instinct is really nothing new, not a conception which should have taken psychoanalysts by surprise. It seems to imply a conception of evolution as a circular, or spiral, rather than a straight line, movement. What is new, and does not seem to fit with the inertia principle (as Freud, 1940a, Chapter 2, clearly acknowledges), is the concept of Eros, the life or love instinct.

I am in essential agreement with Schur (1966a), therefore, when he says: "In *The Ego and the Id* (Freud, 1923a), the role of Eros emerged more distinctly as the disturber of the pleasure principle (which Freud at this juncture equated alternately with the constancy and the Nirvana principles, under the dominance of the death instinct)" (p. 147). Schur calls attention to formulations in *The Ego and the Id* and in "The Economic Problem of Masochism" (Freud, 1924a) which clearly show the emergence of Eros as distinct and different from the constancy principle and the Nirvana principle which are "entirely in the service of the death instincts." And in the latter paper Freud gives a new meaning, conforming to his conception of Eros, to the term pleasure principle, and to the term libido. I therefore believe it is useful to make a distinction between a pleasure principle and an unpleasure principle, as Schur proposes, and that such a distinction is in accordance with some of Freud's most significant later formulations.

I have difficulty, however, in following Schur when he claims that Freud, in his earlier writings, meant withdrawal from *too intense* stimulation, in stipulating the unpleasure principle as the regulatory principle. I maintain that it was Freud's basic premise that *any* stimulation gives rise to unpleasure, that he defined unpleasure not as *excessive* excitation but as any degree of excitation, and that this view was essential to his theory of the workings of the psychic apparatus as then conceived by him. His life instinct, Eros or libido, and pleasure principle as reformulated in "The Economic Problem of Masochism" (1924a), is a breach in this theory—a breach which Freud rather desperately tried to mend, for instance, in some of his speculations in *Beyond the Pleasure Principle* (1920a). To my understanding, according to Freud's theory as formulated in *The Interpretation of Dreams* (1900), the memory of the experience of satisfaction is cathected insofar as it leads to the extinction of instinctual stimulation, and not because the stimuli inherent in this memory are sought for themselves. True: if life instinct has any meaning it must mean that excitation, tension inherent in life processes, is sought and not simply abolished or fended off, that stimuli are sought. This, I assume, is also Schur's understanding of the "approach response." But such a conception (with which I agree) is incompatible with Freud's models, "utilized both implicitly and explicitly in describing the development, functioning, and protection of the mental apparatus, and its 'regulating principles,' " as listed by Schur (1966a, pp. 142-143), including the fifth model (experience of satisfaction, wish, and instinctual drives). Any wish to recathect a memory including certain stimuli was based for Freud on the unpleasure inherent in stimulation (in this context, stimulation by instinctual stimuli). The experience of satisfaction, as far as his model goes, consists in the diminution or extinction of excitation. To quote from chapter 7: ". . . the accumulation of excitation . . . is felt as unpleasure and . . . sets the apparatus in action with a view to repeating the *experience of satisfaction, which involved a diminution of excitation and was felt as pleasure.* A current of this kind in the apparatus, starting from unpleasure and aiming at pleasure, we have termed a 'wish' " (Freud, 1900, p. 598, italics added). Pleasure, the experience of satisfaction, means diminution of excitation. The experience of external fright, which Freud discusses in the same context (ibid., p. 600), is adduced by Schur to show that Freud, in speaking of the unpleasure principle, had excessive stimulation in mind (Schur, 1966a, pp. 133-134), and not stimulation per se. But it seems to me that Freud's discussion of this issue is concerned with the crucial alternative to the experience of satisfaction (as defined by him two pages earlier), in the absence of the possibility of its realization: if the excitation cannot be diminished by an experience of satisfaction or its recathected memory-trace, if unpleasure cannot be diminished or extinguished in this way, then another mechanism comes into play, namely the turning away from, the avoidance of the painful memory, i.e., the prototype of repression (Freud, 1900, p. 600). Freud's discussion of the experience of external fright does deal with too intense stimulation, but it does no more than explain the regulation by the unpleasure principle in this particular and crucial case; it does not deny or revoke the notion that stimulation which can be diminished by the experience of satisfaction is also unpleasurable and that this sequence of events, too, is "regulated" by the unpleasure principle.

My insistence on this issue does not prevent me from recognizing that Freud, even at this stage of his research, was keenly aware of the *phenomena* which have been subsumed under such terms as stimulus seeking, stimulus hunger, approach response, and that they significantly entered into his considerations of the experience of satisfaction. But his explanatory concepts, at this time, were firmly based on the constancy principle and reflex arc physiology, and predicated on the postulate that the psychic apparatus is a system whose function and purpose it is to reduce or, if feasible, abolish stimulation. As late as 1915 this is clearly stated in the introductory pages of "Instincts and Their Vicissitudes" (Freud, 1915a, pp. 118-120). Some doubts are expressed, without being elaborated, pointing in the direction his thought is going to take him in *Beyond the Pleasure Principle* and especially in "The Economic Problem of Masochism," toward the end of this introduction (ibid., p. 121) (see also footnote by Strachey). But I thoroughly agree with Schur that with the emergence of the structural theory and the life instinct, pleasure, libido, and thus a pleasure principle, take on different connotations. This has to do, I believe, with the important change of Freud's views on the significance of object relations in the broadest sense (environmental "stimuli") and the emergence of identification and internalization as crucial psychological processes.

I will have to abstain from a more detailed discussion of Schur's consideration of the repetition compulsion. Difficult, ambiguous, and controversial as the concepts of a repetition compulsion and a death instinct are, I feel that they cannot be easily discarded and deserve further consideration. This is true particularly if, as Schur so convincingly shows in his chapters on the id, the id concept deserves much fuller understanding and elaboration than it has been accorded under the impact of ego psychology. In this spirit, let me say a few words about the daemonic.

I don't think that Freud, when speaking of the daemonic, is primarily concerned, as Schur states, "with the consequences and not with the forces at work" (Schur, 1966a, pp. 168-169). For instance, in his discussion of repetition in "The Uncanny" (Freud, 1919c), published a year before *Beyond the Pleasure Principle*, he clearly is concerned with the daemonic in the sense of the power of early, primal forces and experiences (whether for good or evil as to consequences) which dominate life and which, insofar as they are recognized or intimated, convey the sense of the uncanny. According to Webster (1947), daemon (in Greek religion) is "a deity regarded as a supernatural power rather than as a person; hence, some being never definitely personified, but recognized as exerting power, especially over the lives and fortunes of men." I believe the concern with the daemonic is a reflection of Freud's working up to the concept of the id as something we are lived by. The id concept has connotations implying that we are lived by forces we never fully control or master, forces which thus have an impersonal or not quite personal character; forces which are earlier in time than what we might call the forces or strength of the ego, and which in a sense override all later developments and acquisitions of personal will and control, as though the latter were newcomers, superficial layers of the personality, not the kernel and essence of our motivations and actions. Schur, in his extensive discussion of the id concept (1966a, pp. 11-122) points out the fallacy of current tendencies to reduce the concept id to a purely economic one, although Freud in some ways has contributed to this tendency. It is also implied in a more comprehensive id concept that these forces, in pure culture so to speak, represent both the most creative and most destructive potentialities of the personality. The words "daemonic," Eros, death instinct, must be heard in that sense, too. Such potentialities, this daemonic core, the id (the psychoanalytic concept of omnipotence is related to this), need limitations and discipline to allow the conduct of a human life. But human life ends through illness or self-exhaustion, and in this sense it can be said that it destroys itself, compelled by forces beyond its control to repeat the cycle of life and death. If we look at the death instinct and the repetition compulsion in that light, perhaps the last word has not been said about these concepts and their range and validity. I am convinced that Freud struggled with such ideas, attempting to force them into the rather uncongenial channels of somewhat antiquated scientific-economic concepts and formulations.

When it comes to the examples Freud gives of phenomena and processes which in his view tend to demonstrate the rule of the repetition compulsion as an all-embracing and "impersonal" principle, it is my impression that he was not so much regarding them as "scientific proofs" for his new theory, but that he felt these phenomena contain a residuum of inexplicability in terms of his old theories, which made him grope for different explanations. As suggestive as Schur's explanation of the repetition of traumatic events in dreams is, for me such a residuum remains; and this generally applies, in my opinion, to the "resistance of the id," so closely related to Freud's conception of the repetition compulsion. This does not deny or in any way minimize the ego aspects of post-traumatic dream repetition which Schur so convincingly describes.

The repetition compulsion as manifested, for Freud, in the resistance of the id, leads me to the last point I wish to comment on, namely the relations between id resistance and working through. Working through is an activity in which the ego, but not necessarily or exclusively the conscious ego, works over the old conflictful experiences and their "compulsive" repetitions in current life and particularly in the transference situation. As I have stated elsewhere (1955), I believe that the term working through does not primarily apply to that sector of the analytic work which has to do with the lifting of repressions and the analysis of ego defenses, but most specifically to the work concerned with id resistances, the compulsion to repeat in the clinical sense, with "the attraction exerted by the unconscious prototypes upon the repressed instinctual process" (Freud, 1926, p. 159). There undoubtedly is, in this compulsion to repeat painful affects and conflicts, in the compulsion to re-enact traumatic events in dreams and in the transference neurosis and the "fate neuroses," a more or less prominent component of a "wish to undo the past" (Schur, 1966a, p. 189). But there is likely to be also—and I believe I am here in essential agreement with Schur—a wish for re-doing the past—not exclusively a wish to do away with what happened to the patient by dint of unfeeling parents or evil fates, but also a wish to experience, to deal with whatever happened in a different way. This wish tends to be thwarted by "the attraction exerted by the unconscious prototypes upon the repressed instinctual process." This wish would also be an ego aspect of the compulsion to repeat, not of the primitive ego and its magical operations, but of the more mature part which tends to repeat on higher levels of organization. Repetition is a term which requires further clarification; it should not be restricted to the meaning of mere duplication.

One also gains the impression that frequently there is a tendency in patients to stick to and repeat the traumatic experience just *because* of its age, so to speak, just because of its intensity and primordial quality; one might say: just because of its daemonic quality. If one wishes to speak of masochism here, it could be characterized loosely as a masochistic surrender of the ego to the id. One can sense such things particularly in some young patients: a resistance to having to give up something that is precious, whether painful or blissful, in its intensity and uniqueness—a uniqueness which also has to do with the fact that the event was experienced for the first time, something that tends to give experiences a poignancy never to be attained again, but forever longed for. Working through has to contend with such resistances, among others. If you say that I am talking here not so much of a death instinct in Freud's sense, but more of an urge toward the bliss and pain of consuming oneself in the intensity of being lived by the id, you may be right. Ecstatic states, whether induced by drugs or religious and erotic ecstasies, may have this lure where love and self-destruction, Eros and Thanatos are merged into one. Yet, with regard to Freud's death instinct and repetition compulsion, such things were likely to be in his mind, too, when he brooded over the death instinct and the fusions and defusions of libido and aggression, over primary narcissism and primary masochism and the repetition compulsion.

Working through seems to be the work of the ego to repeat "actively" what was experienced "passively," to repeat on a higher level—a level of more dimensions and further differentiated and integrated experience and functioning. Working through has decidedly to do with re-doing, not with un-doing, the past. The repetition involved here is not duplication or re-iteration, but re-creation, to be distinguished from reproduction. To speak of such re-creative repetition as a "compulsion" means speaking from a point of view which is outside the self, beyond the ego and the id and the superego, overreaching the pleasure and reality principles.

CHAPTER 4

Metapsychological Aspects of Phobias in Adults

Max Schur, M.D.

A series of panel discussions and individual papers have been devoted in recent years to a systematic reformulation of nosological concepts. While interest in ego psychology dominated such attempts, we should not lose sight of the fact that the structural point of view represents only one of the metapsychological points of view, as formulated by Rapaport and Gill (1959). I here apply this broader approach to that group of adult patients in whom severe phobias are the dominant symptom—and the phrase, dominant symptom, shows how unsatisfactory our present nosological labels are.

Let me start with a quotation from Lewin's paper on "Phobic Symptoms and Dream Interpretations" (1952): "Freud said that the manifest content of the phobias . . . . is comparable to the manifest content of a dream, that it is a façade behind which are concealed the latent thoughts that truly call forth the anxiety. Thus phobias are like dreams which fail in their sleep-guarding function and terminate with anxiety" (p. 298).

Dreams of phobic patients frequently give us a clue about the content of their phobias. A young woman I am using as a sample case reported the following dream:

> I sit in a taxi [taxis were one of her many phobic situations]. The driver turns out to be a well-known psychiatrist. He makes passes at me. He wants to take me downtown, to an Armenian restaurant.

Editor's note: This paper was presented before the Boston Psychoanalytic Society and the Philadelphia Association for Psychoanalysis in 1963.

The pertinent associations were: She had been told how hard it was to understand a certain psychiatrist because of his Hungarian accent. She remembered a restaurant where she once had an anxiety attack. Its name, "8 Bells," reminded her of "balls"; 8 = 2 × 4. Four was her "magic" number which, since childhood, she had to repeat compulsively. It stood for the two four-letter words. When asked about an Armenian dish, she remembered "Shishkebab." She now understood this part of the dream. She had a compulsion to pick petty fights with her husband, and had obsessional fears about his having an accident. During intercourse she had fantasies about biting his genitals. After reflecting, she said, laughing: "I had made Shishkebab a few days ago, and I was surprised that my husband liked it."

Obviously, I was the psychiatrist with the foreign accent. To be taken downtown alluded to her sexualized transference fantasies. However, apart from the dig at my accent, what was the meaning of the association, "it is so hard to understand the psychiatrist"? Here we have to make a wide detour and learn more about ego functioning in phobias.

Let us return to the comparison between phobic symptoms and the dream. The condition for sleep and dream formation is a withdrawal of cathexis during sleep which affects what we subsume under the ego to a much greater extent than the id. This withdrawal initiates regression with a resulting shift to primary process, characteristic of the dreamwork. In phobic symptom formation, something happens which is analogous to the partial withdrawal of cathexis from the ego in the dream, namely a regression of various ego functions with relative prevalence of the primary process. We will therefore first examine those manifestations of ego regression which are most pertinent for the formation of phobic symptoms and then try to formulate some of the causes for this regression.

I might interpolate here that when I speak of phobias of adults, I am of course aware that regression is facilitated by or even dependent on some arrested development (a term which I prefer to the term, fixation, when speaking of ego functions). In contrast to psychotics, in phobias neither the arrest nor the regression is ever *global* but is restricted to certain functions.

Most conspicuously affected is the ego's biphasic function of evaluating *danger* and responding to this evaluation. The emphasis on this biphasic aspect has been my main addition to Freud's concept of signal anxiety. Such patients behave, to quote Freud (1926), "as though the old danger-situations still existed, and [they keep] hold of all the earlier determinants of anxiety" (p. 147). Freud (1926) described the hierarchies of danger situations: the mounting tension from nongratification resulting in an economic disturbance, exemplified, for instance, by the birth situation and by hunger; the shift from what we would call physiological danger to psychological danger, from the economic situation onto the condition which determined that situation, namely, separation from and loss of the object, loss of love, castration, disapproval by the superego, etc.

Essential also to an understanding of the problem is Freud's distinction between a danger situation and a traumatic situation. Freud (1926) calls a "situation of helplessness that has actually been experienced, a *traumatic situation* . . . A danger-situation is a recognized, remembered, expected situation of helplessness" (p. 166). For reasons discussed in previous papers (1953b, 1955, 1958), I suggested a further differentiation between situations of potential and of actual, present danger. To a phobic patient, the mere thought of finding himself in a phobic situation represents potential danger. A situation in which he once got frightened represents a situation of actual, present danger which can deteriorate into a traumatic situation.

Both the development of the phobia and the deterioration of a phobic situation into an anxiety attack depend to a great extent—as I will try to show—on ego functioning.

In speaking of dangers, we must distinguish between "inner" and "outer" dangers. What are the inner dangers to which the phobic patient responds with all the gradations of anxiety ranging from a thoughtlike awareness of danger to uncontrolled anxiety in the anxiety attack in the traumatic situation, the dangers which motivate the phobic defense?

When Freud re-examined the case histories of little Hans and the Wolf Man (1926, pp. 104-110), he assumed that the motivation for the defense, the dreaded danger, was in both cases the fear of castration. Much ink has flowed over this statement, specifically over the question of the extent to which dangers linked with the prephallic phase are also partial determinants of the danger and anxiety in phobias. Freud himself implied the answer to the question when he established the previously mentioned hierarchy of situations, and said that *every* anxiety response has a hysterical core. Thus, castration is linked to weaning, the loss of the first teeth, of stool, etc. In Freud's two animal-phobia cases, the fear of being eaten, which Freud partly explained by displacement and libidinal regression, played a prominent role.

The literature on phobias describes innumerable determinants of danger (Bornstein, 1935, 1949; Deutsch, 1929; Fenichel, 1936; Lewin, 1935, 1952). The importance of aggression toward the object as a source of danger in agoraphobia has been especially emphasized by H. Deutsch (1929).

Lewin (1952), giving examples in which elements of the "oral triad" were a source of danger in phobias, summarized his position as follows:

> Accepting Freud's statement that the events of the oedipus complex and the phallic stage determine the anxiety of the phobias, we may nevertheless . . . note many instances where the anxiety is overdetermined and fed by pregenital fears. . . . For anxiety, though a signal, is not *merely* a signal. It has a content and is a sort of "memory." . . . Anxiety attacks not only serve as warnings; they also reproduce earlier life events. . . . I therefore see no difficulty or contradiction in the idea that . . . anxiety, even though it be a signal . . . of a danger of presumed impending castration, *should* also repeat and simultaneously signify some other anxieties, such as a fear of being separated from the mother, or of "being eaten," or of *any* fear that might be appropriate somewhere between birth and the oedipal stage [p. 311, italics added].

In summary: the ego of the phobic patient has lost, or more likely never has acquired, the faculty of evaluating many instinctual demands on the level of reality testing. Both sexuality and aggression mean danger. Castration remains psychic reality. Thought, fantasies, and deed are treated as identical, instinctual danger is equated or rather confused with external danger. It is therefore not surprising that phobics, apart from their main defenses of avoidance, displacement, and primitive identification, also frequently use projection.

So far I have discussed the id aspect of dangers in phobias. Let us now return to ego functioning. Upon awakening from an anxiety dream, one tries to recathect reality testing. This frequently does not take place instantaneously. Anxiety may linger on until ego control is fully re-established. If we compare an ordinary anxiety dream to a nightmare, we are aware of quantitative differences. Let me remind you of Freud's description of the feeling of helplessness in the traumatic situation. What is being experienced, both in the nightmare and in the anxiety attack of the phobia, is the ego's utter helplessness. This helplessness becomes one of the most important sources of *danger* for phobic patients. When we ask a patient what he actually fears in a given situation, he will answer, "I am afraid that I will get frightened." We treat this statement as resistance; we try to show the patient the hidden dangers, and may eventually get to important id material. However, such patients are not *only* "resisting"; they are also right. They are not *only* afraid of the danger of a disguised instinctual demand, they are also afraid of their own ego regression which would result in what I call "uncontrolled anxiety" in the situation of traumatic helplessness. It is this fear of anxiety which makes the anxiety in phobias self-perpetuating. I remind you here of Roosevelt's famous statement, "The only thing we have to fear is fear itself." If, at the proper phase of the analysis, we concentrate on this aspect of ego regression, we can recognize and then show the patient to what degree the relative preponderance of the primary process is responsible for the shift from "controlled" to "uncontrolled" anxiety, and therefore for the deterioration of a mere danger situation into a traumatic one. This shift from controlled to uncontrolled anxiety signifies in most general terms the failure of the ego to restrict certain responses to the "signal" level. We see similar mechanisms in the difference between what I have called "controlled and uncontrolled aggression." Zetzel (1965) has applied this concept to the distinction between the normal depressive affect and depressive illness. Moral masochists and patients with severe depressions cannot restrict guilt feelings to the level of signal guilt, and the obsessive fails to restrict doubting to a signal function. Obsessive doubting may enter into the evaluation of a danger situation. It is therefore not surprising that for this, and other reasons (which will be discussed later) obsessive and phobic symptoms are frequently present simultaneously or alternatingly in the same patient.

An important ego function has been conceptualized as neutralization of sexual and aggressive energy. There is a parallel between the degree to which thought is organized according to the primary and secondary process, and the degree of neutralization of cathexis. I have stated elsewhere (1953b, 1955, 1958) that the desomatization of responses, which is an essential part of development, is tied up with a prevalence of secondary process and neutralization of aggressive energy; that correspondingly, regressive resomatization of anxiety *responses* is linked with a prevalence of primary processes and the use of nonneutralized energy. Consequently we find in every phobia *some* phenomena of resomatization, which may occur in anticipation of the phobic situation; resomatization always occurs when the situation becomes traumatic. It may be restricted to the common discharge phenomena of anxiety, or it may manifest itself in conversion—or in "psychosomatic" symptoms. If resomatization leads to "psychosomatic" symptoms, this serves as evidence to the patient that the danger is real, and such symptoms become *the* danger to him. Failure to neutralize aggression fosters ambivalence and adds to the phobics' fear of their own aggression. Failure of desexualization permits the infiltration of many ego functions with fantasies. It interferes with autonomous ego functioning and contributes in great measure to symptom formation.

Another important ego function is the establishment of object constancy and the formation of stable, conflict-free identifications, which, in turn, are essential for the formation of ego and superego structures. This ability presupposes two interdependent developmental achievements: the child has to pass successfully the separation-individuation phase as described, among others, by Mahler (1968) and also reach a stable, realistic defusion of self-and object representation within the ego, an aspect discussed extensively by Jacobson (1964).

Let us examine this function in our sample case. Some aspects of the patient's ambivalent relationship to her mother and sister might explain why this function was tenuous and prone to regression and also add to our understanding of the genesis of her abnormal anxiety.

The image of her mother emerged as that of a basically kind, immensely devoted, but also ineffectual, confused, frightened woman with phobic and compulsive symptoms. Only after the patient was well advanced in her analysis could she see her mother's many positive aspects. The mother was deeply concerned with the physical well-being of her two girls. She saw life, however, as filled with horrible dangers, and their description constituted one of her main educational tools. The father, who suffered from emphysema and eventually died from a heart attack, was a veterinarian. He, and especially the mother, described most dangers in semimedical terms. The Merck Manual was her Bible. The number of situations in which little children could get hurt or become sick was infinite. Many superstitions were incorporated in her "do's" and "don'ts." The circumstances were reminiscent of Niederland's (1959, 1960) description of how Schreber's delusions repeated his father's manipulations.

It was possible to detect many of the dangers depicted by the mother in the phobias and obsessional thoughts of the daughter. Such environmental factors contribute to deficiencies of the signal function: if every potential danger is magnified, the differentiation between potential and actual present danger fails to develop properly. Therefore, any potential danger—and under the sway of the primary process, dangers are manifold—may create anxiety. For phobic patients the result is confusion. On the one hand they behave like children in a transitional phase where anticipation of danger can be conceptualized only when danger is experienced as present, when the child has to touch something hot and say to himself, "fire burns." In other words, *they substitute anticipatory anxiety for reality testing.* On the other hand, phobics take the registration of their own anxiety as proof that they really are in danger. They may also consider it dangerous not to be afraid of certain situations, as if this would mean to forego reality testing. The same mechanism, is also hidden behind many superstitions.

In her relationship to her mother and her husband, and in her transference behavior, the patient showed her needs for refusion. These needs and the premium put on physical illness explain why, for instance, she presented a severe childhood pneumonia—especially her stay in an oxygen tent—as a wonderful memory. These needs for union with her mother were reinforced by frequent separation from her. During summers and after an illness, the little girl was sent to recuperate at her grandparents' farm. Many anxiety dreams and memories of extreme sadness and longings were linked with this farm. These reactions to the *accomplished* separation made it understandable that illness was preferable, because then mother was always with her, and that separation which could not be mastered by an infantile, or later by a regressive, ego was the ultimate danger. This need for refusion and the fear of separation could best be analyzed both during her pregnancy and the first few months after her baby was born. Thus we could speak of a truly symbiotic state. She dreaded the delivery because it meant separation on every level. Later, instead of feeling *empathy* for her baby's needs, she identified fully with them. Her anguish when she could not guess a momentary need of the baby made her own separation-sadness accessible to analysis. Her difficulty in tolerating any of the baby's frustrations resulted in outbreaks of ambivalence, of deep guilt feelings, alternating with periods of mild detachment and depression, and also in some symptoms in the baby—mainly a sleeping disturbance and occasional manifestations which had to be interpreted as rudimentary depressive reactions. It was fascinating to watch the uncanny way the baby responded to her mother's swings of mood. Only with growing understanding could full refusion change into empathy, and could she permit separation and enjoy the baby's growth and development.

My patient's ambivalence was traceable to early infancy. Although her feeding had been handled with great overconcern, it was only after completion of her toilet training, which was early and compulsive, that she became a serious feeding problem. The patient developed, in the area of feeding, and especially of toilet training, an attitude of mulish stubbornness. (The special importance of this attitude for her symptom formation will be discussed later.)

The bright little girl early discovered her mother's insecurity and that both her father and her older sister were teasing her mother mercilessly. She soon joined the game; one of her most precious memories was that when she was about seven, her father listened with her to a radio program, the main figure of which was a woman who was always confused and always got into trouble. They would roar with laughter and say, "Exactly like mother!" She found great pleasure in provoking her mother, hoping to be punished and spanked. The latter never happened, especially because she was so cute and pretty; the mother just became unhappy, and the girl felt remorseful.

With her sister, five years her senior, she was more successful. She would provoke the sister into hitting her, whereupon she—although not actually hurt—screamed lustily. The frightened sister begged her to hit back, which she always refused to do.

Her relationship with her mother was also pathological. She loved to creep into her mother's bed and be physically close to her. Relatively early in her analysis, she became aware of the sexual character of these needs which returned in her masturbation fantasies; but she also had to listen compulsively when lying next to her to hear whether she was still breathing. This intertwining of her wishes for oneness with her mother, her instinctual needs, her abnormal anxiety, her ambivalence, and her unresolved oedipal conflicts resulted, in her early latency period, in such symptoms as fear of falling asleep, of burglars, of fire, in a severe anxiety attack on an outing at the age of six, but also in obsessive thoughts and compulsions and in certain manifestations which we usually find in anal characters. What brought her into analysis was not her phobias, but her frigidity and her compulsive need to pick little fights with her husband, which in its structure was very reminiscent of the "game" she played with her sister.

Her conflicts about identification with her mother extended to every level and were complicated by the tendency to confuse and refuse self-and object representation. Identification with the mother meant to accept femininity and her own lack of a penis. It meant rivalry on the oedipal level, but also to be as foolish, "unsexy," unsophisticated as mother, to accept her do's and dont's, her threats, her anxieties, not to understand something complicated such as, for instance, an interpretation by the analyst. Identification represented danger and conflict because it meant both the wish and the fear of being submerged and swallowed. The confusing aspect of identification conflicts became most apparent when, after three years of analysis, she started to consider the planning of a pregnancy. To become *a* mother and be her *mother* were to her identical. The alternative to becoming a mother was not being *like* a child, but *being* a child.

It was characteristic how frequently this very intelligent, professional woman frequently talked in her analysis in a peculiar baby-like voice. To be a child meant giving in to symbiotic wishes; but also to cry, to be frightened or angry; to tease, to provoke. All these aspects she acted out in her relationship with her husband and in the transference.

To schizophrenics, refusion of self-and object representation becomes psychic reality—to the phobic, it means danger. This danger contributes in turn to *the* overriding danger, to loss of ego control, which makes control of anxiety impossible. We will see how this influenced the development of individual phobic situations.

Conflicts around identifications also inhibit superego development which, in turn, is essential for normal ego development. I will return to this aspect later.

Finally, a few words about the difficulty phobics have in tolerating what Ernst Kris (1934) has called regression in the service of the ego, and passivity in Rapaport's (1953b) sense. The fear of regression in the service of the ego is manifest, for example, in the phobic's difficulty in following the basic rule and in the ability of most women with extensive phobias to achieve a vaginal, truly genital orgasm. The difficulty in following the basic rule is reinforced by their experience that fantasies and daydreams, in which they indulge so freely, frequently end in anxiety.

Rapaport (1953b) has proposed two sets of models of both passivity and activity. His models of passivity are: (1) The situation of helplessness which ensues when mounting drive tension meets a countercathectic barrier and tension discharge is prevented; and (2) The situation in which the discharge of accumulated drive tension occurs without a contribution by the ego. His models of activity are: (1) The discharge of drive tension by means of the ego's control and executive apparatuses, and (2) the defense and/or control prevention, or postponement of the drive discharge.

The first model of passivity refers to a nonautonomous ego which does not regulate id-tension but rather is regulated by it, since the more the drive tension mounts, the more unyielding the ego's discharge-barring function becomes. In contrast, the second model of activity refers to a relatively autonomous ego, which controls, postpones, or prevents drive discharge in keeping with the demands of its own organization, but also in view of the whole organism and the reality circumstances.

Rapaport implies that transitions between these various ego states occur both in progressive structure formation and in regression. Phobics have both a strong unconscious wish for, and a conscious fear of passivity, which means to be flooded by id demands. Hence, an additional need for constant vigilance. Conflicts centering around passivity contribute to phobias of elevators, vehicles, etc. The relationship of these conflicts to the fear of regression in the service of the ego is obvious.

Let us see how various levels of ego functioning influenced the responses of my patient in phobic situations. First, a relatively simple example. She was afraid of walking in the park beyond a certain distance. On one occasion, she decided to go beyond a certain boundary. Upon entering the park, she saw some men. She was somewhat frightened, but thought, "Oh, again my fantasies of being raped." The anxiety disappeared. This means she could utilize such interpretations which had by now been integrated. She recognized the difference between external and instinctual danger, tested the reality, and therefore a situation of "potential danger" failed to deteriorate. Proceeding on her walk and approaching the spot which she had designated as the outer limit of her excursion, she again grew anxious. She saw some mothers with their infants in baby carriages, became frightened, turned her head, and found that she could no longer see her house. This was too much. In a panic she started to run home. What had happened? She was, at that time, contemplating pregnancy. The perception of mothers and infants occurred at a moment of tenuous equilibrium between dominance of secondary and primary process. The primary process won. On this level, she had only two choices left: Either to become *a* mother—meaning to become *her mother*—or to become an infant. To become mother was inadmissible on every level. She therefore chose to become an infant. But when an infant loses sight of mother-home, it goes into a panic and runs.

A second, more complex example: She was afraid of department stores. However, she decided to be brave and went to buy a new dress. She tried on what she thought was a very sexy dress. When she looked into the mirror, she grew frightened. Trying to understand why, she thought about her exhibitionistic, competitive wishes, which played a great role in her masturbation fantasies and dreams. She re-established a tenuous equilibrium and bought the dress. As she left the store, she thought of her mother and felt frightened and guilty for having bought such a sexy and expensive dress. Control was slipping, and she could not understand why. Only weeks after, she remembered that the department store episode was preceded by a visit to her gynecologist, who encouraged her in her plans to become pregnant. This mobilized even deeper conflicts around her identification with her mother, including, of course, all her oedipal conflicts. She left the store. She tried *not* to think. To be diverted, she bought a newspaper and tried to walk briskly a few blocks before taking a taxi to go home. The attempts to "understand" were abandoned. She now relied on denial and on using activity as a defense. She finally got into a taxi. To sit in the taxi meant to be more passive and increased the anxiety. And when the taxi got stuck in a parade, ego control disintegrated; the situation became traumatic. She got out of the taxi and did what she had never done before (or since); she called me over the phone, sobbing violently. The re-established contact helped her to regain some kind of ego control. However, after this episode her phobias reached the peak of intensity.

A final example: She went to a concert with her husband. She was afraid of concerts, of crowds, of sitting quietly for a long time. She found the music overwhelming and felt small and insignificant. Suddenly she noticed that a woman sitting close to her had fainted. She became very frightened, but managed, helped by her husband, not to leave the concert. Some determinants of this episode were obvious to her. Her sister had just given birth to a boy, and she had ambivalent feelings about it. The woman's fainting spell precipitated a primitive identification process. The overwhelming music added to the feeling of helplessness. It took weeks to understand some of the other determinants of this situation. We had discussed in detail the department store episode, and she was ruminating about her concern connected with a prospective theater party with her in-laws. She eventually remembered that at the concert, she had been wearing, for the first time, the "sexy" dress she had bought. She recalled, too, having the fantasy that her mother-in-law, who was sitting behind her, was jealously watching her hold hands with her husband: a primal scene fantasy in reverse. When she first spoke about the concert episode, she said, "You know, I was repeating to myself what you would tell me, why I got scared when this woman fainted. I knew it had something to do with my sister and my mother, *but somehow all this had no meaning to me*."

Because some determinants of her anxiety were still unconscious, there was no proper inter- or intrasystemic communication. The secondary process could not prevail. There was, on the other hand, no complete loss of control. The situation remained one of actual danger but did not become traumatic.

Now we could understand one element of the "Armenian Restaurant" dream: "The psychiatrist with the Hungarian accent speaks so that one can hardly understand him." This meant, "I cannot yet establish the dominance of reality testing in the evaluation of danger. I have only limited access to my unconscious. Primary and secondary process truly speak in different languages."

Why does the ego of the neurotic keep up its old determinants of danger? Before attempting to answer this question, we must discuss yet one other aspect: which part of the phobic system constitutes the actual symptom? When Freud re-examined the case of "Little Hans" in 1926, he stressed that the hatred of his father and the resulting fear of retaliation were not abnormal. What made it a neurosis was not the anxiety, but the displacement of the fear from his father to a horse. Freud then emphasized the boy's regression to passive, genital, and oral wishes.

Where, however, is the substitute gratification, the return of the repressed, which Freud postulated as the essential part of symptom formation? In terms of Freud's old anxiety theory the answer was simple: repressed sexuality was converted into anxiety. This concept Freud had to abandon. Fenichel (1941), when he discussed the consequences of the "dammed-up state," tried to fill this gap in Freud's definition of what constitutes the symptom in phobias. He spoke of anxiety spells as also having the character of an emergency discharge. For Fenichel, anxiety in anxiety-hysteria was not only a manifestation of defense, it was also a psychoneurotic symptom. This explanation is based on the theory of affect as discharge of drive representation.

Returning to Lewin's comparison between phobias and the dream, in a simple anxiety dream we can usually detect an instinctual wish, which is being declared as a danger by the not incompletely de-cathected ego. To this danger the ego reacts with anxiety. The sexual wish in anxiety dreams can frequently be traced to masturbation fantasies. Freud has shown how intimately conflicts around masturbation are linked with the outbreak of infantile phobias, and Arlow (1953) has called attention to the close relationship of masturbation fantasies and symptom formations.

In each specific anxiety situation of our patient, we could detect a sexual fantasy which usually preceded and precipitated the anxiety. Is, however, this distorted, regressive, dangerous fantasy to which the ego responds with anxiety, the only substitute gratification? I think that, except for the initial anxiety, which so often precedes a phobic attack, *patients with severe phobias derive actual satisfaction from the anticipation of their anxiety response*: they think constantly, often in an obsessive way about their danger situations. They have elaborate fantasies about them; *they play constantly with danger.* This instinctual gratification can best be described as *tension pleasure.* It has many roots in prephallic sexuality, as, for instance, in pleasure from distension of the bladder and rectum and from playing with the danger of loss of sphincter control. (The importance of bladder distention both as source of pleasure and of danger was clear in Bornstein's [1949] description of Frankie's elevator phobia.) Other prephallic sexual pleasures lie in the stimulation of the sense of equilibrium being tossed or rocked and in cutaneous tension pleasure, exemplified by sensations of being tickled, or itching and scratching. Excessive masturbation and/or excessive masturbation fantasies and the prolonged period of extensive sex play without actual intercourse, starting early in adolescence, which is so typical of our culture, is in some cases a contributing factor.

The first-mentioned type of tension pleasure from playing with the danger of loss of sphincter control is probably the most important source. It is not easy to see and even more difficult to show to the patient. We can find it in reconstructed material, in the patient's ruminations about their phobic situations, in the patient's insight after the disappearance of her phobic symptoms.

I have already mentioned our patient's response to her toilet training. She invented all kinds of devices so as not to use the toilet—especially before leaving her home. She always left things to the last moment, first the simple "do's" of her mother, later school assignments, household duties, etc.

After considerable progress in her analysis, we could discern two kinds of responses. One was an automatic "no" with which she would respond to a host of both reality demands and those of her superego. She recognized suddenly, to her own amazement, that this "no" extended also to suggestions to do something pleasant. The automatic "no" preceded the evaluation of the situation. In contrast to this "no," which genetically had all the earmarks of anal stubbornness, was a compulsion to do her household duties in a rigid order, starting with the most unpleasant chores. This compulsion she also extended to making her little girl (15 months) start with the less pleasant things. When interrupted in such compulsive activity, she would get angry. She would, by the way, during each session, say many times, in the midst of some—often quite pleasant—association, "Now I am angry at you!"

Such obsessive-compulsive symptoms are very common with phobic patients. In some symptoms, the return of the repressed is obvious. For instance, my patient's use of the number four as a magic formula represented her preoccupation with four-letter words. When we discussed the problem of tension pleasure, she confessed the following compulsion: she loves hot showers. Toward the end, however, she *has* to turn off the hot water and stand under the ice-cold water for a few moments. Hot showers stood for sexual stimulation, but the defense against it, the cold shower, created a peculiar, anxious tension pleasure of its own. The second compulsion went back far into her childhood and led us directly to the area of tension pleasure connected with sphincter control. For years she had to have a piece of tissue paper in her hand when going to sleep. When she told me about it, she made a slip, saying "toilet paper." This magic device she repeated during sessions by clutching her handkerchief in her hand. Many of her phobias had to do with time, distance, and the control of them: will the door of a subway or bus open before she will get frightened, etc?

I spoke about her teasing her mother. She tried to tease me in many ways. Her mounting tension during long periods of silence, her way of bringing important associations, only to stop the sentence at the crucial point, was most revealing.

It is not surprising that her phobias reached the highest intensity when, after three years of analysis, she finally brought into analysis her frequent masturbation and some of the fantasies underlying it.

After most of her phobias were gone, she felt quite nostalgic. Life was so dull without them. Only after she achieved a normal vaginal orgasm could she understand that one of the reasons she could not have one before was her enjoyment of mounting tension and her fear of letdown. Only then came the tedious working through of her many obsessions and compulsions related to trivial daily duties. Here, too, the pleasure of playing with deadlines and the libidinization of thinking was obvious. The working through of the anal element of the tension pleasure could only be achieved during the period of toilet training of her little girl.

We can now establish a parallel with the hierarchy of situations which we discussed at the beginning. When the phobic patient thinks about the phobic situation, he is not only frightened, he is also playing with danger. This creates a situation of *potential* danger. When he enters the situation, the danger is *present.* The equilibrium becomes precarious. The fantasy has perhaps carried too far, and, for the many reasons discussed previously, the regressing ego cannot cope with instinctual and external dangers. If the controls break down, the situation becomes a traumatic one.

We may now return to the thorny question of the relative importance of preoedipal and oedipal conflicts in neurosogenesis. I think that with our increasing knowledge of ego development and its importance for normal and abnormal development, of the intricate interaction of id, ego, and superego, and of the total structural development and the environment, this has become, to a certain extent, a moot question. To the concepts regression or fixation, we have now to add the etiologic consideration of arrest, inhibition, and faulty development of ego functions and their interdependence.

Development is a continuous process, starting even before birth. Schneirla (1959) recently took issue with the biological concept "critical period" and stressed that every period is "critical." Not only the danger and therefore the content of phobias is overdetermined. In the reconstruction of most adult phobias, it becomes obvious that the patients had entered the oedipal period with a residue of unresolved conflicts. This applies also to those cases in which the development of a phobia could be observed in *statu nascendi* as in Schnurmann's (1949) observations from the Hampstead Nursery, and to reconstructive analysis of childhood phobias. Bornstein's (1949) unsurpassed presentation of Frankie describes the preoedipal components of his anxiety, the danger of the overwhelming sadness he had to suffer after the trauma of having been abandoned by his mother. Erikson (1950) has especially emphasized how the residue of conflicts from each developmental phase influences the fate of the next one, basing his application of the epigenetic concept to psychoanalysis on this fact. (Spitz used the epigenetic concept within a different framework.) All of which emphasizes Freud's thesis about the interdependence of fixation and regression. I do not mean to deny the *crucial* importance of the oedipal phase. Its impact depends, however, on the child's instinctual and ego development when he reaches this phase, in which *the full development of a symptom neurosis* takes place.

Phobic patients often have a long history of early sexual stimulation. This applies to my example and is strikingly apparent in most published cases of severe phobias. Many such cases approach closely the "early seduction" theme which Freud had to discard as the overall explanation of neurosis. This seduction is accomplished at least as frequently by contemporaries as by incestuous figures. I also have the impression that many of these patients, especially females, are themselves quite seductive at an early age. There is accordingly, later on, a prolonged conflict around masturbation, a predilection for foreplay and an inability to achieve genital satisfaction, which is more transparent in a female patient. They not only usually fail to achieve a vaginal orgasm, but often cannot permit themselves clitoral stimulation and masturbation. This in turn is linked with their severe castration conflicts and their image of the genital region as cloaca. *They live therefore in a state of frustration.* This type of sexuality shares with infantile sexuality the lack of real discharge. The constant state of frustration promotes the development of what one could call a pansexualism, and with it a tendency to experience so many situations of daily life in terms of sexual symbolism. The clinical observation of this undeniable fact was the basis for Freud's concept of an actual neurosis, where anxiety and a host of somatic phenomena were the prevalent symptoms. Fenichel had always emphasized the importance of the "dammed up state" for most neuroses. I have seen in my medical practice many cases where coitus interruptus, which in previous decades was much more frequently practiced than nowadays, had precipitated such symptoms, especially in the female patients.

The clinical observation is pertinent, and the importance of the "dammed up state" should not be overlooked. The theoretical explanation, to which Freud adhered with such tenacity, has, I maintain, slowed down our theoretical understanding of the theory of anxiety and more than that, of affects in general. I have suggested in my previous papers (1953, 1955, 1958) that frustration is treated as a danger. To this general theoretical (mainly genetic and structural) statement, I want to add that instinctual frustration may account for *some* somatic-tension phenomena. Frustration-tension phenomena, some discharge phenomena of sexual foreplay, and some discharge phenomena of anxiety, use similar somatic discharge channels, and the ego of the phobic patient can confuse such perceptions and substitute one for the other. Sexual frustration may thus become a danger and promote anxiety, which then can be libidinized.

We can thus discern elements of substitute gratification in most anxiety situations of phobics. Only in the outright traumatic situation has any trace of substitute gratification disappeared. The gamble has failed, and ego control disintegrates. What I have described here has been conceptualized as a secondary libidinization of anxiety. It adds to severe phobias certain characteristics of a masochistic perversion, and constitutes one of the greatest obstacles to their analysis.

Libidinization of anxiety in phobias has its analogy in the libidinization of obsessive doubting in the obsessive-compulsive, a similarity which can be seen clearly when both types of symptoms coincide in the same patient, and in the libidinization of guilt in moral masochism and some types of depression.

Conflicts over sexual and aggressive aims also involve the superego. In the discussion of superego problems we have to be particularly careful to avoid generalizations. I was partly guilty of these when I spoke of "the phobic patient." Let me correct that. Phobic symptoms occur in patients with most types of neurosis and psychosis. What I have discussed here are patients whose phobias were *the* prevalent symptoms—and to avoid generalizations, I discussed the pathology of *individual ego-functions.* While I assume that this pathology always exists, it need not be manifest in other but the phobic areas. The "phobic patient" may have a very realistic evaluation of danger in many other situations. We must be careful to avoid using such generalizations as the weak, infantile, etc., ego.

It is even more common to speak about the "punitive," "corrupt," "defective," superego. Bornstein (1949) and Wangh (1959), who both refrain from such generalizations, have emphasized in their case histories the well-known fact that absence of environmental figures, which provide a clear-cut frame of reference for identification, and seduction by such figures, may explain a lag in superego development. Wangh ascribes to this lag, which, in turn, "is linked to the moral structure of the superego figures" (p. 690), an important etiological role in phobias. However, Wangh remarks rightly that "the acquisition of control of one's impulses which occurs, obviously, before the development of superego function, has important ego aspects" (p. 691). *Specifically*, the impact of identification on the formation of the superego will depend on the development of this function, identification. Let me refer here to the hierarchy of the identification processes postulated by Jacobson (1954) and her differentiation between ego and superego identifications. Any intrasystematic conflicts around identifications, any tendency for refusion of self- and object representation, must therefore have a bearing on the superego development. It is pertinent that Bornstein (1949) emphasized that Frankie's earlier internalized superego configuration was not felt as separate from the ego. In other words, it was not yet separated as a structure. Neither of my patient's parents was lacking in moral qualities for superego identifications. She had in many areas a well-structured superego. She had—especially in "big things"—a proper sense of responsibility and became an excellent mother. There was, however, most probably occasion for primal-scene observation and a lot of childhood sex play with contemporaries. Her lag in superego development showed in her mulishness in small everyday duties, her need for procrastination and postponement, and other "anal" mechanisms which I have described as a source of her tension pleasure. The second aspect was that in certain areas pertaining to her sexual fantasies, and aggressive preoedipal and oedipal aims connected with them, she experienced much less guilt than fear of external retaliation, such as abandonment and castration. The superego was in both instances not yet separated as a structure, and, accordingly, we were dealing with an intrasystematic conflict between reintrojected objects and their representations and self-representations. It is this primitive refusion which accounts, for instance, for acute symptoms arising out of primitive identifications with any outside figures which suffer from an illness or accident. Hence it may often be more precise to describe certain superego defects in terms of the underlying disturbance of ego functions. It was fascinating to observe how the stability of her superego structures developed under the influence of her analysis, but especially also under the impact of the highly rewarding relationship to her little girl.

The persistent inability of phobics to evaluate the danger arising from their instinctual drives is only an exaggeration of a ubiquitous phenomenon. In evolution, especially among vertebrates, mating and fighting are instinctively linked with each other. I, therefore, indulged in an earlier paper (1958) in a speculation that the link between sex and violence, and therefore danger, may be rooted in innate, instinctive givens. Another ubiquitous danger encountered in every analysis is that of being devoured. This danger, too, may be based on innate givens. While we were able to trace these dangers to early libidinal and aggressive strivings, an innate factor may be the matrix of the fear-laden aspect of infantile sexuality. The instinctive roots of sexuality—and I am using the word instinctive in the biological sense, in contrast to instinctual drive (*Trieb*)—may account for the fact that in no other area is symbolic representation so ubiquitous and so indestructible throughout life. It is therefore less surprising that in phobics, who sexualize so many areas of their ego functions, symbolism permeates through processes to such a degree. This is an added cause for ego regression which then may carry to a primitive, automatic, phyletically older type of response, which impresses us as "repetitive compulsiveness," where the executive apparatuses still are or become again passive, relative to the instinctual drive and/or the affect.

Let me draw now *some* technical conclusions from my presentation. Needless to say, analysis of phobias has to follow the rules of classical analysis; we have to analyze the defenses, the resistance, the transference neurosis. Id material usually becomes manifest earlier than, for instance, in obsessional neuroses. The transference neurosis comes early, and acting out is quite common. Only after pregenital material becomes accessible, can we begin to tackle the crucial problem of libidinization of anxiety. I have enumerated those disturbances of ego functions, which I consider an essential part of symptom formation in phobias: regressive evaluation of danger; the failure to neutralize energy; the primitive identifications and the tenuous defusion of self-and object representation; and finally, the difficulty to tolerate passivity and regression in the service of the ego.

Of course, we do not discuss theoretical concepts with the patient. It is, however, essential to analyze and work through the ego disturbances and to show the patient how all these factors contribute to his inability to test reality and to the prevalence of the primary process. We have to show the patient, not only the many *determinants* of his anxiety, but also how and why a given situation gets out of hand and deteriorates into a traumatic situation. The same applies to manifestations of aggression. Each situation has to be worked through from this point of view. This becomes especially important in the phase of the analysis when, following Freud's advice, we occasionally have to insist that patients not avoid their phobic situations. By that time, the *content* of the phobias may have been analyzed *ad nauseum.* But then and there, we can show the patient how everything depends on how well he can retain or quickly regain control. When this is done, we can repeat part of Bornstein's (1949) penultimate sentence of her paper, ". . . Then we knew that the secondary process had won a victory over the primary one" (p. 226).

Let me conclude by summarizing how I have tried to apply the five metapsychological points of view to the problem of phobia.

1. Such concepts as the hierarchy of danger situations and the responses to them, including the inborn mechanisms and discharge channels and apparatuses; the concepts of structure development from an undifferentiated phase; the concepts of desomatization; the concepts of regression express, among others, the genetic point of view.

2. The participation of the id, ego, and superego in the formation of phobias; the interdependence of ego functioning, drive development, and superego structures; the emphasis on various ego functions

and on ego regression; the discussion of economic consequences of ego regression express, among others, the structural point of view.

3. The discussion of cathexis and its withdrawal; the concepts of de- and resomatization of responses, of neutralization, of the primary process and its manifestations express, among others, the economic point of view.

4. The discussion of intra- and intersystemic conflicts; of symptoms as compromise formation; the description of attempts to restore reality testing express, among others, the dynamic point of view.

5. And finally, the discussion of the influence of drive and structure formation on reality testing, on the relationship to the environment, and vice versa; the influence of the environment on the developmental history, including the specific manifestation of symptom formation express, among others, the adaptive point of view.

CHAPTER 5

Correlation of Childhood with Adult Neurosis: Transition from Phobic to Obsessive-Compulsive Symptom Formation

Max Schur, M.D.

My discussion concerns itself with the main theme of S. Ritvo's paper, with certain developmental phenomena which occur between phobic and obsessive-compulsive symptom formation. These phenomena comprise, among others: (1) The phases of sexual development. (2) The transition from a chiefly stimulus-bound existence to one where *thoughts* can both initiate and replace action, a transition based upon the maturation of apparatus and the development of various ego functions. (3) The simultaneous developmental shift in hierarchies-of-danger situations. (4) The parallel development of various signal functions (signal anxiety, signal doubt, signal shame and guilt), of desomatization of responses, the faculty for neutralization of aggression, etc., all enabling the relative prevalence of secondary processes to come about. (5) The developmental aspects involved in the shift of defenses and in various modes of substitute gratification in phobic and obsessive-compulsive symptom formation.

The ability to initiate goal-directed *action* on the basis of thought instead of stimuli represents a crucial step both evolutionally and developmentally. The substitution of thought for action can not only

Editor's note: The case of Frankie, whom Bornstein (1949) analyzed for three years, beginning when he was five, and who returned to analysis 15 years later, was the basis for a discussion at the 24th International Psychoanalytic Congress (S. Ritvo, 1966).

bring about a capacity for delay and make possible the planning of more complex action; it allows for the development of ideation, creativity, sublimation. If thought processes are to initiate *action*, they must include reality-testing, specifically the evaluation of potential danger involved in such action.

Danger can be evaluated and experienced only by the ego. Both the evaluation and the response depend on the ego's developmental level. Anna Freud (1936) has elaborated on Freud's discussion of the danger concept by showing that the ego is faced with danger from the id, from the environment, and from the superego, and how, especially in children, inner, instinctual danger is projected outward and experienced as emanating from without as, for example, in castration fear.

We must, however, also consider an essential ego aspect of danger inherent in Freud's definition of a traumatic situation; namely, the ego's feeling of helplessness when faced with overwhelming danger. This definition introduces a quantitative factor into the danger situation: the relationship between the precipitating situation and the responding organization.

We find in both phobias and obsessive-compulsive neurosis a stratification of dangers originating in the oral, anal, and phallic phases. This also applies to Frankie. What varies at different phases of phobias, and especially in the transition to obsessional neurosis, is the main impact of certain dangers. To the "pre-ego" infant, "danger" is still identical with delay in need satisfaction. In the pregenital phase, inner, "instinctual" danger is *experienced* as a threat of being swallowed, devoured, as a threat of separation, injury, mutilation. In later development, the content of the phobia is extended to situations linked symbolically to these now unconscious sources of instinctual danger.

The prevailing defense against such dangers are avoidance, with displacement and projection of the danger to the outside. With the extension of danger situations, fantasies about various dangers and the experiential and somatic consequences mushroom, and we see how thought processes are increasingly diverted to pathological defenses and to substitute gratifications.

What is paramount in phobias is the fact that the ego's faculty for limiting anxiety to a signal is impaired. Moreover, phobic patients tend to evaluate and measure the reality of a danger situation by their own anxiety response. Their anxiety becomes a confirmation of danger, and finally it seems to them unrealistic and dangerous not to get frightened in certain situations. Thus certain thought processes and affective responses become maladaptive.

The transition from phobic to obsessional symptom formation and its correlation with replacement of action by thought is clearly illustrated in Bornstein's (1949) description of the sequence of Frankie's masturbatory activities: prohibition of touching his genitals → compulsive contraction of pelvic muscles → anal masturbation → playing with various toys → replacement of actual playing by fantasies.

Parallel to the development of thought processes and their importance in the overall mental economy, the following steps can be detected in the transition from phobic to obsessive-compulsive symptom formation:

1. The investment of narcissistic libido is shifted from somatic qualities and physical achievements to thought processes and their qualities. This shift is influenced by the frequency of precociousness and well-above-average intelligence of these individuals.

2. The same shift occurs in the area of instinctual drives having an exhibitionistic component. These shifts contribute to a more narcissistic type of object relationship.

3. Thought is substituted for action in areas of defense and of gratification of libidinal and aggressive aims, with action being retained in the compulsive rituals.

4. Although danger is rooted in the same phases as in phobias it is mainly perceived and experienced in terms of failure of thought processes. We may call this a shift from the soma to mental processes. However, it is also pertinent that thought processes are frequently perceived and experienced in concretely somatic terms.

Those shifts can be traced beautifully in both reports on Frankie's analyses. We can also observe a change from a relatively adaptive to a definitely maladaptive aspect in these shifts. When Frankie first learned to substitute thoughts for his masturbatory activities he was proud of a faculty he could use for substitute gratification, for defense, and also for the development of phase-adequate intellectual activities. Ritvo described a similar development in connection with Frankie's reading.

Thought activities are an essential part of the general function of control. However, we see, in the case of Frankie emphasizing what I called the ego aspect of danger, how this need for control through thought activities became maladaptive and extended to ever wider areas, culminating in the near-psychotic Boo-Boo episode.

The most common and consequential example of maladaptation is the development of obsessive doubt. Doubt, defined as a difficulty or objection brought up for solution, is an essential aspect of reality testing, of learning, of scientific work in the formation of superego structures. In obsessive symptom formation, it is the primary manifestation of the maladaptation of thought processes.

Freud (1909b) discussed the origin, vicissitudes, and meaning of obsessive doubt. Once the obsessive neurosis has been established, we must understand not only the genesis and unconscious content of the doubt, of which Freud has given such penetrating examples, but also the fact that the function of doubting, as such, gains, in the process of the neurosis, a quasi-independent importance and meaning. I have stated that the phobic has lost—or not acquired—the faculty of limiting *anxiety* to a signal; we can now say that the obsessive neurotic cannot restrict *doubt* to a signal. I have said that the phobic considers it dangerous not to be frightened in certain situations. To the obsessive, doubt has become an integral part of self-observation and reality testing. Because of his inability to limit doubt to a signal, and because of its genetic unconscious roots, the obsessive must continue doubting and introduce ever new safeguards. Because any attempt to do without doubt might result in severe anxiety and/or self-manipulated failure in reality, doubt has to be extended in severe cases to ever new areas. What Freud has described as obsessional deliria are the extreme manifestations of this maladaptive thought process.

Freud has spoken of replacement of action by thinking as "a sort of regression." Actually we cannot designate as regression a process which genetically is a sign of progressive development. But we may say that the obsessive patient uses thought processes in a regressive way: by resorting to primary process, by using them "magically," by equating them with action, by treating the thoughts and their results concretely, by resomatizing the whole process. Hence, we can understand that an even more paralyzing restriction of ego autonomy can result from a severe obsessive-compulsive neurosis than from a phobia. Parallel with these shifts, avoidance and projection are replaced by isolation, undoing, and reaction-formation.

A few final words about substitute gratifications in phobias and obsessive-compulsive neuroses. Both papers about Frankie give many examples of fantasies which represent derivatives of unconscious libidinal and aggressive wishes. I have suggested (see Chapter 12, This Volume) that in phobias, "tension pleasure" represents the actual substitute gratification to such pregenital sensations as distention of the bladder and rectum, cutaneous sensations of being tickled, and such stimulations of the sense of equilibrium as being tossed in the air, lifted, carried, etc. Phobics' accounts of all the dangers they might encounter reveal a constant playing with danger. This libidinization of anxiety and the playing with danger are conducive to acting out, and represent a serious obstacle to successful analysis.

In obsessive neuroses we encounter a similar process. Parallel with the transition from experiencing danger in somatic terms to experiencing it through thought processes, we encounter a libidinization of thought, a phenomenon emphasized by Freud (1909b) in his study of the Rat Man. Freud also stressed the fact that not only can the *content* of the process be traced to unconscious drive derivatives, the thought process itself becomes sexualized. He traced this sexualization to such component instinctual drives as exhibitionism, scoptophilia, and to the epistemophilic instinct. Moreover, thought processes and verbalization are treated in concrete terms, as if they were somatic structures. "Touching upon a topic," for instance, equals masturbatory touching.

This libidinization of anxiety, tension, and thought processes can be traced in both reports about Frankie. His hours-long retention is suggestive, not only of an expression of his need for control and an act of defiance, but of masturbatory "playing" with the distention of the bladder. The same applies to the contraction of his pelvic muscles. Bornstein repeatedly emphasized the great excitement with which Frankie talked about his fearful fantasies. Ritvo's account furnishes many examples of the hidden instinctual content of Frankie's thought processes, as well as of the libidinization and the aggressive aspects of his thinking.

Ritvo has told us that he could deal with only a few selected topics out of this rich material. This holds true even more for any discussion of that material. We look forward to further studies which might contribute to our knowledge of the genetic aspect of neurosis.

Part III

Psychoanalytic Theory

CHAPTER 6

The Defense Mechanisms and Activities of the Ego: Some Aspects of a Classificatory Approach

Arthur F. Valenstein, M.D.

The term *defense* was introduced by Freud in "The Neuropsychosis of Defence" (1894) and was subsequently used at about this time in several other papers to specify the effort on the part of the ego (at that time the total psychic apparatus) to rid itself of unacceptable feelings or ideas. Very shortly, however, the concept of defense in the general sense was apparently abandoned, and the particular concept of repression took its place. I expressly speak of the term defense as being "apparently" abandoned because some 25 years later Freud revived interest in this original concept. In the Appendix to *Inhibitions, Symptoms and Anxiety*, Freud (1926) suggested that the term defense be utilized to connote all of the various techniques which the ego might use in conflicts "which potentially lead to neurosis." The concept "repression" became understood as a uniquely important and basic mechanism of defense employed by the ego, but as only one of many succinctly describable techniques which could be used for control of the drives and their derivative representation in unconscious conflict.

However, with the introduction of a systematic ego psychology which assumed that much of ego function is in itself unconscious, in particular the operation of the entire defense organization of the ego,

Dr. Valenstein is Assistant Clinical Professor of Psychiatry, Harvard Medical School.

the concept of repression gained an additional significance. "Repression is the paramount mechanism through which this unconscious ego state is maintained, and the activity of the various defenses kept at an unconscious level" (Bibring et al., 1961, p. 70). This underscores the "unique relationship of repression to instinctual drive, on the one hand, and its dynamic role with regard to the unconscious ego state on the other hand" (ibid.). Given this significance, repression more broadly points up the incorrectness of setting up dichotomies between pathological and normal defenses, as if they were mutually exclusive. What determines whether a defense is normal or abnormal is its functional relevance; is it predominantly in the service of conflict, or is it developmentally phase adequate, reality appropriate, and predominantly in the service of healthy adaptation? I will not here consider a related, often erroneously applied distinction between successful and unsuccessful defenses.

Although from the very beginning many elements of a comprehensive psychology of human behavior—and to some extent human development—were implicit in its theory, psychoanalysis paramountly originated as a conflict psychology, as a psychology of the unconscious with particular significance for the origin and treatment of neurosis. Hence, the singular emphasis for a considerable time upon the pathognomic significance of repression and the defenses. Many analysts considered the defenses to be synonymous with resistance and viewed them as pathological impediments to treatment and health which required their defeat and even their disintegration. Only during the past 20 to 25 years, with the elaboration of an explicit adaptational point of view, has the essential role that defenses play in normal development and adaptation gained acknowledgment. This coincides with the growing tendency to redefine psychoanalysis more inclusively as a comprehensive psychology of human behavior, both normal and abnormal.

Anna Freud (1936), following a suggestion of Helene Deutsch, considered that "possibly each defense mechanism is first evolved in order to master some specific instinctual urge and so is associated with a particular phase of infantile development" (p. 51). This led her into an inquiry regarding the possibilities of chronological classification. But so obscure did early psychic development appear at that historical period, she decided to abandon this approach to classification and instead "to study in detail the situations which call for the defensive reactions" (p. 53). Nonetheless, in drawing a parallel between defenses which are directed predominantly against instinctual breakthrough and those which limit affect expression; in calling attention to the significance for defense of a child's recognition of self in contradistinction to objects and the reality of an outer world; and in separating those defenses which antedate the crystallization of a definitive superego from those which make their appearance thereafter, Anna Freud made a most useful contribution to the problem of classification.

But what are the further formulations which have appeared since Anna Freud's discussion of classification 30 years ago? As a consequence of the widened scope of psychoanalytically oriented treatment of disturbances which originate from trauma occurring during the earliest verbal and preverbal phase, interest in this period of development increased. This led to direct observational studies of neonates and very young children and the collection of additional data. Every ego function heretofore considered largely with respect to conflict and in the setting of neurosis is now considered within the range of a normative psychoanalytic psychology. Hypotheses and stimulating speculations have been offered regarding the development of a relatively autonomous and adaptive ego organization of defenses.[1]

Not only do discretely describable mechanisms of defense apparently unfold according to an epigenetic sequential schema, but the variegated functions of the ego, and the whole psyche, too, for that matter (id and superego as well), can be implemented for defensive purposes. The earliest archaic mechanisms of projection-introjection

[1] In her book, *Normality and Pathology in Childhood* (1965), Anna Freud wrote, "In fact, all defense mechanisms serve simultaneously internal drive restriction and external adaptation, which are merely two sides of the same picture. There is no antithesis between development and defense, since the strengthening of the ego and its defensive organization is itself an essential part of the child's growth and comparable in importance to the unfolding and maturing of the drives" (p. 177).

And continuing in a footnote (p. 177) directed to the limitation of "differentiating between defense and adaptation and labeling the ego mechanisms employed as either pathological or normal," she suggested that "Defenses have their own chronology, even if only an approximate one. They are more apt to have pathological results if they come into use before the appropriate age or are kept up too long after it. Examples are denial and projection, which are 'normal' in early childhood and lead to pathology in later years; or repression and reaction formation, which cripple the child's personality if used too early."

and other typified techniques which are also vicissitudes of the drives themselves, i.e., active into passive, turning about on the object, and displacement (at least as it is first modeled upon the primary process quality of ready displaceability within the id) give way over time, with the structuralization of an increasingly complex but definitive ego, to more evolved, reality-oriented, and sophisticated defense mechanisms and activities. Critical turning points seem to be the establishment of enduring and specific object ties, and the gradual ascendancy of secondary process. With the crystallization of a definitive superego and a turn toward reality in more elaborate social and cultural terms, those defenses which serve social adaptation most particularly, i.e., intellectualization, rationalization, reaction formation, and sublimation take precedence.

If the earliest defenses are closer to the drives as such and to the biological basis for adaptation (closer developmentally to the id-ego matrix and the id), then the later defense mechanisms and efforts are closer to reality and the social basis for adaptation (closer developmentally to the reality world and the superego).

A word concerning the fascinating area of the biologically rooted developmental precursors of defense: In this brief article directed primarily to the issue of classification, justice can hardly be done to the work and thoughts of Greenacre (1958b), Mahler (1968), Mahler and McDevitt (1968), Spitz (1961), Lampl-de Groot (1956), and a number of others whose stimulating contributions are relevant to a classificatory approach based upon the chronology of defenses. One example is the idea of a reflex-organized biophysiological substratum of responses (Greenacre, 1958b) which has protective value (psychobiological protectivity being a probable precursor of defense in the psychoanalytic psychological sense) and which, after birth, ontogenetically takes over where the intrauterine protectivity afforded the fetus by the mother leaves off.

The mother apparently serves very literally as a special "stimulus barrier" for her unborn child, and biologically a state of "quiescence" is thus created as a forerunner of sleep. This leads to the heuristic and exciting speculative possibility that sleep becomes an *Anlage*, prototypical of the earliest defensive response of withdrawal, upon which later may be modeled specific defense mechanisms of avoidance, isolation, denial, and, even in a sense, repression (Greenacre, 1958b; Spitz, 1961).[2] Implicit also is the assumption of a phase of mother-child symbiosis, and its implication for an essential anaclitic condition for the early development of ego functions, including the earliest defense mechanisms and their precursors (Mahler, 1968; Mahler and McDevitt, 1968).

There is much to suggest that constitutional predisposition developmentally influences the qualitative form of the defensive organization of the ego and in this way contributes to what is termed the adaptive style of character. Even though character structure may be diagnostically typified in this respect, for example, as obsessive or hysteric, such dynamic formulations do not necessarily connote substantial unconscious conflict, or clinical neurosis and symptomatology. This ambiguity is attributable to the aforementioned historical fact that psychoanalysis evolved as an abnormal psychology, with its explanatory concepts and terms derived in large measure from the psychoanalytic study of neurotically afflicted individuals. Probably the phrase "character style" has come into increasing favor to underscore that such psychoanalytic formulations may reflect *normal* character which functions within the range of relatively conflict-free adaptation.

In 1965 a scientific panel (Gabe, 1965) took as its topic "The Genetic Determinants of Obsessive-Compulsive Phenomena in Character Formation." The pivotal question was whether there is something particular to character development which antedates intrapsychic conflict and which is relatively independent of it, even though this operationally elusive constitutional factor may be swept up subsequently by conflict and reciprocal defensive response. This coincides with the assumption that there are congenital variations in the ego which significantly contribute to the specificity of character, a hallmark of which is the qualitative form of the organization of defenses as it is structured into character traits.

[2] Spitz cautioned against assuming too literally that psychological defense mechanisms will be derived analogously from neurophysiological precursors. His position is that "in the course of development, physiological functions are psychologically processed and give rise to adaptive mechanisms of defense" (p. 628). However, later ego defenses do not necessarily follow the same pattern as the early physiological prototypes. In fact, in his opinion, "the defense mechanism which eventually develops may acquire a function quite different from that of its original physiological prototype" (p. 628).

However, psychoanalytic developmental theory assumes an initial undifferentiated ego-id matrix from which evolves the coherent ego, within which is the organization of defenses (Hoffer, 1954). And in discussing the functions of the id, Schur (1966b) reminds us that since ego and id mutually influence each other developmentally and functionally, it is appropriate to apply "[the] concept of a continuum, as well as that of complementary series . . . to the participation of id elements in all mental functioning" (p. 48).

Thus the qualitative and quantitative nature of drive endowment is fundamental to ego structure and to the final adaptive form of the defenses and their efficacy in coping with intrapsychic unconscious conflict. Freud (1937a) specified three factors, "the influence of traumas, the constitutional strength of the instincts and alterations of the ego," as being crucial for "the success or otherwise of analytic treatment" (p. 224). And Hartmann (1953), continuing this thesis, speculated that schizophrenia might be the outcome of a constitutional inability to sufficiently neutralize aggressive instinctual energy (Hartmann et al., 1949), thus impoverishing the ego in both its synthetic and defensive capacities while it is simultaneously taxed with a superfluity of archaic aggressivity. The characterological vulnerability under such circumstances is typified by primitive defenses, such as introjection, projection, and splitting of the ego.

"Splitting of the ego" for purposes of defense is encountered in major disturbances and in borderline states, where the regression is extreme. It coincides therein with a basic defect in character structure originating in the preverbal phase of development. In this regard, we have learned to exercise diagnostic caution and prognostic reserve when we encounter a so-called grand hysteric who dramatically splits off major psychic functions through conversion. I will not discuss here this appropriate use of the concept " splitting of the ego" for purposes of defense, in contrast to an overextended and, in my opinion, unwarranted application of the concept to normal development and neurosis, wherein reality testing is relatively unimpaired.

To return more explicitly to the problem of classification. In an earlier publication (Bibring et al., 1961), I suggested that defenses, i.e., defense mechanisms in the sense of typified clinical constructs which in many instances terminologically coincide with their observable specifically connected behavioral referents, might be approximately separated into those which are Basic (first order) (ibid., p. 62) and those which are Complex (second order). The quality of basic irreducibility, in contrast to the complex synthesis of various ego defensive functions, was suggested as the measure. Amongst the complex order which would have higher social significance might be included aestheticism, asceticism, counterphobia, depersonalization, identification, sublimation, and a number of others. Identification as a complex adaptive ego function, as well as a defense to resolve unconscious conflict, is a topic in itself. It was defined as having two roots of origin. The first, which occurs much earlier and more extensively than is usually realized, is through imitative activity, making use of the extraordinary repertoire of ego functional capabilities upon the stage of rich and stimulating possibilities provided by objects in the environment. The second would be in the archaic instinctual modes of incorporation or introjection, and would appear thus to have more to do with the solution of early conflict than adaptation as such, at least *prima facie.* Sublimation also seems to be closely related to ego autonomous potentialities for adaptation through coping and mastery efforts, as well as to the renunciation of direct instinctual satisfaction as the result of unconscious conflict.

This leads us then to the issue of the hierarchy of defenses, as it is encountered both in normal, well-adapted living and under circumstances of regression. The shift in the hierarchical pattern of defenses secondary to such regression may be facultatively in the service of the ego and, being readily reversible in response to reality, is within the range of normality. Or, on the pathological side, it may reflect lifelong continuance of unconscious infantile conflict and neurosis; or the very shift qualitatively to more primitive or more rigidly employed hierarchies of defense may signify regression consequent to the precipitation of latent neurotic conflict, often exacerbated by current emotional trauma or interpersonal exigency.

The conception of a hierarchy of defenses is discussed at some length by Gill (1963). After calling attention to Freud's (1915d) implicit suggestion that defenses are organized according to a developmental hierarchy, Gill reviewed the conception of a hierarchy of defenses as it has been considered by a number of later contributors. Gero (1951) pointed out that defenses might be hierarchically located according to their relative "nearness to the conscious ego"; Glover (1948, p. 342) was concerned "with the variations in distribution of cathexis" of a defense, from which it is logical to infer that variations in cathexis of the different defenses account for the hierarchical organization of the system of defenses. Fenichel (1941a) took up defenses and their hierarchy in relationship to id and ego. After underscoring Fenichel's point that "any behavior simultaneously has impulse [id] and defense [ego] aspects," which signifies the relativity of defense with respect to id and ego, Gill then proposed that such a distinction regarding a hierarchical ordering of defenses would be consistent with Rapaport's (1953b) activity-passivity dimension, which connotes the "degree to which behavior is regulated by the Ego [*activity*] or the Id [*passivity*] respectively" (p. 124; italicized insertions added). Applying this conceptual measure, Gill also writes, "I believe it is probable that defenses lower in the hierarchy are more passive and those higher in the hierarchy more active" (p. 124).

It would appear that Gero's approach is *topographic*, Glover's is *dynamic*, and Fenichel's and Rapaport's are predominantly *structural*; and that all three approaches are complementary and relevant to the hierarchical concept of defenses. Together they take us a fair distance toward a metapsychological formulation of the principle of hierarchies as it pertains to defenses. What is needed to fill it out are the economic, the adaptational, and the genetic points of view.

The conception of an energic or quantitative aspect is probably implicit in the assumption of variations in the strength of the different defenses, in particular, and of the defense organization of the ego as a whole, at the successive developmental phases.[3] Included would be both congenital influences, namely, the diatheses toward the developmental unfolding of defenses, as such innate organizing tendencies are laid down *primarily* in the id-ego undifferentiated matrix, in the "proto-ego"; as well as those determining inclinations acquired *secondarily*, coincident with the emergence of an increasingly definitive ego as development proceeds apace. The latter would also involve the process of adaptation and the moulding of the ego in response to experience and the environment.

[3]Possibly Rapaport's activity-passivity dimension is relevant here as well; perhaps as a more heuristic proposition than the problematical assumption of innate qualitatively disposed psychic energies.

The choice of specific defenses, as well as hierarchies of defenses, in Glover's sense of the variability of cathexis within an organization of defenses, pertains also to the adaptational point of view. The concept of a characterologically structured organization of defenses particular to the individual includes not only his constitutional and experientially acquired disposition toward a personal set of defenses variably cathected so that typified hierarchies are patterned, but also the adaptive quality or fit to usually encountered external circumstances. Defenses are likely to be maladaptive if they are employed in a stereotyped fashion, inflexibly bound to a fixed neurotic characterology, regardless of external circumstance. On the other hand, if there is more resilience, if the individual can draw upon his repertoire of defenses with more versatility, appropriate to his age and to external circumstances, the organization of defenses is certainly more reality adapted (cf. A. Freud, 1965, p. 177n).

If I might use an analogy, I would like to picture the genetic aspect as follows: the child climbs a developmentally contrived ladder of his own epigenetic making as he goes upward chronologically toward a more mature and reality adequate mode of adaptation. In terms of the defenses, normally each rung would correspond to a functionally patterned hierarchy of defense mechanisms and various ego functions used defensively, appropriate to that developmental phase. Under circumstances of neurotic decompensation, the genetic history of the coalescence of an individually specific array of defenses and their improvisation into hierarchically patterned constellations blended with various ego functions used defensively, makes itself known in reverse. As the individual in regression, whether normally facultative or neurotic, descends his personally constructed ladder of epigenetic development, from the very way in which he falls back upon previous defensive modes, and from the behavioral and mental representations of their hierarchical pattern, we can infer a good deal about the nodal points of his development. Insofar as he adheres to or falls back upon particular rungs of his developmental ladder, we learn about the fixations which were established earlier, whether by frustration, indulgence, or combinations of both.

Anna Freud (1936) wrote of "a regular connection between particular neuroses and special modes of defense, as, for instance, between hysteria and repression or between obsessional neuroses and the processes of isolation and undoing" (p. 34). More broadly speaking, it is possible to make a classificatory approach, based not only on the specific mechanisms of defense, but also on their hierarchy in dynamic association with particular neuroses. Such a classification, based on typified character structure or neurosis, is not inconsistent with a developmental or chronological approach, but it is at a more clinical level of conception and usefulness, and highly germane to problems of diagnosis and technique.

One has to ask of a classification of the defensive activities and mechanisms of the ego, to what purpose? Is it primarily for a better psychoanalytical understanding of human development and the process of adaptation in a normative sense? Or is it for a more adequate assessment of intrapsychic conflict, its origin, course, and outcome, and the specificity of the neurosis which evolves from it? Or, finally, is it to enhance our diagnostic acumen and refine our psychoanalytic technique with a more thorough appreciation of its subtleties and therapeutic specificity?

CHAPTER 7

The Relationship of Defense to Affect and Its Tolerance

Elizabeth R. Zetzel, M.D.

A comprehensive psychology must include within its conceptual framework both healthy and pathological aspects of psychic structure and function. From the outset Freud regarded psychoanalysis as far more than a tool directed toward the understanding and treatment of neurotic illness. As early as 1895 for example, he said, "I am plagued with two ambitions: to see how the theory of mental functioning takes place if quantitative considerations, a sort of economics of nerve-force, are introduced into it; and secondly, to extract from psychopathology what may be of benefit to normal psychology. Actually a satisfactory general theory of neuropsychotic disturbances is impossible if it cannot be brought into association with clear assumptions about normal mental processess" (pp. 119-120).

This statement confirms Freud's early recognition of dynamic and economic factors. These hypotheses remain integral to contemporary psychoanalytic metapsychology. Both "The Project for a Scientific Psychology" and "The Letters to Fliess" also demonstrate that affect, its origin and its significance, was an area which Freud regarded as crucial from the time he first began to treat neurotic patients. His initial approach to this subject led him, however, to a conclusion almost diametrically opposed to the thesis that will be developed in this paper. "[I]t is the business of the ego to permit no release of affect since this would at the same time permit a primary process"

Published posthumously. Dr. Zetzel, at the time of writing this article, was Associate Clinical Professor of Psychiatry, Harvard Medical School.

(1895, p. 415). This statement is obviously incompatible with contemporary understanding of the positive creative aspects of primary process thinking subsumed under the concept of regression in the service of the ego. It is equally disparaging of the positive implications of affect, its recognition, tolerance, and mastery, as developmental tasks indispensable for optimal ego maturation.

Many years later (1926) Freud himself posed this very problem: "What we need and cannot lay our finger on is some factor which will explain why some people are able to subject the affect of anxiety, in spite of its peculiar quality, to the normal workings of the mind, or which decides who is doomed to come to grief over that task" (p. 150). It may be suggested that Freud foresaw the approach to this question as early as 1911 when he first made an explicit distinction between ego development (then formulated mainly in terms of the reality principle) and the vicissitudes of libidinal development.

> If . . . each step in these two courses of development may become the site of a disposition to later neurotic illness, it is plausible to suppose that the form taken by the subsequent illness . . . will depend on the particular phase of the development of the ego and of the libido in which the dispositional inhibition of development has occurred. Thus unexpected significance attaches to the chronological features of the two developments (which have not yet been studied), and to possible variations in their synchronization [pp. 224-225].

This statement, like many others, is cited to illustrate the fact that psychoanalysis is a comprehensive developmental psychology. Of special relevance to the present discussion was Freud's suggestion that developmental failure with respect to the ego which had not yet been studied might influence the predisposition to certain types of illness. Such failures could then be contrasted and compared to the already known consequences of significant failure with respect to the mastery of intrapsychic, i.e., instinctual conflict.

It has long been recognized that anxiety and depression are among the most common symptoms encountered in a wide variety of pathological conditions. Both affects have recently been defined as basic ego states which may assume signal functions with respect to the mobilization of ego defenses (Bibring, 1953). Failure to develop, tolerate, and master anxiety has been increasingly recognized as an important factor in determining regressive ego states. Schur (1953b, 1955) has made important and significant contributions regarding the regressive evaluation of danger as the ego fails to control anxiety. Related observations relevant to depression have also been the subject of a recent paper (Zetzel, 1965). Much of our understanding of the significance of such regressive states originally derived from experiences in the practice of clinical psychoanalysis. These findings have been enriched by broad-based observations, ranging from the evaluation of so-called normal applicants for education or training to patients whose affective disturbance has required hospitalization. It may therefore be possible to propose a developmental evaluation of affect and its tolerance within the framework of contemporary psychoanalytic metapsychology.

The author's interest in the potentially adaptive and prophylactic value of anticipatory anxiety and its tolerance under conditions of real external danger was initiated by the unusual opportunities available to an Army psychiatrist during World War II. A preliminary theoretical approach to this subject was made in an earlier contribution (Zetzel, 1949). Soldiers with a history of neurotic symptoms associated with manifest anxiety proved to be less predisposed to serious, relatively irreversible traumatic neurosis than many whose anaemneses revealed a history of overtly uneventful external adaptation with little evidence of subjective anticipatory anxiety. The former possessed to a high degree the capacity to control or tolerate anxiety emphasized by Schur. The latter, conversely, often illustrated the evaluation of danger characteristic of the ego in regression. Additional clinical experience during the intervening years has suggested that depression and its tolerance may be considered in a parallel manner. Separation, disappointment, and/or object loss is inevitable, particularly during the later years of life. There is much to indicate that those individuals who have previously experienced manifest sadness, grief, or some subjective depression prove to be more capable of accepting later life experiences in a progressively adaptive manner than individuals whose life history lacks such overt affective experiences.

Although the statements already cited indicate an implicit structural theory from a very early period, it was only in 1923 (*The Ego and the Id*) that Freud explicitly recognized the ego as the seat of anxiety and other affects. He had nevertheless hinted (1900) at the possibility that the psychic apparatus might, during the course of development, become able to cathect and work-over mental content which had originally been associated with the release of unpleasure or anxiety.

> It seems probable that in the first instance the unpleasure principle regulates the displacement of cathexes automatically. But it is quite possible that consciousness of these qualities may introduce in addition a second and more discriminating regulation, which is even able to oppose the former one, and which perfects the efficiency of the apparatus by enabling it, in contradiction to its original plan, to cathect and work over even what is associated with the release of unpleasure [p. 616].

Anna Freud (1936) made a more general statement to the same effect. "The child must learn to tolerate larger and larger quantities of unpleasure without immediately having recourse to his defense mechanisms" (p. 64). Both statements clearly suggest that successful development involves an increasing capacity to tolerate psychological experiences which elicit painful feelings. Affect, its recognition, tolerance, and mastery, has therefore been at least an implicit major prerequisite to the progressive development of psychic structure from the conception of psychoanalysis as a comprehensive developmental psychology.

Historically it is well known that the term "defense" preceded the term "repression" in Freud's theoretical formulations. While he regarded repression as the mechanism chiefly responsible for the persistence of unconscious mental activity, the relationship between fear, anxiety, and defense remained somewhat obscure. Both *The Ego and the Id*, as already noted, and Freud's *Introductory Lectures* (1916-17) represented an intermediate stage in Freud's thinking. The ego was recognized as the seat of anxiety, and at the same time, the relationship between essentially normal fear of objective reality and the irrational anxiety best seen in phobias was clearly recognized.

Freud still maintained, however, his original correlation between morbid anxiety and mounting instinctual frustration. In *Inhibitions, Symptoms, and Anxiety* (1926) and in his lecture on anxiety in the *New Introductory Lectures* (1933), Freud attempted to integrate his understanding of the defenses against external and internal danger, on the premise that similar mechanisms are mobilized with respect to both. He attributed the emergence of signal, or secondary anxiety to the child's perception of external danger–i.e., object loss and/or castration. Such realistic threats were regarded as the major stimuli which motivated the child toward intrapsychic defenses against his own instinctual impulses. Freud clearly recognized that such defenses might be restrictive. "If the ego succeeds in protecting itself from a dangerous instinctual impulse, through, for instance, the process of repression, it has certainly inhibited and damaged the particular part of the id concerned; but it has at the same time given it some independence and has renounced some of its own sovereignty. This is inevitable from the nature of repression, which is, fundamentally, an attempt at flight" (1926, p. 153). Freud also retained the concept that the human psychic apparatus has limits or thresholds with respect to its capacity to tolerate and master mounting excitation, whether this derives from external or internal sources.

Both Freud, in his definitive theory of anxiety, and Anna Freud in *The Ego and the Mechanisms of Defense* (1936) distinguish between the anxiety aroused by objective reality and the anxiety which mobilizes the ego's unconscious defenses against internal–i.e., instinctual danger. Freud attributes the major problems inherent in human development to the sharp differentiation between ego and id. He cites as a psychological factor response for neurotic problems "a defect of our mental apparatus which has to do precisely with its differentiation into an id and an ego" (1926, p. 155). Anna Freud limits the term "defense mechanism" to the unconscious responses to internal danger. Among such defenses she suggests that reaction formations "appear almost unheralded in the ego in the course of a child's development" (p. 9). At the same time she also raises the possibility that the differentiation between ego and id may only gradually be achieved. Her emphasis, moreover, on avoidance of objective pain and objective dangers as preliminary stages of defense merits careful consideration.

It is well known that the defense mechanisms in their definitive form may be preceded by a wide variety of less permanent defensive efforts. Anna Freud described some of these as attempts to avoid or deny the painful affect aroused by objective perceptions which cannot yet be tolerated. Certain mechanisms, it is widely agreed, take on the function of automatic responses to an unconscious signal only relatively late in the child's psychic maturation. Others, as has already been noted (Freud, Anna Freud, op. cit.), may become unnecessary if and when the child's capacity to tolerate pain increases. This tolerance may be closely related to all that is involved in secondary autonomy of the ego and the emergence of areas of conflict-free activity. It may be added, in this context, that many contemporary analysts would interpose certain forms of objective and/or separation anxiety between Freud's concept of a traumatic situation and the signal anxiety which mobilizes automatic unconscious ego defenses.

The dream as an immediate short-term defensive response to a sleep-disturbing painful signal may be compared and contrasted with the unconscious ego defenses. During sleep, the paths to motility and consciousness are closed. As a result, the ego's defenses are presumed to be less powerful, thus permitting the disguised gratification of certain wishes as a result of successful dream work. In the event, however, that the dream work is not immediate and automatic, taking place outside the sphere of consciousness, its purpose fails, some anxiety is mobilized, and the sleeper wakes up. On the one hand, dreams may be stimulated by an internal signal. Equally, however, dreams of convenience have long been recognized as attempts to deny the sleep-disturbing impact of an external, i.e., affective perception.

The ego's unconscious defenses in waking life have a parallel automatic quality. Insofar as they are successful, they protect the individual from full awareness of some part of either internal or external reality. Anna Freud's discussion of the avoidance of objective pain and objective danger as preliminary stages of defense has implications equally relevant to anxiety and to depression. Certain responses may be attributed to the need for defense against the impact of perceptions which in essence confront the child with his relative helplessness, either physical or mental. Denial and withdrawal, which she notes in this context, were not regarded as comparable with the unconscious ego defenses against signal anxiety with respect to either their automatic quality or their relative unchangeability. They could rather be included within the range of normal childhood reactions to narcissistic injuries concomitant with reality perceptions. The child is confronted with the fact that he is neither as brave, as strong, or as good as he had mistakenly believed. This in essence imposes the type of narcissistic injury noted by Bibring (1953) in his discussion of depression as a basic ego state. If, as he suggested, this affect can assume signal functions, it is some aspect of painful reality, rather than internal instinctual danger, which constitutes the primary motive for the defenses against depression. The child, it might be suggested, would become depressed if he acknowledged his realistic sense of inferiority and inadequacy. Denial, in this context, may be a defense against depression with implications relevant to normal childhood, to situations of realistic stress and helplessness, and to the psychopathology of everyday life. The well-recognized relationship of depression to mania illustrates, in brief, pathological reinforcement of a mechanism which, in its milder forms, may have adaptive functions as well as pathological implications.

"Our developmental hypothesis includes by definition both progressive and regressive potentialities at all times. This statement applies both to instinctual development and to the structured ego-superego system. It is a cardinal feature of psychic life that every important maturational challenge presents highly significant regressive threats" (Zetzel, 1964, p. 153).

It is here proposed that previous recognition and some tolerance of the anxiety mobilized by internal danger increases rather than decreases the ego's definitive capacity to respond adaptively to developmental and/or situational crises and their regressive threats. Insofar as depression is also to be regarded as a basic ego state, it may be suggested that during childhood some capacity to recognize and tolerate sadness and disappointment with regard to realistic limitations and the possibility of failure serves as one motive for learning mastery and adaptive progress. It is also prerequisite to the later capacity to tolerate the more serious blows which will inevitably occur during the course of adult life. Freud emphasized threatened or actual object loss as one realistic basis for both anxiety and depression. Such threats are implicit during the early stages of development when the child first develops separation anxiety. He is directly confronted with his own dependence and relative helplessness. This, on the one hand, is closely related to Freud's definition of a traumatic situation as one of total helplessness. The narcissistic injury implied in such recognition of relative helplessness may in some cases determine the onset of such unconscious defenses against depression as denial and ego restriction.

Insofar as such responses lead to significant limitations in the child's ability to accept reality, his defenses against depression may later have serious consequences. Intolerance of relative helplessness may foster precocious ego development associated with premature defenses against instinctual danger. This not only occurs in certain well-known character neuroses; it is also characteristic of many so-called normal characters whose external adaptation proves to be based on considerable denial of feelings of inadequacy. In such cases, both anxiety and depression have assumed major signal functions. In this context, the more the response is unconscious, automatic, and involuntary, the less the individual has genuinely worked through conflicts equally relevant to adaptive mastery of internal and external reality. Some tolerance of both anxiety and depression is prerequisite to optimal mobilization of neutralized, bound, or sublimated energy in the conflict-free sphere of autonomous ego functions.

It is a well-recognized finding that many of the men who have made important original and creative contributions have undergone periods of both symptomatic neurosis and sadness, grief, or depression before they reached the prime of their capacity. Darwin and John Stuart Mill might be mentioned as outstanding examples. Even more significant, for our purposes, is the history of the founder of psychoanalysis, Freud himself. The fact that Freud suffered from phobic anxiety is familiar to us all. In the Preface to the Second Edition of *The Interpretation of Dreams*, written in 1908, Freud hinted at the importance of grief and depression. "This book," he said, "has a further subjective significance for me personally—a significance which I only grasped after I had completed it. It was, I found, a portion of my own self-analysis, my reaction to my father's death—this is to say, to the most important event, the most poignant loss, of a man's life" (1900, p. xxvi).

Freud not only worked through the depression appropriate to normal grief; he also made the subjectively unwelcome but objectively momentous discovery that oedipal wishes, rather than traumatic incestuous experience, constitute the core of the infantile neurosis. The acceptance of external reality, namely, the death of his father, was thus closely associated to recognition of the internal threats which mobilize anxiety. Passive acceptance of the limitations and losses posed by external reality had increased rather than decreased his capacity to recognize and master the anxiety integral to intrapsychic conflict. This, in his case, involved crucial explorations of the new and unknown.

It is hardly by chance that the dream cited by Freud in his Introduction to Chapter VII is highly relevant to grief and depression, with specific reference to the father-son relationship. I refer here to the dream of the father sorrowing for the son who had just died. In the dream, the boy spoke to his father as if he were still alive. This dream not only prolonged sleep; it also denied a painful reality, the death of the son. Although only partially and temporarily successful, the dream illustrates denial as a major defense against depression. In the boy's reproaches to the father, moreover, the dream vividly portrays the narcissistic injury, sense of helplessness, and implicit feelings of self-reproach ineluctably associated with significant object loss or disappointment, whatever the cause, whenever it occurs, and however inevitable it may have been.

Just as the capacity to withstand realistic danger in adult life has its prehistory in the development and emergence of manifest anxiety, so too the capacity to work through the losses and disappointments to be expected during the course of any productive life has its prehistory in the earlier responses to helplessness and separation. It is not, in this context, necessary to suggest that the child's brief experiences of sadness or withdrawal constitute clinical depression as we recognize it in adults. The affective concomitants of psychic growth may be epitomized by Freud's (1887-1902) description of his own subjective state during the period of self-analysis following his father's death. He described the type of affective experience which precedes the insight achieved during the process of significant active mastery.

> I am now experiencing myself all the things that as a third party I have witnessed going on in my patients—days when I slink about depressed because I have understood nothing of the day's dreams, phantasies or mood, and other days when a flash of lightning brings coherence into the picture, and what has gone before is revealed as preparation for the present [p. 226].

This state of mind includes elements of both anxiety and depression. Tolerance of such affective states is to be regarded as a necessary preliminary to the discovery of appropriate areas of growth and mastery more adaptive than the continued mobilization of unconscious automatic defenses. In this sense, which is relative rather than absolute, the capacity to tolerate affective pain is an important determinant of the degree to which, in effect, where id was, the ego can be.

CHAPTER 8

The Malignant No: A Hypothesis concerning the Interdependence of the Sense of Self and the Instinctual Drives

Heinz Lichtenstein, M.D.

In the Foreword to Max Schur's (1966a) monograph, *The Id and the Regulatory Principles of Mental Functioning*, the editors credit Schur's work with "reflecting the *Zeitgeist*," insofar as it constitutes a "reappraisal of basic psychoanalytic concepts in the light of recent advances in our discipline" (p. 7). Characteristic for this reappraisal is Schur's emphasis on the "concept of a continuum . . . between the structures 'ego' and 'id' " which, as he goes on to say, "is part of the problem of the *mutual* influences in the development of ego and id" (p. 48). The acute awareness of the importance of the continuum between ego and id, together with his stress on Freud's concept of the complementary series, does reflect indeed the Zeitgeist in psychoanalytic thinking in the last decades, representing a dialectical understanding of the interdependence of "the differentiation of psychic structure and relation of the self to external objects" (Hartmann, Kris, and Loewenstein, 1949, p. 27). The present paper attempts to study the dialectic relationship between the ego function of negation and the sense of self and their mutual influence on the manifestations of the instinctual drives. A hypothesis is introduced correlating a specific deviation of the ego function of negation and the predominance of aggressive patterns of object relations. This de-

Dr. Lichtenstein is Associate Clinical Professor, Department of Psychiatry, State University of New York at Buffalo.

viation of the function of negation is referred to as the "malignant No." It is defined as the experience of feeling negated in one's existence as an individual. "The malignant No" not only affects the individual's object relations, but also influences his perception of reality. Some contemporary social phenomena which might be understood as reflecting this dialectic interaction will be discussed briefly.

THE DEVELOPMENT OF THE NO-CONCEPT

The development of the no-concept, of negation, constitutes an important aspect of psychoanalytic ego psychology. In discussing the special characteristics of the system Ucs., Freud (1915d) states: "There are in this system no negation, no doubt, no degrees of certainty: all this is only introduced by the work of the censorship between the Ucs. and the Pcs. Negation is a substitute, at a higher level, for repression. In the Ucs. there are only contents, cathected with greater or lesser strength" (p. 186). This proposition is several years later taken up and elaborated by Freud (1925b) in a paper exclusively devoted to the concept of negation. In this paper Freud declares: "With the help of the symbol of negation, thinking frees itself from the restriction of repression and enriches itself with material that is indispensable for its proper functioning" (p. 236). Instead of repression, according to Freud, the individual has now acquired the intellectual function of judgement, by means of which we are able "to affirm or deny the subject matter of thoughts" (p. 236). He sees the intellectual function of judgement as depending genetically on the acquisition of the no-concept: "The performance of the function of judgement is not made possible until the creation of the symbol of negation has endowed thinking with a first measure of freedom from the consequences of repression and with it from the compulsion of the pleasure-principle" (p. 239). Insofar as freedom from the compulsion of the pleasure-principle would appear a prerequisite for nonambivalent interactions between individuals, it comes as a surprise to read that Freud correlates the function of negation to the destructive instinct: "The polarity of judgement appears to correspond to the opposition of the two groups of instincts which we have supposed to exist. Affirmation—as a substitute for uniting—belongs to the Eros; negation—the successor to expulsion—belongs to the instinct of destruction" (p. 239). If the incapacity to negate characterizes the primary process, indicating the domination of thought processes by the id, is then unlimited affirmation not a sign of ego defect? And if negation ushers in the freedom from domination by the id, is then negation not the prerequisite for an integration of the personality on a higher level of adaptation?

One is inclined to reject Freud's correlation of affirmation and negation to Eros and the destructive instinct as inconsistent with the whole argument in his paper on negation. Freud gives us, however, some clue of what might have motivated him to postulate a correlation between negation and aggression when he refers to the negativism of the psychotics. The aggressive and destructive quality of psychotic negativism has impressed many observers. Insofar as negation may lead to a frustration of needs, it has been singled out as the most important motivation for aggression (Dollard et al., 1939). Sullivan's (1953) concept of malevolence postulates a correlation between denial of tenderness to the child and the malevolent transformation, i.e., aggressive behavior. Negation, it seems, is Janus-faced: one of its faces looks toward the liberation of the individual from the compulsive pressures of the pleasure principles and thus toward the possibility of genuine object relations; the other face, however, appears to menace the very basis of object relations in that it expresses the aggressive potentialities of man. It seems, therefore, justified to investigate the phenomenom of negation and its role in human development. With this in mind, it becomes imperative to review the important studies of infants that have been undertaken by René Spitz (1957) concerning the genesis of human communication.

THE GENESIS OF HUMAN COMMUNICATION AND THE ACQUISITION OF THE "NO"

In the monograph "No and Yes" Spitz (1957) explores the acquisition by the infant of the "No" and "Yes," as word as well as gesture, from evolutionary, ontogenetic, and clinical viewpoints. Following Freud's ideas on the acquisition of the function of negation, Spitz quotes Freud's (1925b) distinction concerning what a negation negates: "The function of judgement is concerned in the main with two sorts of decisions. It affirms or disaffirms the possession by a thing of a particular attribute; and it asserts or disputes that a [mental] presentation has an existence in reality" (p. 236). For Freud (1925b), these two types of decisions indicate important steps in ego development. The first type of judgement is, according to Freud, a more primitive type of decision, indicating a dominance of judgement by a wish. "The original pleasure-ego wants to introject into itself everything that is good and to eject from itself everything that is bad. . . ." The judgement concerning the existence of a mental presentation in reality is seen as an indication of more advanced ego development:

> The other sort of decision made by the function of judgement . . . is a concern of the definite reality-ego, which develops out of the initial pleasure-ego. . . . In this stage of development regard for the pleasure principle has been set aside. Experience has shown the subject that it is not only important whether a thing . . . possesses the "good" attributes but whether it is there in the external world [p. 237].

This affirmation or negation of the reality of a thing Freud considers genetically to constitute a step forward because it "offers a further contribution to the differentiation between what is subjective and what is objective" (p. 238). Spitz (1957) reformulates these ideas of Freud concerning negation as follows: "The acquisition of the 'No' is an indicator of a new level of autonomy, of the awareness of the 'other' and of the awareness of the self; it is a beginning of a reconstruction of mentation on a higher level of complexity; it initiates an extensive ego development, in the framework of which the dominance of the reality principle over the pleasure principle becomes increasingly established" (p. 129). Spitz dates these developments "somewhere around fifteen months of age" (p. 129). Beyond the significance for ego development, Spitz emphasizes the importance of the acquisition of the "No" in terms of its impact on the patterning of object relations: "The child, as an independent person, with a will of his own, confronts the 'other,' who is equally independent, also a discrete person with a will of his own. . . . This raises object relations from the level of instinctual drive to the level of social relations" (p. 132). Spitz uses this as a turning point in the evolution of man, in that "it established man as a species different from all others in regard to the level of his social relations" (p. 145).

How, then, does the child acquire the "No"? Freud (1925b) does not elucidate this question beyond implying that it is the result of the child's interaction with the love object. Spitz (1957) is more specific. He suggests several theoretical possibilities, but the one that he singles out for detailed discussion is based on Anna Freud's (1936) concept of the child's identification with the aggressor. The aggressor is "the frustrating object against whom his own [the child's] 'No' is hurled" (Spitz, 1957, p. 47). Thus, we are again confronting the ambiguous, Janus-faced nature of the function of negation. Just as Freud's postulated correlation of aggression and negation, Spitz' derivation of the acquisition of the "No" through identification with the aggressor seems incompatible with his claim that the function of negation transforms instinctual responses into specifically human, i.e., social relations. It is difficult indeed to consider aggression as the matrix of social relations. Spitz (1965) is not unaware of this conceptual dilemma, when he says that "it should be clearly understood that when I speak of the aggressive drive or of aggression I do *not* mean hostility" (p. 178).

The seeming dilemma can be removed, according to Spitz (1957), if we understand the aggression set free in the child by the "No" of the frustrating adult as a trigger mechanism that sets in motion *thought* processes in the child: "Imitation, turning of the affect against the adult, thought processes—present energy transformations on a large scale. In this transformation of energies the motor expression of the affect 'against' has been subjected to the control of the ego and modified, with far-reaching consequences" (p. 52).

This is a very interesting and ingenious hypothesis. It is based on a hypothetical transformation of aggressive drive energies into ego functions—a metapsychological alchemy by means of which the leaden weight of the aggressive drives is transformed into the pure gold of higher ego functions. It is possible that such transformations do occur. They are, however, very difficult to validate. Spitz' own observations contain possibilities of another approach toward the dilemma of the relation between negation and aggression when he says "the adult's mental processes and the possible rational reasons for his 'No' are completely beyond the fifteen-month-old's capacities of understanding. He cannot understand whether the adult prohibits because of concern for the child's safety or because of anger when the child does something forbidden" (p. 50). This is certainly correct as far as the rational reasons of the adult are concerned. But is it really self-evident that the affective implication of a "No" might not be perceived, even by a young child, as more meaningful than the verbal articulation of it? In the adult the effect elicited by the "No" seems to vary greatly according to the experiental context in which it occurs. The possibility that this may also be true for the child cannot be ruled out without further evidence to the contrary.

THE PERCEPTION OF THE "NO" IN ADULT INTERACTION AND THE CONCEPT OF "DIALOGUE" (SPITZ, 1963)

One example shall suffice to illustrate that the meaning conveyed by a "No" is derived from the human context within which it occurs. If a motorist stops a stranger to ask him whether the road straight ahead leads to Xville, he may receive the answer: "No, you must take the next turn to the right." In this context, the "No" implies neither aggression nor frustration. Rather it indicates that the stranger is *sharing a common world* with the motorist: he understands that the motorist wants to reach a certain place, his identification is with this particular aim, and his "No" protects the motorist from losing his way. It is in acknowledgment of this sharing identification that the motorist expresses his thanks to the stranger. This type of "No" may be described as the "coaching No."[1] It is proposed that the "No" with which a mother confronts the child is—in an ideal, conflict-free relation—intended to be a "coaching No" and is perceived as thus by the child. The mother who tells the child, "Don't play with matches," is coaching the child in how to deal with a shared world that is complicated and often dangerous, and about which she knows more than the child. It is not unreasonable to assume that the child, even if

[1] The term "coaching" is borrowed from Anselm Strauss (1959). In this paper the concept of coaching is, in contrast to Strauss, limited to interpersonal relations based on a protective identification of the coach with the needs of the learner.

he feels frustrated by such prohibition, is more affected by the sense of being coached in finding his way in this strange and new world, shared by him and the mothering person, than by an aggressive implication of the word "No." As a result of this coaching, the area of the world that the child can share with the parental persons is enlarged and enriched. This is true as long as mother and child partake in the "dialogue," as defined by Spitz (1963). This important concept denotes in Spitz' (1965) terminology an essentially nonverbal communication between mother and child, a "specific sector of reciprocity between mother and child" (p. 173) which is described more fully as a "dialogue of action and response which goes on in the form of a circular process within the dyad, as a continuous, mutually stimulating feedback circuit. Actually, it is a *precursor* of the dialogue, an archaic form of conversation. In the human it leads eventually to the acquisition of verbal communication, of speech" (p. 173). Because this is the earliest form of communication, the consequences of a breakdown of the dialogue are considered especially grave by Spitz (1964) insofar as "the deviation will become evident in increasing measure from phase to phase eventuating in a skewed personality" (p. 765). This breakdown of dialogue is not identical with maternal deprivation, maternal rejection, or other tangible forms of maternal neglect. One consequence of such a breakdown might well be the inability on the part of the child to perceive the mothering person's "No" as an aspect of the ongoing dialogue, i.e., as a "coaching No." In other words, the undiscriminating perception of every "No" as aggression on the part of the parental person might be considered an early manifestation of a damaged ego. Only by such children, it is suggested, will the "No" be perceived exclusively as frustrating. Referring back to Freud's (1925b) distinction between the negation (or affirmation) of a particular attribute of a thing, and the negation (or affirmation) of the existence of a thing in reality, it is proposed that there are individuals who perceive the parental "No," not as a verbal negation to them of a particular thing (for instance a piece of candy); rather, they interpret the verbal "No" as expressing a nonverbal negation by the other one of their own existence. Because this interpretation has a disruptive effect on the pattern of the object relations of the individual, it is referred to as the "malignant No." The "malignant No" does, in more severe cases, not only distort object relations, but affects the individual's total interaction with his social environment as well. It is the perception of the verbal "No" as a nonverbal "malignant No" that establishes a correlation between negation and aggression. The nature of this correlation will be investigated further, but it is necessary to state here that it was described decades ago by Erikson (1950), when he declared: "Deprivation of identity, not frustration, leads to murder" (p. 212). It seems indeed likely that the transformation of the "coaching No" into the "malignant No" indicates a damage to early processes of identity formation in the child. It also appears probable that such damage is specific for a certain pathology of the mother-infant dialogue.

THE MANIFESTATION OF THE EXPERIENCE OF "BEING NEGATED" IN CLINICAL OBSERVATION

The experience of "being negated in one's existence" remains unconscious, although affective aspects of it enter the individual's conscious perception. Its unconscious reality is hypostasized on the basis of certain characteristic modifications of the individual's object relations. They consist of an inability to deal with a temporary or permanent denial of their needs, i.e., negation in the sense of nonfulfillment of a desire, regardless of whether this negation emanates from another person, from the social order, or, in the most extreme cases, from the conditions of life itself. Coexisting with the inacceptability of negation, one observes in these individuals a characteristic manifestation of their instinctual drives, which ranges from a coercive sexual approach to varying degrees of aggression in their object relations. A definite correlation exists between the severity of the response toward negation and a shift from a sexual to an aggressive approach in their object relations. While it is not claimed that patterns of sexuality and aggression are *exclusively* determined by the perception of negation, the latter appears to be one determinant of drive manifestation that deserves attention. The following clinical observations attempt to illustrate these points.

Robert, a 27-year-old unmarried male patient, complained about his profoundly unsatisfactory relations with girls and about the difficulties in dealing with his associates at work. In both situations he encountered a rejecting, if not outright hostile attitude toward him which he could not understand because he tried hard to please both his girl friends as well as his employers and co-workers. His feelings about the cold and hostile responses he met with assumed at times a paranoid coloring, but generally left him dejected and depressed about his failure to establish satisfactory relations. In spite of good looks, intelligence, and other assets, he suffered repeated rebuffs from girls he was interested in, and lack of success and advancement in his chosen career.

During the treatment, it became clear that this patient expected an instantaneous and unconditional affirmative response to his verbalized and even to his not verbalized wishes. If he called a girl in order to make a date with her for a certain evening, he expected her to accept his invitation immediately and enthusiastically. If he wanted her to sit very close to him in the car, he was profoundly disappointed, if not angry, if she did not conform to his wish. This same expectation applied to every aspect of the girl's behavior: he wanted a girl to dress the way he liked it, enjoy the same things that he enjoyed. Otherwise, he perceived coolness, rejection, or hostility on her part. His own reaction would fluctuate between anxiety, depression, and rage against the particular girl or girls in general. These emotions reached their climax when a girl did not give in to his sexual advances. He justified the intensity of his disappointment (a disappointment that seemed especially keen when the girl was a casual date) by elaborating with great eloquence and vigor his philosophy of male-female relationships. He believed in total sexual freedom between the sexes, quoting extensively proponents of these views, stressing that any relationship between a man and a woman ought to be consummated sexually without hypocritical moral or religious restraints. A girl who accepted a date, according to his view, had implicitly consented to have sex relations with a man. To refuse the sex act was, therefore, a kind of a breach of contract. In striking contrast to these programmatic statements was his actual behavior in his relation with girls. The almost fanatically held views appeared oddly dissociated from the actually felt affects in a real contact with a girl. What he was trying to do was to enact a fantasy in which the girl was responding to his verbalized and not verbalized wishes like an automaton who had no spontaneity and no desire of her own, but was "coming to life" only through his own directions. He would tell the girl that they were going to his apartment to have sexual intercourse. He sometimes prescribed to the girl how she should dress to excite him sexually, even indicate how she should react to his advances. If the girl refused to cooperate with his instructions, he was disappointed, resentful, and often angry. If, however, the girl was willing to have sexual relations with him, he was disappointed too, because the reality of her spontaneous responses did not correspond to his anticipations in fantasy. He consequently had a let-down feeling even if he was successful, his sexual excitement was not very intense, and at times he had difficulties in performing adequately. Occasionally he met a girl who was just as eager to have sex relations with him as his theories postulated a girl should be. With an especially responsive girl, he admitted feeling bored if not somewhat disgusted. He explained this by saying that this girl just enjoyed *sex* but did not really respond to *him.* There were, however, exceptions which were all the more remarkable because they did not fit his theories at all, nor did they correspond to his fantasies. There were a few occasions when he met girls with whom he became genuinely emotionally involved. These he described as "always cooperative," in the sense that they enjoyed whatever he offered them in terms of entertainment, and were also tolerant of his sexual advances. They did not, however, fulfill his desire for complete freedom from any sexual restraint. These girls, whose company he enjoyed genuinely and for a long time, did not, in fact, consent to have sexual intercourse with him, one girl because of religious scruples, the other because of an unsettled marital status. Although he regretted their reluctance, it did not affect his fondness for these particular girls; in fact, he even contemplated marriage with either of them.

While his relationship to girls appeared thus very complex and full of emotional contradictions, his relationship to his superiors and co-workers was consistently strained. It seemed indeed true that he was thoroughly disliked both by his colleagues and by the people that worked under him. Ideas which he had contributed and developed were handed over to someone else because people expressed unwillingness to work on a project under his direction. Apparently the same coercive approach that estranged most of his girls alienated his co-workers, his secretaries, etc. He displayed an imperious and dictatorial manner, expecting instant execution of any order. This attitude expressed itself in many other situations as well. When required to wait, for instance, in a physician's office, he told the doctor's secretary that his time was as valuable as the doctor's, and that he would be back some day when the doctor could see him. Similar situations occurred when he had an appointment with a person with whom he had to discuss some matter pertaining to his work projects and whose cooperation was important for its success. He often held forth on the subject that certain rules, such as traffic laws, should not be applied to him. He referred to the immunity of diplomats and other high-ranking public officials with regard to speeding, and expected, though he was just a junior executive with a prestigious organization, that such immunity should also be extended to him. When his tactless manner antagonized people, the negative responses puzzled him, made him anxious and depressed, as if he was unable to see the obvious connection between his approach to people and their reaction to him.

The theoretical implications of the reported case for the thesis of this paper shall be stated briefly. In this connection, a quotation from Sandler (1960) seems pertinent:

> The problem of what it means to "feel loved," or to "restore narcissistic cathexis," is one which has as yet been insufficiently explored. What the child is attempting to restore is an affective state of well-being, which we can correlate, in terms of energy, with the level of narcissistic cathexis of the self. Initially this affective state, which normally forms the background of everyday experience, must be the state of bodily well-being which the infant experiences when his instinctual needs have been satisfied (as distinct from the pleasure in their satisfaction). This affective state later becomes localized in the self, and we see aspects of it in feelings of self-esteem as well as in normal background feelings of safety. The maintenance of this *central affective state* is perhaps the most powerful motive for ego development, and we must regard the young child (and later the adult) as seeking well-being as well as

> pleasure-seeking; the two are by no means the same, and in analysis we can often observe a conflict between the two [p. 149n].[2]

The conflict between seeking well-being and seeking pleasure is most obvious in the case of Robert. It is this conflict that seems to account for the inconsistencies and contradictions concerning the patient's coercive sexual and aggressive behavior on the one hand, and the actuality of his relations with girls on the other hand. We think of the sexual drive as a means to experience lust, joy, or ecstasy. In contrast we link the experience of well-being with inner harmony and security. For the gratification of such aims we need a sense of self-esteem based on the acceptance and respect of others and the internalized representations of important love objects in the superego. Well-being in this sense would be a function of the "loving and beloved superego" (Schafer, 1960). This patient appeared bereft of a sense of well-being as a central affective state which only under special circumstances gave way to a more comfortable feeling concerning himself.[3] His efforts to secure a sense of well-being consisted of quixotic attempts to coerce others into the role of a loving superego by means of sexuality and aggression. The function of his coercive sexuality and his aggressive manipulations is not primarily to enjoy sexual pleasure, but to obtain an unqualified and unconditional affirmative response to any kind of desire. This includes not only sexual desires, but many nonsexual wishes as well, such as the permission to drive at high speeds at will. A loving superego, in the interpretation of this patient, is one that says "yes" to whatever he demands. This superego is not fully internalized, but remains at-

[2]See also Nelson (1967). Referring to experiences that "will condition the young organism toward different patterns of feeling 'alive' and 'engaged,' " she stresses the importance of "[S]uch primary modes of awakening of the sense of self . . . in character formation and the individual's underlying perception of the world" (p. 6).

[3]Kubie (1963) has described, under the name of Central Affective Potential, a latent affective state to which he ascribes the decisive formative influence on personality development, object relations, patterns of sublimation, etc. Kubie stresses the diversity of Central Affective Potentials in different individuals. This concept appears applicable to the patients described here. Their underlying Central Affective Potential, as will be discussed more fully later, is a specific form of dread.

tached to a real person who will provide this affirmative, yes-saying attitude toward him. If he finds such an individual, he experiences a sense of well-being that changes his total behavior. This was the case with the girls of whom he grew extraordinarily fond. They were affirmative in their response to him as a total person, able to overlook the peculiarities by which he alienated most people. The striking fact under these circumstances was the disappearance of the coercive sexuality and of aggression as a response to this experience of feeling affirmed by these individuals. In the transference, he displayed a similar attitude toward the analyst whom he apparently perceived as an affirmative figure. Since, however, none of these experiences became truly internalized, he needed, when such relationships came to an end, a new person to take over the affirmative function on which his well-being depended. His method more often than not had the very opposite effect of confronting him with mildly to extremely negative responses to his coercive approach leading to a vicious circle, in that the increase of his emotional malaise made his approaches ever more aggressive, with the expectable negative result. That he failed to understand these predictable responses shows a definite disturbance of his reality testing, since he seemed unable to learn from experience. The use of coercive sexuality and aggression rather than pleasurable gratification in order to bring about well-being appears thus as a defense against the possibility of encountering negation, instead of affirmation. What is perceived as negation in these individuals is so all-encompassing that they appear incapable of distinguishing between shades of negation. What is not considered unconditional affirmation is easily perceived as a total negation—a negation not of *a* specific desire, *a* particular need, but, as became clear from the response of the patients, a negation of the reality of their existence. It is this unusual response to negation that led me to hypostasize the concept of the experience of the "malignant No." The instinctual drives are placed in the service of eliminating the possibility of the dreaded negation of existence, and it is this striving for the elimination of such possibility that maintains their coercive and aggressive force. This pattern proved to be especially destructive in its effect on psychoanalytic therapy.

THE EXPERIENCE OF "BEING NEGATED" AND ITS EFFECT ON THE PSYCHOANALYTIC SITUATION

It should be emphasized that the coercive sexuality and/or aggression of individuals who have experienced the "malignant No" does not invariably lead to acting out of sexual coercion and/or aggression recognizable in the individual's manifest behavior. This can be the case, but there are many other outcomes of the coercive sexuality and aggression that depend on numerous factors, for instance, on the anxieties aroused in the ego by the pressure of sexuality and aggression. Thus, the actual behavior of these individuals may range from subtle but pervasive seductiveness with anxious withdrawal when this seductiveness meets with response, to a pattern of "sexual addictiveness," where the consummation of the sexual act is experienced as the only means of feeling affirmed. If the individual feels, however, that the sexual partner is interested in his own sexual pleasure only, and does not respond to him as a total person, the ecstatic quality of sexual experience may give way to an even greater sense of having been negated in his existence. Such disappointment may be followed by a new attempt to find affirmation with another sex partner. Thus a vicious circle may develop, with all kinds of destructive results, including psychotic withdrawal.

These consequences of the experience of the "malignant No" manifest themselves in a characteristic way in the transformation of the transference into a battle for total affirmation, in which the affirmation is acceptable to the patient on his or her terms only. This type of transference may prove unmanageable because the therapeutic process in itself implies to some of these patients a repetition of the experience of "being negated," in that the abstinence which is inherent in the psychoanalytic process is perceived as a negation of their reality.

The perception of the therapeutic process as an experience of being negated was most poignant in some women patients who responded with an initial development of a seemingly intense, at times clinging, transference. This positive transference coexisted with a violent rejection of the analytic process. On the contrary, the more positive the feeling toward the therapist, the more negative the reaction to interpretations that were offered. They were belittled as mere empty words, or worse, as criticism or even insults. It was very clear, however, that it was not the particular content of the interpretation that these patients found so unacceptable, but the disappointment in not having obtained a total affirmative response to them as individuals. It was quite obvious that an acceptable response implied to them unconditional affirmation. Mrs. N., for instance, became very abusive and vehemently criticized the stupidity of the interpretations. She would then become very distraught, anxious, and depressed, sometimes leaving the session abruptly with the remark, "You do not perceive me at all." Sometimes she returned, or telephoned, apologizing for her intemperate language. Such sessions often left her anxious and depressed for many hours afterwards. She denied most emphatically that she expected anything from the therapist beyond help with her personal problems. She wished that the therapist would take the initiative, start talking, not wait for what she had to say, not just listen and give interpretations. This she interpreted as lack of communication. References to statements that she herself had made, and which appeared meaningful in a certain context, she perceived as negative comments; "Now you are throwing this up at me," was one of her remarks on such an occasion.

Mrs. G. had a tendency to respond to every interpretation with an almost automatic "No." The suggestion that her marital difficulties were due to a particular type of interaction between her husband and herself, one which was very threatening to both of them, she saw as intolerable criticism. When the point was illustrated by reference to certain specific situations which she had mentioned, she could only conclude that she was blamed for everything that had happened. In one such context she burst out: "You always negate me. I cannot endure to be negated." Both of these patients, after many years of treatment, came to the conclusion that the total affirmative response on their terms was not forthcoming. It led in both to a most conflictual ending of the treatment, an ending neither of them truly wanted. For both of them, the treatment implied a degree of feeling negated in their existence which they perceived as intolerable.[4]

[4]See also Schur's (1966a) important discussion of certain patients whose resistance is impervious to working through. Especially pertinent in the context of this chapter are Schur's comments on patients with "masochistic character disorder with a tendency to depression" (pp. 188-189).

In male patients, extreme fluctuations in the relationship to the therapist are common too, as was the case with Frank, a young business executive. He had consulted several psychiatrists before entering psychoanalytic treatment; for both of them he felt an unrelenting loathing because of certain questions they had raised. In one case the question pertained to the patient's emotional capacity to deal with his managerial responsibilities under the pressure of his often intense anxiety. This he perceived as a total negation of his competence, his intellectual abilities, and his personal qualities. He devoted himself to endless tirades on how one day he would "fix that guy," followed by streams of invective, which were probably intended to intimidate the therapist. In a similar manner he would talk about business associates, employees, and customers who had in one way or another differed with his judgement or displeased him by not cooperating with him. He was in business with many relatives, among them a brother who was his favorite. Nevertheless he had frequent fits of rage that led to repeated threats of physical violence. In college, he had once threatened his brother with a knife because of a disagreement between them. At the same time, he could be very solicitous and almost fawning when he aimed at being "recognized" by a person whose good opinion and respect were important to him. With girls, he was aggressively seductive, passionate in his lovemaking, which once he described as the "only moments of happiness" in his life when he felt free of anxiety. It was all the more striking that after he married a girl who was most responsive to him as a sexual partner, he felt uneasy about their frequent sexual relations and particularly about the fact that his wife seemed to enjoy sex so much. His verbalizations suggested that total affirmation—in this case expressed as willing surrender—was giving him happiness only when he could interpret it as affirmation of himself by someone he perceived as a potential "negator," someone he had, at least in fantasy, coerced—by seduction, or, as in the case of his business affiliates, by aggressive threats—into affirming his existence. He was at first very pleased about his experience in analysis. He was rather fulsome in his praise. How much better analysis was than the treatment he had before. As the treatment progressed, however, he was often profoundly bored with it, expressing the desire to cut the hour short, or to end the treatment altogether, or complaining that he had to come to his appointment when he was really too busy. It seemed he had anticipated being negated as a person, was at first delighted to feel "affirmed," but when the affirmation lost the quality of having been "won" from the therapist by coercion or seduction, he felt depressed, bored, fatigued, and often extremely anxious. He did continue treatment in spite of great fluctuations in his sense of relatedness, of self-esteem. He, like the patient Robert, appeared to use the analyst as a "loving superego" which he needed to sustain him. His fear of "feeling negated" in his existence functioned in him also as a challenge to which he would often rise, in his own aggressive way, by performing successfully. This was also true of Mrs. N., whose dread of feeling negated—"I shall never want to live as one of those grey people of whom nobody is ever aware"—acted as a constant stimulus to achieve success in her chosen field.

There are certain striking similarities concerning the patients who, according to the thesis of this paper, had experienced the threat of the "malignant No" in their early life. None of these patients could be said to have suffered gross emotional deprivations. Not one of them came from a broken home. Neither were they only children; a number of them were middle children. Some of them came from affluent families, with parents trying to give them many advantages such as private schools, summer camps, expensive clothing, etc. None of them came from poverty-stricken backgrounds. All of them, however, remembered their childhood as a period of profound loneliness and inner isolation, even though they often remembered having been a favorite child. Mrs. N. spoke of her childhood as "endless periods of silence." She spoke with great warmth of her father, who never failed to hug her, but added: "I cannot remember, though, that he was ever talking to me or I to him. My closest companions were my pets." Frank was sent each year to an exclusive camp. He remembers his loneliness there and the conviction that nobody would come and bring him back home. The same was true of Robert. He never felt that anybody communicated with him, although he was given many material and education advantages. These facts must be taken into consideration in an attempt at a genetic reconstruction of these patients' development.

GENETIC RECONSTRUCTION OF THE EXPERIENCE OF "BEING NEGATED" IN ONE'S EXISTENCE

In view of the absence of any gross emotional deprivation in these patients, it seems appropriate to apply Spitz' (1963, 1964, 1965) concept of the derailment of dialogue to a genetic reconstruction of the pathology. The concept of the derailment of dialogue is suggested here as constituting at least a major contributing factor to pathological development, but a factor within a "complemental series" (Freud, 1916-17, p. 347). This must be emphasized particularly with regard to the development of the instinctual drives, where it is known that other genetic and maturational factors cannot be neglected. Important as the concept of derailment of dialogue is, its exact nature is not yet fully known. It is likely that Spitz' (1964) theory of the stimulus overload is true for some cases. Brodey's (1965) description of the image-pattern of mother-child relationship can also lead to a derailment of dialogue, but perhaps of a different type than that which Spitz (1964) observed. The disturbance in mother-child communication which is referred to in this paper as the "malignant No" may not be identical with either of these situations.

In the cases reported here, there are so many variations in the degree of pathology that the disturbance of dialogue must be assumed to occur in varying degrees of severity. They have, however, in spite of great differences, certain common characteristics, such as the tendency to respond to negation in the previously described intolerant way, culminating in the coercive-aggressive drive pattern. There thus remains enough specificity to justify a proposition concerning the particular developmental origin of this disturbance of dialogue. The strong sense of being alone and isolated in their childhood, as well as the transference phenomena encountered in the psychoanalytic treatment of these patients, makes it particularly suggestive that they suffered a disturbance of their "mirroring experience" (Lichtenstein, 1964): "The child, while not capable of perceiving the maternal object or of possessing a sense of self or of identity, experiences its existence as reflected by the libidinal cathexis of the mother. The mother, in contrast to the non-human environment, reflects back to the child a configuration of its own presence" (p. 54). Insofar as this mirroring experience was considered essential for the later development of a sense of self, it would be consistent with this hypothesis to assume that the patients who perceive the verbal "No" as a nonverbal negation of their existence suffered from some disturbance of the mirroring experience.[5]

This hypothesis, if confirmed, could have interesting implications for certain assumptions of psychoanalytic theory. In a restatement of Freud's thesis (1900), Gill (1963) has postulated that a "mental content can stimulate the sense organ [consciousness] only if it possesses . . . 'quality,' and that 'quality' can be derived only from perception or from sensations of pleasure and pain from within" (p. 63). But, as Gill points out, Freud considered the possibility that contents possessing great sensory intensity may also excite consciousness directly. Freud (1900) considered the sensations of pleasure and unpleasure as directly expressing the state of instinctual drive tension. (See also Schur, 1966.) In Sandler's (1960) previously quoted opinion, the sensations of pleasure-unpleasure and those of "well-being" should be distinguished from one another. Does this perhaps imply an additional "quality" of mental contents (Gill, 1963) or primitive thought processes (Schur, 1966a) which is capable of stimulating consciousness directly, a consciousness of "well-being" rather than one of pleasure or unpleasure? The subjective consciousness of the patients who, according to the hypothesis presented in this paper, have experienced the "malignant No" seem to lack a basic sense of "well-being." It was suggested this could be due to their not having experienced the subjective affirmation of their reality by a disturbance in the "mirroring" experience. This would make it probable that "mirroring," i.e., the experience of one's own reality as affirmed by the other one, endows mental contents with a "quality"—we may call it "subjective affirmation"—which becomes conscious as the affect of well-being, which, for Sandler (1960), is the underlying experience of being loved on the part of the child. If this were so, we would have to consider the possibility that affirmation and negation do not primarily, as Freud (1925b) thought, confirm or deny whether a thing has the good or bad attribute, but whether

[5]The mirroring experience of the child through its reflection in the mother may be the genetic precursor of the Mirror Stage described by Lacan (1953).

there is an experience of feeling subjectively affirmed or negated. The development of the judgement of affirmation and negation, as Freud (1925b) describes it, would differ according to whether the child has previously experienced himself affirmed or negated in his existence. Because the ego functions of negation are important aspects of reality testing, it would be understandable that the hypostasized experience of the "malignant No" affects this function to a remarkable degree in the patients described previously. But the most striking feature in the symptomatology of the patients was the coercive pattern of their sexuality and the tendency toward aggression in their object relations. This would speak in favor of the assumption of a genetic interdependence between the drive tension of the individual and his capacity for the affective state of well-being due to the experience of subjective affirmation by the other one. A shift toward coercive sexuality and/or aggression would occur as a result of the absence of that "quality" in their mental processes which brings about the conscious affective state of well-being. This suggests that the instinctual drives might serve, in case of absence or deficiency of the experience of subjective affirmation, as an alternative means constituting a kind of reserve against the threat of feeling negated in one's existence.[6] Through this regressive use of the sexual and/or aggressive drives, the aggressor manages to perceive the object's response to them as an affirmation of his existence.

THE AFFIRMATIVE FUNCTION OF THE INSTINCTUAL DRIVES

With the last remarks, we return to the question of a correlation between negation and aggression. It does not appear that the ego function of negation is genetically derived from the aggressive drive as Freud had suggested (1925b). Rather, there seems to exist a correlation between the experience of feeling negated in one's existence

[6] The absence of the experience of subjective affirmation can become conscious as an affect of dread. This affect has been described by various authors under different terms and has been conceptualized in accordance with the theoretical approach of the author. Jones' (1927) concept of aphanisis should be mentioned here, as well as Eidelberg's (1957, 1962) concept of "narcissistic mortification." Sullivan's (1953) "personification of not-me," characterized by the break-through of "uncanny emotions," which he lists as awe, horror, loathing, or dread, and of which he furthermore says that they are "practically beyond discussion in communicative terms" (pp. 163-164), seems to refer to the same class of experience.

(a disturbance in the "mirroring experience") and the dominance of aggressive drives in the individual's object relations. More generally stated, both sexuality and aggression can be employed to *ward off* the "dreadful" affect of feeling negated in one's existence. Sexuality and aggression thus appear as the means of ultimate resort for undoing the very possibility of negation and for assuring instantaneous, total, and unconditional affirmation of one's existence from the object that is sexually or aggressively pursued. This implies that sexuality and aggression are perceived as capable of establishing object relations which, in contrast to all other forms of object relations, are exempt from the possibility of negation. According to Spitz (1957), the acquisition of the "No" which enables each individual to affirm or negate, is the developmental prerequisite to raising "object relations from the level of the instinctual drive to the level of social relations" (p. 132). The capacity to affirm or negate—making possible the acquisition of the function of judgement (Freud 1925b)—leads to the emergence of thought, separation of I and Not-I, autonomy, and awareness of self, all of which form the developmental prerequisite for object relations on the human level. The implication here is that human object relations are dependent on a functioning ego. It is the ego that has acquired the capacity to negate, but the id remains beyond negation. Insofar as the instinctual drives are an aspect of the id, they can only affirm, but not negate. An individual able to stimulate by his sexuality and/or aggression the sexuality or the fear of another individual perceives instantaneously a response to his existence from the other one that constitutes an unconditional affirmation of his reality. The individual who reacts to the sexual desire or the aggressive threat of the other person may mobilize his ego and superego defenses. These defenses can restrain his own sexual responses from being expressed or acted upon. The individual cannot, however, *negate* having been sexually stimulated or threatened by the perception of an aggressive threat. If one would paraphrase the nonverbal dialogue between two such individuals, one would have to say that it leads to an answer on the part of stimulated object of "Yes, but . . ." The "yes" would imply that there has been an affirmative response, the "but" would be a negation made possible by the ego and superego defenses that enable the individual to refrain from action such as sexual intercourse.

Nothing, however, can transform the affirmative response of the instinctual drives into a negation. The affirmation may become apparent to the sexual pursuer or the aggressor by blushing on the part of the person to whom the sexual message has been communicated, or by trembling, as a response to aggression, and by numerous other "affirmative" somatic manifestations. It is, therefore, possible to undo by means of sexuality and/or aggression all the developmental steps that have been acquired by the emergence of the capacity to negate. The more coercive the sexual approach and the more violent the aggression, the more obvious will be the affirmative response—affirming, that is, the existence of the aggressor—on the part of the chosen object. Everybody's capacity to negate, with all its developmental consequences, will indeed collapse under threat of violence and aggression. Even heroic individuals cannot conceal their pain in the face of torture. Thus, the individual who insists on coercing another one to respond to him with instantaneous and unconditional affirmation will always triumph by the use of coercive sexuality and/or aggression. What he will not obtain by aiming at the inherent psychic vulnerability of the other one is a genuine object relation on a human level which can only be obtained by two individuals permitting each other to affirm or negate the uniqueness of their individualities in an act of autonomous choice. One could paraphrase Kris' (1934) formulation of "regression in the service of the ego" by speaking of a regression of object relations in the service of clinging to the certainty of one's existence. Thus, the triumph that coercive sexuality and/or aggression may achieve in terms of unconditional affirmation of an individual's existence by another one, is always a Pyrrhic victory. The victory has been won at the price of having lost the yearned-for affirmation of the individual, not as just existing for another one, but of having been freely acknowledged by the other person's total personality. This is the tragedy of the individuals who have suffered the experience of the "malignant No": their victories always end up in a more profound sense of feeling negated in their existence.

Nevertheless, there exist forms of feeling negated in one's existence that reach such extremes of dread that only the most violent aggression affords them the means to compel the other one to recognize their existence as real. Edward Albee (1959) has powerfully presented a variation of this theme—in that the victim coerces the murderer to acknowledge his existence—in one of his plays. But in order to fathom the full implications of the fateful interdependence between the experience of feeling negated in one's existence and the malignant transformation of the instinctual drives, one has to turn to the writings of the Marquis de Sade (1740-1814). Psychiatry has failed to acknowledge any debt to de Sade beyond its appropriation of his name in the adjectival sense. What de Sade has to say about the relationship between the experience of feeling negated in one's existence and the recourse to unlimited sexual coercion and murderous violence constitutes, however, one of the most lucid and intellectually forthright confrontations with the problems of human relations whose primary aim has become the unconditional affirmation of one's existence by the other one. It is impossible to do justice to the implications of de Sade's ideas within the limits of this paper. The remarks which follow can therefore only aim at demonstrating the relevance of de Sade to the work of the psychoanalyst who attempts to deal with the emotional problems of "the age of alienation."

THE USE OF SEXUALITY AND AGGRESSION AS A DEFENSE AGAINST THE EXPERIENCE OF "FEELING NEGATED" IN DE SADE

Since their appearance, the writings of the Marquis de Sade have been considered as among the most notorious examples of pornographic literature. De Sade's claim that they were didactic treatises expounding a revolutionary philosophy of the human condition was taken seriously by few in the last part of the nineteenth century. A philosophical re-evaluation of de Sade on a large scale has been in progress only in our own era. Among the outstanding contributions on the part of philosophers regarding de Sade's place in the history of ideas is a study by Simone de Beauvoir (1951-52), on which the following remarks are based. The direct quotations from de Sade are taken partly from de Beauvoir's essay, and partly from an American selection of his writings (Dinnage, 1953), which appeared together with the English translation of de Beauvoir's study. "The curse which weighed upon Sade" de Beauvoir characterizes as his "autism," which she defines as his incapacity for "ever forgetting himself or being genuinely aware of the reality of the other person" (p. 33). What de Beauvoir calls de Sade's autism is interpreted here as the affective state of an individual who has, in a most extreme way, experienced the sense of being negated in his existence, i.e., the experience of the "malignant No." This proposition is derived entirely from statements found in de Sade's writings. In these writings one of the recurrent themes is de Sade's horror concerning the silence and total indifference of Nature. For de Sade, as an eighteenth-century atheist and mechanist, Nature is the only reality, but he perceives Nature, which he calls "the mother of the human race" (p. 31), as truly murderously hostile and destructive to her creatures. "Man is isolated in the world," he asserts (p. 66), and he conceives as man's greatest torment "the impossibility of offending Nature" (p. 70). When de Sade describes the atrocities that his protagonists commit, he lets them express again and again their impotent rage against Nature's indifference and silence. "We have reviled, dared and defied Nature. . . . Oh, rest assured, no crime in the world is capable of drawing the wrath of Nature upon us" (p. 198). It is obvious that by describing Nature as indifferent, cruel, and murderous, even attributing to her "concealment of motives" (p. 70), de Sade anthropomorphizes Nature. This is logically incompatible with his mechanistic view of Nature, which he emphasizes repeatedly. Reading these resentful, bitter tirades hurled against Nature—"I abhor Nature . . . I loathe her" (p. 70)—one is reminded of Sullivan's (1953) concept of the "not-me," which is marked by the breakthrough of "uncanny emotions," consisting of "awe, horror, loathing and dread" (p. 163).

It appears justifiable to interpret all this bitterness and hate as the response of an individual who desperately attempts to establish a dialogue with someone who refuses to answer. It is proposed that de Sade responds to the silence of Nature as if he has encountered a cosmic "malignant No." It is not surprising then to find that his reaction to this "malignant No" shows a most striking resemblance to that of the patients previously described. De Sade's reply to Nature's "malignant No" is his proclamation of a new morality, in which the most violent forms of coercive sexuality and the most destructive methods of aggression toward any potential love object are hailed as the only means to establish genuine contact between two individuals. Thus, de Beauvoir states, "Eroticism appears in de Sade as a mode of communication, the only valid one" (p. 79). But this eroticism is characterized by coercive sexuality and aggression: "At the basis of de Sade's entire sexuality, and hence his ethics, is the fundamental identity of coition and cruelty" (p. 31). "What the torturer demands is that . . . the victim recognize . . . that his destiny is the freedom of the tyrant. He is then united to his tyrant by the closest of bonds. They form a genuine couple" (p. 78). The "freedom of the tyrant" is nothing other than the total, instantaneous, and unconditional acknowledgement of the existence of the torturer as the only person who is real for the victim. In the name of this freedom, de Sade demands the total elimination of any possibility of negation in the relationship of the individual and the object of his sexual and/or aggressive desires. The "new citizen" must be "free to vent (on the objects of his desires) all those passions prescribed in him, without ever being restrained by anything. . . . The lightest refusal (of complete subordination) will be punished immediately" (pp. 132-133). By becoming thus the victim's destiny, possibly his death, the torturer has gained his "freedom," i.e., he is no longer negated in his existence, he is, for that one moment, totally real. In de Sade's words: "What does one want when one is engaged in the sexual act? That everything about you give you its utter attention, think only of you, care only for you" (p. 16). This total acknowledgement of one person's existence by the other one is for de Sade incompatible with giving pleasure to the sexual partner. "If the objects who serve us feel ecstasy, they are then much more often concerned with themselves than with us, and our own enjoyment is consequently impaired" (p. 33). For individuals who have not suffered the experience of being negated, the ecstasy of the partner enhances their own gratification. De Sade's objection to the sexual pleasure felt by the partner is almost verbatim the argument used by the patient Robert to explain his annoyance with a girl who gave every indication of enjoying intercourse with him. De Sade, however, takes one more step: the sexual object must not enjoy the sexual act, but must submit to it while suffering, because "No kind of sensation is keener and more active than that of pain; its impressions are unmistakable" (p. 34). In the terminology of this paper, no acknowledgement of their existence for individuals afflicted with the dread of being negated, no "affirmation" is more convincing, more "unmistakable" than the evidence that the other one is reacting to the pain caused by the aggressor. It should be noted, however, that not only the aggressor, if he suffers from the sense of being negated, feels confirmed absolutely in his existence by becoming another person's destiny. The victim too, if he has suffered from the experience of the "malignant No," may perceive it as an acknowledgement of his existence if he is able to coerce the other one into a frenzy of violence directed toward him (see above reference to Albee, 1959).

In summary, de Sade's writings seem to support the thesis proposed in this paper that "feeling negated" in one's existence interferes with the development of a sense of well-being and makes the individual prone to an affective state of dread or horror. Against this dread the individual mobilizes the instinctual drives as a means of obtaining total and unconditional affirmation of his reality from another one. The more severe the sense of "feeling negated," the more aggressive become the means of obtaining unconditional affirmation. The writings of de Sade would be remarkable if they did nothing else but state this interdependence in a most explicit manner. De Sade is important, however, for numerous other reasons that are relevant for psychoanalysts who attempt to deal with the psychological complexities of our present age. De Sade is perhaps *the* philosopher of alienation. For him, alienation is a new, radical, philosophical, and moral position, the only one that modern man, existing in a godless universe, could support with intellectual honesty.

DE SADE ON THE NEW MORALITY AND NEW FREEDOM FOR ALIENATED MAN

It would be a fallacy to understand the outrageousness of de Sade's philosophy as nothing but a rationalization of the personal sexual aberrations of an individual who had suffered a severe disturbance of his sense of self. It is true enough, as de Beauvoir says, "that his vices condemned him to solitude. He was to demonstrate the necessity of solitude and the supremacy of evil" (p. 65). What makes de Sade important as the most articulate representative of a new ideology is the fact that "he ascribed to his situation the value of a metaphysical inevitability" (p. 65). "His situation" does not only refer to his sexual perversions. Rather, it defines his existence within a universe which is perceived as indifferent if not hostile toward life, and within a social order that is seen as inherently opposed to the interests of the individual. He had no illusions about the oppressive character of the old aristocratic order into which he was born. He had hoped that the new order, brought about by the French Revolution, would integrate him into a collectivity. But the Terror, which he was to witness "with the guillotine before my eyes" (p. 26), convinced him that the "body politic . . . considers men a mere collection of objects" (p. 26). His new morality, which has been referred to as the Ethics of Criminality, is based on the conviction that crime (i.e., destruction) is the supreme Law of Nature and therefore the only natural law of conduct, and that every society is criminal (destructive) in its relation toward the individual. Therefore "In a criminal society one must be a criminal" (p. 75). This is not meant as a submission to society, but as a refusal "of any complicity with the evils of the given situation" (p. 76). Thus, total alienation from society is the only way to assert one's existence as a person: "The most perfect being we could conceive would be one who would depart most radically from our conventions and consider them most hateful" (p. 202). We are confronted here, therefore, with a *threefold* sequence of the experience of feeling negated in one's existence. In this paper, only the first psychological layer of these experiences has been considered. It was assumed to have its roots in a miscarriage of the processes of individuation. Now, however, we discover in de Sade experiences of feeling negated in one's existence by a malevolent conception of Nature and Society. Neither of these can be said to have its roots in the vicissitudes of individual psychological development. Conceptions of nature are shared aspects of the sense of reality in a given society. The same is true to a large extent of the concepts an individual forms about the society to which he belongs, or about the role of any social organism. While in the latter case different classes have greatly varying conceptions of the society in which they live—an individual belonging to the underprivileged class will have a vastly different conception of society than one belonging to an affluent or a ruling class—it is nevertheless true that these conceptions are shared by a group so that they too partake in the formation of the sense of reality of the individual. The interdependence between the *individual* experience of feeling negated—the "malignant No"—and the *shared* experience of feeling negated by Nature and/or Society is a complex one. In the era of de Sade, he was isolated insofar as his social and moral philosophy was concerned—so much so that the new Republican Society confined him to a mental hospital. His conceptions of Nature were, however, shared by many philosophers of the age. His critique of Society, although more extreme than most, was not unique in that period. But no other contemporary philosopher arrived at an Ethics of Criminality comparable to that of de Sade, nor at the conceptualization of total alienation from any social organization as the only true form of individual freedom—the new freedom of the libertine and criminal—thus consciously promoting "an apocalyptic condition which constrains all individuals to ensure their separateness, and thus their truth, in a state of constant tension" (de Beauvoir, 1953, p. 76). Does this imply that only when all three experiences of feeling negated—the individual one of the "malignant No" and the shared ones of feeling negated by Nature and Society—coincide in the total experience of an individual, that only then a radical transformation of the personality results in which the freedom to engage in coercive sexuality and aggression characterizes the individual's object relations because there is no other way to be certain of one's reality? For the answer we have to turn from de Sade to the contemporary world, because de Sade's apocalyptic vision has become the existential truth for a whole generation of intellectuals, artists, writers, and "alienated youth" (Keniston, 1965). While not all of them would accept all of de Sade's theses, they all share essential aspects of his ideology. The relationship between de Sade and the contemporary mode of experience has not escaped the attention of other observers. Thus, Steiner (1965) states: "There may be deeper affinities than we as yet understand between the 'total freedom' of the uncensored erotic imagination and the total freedom of the sadist. . . . Both are exercised at the expense of someone else's humanity, of someone else's most precious right—the right to a private life of feeling" (p. 76). In the context of this paper, one might say: someone else's right to affirm *or* negate. Susan Sontag (1966) defines the sensibility of the modern artist as one "which disclaims ideas, which situates itself *beyond negation*"

(p. 229, italics added). In its more extreme forms, this new freedom is encountered in the cult of sex and violence by such groups as the Hell's Angels (Thompson, 1966) and in many of the radical revolutionary ideologies which extoll violence as the only means of countering the threat of "existential negation" (Fanon, 1963). These themes can only be hinted at within the limits of this paper. They raise more questions about the condition of man in a technological society than it is yet possible to answer. It might well be possible that it is modern technology itself which creates conditions under which the psychological experience of the "malignant No" becomes a dangerous factor in child development. Perhaps this is the result of radical changes in the pattern of family life, as Mitscherlich (1965) has suggested. Keniston (1965) has raised the question of the effects of the "technological ego" on personality development. Together with modern man's perception of existing in an impersonal universe and feeling threatened as an individual by a depersonalizing social system, the sequence of a threefold negation of personal existence may thus be a far more universal experience than in previous ages.

If it should be borne out that this threefold sequence of existential negation is able to bring about a profound change in the structure of modern man's personality, the study of the hypothesis of the "malignant No" has more than a theoretical significance for the understanding of human individuation. It would raise issues of relevance for our age of violence and existential despair, urgent issues that the psychoanalyst least of all can shirk. When Freud discovered the Unconscious as a dynamic concept, embodying for him, at first, the instinctual drives, he laid the foundations for a new science of the human mind. His ideas were, however, relevant beyond the field of psychiatry. They contributed to a new self-knowledge of an era. As psychoanalysis developed and was amplified by the discovery of the unconscious aspects of the ego and the superego, it became a general psychology whose influence has touched profoundly the social sciences, the moral climate, and the arts of a whole generation. Today, psychoanalysis appears to many to have lost touch with the problems and agonies of the technological and social revolution through which we are living. This revolution which touches all aspects of human life has, to use the language of St. Augustine, made man a question to himself. By raising the issue of the unconscious aspects of the human self and their dialectic relationship to the possibility of man's relatedness to the other one, within the context of nature and the society of which he is a part, psychoanalysis addresses itself to the phenomenon of modern man's alienation. The hypothesis of the "malignant No" is an attempt to uncover the roots of a regressive, dedifferentiating process that deserves to be called a malignant transformation of the human potential.

ADDENDUM

The reader will be aware of the fact that this paper was written at a moment of contemporary history very different from that of the present. While the late months of 1966 belong to a relatively recent past, the "revolution" had yet to occur. Neither the student uprising in Paris, nor those at Columbia, Harvard, and elsewhere had taken place. The flood of publications on the Counterculture, the New Morality, and the like, which constitutes a library in itself, was just beginning to emerge. The various commissions on violence were still in the process of gathering material which has since been published in a variety of reports. The author is fully aware of the fact that since the formulation of this paper both events and their sociological and psychological interpretation have gone rapidly beyond their original frame of reference. The writer has nevertheless decided to let the text stand. An attempt, he feels, to bring it up to date would shift the emphasis from the basic psychoanalytic propositions which form its nucleus to a psychoanalytic study centering on the psychohistorical dimension for which the time, in the writer's opinion, has not yet come. Some of the psychoanalytic propositions have been further elaborated by the author (1970).

CHAPTER 9

Transference and Structure

Harold P. Blum, M.D.

Since Freud (1901) described transference in the "Dora" case, the scientific study of this phenomenon has resulted in enormous theoretical and technical advances in psychoanalysis. This paper applies the structural viewpoint and ego psychology to some of the complexities of transference. Transference will be viewed in terms of the infantile mental organization, the primary process, and the interplay of both development and structural regression. Transference is pursued in a multifaceted survey which includes a clinical and theoretical note on erotized transference. The paper further explores the relation between transference and resistance, and aspects of reality, autonomy, and adaptation.

Transference is a universal, usually unconscious, automatic archaic phenomenon which arises spontaneously. Stern (1957) saw the biological matrix of transference in the conditioned response in which reaction to a previous experience is transferred to a perception symbolizing it. New situations derive meaning from and reactivate previous experiences. Stern compared transference to the unextinguished conditioned response; there is a fixation to past response instead of objective evaluation of the present.

Following Nunberg (1951) I shall define transference as the displacement of aspects of an unconscious mental representation of an object onto a mental representation of a current external object.

Dr. Blum is Assistant Clinical Professor, Division of Psychoanalytic Education, Department of Psychiatry, State University of New York, Downstate Medical Center, Brooklyn, New York.

Transference depends on memory and mental representation. Memories (and fantasies) of significant past objects are transferred to current object representations (or their symbols), investing them with qualities of the archaic object representation and attempting to repeat or restore the past relationship in the present. The present is misunderstood in terms of the past; the past is repeated in the present. Transference utilizes the primary process, achieving a timeless perceptual identity between the past memory image and the current object percept. The perceptual identity is related to unconscious wish fulfillment and reflects the mechanisms of displacement and symbolization. Unconscious perception rapidly undergoes primary-process transformation. Percepts registered outside of awareness are readily invested with transference from the infantile drive organization of memory (Fisher, 1954).

At the time of its discovery, transference was immediately conceptualized according to the prevailing drive orientation of psychoanalysis, with emphasis on the presence of positive or negative transference depending on whether the investment was of libidinal or aggressive energy. With the advent of structural theory, complex ego and superego aspects of transference were gradually recognized. Even in 1901 Freud realized that not all transference was an unmodified reprint, that developmental influences resulted in a revised edition of the past.

Where emotions were studied in structural terms of complex affective states of trust and confidence, suspicion and hate, affection and resentment, the description of positive or negative transference in terms of drive investment did not do justice to the affects involved. Not only were drive derivatives, affects, and attitudes transferred, but defenses against them as well; and, in structural terms, infantile modes of adaptation and superego demand and ideals. (I have already related transference to such ego functions as memory and object representations.) Analytic transference evolves as a complex unconscious repetition which involves regressive patterns of structure and function, utilizing the primary process and projection.

TRANSFERENCE AND TRANSFERENCE NEUROSIS

Psychoanalysis does not create transference, but permits its observation and promotes its development and concentration within the analytic situation. The patient perceives and reacts to the analyst in terms of the crucial infantile object-representations, allowing a re-experiencing of the distorting influences of the past upon the present. The intense revival, the concentration and continuity of the transference of neurotic conflict in psychoanalysis, constitutes the transference neurosis.

I use the term transference neurosis here in the clinical sense of the transference that is created in classical psychoanalysis, not as opposed to Freud's "narcissistic neurosis." The transference neurosis is a treatment illness with symptoms invested with transference meaning. These transferred symptoms are derivatives, but not necessarily duplicates, of symptoms of the infantile neurosis. Transference and symptoms do not have a direct or constant relationship during psychoanalysis. To define the transference neurosis solely in terms of symptoms would be conceptually regressive. Today, neurosis means character neurosis. Transference neurosis includes neurotic character attitudes such as compliance or petulance, and the transferences emerging in free associations and fantasies as well as in symptoms. Transference analysis is directed at unconscious conflict rather than manifest symptomatic disturbance. Anna Freud once stated (1946) that only in a transference neurosis is the original neurosis given up during treatment and replaced by a new neurotic formation in which the analyst has taken the place of the original objects in the patient's emotional life. I do not believe that transference neurosis precludes generalized neurotic behavior or that it totally replaces the original neurosis. The patient's neurosis is probably never exclusively or ideally confined to the analytic situation.

The analysis of the transference neurosis has become the cornerstone of adult psychoanalytic technique and distinguishes psychoanalysis from all other psychotherapeutic methods. The patient arrives with transference readiness, depending upon his fantasies and expectations and his knowledge of the analytic situation. The initial transference, for example, may be related to a real or fantasied object loss. A severely depressed woman arranged to begin her analysis on the anniversary of her father's death, in confirmation of Lewin's (1950) observation that initial transference can be an attempt at restitution of object loss.

In contrast to the spontaneous appearance of transference phenomena, the development of the transference neurosis is partially dependent on the analysis of initial resistances and defenses resulting in the loosening of defenses and character. The benevolent neutrality and abstinence of the analyst are vital. The patient's typical personality reactions to people are at first also displayed to the analyst, but as transference attitudes press against old defenses, the personality integration begins to shift, and the transference neurosis becomes apparent.

A generally infantile male adult patient who is demanding, provocative, cajoling, and coercive with his parents, sister, and wife, initially displays the same character to his analyst. Glover (1955) has defined this type of treatment relationship as spontaneous transference, referring to the potential attachments, aversions, and reactions which govern the person's current object relations. What Glover describes as "spontaneous transference" is primarily a manifestation of character. Stone (1961) and O. Sperling (1965) show the interrelation and difference between transference and character. The transference neurosis selectively presents personality components which were amalgamated in character patterns. In the transference neurosis, urges and defenses underlying symptom and character reappear in renewed conflict concentrated in the analytic situation. The concentrated revival of infantile fantasies, attitudes, and moods requires the synergistic operations of synthesis, discrimination, and many other ego functions.

The "transference potential" which Glover (1955) referred to as a measure of accessibility, and the "transference readiness" of Macalpine (1950), pertain to the potential for transference neurosis. I would recognize that there are degrees of transference development and of partial formation of a transference neurosis. In the adult, the greater the postoedipal structure of transference conflict, the more the likelihood of successful psychoanalysis. The transference neurosis is not necessarily always oedipal in content, but requires oedipal-phase and superego development. The capacity for transference neurosis is dependent on relatively advanced psychic development.

TRANSFERENCE AND THERAPEUTIC ALLIANCE

Transference phenomena are relatively universal, while both transference neurosis and therapeutic alliance are products of psychoanalysis. The analytic situation fosters the appearance of transference derivatives, but the development and toleration of the transference neurosis is dependent upon the therapeutic alliance. The therapeutic alliance preserves the realistic doctor-patient relationship from becoming eclipsed by the revived infantile object relations of the transference neurosis.

Fenichel's (1941a) "rational transference" and Stone's (1961) "mature transference" should not be confused with the irrational archaic nature of transference, or with the current concept of the "therapeutic alliance" (Zetzel, 1956), or the "working alliance" (Greenson, 1967). In a sense, the therapeutic alliance and the transference neurosis are reciprocal analytic structures built on the conflict-free and conflicted spheres of the ego respectively. A positive transference involving basic trust (Erikson, 1950) or confidence in the object (Benedek, 1956) is essential for the formation of both a therapeutic alliance and a manageable transference neurosis. While components of positive transference are now recognized in both therapeutic alliance and therapeutic defiance, the contributions of Hartmann (1951) and Kris (1956b) on technique indicate that insight can also be achieved in a state of negative transference. They emphasize the paramount importance of structural considerations and the participation of the autonomous ego in the controlled regression of an analyzable transference neurosis. The maintenance of the therapeutic alliance theoretically allows the sustained analysis of hostile transference.

Early in the analytic relationship the patient internalizes the relatively permissive superego of the analyst. He also projects his own magical controls and superego attitudes onto the analyst. The analyst may be seen as punitive, controlling, permissive, etc., but this is concurrent with some perception of and gradual identification with the real analytic attitude of autonomous neutrality and impartiality. This promotes the therapeutic alliance, the secondary autonomy of the ego, and structural development. The analyst's calm in states of panic, his tolerance of anger and passion, may be silently therapeutic, facilitating exploration and permitting deep transference regression in the service of analysis. The therapeutic commitment of the analyst and his insightful understanding are vital transference gratifications. Whether a true transference neurosis can develop or be sustained in an analysis conducted purely as a scientific experiment or by an uncomprehending therapist is doubtful.

TRANSFERENCE AND RESISTANCE

Waelder (1956) noted three views of transference in the history of psychoanalysis: 1. as an obstacle to treatment; 2. as the most important vehicle of treatment; 3. as an opportunity for direct influence through identification or re-education. At the time Freud was regarding transference as a resistance to remembering, psychoanalytic technique was preoccupied with the recovery of memories and the undoing of infantile amnesia. Freud also recognized that transference itself was a way of remembering and reliving, and sometimes the only way in which the past might be reproduced. Transference was both memory and resistance to memory. Freud's (1912) early idea of transference serving as resistance was paradoxically associated with the concept of positive transference as the necessary agent to overcome resistance and induce memory recall. Affectionate and attachment components of transference were differentiated from all transference as resistance. Transference was later (1926) regarded as a regressive repetition which included patterns of defense. Further, any regressive aspect of transference (e.g., magical thinking) may function as a resistance to insight. And so transference primarily as resistance was replaced by the analysis of resistance and content within the transference; and transference, originally viewed as a hindrance or help to analysis, became the focus of analysis.

There are resistances to the development of the transference neurosis, and further problems may arise in terms of splitting, acting out, and displacement of transference outside the analytic situation. But the basic technical difficulty in classical analysis lies in the management of the transference resistance, particularly in the analysis of the infantile pathological defenses and defensive reactions which are repeated in the transference neurosis. The analysis of defense may intensify transference reactions, illuminating the role of defense within the transference neurosis. Far from being simply a means to memory, the analysis of the transference resistance becomes an opportunity to alter the immature organization of the ego and remove those pathological modifications and distortions resulting from primitive defensive structures. Memories, fantasies, symptoms, and behavior are now studied in the dynamic context of the transference neurosis. The sources and sequellae of trauma can be viewed in their complexity in their transference recapitulation. The revival and reexperiencing of the past in transference adds to the affective conviction of analytic work, which in turn furthers the mastery of conflict and resistance through insight.

TRANSFERENCE AND REPETITION

Freud (1920a) ascribed the repetition in the transference of the painful past to the repetition-compulsion, a theory which has persisted side by side with the primary-process theory of transference in which the instinctual demands are linked with objects originally associated with gratification. These early drive-oriented strivings may be experienced as painful in relation to later ego and superego development. Schur (1966a, pp. 182-183) has delineated objections to the transference neurosis as an example of daemonic repetition of unpleasure. The adherence to primitive patterns of discharge and seeking "identity of perception" is concordant with primary process and the pleasure principle. As a repetitive phenomenon, transference is related to recurrent instinctual wishes and to infantile automatisms of primitive structure. As an unconscious revival of unresolved conflicts, transference neurosis is also a mobilization and "return of the repressed."

Stern (1957), highlighting the ego activity as well as the recurrent demands of the instinctual drives, advanced the possibility of transference as reparative ego mastery of infantile traumata. In this view, the repetition serves the undoing and the ego mastery of traumatic experience; it is within the pleasure-unpleasure principle rather than beyond that principle. I suggest the transference neurosis is adaptive as a mobilization for mastery in the context of the therapeutic alliance and analytic process. The transference neurosis is not inherently therapeutic, but regressive, although in the service of analysis; it is the analytic process and the analytic work that provide for progressive resolution and the achievement of higher levels of functional organization.

TRANSFERENCE AND INFANTILE RELATIONSHIPS

Transference involves the reproduction of archaic structural states with regressive patterns in such ego functions as object relations, defenses, affects, and body image. Not all transference can be conceptualized in terms of displaced object representations. In analysis, projection of forbidden id impulses or aspects of the self or ego ideal occurs in the externalization of intrapsychic conflict. Anna Freud (1965) refers to these phenomena as a subspecies of transference. I regard the phenomena as universal components which amend the earlier definition of transference in terms of object representations. These externalized reactions frequently reveal important object relations and identifications, repeating externalizations with the original objects.

The understanding gleaned from earlier analytic instinct-oriented studies of the libidinal phase manifestations of transference has been brought into the broader sphere of structural concepts and modern ego psychology. From the classical analytic transference of the oedipal phase there has been a growing awareness of preoedipal factors and their influence on subsequent development. Similarly, the influence of postchildhood experiences has been increasingly recognized, and not only are the identifications and object relations of infancy reconstructed, but those of the adolescent period as well.

PRIMITIVE TRANSFERENCE

The core of a transference relationship is essentially an archaic object relationship. The study of early object relations contributed to the understanding of primitive transferences. Spitz (1965b) and Greenacre (1954b) have stressed the paradigm of the mother-infant relation in the primary transference and, with Stone (1961), have illuminated the derivation of all later transferences from the primal object relationship. There has been fresh consideration of the analytic situation paradoxically fostering the transference of both fusion and separation. Greenacre regarded the matrix of transference as the mother-infant quasi-union of the first months of life, before differentiation of self and object occurs. Tarachow's (1962) formulation of the constant desire for fusion with the analyst, with separation through interpretation, is descriptive of a basic layer of primitive transference usually not active in the classical analysand with advanced structural differentiation. With more regressed, orally fixated patients, fusion of self-and object representation may become a central transference conflict. Keiser (1952) has shown that such patients are fearful of body-ego disruption.

Stone (1961) has elucidated the converse of fusion, the "intimate separation" of analyst and patient, a situation which reactivates the mother transference of the repetitive phases of separation during which speech increasingly replaced physical contact. The later, more mature types of transference require maturation and separation from the original objects. Stone's formulation of "mature transference," a correlate of biological maturation and tendency to individuation, is also opposed to the primordial transference of fusion. Stone's (1967) "primordial transference" is derived from the effort to master the series of crucial separations from the mother. The concept of "mature transference" (closer to aspects of the therapeutic alliance) should be demarcated from the usual definition of transference and infantile repetition.

Emphasis on the early infantile states of fusion and symbiosis, or an anaclitic-diatrophic transference relationship, tends to overshadow the oedipal and later development. There are mature demands upon the classical analysand from the outset of treatment. Primordial transference should not be confused with later analytic transference in a genetic fallacy which ignores structural change.

The child does not give up his reality strivings with his parents, who participate with him in conflict and autonomy, defense and discharge, while treatment proceeds. But the continued interaction with original objects does not preclude transference, which is based on object representation. Theoretically, one could postulate transference to a parent. Anna Freud (1965) distinguished between the child's transference, transfer of current conflicts, and the use of the analyst as new object during treatment. Fraiberg (1951) illustrated the difference between extension or transfer of the symptom into child analysis. These observations refine the perception of the child's transference and also of similar phenomena in the adult. Anna Freud and other child analysts have enormously enriched our parallel understanding of pristine transference and the development of object constancy and object relations. Mahler and Gosliner (1955) and Winnicott (1953) conceptualized the phases of symbiosis and transitional-object relationships, which further integrated child development and pioneer investigations of therapy with psychotics. Freud's original idea of a narcissistic neurosis as opposed to a transference neurosis has been modified in the sense that psychotic narcissism is not absolute, and psychotic transference is now recognized; but it is tenuous, shifting, unstable, charged with aggression, and characterized by incomplete differentiation, as well as fragmentation and fusion of representations of self and object (Jacobson, 1954). A transference psychosis may also repeat an encapsulated infantile psychosis, or may represent a regressive reaction in a psychotic character (Frosch, 1967). Transference is not absent in psychosis, but its pristine distortions are further complicated by the relative inability of the ego to maintain a therapeutic alliance. With interpretation, the neurotic patient is able to recognize the difference between the real analyst and his fantasy about the analyst, between the self and the object.

EROTIZED TRANSFERENCE

A situation related to the differentiation of transference and reality arises in the charged atmosphere of so-called "erotized transference." The patient clamors for direct erotic gratification, insists on the reality of transference fantasy, and attempts to seduce the therapist into mutual living out. Such a transference may be so intense and impervious to ordinary interpretation as to approach delusional proportions. The maintenance of a therapeutic alliance, rooted in the autonomous functions of the ego, then decides the limits of transference analysis and synthesis. The question of erotized transference must be considered in broad structural terms, referred to in the following discussion.

A married mother in her thirties announced during an early phase of analysis that she had fallen completely in love with her analyst. She was ready to leave her husband and "drown her children" if only he would eliminate his family and marry her. At first coquettish and flirtatious, she became openly seductive. She thought only of the analyst during sex play; he replaced all prior objects in conscious erotic fantasies. She complained that analysis was useless because she loved the analyst too much to talk about her feelings or objectively consider interpretations. She reported an altered state of mood and awareness during her analytic sessions. Any external noise was an unpardonable intrusion on an intimate tryst, breaking a magic spell. On the couch she became sexually aroused with vaginal sensations, and cherished the hope that she would sleep with her analyst at least once in her lifetime. Her husband was cold, insensitive, mechanical; her marriage, a mistake. The analyst was empathic, understanding. She should have married him.

At first she resisted all attempts to interpret the transference, refusing to accept any formulation related to the revival of the past. This love was a development, a discovery, not a repetition.

This patient was not psychotic and, despite severe regressive and acting-out tendencies, was gradually able to acquire insight into her transference love. Through her fantasies and dreams, it was possible to reconstruct her oedipal love and disappointment. She was attempting to live out a masturbation fantasy of being surrounded by admirers and then having simultaneous rectal-vaginal intercourse with two men. These men were analytically unmasked as her analyst and husband, genetically representing her father and grandfather. After visiting her father's grave she dreamed of having intercourse with X, whose penis was ice cold. X had her father's name, and the associations to ice cold were also to a cadaver, her father. There was an unconscious fantasy of incestuous reunion through necrophilia. But the dream also referred to her husband, an ice-cold lover, whom she wished to entomb in exchange for her adored father, in the same way she wanted to transform the cool objective analyst into a warm paternal lover. Her husband's cold rejection pushed her toward another man, unconsciously her father, to whom she was delighted to go. The erotization, as seen by Rappaport (1959), means a demand for infantile love. For her, these were oedipal demands rather than oral hunger. The concrete feelings about her father should be noted. Her incestuous fantasies had been partially acted out by toileting with her grandfather, by exhibiting and excreting in her grandfather's and father's presence. She would lie next to her father in bed, and he was fond of petting her buttocks under her clothes. This behavior continued until her wedding day, when she urinated in her father's presence. Consciously this behavior had been accepted in the family situation as one of benevolent intimacy and was never questioned until she entered analysis. What I wish to emphasize here is the reality of incestuous activity in both parent and child, in fact, in three generations together. This feeling of vivid reality is repeated in the transference and does not require that the analyst elicit it through accidental resemblance to the infantile object, countertransference conformity to the patient's wishes, or psychotic loss of reality testing in the patient. The transference reaction repeats a fantasy verified by reality. If there has been mutual seduction with the parent, the patient may well expect such overt behavior with the parental surrogate in transference. The difference between transference fantasy and the repetition of real events in transference is comparable to the distinction made by Greenacre (1954b) between fantasies and traumatic memories in the process of working through.

During analysis the inherent resistance of erotized transference gradually became apparent to the patient. It was resistance to analysis of any painful emotion without any responsibility or requirement for change. She expected the analyst to fall in love with her and to change himself and exchange love objects for her.

The special quality of the reality sense in this erotized transference is also due to the repetition of the altered sense of reality of masturbation. There is a different organization of both awareness and defense, along with increased narcissism and omnipotence during such a masturbatory transference. The important defensive alterations of consciousness described by Dickes (1965) in this situation, I would suggest, may ward off impulses to masturbate. Here, structural considerations indicate the presence of an altered ego state originally concomitant with childhood masturbation. This is a *pars-pro-toto* defense where the altered awareness wards off the masturbatory act it originally accompanied. The mood of masturbation may dominate the transference, divorced from any awareness of masturbatory activity. The insistent urge toward an altered consciousness then derives from conflict over masturbation. The possible reproduction of the intrapsychic structural shifts associated with masturbation should be considered in evaluating the special quality, intensity, and tenacity of erotized transference. Freud's awareness of the reverie states associated with masturbation was noted by Stein (1965) in tracing the implications of change of reality function in sexual activity, orgasm, and traumatic experience.

Further analysis revealed that the patient's extreme paternal transference love was a defense against a violent negative maternal transference. Her mother had tried to abort her, and this patient literally regarded her father as the less ambivalent parent, rescuer from the lethal rivalry with the oedipal mother. The erotic transference was both a screen and a plea for protection against sadomasochistic castration and destruction. Her omnipotent triumph was overshadowed by her anxiety and guilt as the surviving twin of the attempted abortion. In her masturbation fantasy, she identified with her mother in guilty search for her lost twin. She sought constant reassurance and both offered and demanded undying affection. She needed and expected special love as both unwanted and chosen, rejected and irresistible.

This patient's erotized transference illustrates the importance of ego considerations in transference and the interweaving of fantasy and reality. Reality may reactivate or reinforce fantasy, and fantasy may incorporate reality. Erotized transference, in this case example, indicates infantile incestuous fixation, but also suggests considerations of real childhood seduction, the revival of the altered sense of reality connected with masturbation, defense against destruction of the object, and restitution of the lost love object. This case further demonstrates a phase of erotized transference in a nonpsychotic patient without marked pregenital fixation. Oral conflicts and global ego regression are not invariable causes of erotized transference.

Nunberg and Tarachow have discussed problems closely related to erotized transference. In his classical paper, "Transference and Reality," Nunberg (1951) reported what I consider a variant of "instinctualized transference." Nunberg referred to a female patient's insistence that he act like her father as "readiness for transference." "This readiness obviously produced two attitudes in her: first, an expectation of finding her real father in the analyst; secondly, the wish to change the real person of the analyst into the father as she imagined him. . . . It is evident that she did not transfer her emotion from her father to her analyst, but rather that she attempted to transform her analyst into her father" (p. 1). (Nunberg's "readiness for transference," a concept of failure of true transference, should not be confused with Macalpine's [1950] "transference readiness.")

Tarachow (1962) viewed this phenomenon as "resistance to transference." "Nunberg's patient, although she seemed to demand that the analyst be her real object, had not really turned to the analyst. She was actually fixated to the original and real father, did not abandon that, and demanded that the analyst step into her system and actually conform to her infantile object representations. This is a psychotic system, not even acting out" (p. 384). Yazmajian (1964) offered a similar explanation for the undisguised appearance of the analyst in the first dream. This was "an attempt to treat him as a 'real' person, and thus avoid investing him with symbolic importance; in effect a resistance to transference formation" (p. 550). Tarachow's concept of resistance to transference formation is important to the general problem of transference and its manifestations in borderline and psychotic states.

I suggest that manifest dreams of the analyst undisguised usually do represent transference resistance, but not a resistance to the formation of transference. (Of course the manifest content alone does not distinguish between identification with the analyst, the analyst as important new real object, or as an object of transference.) Given an ego organization beyond primary narcissism, there will be an unconscious tendency toward "identity of perception." Assuming constancy of self-and object representations, and symbolic capacity, the manifest picture of "resistance to transference formation" represents a rigid resistance to the awareness of transference which may be linked with impaired ego autonomies. The unconscious transference may be intense, accompanied by tendencies to act out the transference without regard for present reality. However, such difficulties do serve as resistances to a workable transference neurosis which is to be distinguished from the concept of resistance to transference formation. The lack of therapeutic alliance or inability "to split" the ego for autonomous contemplation of transference should also be distinguished from resistance to transference formation or absence of transference. Manifest insistence on the reality of the analyst or obliteration of the reality of the analyst proclaims the latent symbolic importance of the analyst.

FURTHER CONSIDERATIONS OF TRANSFERENCE AND REALITY

Nunberg's patient, probably a borderline psychotic, demanded the living-out of her unconscious transference fantasy with the support and participation of the object. Fantasy was to replace reality. The analyst was to join the denial of reality in her game of "let's pretend." The father transference to Nunberg was present, but remained unconscious. Had he responded to the patient's coercion, she would still have been able to defend against the awareness of the incestuous transference because the relationship would then be one of pretense, akin to the dynamics of pseudologia fantastica. The use of massive denial, the need for concrete literal symbols, the intolerance of frustration, the omnipotent demands, all indicate primitive ego functioning. Nunberg's patient seemed to have sufficient reality testing to recognize the difference between the current object and the infantile object; but she demanded conformity with her infantile wishes and magical alteration of reality to produce an identity of perception. In the "corrective emotional experience" advocated by Alexander (1954), the transference would be made real by the therapist's role-playing with the patient, as Nunberg's patient demanded.

Neurotics may also clamor for paternal behavior by the analyst, but do not insist on creating a misperception, on immediate wish fulfillment achieved by denial in action and magical manipulation of external reality. Nunberg's "readiness for transference" is a species of unconscious transference reaction associated with more general ego impairment.

The usually unconscious transference relationship may emerge into consciousness without the patient's distinguishing it from reality. This can be seen clinically in dreams and psychosis. A psychotic adult patient addressed his therapist as father, confusing symbol and referent as he did with words. He asked his therapist to read to him and play games with him. When the therapist announced he would be leaving the hospital staff, the patient went into a semistupor, murmuring, "Father is dying, Father is dead." Unlike this schizophrenic, Nunberg's patient distinguished the real analyst from her father and was apparently not aware of her unconscious father transference.

TRANSFERENCE AND AUTONOMY

The awareness of transference as such is structurally dependent on the autonomous ego. As described in reference to hypnosis, with all transference, there may be more than one subordinate state of awareness, associated with a coordinate ego state or subsystem of the ego. The various psychic vectors which Gill and Brenman (1959) identified in the hypnotic state are applicable to the analytic situation: the regressive core of the transference relationship, the alternations in general ego-functioning, and the maintenance of a significant degree of reality attunement. There is a selective rather than a global structural regression, and the development of a workable transference neurosis in the service of the analytic compact is a sign of ego strength. Intrasystemically, it is a regression of part of the ego in the service of therapy. The depth and intensity of regression are regulated by the overall ego, particularly by autonomous ego functions.

The opposite effects of transference on autonomy may also be significant. The transference regression may involve the more fragile secondary autonomies, and, at times, sublimations may become impaired. The pianist, for example, may be inhibited by the revival of masturbatory conflict. On the other hand, transference is a potent force in the acquisition and refinement of sublimations. Indeed the transference of an artist to sponsor and audience may be a variable in his sublimation. Transference analysis aims at the stable restoration and creation of adaptive secondary autonomies.

Counter-regressive forces in the analytic situation, such as autonomous observation and the secondary-process verbalized dialogue of analyst and patient, aid the regulation of transference regression. There is a circularity between free association and interpretation, superimposing secondary process on primary process, promoting ego development and controlled transference regression. With reorganization and synthesis on a higher level of awareness, and neutralization, primitive transference images are attenuated, and there is a heightened perception of analyst as understanding object. Some perception of the analyst as a real object is necessary from the outset for the analysis of transference fantasy, and then transference analysis further improves reality testing. The therapeutic alliance and the process of interpretation are essential counterpoints to regression and transference.

Transference recapitulation is not chronologically stratified, but undergoes displacement, condensation, and reorganization. There are layers of transference, however, in terms of conflict dynamics and closeness to present reality. Kanzer (1953) and Loewenstein (1951) have underscored the role of the present in shaping the transference, and the regressive representation of concealed current conflicts in transference. Inasmuch as transference is a revival of the past, it does not apply to the purely current, but to current conflicts which have become invested with transference. The analyst may represent a patient's wife, child, or employer, but they in turn may be transference objects. The transference is a guide to the infantile past, but also to the "reconstruction upward" of the later derivatives of early conflict, and the activation of latent conflicts by reality. In states of sudden decompensation, the precipitating situation and point from which regression occurred can be retraced in transference.

In transference, the coalescence of images and experiences is comparable to a dream image, deriving from contemporary day residues and the memories of prior developmental stages (Kanzer, 1953). Freud (1914d) stressed present reality when he pointed out that the transference neurosis was an artificial illness produced in the analytic situation at a particular time in the patient's life and that not all latent conflicts and psychopathology were reproduceable in any particular transference (1937a). Any elucidation of Freud's view of transference neurosis as an artificial illness would explore the possible artificial introduction, changes, or exclusion of component elements. As a new development, the transference neurosis is a revised edition of the adult neurosis, just as the adult neurosis is a modified derivative of the infantile neurosis. Transference neurosis conflicts may also present departures from childhood conflicts or symptoms.

Apart from countertransference which can obscure, distort, or preclude a transference neurosis, the transference is probably influenced to a degree by variables in the therapist, such as age, style, and sex. Real attributes of the therapist and analytic situation may color the developing transference, hopefully to a minimal degree. The possible developmental influence of the therapeutic alliance and analyst as new object must also be considered. The transference is not an entirely spontaneous endogenous development, and entirely new symptoms may appear. The awareness of an "artificial illness" will not invalidate analytic theory, as critics have claimed, but will deepen our investigative insight. Awareness that psychoanalysis fosters regression will not be confused with analysis as a "regressive evasion" of later conflicts, nor with the major regression inherent in the patient's illness. The analyst is encountered not only regressively, as an object of transference, but also as a "consistently mature new object" (Loewald, 1960), with an unwavering analytic attitude. During analysis, revival of the past is concurrent with new development and structural reorganization.

TRANSFERENCE AND ADAPTATION

The transference neurosis is adaptive in the sense of regression in the service of analysis, mobilization of the repressed, and ego mastery of trauma through repetition. The utilization of unanalyzed transference may also be a powerful psychotherapeutic tool. The symptomatic "transference cure" derives from unconscious needs to please or spite the therapist, magical introjection of therapist, and/or the restoration of a needed infantile object relationship. Transference to a hospital or clinic, abstract objects often representing a nurturing mother, may contribute significantly to their therapeutic achievements. Transference to significant objects and institutions is a factor, not only in "cure," but in the constant maintenance of emotional equilibrium. In psychoanalysis, transference neurosis is resolved through integrative insight. Loewald (1960), noting the emotional impoverishment resulting from pathological transference distortion, stresses that the dissolution of transference neurosis does not remove all transference. It is not accidental that Freud (1900), also through the term "transference," connected the past memory to the day residue of the dream. Transference may not only support but enrich current object relations, adaptively providing the substrate for new emotional ties.

Transference depends on self-object differentiation and the development of object constancy. Activated by the search for perceptual identity, transference eases the pain of separation, and may facilitate new object relationships. The strange and new become latently familiar, potentiating adaptive, object-oriented responses. As a corollary, stranger anxiety, indicative of object differentiation, may be related to the early manifestations of ambivalent transference reactions. There are interrelations between object loss, object hunger, and transference. Identification resolves object loss through internalization, while transference restores loss through fantasied external restitution. Transference permits the appreciation of the present incorporating the past, and of the old within the new. The concentration of transference and its relation to restored love is beautifully described by Shakespeare (sonnet 31):

That due of many now is thine alone.
Their images I loved I view in thee,
And thou, all they, hast all the all of me.

CHAPTER 10

The Psychoanalytic Unconsciouses

Samuel Abrams, M.D.

There are terms in psychoanalysis which could well serve as day residues for a lexicographer's nightmare. Too many are difficult to delineate with any precision. Partly this derives from circumstances in the history of psychoanalysis; partly from the complexity of the subject matter; partly from the special cognitive strain imposed by its many hierarchically diversified abstractions. In certain cases, stating even simple definitions may pose problems. Some terms are obscure because they also happen to designate related concepts found in ancillary disciplines; "instinct" is one such word. Some evoke uncertainties because they have gradually come to assume multiple meanings within psychoanalysis itself; "ego" is a good instance. And some are vague because of the weighty burden of casual usage; "transference" is a spectacular example.

The term "unconscious" owes its ambiguities to all these sources. Initially, this word was conceived in various ways in the fields of philosophy, psychology, literature, and medicine. Within psychoanalysis, it came to be applied to phenomena and to hypotheses of markedly disparate natures. Through it all, pragmatic usage derived from attempts to integrate new clinical discoveries impeded attempts at specific differentiation. Nevertheless, "unconscious" burned itself deep into Freudian argot—as adjective, adverb, verbal- and multiply-defined noun. Despite all the difficulties of origin, assignment, and implementation, no other word is more firmly welded to psycho-

Dr. Abrams is Assistant Clinical Professor, Division of Psychoanalytic Education, Department of Psychiatry, State University of New York, Downstate Medical Center, Brooklyn, New York.

analysis (e.g., Freud, 1940b, p. 286). Late in life Freud (1940a) wrote that the term appears "... likely to be a source of limitless confusion rather than a help towards clarification" (p. 161). Recreating the development of the different psychoanalytic unconsciouses might help set some limits to that confusion.

QUALITY

To begin with, "conscious" and "unconscious" are words which define a quality of mental activity. This quality is adjudged from the vantage point of a person's subjective recognition; hence, "aware" and "unaware" would be appropriate synonyms. Today, this designation seems unlikely to find its disputants, but the psychologists of the nineteenth century differed in what they regarded as the legitimate limits of their inquiry. Some held that the "psychological" ought to be strictly equated with the "conscious." Freud and Breuer, however, committed themselves to an alternative position.

To Breuer, the existence of nonrecognized or unconscious ideas was a simple empirical proposition, an obvious fact of everyday life (Breuer and Freud, 1893-95, p. 222). The word, "unconscious," was an adjective or an adverb, pure and simple. In speech, it might be used as a substantive noun, but in conceptual reality, "the unconscious" did not exist. Despite this view, Breuer was destined to be the first to introduce the phrase into the psychoanalytic literature (p. 45). He ushered it in cautiously, within quotation marks. Later this qualification appeared:

> It is only too easy to fall into a habit of thought which assumes that every substantive has a substance behind it—which gradually comes to regard "consciousness" as standing for the actual thing. . . . All our thinking tends to be accompanied and aided by spatial ideas, and we talk in spatial metaphors. . . . If, however, we constantly bear in mind that all such spatial relations are metaphorical and do not allow ourselves to be misled into supposing that these relations are literally present in the brain, we may nevertheless speak of a consciousness and a subconsciousness. But only on this condition [pp. 227-228].

The editors of the Standard Edition contend that Breuer's use of quotation marks may have been his way of attributing the concept to Freud (p. 45n). More likely, however, it reflects Breuer's objections to the substantive noun.

To Freud, the whole question of qualities had broader significance. The existence of unconscious mental processes provided a theory which could establish a foundation for a systematic investigation of all of the mind. Influenced by the existing *Zeitgeist*, Freud held the view that a scientist's field of study was the laws of nature; his goal was to discover the logical sequences in all phenomena. When mental activity was viewed only from the perspective of subjective awareness, all sorts of "unintelligible gaps" in memory became manifest (1915d). By severing the link between "conscious" and "mental" those gaps might be bridged. Freud tried two approaches. First, he conceived of some hypotheses about brain structure and physiology, and restricted consciousness to a single function of the brain. As such, it was simply a manifestation of some underlying somatic process, linked logically to other somatic processes of the central nervous system (Freud, 1895). Limits in the knowledge of neurophysiology and neuroanatomy made this approach hazardous; in any case, it was impractical from a therapeutic point of view. Freud selected a more fruitful path. Limiting himself to a strict psychology and applying the substantive boldly, without quotation marks, he suggested the postulate that what is mental is in the first instance what is unconscious. Consciousness, therefore, was only one aspect of the larger sphere (1900, pp. 611-613). Freud put neurology aside after this; however, more than a trace of his original disposition persisted in the metaphorical descriptions of the mind which he offered. In addition, the imagery continued to emphasize spatial relationships and localizations. Furthermore, some of Freud's constructs were shaped out of neurological hypotheses, e.g., Hughlings Jackson's concept of hierarchal layers (Freud, 1891).

Although Freud and Breuer came to the unconscious from distinctive vantage points, they were able to agree on the significance of establishing the idea of the existence of "the aware" and "the unaware." Important differences were destined to strain their alliance. But, for the moment, the word "unconscious" had survived its first conceptual offering. The view that mental equals conscious had been changed to mental—to begin with—is *un*conscious. There were casualties. Henceforth, for some, interest in "consciousness" was to be viewed with suspicion or disdain, despite Freud's view of it as the "beacon-light" of depth psychology (Freud, 1923a), and the substantive was to reign, overriding all considerations of grammar.

DYNAMIC

Freud was not unmindful of the problem of substantives and substances. But his substantive was to prevail because, in fact, it contained substance. Implied in it was not merely a degree of awareness, but a degree of access to awareness. This is a more complex issue, for, obviously, many kinds of factors may facilitate or impede access. To emphasize this distinction, eventually Freud divided his unconscious into two parts, one which was more readily available to conscious awareness, the "preconscious," and another which was less available or even inaccessible altogether, the "unconscious proper" (e.g., Freud, 1915d, 1940a). The "unconscious proper," however, was not merely the inaccessible unaware. It had additional characteristics: it was a determinant of behavior, and its contents were grouped in a fashion quite unlike conscious ones.

The observations which had led to such a cataloguing seemed well documented. Breuer and Freud (1893-95) had examined hysterical symptoms and arrived at the conclusion that they reflected incidents in the forgotten past. A central core experience in that past often appeared to be a sexual trauma, especially to Freud. Emanations from such an experience, now unconscious, seemed to provide the motor force for the symptoms, i.e., produced the impelling or dynamic effect. The memories of various related happenings, past and present, real or imagined, were affected by the core reminiscence. Symbolic distortion was common, all tended to fuse together, and each was readily displaceable on the other. What could account for the dynamic effect and the curious assemblage of certain unconscious processes? Both men sought hypotheses, along the lines of their own predispositions.

Breuer postulated qualitative distinctions in the energic constituents of the etiologic memories, and he conceptualized these in psychological terms. Hysteria, he suggested, resulted from experiences which had occurred during altered states of consciousness, "hypnoid states." Memory-traces of experiences occurring in such states were automatically imprinted with a strange quality, a "mobile" cathexis. Mental processes, so fashioned, he theorized, tended to group themselves along lines of condensations and displacements, precisely by virtue of this energic condition (Breuer and Freud, 1893-95, Chap. III). Hence, to Breuer, the experiencing state was more significant than the subject matter of the etiologic episode; he acknowledged, however, that sexual traumata might be implicated because they were frequently accompanied by powerful altered mental states (p. 248). Breuer ingeniously accounted for all of the phenomena which he had examined: the lack of subjective recognition, the difficulty in achieving awareness, the dynamic effects of the unconscious memories, and the special organization to which the reminiscences were subjected. And he did it all without ever having to make his "unconscious" anything more than a modifier. The substantive was unnecessary, even misleading.

Freud's solutions were different; but his project was a more ambitious one. In part of the neurologically based psychology which he had devised, it had been asserted that the aim of the central nervous system was to effect discharge of all stimuli which impinge upon it. To do so, Freud assumed that it had originally been equipped with a primary system which contained a method of organization to effect this optimally, i.e., a primary-process mode involving condensations and displacements of the imposing stimuli. But, since no complex living organism could long endure with only such a primitive structure, a second one evolved, hierarchically layered over the first. This second system organized mental contents differently; it could delay discharge and direct events along specific goals. And to accomplish all of this, it was equipped with appropriate functions (Freud, 1895).

From out of this complex general psychology, Freud extracted an explanation for the strange organization of certain unconscious memories and for their dynamic effects in hysteria. The etiologic experience had always been a sexual seduction during childhood. Such an incident induced an impelling effect, Freud contended, because it evoked a sexual excitation in the brain of a child—a brain which was unprepared to deal with it appropriately, precisely because the experience was a premature one. The prematurely evoked stimulus naturally sought discharge; this accounted for the dynamic or impelling quality. Under such an energic stress, the brain, in the fashion of one of Hughlings Jackson's theories, automatically reverted to an earlier form of activity, a primary-process mode. Thus, it attempted to deal with the excess, and it was this regression from the secondary to the primary system which accounted for the clinical presence of an archaic mode of organization (Freud, 1895, Part 2). Breuer's view had been a strict energic one; Freud's was based on structural and dynamic lines. The clinical issue upon which the theory rested was the innocence of children. To get the neurosis going, the core sexual experience in childhood had to have evoked a *premature* excitation (p. 357).

Then Freud made the discovery that sexuality was natural in childhood. Breuer's theories were relatively unaffected by this new insight; nevertheless, thereafter, he abandoned psychoanalysis for other reasons (Freud, 1914a, 1925a). Freud's concept of neurogenesis was crushed, and his whole structure teetered on the brink; but he persevered. If childhood sexuality was a fact of life, however, the specific dynamic effect of unconscious memories in hysteria could no longer be accounted for along the lines which he had proposed.

Freud originated a new frame of reference for psychoanalysis, an independent dynamic one, his theory of instinctual drives (1915a). He postulated the existence of special stimuli to the mind which arose from within the body, achieving representation in an archaic form especially through the function of sexuality. It was the mental representative clusterings of the ungratified infantile sexual function which was unconscious, and it was this function, with its endogenously derived drive energy which provided such an impelling effect. This special dynamic unconscious was a discovery of unimagined richness, although it tended to overwhelm Freud's earlier general views about dynamic unconscious processes. Other inaccessibly unaware determinants of behavior which had been highlighted before, such as affective trends or defensive operations, were crowded out by this monumental intruder. "The" unconscious, heretofore a general statement of the existence of dynamic unconscious processes, was for some time thereafter to imply that special variant derived from infantile sexual sources.[1]

TOPOGRAPHY

Emphasis on that special unconscious had a profound effect. Awed by the discovery of infantile sexuality and by the vitality of the drive theory, Freud's interest turned from the structure-and-functions aspect of his general psychology. To provide an organizational scheme, he offered a new hypothesis, couched in pure psychology. It permitted more of a focus on his new discovery. Thus, another "unconscious" was added to psychoanalysis and, although this one was to be abbreviated most of the time and set apart with capital letters to distinguish it from the others, the word braced itself for a fresh conceptual onslaught.

Using the reflex arc as a model and neurological prototype, Freud mapped out three locales within the mind: the system Unconscious (Ucs.), the system Preconscious (Pcs.), and the system Conscious (Cs.) (1900, 1915d). With only minor terminological alterations, he was able to retain his earlier postulates concerning mental principles. The psychological representatives of the instinctual drives, as well as environmentally derived stimuli, moved from the "deep" Ucs. through the higher Pcs. and eventually rose to the surface Cs., the discharge point. In the course of such a procession, mental contents came under the influence of the ordinances of each of the systemic locales. The Ucs., at the "sensory" end, functioned in a primary-process mode with mobile energy, according to the regulatory law of the Pleasure Principle. Its contents were linked according to conditions of temporal or spatial contiguity or along lines of assonances. It was "timeless." In that locale, "no" did not exist. At the "motor" end, the Cs. system functioned in a secondary-process mode. Hence,

[1] Eventually the "general" unconscious was to be highlighted anew. Adaptive trends in the personality were unconscious and influenced behavior (Hartmann, 1939). Progressive developmental processes, a consequence of maturation, were also unconscious, and clearly they too were determinants of character and symptom formation (e.g., A. Freud, 1965), in a manner analogous to repressed fantasies. In addition, certain other pathological states, i.e., some of the psychosomatic disorders, were evidently expressions of subjectively unrecognized regressive processes, and not only a product of erotic and aggressive trends (M. Schur, 1955).

its contents were arranged more with consideration for logic and coherence. It functioned with bound energy and according to the Reality Principle. "Things" had established verbal links in the Pcs. prior to arrival in the Cs. locale. The system Cs. was enjoined to discharge under circumstances which afforded appropriate gratification, according to issues in reality. Hence, it was empowered to delay discharge, and it contained many valuable functions so that it might implement its tasks. The Pcs. system showed qualities of both systems; its special function, however, was supplying verbal designations to "thing" presentations. Censors, in part precipitates of the prevailing social mores and customs, existed at the common borders of the three locales. They were empowered to arrest progress under a variety of circumstances. Furthermore, Cs. contents could be drawn back into the Pcs., at the behest of these censors or even into the Ucs., if experiences touched upon certain tabooed elements. All mental functions could be linked developmentally to instinctual drives as well as being energically driven in one way or another by their power source. (See, e.g., Rapaport, 1951b, 1960.) Different pathways of discharge were suggested for ideational as opposed to affective representatives (Freud, 1915d, p. 178).

The Topographic Hypothesis offered Freud the advantages of retaining an organizational scheme which emphasized the new discovery and the new theory. Now with topographic, dynamic, and economic points of view, Freud had his first comprehensive metapsychology (1915d, p. 181), along with his third unconscious.

WHAT LEVEL OF ABSTRACTION?

Freud set about classifying his various unconsciouses, and he did so with reasonable care. There was a descriptive, a dynamic, and a systemic one (1912b, 1915d, 1923a). The first was simply a quality of mental activity; the second was a substantive with dynamic and economic substance; the third was a noun in its own right. But was it a noun with a concrete existence?

There was an image which Freud used in contemplating the development of his science. Recognizing the necessary interrelationships between theories and discoveries, he distinguished between the two groups metaphorically. In words echoing the spirit of Breuer's "substantive-substance" qualification, Freud (1900) introduced his topography:

> Analogies of this kind are only intended to assist us in our attempt to make the complications of mental functioning intelligible. . . . We are justified, in my view, in giving free rein to our speculations so long as we retain the coolness of our judgement and do not mistake the scaffolding for the building [p. 536].

These postulates of metapsychology are "scaffolding," i.e., higher-level abstractions. They are designed to facilitate the creation of the real structure: empirical propositions and explanatory clinical theories. The word "unconscious," used to designate a quality of mental process, is clearly a part of that structure; the existence of certain unconscious processes which exert a dynamic effect is probably that structure's very foundation. But as for topography, that is scaffolding. In commenting on the differences between his unconsciouses, Freud did not do justice to these distinctions in levels of abstraction. The descriptive unconscious is an empirical proposition, the dynamic is a discovery with features of an explanatory and not merely of a descriptive nature; but the systemic Ucs. is part of meta-theory, no concrete reality at all, despite the fact that much of the phenomena from which it is derived are real enough.[2] It was precisely this which led Rapaport and Gill (1959) to assert that, while it was impossible to deny the fundamental significance of unconscious processes, it was appropriate, nevertheless, not to accord them metapsychological status. Their authority for such an assertion was Freud (1914a, pp. 16-17).

USAGE

The Topographic Hypothesis was found to be conceptually tortuous and theoretically inadequate to encompass further developments in clinical psychoanalysis (Freud, 1923a, 1940a; Kris, 1951; Hart-

[2] For more on such distinctions in level of abstraction see Rapaport (1960), Waelder (1962), and Rubenstein (1967).

mann, 1956; Gill, 1963). Those two censors, especially, were strange hypothetical fellows to manage. It turned out that they too had unconscious representations, were determinants of behavior, and came under the influence of the primary process. How could what was empirically and dynamically unconscious be pictured outside the system Ucs.? Freud, the cartographer, had the problem of isolating the borderlands between several regions within the confines of one. After an extensive effort to account for the new phenomena by a massive extension of drive theory, he attempted to drop the Topographic point of view and substitute the Structural Hypothesis. Id, Ego, and Superego became the new nuclei for an organizational scheme in psychoanalysis—a scheme not very dissimilar from the earlier neurologically based theory. With this, one of Freud's unconsciouses, the system Ucs., receded in prominence. But the word had enjoyed its metapsychological fling and its display of vivid spatial imagery. It was reluctant to yield its position. In the guise of Topography it had wooed and won the clinicians (also see M. H. Stein, 1965).

Several factors contributed to this alliance of clinician and Topography. For one thing, Freud's therapeutic capacities flowered, following his discovery of infantile sexuality. Because the systems focused on instinctual drives, clinical work naturally became linked with the language of Topography (Arlow and Brenner, 1964).

In technique, for example, the significance of putting "things" into "words" matched the systemic distinctions between Ucs. and Pcs. Furthermore, "interpretation" was the basic implement of the analyst, and the "art of interpretation" was understood as a kind of "translation" from one language to another (Freud, 1904, p. 252). This further supported the imagery of alien locales. Some of the metaphors which Freud used with his patients accented this even further. He formulated instructions on the fundamental rule of psychoanalysis in this fashion, for example: "Act as though . . . you were a traveller sitting next to the window of a railway carriage and describing to someone inside the carriage the changing views which you see outside" (1913a, p. 135). Shengold (1966) has suggested possible unconscious dynamic motives for Freud's propensity for this kind of imagery. But whatever the origins, clinicians passed along attitudes with the aphorisms.

The concept of cure showed this as well. "Make the unconscious conscious" became a favored therapeutic slogan. Freud (1916-17) wrote:

> Symptoms are never constructed from conscious processes; as soon as the unconscious processes concerned have become conscious, the symptoms must disappear [p. 279].

And:

> The task of a psychoanalytic treatment can be expressed in this formula: its task is to make conscious everything that is pathogenically unconscious [p. 282].

These are facile formulations; they easily lend themselves to confusing means and goals. This confusion was surely enhanced by another famous clinical metaphor which Freud (1909b) offered in one of his well-known case histories:

> I then made some short observation upon the *psychological differences between the conscious and the unconscious*, and upon the fact that everything conscious was subject to a process of wearing-away, while what was unconscious was relatively unchangeable; and I illustrated my remarks by pointing to the antiques standing about in my room. They were, in fact, I said, only objects found in a tomb, and their burial had been their preservation: the destruction of Pompeii was beginning now that it has been dug up [p. 176].

Naturally, such a description does not do justice to the kinds of active dynamic processes involved in such a disintegration, just as it understates the dynamic psychoanalytic processes of cure. Freud himself recognized the distinctions between task and techniques despite his metaphors (e.g., Freud, 1919a, p. 159 ff). However, his imagery was attractive, and it emphasized the qualitative rather than the dynamic and structural.

Topography even offered the clinicians a nosology of sorts. Different clinical entities could be understood in relationship to the dominance of one or another of the systems. Consider, for example, that remarkable last sentence in "The Metapsychology of Dreams" (Freud, 1917b). "In dreams the withdrawal of cathexis . . . affects all systems equally; in the transference neurosis, the *Pcs.* cathexis is withdrawn; in schizophrenia, the cathexis of the *Ucs.*; in amentia, that of the *Cs.*" (p. 235). It is an ambitious nosological project and couched in pure Topography.

To summarize: technique, a concept of cure, a classification—these were the seductions. Draped in vivid imagery, in a style which made the drives dazzlingly prominent, it was no wonder that the systemic Ucs. was welcomed so eagerly, accepted so elaborately, and set aside only with such reluctance.

THE PRECONSCIOUS UNCONSCIOUS

Another "unconscious" remained: that which encompassed processes which came to be known as "preconscious." What of the descriptive, dynamic, and systemic classification of this term? Freud had specified that a descriptive preconscious was a desirable concept. To this substantive was assigned those unconscious processes which were easily available to conscious awareness. On the other hand, by definition, a dynamic preconscious was a conceptual impossibility. And as for a systemic Pcs., it had been offered, but was discarded as a viable system when the Topographic Hypothesis was dropped. However, the new Structural Theory kept a preconscious alive; in fact, it infused it with a new conceptual vitality. Freud (1940a) devised the following equation in 1938: Ego and preconscious are "intimately" linked, almost exclusively so (p. 163).

Ego equals preconscious. What could this mean? The "Ego" was a construct derived from a new metapsychological postulate, on the same level of abstraction as the system Ucs. But "preconscious" was a pure empirical proposition. Was it possible to equate such nonequivalent levels of abstraction?

The functions of the personality are something else again. These, unlike the concept Ego, are more concrete entities, akin to dynamic unconscious processes. If Freud meant to equate "preconscious" with those functions which were to be assigned to the interior of the ego, i.e., the former preconscious *system*, then his link was conceptually legitimate. However, such an equation could hardly go unchallenged. Many ego functions specifically are dynamically unconscious, as Freud (1933, p. 71) himself indicated. There have been many attempts to unravel the dilemmas derived from this mixed equation, apparently aimed originally to bridge Topography and the Structural Theory. They remain unsolved (Markovitz, 1963; Arlow and Brenner, 1964; Schur, 1966a).

Despite the peculiarities of its origins, the word "preconscious" continues to cling stubbornly to life. Suggestions have been made that it be officially and permanently dispatched (Arlow and Brenner, 1964, Chap. 8), but it remains viable, partially on account of clinical customs, but also because it has attached itself to another complex set of phenomena. These phenomena encompass the spectrum of mental processes involving altered experiential states. A short sampling of some psychoanalytic contributions might serve to illustrate this issue.

Originally, Breuer (Breuer and Freud, 1893-95) made much of what he called a "hypnoid" condition. He related it to the etiology and the psychopathology of hysteria. Freud favored an approach which focused on conflict and on structure; hence, he rejected Breuer's concept as well as the use of hypnosis as a therapeutic tool. In these repudiations, the slighting of the issue of altered states was begun. Other phenomena within which it was concealed took dominance; however, the "states" question was not neglected entirely and was destined to slowly regain its foothold. For example, commenting on the fundamental rule of analysis, Freud (1900) wrote:

> What is in question, evidently, is the establishment of a psychical state which, in its distribution of psychical energy . . . bears some analogy to the state before falling asleep—and no doubt also to hypnosis. As we fall asleep "involuntary ideas" emerge, owing to the relaxation of certain deliberate (and no doubt also critical) activity which we allow to influence the course of our ideas while we are awake. . . . In the state used for the analysis of dreams and pathological ideas, the patient purposely and deliberately abandons this activity and employs the psychical energy thus saved (or a portion of it) in attentively following the involuntary thoughts which now emerge, and which—and here the situation differs from that of falling asleep—retain the character of ideas [p. 102].

Freud (1923b) noted that something akin was required of the analyst as well:

> Experience soon showed that the attitude which the analytic physician could most advantageously adopt was to surrender himself to his own unconscious mental activity, in a state of *evenly suspended attention*, to avoid so far as possible reflection and construction of conscious expectations, not to try to fix anything that he heard particularly in his memory, and by these means to catch the drift of the patient's unconscious with his own unconscious [p. 239].

The analytic situation was to proceed with both participants "equally awake" (Freud, 1904, p. 25), but apparently not fully awake.[3]

In one of his last statements on the subject, Freud (1940a, p. 63) again raised the question, but still it was tied to other issues. He suggested that the economic route originally offered by Breuer still best differentiated "unconscious" and "preconscious."

Thus had been established the ingredients for a new confusion: Freud had acknowledged the significance of "states," but buried the issue in ancillary matters; nevertheless, the word "preconscious" bobbed up and floated over these diffuse issues.

Kris gave these ingredients a significant stir. In his well-known paper, "On Preconscious Mental Processes" (1950), he explored altered states along with other processes, but without specifically labelling them as such. Like Freud, he loosely applied the term "preconscious" to include them all. The Kris paper emphasized altered experiential modes and the spectrum of sleep-wakefulness. Kris justified calling these processes "preconscious" by citing and supporting the equation, "Ego equals preconscious." The Topographic spectre had been roused.

Fisher's (1954) important work highlighted the conceptual problems afresh, even as it contributed to them. Working with experimentally induced dreams, he observed perceptual phenomena and decided to call them "preconscious," citing the Kris article to justify such a labelling (p. 424). Fisher stressed such phenomena as images being perceived as concrete things and assemblages of perception along a primary-process mode. He revived the Topographic Hypothesis and even extended it a bit, e.g., he theorized that the "Pcpt." function belonged to the system Pcs. and not only to the Cs. as

[3] Dickes (1965) and Stein (1965) have demonstrated that excesses of such states can constitute subtle but significant obstacles in treatment.

Freud had suggested. In effect, Kris had used Freud's "Outline" (1940a) as a bridge to cross over to Structural Theory, while Fisher used it to cross back to Topography.

George Klein (1959), involved in a similar area of research, chose to focus his attention specifically on the question of the experiential condition, i.e., "the distinctive qualities in which we can become aware of ideas" or the "modes of experience." He noted differences in natural and experimental settings. His work has all kinds of implications for the study of "frames of mind" or "conditions of consciousness" or "states." Klein felt the term "Preconscious perception" might promote further confusions (p. 31) and generally avoided Topographic considerations in favor of Structural ones. Gill and Brenman (1959) similarly attempted to account for altered states with a metapsychological profile which excluded Topographic systems.

Eissler (1962) supported Topography in addition to, and not as a substitute for, Structure. His Topography was specifically designed to highlight "states" and altered conditions of awareness. He offered a theory of "medial" processes, conscious and preconscious, which were interspersed with "nuclear" processes, id, ego, and superego (p. 14). Eissler suggested that mental processes moving between nuclei were interspersed with "nuclear" processes, id, ego, and superego (p. late would account for differences in the experiential states. Whether it is necessary to offer such a theory or whether it is still possible to encompass the accumulating data under existing frames of references remains to be conceptually decided.

Gradually, therefore, the word "preconscious" has managed to become explicitly attached, not merely implicitly linked, to the question of differences in the nature of mental processes. Like Breuer's original designation, this unconscious is a modifier again, but unlike his, more significant qualitative differences are at stake than simply the question of degrees of awareness. The equation "Ego equals preconscious" has led to fresh polarities. Perhaps something is to be said in defense of this. There are still much data to accumulate, and postulates which have a preemptory effect fail in their "scaffolding" function (Loewald, 1966).

The "unconscious" continues to hover over some of the past achievements of psychoanalysis and over some of its future prospects.

Part IV

Clinical Contributions

CHAPTER 11

The "Real" Relationship between the Patient and the Psychoanalyst

Ralph R. Greenson, M.D.

INTRODUCTION

This presentation is an attempt to explore further into the nature of the therapeutic processes which occur during psychoanalytic treatment. It has been the hallmark of psychoanalysis to emphasize the occurrence of transference and resistance during psychoanalytic therapy and to stress the decisive importance of interpreting these phenomena. This has led to a widely held view that all the patient's meaningful reactions to the person of the analyst are transference manifestations and the only important interventions are transference interpretations, a view common among Kleinian as well as the more "conservative," classical analysts. These analysts may concede that other kinds of personal interactions take place in the analytic situation, but they are considered irrelevant and awkward impediments which are either to be circumvented or ignored. I base this last statement on the fact that I have never read a paper by an "Orthodox" or Kleinian analyst which indicated that any intervention besides interpretation was important in the patient-analyst relationship.

On the other hand, a survey of the recent psychoanalytic literature reveals that a significant number of psychoanalysts, a group too heterogeneous to be classified, do not deny the special value of transference phenomena and transference interpretations, but maintain

Dr. Greenson is Chairman, Scientific Advisory Board, Foundation for Research on Psychoanalysis, Beverly Hills, California, and Clinical Professor of Psychiatry, U.C.L.A. School of Medicine.

that the total object relationship between the patient and the analyst must be taken into account in order to fully understand and handle the vicissitudes of the psychoanalytic situation. They believe that a wide assortment of object relations, other than transference, takes place in the course of an analysis in both the patient and the therapist. It is their contention that the proper handling of these "non-transference," "extratransference," or "real" interactions are ar indispensable ingredient for successful psychoanalytic treatment. I want to interpolate here that in this discussion I am emphasizing object relations including and beyond the scope of the concept of the therapeutic or working alliance as described by Zetzel (1956) and Greenson (1965). Stone (1961, 1967) and Fairbairn (1957, 1958) are the most outspoken on the subject of total object relations, but Anna Freud (1954a, 1965), Gitelson (1952), Knight (1953), Winnicott (1955, 1965b), Loewald (1960), and Erikson (1962), to mention only a few among many, have also pointed in this direction.

I want to quote from a few of the authors mentioned above in order to illustrate the areas of agreement despite the sharp differences in theoretical and technical points of view. Let me begin with the clearest statement of the problem, some remarks by Anna Freud published in 1954:

> Just as "no two analysts would ever give precisely the same interpretations," we find on closer examination that no two of a given analyst's patients are handled by him ever in precisely the same manner. With some patients we remain deadly serious, with others humor, or even jokes, may play a part; with some the terms in which interpretations are couched have to be literal ones, others find it easier to accept the same content when given in the form of similes and analogies; there are differences in the ways we receive and send off patients, and in the degree to which we permit a real relationship to the patient to coexist with the transferred, fantasied one; there is, even with the strictness of the analytic setting, a varying amount of ease felt by analyst and patient. These wholly unintended and unplanned variations in our responses are imposed on us, I believe, not so much by the patients' neuroses but by the individual nuances of their personalities which may escape unobserved otherwise. If we become aware of these often minute variations in our own behavior and reactions, and cease to treat them as unimportant chance occurrences, their observation and scrutiny

leads us directly to important findings. In the personal pressure which the patient exerts on us in this manner, he betrays the subtleties of his healthy personality, the degree of maturity reached by his ego, his capacity to sublimate, his intellectual gifts, and his ability to view his conflicts at least momentarily in an objective manner. In the variations of the analyst's "acting out" in technical behavior, we may, therefore, find new clues for the systematic study of character structures and personalities [pp. 609, 610].

Later on in the same paper Anna Freud goes on to say:

> Further, I refer briefly to Dr. Stone's remarks concerning the "real personal relationship" between analyst and patient versus the "true transference reactions." To make such a distinction coincides with ideas which I have always held on this subject. . . . We see the patient enter into analysis with a reality attitude to the analyst; then the transference gains momentum until it reaches its peak in the full-blown transference neurosis which has to be worked off analytically until the figure of the analyst emerges again, reduced to its true status. But—and this seems important to me—so far as the patient has a healthy part of his personality, his real relationship to the analyst is never wholly submerged. With due respect for the necessary strictest handling and interpretation of the transference, I feel still that we should leave room somewhere for the realization that analyst and patient are also two real people, of equal adult status, in a real personal relationship to each other. I wonder whether our—at times complete—neglect of this side of the matter is not responsible for some of the hostile reactions which we get from our patients and which we are apt to ascribe to "true transference" only. But these are technically subversive thoughts and ought to be "handled with care" [pp. 618-619].

Fairbairn (1957), whose theoretical and technical orientation differs considerably from Freud's, wrote the following:

> The relationship existing between patient and analyst is more important than details of technique; and it would seem to follow that the role of the analyst is not merely to fulfill the dual functions of (1) a screen upon which the patient projects his phantasies, and (2) a colourless instrument of interpretative technique, but that his personality and his motives make a significant contribution to the therapeutic process [p. 59].

It is interesting to observe how the different participants of a panel on "Variations in Classical Psycho-Analytic Technique" (Loewenstein, 1958) dealt with the problem of the nontransference relationship. Loewenstein (1955), Eissler (1958), and Rosenfeld (1958) look askance at any intervention other than interpretation and make no mention of any form of interpersonal relationship other than transference. Bouvet (1958) talks of the need to "manage" the relationship of patient and analyst. A. Reich (1958) describes helping her patient analyze her mother's behavior in order to free the patient from a crippling fixation. Nacht (1958) warns against taking the rule of neutrality and anonymity too rigidly and makes a plea for recognizing situations requiring the analyst's "*presence*" in the analytic situation.

Erikson (1962), pondering the issue of reality and actuality in the psychoanalytic situation, turned his attention to Freud's treatment of Dora in 1905. He raises the question which I would paraphrase as follows: What was it that Dora really needed from Freud that Freud would not or could not give her?

Stone (1967) writes the following:

> The analyst is first perceived as a real object, who awakens hope of help, and who offers it, on the basis of his therapeutic competence. This operates in the patient's experience at all levels of integration, from that of actual and immediate perception, evaluation, and response, to the activation of original parental object representations and their cathexes.
>
> This view does place somewhat heavier than usual emphasis on the horizontal coordinate of operations, the conscious and unconscious relation to the analyst as a living and actual object, who becomes invested with imagery, traits, and functions of critical objects of the past. The relationship is to be understood in its dynamic, economic, and adaptive meanings, in its current "structuralized" tenacity, the real and unreal carefully separated from one another [pp. 40, 41].

Roland (1967), emphasizing the need to activate a real reparative object relationship with the patient in order to overcome severe character resistances, quotes a hitherto overlooked contribution of Menaker in which she stated (1942):

> It seems to us, however, important to distinguish between that part of the analytic experience which is relived *as* "real" (not to question the genuineness of this experience), and that part which *is* real, that is, which constitutes a direct human relationship between patient and analyst, which has an existence independent of the transference, and which is the medium in which the transference reactions take place [pp. 172, 173].

Finally, I want to quote one sentence from Freud himself which was brought to my attention by Anna Freud after I had already submitted the original draft of this paper. Freud is referring to his relationship to Ferenczi in "Analysis Terminable and Interminable" (1937a, p. 222): "Furthermore, he added, not every good relation between an analyst and his subject during and after analysis was to be regarded as a transference; there were also friendly relations which were based on reality and which proved to be viable."

Different as their styles, their theoretical and technical orientations may be, all the authors cited above seem to be in accord with the idea that (1) personal interactions other than transference occur in the course of psychoanalysis, and (2) it is important to differentiate between the transference and the "real" relationship.

WORKING DEFINITIONS

At this point, I want to attempt to briefly define the terms transference and the "real" relationship. Transference is the experiencing of feelings, drives, attitudes, fantasies, and defenses toward a person in the present which do not befit that person, but are a repetition of reactions originating in regard to significant persons of early childhood, unconsciously displaced onto figures in the present (Greenson, 1967). The two outstanding characteristics of a transference reaction are: (1) it is an undiscriminating, nonselective repetition of the past, and (2) it is inappropriate, it ignores or distorts reality.

The term "real" relationship is much harder to define. At best I can only describe what I mean by the concept. Like all object relations, it also consists of repetitions from the past; however, it differs from transference in being selective and discriminating in terms of what is repeated. Furthermore, a real relationship is modifiable by internal and external reality. In a real relationship between a husband and wife, for example, the wife may resemble the husband's mother in some bodily feature, but the resemblance does not bring with it all the instinctual and emotional components which were originally bound up with the mother. In addition, the wife will have traits that resemble other people in the past, both remote and recent. Consequently, such a wife becomes a unique entity, free from the fearful and guilt-laden infantile connections to the past. Finally, the real relationship to the wife will be influenceable and modifiable by changes occurring in each individual and the world they live in.

I must add that in all transference reactions there is some germ of reality, and in all real relationships there is some element of transference. *All object relationships consist of different admixtures and blendings of real and transference components.* Although transference and real relationship are relative terms, they can and, as I hope to show, should be separated from one another. I also want to specify that the meaning of "real" in real relationship implies (1) the sense of being genuine and not synthetic or artificial, and (2) it also means realistic and not inappropriate or fantastic. In ordinary usage, the term "real" has been employed for either genuine or realistic. I shall use the term "real relationship" only when I mean both.

Perhaps I can clarify these definitions if I point out that transference reactions are essentially unrealistic and fantastic, but they are felt as genuine, authentic, and sincere. Yet, here again this is only relatively true. Some transference reactions feel more genuine than others. When most of the ego is immersed in the experiencing of the feeling and only little of the rational ego is left untouched, the patient experiences the feeling as genuine. Other transference reactions may be experienced with "tongue in cheek," as though they are a "serious make-believe" (Stone 1967). In such instances, the experiencing ego and the observing ego are more or less of equal strength.

The working alliance, on the other hand, is essentially realistic, but more or less synthetic, artificial. In the analyst, the working alliance becomes part of his therapeutic character and personality, and in that sense it is genuine. But situations do arise when a strong countertransference will make it necessary for the analyst to call forth a therapeutic attitude by a conscious act of will. This state of affairs is even more likely to occur in a patient when he is in the throes of an intense transference reaction.

At this point I find it necessary to clarify the relationship between the working alliance and the real relationship. I described in an earlier paper how the patient and the analyst contribute to the working alliance (Greenson, 1965). The patient must have the capacity to form a relatively reasonable object relationship to the analyst and also fulfill the special requirements of the analytic situation. I also stated that certain transference hopes and longings contribute to the alliance.

As for the analyst, I wrote then that his consistent and unwavering pursuit of insight, as well as his concern and respect for his patient's predicament, contributed to the working alliance. His transference reactions, too, may support the alliance. I want to emphasize that the reliable, enduring core of the working alliance is the "real relationship" between the patient and the analyst, using the term as I defined it, the realistic and genuine relationship. The transference feelings, loving or hateful, from the most infantile to the most mature, may be helpful, but transference is an erratic and treacherous ally.

CLINICAL MATERIAL

It is an impressive clinical finding that in some patients the real relationship remains vaguely in the background and rarely becomes a noticeable issue in their psychoanalytic therapy. In other patients, the real relationship becomes a burning and crucial issue from the beginning to the end of treatment. In part, this may be due to the differences in the specific pathology and therapeutic needs of a given case. The situation is parallel to what one meets with in problems of identity. Patients in whom this issue is in the foreground are those who have had special difficulty in establishing an identity. The role of the real relationship in therapy may be determined by the patient, but also by the therapist's sensitivity or blindness to the issue of the real relationship. The personality or the theoretical orientation of the analyst may be the determining factor.

I shall first present clinical material demonstrating some of the difficulties patients have in dealing with their nontransference reactions to the analyst.

A young man, in his fifth year of analysis, hesitates after I have made an interpretation and then tells me he has something to say which is very difficult for him. He had been about to skip over it when he realized he had been doing just that for years. Taking a deep breath, he said: "You always talk a bit too much. You tend to exaggerate. It would be much easier for me to get mad at you and say you're cock-eyed or wrong or off the point or just not answer. It's terribly hard to say what I mean because I know it will hurt your feelings."

I believe the patient had correctly perceived some traits of mine and it was indeed somewhat painful for me to have them pointed out. I told him he was right on both counts, but I wanted to know why it was harder for him to tell it to me simply and directly as he had just done than to act in an angry fashion. He answered that he knew from experience I would not be upset by an exhibition of temper, since that was obviously his neurosis and I wouldn't be moved by it. Telling me so clearly about my talking too much and exaggerating was a personal criticism, and that would be hurtful. In the past he would have been worried that I might retaliate in some way, but now he knew it was not likely. Besides, he no longer felt my anger would kill him (Greenson, 1967, pp. 217, 218).

Here the difference between transference and nontransference reactions becomes clear. The patient had correctly perceived some characteristics of his analyst's way of working and had also quite realistically predicted that it would be painful for the analyst to have them pointed out. These are nontransference phenomena; they are contemporaneous, appropriate, and realistic. His earlier fantasies about a potentially retaliatory anger that might kill him were historically rooted carry-overs from his childhood anxieties: inappropriate exaggerations, and therefore transference distortions. The patient had developed a good working alliance in relation to his temper outbursts at the analyst, but this alliance could not maintain itself when it came to more realistic criticism. This development occurred only in his fifth year of analysis.

In the example cited the patient tried to hide his realistic perceptions and judgments by resorting to transference distortions. Other patients cling to some of the realistic traits they perceive in the analyst as a screen to ward off the awareness of other realistic traits or transference fantasies. One patient who felt I was annoyed in an hour insisted that it was a transference distortion. She "knew" I was a man of compassion and in good control of my emotions. I asked her what she would feel if I had really been annoyed with her. Only then did she realize how frightened she was of my being angry. She equated it with the rage of her brutal father. This patient tried again and again to keep me a "mirror-type" analyst whose every reaction was mild and benign. She either did not perceive reactions or traits in me which contradicted this or considered her perceptions to be inaccurate.

A male patient "knew" I was against sexual infidelity in marriage. He "knew" it because he felt a good analyst "must be" well analyzed, and if you are well analyzed you have a good sex life and a happy marriage and therefore don't need extramarital affairs. I responded to this somewhat stuffy portrayal of a psychoanalyst with a teasing question something like: "Why do you insist that I'm such a goody-goody?" This led to insight revealing the patient's need to use this image of me as a bulwark for his faltering superego because of his own promiscuous impulses. It also eventually uncovered another picture of me as Zorba the Greek, a man of great passions. In fact, it was the Zorba image he had perceived in a public lecture of mine which made him seek me out as an analyst in the first place. The Zorba image was subsequently camouflaged by other perceptions and transference distortions. Only later did the patient acknowledge that to him I was "really" more of a "Zorba" figure than a "goody-goody."

Lest you feel it is mainly the sexual and hostile reactions which are isolated or denied by the patient, let me cite the following illustration. A young man I sent into analysis with an analyst newly arrived from Europe told me how much he loved the "cute" mistakes in English and the bumbling physical clumsiness of this analyst. I knew the analyst personally and could verify that the young man had made accurate perceptions about him. I therefore asked him if he had brought this up in the analysis, to which he replied: "Hell, no. It's too embarrassing." I told him that it should be brought up, it belonged in the analysis. The young man said he would get around to it "sooner or later." Years later I asked if the cute errors and clumsiness had ever come up during treatment. He sadly said no. It became apparent to both of us at this point that these realistic perceptions and the loving and hostile transference derivatives had never entered his analysis.

I would now like to turn to the analyst's problems in dealing with the real relationship in our patients and ourselves. One source of error is the fact that a transference interpretation is not a neutral designation but our subjective judgment of the patient's behavior, a point Szasz (1963) has stressed. We have to know ourselves and our patient very well to be able to determine whether we are dealing with a transference or a realistic reaction. There is always the possibility that we are blind to some painful characteristic or behavior in ourselves. Furthermore, we may assign different values to certain traits than our patients do. For example, it may be that what I call straightforward speech may be perceived realistically by a patient of a different background as harsh and vulgar. It is not easy or always possible to determine which is correct.

It is important to keep in mind that our patients know us really far less than we know them. Their beliefs and judgments are based on much less evidence than is available to us. Yet, everything we do or say, or don't do or say, from the decor of our office, the magazines in the waiting room, the way we open the door, greet the patient, make interpretations, keep silent, and end the hour, reveals something about our real self, and not only our professional self.

Understandably, we analysts might be tempted to consider as transference manifestations all hurtful remarks made by the patient. In that way, we defend ourselves against recognizing our painful traits or behavior and our faulty interpretations.

I would now like to describe a flagrant example of the neglect of the nontransference relationship. Some years ago, I sent Mrs. E., a young woman I knew socially, into analysis with a psychoanalyst of another city whom I believed to be competently trained and a man of personal integrity. Although I continued my social relationship with Mrs. E., we did not discuss her analysis. About five years from the time I had recommended psychoanalysis to her, we had occasion to talk alone. She told me she had finished her analysis and that she had the greatest respect for psychoanalysis as a therapy and as a science despite the fact that her major symptoms had remained unchanged. I was puzzled and asked Mrs. E. why she had stopped treatment. She replied that, although her analyst was a brilliant man, an impeccable scientist of incorruptible character, she had found the analysis extremely painful from beginning to end. She had hated almost every minute of it. She believed her analyst had tried to help her, but something was wrong, something was missing. For example, she once asked if it were possible to stop the hour ten minutes early because she had an appointment with her child's school teacher. The analyst said nothing, and when she fell silent he repeatedly asked her just to say what came to her mind. He gave no indication that it was permissible for the patient to leave early, so she remained. He behaved in the same way when she occasionally asked for a change in the time for her appointment. He would either remain silent, ask her for associations, or inquire when had she done such things in the past. At the end of such an hour, he would usually interpret that it was her feelings of anger, hostility, or resistance, etc., transferred from some figure in her past, that were responsible for her request, and that would end the discussion. Mrs. E. felt that, although he was right, something was missing. I asked Mrs. E. if she had ever told her analyst of these feelings. She replied that she had, particularly in the beginning. "He only interpreted, he never conceded that my feelings or wishes had some merit. When I complained about it, he would interpret that, too, as transference. I finally gave up. I thought that is how psychoanalysis is supposed to be. I recently spoke to a friend who was analyzed and was struck by how different her experience had been. I know I need more analysis and I want it, but please send me to another kind of person."

No doubt Mrs. E. was an unusually submissive and masochistic patient. Nevertheless, I submit this material as an extreme example of the analyst's neglect of the real relationship between the patient and the therapist. I believe Mrs. E.'s analyst tried to interpret and dig out the original sources of the patient's transference resistances, but he neglected to recognize or acknowledge reality factors or his own contribution to some of the patient's resistances and hostile reactions. By "only interpreting" or "only analyzing," he interfered with the formation of a strong working alliance. His way of working signified to the patient that he was essentially detached and impersonal, there was little indication of concern or compassion (Stone, 1961). As a consequence, the real relationship remained thin and narrow, as did the working alliance and the transference neurosis. I believe that the whole school of analysts which believes that psychoanalytic treatment consists of "only interpreting" is guilty of using transference interpretations as a defense. Some of them seem to interpret the transference so frequently in the course of an hour because they are afraid of the painful affects that they or their patients might otherwise develop. Others of this group ignore the patient's correct and painful perceptions and judgments concerning the analyst and remain silent or pick up some interpretable material, no matter how trivial.

The harmful consequences of such a technique are many. At this point I want to stress three possibilities. By focusing constantly on the patient's transference distortions and ignoring the reality elements, we undermine his self-esteem and make him feel he is always wrong, sick, or crazy, beliefs which he has brought with him into the analysis. By acting as an ignorer of reality, we tempt the patient to live in the outside world as though all of life were lived on a gigantic psychoanalytic couch and people at large were either patients or psychoanalysts. By "only interpreting," we constrict the unfolding of the patient's transference neurosis and limit its development in accordance with our own theoretical biases.

If the patient has made a correct and accurate perception about the analyst, it should be acknowledged some time in that hour or in a subsequent hour. I am not claiming that this acknowledgment should precede or preclude interpretation of the patient's material: that will depend on many different factors. I do maintain that the analyst's confirmation of a patient's correct perception in regard to some trait, fault, or error in himself helps the patient learn to discriminate between reality and fantasy, something all our patients have difficulty with. It also helps break down the patient's infantile wish for us to be omnipotent and omniscient. Furthermore, it can keep the analyst from falling into the God-like conception of himself our work makes so easily possible. Acknowledging the correctness of a patient's perceptions or beliefs helps strengthen the patient's healthy capacity for object relations. Finally, an admission of fault or error indicates honesty, a basic and vital component of a "real relationship."

I have had many patients report to me that when I or their previous analyst responded to a complaint about our person by "only interpreting," we were saying to the patient, in effect, "Your perceptions or judgments are false, distorted, infantile, or unworthy of discussion." This was surely not the analyst's conscious intention, but the failure to acknowledge the correctness of the patient's perception in some way resulted in the patient's feeling humiliated and demeaned. There are analysts who behave as though the discovery of some interpretable unconscious material nullifies the possibility that the patient can also perceive and judge correctly.

Correct perceptions and beliefs can lead to transference reactions or to nontransference reactions or both. Let me illustrate how transference and realistic reactions may appear in an analytic hour. In the second year of his analysis, Mr. C., a 35-year-old sensitive and perceptive writer, begins the hour by attacking his wife verbally for her disorganization, forgetfulness, and irresponsibility, all of which lead him to jealousy fantasies concerning her sexual flirtatiousness with "some third-rate artist." My patient admits his fantasies have little basis in fact, but of late he cannot stop them. Mr. C. then goes on to talk about his wife's analyst, Dr. Z., whom he hates but admires and about whom he also has jealous fantasies. He feels that Dr. Z. considers him a bad husband for Mrs. C. and, further, that Dr. Z. would never tolerate his present behavior if he were in analysis with him. Mr. C. says that I put up with it because: "You are weak and full of shit. You like me, and you are wrong." I point out to the patient that he wants me to be tough like Dr. Z. so that I would control his bad behavior as his harsh father had done. When I am lenient, I become his mother, weak, full of shit, liking him, and wrong.

Mr. C. responds with an attack upon my "wishy-washy" attitudes, my repeatedly saying, "Let's try to understand this behavior," and my willingness to "wait and see." He shouts that he would rather have an answer about what to do, and no interpretations. He imagines Dr. Z. would give him a direct answer. I remain silent.

Mr. C. goes on. He does not trust psychoanalysis. There are no absolute standards for right and wrong. He pauses. Actually, he has been surprised about how well I understand him. He has the feeling, sometimes, that I must be a little bit like him to be so accurate about him. This embarrasses him, and it is probably wrong. Then Mr. C.'s tone changes: "Anyway, you can be fooled. You took me as a patient. You are supposed to be a big-shot analyst, it was so hard to get an appointment with you, and yet you accepted me as a patient. At first, I decided to fool you because I felt you would throw me out if I stopped throwing sand in your eyes. Why *did* you take me as a patient? You must be shit if you chose me. My God, I have felt this toward everybody who has ever liked me."

At this point, I say: "Yes. You felt this way toward your mother, your wife, and now toward me. A mixture of contempt, loving-closeness, and guilt." The patient then adds: "And I admire tough men who frighten me. I know you are not weak. There *is* a difference between warmth and weakness, only I forget sometimes. Now I recall something you have often told me: that I am afraid of warmth. It will make me like you too much, and I will become too dependent on you. I guess I am really more afraid of that than of the tough guys."

I intervene and tell the patient that I feel his last point is right. He was much more afraid of the warm me than he was of me as tough Dr. Z. He wishes I would be tough, then he could fight me and keep me at a distance. Loving me made him vulnerable, dependent, and also full of jealousy. Mr. C. replies that he wished I would not use the word love, it made him feel squeamish: "But I know you. That is probably why you used it." He pauses, reflects and adds: "I suppose you are the third-rate artist I am jealous of."

I have chosen this clinical fragment to demonstrate how interwoven the transference relationship and the real relationship can be in a given hour. The main lines of the transference are quite obvious, and I shall condense my remarks. Mr. C. is jealous of me, a third-rate artist. He also fears and admires me as a tough, harsh analyst. He would like me to act the role of his severe father and control him.

But he knows I will not, and then I become weak, full of shit, wrong, and "wishy-washy" like his mother and himself. From this point, Mr. C. goes on to speak of how I am a fool and a shit to have chosen him as a patient. He also recognizes how afraid he is to love and need me. It seems clear that all the above reactions are for the most part transference distortions.

In addition to these transference reactions, however, Mr. C. also indicates some realistic awareness of me as a person to whom he is relating. He knows that I like him, that I keep trying to understand him, and that I am persistent and patient. He is also aware that I can be fooled, I can be wrong, and at times harsh. Yet he senses I have a good grasp of his underlying feelings and impulses, I must resemble him in some way; I am warm, not weak, and also not afraid of upsetting him by choosing words which get to the heart of the matter. Furthermore, he also realizes that psychoanalysis has no absolute standards for right and wrong. I submit that these are not distortions, but accurate perceptions and judgments based on his observations of me and my work during the 18 months of treatment. They coexist with the transference reactions and do not negate them.

Correct perceptions may lead at first to realistic reactions and later to transference distortions. Let me turn now to another patient in whom the real relationship came into focus unusually early in the treatment. The main reason for this was that I had great doubts about the patient's motivation and suitability for psychoanalytic treatment which impelled me to confront him in one particular hour. Mr. D., a businessman in his mid-fifties, consulted me at the instigation of his young girl friend who told him he was sick because he was unable to commit himself to anybody or any activity he liked, for any length of time. His only loyalty was to business and to making money. The preliminary interviews confirmed the girl's main findings, and I was able to demonstrate to Mr. D. that this was a lifelong pattern which prevented him from enjoying a rich and full life. He seemed eager to embark upon treatment, and although I found him bright, psychologically minded, youthful in spirit, and interesting, I still wondered how much of his motivation was essentially a wish to please his lady friend and would evaporate when and if the love affair disintegrated or the hostile transference came into the foreground.

During one session in the third month of the analysis, Mr. D. spent a good part of the hour talking about various people he knows and kept coming back to the theme that people give one impression upon first acquaintance and later turn out to be quite different. He included in this portrayal his recent girl friend, two unhappy marriage partners, several friendships, and a few hostile business partnerships. He ended this part of the session by stating: "You can't judge people by appearances, you never get to know anyone until you've lived with them." This prompted me to ask: "You have been living with me for three months now, what do you think of me?" Note that I did not ask him for free association, nor did I interpret that he was talking about me, the more traditional approaches. I wanted to highlight his nontransference reactions because of my concern for the working alliance. Although Mr. D. had brought into the analysis several fantasies and dreams about me as a transference figure he feared, resented, and idealized, he was taken aback by my question. He was silent a few moments, coughed uneasily, and then hesitantly replied: "When I first met you, you seemed very competent and sure of yourself, a little cocky perhaps, but straightforward. Now I would also describe you as essentially a kind person, but I still think you are too outspoken at times." The patient paused and then jokingly added: "Well, how did I do? Did I guess right? Or are you going to tell me this is also what you call transference?" I replied that I would not answer him directly, that we would first have to explore the evidence on which he based his assumptions. Only then could we determine whether his reactions were realistic or transference.

Mr. D. was quite obsessional and very organized; thus, in the next several hours we uncovered material which explained how he had arrived at his opinions and attitudes. I am deleting other data in order to clarify my point. Mr. D. brought out that in the first sessions he found my approach to his complicated problems rather astute and my explanations very understandable. His previous sporadic exploratory experiences with psychiatrists had left him confused and unconvinced. Above all, he was surprised that I greeted him in my shirtsleeves and that I have no diplomas on my walls. This he interpreted to mean that I must be very sure of my professional status.

Mr. D. continued to pursue the question I had set before him. He felt I was generous because of my ample explanations and because I often permitted sessions to continue a few minutes beyond the 50-minute period. He considered this last trait poor business organization but good public relations. The patient did feel I was too outspoken and cocky because I talked of hate so readily, and besides I tended to use obscene words like "shit" and "fuck" more often than he considered to be in the best of taste. It was true he used such words upon occasion, but he believed it was not appropriate for a distinguished professional man.

In the course of the ensuing analysis, Mr. D. developed many different transference and nontransference feelings and attitudes toward me, some of which were triggered by the above-mentioned traits he had so early correctly detected.

Let me cite a few examples: What he once saw as competence and self-assurance, he later experienced as smugness and arrogance. My straightforwardness, outspokenness, and cockiness became the source of fantasies of me as vulgar and exhibitionistic, using interpretations as a brutal form of shock therapy and one-up-manship. The generosity he once admired turned into contempt and disgust for my homosexual seductiveness and my Jewish motherliness. What he once considered patience was only a façade for incompetence, slothfulness, senility, and timidity.

Mr. D., of course, experienced different varieties of love, dependency, and trust, as well as hostility, hate, and fear toward me. Sometimes the former took precedence, sometimes the latter; at other times both went on simultaneously. But Mr. D. did not remain in his analysis because his loving transference "neutralized" his hostile transference. I contend that in addition to his transference feelings, Mr. D. also had a real relationship with me which I think kept him in the analysis and which enabled us to work effectively.

The importance of the real relationship can be seen in the rigors of working through. A patient will break off an analysis of long standing when driven by a sudden eruption of an intense hostile transference. This may be understood as a failure to make the correct interpretations. Yet I have made many false interpretations which my patients knew or sensed, and they did not run away. The decisive factor was the relative strength of the real relationship existing between us, how much genuine and realistic liking and respect there was between us. Again I want to stress that the real relationship does not have to be verbalized or conspicuous, but it must be present to a sufficient degree for the analytic situation to endure the long and painful process of working through. A patient or an analyst will consider interrupting treatment if either realizes some basic aspect is not being properly understood. But this decision will be arrived at mutually. Unexpected crises or failures in psychoanalysis are the result of both incorrect interpretations and a failure in the real relationship. By and large, technical errors may cause pain, but they are usually repairable; human errors are much harder to remedy.

I would add that there are many indications which signal a change in the nontransference relationship. One typical clinical sign of a change in the patient's real relationship to the analyst is when a patient who has been coming to your office for months or years "sees" something for the first time. A patient in his fourth year of analysis will suddenly ask as he enters the treatment room, "Is that a new chair?" That chair was there, unchanged, from the first day he came to see me. What changed was something in his awareness of me and of himself as real persons.

FORMULATIONS, HYPOTHESES, AND CONCLUSIONS

At this point, I would like to state some additional formulations and hypotheses which I have derived from my own clinical experience and the writings of others. In the course of a successful analysis, a patient will experience a wide range of *transference reactions* to his analyst from very primitive to quite mature, in terms of love, hate, sex, and aggression. In addition, the patient will also experience realistic and genuine reactions towards the analyst and form a real relationship. I believe this must be present, to some extent from the beginning, in order for the patient to "get into" analytic treatment. All the qualities of the patient, realistic and unrealistic, genuine and synthetic, will play a role in determining the development and course of the transference and the real relationship. Intelligence, sensitivity, humor, empathy, education, temperament, and taste all play a part in shaping the transference and nontransference reactions. I believe all of this is true, albeit unequally, for both the patient and the psychoanalyst.

I furthermore believe that all patients have transference reactions, but only those who have the capacity for forming a real relationship to the analyst are analyzable. I contend that borderline and psychotic patients are analyzable only if and when they have the ability to form a real relationship to their analyst. (For a contradictory point of view see, above all, Rosenfeld, 1965.) In my opinion, most of them require preparatory therapy which consists essentially of *building* an object relationship. The reader is urged to refer to the writings on severely regressed adult patients by Federn (1952), Winnicott (1955, 1965b), Fairbairn (1957, 1958), Wexler (1951, 1952, 1960), and Searles (1965). With regard to symbiotic or autistic children, see Mahler (1965) and Bettelheim (1963) and for borderline and neurotic children, Anna Freud (1965).

My clinical experience leads me to believe that the final resolution of the transference neurosis depends to a great extent on the transference neurosis being replaced by a real relationship. I do not share the traditional psychoanalytic point of view that interpretation alone can resolve the transference neurosis. Interpretation has to be supplemented by a realistic and genuine relationship to the person of the analyst, limited though it may be, for the transference neurosis to be replaced. This last subject deserves more elaboration but exceeds the boundaries of this presentation.

These deliberations concerning the importance and the role of the nontransference relationship between patient and analyst imply a significant reevaluation of some of the theory and technique of psychoanalytic therapy. I have only hinted at some of the possibilities in the clinical part of this paper. This will be pursued further and in greater detail when time and space permit.

I want to conclude this discussion by referring to the question of selecting certain therapeutic elements in accordance with the diagnostic category of a case (A. Freud, 1965). Most of our neurotic patients come to us with a mixed clinical picture. We ought to offer them the broadest range of therapeutic possibilities and not limit the changes of therapy to any single factor. I believe that "only interpreting" or "only analyzing" is insufficient for most of our patients.

CHAPTER 12

On Time and Anniversaries

George H. Pollock, M.D., Ph.D.

Anniversary phenomena are frequently observed in uncompleted or pathological mourning processes. In some instances anniversary reactions trigger latent pathology which can result in severe phobic responses, psychosomatic responses, anxiety, depression, or melancholia with or without suicide. Anniversary responses may be nonpathological as well as pathological, conscious as well as unconscious, and may be more frequent than is realized. The importance of time in anniversary phenomena is significant at different levels. This essay will present some of the early psychoanalytic observations that link time with anniversaries, some developmental and clinical aspects of time and its pathology, and some theoretical psychoanalytical considerations of time.

EARLY PSYCHOANALYTIC OBSERVATIONS OF ANNIVERSARY PHENOMENA

Anniversary phenomena can be traced historically to the very beginnings of psychoanalysis. In the midst of the clinical description of Fräulein Elisabeth von R., in the *Studies on Hysteria* (Breuer and Freud, 1893-1895), Freud characteristically presents us with insights that go beyond that of the topic he is discussing. He mentions "... traumas accumulated during sick-nursing being dealt with subsequently, where we get no general impression of illness but where the mechanism of hysteria is nevertheless retained" (p. 162). Freud

Dr. Pollock is Director of the Chicago Institute for Psychoanalysis.

digresses briefly with a clinical account of "a highly-gifted lady who suffers from slight nervous states and whose whole character bears evidence of hysteria, though she has never had to seek medical help or been unable to carry on her duties" (p. 162). He emphasizes that the "woman is not ill; her postponed abreaction, was not a hysterical process, however much it resembled one" (p. 164).

From what clinical observations do these conclusions stem? Freud tells us that this woman

> has already nursed to the end three or four of those whom she loved. Each time she reached a state of complete exhaustion; but she did not fall ill after these tragic efforts. Shortly after her patient's death, however, there would begin in her a work of reproduction which once more brought up before her eyes the scenes of the illness and death. Every day she would go through each impression once more, would weep over it and console herself—at her leisure, one might say. This process of dealing with her impressions was dovetailed into her everyday tasks without the two activities interfering with each other. The whole thing would pass through her mind in chronological sequence. I cannot say whether the work of recollection corresponded day by day with the past. I suspect that this depended on the amount of leisure which her current household duties allowed [p. 162].

Here, the Editors of the *Standard Edition* note that in this 1895 "account of the 'work of recollection' Freud seems to be anticipating the 'work of mourning' which he described much later in *Mourning and Melancholia*" (1917c).

Freud continues with his clinical account,

> [I]n addition to these outbursts of weeping with which she made up arrears and which followed close upon the fatal termination of the illness, this lady celebrated annual festivals of remembrance at the period of her various catastrophes, and on these occasions her vivid visual reproductions and expressions of feeling kept to the date precisely. For instance, on one occasion I found her in tears and asked her sympathetically what had happened that day. She brushed aside my question half-angrily: "Oh no," she said, "it is only that the specialist was here again today and gave us to understand that there was no hope. I had no time to cry about it then." She was referring to the last illness of her husband, who had died three years earlier [pp. 162-163].

Freud goes on

> I should be very much interested to know whether the scenes which she celebrated at these annual festivals of remembrance were always the same ones or whether different details presented themselves for abreaction each time as I suspect in view of my theory. But I cannot discover with certainty. The lady, who had no less strength of character than intelligence, was ashamed of the violent effect produced in her by these reminiscences [pp. 163-164].

In a footnote to the above clinical vignette, Freud describes the case of Fräulein Mathilde H. The anniversary of her engagement, whose dissolution precipitated her depression, proved crucial in her successful hypnotherapy and symptom removal. It is in this brief account of Fräulein Mathilde H.'s treatment that Freud uses the term "anniversary."

Before discussing the further implications of Freud's ideas as noted here, particularly as they related to reminiscing and working through, mourning, trauma, and anniversary-holiday reactions, I wish to call attention to one aspect of Breuer's account of the treatment of Anna O., the first case in the *Studies on Hysteria.*

In this clinical report, Breuer notes that Anna O. (Bertha Pappenheim) became ill in the middle of July 1880, when her father fell ill of peripleuritic abscess.

In describing the alternation of Bertha Pappenheim's mental states, he says,

> in the first she lived, like the rest of us in the winter of 1881-2, whereas in the second she lived in the winter of 1880-1, and had completely forgotten all the subsequent events. The one thing that nevertheless seemed to remain conscious most of the time was the fact that her father had died. She was carried back to the previous year with such intensity that in the new house she hallucinated her old room, so that when she wanted to go to the door she knocked up against the stove which stood in the same relation to the window as the door did in the old room. The change-over from one state to another occurred spontaneously but could also be very easily brought about by any sense-impression which vividly recalled the previous year. One had only to hold up an orange before her

> eyes (oranges were what she had chiefly lived on during the first part of her illness) in order to carry her over from the year 1882 to the year 1881. But this transfer into the past did not take place in a general or indefinite manner; she lived through the previous winter day by day. I should only have been able to suspect that this was happening, had it not been that every evening during the hypnosis she talked through whatever it was that had excited her on the same day in 1881, and had it not been that a private diary kept by her mother in 1881 confirmed beyond a doubt the occurrence of the underlying events. This re-living of the previous year continued till the illness came to its final close in June 1882 [p. 33].

The account of Bertha Pappenheim's illness as it related to Breuer's psychic life has been discussed elsewhere (Pollock, 1968). The present focus is on the anniversary aspects of the course of Bertha Pappenheim's treatment. Breuer proceeds to describe how these "revived psychical stimuli" of 1880-81 made their appearance in the more normal year of 1881-82.

> [O]ne morning the patient said to me laughingly that she had no idea what was the matter but she was angry with me. Thanks to the diary I knew what was happening, and sure enough, this was gone through again in the evening hypnosis: I had annoyed the patient very much on the same evening in 1881. On another time she told me there was something the matter with her eyes; she was seeing colours wrong. She knew she was wearing a brown dress but she saw it as a blue one. We soon found that she could distinguish all the colours of the visual test-sheets correctly and clearly, and that the disturbance only related to the dress-material. The reason was that during the same period in 1881 she had been very busy with a dressing-gown for her father, which was made with the same material as her present dress, but was blue instead of brown. Incidentally, it was often to be seen that these emergent memories showed their effect in advance; the disturbance of her normal state would occur earlier on, and the memory would only gradually be awakened in her *condition seconde* [pp. 33-34].

Breuer notes that with the "verbal utterances" of the psychical events, the symptoms disappeared. Bertha herself described the therapeutic procedure as a "talking cure," or in a more joking fashion as "chimney sweeping." This discharge through verbalization of what was recalled corresponds to the importance of verbal discharge in the normal mourning process.

The questions posed by these anniversary phenomena are many, and only in recent years have we begun to consider them.

DEVELOPMENTAL ASPECTS OF TIME

In his paper "On Narcissism" (1914c), Freud states that the time factor has no application to unconscious processes. He elaborates on this in 1915 when he writes, "the processes of the system *Ucs.* are *timeless*, i.e., they are not ordered temporally, are not altered by the passage of time; they have no reference to time at all. Reference to time is bound up . . . with the work of the system *Cs.*" (p. 187). In *Beyond the Pleasure Principle* (1920a), he repeats this topographic conceptualization, adding, "our abstract idea of time seems to be wholly derived from the method of working in the system Pcpt.-Cs. and to correspond to a perception on its own part of that method of working" (p. 28). This latter idea is reiterated in the paper on the "Mystic-Writing Pad" (1925c). In the *New Introductory Lectures* (1933), Freud related his ideas about time to his later structural hypothesis.

> [T]here is nothing in the id that corresponds to the idea of time; there is no recognition of the passage of time, and . . . no alteration in its mental processes is produced by the passage of time. Wishful impulses which have never passed beyond the id, but impressions, too, which have been sunk into the id by repression, are virtually immortal; after the passage of decades they behave as though they had just occurred. They can only be recognized as belonging to the past, can only lose their importance and be deprived of their cathexis of energy, when they have been made conscious by the work of analysis, and it is on this that the therapeutic effect of analytic treatment rests to no small extent [p. 74].

What Freud means here is that the id, operating according to the primary process, seeks immediate present discharge and the accompanying pleasure through release—thus timelessness reigns. Freud continues, "the relation to time, which is so hard to describe, is . . . introduced into the ego by the perceptual system; it can scarcely be doubted that the mode of operation of that system is what provides the origin of the idea of time" (p. 76). In other words, the ego with its functions of memory and reality orientation operates according to the reality principle, and the secondary processes (e.g., delay, detour) regulate discharge in accordance with adaptive needs.

Brown (1959), addressing himself to the psychoanalytical meaning of history, suggests that repression and the repetition compulsion generate historical time. He writes, "[R]epression transforms the timeless instinctual compulsion to repeat into the forward-moving dialectic of neurosis which is history" (p. 93). Fixation to the past is crucial, and one might classify this as superego-time in comparison to id-time and ego-time. We must, however, distinguish the perception of time from the retention of the past through repression and fixation.

Anna Freud (1965) has written about the different evaluations of time at various age levels:

> The sense of the length or shortness of a given time period seems to depend on the measuring being carried out by way of either id or ego functioning. Id impulses are by definition intolerant of delay and waiting; the latter attitudes are introduced by the ego of which postponement of action (by interpolation of the thought processes) is as characteristic as urgency of fulfillment is of the id. How a child will experience a given time period will depend therefore not on actual duration, measured objectively by the adult, by the calendar and by the clock, but on the subjective inner relations of either id or ego dominance over his functioning. It is these latter factors which will decide whether the intervals set for feeding, the absence of the mother, the duration of nursery attendance, or hospitalization, etc. will seem to the child short or long, tolerable or intolerable, and as a result will prove harmless or harmful in their consequences [pp. 60-61].

It is in the progression "from primary to secondary functioning that we get anticipation of the future, between wish and action directed towards fulfillment" (p. 92).

Concepts of time do not develop suddenly into final form, but follow a developmental pattern of evolution. However, as is true with so many psychic evolutions, the old patterns are not totally abandoned. Under duress, regression can occur, and earlier conceptualization referable to time may reappear, e.g., loss of ability to gauge duration, to detect succession and temporal association, or to note seriation. These internal psychic processes related to time, proceeding on a developmental time-axis, serve to facilitate the outward adaptation to external reality. Unlike other psychological concepts which have a tangible and material basis, however, time is one of the most abstract of all concepts. In an attempt to link it with some thing, early in development the clock or another time-measuring device becomes the base for the thought. But the abstract concept of time, involving internal and external instants, intervals, sequences, requires more advanced thinking processes, described under the rubric of the secondary process.

Boring (1936) has described five bases for time perception: (1) the child gets some perception of succession, or how stimuli follow one another through play, e.g., running his fingers over the teeth at different rates; (2) the child acquires some perception of continuity when he observes some action continuing until it stops, e.g., a moving wheel which slows and stops; (3) the child obtains an idea of temporal length from perceiving differences in particular sensory stimuli, e.g., hearing long or short musical sounds; (4) the child learns to perceive and respond to present visceral stimuli, e.g., hunger, pain, tension (these are aspects of the immediacy associated with primary-process discharge, and biological rhythm associated with id activities); and (5) the child acquires the ability to perceive patterns of successive stimuli, to feel and respond to physiological rhythms. This latter is a more advanced stage in the developmental line of time conception than that of the id—primary process—time conception.

Lovell (1966) has called attention to the words used in primitive societies to express time. He notes that the terms used frequently reflect the main events of the day or the season, e.g., watering-time, milking-time, planting-time, harvesting-time. These descriptive periods deal with biological activities necessary for life adaptation. Lovell observes that time for the young child is also linked with a series of events that are task- or tension-relieving activities and biologically related.

As development proceeds, the adult concept of time gains ascendancy, and personal time becomes more closely linked to objective time which relates to events in the external world (hours, dates, holidays, anniversaries), and less linked to biological rhythms and id-time. There is a gradual ability to differentiate past, present, and future; there is the acquisition of a time vocabulary that has meaning; and there is a growth of understanding of clock and calendar.

Lovell (1966) has observed that up to about age five, the child may fuse time and space, with a linkage to certain concrete objects and events. Onward from that age, the ordering of events into earlier or later begins to emerge, and the past gets structured into a succession of events. The learning and usage of time-words precedes the child's grasp of differentiated time relationships. Ames (1946) found that the understanding of time-words and their use came in a fairly uniform sequence which was generally the same for all children, although the age at which a particular child could understand or use a specific term varied. Children in the United States were able to use the terms morning and afternoon by four years of age, knew what day it was by about five years of age, and could tell time by seven years of age. The child could use terms like winter-time or lunch-time before the word time itself. Lovell suggests that a vocabulary of time-words is built up by association. For example, when it is light, it is day; when it is snowing, it is winter. These linkages of words with time or season are also related to drive satisfactions and to need-fulfilling objects. Thus, breakfast and morning, sleep and night may become linked. Gradually the more global morning or night becomes differentiated and associated with certain measured time, first linked to whole hours, but later divided into half and quarter hours, and finally into minutes and seconds (Springer, 1952). What was directly associated with need tension and its satisfaction becomes a relatively conflict-free development of the autonomous ego. Time becomes a cognitive acquisition which takes on its own meaning and adaptive function.

Bradley (1948) has observed that in children below the age of nine time perspective for the past is very shallow, becoming nebulous beyond the span of a generation or so. By six years of age, however, time can be related to personal experience, e.g., morning, child's own age. By eight years there is increasing understanding of the week and of the calendar. Development progresses with increasing comprehension of the week, month, and year, until finally there is a gradual extension of the understanding of time in relation to both space and duration, e.g., time elsewhere, and time between holidays. As children get older they can increasingly differentiate between objective and subjective time, and, as Lovell (1966) has demonstrated, the concept of time in its more adult form is available to the majority of children by nine years of age. It is at this age that there may be sufficient integration and consolidation of internal psychic structures to allow for conflict-free, autonomous ego activity to deal with objective time per se.

Time is one of the most complex perceptual abstractions derived from sensory data. Stimuli are ordered into the temporal properties of succession and duration. These then become conceptualized and capable of being communicated. In order to facilitate adaptation the psychic apparatus must integrate sequence and order, interval and duration. This involves the perception of the current and present, the memory of the past and the historical, and the capacity for the consideration of the future.

> Only man has an elaborately organized and systematized world of time which can be perceived and communicated directly. This taming of the merciless savage, *time*, into a refined and useful social being has enabled the human partially to liberate himself from the bondage of mortality. Language and reason, history and education, theology and philosophy, science and technology, and the arts are the spoils of man's limited but profound victories over *time* [Goldstone and Goldfarb, 1966, p. 449].

The human infant is not born with a developed sense of time and history. At birth, the human organism is little more than a physiological clock involved with the regulation of basic biological rhythms. This corresponds to id-time, which has no awareness of past or future, but is involved only in present attempts to seek discharge and tension reduction. Sleep and feed-excretory schedules appear as the initial biological temporal events which take on later social significance. The parents, especially the mother, become attuned to the infant's physiological clock, and in this way there is gradual regulation which allows for delay, postponement, and socially accepted gratification. These experiences are the beginning of ego-time. The young child, through this mechanism, gradually shifts from pleasure-pain functioning to reality-principle, secondary-principle operations. Regression to the earlier primary process is always present in the most mature. When the before, now, and later can be conceptualized, we have evidence for the completion of the line of development of the time sequence. The clock, calendar, and other objective measures of time allow the adaptation to progress to the point where internal perceptions link with the outside in such manner as to permit social adaptation.

Goldstone and Goldfarb (1966) have reviewed the literature referring to children's conceptions of time from four separate points of view. *First*, the maturation and development of the capacity to perform temporal conceptual operations. *Second*, the maturation and development of the use and comprehension of temporal language. This involves the various developmental stages of the child's integration of the expression and understanding of time concepts, temporal relationships, and temporal language. The integration of succession and duration with language describing these concepts is a necessary precursor to conceptualizing historical information. Children's time concepts proceed from the specific to the general, from the concrete to the abstract, with a gradual reduction in the frequency of inaccurate tenses and inappropriate temporal expressions. This development corresponds to the gradual appearance of secondary autonomy of ego functions and the decrease in drive tensions that allows for the more abstract thinking and conceptualization. Ames (1946) has observed that words indicating the present appear first, followed by representation of the future, and finally by those indicating the past. Ames presents a detailed developmental schedule of the unfolding of this sequence of acquisition, noting the gradualness of the process, the close connection between personal activities and concrete experiences and marks of time, and the importance of understanding chronology and historical epochs which go beyond the ordinary usage of time language.

Third, the relationship between temporal conceptualization and intelligence, especially as observed in mentally retarded youngsters. The retarded child has little conception of sequence, relativity, or historical time, and cannot comprehend the world beyond his own activities.

Fourth, the relationship between temporal conceptualization and personality. Few researches have been undertaken to study this correlation. It is in this area that the child psychoanalyst can contribute empirical and clinical data which can form the basis of more systematic studies. We assume that pathogenic processes interfering with emotional development, internalization, and normal structure formation will affect temporal conceptualization. Thus, ego distortions or defects should show pathological manifestations of the temporal conceptual system. In adults with various types of psychopathology, such time distortions and disorientations occur.

Bromberg (1938) has found that the development of a time-sense in children does not occur until after the age of five or six. It develops slowly until about age 10 or 12 and parallels the development of abstract thinking. Children, he observes, have a better idea of age than of years. Schecter and his collaborators (1955), studying children of three to six years of age, found that in the younger age-groups there is a greater emphasis on time related to immediate personal experience, at first physiological, and later on, interpersonal and play activities. With increasing age, especially in six-year-olds, external factors become more important, i.e., there is an increase in abstraction with respect to the concepts of clock, days of the week, months, and years. This development regarding time sense parallels the development of the self and the ego, i.e., from the autistic, pleasure domination of the infant with obscure boundaries of self and external world, to the more interpersonal, consensually validatable social world of the older child, where frustration of needs, development of routine and purpose is seen. In other words, as reality-oriented ego becomes more firmly integrated, perceptual time and conceptual time can be conceived by the child.

Cohen (1967) has distinguished between perceived time and conceived time. He agrees with other writers in differentiating three levels of adaptation to time: (1) perception of the rhythms which are set to the periodicities of nature; (2) capacity to register duration and sequence; and (3) with the aid of memory, the ability to reconstitute the succession of changes that have been experienced, and by anticipation, the acquisition of a new perspective for future activities. Piaget (1955) also distinguishes between time perception and time conception in the child. Time as a logical concept, for Piaget, has two aspects: the order of the succession of events (before, after, at the same time), and the duration of intervals separating successive events which can be measured in chronometric units.

CLINICAL OBSERVATIONS OF TIME PATHOLOGY

Browne, in 1874, discussed time amnesias and distortions in various mental diseases of children and adults. He presented no theoretical explanations for his observations. When Breuer and Freud (1893-1895) made observations of anniversary responses, they, too, did not link these to a theory of time perception and conception.

Stekel wrote about time and neurosis in 1912.

> [T]he significance of time for the neurotics is most clearly seen in their unconscious calendar. Their dreams betray the fact that in their minds they are continually juggling with certain numbers, especially the years of the birth of certain persons, the years of their death, the days of certain traumata, etc. Gloom and depression on certain days prove on analysis to be the anniversaries of certain important occurrences [p. 97].

Ferenczi's (1919) and Abraham's (1918) papers on the Sunday and vacation neuroses relate to this theme. Freud, in the paper *On Narcissism* (1914c), suggests in a footnote that "the developing and strengthening of this observing agency might contain within it the subsequent genesis of (subjective) memory and the time-factor, the latter of which has no application to unconscious processes" (p. 96). Time references seen clinically by Stekel (1912) and others did not refer to time as such, but served as a symbolic condensation, displacement, or day residue for the emergence of unconscious conflictful impulses.

As early as 1900, in *The Interpretation of Dreams*, Freud (1900) noted that there is a lack of a sense of time in the dream. In 1913 he observed (1913c) that the time of day in dreams often represented the age of the dreamer at some particular period of his childhood. Although he did not elaborate on this statement, it can be inferred that Freud meant that time and age referred to a repressed conflict from childhood, but did not relate directly to specific time perception or conception. He again comments in the *New Introductory Lectures* (1933) on the dream work's changing temporal relations into spatial ones and being represented by these, e.g., smallness and spatial distance in dreams signifying remoteness in time. Gross (1949) studied the sense of time in dreams and concluded that time references in the manifest dream were correlated with a specific thought content which involved a specific task for the dream work and did not relate to objective time as such.

Yates (1935), extrapolating from clinical observations, was one of the first psychoanalysts to write that the earliest time sense is based on bodily needs, intake, and excretory tension-reductions. Later comes the need to "perform on time" (excretion), and then periodic biologic events, e.g., menses. She suggests that most fundamental to a person's later appreciation of musical time and rhythm is the sense of time and rhythm originating in the "breast period," when the body supplied the rhythm. Furthermore, she describes how one may break all contact, including independence of time, in a state of acute anxiety, by regression to an early state where there is the loss of the sense of reality and the awareness of the passage of time.

Difficulties in time awareness and discrimination may be noted in narcissistic disorders. Time for these individuals is closer to the id-time and that of biological rhythms. In the transference neuroses, time awareness and discrimination are intact, although in conversion hysteria the "suffering from reminiscences" is split off from consciousness, and in the obsessional-compulsive we find time symbolically becomes part of the symptom complex in the service of control, conformity, and isolation.

I have seen individuals who can always tell time quite accurately without seeing a watch, or who can awaken at a certain time without an alarm clock. In these people the ego is constantly vigilant and, in order to avoid anxiety, anticipates and controls time perception. They usually have some obsessive-compulsive character traits. In several instances, they were quite musical, played instruments, had good pitch, and a sense of time or rhythm.

Some "accurate time-tellers" have a very competent and secure ego which delights in its control for reasons of narcissistic gratification rather than to avoid anxiety. Such people are often very good sleepers, able to fall asleep at will at a moment's notice, and awaken, relaxed and rested, after a short nap. The more anxious group of "accurate time-tellers" are usually poor sleepers.

Schilder (1936), Straus (1947), and Oberndorf (1941) discuss disorders of time in other psychopathological states. Schilder explains the depressive's complaint that time no longer moves, as a manifestation of the attempt at inhibition of aggressive-murderous impulses. Straus explains the "stood still in time" phenomena, so often described by his depressive patients, as an inability to experience the present as a completion of the past. Thus the stoppage of time, the dragging of time, the hesitation of time seem to be manifestations of hopelessness. The present does not go anywhere, the past seems "ages ago," and the future is not contemplated or is remote. Straus writes that "every experience receives its specific significance, its special value, from its temporal position. Even in its content each moment is determined by its place in our life history. We all know that we will have to die" (p. 256). In the depressive patient, however, overwhelmed by the impact of the guilt of the past, the past is revived with its punitive judgments, and then its retribution emerges. Here the past emerges, not as objective- or clock-time, but as "the time of personal history," which the patient seeks to avoid.

Dooley (1941) has observed in her clinical work that the conscious perception of time may serve as a defense against overwhelming anxiety; that is, those who fear the retreat into the unconscious as a threat to survival of the ego cling to the concept of time as a means of preventing such a retreat. Her three skillfully described adult cases of childhood parent loss offer a mirror image of what has been found in the anniversary reactions described elsewhere. Dooley's patients watch time as a defense against ego disintegration and the emergence of threatening id impulses. Instead of denying or disavowing time, as is sometimes seen, her patients hypercathect time and reality testing as a defense. These people fear anesthesia, because it represents a loss of control of time, and they expect death and disintegration. In many ways this hypercathexis of time perception is similar to the anniversary mourning rituals where there is a hypercathexis of time and of death. Rationalized to take into account the religious beliefs, essentially what is stated is: "Be aware of the time and the event, and then you shall be safe." In other words, focusing on the external defends against the internal dangers. Several statements made by Dooley's patients are worth quoting. The first patient's mother died in childbirth when he was 10. He watched time closely. He stated, "Things have to happen in time and I must be on hand to see what happens. . . . Death and birth can't happen in the same instant. If there is time then I am alive. If there was an interval without time I wouldn't be there! If time ceased, God knows what would happen, I'd be blotted out" (p. 16). The second patient's father died when he was six years old. He said, "I have some idea that I caused the death of my father . . . and I shall be killed. Someone kills you for revenge. . . . Keep your consciousness, know what you are doing" (p. 17). The third patient's mother committed suicide when the patient was 17 years old. The patient developed hyperthyroidism at that time. She said, "I must never forget myself for a single minute. I watch the clock and keep busy, or else I won't know who I am" (p. 17). The danger here is from the failure of repression of the internal forces that threaten the individual, the attention to time being a secondary defensive operation.

I have seen a man in psychotherapy who kept a calendar on which he entered "death days" for the entire year. To him these were more important than birthdays. When asked whose "death days" appeared on his calendar, he listed relatives, friends, and significant (to him) cultural, historical, and political figures. As a child this man had witnessed the sudden and traumatic death of his adolescent brother which consciously affected his entire subsequent life. He observed that in his conversation he frequently used the term "dead-line," to refer to time limits. Unlike the obsessional patient who uses isolation and punctuality for control of internal instinctual conflict, this patient, similar to Dooley's cases, controlled internal tensions through the hypercathexis of "death times." He did have difficulty in going to sleep, which he equated with death.

A variant of these patients who hypercathect time is the patient who is always convinced that he will not have enough time. In one such instance the roots of this anticipation were traced to the patient's childhood, when his next younger sibling was born. He felt cheated, deprived, "hurt," and the anxiety over his murderous rage to the sibling and the mother was displaced onto time. In analysis he paid particular attention to the length of each analytic session, and the termination phase was characterized by a stormy reworking of the theme: "I have not been here long enough," "You want to fill my place with someone else," and "I want to kill you and your next patient." The hypercathexis of time and duration was a defensive maneuver designed to ward off the more basic anxiety related to his rage and death wishes at the time of the sibling's birth, as well as his feeling of helplessness.

Dooley (1941) makes a distinction between those patients to whom the fear of losing track of time means fear of loss of the world of objects, loss of a portion of the mind, loss of the body, death, being thrown back into the past where one was defenseless against internal drives, and loss of identity, and classical obsessive patients who use time defensively as part of the mechanism of isolation. Orgel's (1965) patient had to control time literally as a means of controlling life and death. This patient showed impairment in object relationships, self-observation, memory, and perception, and had to remain permanently young in order to halt time. Past and future were isolated from the present, reality-principle functioning was impaired, and the strong compulsion to repeat rather than remember served to avoid the reality of death.

Scott (1948), Eissler (1952), DuBois (1954), Eisenbud (1956), Jaques (1965), and Deutsch (1966) have described clinical aspects of time-feeling, time-sense, and time duration-impairments as they are related to distortions in ego development. Gifford (1960) has been particularly interested in "Sleep, Time and The Early Ego." He suggests that

> the adaption of the sleep rhythm to the 24-hour periodicity of everyday life represents the first primitive experience of time, as a restriction imposed by the outer world on immediate gratification. These experiences may be the precursors of later attitudes toward time, as a stern agent that curtails pleasure and demands compliance with adult responsibilities [p. 27].

The reality principle impinges on the pleasure-discharge needs of the young infant as an adaptation to the mother's periodic availability and the quality and quantity of her care and attention. The capacity to delay and postpone the immediate need for food in the expectation of future gratification is the first differentiation of past, present, and future, and may be the earliest manifestation of memory as it applies to regulation of personal time. Chambers (1961) has approached the area of early ego-time perceptions through her study of maternal deprivation and its effect on time conceptualization in children. Her formulations, closely following Freud's theoretical ideas, also include some of Piaget's concepts. Chambers' experiments confirm her hypothesis that the group of maternally deprived children were less mature or advanced in the development of temporal concept than a parallel "normal" group.

None of these reports bears directly on anniversary phenomena as such, but do suggest that although objective time is used as a day residue for anniversary reactions personal time linked to unconscious internal conflict is the pertinent consideration in the understanding of this exacerbation of old anxieties and defenses. The experience of time is very subjective and varied, with many different conscious meanings and attitudes attached to it. It is only through the intensive study of individual patients that we can appreciate its meaning structurally, dynamically, genetically, adaptively, and economically.

METAPSYCHOLOGICAL ASPECTS OF TIME AND ANNIVERSARIES

Philosophers and psychologists have discussed time from various points of view. Physical, objective, social, categorical, measured time is distinguished from personal, subjective, existential, experiential time (Weisman, 1965; Eissler, 1952; Meerloo, 1948). Perception of temporal duration, sequence, and other such considerations vary from person to person, and from period to period, developmentally speaking, for the same individual. In connection with this last point, mention has been made of development of a sense of time from youngest infancy to later childhood and adolescence. Jaques (1965) has recently written about the mid-life crisis and its relationship to death. He believes that the central and crucial feature of this crisis is the "psychological scene of the reality and inevitability of one's own eventual personal death [and] one's own real and actual mortality" (p. 506). Here the reality principle operates to potentially create a situation of tension and anxiety. Jaques (1965) suggests that the unconscious wish for immortality may be manifested in various ways, e.g., denial of mourning, ideas of immortality, notions of reincarnation. He further suggests that ideas of immortality, conscious and unconscious, are the counterparts "of the infantile fantasies of the indestructible and hence immortal aspect of the idealized and bountiful primal object" (p. 507), with the accompanying demands for absolute perfection in behavior, as well as the omnipotent and omniscient fantasies of the object and of the self. I would suggest that, viewed retrospectively, the anxiety may not be about death and nothingness, which cannot be conceptualized, but the fear of absolute helplessness that does characterize the very early state of existence. The omnipotence-omniscience of the child and his parent is a protective device against this very threatening state. The counterpart to this early omni-parent is the omnipotent, omniscient God who will take care, control, protect, and insure perpetuity, instead of separation and helplessness which hold such terrors for the child. As an extension of this idea, I would further suggest that the "immortality" fantasy is a reversal of the separation-individuation, with the wish for a symbiotic reunion with the powerful mother who gave life, direction, protection, and gratification. The mid-life crisis can thus be viewed as a reactivation of unresolved conflicts from infancy, childhood, and adolescence as they relate to survival, separation, and creativity. As the adult approaches mid-life, his defensive coping devices may lose their effectiveness, especially when there is accompanying failure of bodily functions and abilities. If depression occurs, suicide as a magical reunion may be attempted.

In Dooley's (1941) cases, cited above, we see the counterpart to the denial mechanism, namely, the hypercathexis of reality, reality testing, and especially of time. Some individuals may show the "nemesis" notion of Chapman (1959). Stein (1953) has written about premonition as a defense. In his clear and concise clinical report of an anniversary reaction which appeared with an accompanying dream during psychoanalysis, he was able to link the premonition with the temporal coincidence of the anniversary and the ongoing transference relationship to the analyst. Premonitory experiences can be used defensively to deny intolerable, conflictful, guilt-laden wishes.

Meerloo (1950) has described the "preparation or anticipation neurosis" in which one finds the traumatic episode imagined and experienced before the traumatic event is provoked. An initial primary trauma may cause a "conditioning of our memorization" by setting up memory traces or internalizations which emerge in the anticipatory fantasy. "The anxiety involved in the new trauma uses the past as defense in order to avoid future traumatic experiences" (p. 662). New defense mechanisms may overemphasize the past, or the fear of dangerous future reality may be warded off by the fantasy that it has already happened. The future, though implying danger and anxiety, is an activation of older internal traumatic experiences.

Spiegel (1966) has recently approached this topic from another avenue. He emphasizes internal anticipation rather than anticipation of external events as a means of adaptation. In his conceptualization, "the superego, when 'finally' established, significantly assists, perhaps (partially) replaces the ego as the chief internal sensory organ of the mental apparatus. . . . this assistance results in a finer calibration of the function of anticipation than has existed before" (p. 315). Related to this idea is that of Bergler and Roheim (1946), who have suggested that the "part of the unconscious personality which watches over time perception is the unconscious part of the ego, under the influence of the superego" (p. 197). According to Spiegel (1966), the superego operates along two interwoven paths: the finely calibrated internal perception of id impulses; and as "a protection of the ego against the traumatic effect of large amounts of drive energy. In these ways, it functions analogously to the protective barrier against external stimuli" (p. 317) thus achieving equilibrium. He describes a "traumatic syndrome" for a class of patients reacting as if they are traumatized, but, unlike the true traumatic neuroses, there is no indication of a recent trauma. Trauma did, at one time, play a part in the genesis of the "traumatic syndrome." The ego of the "traumatic syndrome" reacts as if a recent trauma had occurred, with a resulting psychoeconomic imbalance, but no recent trauma occurred. Spiegel's formulation may be applicable to the understanding of the anniversary reaction. The anniversary reaction can be viewed as a variant of the "traumatic syndrome." The anxiety related to the anticipatory function of the superego has a quality of futurity attached to it. In pathological forms, there is an emphasis on future impending disaster. In the anniversary reactions there is the anticipation that "this will happen because it once happened, and I am helpless to do anything about it." The reality-principle awareness seems incapable of handling the situation because the process is internal and unconscious. The anniversary date or age correspondence may serve as a trigger for the emergence of the latent repressed unconscious, which is not time-bound, but related to repressed instinctual conflict that seeks discharge and resolution.

Cohn (1957) has emphasized the ego as the crucial agency dealing with the time sense. Ego functions include time orientation, coherence, relatedness, and control. "The idea, or illusion of the past, of things gone by, is often unconsciously associated with death, and the ego's effort to materialize the present" (p. 173) includes a "purging" of the past. Time psychologically reflects the assurance of life or existence. By arresting time we avoid death. Again I would consider death in this context to mean total helplessness. The ego develops a capacity to realistically discriminate time, i.e., it has a historical sense. Cohn believes that the ego

> maintains the relation to qualities of ancestral origin apparently through superego reaction. It is incessantly occupied with the "traces of yesterday." Whenever a concept is formed and fleeting experiences are thus brought to a standstill, time is conquered and replaced by form. The time quality of passing and loss is thereby reduced to a latent state . . . [and time is] brought to a standstill, stretched to infinity (unaccountability), and the pleasant illusion of eternity created. When, however, time becomes God, the threat of mortality returns (God lives forever, but Christ is man dying forever), though God can be made to take care of life in the hereafter [pp. 178-179].

God here becomes the omnipotent parent who can protect the helpless child. Through religious ritual, man

> betrays his qualms of doubt in his never-ending labors of worship, by which he hopes to banish fatal time to the outermost regions . . . He also undertakes to organize the world into an unchangeable timeless pattern, and by continuously remaining in touch with his ancestors he creates a strenuous lifetime schedule that becomes a timepiece in itself. He wants to gather past and future securely in his hand. Obviously he cannot take death and annihilation for granted, and thus he lives in constant argument with the dead of his ancestral world. His rule over the times is aimed at making him the eternal survivor, and indeed, out of his narcissistic creation and manifestation of vitality in ritual arises the sublime image of universal mankind. Though his ritual was only meant to mark a standstill of time, it implicitly guarantees an endless future and the conviction of power to survive and to hold the world together [p. 180].

In other words, the rituals tend to be of an unlimited energy and variability in order to avert finality, the symbol of death, or total helplessness.

Marie Bonaparte's paper on *Time and the Unconscious* (1940) is a classical psychoanalytic study of time. In addition to the many insights she offers us regarding this topic, her discussion of time distortions and time symptoms in obsessional neurotics, psychotics, and psychopaths is quite useful. Following Freud, she writes,

> [T]he negation of one's own existence has no meaning for that reservoir of our primitive instincts, the unconscious. Life can only visualize itself in terms of living; in the unconscious of each individual it is depicted as outside time, which does not exist for the unconscious, and without limitations of any kind. It has required all the power of abstraction and generalization of which the conscious human mind is capable to evolve a conception so opposed to life as the idea that death awaits all living things and to enable man to recognize that one day he himself must die [p. 445].

Among the animals, man alone knows that he must die, and the idea of death seems peculiar to man. Furthermore, as Unamuno (1954) has said,

> What distinguishes man from other animals is that in one form or another he guards his dead. . . . And . . . from what does he so futilely protect them? The wretched consciousness shrinks from its own annihilation [p. 41] . . . .
>
> The gorilla, the chimpanzee, the orang-outan and their kind, must look upon man as a feeble and infirm animal, whose strange custom it is to store up his dead [p. 20] .

I might also add, to ritualize death in order to preserve immortality. This last institutionalization through religious belief, with its bipartite division of man into body and soul, with its emphases on perpetuity and eternity, defends against the anxiety of dying or being totally helpless. The narcissistic investment in survival in this world extends beyond religious belief and practice. It includes the narcissistic investment in one's children, one's work, one's ideas, forming a basis for understanding kinship patterns, significance of names and naming, and the wish for preservation through books, theories, monuments or memorials of many varieties. The vision of Paradise or the Garden of Eden is a thing representation of the timeless primary narcissistic unconscious. Bonaparte's synthesis clearly expresses these ideas when she writes,

> A sense of reality and a sense of time appear simultaneously in the system of perceptual consciousness alone. Neither exists for the timeless unconscious, which remains independent of the secondary process dominated by the reality principle and continues wholly subject to the primary process regulated by the pleasure principle [p. 464] .

The pleasure principle takes advantage of every favorable opportunity to forget time.

> It demands the highest effort of which human intelligence is capable to induce us to pay attention to time, just as to reality. Thus time does not appear to form an integral part of our fundamental nature but seems to belong solely to our dawning perception of the reality of the world outside of us [p. 465] .

Maria Bonaparte undoubtedly did not become interested in the problem of time by accident. Her mother died when Marie was one month old.

Marie, who was named for her dead mother, was repeatedly told how her birth had been paid for by her mother's life. Throughout her childhood, she imagined she had really seen her dead mother. At 17 years of age she gradually became convinced, that, like her mother, she had tuberculosis and that this fact was being kept a secret from her. Her mother had died at 22, and Marie expected that she, too, would die of tuberculosis at 22. Her symptoms began to mimic TB; she lost appetite and weight, and had frequent respiratory infections. At 20, the age at which her mother married, her illness became worse; she had a bloody mucus in the throat and began to waste away. Since her mother had died at 22, Marie felt she had to pass this age before she would know whether she could live. Her sickness had the important function of discouraging her from marrying. If she did not marry, she would not become pregnant and therefore would not suffer her mother's fate. When she was 22, her father pointed out to her that it was high time she found a husband and forget her imaginary illness. . . . From then on her symptoms began to wane [Bonaparte, 1928, in Hilgard and Fisk, 1960, pp. 55-56].

In her 1940 paper, Bonaparte shares with us further personal information, not about her anniversary symptoms, but of her growing awareness of time and its relationship to death.

I recall an impression from my childhood years. I was perhaps eight years old at the time and was thus still possessed by the more or less shadowy notions of time characteristic of childhood. I had been taken on a visit to the mother of my father's secretary, who had expressed a desire to see me. She had just completed her hundredth year. I see her to this day, covered with wrinkles, her skin shrivelled and her eyes without lustre, holding out to me her little emaciated hands and I seem still to experience the mingled feelings of terror and respect which she inspired in me then. My mother had died in the full bloom of her youth in giving birth to me: accident! evil design! But here I was confronted with the opposite extreme, a complete contrast in the procedure of dying. To be sure, a hundred years seemed to me an eternity, but I had after all been told that I should have to make haste to go and see the old lady as she was very soon going to die. At that moment I acquired a fully developed sense of death as a natural and inevitable consequence of old age and decay, of the dread inexorable law that we must die [p. 448].

Bergler and Roheim (1946) have noted that the passage of time emphasizes the period of separation, and that timelessness may have an underlying fantasy in which the mother and child are endlessly united. The calendar becomes the symbolic representation of separation anxiety and exposure to the return to a potential state of helplessness and aloneness. This may explain the preoccupation of some patients with anxiety about chronometric instruments.

Mintz has kindly let me read his as yet unpublished paper on "The Anniversary Reaction: A Manifestation of the Unconscious Sense of Time." He differentiates two types of anniversary reactions, only one of which, he feels, reflects the presence of the ego's unconscious sense of time. There is conscious awareness of a date or event which produces a specific ego response "which is then associatively linked to specific earlier conflict with revival of the conflict via symptoms, behavior, dreams, etc." The conscious time symbol reawakens the repressed, unresolved earlier conflict, and the resulting anniversary reaction is a "reproduction of an adaptation to that conflict on a specific date." In the second type of anniversary reaction, Mintz suggests, there is no specific current conscious stimulus to which the ego may respond. He believes the stimulus is unconscious, and there is an unconscious sense of time which is used to initiate the reproduction of the conflict. Because of the unconscious time sense and its linkage with death, defenses are weakened, and there is a compulsion to repeat in order to master the anxiety. The anniversary response may not require an ego sensing of time, but time, age, season, or holiday may serve as a trigger which permits repressed instinctual conflict to emerge from the unconscious into the preconscious, and then gives rise to the symptoms, reactions, behavior, or affect connected with the original conflict. Various defenses may be used to avoid this anniversary emergence (avoidance or hypercathexis of potential triggers). Once the emergence occurs, it may be dealt with in a variety of ways, depending upon the integrative ability of the ego to seal, deal, or work through the disturbing situation. If the emerging forces are too strong or the ego is too vulnerable, no sealing off can occur, and regression with symptom formation takes place. Cultural and religious practices have attempted to handle such crises through various rituals and practices. These alloplastic devices may be helpful to some in coping with the situation; however, the crucial determinant is the individual's internal psychic structure.

Fundamentally the anniversary response reflects the anxiety related to the sense of absolute helplessness which can result in a nothingness or destruction to the self. It is for this reason that anniversary reactions are so frequently connected with death and mourning. Mourning is an adaptation to loss which requires internal rearrangements so that the integrity of the ego and the self are maintained at a nonhelpless level and further progression can take place.

CHAPTER 13

Factors in the Development of Male Homosexuality

Robert Dickes, M.D.

This report will be confined to a consideration of only a few of the problems presented by perversions in general and homosexuality in particular, a limitation based not on my belief that the topics to be concentrated upon are necessarily the most crucial in a consideration of homosexuality, but upon the nature of the clinical material I have been able to collect. This material involves, among other things, certain deeply unconscious beliefs concerning the body and its mental representations and was obtained through the analysis of two obligate male homosexuals. Both patients were convinced that they and other male homosexuals possessed both male and female sexual organs. Both told me that several of their friends held similar convictions. To the best of my knowledge, no previous report of such distorted beliefs has been presented in the literature. I hope to shed some light on the still shadowy sources of homosexuality as well as to present the value of a genetic approach to the problems of this perversion.

Freud (1919b) and many others have stressed the crucial significance of the oedipal conflict to the development of perversion, and, while aware of oral and anal elements, have tended to see these as regressive and defensive rather than as primary. Loewenstein (1935), for example, paid particular attention to the phallic phase and im-

---

Dr. Dickes is Professor of Psychiatry, Division of Psychoanalytic Education, Department of Psychiatry, State University of New York, Downstate Medical Center, Brooklyn, New York.

plicated a passive phallic phase as responsible for a special type of homosexuality. He therefore also stressed the oedipal conflict, especially the negative oedipal complex. Nunberg (1938) noted behavior and fantasy of an oral and anal nature in a male homosexual, but he too considered the problem of inversion mainly from the oedipal point of view.

Other approaches to the problems of homosexuality exist. For example, Bergler and Eidelberg (1933) have emphasized the primary significance of the oral period, a point of view later amplified by Bergler (1947, 1951). In view of the differences of opinion concerning phase specificity, Gillespie (1964) stated that the determination of the importance of oedipal factors relative to preoedipal factors is a central theoretical issue. What has remained unsettled therefore, according to this essentially instinctual developmental approach, is the question of which phase-specific disturbance is most important. If primarily phallic (oedipal), then earlier phase disturbances could be absent or, if present, be of minor significance. If primarily oral, and/or anal, then one should find marked preoedipal disturbances antedating the oedipal difficulty. This would require assigning greater significance to the preoedipal phases than has hitherto been the case. The decision as to the primacy of phase disturbance cannot, however, be made on theoretical grounds. It must await the full clinical elucidation of appropriate data, based on the study of not only adults, but of infants and children as well. Some of the data obtained from my patients are pertinent to the above mentioned points and will be discussed.

The structural point of view must also be considered. Freud (1914c) was pointing in this direction when he wrote, concerning object choice, that the homosexual's object choice was based on narcissistic considerations. Reference was also made to identification. Freud also pointed out the predominance of archaic factors and the presence of primitive psychic mechanisms in the perverse individual. Since the development of the structural theory, the writings of many, Bychowski (1945) for example, utilize structural concepts either implicitly or explicitly, but mostly in relation to the ego and the superego. Little has been written concerning the id, where biological forces enter the mental realm as drives and their mental representations. It is my intention to comment later concerning the id in the light of Schur's work (1966a). Problems of identification and object choice will also be considered, obviously, in a tentative and incomplete way. I will also discuss the problem of when a homosexual's difficulties begin, and I will briefly consider aspects of the parental behavior, the ego, and the superego.

CLINICAL MATERIAL

While some homosexuals demonstrate a fair degree of object constancy and a rather stable, moderately well-adapted behavior pattern close to society's norm, others display bizarre patterns and little object constancy. The patient I will describe (the second patient's pathology was so similar, little would be gained by describing him) falls into the second category. When I first saw him, he minced into the room, spoke in a feminine way, and told a story of numerous shifting affairs and compulsive, repetitive street "pickups." Many times he had been placed in danger by one or another of the parade of "faceless" men who robbed or beat him. Desperate, finally, not over homosexuality, but because of some narrow escapes and because temper tantrums were resulting in his losing work, he sought treatment. It was with considerable hesitation that I took him into analysis, but he was intelligent, psychologically minded, and motivated through suffering. A long analysis led to major changes in his behavior and life situation. At the termination of treatment, he was still homosexual, but was able to live in harmony with another man, hold an executive position of considerable responsibility, and give an outward appearance similar to that of any normal man. During the course of treatment, I learned a great deal concerning his early life, including the second year. The patient's recollection of comments by his parents and older sisters illuminated the first year of life as well.

The "stamp" of orality, manifest in the earliest period of his life, remained etched into his character and symptomatic behavior. Extremely impatient and unable to wait for anything, if he visited a friend for dinner, he had to go to the kitchen and sample the contents of the pots because he couldn't wait for the meal to be served. The same impatience led him, when he prepared meals, to serve partially cooked food. He was conspicuously envious, not only of derivatives of his father's "big" penis, but of his mother's organs as well. Depressive features were present and extended well back into the latency period. When he spoke of his depression, it involved the expectation of an early death as well as direct suicidal thoughts. He was unable to eat when severely depressed. His mother and sisters often told him how difficult it had been to wean him and how he had refused to eat new foods. In fact, a lifelong struggle with his elders concerning his food intake began in his first year.

Much orality was also manifest in his sexual behavior and general symptomatology. He reported masturbating with the fantasy of sucking his own penis—a fantasy he attempted to put into practice. He also told me that even up to the age of eight he sucked his toes. On occasion, while masturbating, he would allow his saliva to drop onto his penis and imagine a baby drooling after a breast feeding. Fellatio as a recipient, but primarily as the active partner, was a favored activity. When telling about his pleasure in fellatio, he recalled having once gone out with a woman and making an abortive, unsuccessful sexual attempt. He found the nipple of a woman's breast extremely disappointing; it was much too small, compared with a penis which thoroughly filled his mouth. The patient preferred uncircumcised men because there was more flesh and the penis felt softer. He particularly enjoyed fellatio when his partner had a partial erection. The consistency of the penis, according to him, then more closely approximated the consistency of the nipple. In the same context, he said that the only kind of woman he found attractive was one with very large breasts. In fact, he wished breasts were about one third the size of his body. (The ratio suggested by this idea indicates a ratio that would approximate the size of the breast to that of an infant's body.) He still wished, as an adult, that the nipple were large enough to fill his mouth as it had when he was an infant. Cannibalistic wishes and their derivatives were prominent. He was noted for his biting wit.

Oral features were carried over to the anal phase, and oral-anal combinations as well as purely anal features were present. Bowel training, begun at about the age of one, was a period of prolonged and bitter struggle between him and his mother and sisters. He would sit on the pot for hours without defecating, only to do so as soon as he was removed. His mother was as aggressive in her determination to wrest the stool from him as he was to withhold it. Laxatives, enemas, and invective were commonplace until close to the termination of latency.

Derivatives of this struggle were apparent in many aspects of his daily life. He was a great procrastinator. For example, he decorated the living room and dinette of his apartment, but could not bring himself to complete the kitchen and bathroom even after a number of years. He fought constantly with his parents about money. He remembered that his father refused to give him an allowance. He had to beg his mother for a few cents for candy, money for movies, even for necessary school supplies. Much of the time his mother screamed at him for his requests, as if he were indulging in an anal rape and a cannibalistic tearing of her flesh. He recalled many of her remarks attesting to this, such as, "You'll tear my flesh out, you animal."

Another result of the fierce struggle of the anal period was to leave the patient's anal zone highly charged with both libidinous and aggressive energy. His mother's aggression and the repeated enemas strongly enhanced his passivity. He recalled his many experiences with the enema tube nozzle, how he first fought but finally yielded and experienced the entry as pleasurable. This pleasure highlighted his capitulation and the role enemas played in his eventual homosexuality. It is noteworthy that they occurred prior to the phallic period.

Phallic-phase material was abundant and pertained to the positive as well as negative Oedipus complex. The theme of castration was particularly prominent. He shared a room with his sisters until he left home to go to college and could not remember a time when he did not see his sisters nude. His mother, to whom he was deeply attached, also exhibited herself regularly. Coupled with his castration anxiety was his fear of the barber. It took much courage on his part to present himself for a haircut; a barber's shave was out of the question.

His positive Oedipus complex was powerful but deeply repressed. Eventually, he recalled being in bed with his mother and lying on top of her when he was two years old. Every afternoon when his mother lay down for a nap, he would join her. This continued through the age of nine or ten. He remembered feeling his mother's pubic hair with his hand. After confessing almost humorously that he would use almost any stunt to get into bed with mother, he suddenly recalled an old fear of thunder and lightning which made him run to his mother's bed as the only safe place. Immediately his associations moved to his father—his angry voice, his fear of him.

With regard to the negative Oedipus complex, the patient recalled entering his parents' bedroom, when 15, and finding his father and mother in bed. His father seized him, pulled him into bed with them, "accidentally" handling the patient's genitals. Added to this was information that his father would pinch or stroke his penis playfully when the patient was little, and insisted on kissing him on the mouth even when the patient was well into his teens. The patient also remembered being invited into bed by father who again "accidentally" handled his genitals. It was shortly after this event that the patient had what he claimed was the experience which was decisive for his final acceptance of homosexuality. He was picked up by a stranger and taken to a hotel bedroom where his genitals were handled and fellatio practiced. The patient's father, whom the seducer represented, also took the patient to Turkish baths and insisted on having the boy receive rubdowns while he watched and made comments about his puny physique.

Special note should be taken of his object relationships. Identification remained, for him, a most important way of relating to others. Conceiving of others as independent entities with their own needs was a most difficult task for him, and no full maturation of his ability to relate was noted. In fact, the patient showed little progression beyond the level of viewing people as intermittent or need-satisfying objects, a stage in the development of object relationships discussed by A. Freud (1952).

His primitive relationship to others was also noticeable in the patient's choice of sexual partners. His men were strangers picked off the streets. Sometimes he did not even have so much as a good look at them. This was exemplified by his description of a visit he once made to an area, notable for homosexual activity, which had a special place known as the "meat-rack." Here one could pick a partner in the dark and, without a word being spoken, perform fellatio and other activities. The transient partner could then be discarded. The patient stated repeatedly that he cared for men only as big penises; that they could have no face so far as he was concerned. The less he knew them the better.

Many of his relationships were predicated on identifications, and at times he behaved in the "as if" manner described by H. Deutsch (1942). I wish, however, to emphasize his feminine identification. From his earliest years, the patient behaved like a little girl and recalled no real protest against his mother dressing him as a girl or treating him as though he were actually female. As he grew older, he continued associating with girls and demonstrating an interest in feminine affairs. In his teens, he used the same perfume and peroxided his hair as did one of his sisters. His parents offered no objection to this aberrant behavior. This sister was a nymphomaniac, and her parade of men was equalled only by his own. His favorite masturbatory position resembled a woman's in intercourse or, even more accurately, his mother's. He would lie on his back, legs in the stirrup position with knees apart and bent, and have a fantasy of being penetrated by a man. A curious feature of this act and position was the spreading of newspapers on the bed and lying on them. This practice was discarded only when he was able to recall that his mother used to place newspapers under her mattress. He was thus able to hear all the movements of his parents when they went to bed. As he lay on his own bed listening, he fantasied himself in his mother's role. Thus not only did he identify with his sister, but also with his mother. Once he masturbated with a candle in his rectum and said: "I was doing it just like a girl." This isolated act was related to two separate fantasies, the first of which was that a girl's penis was still there, but only pushed in so that she had to masturbate via the rectum, the vagina itself being blocked. The second fantasy involved the idea that his rectum was the equivalent of the vagina.

It was only after much resistance had been overcome that certain of his deeply hidden convictions concerning his anatomy came to light. He believed himself the possessor of both male and female sexual organs. At times, he conceived of his anus as his vagina. At other times, he considered the area between his apposed thighs close to the body trunk in the perineal area, where he could form a hollow, as his vagina. He believed that this same anatomical situation held true for his various homosexual partners. He also expressed his conviction that many of his friends held these same beliefs. His circle of men all took female names and called one another Miss. All would speak quite openly of their anus as representing their vagina. Thus each, as a female, possessed a penis. Not only did this type of fantasy deny castration; it also represented a deep and early feminine identification. The type of identification belonged to that period of life when knowledge of the differences between the sexes is obscured by the belief in the phallic mother, the perfect possessor of both male and female organs.

DISCUSSION

Gillespie (1956) reviewed the then current thinking on perversion including the idea that the elements of infantile sexuality provided the materials for a perversion and that a perversion represented a defense against the Oedipus complex and castration anxiety. He stated: "The defense involves a regression of libido and aggression to pre-genital levels, so that there is an increase of sadism, leading to further anxiety and guilt feeling and to defenses against them designed to protect both the self and the object" (p. 402). He then considered the ego's role, pointing out that the ego could adopt a certain piece of infantile sexuality, first because the superego was specially tolerant of this particular form of sexuality, and secondly because of a split in the ego and in the object. Gillespie stressed the significance of the oedipal conflict and considered regression responsible for the prominence of preoedipal factors. The stress on the pre-eminent role of the phallic phase and the oedipal conflict in the etiology of perversions, including homosexuality, is the prevalent but by no means universal opinion.

According to Gillespie (1964), the key question is whether homosexuality is the direct outcome of a primary oedipal failure or a primary failure in the preoedipal period. I believe that instead of restricting our thinking to the two alternatives proposed by Gillespie, it would be more fruitful to approach the problem in terms of evaluating the pathology found in each developmental phase and the genetic effects of this pathology on the development of the personality. Such emphasis avoids the artificial issue of whether the preoedipal or oedipal phase is more important, and illuminates rather than excludes consideration of the development of object relationships, and the maturation of the personality.

The consideration of phase-specific involvement also raises the question of whether or not perversion can occur in the absence of preoedipal disturbance. Rephrased, it may be stated as a proposition that each phase must manifest phase-specific difficulties, and that the final outcome in homosexuality is dependent upon an accretion of the many developmental failures attendant upon initial preoedipal failures. The reason the Oedipus conflict and its attendant castration anxiety cannot be mastered is to be sought therefore in earlier difficulties as well as in phallic difficulties. Thus the hypothesis may be advanced that a severe illness such as perversion cannot occur without disturbances in the preoedipal period as well as in the phallic period.

While I cannot validate the concept that *all* severe emotional illnesses require disturbances in all phases, I can at least suggest this concept as a proposition requiring further testing. I can also review this proposition in the light of known clinical data with special reference to perversions in general and to inversion in particular. I have reported elsewhere (1963) on early events in fetishism, as has Bak (1953).

Let us return to my patient, who was in difficulty from the very beginning of his life. An unfortunate and obvious injury to his leg was overlooked, not only by the physician who delivered him, but by the hospital staff as well. His mother was equally neglectful and left the child crying in pain for hours at a time. The leg, which had been broken, required setting, and operative intervention several years later, before a good result could be obtained. In addition, feeding was irregular and at the mother's convenience; one might call it "demand feeding"—but at the mother's demand, not the child's. It was a long time before this information, obtained partly by recall, could be verified, but the family remembered all the stories involved in the child's care and frequently spoke of how much trouble "he had caused." It was as though he rather than the doctor were to blame for the birth injury. That he required special care taxed all the family members, and they told how he would "howl for hours" before they could find the time to feed him, again placing the blame on him. These events, leading to considerable frustration, augmented the child's cannibalistic aggression and oral demands. His ability to form object relationships was interfered with, and incorporative needs influenced identification. Feeding became a major problem, so that by the time of weaning he was already recalcitrant to giving up the breast. This recalcitrance was much greater than that of the average child because the aggression was much greater. A struggle centering on food and the mouth continued throughout later phases of development. The loss of food and the uncertainty of feeding are to be viewed as contributing to the later castration anxiety based upon the symbolic equivalence of the penis and the nipple. The significance of the leg need only be mentioned in this connection.

The recalcitrance and aggression, already so heightened in the oral phase, persisted into the anal phase. The mother's aggressive determination to win control over her son was manifest in her effort to control his bowels. His stool was inspected and unfavorably commented upon. Enemas were frequent, the contest over the stool remaining as unsettled as that over food. His mother was as dissatisfied with his bowel habits and stool production as she was over his feeding habits. Her preoccupation with the stool re-emphasized the loss of the nipple by focusing on the stool and its loss. In the light of later castration anxiety, it can be noted that the anxiety alluded to in the oral period was again augmented. The symbolic equivalents for the penis now included the stool.

Attempts were made to maintain control not only over the patient's sphincter but over his entire musculature as well. His mother prevented him from exercising vigorously and continuously interfered with all his attempts at individuation. The enforced muscular inhibition enhanced passivity and reduced the outlets normally available for discharging aggression, thus further increasing the patient's frustrations and store of aggression. The stamp placed upon the boy's developing character structure now included characteristics resulting from interferences in the anal period as well as the oral. The number of solutions available to him as he entered the phallic phase was thus considerably reduced.

Much has been written concerning the importance to homosexuality of the oedipal conflict and the phallic phase, and I make no attempt to deny their crucial significance. Freud's formulations with regard to the solutions of the phallic phase remain valid, and in view of the extensive treatment already accorded the subject, I will refrain from dwelling on it here. The emphasis I have placed on prephallic material is to demonstrate that the fateful events of the preoedipal periods set the stage for the phallic phase difficulties by limiting the solutions available to the developing child. I do not intend therefore to encourage an either prephallic or phallic approach. The intention is to emphasize the contributions of all phases to the developing pathology. The genetic point of view would indicate that severe disturbance in the oral phase, unless remedied, mandates a disturbance in the anal phase. Without appropriate care, further libidinal and aggressive disturbances occur. In terms of the structural approach, further warping of the ego is inevitable. Thus a stage is set for the confrontations of the phallic phase wherein the child is no longer capable of solving the attending problems.

The course of events in my patient as described in terms of libido, aggression, and phases of development are in themselves insufficient to account for the outcome in overt homosexuality, although the events were probably decisive for severe illness. I will therefore turn to a consideration of some other factors which may be implicated in the development of homosexuality.

Maturation is, from the beginning, much influenced by the attitudes of the mother. These attitudes, conscious or unconscious, are of critical importance to the development of the ego and the formation of object relations. The earliest type of relationship, the symbiotic, is succeeded by a primitive identification with the mother. This is of significance for male homosexuality. Jacobson (1964) mentioned fantasies of fusion persisting for an unduly long time and considered them indicative of the strength of the child's wish to maintain the mother as part of himself, of merging with her without distinction. She also commented that, in some homosexuals, sexual and ego development had been determined mainly by identifications with a loving but dominant, active, "phallic" mother. No clinical evidence was presented for this comment. My own observations would not permit me to classify these women as loving. They are far more aggressive and controlling than loving. What is of more significance, however, is the fact that a conditioning toward homosexuality may already be noted prior to the establishment of the oedipal triangle and prior to the earliest bisexual identification.

A disturbed mother fails to provide a favorable environment, and, therefore, skewing of future growth occurs—a skewing which forces the infant into aberrant paths involving many of the ego's functions. This includes interference with the ability to form interpersonal relationships. Early stricture and fixation on the mother narrows the choices available later in development. Appropriate object cathexis fails to take place, and the person remains inappropriately fixed to an early mode of cathecting objects. Thus, in certain cases, as in the patient described, it can be noted that identification and part-object relationships predominate over more mature patterns. Because normal maturation does not take place, the child enters the phallic phase in a damaged state and cannot correctly identify with the proper parent to reach a satisfactory solution to the oedipal conflict. The existence of an unduly powerful identification with the mother, present from the early months of life, enhances the probability of a secondary identification with the mother in the phallic period. At the height of the oedipal complex the power of the negative Oedipus complex is thus reinforced, creating a situation most favorable to the choice of homosexuality as a solution. It therefore seems appropriate to say that major determinants in the choice of homosexuality occur prior to the phallic period, and that, owing to early stricture in development, certain people are, very early, prone to a homosexual solution. This awaits only the appropriate precipitating factors which usually occur in the phallic period, although the possibility exists that the choice of the sexual object can antedate the oedipal situation. Stoller (1968) alluded to this when he pointed out that in certain children one can note the establishment of gender identity long before the ascendancy of the phallic phase.

Another factor in maturation and identity formation requires discussion. The discovery of anatomical sexual differences under normal conditions aids the child in establishing an identity and separateness from the mother and is important in the development of object relations. Unless appropriate anatomical distinctions are made and a proper body image developed, early identification will unduly influence all later development, and the ego, based on a body ego, will be unable to proceed to the establishment of a normal identity. Mahler (1963) has pointed out that image representations emerge from pregenital libidinal positions and bisexual identifications. She indicated that the disturbed child cannot "emerge" from its bisexual identifications and make the transition to normal relationships. Greenacre (1958a), when discussing fetishism, wrote that frequent and early exposure to the genitals of others may influence later problems of identification more than when such exposure has been limited to the anal and phallic periods. She considered that some degree of fusion of the subject's own organs with that of others is universal and that only later does the conventional image for the person's own sex emerge.

Exhibitionism was a way of life for my patient's family. His mother and sisters exposed themselves to him constantly and from the very beginning. This increased his difficulty in forming an appropriate body image of his own. His confusion concerning his own genitals as well as that of women can be noted in his persistent bisexual identification and in his fixed belief that he possessed both a vagina and penis. This belief is indicative of an early type of identification with the mother and belongs to that period during which a child views the mother as the perfect possessor of all valuable attributes. The phallic mother, so often described as frightening, may actually be a reassuring object. Castration fear does not exist at this stage; object differentiation has not been achieved. It is only later that the mother is conceived of as penisless. What is wanted is the missing set of organs.

Another factor may be considered as contributing to male homosexuality. Lichtenstein (1961), writing about the development of the sense of identity and its relationship to sexuality, stated that the sense of identity is not innate in man and must be acquired over a long period of time. He believed that

> the child is the organ, the instrument for the fulfillment of the mother's unconscious needs. *Out of the infinite potentialities within the human infant, the specific stimulus combination emanating from the individual mother "releases" one, and only one, concrete way of being this organ, this instrument.* This "released" identity will be irreversible, and thus it will compel the child to find ways and means to realize this specific identity . . . [p. 208].

It is possible to conclude from the above that Lichtenstein considers this earliest period as decisive for the future course of the child's growth, and that this is determined, in part, by the mother's needs. Lichtenstein also stated that his female patient sought a homosexual "symbiosis." In like manner, it may be reported, concerning homosexuals of the type I have described, that they do not wish to have the mother, but to remain fused with her. Significant for homosexuality is a symbiotic phase which does not permit appropriate individuation and leaves the child fixed in a primitive identification with the mother.[1] Feelings of separation induce efforts at reunion, and these reactions are impressed upon the child at the very beginning. From the adaptive point of view, it may be stated that a successful adaptation to the environment provided by the mother becomes unsuccessful as the original but abnormal environment gives way, as the child grows to a more varied and normal environment.

The importance of both parents in creating an environment suitable for the development of homosexuality is attested to by the writings of Kolb and Johnson (1955), Litten, Griffin, and Johnson (1956), Bieber and his co-workers (1962), and others. The parental encouragement to my patient was also clear from his history. At no time did his parents object to his use of perfume and other feminine appurtenances. They did object to whatever masculine strivings they observed. They frowned on dating. They encouraged him to associate only with boys. Defects of the superego as well as of the ego have also been attributed to parental attitudes. This may be noted in my patient. Superego formation was warped by the parental insistence on the aberrant behavior which led to the perversion. It should be noted that the patient had no objection to his homosexuality. Neither did his parents. Freud's formulations concerning the development of the superego are pertinent to this point.

Major emphasis has been placed on the earliest months of life when, in terms of the structural theory, the id and ego are in the process of differentiating from their *Anlagen*. It was in the *Outline* that Freud (1940) finally wrote of an undifferentiated ego-id. Recently Schur (1966a) has contributed, in a carefully reasoned account, his understanding of this early period. He stated that: "Every development takes place in interaction with the environment and is

[1] This particular point was also developed by Socarides (1968) but with a somewhat different emphasis although he also stressed the importance of this early phase. Socarides' article was published after this article was submitted.

also dependent on it. If this is so, the id must have its role in adaptation. It certainly mediates in the adaptive function of the ego through the 'pressure' of the instinctual demands" (p. 49). He reminds us that the organism starts at birth with an *Anlage* and innate apparatuses. These latter, usually considered from the viewpoint of the ego, may also be viewed as available in a special way to the id. Inasmuch as the id is a product of development, it is also affected by the interaction of innate, maturational, and experiential factors. The id also has a role in the choice of objects. Schur's comments reiterate the importance of the earliest formative stages of the developing ego-id differentiation and are directly applicable to homosexual object choice.

The persistence with which most inverts cling to their homosexual mode of object selection is well known. This was true of my patients, even though profound alterations in character and general behavior were observed and free association and the lifting of much infantile amnesia occurred. The incompleteness of results in these cases requires explanation, other than the obvious one that the patients were ineptly analyzed. Such explanations avoid the important theoretical implications involved in assessing the causes of incomplete results in a properly conducted analysis.

Cases involving extensive reconstructions are also omitted from these considerations because reconstructions, no matter how accurate, are used in place of memories which represent actualities. Reconstructions, therefore, may not have the same force of conviction for the patient as would full recovery of the actual events. Further, a reconstruction may appear accurate, and yet the possibility of error cannot be ruled out. Under such circumstances it is not surprising that an analysis may, in a certain measure, fail.

There are, however, some people who seem excellent candidates for analysis, whose well-conducted analyses fail to reach a desired degree of resolution of the difficulties. The situation under discussion, therefore, involves those cases in whom, quantitatively at least, amnesia seems to have been sufficiently lifted and in whom the transference neurosis seems largely resolved. In short, the reference is to patients who seem to have been well analyzed and who yet retain an amount of difficulty not compatible with good health. These patients must be contrasted with those who do well in treatment.

The best results are obtained in those patients whose major difficulties stem from developmental periods arising after individuation and after verbal responses have developed. Typically, in the neurotic, the major crises occur in the oedipal period so that, from the economic point of view, the preoedipal difficulties are of lesser magnitude. The obsessive-compulsive patient's difficulties, for example, have their origin in the anal phase and elicit an ego defense system, from the structural point of view, different from that of the patient whose major difficulties stem from the phallic period. The anal symptomatology in these patients, though primary to a certain extent, is in the largest measure a regressive attempt at solution of the Oedipus complex. Thus, anal difficulties yield, as they are analyzed, along with the major phallic difficulties.

The situation is entirely different when problems stem primarily from the earliest period of life, prior to appropriate self-object differentiation and verbalization. Unfortunately, the importance of the early preverbal difficulties may become apparent only after the patient is well into the analysis or sometimes only late in the treatment. It then becomes clear that it was the earliest difficulties which played the most significant role in the creation of the patient's illness. These occur so early, it may be postulated that the early id-ego matrix is influenced adversely and the resultant skewing is present, not only in the developing ego, but also in that special portion of the id which is contiguous to the ego and significant for the formation of proper object choice. The defects which occur so early and affect so many ego functions, including complex functions such as reality testing and synthesis, may also affect various portions of the id. In such cases, it is not sufficient to rely on making matters conscious in the expectation that the patient's ego and especially the synthetic function will initiate a correction in the ego's structure and therefore in its adaptation to reality. Thus our reliance on the power of the ego's synthetic ability and the secondary processes is not always justified. Certain patients will remain sick in spite of their genetic understanding of their illness and even in spite of experiencing correct emotional responses. It remains beyond the ego's capacity to effect the beneficial changes. This is characteristic of patients whose difficulties date from the earliest days of life and whose reactions are often somatized as well (Schur, 1955). Homosexuals such as I have described fall into this latter category, and it is sometimes necessary for the analyst to settle for less than a full measure of health.

CHAPTER 14

Regression and Displacement in the Development of the Body-Phallus Equation

Jules Glenn, M.D.

Certain unusually striking psychoanalytic observations have impelled me to re-evaluate aspects of the well-established fantasy that the body is a phallus (Abraham, 1924; Bunker, 1943; Deutsch, 1925; Fenichel, 1936; Ferenczi, 1926; Harnik, 1924; Lewin, 1933; Sandler, 1959; Shevin, 1963; Tausk, 1919). In particular, the appearance of bodily sensations derived from this unconscious idea occurring in conjunction with the Isakower phenomenon (1938) has shed additional light on the use of regressive processes in the formation of the body-phallus equation. Further, examination of clinical details clarified the importance of displacement of cathexis from the phallus to the rest of the body, and revealed significant variants of the classical equation. Instead of the usual formula, several patients used the body without a phallus or without male genitals to symbolize the phallus. To put it in mathematical terms, they imagined:

Body minus phallus = phallus; or
Body minus male genitals = phallus.

Dr. Glenn is Assistant Clinical Professor, Division of Psychoanalytic Education, Department of Psychiatry, Downstate Medical Center, State University of New York, Brooklyn, New York.

The author thanks Dr. Herbert Urbach for his helpful criticisms regarding the organization and content of this paper.

In this presentation, clinical and anthropological data illustrating the existence of these variants constitute the basis for a discussion of the determinants of the body-phallus equation in its several forms.

CLINICAL MATERIAL

CASE I. MRS. E.

Mrs. E., a 22-year-old woman, experienced the Isakower phenomenon several times while on the couch during the second year of her analysis. She had had similar experiences as a child. During these episodes she would feel as if her body, especially her legs, was melting into wax and that wax flowed into her mouth. No auditory or visual hallucinations occurred. She was not sure whether she could distinguish what was inside her from what was outside.

Associations made it clear that this experience was a regressive oral phenomenon, a hallucinatory memory of the hungry, deprived child being nursed. Her first thought, that she often wished to be satisfied immediately, was followed by the memory of holding a cloth in her hand, when she was a child, as she sucked her thumb. After saying this, she observed with surprise that she was grasping Kleenex and said: "It has to do with oral satisfaction." After mentioning that her husband sucks her breasts, she added that her grandmother, a strict woman who played a major role in her upbringing, was "against breasts and penises."

In a later session, which I will describe in detail, Mrs. E. experienced this type of oral regression after becoming sexually excited; feeling that her body was like a swollen phallus developed along with the Isakower phenomenon.

Mrs. E. talked about her fear of punishment for greediness and for having become pregnant, at the start of this session. She then gave examples of pleasurable activities for which women would censure her: talking too much; interest in her alcoholic father; masturbation; reading medical books at six or seven. Her father had scolded her when she was a child because she drew a picture of him urinating. As she recalled this she became anxious and stated that she feared hurting her unborn baby. When I asked if her pregnancy made her feel guilty, she described a childhood masturbation fantasy: "I am a nun and restrained. A sensuous man rapes me. As I near the climax, I give up inner restraint, am liberated and have an orgasm."

As she spoke, Mrs. E. once more developed the Isakower phenomenon. Her mouth became dry. She felt as if her tongue, the roof of her mouth, and her body in general were swollen. Her hands, especially the fingers in touch with the couch, felt enlarged. The sensation was pleasurable, connected with a warm feeling; it reminded her of "swollen breasts and vagina." As she mentioned swollen parts of her body, I observed that she omitted one part. *She replied that her clitoris was the only part of her body that didn't feel swollen.* She agreed with my comment that she denied being sexually excited by having her body swell rather than her clitoris; instead she becomes a baby at the breast. Mrs. E. then added that her "clitoris should be ignored, not be there."

Here we see regression from oedipal excitement to a preoedipal, oral level of satisfaction and the associated ego state. At the same time there is displacement of cathexis from the clitoris to the rest of the body. Through her wish to rid herself of her clitoris, she could simultaneously avoid sexual excitement and be punished for it. Her swollen body compensated for the lost phallus.

Confirmatory evidence that this patient harbored the fantasy that the body was a phallus emerged in later sessions as she equated herself, the baby within her, and a penis. Numerous overdetermined meanings of the patient's feeling like a baby as she experienced the Isakower phenomenon appeared. She understood the change in her body image to be the result of her wish to be an infant, and even exclaimed on one occasion when her mouth and hands felt swollen, "I'm becoming a baby!" She preferred being an infant who is cared for to being a grown-up mother who has to look after her child. Imagining herself an infant being fed, she could avoid the rage that accompanies deprivation.

As the analysis progressed, she felt a need to keep the baby inside her. To lose control and let the baby be born meant to be punished for her wicked sexuality, to lose a valuable part of herself, to lose her mother from whom she would be separated. For several sessions she worried that the baby might not be able to leave her body when she entered labor. She felt like "rebelling against the uterus," holding back. Again experiencing the Isakower phenomenon, Mrs. E. felt so large and swollen that she thought she would no longer be able to pass through the office door as she left. An important anal factor in the desire to retain became apparent as she recalled being harshly toilet-trained by her grandmother. Even as an adult she held in her bowel movements for 15 to 20 minutes after she had the urge to go to the toilet. Stubborness and rebellion appeared in other areas as well as in her need to keep the baby in. She refused to write a paper for school, to telephone her aunt, and to produce material for the analyst. Like a two-year-old who says no, she disliked rules and wanted to rule.

Eventually the phallic significance of the baby within her, the baby with whom she was one, became clear. Mrs. E. complained that as a woman she was empty, that her vagina was nothing. The baby inside her filled her, she said, as a penis; hence she struggled against losing it.

CASE II. MR. B.

In the course of the analysis of the impotent 33-year-old Mr. B., a specific sequence occurred at least 20 times. He would get involved in what he pictured to be—and sometimes was—an argument with the analyst. Imagining that he had been insulted or that something incorrect or unjust had been said or done to him, he would argue angrily and violently. When the altercation terminated, he would relax and experience certain sensations: he felt small, compact, and very heavy, the space around him seemed empty and all objects distant; sometimes he became thirsty.[1] These experiences could be interpreted to him as substitutes for orgasms after a sexual fight. He associated the arguments with similar verbal exchanges with his mother with whom he had enjoyed a sadomasochistic relationship.

Sadomasochistic ties to his mother, wife, employers, and analyst stemmed from particularly fateful events at the age of five. Up to that age, he had been allowed extreme intimacies with his mother, even to the point of lying on top of her and sucking her breasts. At

[1] These experiences seem related to the complex described by Isakower (1938), but it was not until later that a definite Isakower phenomenon appeared.

the age of five, after a traumatic operation (probably without anesthesia) for a retropharyngeal abscess which saved his life, Mr. B.'s personality changed. He became openly sadistic as he turned the passive experience of the operation into an active one in which he himself became the attacker. He jabbed a scalpel through pictures of people in magazines. He tore wings off insects, or imagined shooting people. Teasing his mother by calling her a hypocrite had a masochistic quality as well as a sadistic one. He provoked his mother to chase him around the table on which the operation had been performed. She would get excited, become red, and scream, "I'm going to *platz* (explode)." His behavior with the analyst was designed to duplicate that with his mother. In addition to reproducing the operation with himself in control, Mr. B. could achieve sexual satisfaction on a sadomasochistic level. The operation had so frightened him that he avoided affectionate and genital contact with his mother or other women.

All this was clear to the patient, at least intermittently, as he badgered the analyst, distorting what he said, asking unanswerable questions, demanding replies, and insisting that the analyst was robbing him.

It was in this setting that an altercation led to a feeling that his body was like a penis. Mr. B. started the session with one of his unanswerable questions. Why, when he lay on his side during sexual foreplay with his wife, did his stomach contract and he have to belch? He added that he understood from the previous session that through his impotence, which the analyst could not cure, he was making the analyst impotent. When the analyst explained that he enjoyed such a relationship and tried to maintain it, Mr. B. grew angry. He denied getting pleasure and insisted that the analyst was accusing him. He eventually agreed that he was attached to the analyst, but then berated him because he would not promise to continue the treatment after he was cured of his impotence. When the analyst underlined Mr. B.'s fear that the treatment would stop if he became well, the patient belligerently agreed, but again started to argue. He insisted that he had never said this because he had never been asked. At this point Mr. B. started to experience the Isakower phenomenon.

He felt (but did not see) something like a balloon on his face.[2] He recalled the same sort of fights with his mother. He said that he was addicted to the analyst. Then he became furious again and said it cannot be *just* attachment to the analyst that makes him fight. At this juncture his entire body, with the exception of his penis, felt tense. He felt as if he were an erect penis. The analyst observed that instead of his penis, the rest of his body became tense. Mr. B. suggested that when he was operated on as a child he must have thought they were operating on his penis. In response to an interpretation that the displaced erection resulted from sexual excitement, he blamed his mother for letting him suck her breasts as he lay on her, prior to the operation. When he was an adolescent she undressed in front of him, but he did not develop an erection. He did not experience the rigid feelings over his body when he was small or when his mother was naked, but did have such sensations when he fought with her during adolescence. He thought his worry that the treatment would terminate if he recovered had its antecedent in the fear that he and his mother would separate when he grew up. He remembered that his parents had fought. His mother repeatedly accused his father of having caused her operation (an episiotomy) by impregnating her.

With Mr. B., as with Mrs. E., sexual excitement resulted in regression to a preoedipal state, evidenced by the experience of the Isakower phenomenon. Again there was displacement from the phallus to the rest of the body, which was fantasied an erect penis.

CASE III. MR. H.

Mr. H., a 45-year-old married borderline psychotic began his analysis with me shortly after his first analyst died after a year of treatment. About three weeks following the start of his first analysis, he had developed the peculiar sensations later associated with the fantasy that his body was a phallus. These feelings included a heaviness

[2] On another occasion Mr. B. added details to the description of this phenomenon. A balloonlike mass, six inches in diameter, which he felt but did not see, was pressed over his face so as to fit its contours. The mass did not appear to enter his mouth, which was dry. A rigidity developed throughout his body as he experienced the mass. Confirming the oral implication, Mr. B. said the mass reminded him of his mother's breast.

which started in the lower part of his body and moved in waves up into his head. He would also experience "gyrations" in his head, i.e., waves proceeding from the neck up and then forward, as though something were escaping through a hole in the middle of his head, through his eyes, which blinked and teared, or through his mouth, in which he occasionally noted a white discharge (probably phlegm) or white coating on the tongue. When I asked him specifically about the parts of the body in which he experienced these waves, he included his entire body *except his penis and testicles.*

In association to these sensations, Mr. H. mentioned several times that a friend had called him a prick. He had a distinct feeling that his body was like a penis. When I pointed out the displacement of feelings from his genitals to the rest of his body, he developed a delusional belief that there actually was a tube through his body connecting his genitals and head. He believed that the white fluid in his mouth was actually semen. Mr. H. also imagined that anger actually escaped through the hole in his head.

Clinically, it is clear that this man fantasied that his body was a phallus, but the sensations deriving from this conception did not include the genitals. The equation *body minus penis and testicles = penis* applied.[3]

ANTHROPOLOGICAL DATA

Anthropological confirmation of the equation of the phallus and the aphallic body is afforded by examination of the Maori *tiki.* It has been determined that the *tiki*, which are stylized human figures worn as neck pendants by the members of this New Zealand culture, symbolize phalli. Best (1924) and Reed (1963) stated that *tiki* is an old sacerdotal term for phallus, and Buck (1950) added confirmatory evidence when he noted that "some creation songs . . . in describing the act of coitus between Tane [a god] and Hineahuone, definitely refer to Tane's phallus as *tiki*" (p. 295).[4] The *tiki* are ornaments

[3] Possibly the formula *body minus male genitals = phallus* applies to both cases. I did not specifically ask Mr. B. whether his testicles as well as his penis were excluded.

[4] Buck nevertheless rejected the idea that the *tiki* is a phallic symbol on grounds I believe are inadequate. He states that because "tiki" is also the name of certain architectural features, a *tiki* cannot be a phallic symbol.

approximately seven inches long,[5] usually made of jade, and representing human beings. Although the figures are naked, the sex is indicated in only one-third of the specimens. Except for one figure with a large phallus, the sex is female and is rendered by a small grooved ellipse. It is apparent then that with one exception the *tiki* is a phallic symbol consisting of a body without a phallus. In the one specimen with a penis, the equation would be: body = phallus; in all others the equation is: body minus phallus = phallus.

Figure 1. Maori *tiki* pendant. Drawn by Sylvia Glenn.

DISCUSSION

In each of the patients cited, the development of the bodily sensations associated with the equation body minus phallus = phallus[6] occurred as a result of defenses mobilized to deal with unconscious

[5] The only *tikis* whose measurements I found stated were 6, 6-3/4, and 7-3/4 inches long. They appear in pictures to average 7 inches in length.

[6] Lewin (personal communication) confirms the existence of this variant. He states that he took for granted that the body in the body-phallus equation is "a smoothed-out one" without a penis "like Natalja A.'s influencing machine body" described by Tausk (1919).

conflict, but no single conflict common to all was involved. Aggressive and/or sexual wishes were defended against to varying degrees in different patients. Mrs. E.'s masturbatory desires, which involved predominantly oedipal wishes, ran counter to her superego prohibitions. Mr. B.'s apparent homosexual longings of a sadomasochistic nature, which were repeatedly satisfied in the analytic situation, could be traced to a regressive defense against sexual desires toward his mother. Tender, affectionate oedipal feelings conflicted with his superego standards, resulting in defensive sadomasochistic attachment to objects, which, in turn, had to be defended against. Fear of injury to his love objects complicated Mr. B.'s pathology. His desire for revenge against the surgeon, whom he thought of as an aggressive father who injured him, made him wish to attack those around him sexually (and in other ways); impotence occurred as a result. The aggressive element was more prominent with Mr. H. A strong desire to attack his depriving mother was displaced onto his wife, whom he feared injuring with his penis in the sex act. The fantasy of his body (without genitals) as a phallus served to guard against the aggressive use of his penis.

In each case prohibitions against the development of erections resulted in a shift of cathexis away from the phallus to the rest of the body. The first two patients also regressed and developed the Isakower phenomenon. Isakower (1938) postulated in a "schematic illustration" that masturbatory impulses on falling asleep may lead to regression, the Isakower phenomenon, and the body-phallus equation.

Ferenczi, who used the term "genitalization of the body" (1916-17), described in "Gulliver Fantasies" (1926) a "sudden displacement of genital sensations or sexual excitation to the whole surface of the body" (p. 48). He noted: "Patients have told me that instead of an erection they experience a sudden rigidity of all their muscles" (p. 48). This statement leads me to believe that Ferenczi was dealing with the variant I have described—a variant which I assume to be similar in its structure to the body-phallus equation. Obviously, since the penis is not a muscle, and since the patients did not have erections, the rigidity did not include the phallus. Sandler's (1959) patient clearly manifested the fantasy I have described inasmuch as he felt castrated and experienced being a phallus at the same time. Similarly in men who picture themselves "phallus girls" (Fenichel, 1936; Shevin, 1963), the appropriate equation is often: body minus male genitals = phallus, an exception occurring when the phallus girl is imagined as a female with a penis.

Specific defenses used in developing the body-phallus equation, particularly regression to the oral libidinal stage, have been discussed in the analytic literature. Ferenczi, as we have seen, emphasized displacement in the body-phallus equation, sharing this position with H. Deutsch (1925) and Harnik (1924). Others have felt regression to be the basic mechanism: regression "to an early infantile stage in which the entire body is a libidinal zone" (Tausk, 1919, p. 85), to a narcissistic state (Tausk, 1919), to orality (Abraham, 1924; Lewin, 1933; Fenichel, 1936), or to the symbiotic state (Mahler, 1952; Shevin, 1963). Sandler (1959) describes the use of displacement,[7] inhibition of affect, and dissociation among the important relevant defenses, dissociation being especially noteworthy when his patient considered his body and penis to be two different entities. Certainly these findings, confirmed in this paper, are not mutually exclusive. Indeed, as I will demonstrate, they complement each other.

Lewin (1933), although he did not observe the Isakower phenomenon in his patients, demonstrated that "The fantasy [of the whole body being a phallus] is a passive counterpart of the fantasy of eating the penis and represents an identification of the body with the penis" (p. 46). In his cases, castration anxiety resulted in a regression to all component strivings, but especially to oral ones, a "postphallic reorganization of the component impulses into an organization whose main aim is oral" (p. 37). The oral regression is particularly clear in my first two patients, confirming an essential of Lewin's thesis. Evidence that the penis is orally incorporated will be considered later, but here I can state that Lewin's remark that "the equation one's own body is one's own penis is not, I believe, found in the neurosis" (p. 43) does not receive support in the material presented. Two of the patients cited in this paper were not psychotic.

My material indicates the importance of several additional interrelated factors in the development of the sensations involved in the equations described.

[7]Sandler (1959) writes of "spreading of the cathexis of the penis to the whole body" (p. 197).

The change in the self representation that accompanies the defensive regression to the oral libidinal level is experienced as an apparent increase in the size of the head, mouth, and hands, which are relatively larger, compared to the entire body, and more highly cathected in infants under one year of age than in adults. In addition, because the genitals are less highly cathected in the infant than in the adult, there tends to be a diminution of awareness of the genitals as the regression occurs. The change in the self representation resulting from the regression coincides to a great extent but not completely with the changes that occur as a consequence of the defensive displacement of cathexis from the genitals to the rest of the body. Because of regression and displacement, instead of the genitals' becoming large and erect, the rest of the body feels that way, especially the head and upper extremities.

The capacity to substitute one set of fantasied enlargements for another is related to the fact that oral and phallic erotic gratifications may be substituted for each other in order to achieve comfort and drive discharge. Mrs. E.'s early achievement of gratification through the use of a transitional object was replaced by satisfaction through manual clitoral masturbation, but she could later regress and rely on a washrag or Kleenex for satisfaction.

There is evidence in my clinical material that the fantasied incorporation of the phallus was active in the development of the body-phallus equation. The sequence: sexual excitement–Isakower phenomenon–sensations of body (minus the phallus) as phallus, strongly suggests that the patient regresses to the oral level where he feels fused with the object or, in terms of Lewin's oral triad (1950), eats (and is eaten by) the object[8] which is equated with the phallus.

Mr. B.'s oral regression did indeed satisfy a wish to be united with his analyst from whom he wanted care and supplies as from a good preoedipal mother. And Mrs. E., who in infancy had been inadequately bottle-fed so that she did not gain weight for a long period of time, and who later was insufficiently cared for by her working mother, wished that her analyst would look after her. She wanted him to advise her regarding the care of her baby and became angry when he did not. She experienced the Isakower phenomenon several

[8]Lewin developed these concepts more fully (1950) after the publication of his article on the body as a phallus.

sessions after the one reported above, in order to quell her rage by introjecting the analyst in fantasy, and imagining that he filled and satisfied her. In fantasy, both of these patients experienced a fusion with the analyst-mother, eating her and being eaten.

In the course of the child's development there are shifts of cathexis from the *oral* zone (which includes the mouth and peri-oral region, the hand, and the body's surface as well as images based on visual, tactile, and other perceptions of the mother whose representation is poorly differentiated from the self-representation of the infant) to the *anal* area, including the lower part of the gastrointestinal tract, the surface of the abdomen and the buttocks, to the *genitals*, especially the phallus. In the course of these cathectic shifts, the hand is used to stimulate first the mouth and other hand, then the anus and eventually the genitals.

The retention of intense oral narcissistic cathexis into the phallic phase facilitates the identification of the idealized image of the parent (originally the mother, but later the father) with the idealized phallus, as described by A. Reich (1953, 1954). In such cases reliance on transitional objects, which at first substitute for the mother, parts of her, and the infant in contact with her, may, in a pathological line of development, lead to the use of a fetish which symbolizes the phallus (Dickes, 1963; Winnicott, 1953). Or, as we have seen, the Isakower phenomenon, a hallucinatory experience which originally served to satisfy oral needs to be filled and fused with mother, to eat and be eaten, may be used as a basis for the body-phallus equation variant.

During sexual excitement, especially orgasm (Keiser, 1947, 1952), ego and id regression from phallic to preoedipal phases, including the oral state, occurs. When regression characteristic of analysis was intensified by sexual excitement, phallic and oral wishes and derivatives appeared simultaneously.

Factors leading to prolongation of intense oral cathexis into the phallic phase are well known. Mr. B., with prolonged satisfaction (mother permitted him to suck her breasts when he was five) was important. Mrs. E.'s marked deprivation (she had been inadequately fed in early infancy and left by her mother later) also had a fixating affect. Fear of punishment—which appeared in both these cases, Mr. B., for instance, having undergone a dangerous operation at the height of the phallic phase—may foster regression as a defense.

Another experiential factor leading to the body-phallus equation: adaptive compliance with the mother's wish that her child be a phallus, was important in Shevin's case, but not conclusively demonstrated in mine.

Displacement and regression to orality involves instinctualization of the body, but not in the sense described by Ferenczi (1916-17) who agrees with Freud[9] that actual edema, turgescence, and hyperemia of *genitalized* parts of the body occur. My patients exhibited what may be called *central* or *perceptual cathexis* rather than *peripheral cathexis* of the body. There is no evidence that with the change in self representation, the libidinization of the body is accompanied by the actual tremendous swelling experienced by the patients. The genitals of course do enlarge considerably during sexual excitement, but the changes observed throughout the body by Masters and Johnson (1966) do not include swelling of the extremities, head, or mouth. The breasts do become enlarged, and in many subjects erythema of parts of the body, including the chest, is noted.

The Isakower phenomenon and the impression that the body is a phallus are transient hysterical symptoms in which the mechanism of conversion plays an important role.[10] As is classically true of hysteria, displacement accompanies the conversion, and memories of significant events may be incorporated into the symptomatology in disguised form. In my first two cases the memory of the nursing experience is clear. In addition, Mr. B's traumatic experience of the retropharyngeal abscess, which was carried out through the mouth, apparently without anesthesia, is represented in the oral and peri-oral sensations of the Isakower phenomenon. Here, a wish for a homosexual penetration determined in part the appearance of the memory. In still another patient, the Isakower phenomenon involved the wish-fulfilling memory of being repeatedly anesthetized during childhood by a beloved uncle. It is interesting that patients who underwent surgery or anesthesia regressed to an earlier, safer experience, nursing, to avoid the operation trauma. At the same time they regressed to an experience which was similar to that during the surgery.

[9] Quoted by Ferenczi (1916-1917).

[10] I am indebted to Mark Kanzer for pointing this out and to Frederick F. Shevin for a similar observation.

The superego contributes to the formation of the equation: body minus phallus = phallus. Along with the reassuring fantasy, *my body is a phallus*, a fantasied self-punitive castration occurs, affording penalty for transgressions and guarding against injury by others.

According to the dictates of my clinical material I have emphasized the individual's conception of himself as a phallus. A few words should be added about people who imagine other persons to be phalli, the classical example being the mother who considers her child her penis. In such cases displacement from one externally perceived object to another occurs. Projection may also be vital in the development of this wishful fantasy. After picturing oneself as a phallus consequent to the regression, incorporation, displacement, etc. already elucidated, this characteristic is projected onto others (see Tausk, 1919). In addition we can see the importance of regression to the early oral, narcissistic, symbiotic stage where self representation and object representation are fused and confused. One's own body is considered a phallus, and therefore the object is considered a phallus. Shevin's (1963) patient's defensive reversals, in which he considered himself and then his analyst-mother a phallus, seem to be based on the regressive state under consideration.

CHAPTER 15

Termination of Analysis: Graduation-Initiation Rite and Mythopoetic Aspects[1]

Jerome S. Silverman, M.D.

In this presentation I examine the influence of myth and rite on the termination period of a patient's analysis. Róheim (1942) has spoken of the ubiquity of separation problems as a constituent of myths and rites. My special emphasis is on the problems over separation which my patient experienced, elements of which I do not believe have been described in the literature.

The formulations by Freud (1908, 1910b, 1913e) and Abraham (1909) with respect to the role played by myth and rite are well known, and there have been many others since. Contributions to the subject incorporating advances in our understanding of ego psychology were presented at a panel (1964) on "Mythology and Ego Psychology." Fantasies have long been known to assist in the assimilation of painful experiences, by making possible their intrapsychic repetition. Similarly, myths have been recognized as attempts to master anxiety-laden situations, by making reality easier to accept than it would otherwise be; they thus help to accomplish the transition from

Dr. Silverman is Assistant Clinical Professor, Division of Psychoanalytic Education, Department of Psychiatry, State University of New York, Downstate Medical Center, Brooklyn, New York.

[1] The author is grateful for the helpful contributions to this article made by the members of the Workshop on Scientific Methodology of the Advanced Studies Program of the Psychoanalytic Association of New York, and particularly by Drs. M. Kanzer and J. Arlow.

the dominance of the pleasure principle to that of the reality principle. In this sense, my patient's fantasy/myth—created specifically in relation to termination of analysis—was at one and the same time the product of his unconscious ego-functions and a revelation of his strengthened awareness of reality.

The developmental and adaptational roles of myth and rite in relation to aspects of ego functioning have already been recognized. Róheim (1942) has written about myth and rite in relation to transition states. According to Tarachow (1964), myths provide "focal points about which the individual can organize his fantasies for identification processes" and thereby "ease the burden of ego synthesis and/or development . . ." (p. 11). Of relevance here is the statement by Annie Reich: "It is not simply society which patterns itself on the idealizing myths, but unconsciously it is the individual man as well who is able to structure his internal clamor of identities in terms of the prevailing myth. Life produces the myth and finally imitates it" (see Arlow, 1961, p. 389). "Both the dream and the myth," says Kanzer (1964), "create symbols which expedite the transition between inner and outer reality" (p. 31). Insofar as the myth "tends to perpetuate and represent the demands of society," he adds, it is "of inherent importance in superego formation . . ." (p. 32). Finally, Arlow (1961) states that to the extent that the myth "serves to bring the individual into relationship with members of his cultural group, on the basis of certain common needs . . ." it constitutes "a form of adaptation to reality and to the group" (p. 375).

The clinical vignette to be reported here confirms, I believe, these general observations. At a significant moment in analysis, the start of the termination period, my patient's fantasies fused with and were served by the modern myth of the gooney bird which he had heard in his teens. This interesting process not only appeared to draw on certain perennial id symbols, but also constituted a significant expression of the ego's problem-solving capacities, as these had been strengthened through analysis. The myth helped solve separation problems in this patient's termination, and it expressed various solutions, thereby facilitating further working through of conflicts.

The patient was a highly intelligent and ambitious scientist. His presenting symptoms had included vague complaints about "personality problems," dissatisfaction with his work, his social relations, and himself. He expressed serious concern over work inhibitions and sexual inhibitions, such as occasional loss of erection. There were also episodes of mild depression, occasional sleeping disturbances, and hysterical and obsessional trends. During analysis, evidences appeared of phobic tendencies—in particular, a fear of falling.

His childhood had been marked by constant strife between his parents. For several years, from the time he was about four, his mother occasionally and without notice left her husband for short periods. Once she took his older brother with her, once she took him. His parents separated several times thereafter and were divorced during his early latency. He subsequently lived with his father and grandmother. He remembered his parents' expressing concern as to his future security and had the guilty feeling that his having been born was somehow responsible for their dissension—he felt "caught in the middle." Circumcision had resulted in some ceruminous material accumulating in an anatomic residue like a sinus or hole. On the advice of a physician, his father had tried to squeeze out the accumulation by manipulating his penis. All this, coupled with exhibitionistic behavior on the parents' part, had the effect of stimulating his infantile curiosity and sexuality, as well as exercising an influence on his later researches and personality.

The episode began when, after nearly four years of analysis, I accepted the patient's request for a *specific* date to terminate—three months hence, at the start of the summer vacation. He had been discussing termination for some time, and in a way clearly indicating progress rather than resistance. Termination at this point, therefore, did indeed seem feasible.

After agreeing on an actual date for termination of his analysis, the patient behaved as one undergoing the painful ordeal of a puberty rite or of graduation-initiation ceremonies. In so doing, he employed characteristic modes of the mythopoetic (mythmaking) tradition. In describing the session of the week following the decision to terminate, I have, in the interests of clarity, taken the liberty of reversing the order of presentation of the last two sessions.

Session 1: The patient who came a little late, brought up the subject of *specific*[2] termination, as he had a number of times shortly before (and, of course, in the past). After calling attention to his

[2]Italicized portions denote words or phrases actually used by the patient.

lateness, he wondered again when he would indeed finish, and referred as he had on previous occasions, but this time, in terms of a *specific date*, to his wife's desire to join him on a trip to a scientific meeting to be held in about three months. Concerned as to exactly how termination could be effected, he added: *Maybe we would finish by gradually reducing the number of sessions.* I agreed that it might be feasible to terminate at the time he had suggested (but not by gradually reducing sessions) and offered to discuss his feelings about this. (Once the possibility of termination has been agreed upon, an assessment, similar to the one that occurs during the trial period at the beginning of analysis, is in order. It is in the very nature of the analytic process to contain a built-in aspect of the examination or ordeal, which becomes manifest during the termination period.)

The patient thereupon declared that he felt *scared, squeezed out, and that he would be happy to stay forever.* I surmise, on the basis of the content of previous sessions, that this willingness "to stay forever" reflects a mother's-womb fantasy, set up as a defense against the anxiety-laden terminal birth fantasy of separation.

The patient indicated his recognition of the fact that he was perhaps *reluctant to see the analysis finished, to be cut off from father and mother and become an independent adult*, to lose the assistance of explanations from the analyst. From there, associations moved on to a recollection of having seen, at the age of eight, a film about a primitive tribe engaged in an initiation-circumcision-puberty rite. He had seen it with his grandmother—a film of *an adolescent puberty rite in which, as the result of the circumcision ceremony, one became a man of the tribe, was admitted to the circle of adults.* Then he recalled that, as a child, *father did manipulate my penis, causing pain. Is the end of analysis like a sexual experience, like intercourse, like castration?* The film and termination reminded him of a joke about circumcision and castration, indicative of his ambivalence and his denial: A man who has been castrated awakens from anaesthesia and sees in the hospital bed next to him another man in pain. "Why are you in pain?" he asks. "From my circumcision," says the second. "Oh, *that* was what I meant to ask for!" says the first.

It was clear that the patient regarded the impending termination as an "examination ordeal"—an ordeal he knew he would have to undergo some time. But because he doubted his ability to go through it successfully, he dealt with it by means of denial. Both film and joke are vehicles of denial mechanisms, adopted in order to undo the reality of the termination actually about to take place. Separation and castration fantasies emerge. An insight into circumcision and tribal ritual thus appears. The individual, with the compromise of circumcision, accepts the symbol of maturity; yet, what with his uncertainty, especially at puberty, he does altogether not want maturity. To the patient, termination is like being "squeezed out" or castrated, in that it means a final confrontation with the analyst, during which *the secrets of sexual life, of intercourse, will be explained.* In his further associations to the meaning of termination, he brought up the question of which of us would be castrated, killed, burned, made to disappear. This was the beginning of a painful (and typical) period, during which death wishes (and disappearance wishes) for the analyst began to appear, along with the fear that he himself might disappear.

Session 2: The idea of a gradual "tapering-off" of the analysis ushered in the next session. The patient, who came late for the second time in a row, began at once by saying that he was *getting to be later and later, until I finally disappear altogether.* This theme of "gradual disappearance," already set forth in the previous session, was his attempted compromise between leaving and not leaving, just as circumcision represented to him a compromise between masculinity and castration. It was to play a part in his mythopoesis.

After acknowledging that he had been trying to find ways of delaying termination—including the bringing up once again of previous symptoms—the patient nevertheless asserted that he was feeling *reborn, new, and different.* He went on to say that the idea of rebirth also brought to mind homosexual ideas. This indicated that, for him, termination meant that he would no longer have fantasied sexual gratifications—the interpretations—from me. Finally, he expressed an interest in *just how an analysis is terminated.*

One significant feature of this second session was the patient's revelation that he felt that he needed contact with my phallus, in order to keep himself from disappearing—a conflict which was worked through further, along with his anxiety about the analyst's disappearance, during the weeks that followed. This led back to the circumcision, which led in turn to paternal manipulation of his penis—a fixation point in his development.

It was this experience, with its masochistic homosexuality, that he had now come to compare with analysis (*You're cleaning out my mind!*). Just as father had manipulated his phallus, so in analysis, I had his mind. It was in this respect that the masochistic homosexual gratification he had earlier experienced had come to be attributed to his relations with me. And that was why he saw termination—the cessation of interpretations—as the ending of fantasied sexual gratification. Further, this unconscious gratification was in part a defense against separation anxiety; if there were no further analysis—that is, no further such gratification—then, he feared, he would disappear. It was as if he needed continuing contact with the analyst's phallus, through the continuation of analysis, in order to keep his own phallus (himself) from disappearing. This fear of becoming a disappearing phallus had been a continuous feature of the analysis: he connected femininity not only with castration, but also with death. Of equal importance with the fear that he might disappear was his need to make the analyst disappear (and yet retain his own penis). These death wishes were subsequently analyzed, however, as a typical "end-of-analysis" fantasy: anxiety was not an indication for more prolonged treatment, but a terminal phenomenon.

In asking how an analysis is terminated, on the other hand, he was bringing up the question of how one is born or reborn, which was comparable in this context to the rites he knew (from the film he had seen as a child) had to be undergone in order to become a man of the tribe. Circumcision was in this sense the prerequisite for being admitted or reborn into the circle of hitherto feared competitors, the adults; but it also offered a combination of sexual gratification with mitigated castration punishment. Arlow (1951) compared an aspect of the Bar Mitzvah ceremony with the marriage ceremony—the initiate is known as the "groom of the Torah." As one part of puberty rites, intercourse, an adult prerogative, serves as a reassurance against castration, the symbolic meaning of circumcision. Light can thus be shed upon the Bar Mitzvah ceremony as well. As with puberty rites, in imparting secrets, it teaches about sexuality. Education is very important in Bar Mitzvah preparation and in puberty rites, and it figures as well in this patient's "graduation ceremony." The question of how an analysis is terminated was thus also a reflection of the child's psychosexual questions: how does intercourse take place; does the penis disappear (forever) in the vagina, or with ejaculation? While all these questions had arisen frequently during his analysis, they were literally repeated again at this time and again worked through within the current separation context.

At this juncture, the following elements have been established: the theme of gradual disappearance; the rebirth fantasy; the view of castration as being the equivalent of birth; the defensive satisfaction of being manipulated by father; the patient's desire to retain his penis; the fixation points from past experience; and the fact that circumcision also represented to the patient castration of father and identification with the aggressor: *he* will manipulate father's penis (analyst's brain), and he will hurt *him.*

Session 3: It was in this session that the link between rites and fantasy, as well as their relation to the myth, became clearly established. In discussing primal-scene material, the patient brought forth childhood masturbatory games and accompanying fantasies reflecting his curiosity about the sex act and the birth process. He spoke of how he had tried to figure out *how it's done; what comes out in masturbation; how you push in, in intercourse, and so on.* Remembered information about the gush of waters preceding birth (as communicated to him by his mother) was now occupying his fantasy; it was correlated with the idea of ejaculation, in which he played both the paternal and the maternal roles in the production of the child. (Sublimations taking place at this same time included a "gush" of long-delayed scientific papers, finally prepared for publication.)

A problem of intellectual origin which was to play a part in the development of his own mythopoesis also emerged. It was a conundrum, obviously related to the riddle of the Sphinx, and it had to do with whether a *spiral*, cut from a paper cone, would lie flat or double over on itself. This seemed to be related to whether the penis, after detachment from the father, would remain erect or curve back. And now came the myth portended in the preceding sessions. The problem of the spiral reminded him:

> *. . . There's some kind of mathematical theorem . . . about getting to a point and disappearing . . . and I recall a story many*

servicemen [World War II][3] *mentioned. It was about gooney birds .... the gooney bird flies in ever-decreasing spirals until it gets to a point and finally disappears!*

The introduction of this modern myth was to externalize, from this point on, the patient's fantasies about the significance of termination. The mythopoetic element involves a "totem figure" in the form of the gooney bird. The bird itself is a Laysan albatross (Aldrich, 1964), which flies away in spiral fashion; by flying in concentric circles, it is easily able to go either up or down, extracting energy from the velocity gradient of the wind. Its "take-off" is accomplished by running a great distance against the wind, awkwardly at first and looking somewhat foolish. Its mode of flying, which is apparently accomplished by a series of narrowing spirals, had given rise to the widely circulated gooney bird myth.

About a month later, when the patient appeared without a necktie, he again drew the gooney bird into his (birth, rebirth, immortality) fantasies. Comparing his forgetting his tie with cutting of the umbilical cord, and referring to the increasing imminence of termination (or birth), he said:

It means I cut the cord here. I'm thinking of the gooney bird; it flies in ever-decreasing circles until . . . [At this point, he added the last detail, thus completing the bird story] *he finally disappears up his own asshole.*

He thought of this with amusement as an (anal) counterpart to the snake that swallows itself. In this allusion to another (the "ourobouros") myth were condensed oral and anal images of birth, defenses against separation, along with the undoing mechanism of being able to fold back on oneself and return to the point of departure. (The

[3]The specific complete bird myth itself seems to have arisen during the terminal period of a terrible ordeal, during World War II, amongst servicemen separated from home (especially on the Pacific Isles, habitat of the gooney birds); they were immobilized and endangered by their wartime duties, and bound together in their anxious hope for survival. Their identification with the bird, which always returned home (safely) after dangerous and lonely trips, was understandable.

fact is that after taking off, the bird does return some months later to the original site.) This could be construed as a fantasy of narcissistic sexual satisfaction, designed to safeguard the patient against the threatened loss of the self, as well as of the object. Moreover, the gooney bird up his own anus defends against the analyst's penetration. It is interesting that, following termination, the patient was planning to go to a scientific meeting at a place whose name contained the word "hole." In entering that hole, he was exiting from another.

When viewed in light of the myth, the contents of the previous two sessions become clearer. He had suggested a *gradual decrease* in the number of sessions. His "*later and later, until I disappear*" suggests that, to him, coitus to the point of ejaculation represents disappearance. Correlations between myth and fantasies also become clearer: does the gooney bird (phallus) disappear forever? Will I be castrated—that is, lose my penis at the end of analysis (the ritual)?

His conundrum related to the riddle of another bird figure—the Sphinx. The gooney bird seemed in many ways to be a symbol of the patient himself and his problems with termination—gradual disappearance; awkwardness at take-off; descriptions of the actual sex act; the spiral as the back-and-forth of the penis (and of the analytic process). The gooney bird was the sex act itself, and not only the phallus. The bird myth may thus be taken as symbolizing the fusion of self and object, as in the symbiotic phase of mother-infant unity.

There had indeed been other early traumata, which had contributed to the intensity of the patient's present separation problems: early separations from a mother who appeared to be, during his earliest years, somewhat depressed and who periodically flew away and disappeared, so to speak; inconstancy on the part of both parents constantly quarreling. Various themes regarding these episodes frequently repeated themselves in his analysis, particularly with reference to separations and ideas about who was loved more and claimed, which parent or parental substitute cared more, curiosity about mother's and father's relationship, reasons for her flight. As for the latter, he too, shall I say, in a "spiral" and personalized way, was interested in the problem of flight—much as Leonardo da Vinci had been (Freud, 1910a). He had once entertained the idea of becoming a sky-diver. His associations made it obvious that flying away, so filled with various levels of meaning, also meant being capable of sexual performance.

Further influencing his choice of bird were other elements. He always had naturalist and scientific interests, having lived in rural areas in childhood, and had been a bird-watcher during puberty and adolescence. His professional work reflected these interests. In screen memories he recalled hunting for bird eggs, curiosity about woodpecker holes, and once getting his hand caught in a nest-hole while searching for eggs or birds. His father, too, was a scientist. One sublimated activity of note was the patient's talent as an expert gymnast (for which he had won awards). Of interest, though not surprising, is that he considered himself something of an aerialist. Some proclivity to visual imagery, a tendency to action, to certain problems in differentiating percepts was accounted for by his early overstimulation, early visual sensitization, by seductive exhibitionistic parents who frequently exposed themselves, performed toilet functions before him. With great anxiety in analysis, there was an occasional initial tendency to regressive visual imagery (which also had synthetic developmental aspects).

Pertinent to his use of a bird myth, during analysis the patient described an upsetting nighttime imagery fantasy, or obsessional idea, of a phallus or phalli coming toward him, toward his mouth, which he'd fantasy cutting (biting and incorporating) in order to fall asleep. This was analyzed at different times in terms of Lewin's triad; on the deepest level, as a wish that the analyst put him to sleep by letting him suck, bite, and incorporate the analyst's phallus. At the end of analysis, with the typical termination onset of transient, mild phobic (falling) manifestations, this was further associated with his fear of falling, as into the "cavity," analyzed on various levels as into sleep, the breast, or as his projected sadistic orality.

Both the bird myth and imagery, at termination, had condensed in them various meanings according to phasic stratification (i.e., phallic phase; penis, vagina aspects). One notes, in view of his nighttime fantasy, that the anus also represented the mouth. The myth therefore also incorporated a narcissistic solution of the problem of refusion with mother and, as another solution, represented his attempt at incorporating the analyst permanently before his departure. These, taken together with the overstimulation of his voyeuristic (and other) impulses as a result of the exhibitionistic practices of the parents, and the physical trauma of circumcision, specifically contributed to the patient's need for a myth as an aid in the resolution of his termination-separation problems.

Session 4: In this next-to-final session of the week the patient reported a dream that involved a difficult birth. He was trying to squeeze out of a narrow orifice, pushing against the walls of a rocky crevasse with his back, hands, and feet, as if he were climbing up a mountain. Some people were going ahead; others were following him (*as in psychoanalysis*, he commented). He said that, for him, birth represented being squeezed out through some small orifice. Associations indicated that this dream represented a fantasy of a difficult birth—and from a man, from father's penis. In other associations, the analytic termination was seen also as a release, as permission to "go to the woman." (He planned to "celebrate" termination by taking his wife away with him on a special trip. Indeed, at his very last analytic session [which he called both a "graduation day" and a "birthday"], his wife was waiting for him, literally to fly away with him.) In material worked on earlier, his wife had also represented the analyst: she thereby defended him against object loss. Significantly, however, his associations to pushing out through an orifice also referred to an important problem which had been dealt with during the course of the analysis—his difficulty in ejaculating. It was obvious, of course, that he saw this difficulty as analogous to his difficulty in ending analysis.

In another dream reported in Session 4, the patient's father gives him a new car. I interpreted this as representing his wish for a new phallus—one that can't be lost in the end; a real one, father's. Many of his associations made it evident that the idea of termination constituted for him either his losing his phallus or getting mine. It was as though he were saying, "At the end of this analysis, one of us will be castrated; the other will be male—me, I hope." Circumcision, in which one loses a part, but not the whole, is the compromise.[4]

[4]Nunberg (1947) has indicated that with circumcision a person's feminine part is removed. Notwithstanding this anxiety, and sarcasm, this patient was also confident and pleased about termination and as if thereby he had "come into full manhood," i.e., gotten rid of his feminine homosexual part, as it were, this time with a successful complete circumcision ritual as compared with the first, which left a residue.

Furthermore, from this dream fragment, we see that the patient is given another organ as a substitute—which is reminiscent of what occurred with Freud's (1909a) Little Hans. (It is of interest that Reik [1962] reports how the candidate, as a part of primitive puberty rites, is often symbolically given a substitute organ.) For this patient, it was *father's* organ that he received, since historically his father had not only previously helped him get a car, but in his teens had lent him his own. Furthermore, the patient's "hot-rod" cars, during his adolescence and after, had had much phallic significance for him.

In the second session of that week (described here so as not to interrupt the continuity of themes), still another dream was reported. In this, a mother calls her baby's physician (the latter very clearly, from the patient's associations, represented both a mother and also the analyst) to say that her baby, who had died following burns, was all right. The physician is annoyed with her for doing this. In the dream, the patient, meaning to defend the baby's mother for saying what she knew to be untrue, instead says: *I'm perfectly willing to say my mother has died* (as in reality she had). Ambivalent about the forthcoming termination, the patient was saying that, despite his burning anger (against the analyst), the latter ought not to accept so readily the loss of the patient. He ought instead to recognize that, for the patient, giving up the analyst was equivalent to dying—it involved castration, separation, and (hopefully) rebirth. The question of burning recalled an upsetting fire fantasy he had had during latency—that his father and grandmother with whom he then lived would somehow burn up the house with him in it. He had first recalled this fantasy when, during his analysis, he was under pressure from his wife to have children (fire = birth). At that time, this rather erudite patient lent support to the hypothesis that fire and birth are connected, by recalling the story of another mythological bird, reborn in its immolation—the Phoenix.

The significance of the gooney bird thus continued to widen. It had now become a Phoenix, a mystery figure related to both rebirth and intercourse, and with anal as well as other implications. The strong resemblance cannot be overlooked between the gooney bird myth, the myth of the Phoenix, and other myths (such as that of the Sphinx, another mystery figure—whose attributes include wings, by the way) which contain unmistakable imagery of birth and death.

Nor can one ignore the presence of obvious conflicts over the impending separation (from father as well as mother), one attempted solution of which would be his taking father's phallus with him (the bird—his own penis—*disappears up its own asshole*). Complicating the problem of separation from father was his oedipal fantasy that father has to be killed for him to have mother—that he would have to castrate father in order to be able to use father's organ for that purpose. In "The Future of an Illusion," indicating a parallel between the hidden truths in religious doctrine and the latent truths of the dream, Freud (1927) tells of the fairy tale or myth of the Stork that brings babies: "Here too we are telling the truth in symbolic clothing, for we know what the large bird signifies" (p. 44).

There was a final fragment to the dream of the burned baby: at his parents' home, the patient starts to bite a long-stemmed vegetable that he has taken from the refrigerator, but thinks he's full. He associated to this by saying that he had had enough—enough of *father's penis,* of *analysis.*

In these two facets of the patient's response to termination—the fantasy of circumcision rites and the myth of the gooney bird (a fused castration and oral incorporation)—one can see the two poles of the separation anxiety that the analyst's acceptance of his suggestion evoked. On the one hand, there is the sense of an inescapably necessary, yet painful departure from a world of dependence into one in which he would be the man he wished (and feared) to be. On the other hand, we see the hope that there need not be any crossing of thresholds, after all, but rather a disappearance, a "fading-out." But there is another aspect of the gooney bird myth that is illuminated by the patient's joke about circumcision. When I took up his suggestion that the number of sessions be gradually reduced, and thus transformed it into my own decision in favor of termination, it was as if the patient felt that I had misinterpreted his suggestion to "ease off" the continuation of the analysis in the same way as the intended request for circumcision had been misinterpreted in the joke. Obviously, neither the surgeon in the joke nor the analyst in reality could say, at this point, "Oops, sorry!" and then proceed to undo what he had just done. Both of them had, so to speak, *pushed the patient across a threshold.* His later reference to the nature of the gooney bird's reputed form of flight—that he flies around in ever-narrowing circles, until at last, he disappears "up his own asshole"—also furnishes a picture of how the patient conceived of the "falling-off" period he had hoped to initiate by his suggestion. This was not only to be a situation that *he* initiated, rather than the analyst; it was also to be a kind of "fadeout," that is, termination without termination, without a threshold to cross, without a developmental crisis. This was one striking way of presenting his struggle.[5]

I have not stressed preoedipal factors, but the weaning aspect was significantly involved: in the patient's identification with the resultant imposed delays; in his adaptational response, as shown in his incorporating the ability to delay; in his accepting separation, and in his subsequent turning outward toward the world with the now available sublimated energy.

As Bunker (1951) has suggested, in the puberty rite (which he compares with a crucifixion) the individual is made to feel that it is only after having fulfilled certain conditions—including symbolic castration for having harbored incestuous and patricidal wishes—that one can enter into "real life" (the Kingdom of God). Only thus can the boy enter into his father's generation. For this purpose, he must also be weaned away from the mother (the earlier "real life" out of which he must pass by way of descent from the totem, birth from father, as in primitive rites).

The patient's "homecoming"—his joining the adults after his analytic *Wanderjahr*—involves his possession of a new tool, analysis. Now that he, like St. George, has slain the infantile dragons (with wings, by the way) that have tormented him, he is granted the penis. He now has the ability to use all aspects of ego functioning, not only sexual. The analyst's figure of reality testing is not now an instinctualized one.

The sequels to the announcement of termination served not only as indicators of the development of various ego and superego functions and of the patient's identification with a group of adults, but also as representations of socialization, of development in his object relations, and as condensed expressions of the effort to resolve various conflicts.[6] In termination, more occurs than being weaned, wiped clean and squeezed out, and being in a state of loss and mourning.

[5] Myths can also reflect ego ideals, as well as anxious conflicts.

[6] One wonders if the relative absence of a satisfactory mythos-schema, or idealization does not contribute to the problems of adolescents searching to consolidate their identifications and thus to navigate satisfactorily the transition to adulthood.

His newfound powers manifested themselves in his preparation for publication of numerous important scientific papers, all finally completed in the terminal phase. His infantile omnipotence had been resolved, facilitating his scientific and other sublimations. He was able to acknowledge his superior's help in this, as well as accept the gifts of analysis from a man (the analyst, father). This, despite his earlier experience of seduction by father (and mother)—and it took place without the destruction of father. He no longer felt that his superior had to die or be fired, and he worked through a similar dread with regard to the analyst and the problem of termination. This working through was, in fact, marked by his taking new significant steps toward achieving better relations with his professional group. By the end of his analysis, he had himself begun to notice that he was getting along better with everyone, that he seemed to have many friends—all of which, according to reports, was something quite new for him. *He was absorbing his analysis into new relations, and in that way his termination was becoming a "continuing."*

The renunciation of oedipal wishes is generally followed by ego and superego development and new identifications. It must not be forgotten that the patient's fantasy and associations to rites emerged during the terminal phase when he was struggling to cope with problems of separation at various levels. It was then that this process took on its "graduation" aspects. In the session following establishment of a termination date, the patient said he had spent the same number of years in analysis as he had in college, and his college years had ended in graduation. He felt that his last day in analysis was a mixture: it included both a sort of special birthday and a sort of graduation—*my graduation day.*

Having first met certain requirements implicit in a satisfactory psychoanalysis, he feels initiated, by way of this rite, into the external world, where he may assume his share, as a man, of the mysteries and privileges that are proper only to men. Once the rite has been initiated symbolically, by way of the analyst's announcement of agreement with a specific suggested date for termination (graduation), he has in effect gained his penis; in terms of his fantasy, he has produced his solutions to the riddle of the Sphinx. As Beres (1962) has said, fantasies help structure unconscious ego functions; they also help in the assimilation of a trauma. Children, by the way, use play and games for the same mastery and structuralization.

As Stern (1964) has said, "Myths arise from the verbalization of unconscious fantasies in the rite. . . . They [not only provide] the group with its identity [but also] dialectically foster in its members—via identification with the hero—the emergence of personal identity" (p. 91). Arlow (1961) has stated that man's capacity and need for myth-making, a shared experience, serves as an instrument for socialization (the patient's ever-widening circle of object relations), bolstering instinctual renunciation by way of sublimated activities.

In *Totem and Taboo*, Freud (1913e) notes that every totem was originally an animal, which was regarded as the ancestor of the clan, and was, in that sense, an ambivalent representative of the father. He described the connection between the child's thinking and "animistic magic," and the nature of the mysteries and myths by which animism sustains itself. Patients utilize, analyze, and sublimate a similar animism in the terminal phase. My patient adopted and used constructively a group fantasy and endowed it with the qualities of a totemistic animal. This significantly helped him work through the terminal phase and to achieve maturity as an independent adult member of society. I suggest that the patient identified with the bird so as to evoke birth at various levels—from the mother, from the totemistic father, and finally from the analyst. As with his jokes, here, too, the mechanism of reversal made its appearance. Thus, he saw birth taking place at one time with his being extruded from the analyst during the transference, at another time with the analyst's being extruded from him. The opposite idea was also represented: the idea of "entering into" the body, a sort of "squeezing into" by a large penis.

This patient also struggled to work out problems of birth and death, just as is done in totemism. At that time, so to speak, the son of the eagle, as such, thereby confirms his descent from the totem (the male, father) and thus, by rite and myth, animistically, attempts to solve the problems of death, birth, incest, patricide, and integration into the tribe. This patient, by rite and myth, depicted his struggle in termination to get in, to get out; to penetrate the analyst, to be penetrated by him; to hold on, to let go.

The idea of the gooney bird took shape partly as a need to control the end of analysis. The gooney bird disappearing into his own anus represents a compromise formation between his desires to penetrate and be penetrated by the analyst. But another compromise occurs—the father is neither completely left nor completely retained; through participation of both wishes in the totem animal image, a superego bond is set up to absorb part of the former dependency while other realistic relationships can still be retained.

Just as the patient came up with the image of the gooney bird, the puberty initiate often has a dream—frequently induced by fasting or drugs—in which the totem figure appears.

The role of the bird is intriguing. Interaction in the analytic sessions culminated in a trend which, starting with Session 1, began to portray analysis as an ordeal, preparing at once as if for final (sex) contact with the analyst, for birth, and for castration (death). Not only is this similar to the mental state that prepares for emergence in adolescence (a phase wherein group identification, myths, idealogies are needed and sought) from the shelter of the parents to early adventures in actual sexuality, but it is also similar to that state the primitive (and in their own way, civilized) cultures have treated with instinctualized rituals and with tribal legends. Analytic procedures (regular scheduling, repetition of person and place, etc.) are drawn in, seen as rituals, and treated by interpretation. Following Arlow (1951), we could say that the affective turmoil around termination was structuralized by myth and rite (termination as such) as occurs in society. The gooney bird was chosen to carry further a disposition on the part of the patient to create his own termination ritual (already foreshadowed in the film mentioned in Session 1, suggesting sex with mother-grandmother, and heightened in Session 3 where, after creating his own "examination situation" (will a spiral lie flat?), he recalls the bird in a spontaneous invocation of the confrontation with the Sphinx. A humorous solution is propounded a month later: he "disappears up his own asshole." With this solution, the bird himself was dissipated in the analysis. As in the dream, whose function is largely dissipated in the experience, so does the myth fade with analysis.

I suggest, then, that the fantasy-myth created during termination-separation struggles constituted an expression of the synthetic, integrative functions, insofar as it gave adaptational expression to gains made during the course of the analysis. The expression was significantly helpful to the patient, both as catalyst and as organizer in the reformulation of ego and superego functions during terminal-phase reactions which showed a marked correspondence to puberty rites. Finally, through the bird fantasy, the patient indicates the expectation that, at the end of his analysis, his infantile and adolescent sexual probings will be answered, the principle of "similarity" (Freud, 1913) among them. My contention is that both fantasy and rites perform structural ego functions, and thereby embody superego development as well. This is in accordance with Waelder's principle of "multiple determinants." The patient's termination fantasy, then, is also a product of unconscious ego functions and, seemingly paradoxically, of a newly strengthened awareness of reality.

CHAPTER 16

Hallucinations in Children

Helen Schur, M.D.

Hallucinations have been alternately defined as perceptions arising without a corresponding stimulus from the outside; as internal processes experienced as if they were occurring in the outside world; as regressive phenomena expressed in the perceptual sphere.

This baffling phenomenon has challenged many investigators of the adult human mind. In the last two decades there have also been several papers published about hallucinations in children. While hallucinations in adults are almost universally viewed as psychotic phenomena, this is not the case when they occur in children. Aside from organic, C.N.S. disorders, or toxic and infectious conditions, hallucinations have also been reported in children diagnosed as normal, neurotic, or suffering from other functional psychiatric entities (Bender, 1954; Despert, 1948; Sachs, 1962; Katan, 1952; Wilking and Paoli, 1966; and others).

My interest in children's hallucinations was aroused by observations of a great number of children who had such experiences, but who did not seem psychotic. Moreover, the clinical picture and/or reaction of the children who had predominantly visual-kinesthetic hallucinations differed strikingly from that of children whose hallucinations were predominantly auditory. No such distinction has previously been made between the two types.

Dr. Schur is Assistant Professor of Psychiatry, State University of New York, Downstate Medical Center, Brooklyn, New York.

The author expresses her appreciation to those members of the staff of the Kings County Child and Adolescent Psychiatric Service, and of the James Weldon Johnson Mental Health Clinic, who let her use some of their clinical material.

I believe that an understanding of the puzzling problem of hallucinations can best be achieved through a detailed discussion of various ego functions which must be disturbed for this symptom to develop; specifically the investigation of reality testing, reality constancy, object constancy, differentiation of self- and object representation, prevalence of secondary as opposed to primary process thinking, failure of repression, of frustration tolerance, of control of anxiety and aggression, all of which would impede the normal functioning of the mental apparatus. Such an analysis should focus on the development of these functions as well as on their regressive aspects. An approach of this kind may enable us to formulate the different factors which lead to either auditory or visual hallucinations. A detailed study of hallucinations occurring in children may be particularly illuminating because many of their ego functions are still not yet stabilized and transitions among fantasy, play, make-believe, and reality testing are fluid even in the normal child.

Perception is one of the most essential parts of reality testing. We usually distinguish between perceptions arising from external stimuli and perceptions arising from stimuli within the organism. "Inner" perceptions are not restricted to awareness of physiological processes and bodily functions, they also include the awareness of psychological processes, i.e., of needs, wishes, emotional states, all of which involve variously organized thought processes. We also know from neurophysiological and experimental studies that perception is not just a passive process or a switching and transmission system; it includes, as well, an active and most complex process of screening and scanning which reflects and is influenced by the state of all the structures of the mental apparatus (Granit, 1955; Galambos, 1956; Fisher, 1956). It is therefore not surprising that a distortion of perception can be caused by a multitude of physiological and emotional factors. Cultural and social factors can also influence perception. "Where the culture expects its members 'to have visions,' individuals in that society will perceive as real entities which have no tangible existence" (Kidd and Rivoire, 1966, p. 191).

Through the interaction of innate apparatuses and multiple experiences, through growth and development, a maturational phase is eventually attained where stable distinctions are made between percepts arising from the environment, percepts arising from within the soma, and percepts originating within the mental apparatus. It is the stability of this function which is considered essential for reality testing. Therefore any interference with this stability—be it immaturity, a lag in or failure of development, altered somatic or psychological states—may impair this particular aspect of reality testing either temporarily or permanently.

Hallucinations have been discussed in the literature from the phenomenological point of view; from the viewpoint of the relationship of hallucinations to other aspects of normal and abnormal behavior, including genetic and developmental factors; as a symptom (within the framework of a great variety of nosological entities) with a specific onset, content, and metapsychological implications; as they occurred in various experimental setups; and according to their etiology. I will restrict myself to a discussion of those studies which are pertinent to my topic. What seems striking to me is that most studies have concerned themselves with *why* hallucinations happen rather than *how* they happen.

Freud's formulations about hallucinations reflect and parallel the development of, and changes in, his general theoretical framework. In the "Project" (1895) he linked hallucinations with his earliest theory on dreams and the characteristics of primary process. He states, for instance, "Dream ideas are of a hallucinatory kind, they awaken consciousness and meet with belief. This is the most important characteristic of sleep. It appears at once when there are alternating spells of sleeping [and waking]. One shuts one's eyes and hallucinates; one opens them and thinks in words" (p. 339). This passage clearly illustrates the fluid transition between different states of consciousness which led Freud to conceptualize the difference between a percept and an idea, a fantasy and reality. The prevalence of primary- or secondary process thinking was seen as the essential differentiating factor.

In 1896 Freud discussed hallucinations as a symptom and pointed to their genetic determinant, namely, a repetition of a childhood experience, the return of the repressed. He expressed a similar opinion in "Dynamic of Transference" (1912a, p. 108), and in "Construction in Analysis" (1937b, p. 267). The same point was convincingly exemplified by Niederland (1959) when he established the connection between Schreber's hallucinations and real events in the latter's childhood, and by Coren and Saldinger (1967).

In "Formulations on the Two Principles of Mental Functioning" (1911a) Freud pointed out the importance of perception, attention, judgment, and periodic examinations of the external world for reality testing. In the "Metapsychological Supplement to the Theory of Dreams" (1917b) he examined specifically the similarity and the differences between dreams and hallucinations and suggested that the concept of *regression* could also apply to the ego. The state of sleeping and dreaming cannot be understood without the assumption of a temporal ego-regression. However, this regression is never a total one: complex thought processes go on, including the perception of inner and outer stimuli.

According to Freud, dreams and hallucinations also show the following similar characteristics: they are *projections*, "an externalization of an internal event"; both represent a wish fulfillment, albeit the latter is mostly unconscious in both instances and can actually be experienced with negative affects of great intensity. Both dreams and hallucinations to varying degrees are characterized by an element of conviction; finally, both show partial temporal ego-regression. The concepts that hallucinations are a sign of regressive ego functioning and that they are an externalization of internal processes are crucial to my theme.

Regression is a developmental concept. Instinctual regression represents a regression to a point of fixation of earlier instinctual development. If we speak of ego regression, we understand a backward movement of functions to an earlier state of development. We must consider the possibility, however, especially when dealing with children, that owing to the immaturity of the mental apparatus, or to pathology, certain ego functions have not yet developed. Hallucinations have been discussed in the literature for the most part as a regressive phenomenon. We must also consider, however, the possibility of developmental arrest, analogous to libidinal fixation on an early phase of development.

This brings us again to the central problem: which functions must be absent or disturbed to produce this specific phenomenon, namely, the externalization of an internal perceptual process? Freud's explanation, of a withdrawal of cathexes from the "system of perception Cs." is incomplete. It deals with the phenomenon only in topographic-economic terms and does not take into consideration the various complex ego functions which guarantee the ability to distinguish external from internal stimuli.

In his paper on "Negation" Freud (1925b) relates the function of judgment to the development of the reality ego, out of the pleasure ego, which in turn depends on the distinction between external and internal.

> It is now no longer a question of whether what has been perceived . . . shall be taken into the ego or not, but of whether something which is in the ego as a presentation can be rediscovered in perception (reality) as well. It is . . . a question of *external* and *internal.* What is unreal . . . is only internal; what is real is also there *outside*. . . . The first and immediate aim . . . of reality-testing is, not to *find* an object in real perception which corresponds to the one presented, but to *refind* such an object, to convince oneself that it is still there [pp. 237-238].

In considering the concept of the externalization of an internal process, we must first define the concept of internalization. Internalization is the result of a complex developmental process. It encompasses processes, described by ego psychologists and such genetic epistomologists as Piaget (1967), involving such mechanisms as introjection, various levels of identification, and the development of the superego. It results in such diverse structural changes as the development of self- and object differentiation, the development of object and reality constancy, and separation-individuation. Internalization is essential for the development of abstract thought and concept formation, for thinking on a secondary-process level, and for other ego functions (Freud, 1965; Mahler, 1965; Jacobson, 1964; Hartmann, 1950a; Hartmann, Kris, and Loewenstein, 1949; and others).

We may therefore postulate that the lack or loss of the ability to differentiate between inside and outside (resulting, in the case of loss, in externalization or projection) can only come about if some of these essential functions either have not reached a stable state or have lost that stability due to organic or severely traumatic psychological noxae. This applies most of all to object constancy, identification, especially with regard to gender identity, and a differentiation of self- and object representation. The treatment of children offers an excellent opportunity to observe the unfolding and development or the arrest of all these functions.

Brenner's paper "On a Case of Childhood Hallucinosis" (1951) is pertinent. As with the cases of visual hallucinations described by Esman (1962), Coren and Saldinger (1967), and those encountered in my observations, the hallucinations in Brenner's case started with a night terror. The visual hallucinations of most of these children were coupled with a tactile sensation of bugs crawling over them. Almost always, the night terror extended into the hallucinated state, during which the panic continued to be felt.

In Brenner's case the episode occurred when the patient was three-and-a-half-years old and in the midst of very lively oedipal fantasies. The night terror and hallucinatory experiences could be traced directly to fantasies about impregnation following the child's "enlightenment" by her older sister.

Here I want to refer to Kluever's statement (1933) about the close and transitional relationship between percept and memory, eidetic imagery and phenomena, such as after-images, projected memory-images, subjective visual sensations, illusion, hallucinations, hypnagogic images; and subjective visual phenomena produced by hypnosis or drugs (see also Isakower, 1939; Silberer, 1909; Varendock, 1921). Werner (1957) states that primitive man is certain that there is no fundamental difference between subjective and objective phenomena. It is essential to bear in mind also the continuum along which lie anxiety dreams, pavor nocturnus, and night terror (Jones, 1931; Stern, 1951).

A similar fluidity between internalization and externalization occurs in the auditory sphere. According to Piaget, young children are inclined to identify thought with the act of speaking. Thought is a material event rather than an inner, psychological process (Flavell, 1963). The fluid boundary in an auditory hallucination between a thought and a voice was described by Levin (1932). The child said: "My mind tells me to do different things. Sometimes I hear a voice and it says do it, and the other side says don't do it." Sherman and Beverly (1924) were also able to trace hallucinations through several stages of regression. The child would first argue with himself about "being good," then would recognize vague images, one of which was telling him to be "good" while another was telling him to be "bad," and finally he would see the images of God and the Devil. What is also interesting in this latter case, as in almost all of the others, is that the "good" voice telling the child what was right to do was perceived in the right ear, while the "bad" voice was heard in the left.[1]

Apparently these fluid stages between externalization and internalization are intimately and reciprocally connected with contact with reality. Geleerd (1946) coined the term *reality span* when discussing children whose hold on reality could be maintained only in the actual presence of an adult, and who lost contact with reality as soon as they were left to themselves. Obviously those children had not achieved reality constancy (Frosch, 1966), i.e., a stabilized internal representation of the environment.

The close relationship between dreams, hypnagogic and hypnopomic hallucinations, eidetic imagery, imaginary play objects and companions, "isolated" hallucinations and hallucinosis, delusion, illusion, and percepts has also been pointed out by Weiner (1961) and Despert (1948). Weiner defines hallucinations as an adaptive mechanism, an attempt to deal with internal emotional stimuli by translating them into concrete perceptual material. Coren and Saldinger (1967) have discussed the close relationship and shifts among visual hallucinations, paranoid delusions, and phobias in children; they explain these phenomena in quantitative terms and view the shift from phobias to hallucinations as a topographic regression, a response to acute psychological stress. Esman (1962) has stressed the impairment of ego functions in hallucinated children, especially in the area of reality testing and impulse control.

My own contribution is based on the clinical observation of several hundred children seen in a psychiatric hospital, a child guidance clinic, and in private practice. The children observed had auditory and/or visual and tactile hallucinations. I have selected three cases for detailed discussion. The first, that of Alice, was of the kind usually described as acute hallucinosis.

[1] The equation of the right side with the "right" thing and the left with the "wrong" is found in many languages; for instance: German: *rechts* (right); *Recht* (law, justice); French: *droit* (right); *Droit* (law); Italian: *destra* (right); *sinistra* (left, sinister, ill-omened); Latin: *dexter* (right, proper); *sinister* (left, bad, evil); Polish: *prawy* (right); *Prawo* (law).

Alice

Alice was brought to the Clinic when she was not quite eight years old. Ten days earlier, she had awakened at three o'clock on a Sunday morning because of a bad dream and had been unable to fall asleep again. She showed no effects of this on Sunday, but on coming home from school the next day she complained of feeling warm all over her body, with a tingling sensation around her legs. A physical examination by a doctor was negative. During the next few days, however, she frequently looked at her legs, complaining that she felt something crawling on them. These sensations occurred only in the late afternoon and when she was in bed.

A few days later she awakened at five in the morning, extremely agitated, screaming that there were insects all around her and she was afraid that they would bite her. She remained in this panic state for several hours. By the time the mother brought her to the clinic she had calmed down and was able to talk about her experiences of a few hours earlier. An organic work-up was again negative and tranquillizers were prescribed. The next few nights Alice was afraid to go to sleep, and the mother had to lie down with her.

Alice's parents had been separated for the past four years. She and her sister, one year younger, lived with the mother, but visited the father every Saturday. The father had other women and evidently did not sufficiently conceal from his daughters his sexual relationships with them.

The mother described Alice as a friendly, outgoing girl, who was doing well at school and had several friends. On the whole, she was easy to handle. Occasionally, when she was stubborn, the mother would whip her, and the child would then quickly comply with the mother's demands. During her illness, however, Alice was stubborn, had frequent temper tantrums, and cried easily. While she had previously liked going to school, she now made a fuss in the morning and fought with her younger sister, accusing her mother of preferring the sibling.

She had a habit of scratching her protruding navel (she had an umbilical hernia), for which she had been severely criticized and threatened, and this increased markedly during the acute phase of her illness. The mother was at a loss at how to handle her. She reluctantly agreed to the suggestion that she stop the whippings and postpone looking for a job. When seen two weeks after her original clinic visit, Alice was reported to be sleeping well.

Smiling shyly and talking in a babyish voice, she denied having seen "insects." She nevertheless talked about "things" she was seeing which she said she could not describe, but she eagerly complied with the suggestion that she draw them. An egg-shaped form represented a white ghost which she said touched her and felt hot but didn't hurt. The next two drawings represented monsters. One looked like a penis and the other like an arm with a four-fingered hand. Alice said that these monsters bit her (see figure 1).

The following week Alice's behavior at home had much improved, but she was still seeing monsters, and this time she drew three of them. Again one looked like a penis and was flanked by a two- and a three-fingered hand and arm, respectively. She remarked that they bit with hidden teeth, and that the bite hurt (see figure 2). On her next clinic visit she said that she could still see the monsters when lying in bed at night, but only with her eyes closed. Her drawings now represented the upper part of a person with head and arms. The hands had two fingers each, which, she said, pinched her arms, but only if she kept them outside the covers (see figure 3).

This case is typical in many respects for an acute hallucinosis. However, unlike the cases of Jane and Richie (see below), who were in treatment for a long time, the information about Alice is scant. It would therefore be too speculative to assess the disturbances of various ego functions as I will try to do for the other two cases. We can nonetheless draw certain conclusions from Alice's history, symptoms, hallucinations, and description and drawings of the monsters. Alice had been exposed to prolonged dissension between her parents, as well as to repeated separations and reconciliations. She had been exposed to her mother's severe depressions and treated inconsistently. She had further been exposed to sexual overstimulation by witnessing the various affairs of her mother and her father.

The development of Alice's symptoms shows the close relationship, already postulated by Freud, between dreams, phobias, and hallucinations. We would not hesitate to offer interpretations, even without further associations, had Alice presented us with a series of anxiety

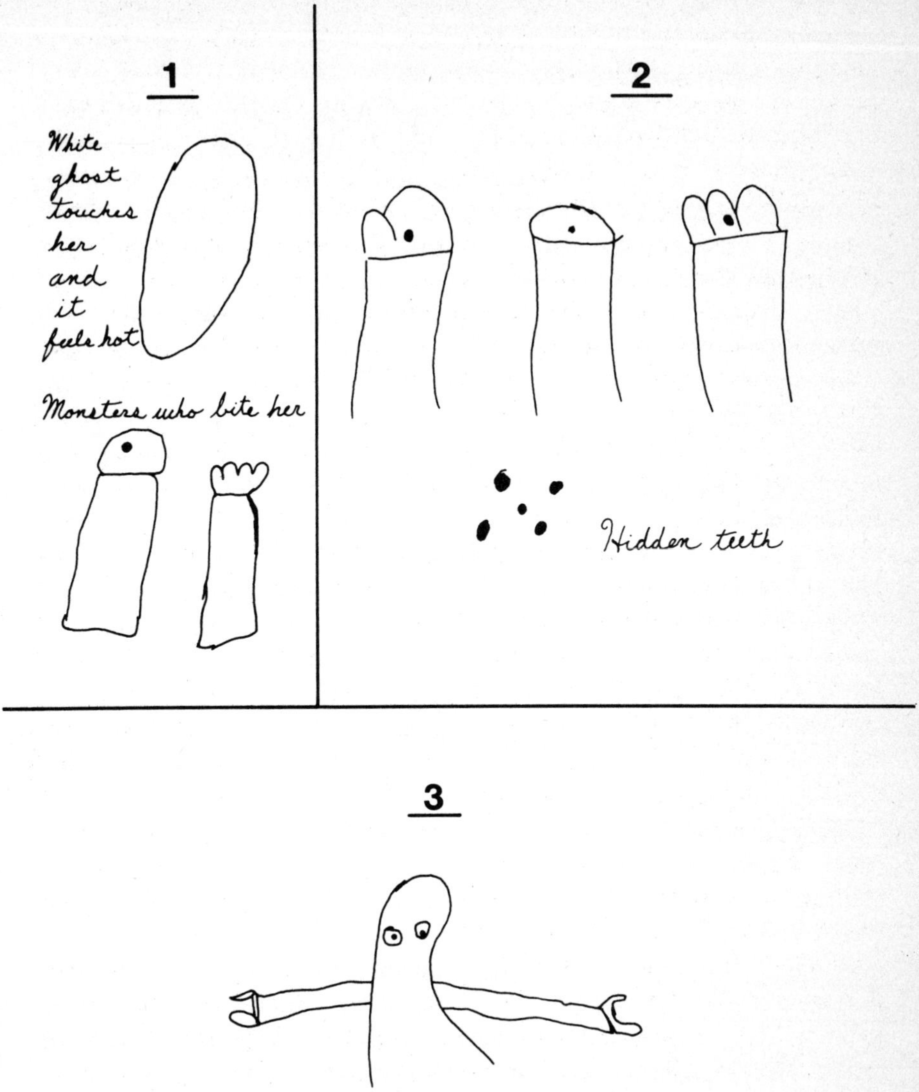
1
White ghost touches her and it feels hot
Monsters who bite her
2
Hidden teeth
3

dreams whose content was bugs crawling or biting, monsters touching her, and penis- or fingerlike structures biting her arms or pinching her. We would similarly have no difficulty understanding the structure of symptom formation which started with sensations of heat and tingling of the legs, followed by a fear of insects, and accompanied by sleep disturbance. We would diagnose this as a combination of conversion hysteria and phobia. In Alice's case, however, the externalization went one step further, and here we can again recognize, in confirmation of Freud's assumption, both the "historical truth" returning in the hallucination and the importance of visual sexual stimulation for the development of visual hallucinations. We must, of course, assume that we are dealing with qualitative and quantitative differences when the externalization includes the perceptual system.

The gradual improvement in Alice's symptoms and the changes shown in her drawings, without any kind of interpretative psychotherapy, resulted mainly from the fact that the mother had become more accepting and less punitive, and that the child had developed a positive transference. There was an interesting parallel between the improvement in the symptoms and the change in the drawings. We saw the monster hallucination change into a hypnagogic phenomenon with a complex meaning. If she kept her hands outside the cover, thus avoiding masturbation, the monster pinched the exposed hand. In this way Alice was expressing the compromise between regressive wish fulfillment and punishment. Then too, the last drawing was much better organized than the others, pointing to the beginning of more adaptive repression.

There is surprising uniformity in the phenomenology and type of onset in my cases, and in the cases reported in the literature. As mentioned before, they nearly always start at night and are first hardly distinguishable from a night terror. Night terror, an altered state of consciousness, differs from sleep in that there is in it greater access to motor discharge. The children have their eyes open, they point at the images of their dreams, verbalize them, and scream in terror. Mostly, when they overcome the panic, they return to the state of full sleep and have no memory of such an occurrence.

Such attacks of night terror are the result of acute or chronic traumatization, and while they leave no immediate conscious memory trace, they can become the nucleus of more or less severe pathology. In some cases, however, the night terror either extends directly into the waking state, or erupts, after a short interval, in the form of a hallucinosis. Characteristically, the process of externalization, which is typical of all dreams, remains unchanged, and these children then repeat in their hallucinations the images experienced in the night terror. Here, too, the uniformity might sound perplexing unless we remind ourselves of the universality of such symbols as small crawling and flying insects and snakes, which are the most frequent contents of these hallucinations. These are the cases which are frequently brought to hospitals and clinics, because of the panic of the child and of the parent, hallucinations being the presenting symptom overshadowing all other difficulties. Because these usually improve quickly through hospitalization or medication, relatively few thorough studies have been made or published.

A second type of visual hallucination is represented by the case of Richie. In cases such as his, the hallucinations are rarely the presenting symptom. They are brought up incidentally either in the process of the diagnostic interview or during treatment.

Richie

Eight-year-old Richie was referred because he was extremely aggressive, preoccupied with sex, often drew pornographic pictures, and bothered the girls in the classroom. His peer relationships were poor. He was constantly fighting for no apparent reason. He also had frequent nightmares and many fears.

Richie was the eldest of three siblings. His mother was a young, attractive, intelligent woman. She was severely disturbed, lost her temper easily and often, and had numerous somatic complaints. At times she appeared delusional. The father, who looked like a prizefighter, was employed out of town, coming home only on weekends. The mother thought this arrangement very satisfactory and considered her marriage a happy one. The father would have preferred to live with his family. He often accused his wife of being unfaithful. This led to arguments and physical fights which stopped when Mrs. X. attacked Mr. X. with a wooden plank.

Richie was a hyperactive child. At nine months, a fall from his high chair, the first of a long series of accidents, required three stitches on his head. At two, he developed asthma which at times required adrenalin injections. When he was five, his father accidentally dropped him while playing. On that occasion he had allegedly lost consciousness for a few minutes, but examinations proved negative.

Richie, when first seen, was an appealing, slightly-built boy, looking more like a six- than an eight-year-old. He talked rapidly as if his words could not keep pace with the pressure of his thoughts. What he said was often confused and contradictory. Noticing the dollhouse, he commented that he liked to play dollhouse with his sister. Asked how they played, he quickly shifted to fantasy. He was the father, and his sister the husband. Here he corrected himself. The father was coming home, the wife had not cooked. Then the father did not come back for several months, and when he did, he was old—100 years—and wanted a divorce. Richie then switched to playing with a fortress. He was concerned about where the drawbridge was; finding it, he wanted to know where it fit. Becoming more anxious, he wondered why it had no roof and how the soldiers would come down. He solved the problem by pulling the fire engine up and using a ladder. Becoming even more anxious, and panting slightly, he explained that the fire engine had to be pulled by a tow truck because it had run out of gas. There was an emergency, but no one knew what and where. A house was on fire. The mother had lit the oven and forgotten it. The baby was in the house. The mother had smoked in bed. She was killed already. Richie informed me that he had seen a fire, and went on to say that he had dreamed about fire. But what frightened him more were dreams about monsters. He could see them during the day, but only at home. He was quite willing to draw them, commenting that he could not understand how they could choke him as they had no hands. He went on to demonstrate how he thought they could do this. They had been with him since he was born, and would go to another person when he was dead. He could throw acid at them, but this might go through them and so get to him and dissolve him, though pouring water over him might help. He would ask his father to take him far away so they couldn't find him. At home the monsters called his name. At school he didn't see them but heard them telling him to throw things, threatening him if he didn't comply.

Asked who made up the story when he played at home with siblings, he said: "I do, but everything I told you just now is true." He wanted to become a fireman when he was grown up, and when he got old—30 years old—he would get himself a big house to live in with his husband. (This time he did not correct himself.) He would have three children, like his mother.

Richie revealed most of his pathology and underlying conflicts in the first interview. At the beginning he was able to exert some control, but almost immediately his brittle defense broke down and he became overwhelmed by almost undisguised instinctual wishes. He responded to these with increasing anxiety and a breakdown of his reality testing. Fantasy revealed confusion about sexual aim and sexual identity.

The fantasy, with its scarcely disguised primal-scene connotation, ended with the mother being killed. The monster fantasy expressed a failure of differentiation of self- and object representation: the monsters had been with him since he was born and would go to another person only after he was dead. They revealed, too, the fluid transition between dream, fantasy, visual, and auditory hallucinations. His dreams of the monster expressed both castration fear and/or his self-image as castrated. This was in line with the feminine role which he assumed in games and fantasies and which was apparent in his parapraxis. Any attempt to destroy the monster (throwing acid at him) would end with his own destruction because the monster was part of him. In his feminine identification, the father who injured him by "playing" was also the threatening monster.

At his next interview, he again said that there was a fire in the dollhouse caused by someone's smoking in bed. Richie reached into the window of the house and took out a small wooden figure of a woman. He said he couldn't get the ladder up there and wondered aloud what he should do. He thought of a net, and had the woman jump into it. After this, he reached in to bring out the furniture, saying that it was causing the fire to spread. Then he turned the hose on the house, and threw the remaining pieces of furniture out of the dollhouse. What concerned him most was getting all the beds and sofas out. He said it was something like his house where he slept in the top bunk while his brother slept in the bottom one. Mother and father had a studio couch in the room. The studio couch opened up and shut with a button "and it's always ready for sleeping; the sheet is always on the bed. One day I was in the bed and my mother didn't notice it when she was straightening it. She pushed the button, and I was locked in the bed. I had a terrible time reaching my hand around for the button. It was pretty dark in there, and I didn't like it at all." When I asked why he hadn't yelled, he explained: "There wasn't room to open my mouth." He insisted that this really happened.

This session, which followed a weekend his father had been home, was clearly a response to a primal-scene observation. It is highly improbable that Richie could have been caught inside the bed as he described. The story shows the ease with which he confused fantasies and reality.

The content of the fantasy seemed to be a symbolic representation of intercourse, a full return to the womb, and being trapped there.

Shortly thereafter, Richie elaborated on the monster theme in a story which he dictated:

> I was sleeping in bed. Then I woke up and fell out of bed on the floor and saw a monster on my bed. Someone tried to stab me with a knife. It was a nightmare. I called my mother and she came in the room. Then my father came in. My father asked me if I was scared and I told him I was, so he stayed in my room and slept on the bottom bunk. Junior went to sleep with Mom. Anyway, I had the nightmare again and fell out of bed and hurt my head bad. In the morning my father took me to the hospital and I had to have five stitches. This happened last year. After that I never had any more monster dreams.

Then Richie tried to play the trombone. He looked and looked into it, almost trying to push his head in, remarking that in a circus, a balloon had come out of a trombone, and he thought he could make that happen too.

The "monster" story represented a condensation of many events: the first accident at the age of nine months, which had required stitches (his mother had told him about this); the accident during play with the father, when he had fallen and remained unconscious; and his passive, feminine identification in the primal-scene observation. He had ended up by sleeping with his father and relegating his brother to his mother's bed. His fear of the mother as the primitive whipping object makes it likely that the monster represented both the father and the castrating phallic mother.

A few months later Richie had another accident which resulted in a skull fracture, requiring a few days of hospitalization. It had, however, no further consequences.

The occurrence of magical thinking and externalization was demonstrated during a session in which he was angry and throwing darts at a board, talking to them, telling them threateningly to stay in place. In response to a remark that this seemed like a good way to handle his anger, Richie agreed, "That's right, because you can't hurt the dartboard; it's not human." A comment on how amusing his play was because he talked to the darts and the bat almost as if they were people elicited a laugh and an assertion that it was just a game. He went on to say that the bat couldn't put itself away because it didn't have any legs with which to walk to its corner; it wasn't a person.

During the next months the sessions were concerned chiefly with Richie's attempt to establish reality testing and reality constancy, a process subject to many strains and stresses. One session following the hospitalization of Richie's sister was typical. Richie manipulated the play-dough, referring to it as the blob, a monster which dissolved everyone around. Out of the "blob" he fashioned a head which he said was himself, declaring that if he were writing stories he would write about real people, not monsters and blobs or other such things, as they do in movies or on TV. If the blob ever came, he would go to California, and if the blob reached California, he would use tear gas. When it was pointed out that he seemed to be a little confused about whether the blob really did exist or was just a story, he repeated over and over that this was just a story and he was just pretending. We can see here a move in a direction away from that of hallucination formation. The sequence now is one of hallucination-fantasy-make-believe game, or at least the pretense of a make-believe game.

Two examples of Richie's concrete thinking and faulty reality testing follow, the second pointing to his confusion about self representation. Richie drew a two-part picture. One was full of sunlight and showed a happy-looking figure whom Richie said was himself. The other half was a night scene, except that the sun was red and hadn't quite gone down. In response to a comment that the night part seemed to be so much shorter than the day, Richie explained that this was because the night went very fast when you slept. He added that the days were getting shorter and the nights longer, so that next time he would reverse the proportions.

He wrote a letter to his teacher asking her how everything was going in his absence. He then asked about John, Arthur, Curt, and Eric, and signed the letter, "Love, Richie." When he finished, he counted the names, saying that they included everyone except himself, because he wasn't there.

The following is an example of the fragility of Richie's representation of his body image. On his birthday he was given a magnetic checker set which quite intrigued him. He commented over and over that something was happening to the checkers which were getting smaller and smaller and would soon disappear altogether. This fantasy of dissolution was taken up and the discussion brought back to the reality level by the explanation that the checkers were small so that they could be taken on planes, buses, trains, and to camp. Words to this effect on the cover were brought to his attention, but he had a difficult time reading them. He knew about the magnets, and, after a discussion of why the pieces were small, he was willing to play checkers with them. Jones's (1931) concept of aphanisis applies to such fears of dissolution.

Richie's next visit highlighted his tenuous equilibrium and intense fear of his father. He rambled on about how hard it was to be in this world, which was too crowded—a displacement from his rather crowded apartment and his mother's announcement that they would all move to where father lived where they could get a bigger apartment. Richie said he wouldn't go. He moved to a friend's so as not to have to live with his father every day. "He's too difficult." Richie wasn't afraid of a new place, just of father. But if he were to be forced to go, he would rather die and live on another planet, etc. Maybe he could suck blood, and this would help him.

Richie's wish to establish his own identity, and also for an end to his exposure to the primal scene, was contained in a dream, in which the family moved to the 11th floor on June 29th and to the 12th floor on July 29th, to a bigger six-room apartment. He and his younger brother would share one room, his mother and sister would share another, and father would have a room to himself. When told that this was a rather unusual idea, Richie responded that most mothers and fathers slept together but that when he, Richie, grew up he would have his own room.

It then became certain that Richie really had to move to another city. At one of his last sessions he dictated onto a record. He accepted the fact that his medication would be increased. Before he left, however, he said that the medicine was good, but "it doesn't talk to me like you do." At this point, as though expressing his wish to hold on to the object, he asked to take the record with him. Richie responded to the impending separation from the therapist with great sadness and a severe asthmatic attack, but he did not lose his hold on reality and never again had a monster hallucination.

Richie's pathology was severe and extensive: he lacked impulse control and his judgment was poor. In addition to his somatization in the form of a quite severe asthma, he was accident prone, a symptom which, aside from the "aggression" turned against the self, also implies, as in suicide, the lack of differentiation of self- and object representation. By having the accident, he injured himself as well as the object—another example of externalization. His fear of both parents was overwhelming. His object relationships were even more pathological than those of Jane.

Jane

It was Jane's mother who asked for help with her eight-year-old daughter. The oldest daughter, Debbie, had been in treatment for some time. The mother saw Jane as rambunctious and defiant, constantly getting into trouble with other children and with her sisters, and complaining that she was not loved.

Jane often stuttered, had an eye tic, and her speech was frequently garbled. She was a bright child, did very well academically, and was well liked by her teachers, although she was a disciplinary problem. Once when she accompanied Debbie to her therapist, Jane shrieked that she was seeing bugs and cockroaches on the wall of the office.

Jane was the youngest of four children—one boy followed by three girls. The parents' marriage had been satisfactory until Mr. Y. went into military service where he apparently suffered a psychotic break. He returned home depressed, unwilling to work, and started drinking excessively. The marriage deteriorated. There were several separations and reconciliations—Jane, the product of the last of these. Mrs. Y. refused, shortly after Jane was born, to continue living with her husband, but there was still close contact between the children and their father.

When Jane was seven years old, Mr. Y. was stabbed to death in a drunken brawl. The precise circumstances were never clear because Mrs. Y. refused to get involved, would have no contact with her husband's family, and avoided the police as far as possible. Shortly before Jane came for treatment, the mother fought off all pleas that she participate in the murder trial.

Mrs. Y. was a bright, articulate, vivacious semiprofessional woman, active in the community. At the time of the referral, she was dating three men, each of whom wanted to marry her. She, however, did not want to marry again.

Aside from her complaints, she regarded her daughter as bright and cute, and as the baby of the family. Like Jane, she stuttered occasionally and had a facial tic. Jane was the lightest-complexioned member of this Negro family, taking after her father; she sometimes thought of herself as white. Apart from the therapist's observations, there was no mention of Jane's having hallucinations. Only those aspects of Jane's two-year treatment which are pertinent to my thesis will be dealt with here.

During the first session she talked continuously and rapidly, swallowing and mispronouncing words, and correcting herself. She played with a doll she had brought along. This was her favorite doll, obviously one she identified with. It was dirty and disheveled; its nose was deformed, and its name was Miserable Pearl. Jane said she did not want her mother to have another child. She would have to kill any other children that were born because *she* wanted to be the baby. What she really didn't want was for mother to remarry because she, Jane, wanted to be true to her dead father. A little later, she related, in an increasingly confused way, incidents about a friend's mother who was drinking. She commented that when she was anxious she talked continuously, and that her mother complained about it. She confided a secret which she did not want her mother to know, namely that she had a pet puppy, a female dog which she had boarded at a friend's house because her mother only liked boy dogs. The dog had "made dirty" on her friend's rug. As she told this, she excluded "Pearl" because "she's not supposed to listen in."

As so frequently happens, Jane, like Richie, revealed a great deal during the first session, both by her behavior and the content of her talk. Clearly, she was flooded by fantasies and in deep conflict. She revealed multiple levels of identification: she identified with the dirty, mutilated doll-baby but was also the mother of this baby as well as of the not-yet-toilet-trained puppy. She was also taking the mother's place when she wanted to remain true to the dead father, expressing, at the same time, the wish to retain the mother and to remain "her baby." She expressed envy and jealousy of her brother, who was mother's favorite, and denied her wish to be a boy by having (secretly) a female puppy. She expressed her murderous impulses (she would kill a younger sibling) and also expressed her horror of drunkenness, displacing this from her father to her friend's mother.

Jane's remark about the doll listening in was not only a sign of confusion between animate and inanimate objects, but the first indication of externalization (thus far in a manner not uncommon in children).

A few sessions later she talked at length about the rules and regulations she had set herself and those which mother set up for her. She mentioned that a cold had prevented her from going to the swimming pool and that her mother had prohibited her from going lest she catch another cold. She then spoke of her fear of going to the pool, as young girls got "raped" there. This fear was substantiated by her reference to a girl who, according to her mother, had actually been raped at the pool. This led into an account of two girls who had had children out of wedlock, although they had them before Jane herself was born. At one point in her story of the pregnancies, she stopped herself, fearful that she had revealed too much for her mother's liking. It is possible that the rape fantasy had been stimulated by a tooth extraction performed the day before, an incident which she described at great length, with particular emphasis on the long needle.

Her preoccupation with rape was greatly exaggerated and pointed to the existence of the fantasy wish behind this fear which played a persistent role in therapy. Her obsessive-compulsive mechanisms were not signs of an integrated superego, but rather a dependency on prohibitions by the mother. Her self representation and representation of her mother were not well differentiated. We see, therefore, on the one hand a primitive identification with the mother, and on the other, a struggle against such identification. It was also pertinent that she made a quick shift from an external prohibition to a prohibition by the mother, and from a fear of a cold to a fear of rape.

A few sessions later she mentioned that her mother had gone to a therapist because she was "crazy," not just "nervous," and quickly added that she was glad that she herself was not crazy, although at times it worried her that she might be. She then complained angrily that the school psychiatrist had asked her whether her father had been drinking.

After discussing her sibling rivalry and her need to be the youngest in the family, she expressed the thought that she would not have to worry as long as her mother was not married, but then realized that her mother could become pregnant out of wedlock too. Jane then made a baby rabbit out of clay which she called "she." She wondered whether the body should be made out of two parts—a left and a right one. It is interesting that Jane expressed her conflict about bisexuality in terms of bilaterality. In these few sessions, Jane revealed her underlying concern about being crazy, confusion about body image, her sexual aims and sexual identity, and her masturbation and castration conflicts.

Shortly afterward, Jane was concerned about a pimple next to her nose which came from "heat"—that is, from getting hot by playing excitedly with her friend. She had had the urge to scratch it, and let it "burst out," but her mother had told her not to. She had a scar on her chin from having scratched once before.

It is significant how easily her masturbation conflict and castration fear came into therapy with so little disguise. This also applied to the use of the words "heat" and "hot," and her connection of these with sexual excitement.

Many of the ensuing sessions dealt with sexual curiosity, differences between the sexes, highly exciting observations, and also the sadomasochistic aspect of her sexual fantasies. Her confusion about the anatomical differences between male and female were remarkable in a girl who had had numerous occasions to observe such differences. She also gave the impression that difference in color and its "value" was being confused with the "value" of the differences in sex.

Around this time she wrote the following composition at school:

> There was once a lad that didn't listen to his mother and so something happened to him. His mother warned him not to go near the tracks, but he didn't pay any attention to her. Thus he went walking on the tracks with Lefty.[2] Along came a train. All that he did was stand staring. You must know what happened. He was smashed like mashed potatoes. So was Lefty. What a sight. The whole neighborhood felt bad, but not Sally Goodman. She was happy because Samuel Woodwel, who was killed, always annoyed her. She should not have been happy that Samuel was killed.

Pertinent here was not only the blatantly sadistic fantasy about the boys who had annoyed her, but the fact that in the last sentence she treated the fantasy as if it were reality. Probably only in this way did she come close to guilt feelings (internalization).

Using puppets, she dramatized a fantasy about a family consisting of both parents and two children. There was fighting between the parents, with the mother first knocking the father unconscious and then a reversal of the roles because "this couldn't really happen." Mother and father were very angry with the children, hitting them when they made any request. But in the end everyone made up. This led into a discussion of Jane's father, whom she missed. She spoke of being to some extent like him, i.e., lighter than the rest of the family, but without his nice hair. This was the first time she expressed her longing for her father. However, she did so in the framework of a sadomasochistic primal-scene fantasy. She also indicated her identification with her father.

A few weeks later, Jane seemed quite restless, pacing up and down or looking out of the window. First she wanted to know whether she had asked me to remind her of something. She thought she had not. Then she took the gun, angrily fantasizing shooting an old man across the street, "even if it cost her four fingers and maybe the tip of her little finger." She told of having gone bike-riding with a boy, although her mother had forbidden it, how she lifted her legs, broken

[2] See my discussion of the concept "left and right" above.

the spikes, and hurt her leg. Jane went on to say that her mother was sick, but she didn't know why. Her mother had cramps every month. Asked if her mother were menstruating, she replied that she did not know what that word meant. But some time after, she spelled the word menstruation spontaneously. She said that her mother had explained it to her sister but not to her, because she was considered too young. But her mother had given her sister a book, and Jane had read it too.

A characteristic feature of this session was the "flood" of scarcely disguised id derivatives. The danger lay not only in their content, but in the possibility of Jane's being overwhelmed by them and by her need for motor discharge. It was typical that Jane fluctuated between knowing and not knowing, and that she included menstruation in her sadomasochistic concept of sexuality. Also significant was the weakness of the child's defenses and the externalization of her conflicts. In structural terms, the ego was not in conflict with the superego but with the environment.

A few weeks later, in a mixture of a movie story, dreams, and fantasies about a beloved person dying and being bandaged up, Jane introduced her fear of mummies. The mummy had loved someone who was killed and took for a substitute love-object a relative living many generations later—for example, Jane. This person of the present generation would "wither, her teeth would get long, she would become ugly, and the mummy would drag her down into the sea so that she would die." But the mummy would also kill the person who had destroyed the beloved many generations before. The mummy in turn was killed by the person who loved the mummy's new love. Jane would dream that she was coming home from a party with her mother, that there were secret passages where the mummy was waiting. She would hide in the bathroom with the mummy outside, but mother would open the bathroom door.

From additional material it became obvious that the killed and bandaged person was the father. The rest of the fantasy, which she told in a highly excited manner, illustrated utter confusion about her identity and her role in the oedipal conflict. The mummy was the lover of the father, and the avenger. However, as a lover, he or she was also a killer, as well as the lover and killer of Jane. In the dream, the mother seduced and failed to protect. Apparently Jane created distance by placing herself a few generations away from the father.

Jane went to the toy shelves and picked out the black and white babies. This time, she said, she would give me the white one. "How easy babies have it," she remarked while we fed them, "everything is done for them; it's a good thing we're not dolls and can live longer; we can't be given to a careless girl who just drops us and breaks us." There was apparently no safety other than that of being a baby, which is completely taken care of.

Two sessions later, Jane complained that she was hot, then commented that she had been given a game by a friend of her mother's—"a boy friend who isn't stingy." She hoped they would marry. "She needs a man; she's kind of hot." Her immediate transition from feeling hot to the mother's being hot and needing a man, offered another example of the fluidity of the differentiation between self- and object representation.

Her concern that she, her sister, and her mother might be crazy, and that a hereditary factor might exist, came up again and again. However, she excluded herself by the fact that she, her brother, and her father were the lighter ones in the family. "We have less of a substance in our blood. It is better that way." A later session took place in another room. To this she responded by concern that I might leave the clinic. She wondered about my age and then talked of worrying about being bad. Her mother was always saying that Jane would kill her, as she was a nervous woman. In the immediate context of this, she related how she had been the last person to talk to her father. He had inquired on the telephone whether mother was in, and she, on mother's instructions, had told him a lie, saying that mother had gone to work, when really she had gone shopping. The reason for this was that if father knew mother had gone shopping he would return to bother her. Jane denied ever thinking that if she had told the truth things would have happened differently. She also expressed her own fear of dying.

The theme of the father continued to come up in various ways. She used to be blond and still had some blond hair like her father had. (In reality she had dark, kinky hair.) Prepuberty problems made their appearance. Jane was concerned about her developing breasts and thought she should diet now. Her budding physical development was increasing her conflict about sexual identity. But it was mainly her conflict with her mother which was troubling her. She also wondered who was, or had been, crazy—she, mother, or father.

A mere change of environment could precipitate fear of object loss by abandonment, death, or being killed. This rapid shift was understandable because her conflict was, at least for the present, insoluble —was she responsible for her father's death, or was the responsible party the mother who made her lie? Did she really want to kill her mother as the latter was implying? With whom could she identify?

And then a new threat precipitated a crisis. The session started ordinarily enough. Jane asked me to show her some math tricks I had shown her once before. Then she went for a spin on the chair. She loved to get dizzy. She then expressed her fear of having her tonsils taken out; her mother said this was necessary because she had frequent laryngitis, but she had a "premonition" that she would die from the anesthesia. She had had the same feeling once before, at the time her aunt, who had cancer, had died. She also had "known" that her uncle would die, and she was the last in the family to talk with her father. She had had a dream, and a voice had told her not to go downstairs, although her mother had said that she could. There had been a shooting gang-fight at that time. Another time the voice had told her in the dreams not to eat fish. She had done so anyway and had almost choked. She felt that the voice gave her warnings, and if she told me whose it was, the voice would not warn her anymore. She gave me the impression that it was a protector's voice. She had started to hear it after her father's death. Here the transition from the dream to the hallucination is quite clear.

A few days later Jane said she had had a dream but could not tell it to me. She was also hearing the voice. She could not reveal whose it was, but it was telling her to go straight home. Something would happen to her today. I said that we would try to understand why she needed the voice, so that in the future she could help herself. Jane replied: "My father just said—oh now I said it and I won't hear him any more." She strained to listen and became desperate. She talked about her father's being like God, God's servant. He was immortal, and therefore she was immortal. She really had two children—one girl (Jane) and a boy, and they were in Paradise. Paradise was something different from Heaven. Father's soul would enter another man and then it would enter her. Would I come to Paradise with her? She did not want to live at home any more; maybe at a boarding school or in the West Indies. If she concentrated, she could fly from the 14th floor. That evening she would go up on the roof and take along Mary and John (two small children who were temporarily staying with Jane's family). These children had broken a radio, but Jane had been accused of doing it. Jane insisted that she could fly and that she was going to do it. I told her that I would not let her harm herself, and that I would call her mother so that she could protect her. Jane agreed. She refused an appointment for the next day, as she would not be here. I arranged with her mother to meet Jane and discussed the possibility of hospitalization. Jane replied that she would go to the hospital anyway for a tonsillectomy the next day. The operation did not worry her because by that time she would be in Paradise. Jane's fear of the tonsillectomy, especially the anesthesia *which meant loss of control, mutilation, and death*, had precipitated the crisis.

Her fantasies about her father, her failure to reach object constancy, to go through the normal separation-individuation process (Mahler, 1965) which was paralleled by a confusion of self- and object representation, were all interfering with normal progress which would entail accepting in prepuberty a feminine role and choosing a new love object. The violent death of her father and her guilt feelings about it had made such a transition impossible.

Her conflicts had interfered with the normal mourning process for her father. She had therefore regressed to a state of complete refusion of her self- and object representation. The father had really become part of herself, because she was the last one to hear him. She could also hear now, in her hallucinations, his protecting voice, so that inside and outside could no longer be distinguished. To admit her hallucination and to confess to the therapist whose voice she was hearing meant to her the threat of giving up the father by exposing her fantasy to reality testing. Verbalization in therapy would also mean the transition from primary to secondary process. In her hallucinatory fantasy she could preserve her oedipal wishes.

The two children she "had" confirmed her bisexual self-image. In the transference, she both dreaded and wished to be freed from the fusion which threatened to engulf her to the point where she would give in to the wish for refusion by committing suicide. But into this wish was woven the omnipotent fantasy of being able to fly and the wish to replace her fantasy father by the therapist in the role of the protector.

In the sequence trauma-response-hallucination which characterizes all hallucinations, we can recognize a distinction between predominantly auditory and predominantly visual hallucinations. Both auditory and visual hallucinations represent an externalization of percepts and thoughts, a lack of distinction between inside and outside, and therefore also a break with reality. There is, however, a basic difference between the two types. Auditory hallucinations are linked with word representations and therefore indicate a higher level of organization. They are more complex, and their content mirrors, as already mentioned, all structures of the mental apparatus. Auditory hallucinations express in words libidinal and aggressive demands that we attribute to the id derivatives, compromise-formation under the influence of defenses, and verbalization of what we assume are demands of the ego, or of objects who function as supplementary egos, and of the not-yet-internalized superego. Their content can therefore be punitive, seducing, comforting, threatening, etc. All visual hallucinations are more primitive. They are less ego syntonic, and express a more regressive state. The most severe regression is seen in "hallucinosis," in which the break with reality is total, thus representing overwhelming danger and resulting in outright panic.

Most of my observations of hallucinations in children stem from diagnostic interviews or short-term evaluation. Auditory hallucinations have been the type by far most frequently reported. The content of the hallucinations has shown little variation and been more or less stereotyped. A few examples:

Richard, a nine-year-old boy, hears a man's voice "just outside his ear" which tells him to throw stones, do bad things, and jump out of the window.

Michael, nine years old, says, "I hear a voice that tells me to kill myself, but I don't do it, I don't listen to it; it tells me to kill my mommy, but I don't do it.

Alexander, nine years old. The voice tells him to steal, to do bad things. At times he has to obey the voice, at other times he doesn't have to. He also hears a good voice inside of him telling him, for example, "put it back."

Gerald, nine and a half, hears the voice of a man who teaches him spelling, helps him with geography and comments on what he does.

Arthur, eight and a half, hears the devil's voice "all the time." It tells him to set fires, and not to talk. He *has* to do what the devil tells him.

Ronald, ten years old, has been hearing the devil's voice since the age of four telling him to curse and steal. If he doesn't obey the voice he gets a pain in his head until he does so. If he keeps himself very active he doesn't hear the voice.

Chester, nine years old, says, "I can hear a man's voice. It speaks to me on Monday and Tuesday. It tells me to stay away from school. I don't have to listen to the voice, but I do."

Thus, the voices could be seductive, urging the child to perform forbidden acts, but they could also be protective and benevolent.

Some of these children also reported visual hallucinations. Richard saw monsters coming through the curtains at night; Gerald saw "a little old white man" with a long, white beard, tall green cap, and pink hair; Ronald saw a small red devil and big monsters in the dark that touched his head.

Unlike the cases of acute hallucinosis, these hallucinations did not produce panic; they were rarely among the presenting symptoms and were usually elicited only by direct questioning. The children would say that monsters and ghosts scared them so they hid under the covers. The appearance of the devil or of people was rarely connected with panic, and seemed rather an attempt to give the voice heard a concrete source (see Gerald and Ronald).

While I could not, on the basis of such short-term observations, convincingly elucidate all the underlying disturbances in ego function, these children showed a certain uniformity in their family histories and presenting symptoms. Most of them came from broken homes. They had been exposed to violent quarrels and fights. They often had siblings fathered by different men. Their mothers were frequently unable to take care of them because of depression, psychotic illness, or the need to work. They were partly brought up by their grandmothers or placed in foster homes or institutions for various lengths of time. Praise and punishment, what was permitted, and what was forbidden, were handled arbitrarily. Severe corporal punishment was the rule. All of these experiences were conducive to the kinds of ego disturbances already described for Jane and Richie. The usual presenting symptoms were stealing, lying, fighting, poor achievement in school, obscene language, truancy, running away from home. Almost typically, the hallucinations disappeared after a few days of hospitalization.

DISCUSSION

As stated above, hallucinations can occur only when certain ego functions are impaired. I have chosen from my case histories material which illustrates such disturbances.

That hallucinations are in the first place a disturbance of perception is a truism. In "The Unconscious," Freud (1915d) stated that the understanding of hallucinations must begin with an understanding of negative hallucinations. Implicit in this statement is the fact that perception must be, at least partly, an active process.

Which part of the external stimulus is perceived and which part of such a percept is stored as a memory is the outcome of a complex intrapsychic process. The functioning of the perceptual system is under the influence of an endless variety of memories. It is therefore understandable that some distortions of perception are more or less universal and that memories hardly ever represent a photographic replica of the external stimulus. A certain amount of perceptual distortion is apparently acceptable without disruption of the inner equilibrium. In hallucinations this equilibrium is seriously disturbed. Achievement of the constancy of perceptual differentiation, especially between inside and outside, is much more complex than the maturation of the functional apparatuses.

An intrinsic part of the learning process is based on the integration of perception, memory, language, and the motor apparatus. The work of Piaget (1951) and his school, J. Bruner (1966) and his collaborators, Granit (1955), Galambos (1956), and others has contributed to our understanding of these processes. We are now relatively well informed about the timetable for the development of cognitive functions in which the differentiation between self and nonself is an essential step. The work of A. Freud (1965), Mahler (1963), Spitz (1966), Winnicott (1965a) and others has centered on other aspects, such as the capacity for and development of object relations, the achievement of object constancy—which in turn is essential for phase-adequate identification processes—for the normal course of individuation-separation, for self-object representation, and therefore also for a normal development of these perceptual processes which guarantee the vital differentiations between inside and outside. Pathological development of these processes is the result of innate and environmental factors.

Can we pinpoint the pathology of such functions, essential for the development of hallucinations, and can we detect this in the case material I have presented?

I must first emphasize that *some* of this pathology can be found without the occurrence of hallucinations.

All my cases show a severely disturbed, highly ambivalent relationship to the mother. They were, on the one hand, consciously afraid of their mothers and, on the other, desperately desirous of their mother's affection and deeply afraid of separation. The fear of the mother was justified, insofar as most of the mothers were punitive, frequently resorting to severe corporal punishment. The mothers, who frequently had been deserted by their husbands, were often severely depressed; some were psychotic. The inconsistency in their behavior, in their "do's and don'ts," made it difficult for the children to predict their mothers' responses. The unconscious fearful fantasies thus found reinforcement in reality. The highly ambivalent relationship to the mother colored all the children's other relationships. Sibling rivalry, envy, and jealousy played a tremendous role. This attitude extended to peers and teachers as well.

Most of the children had been exposed to excessive sexual stimulation. Primal-scene observation was the rule rather than the exception. Uninhibited sex play was frequent. In addition, there was "violence in the air." Loud arguments and physical fights between adults was a regular occurrence. Sexuality was therefore almost automatically seen as an aggressive act. Early overstimulation resulted in an intense need for masturbatory activity. Because sex and violence were inseparably linked, castration fear was markedly heightened. Extensive sexualized and aggressive fantasies disrupted the development of phase-adequate ego functions.

The relationship of these children to their fathers was even more abnormal. Neither sex could develop the type of oedipal conflict one encounters in an "average expectable environment" (Hartmann, 1939). Separation, divorce, remarriage, and abandonment were frequent.

Because of the highly ambivalent relationship to the mother and the distorted, disruptive influence of excessive early sexual stimulation, the normal process of identification had been impeded. Confusion of sexual aim was compounded by confusion of sexual identity. Penis envy in girls and castration fear in boys were excessive. An alternation between "identification with the aggressor" and passive surrender was prevalent. Parallel with this, we encountered highly exciting sadomasochistic fantasies which were frequently acted out.

Not only anxiety dreams, but nightmares and night terrors were frequent. We know from Freud (1918), Jones (1931), and Stern (1951) that night terror can by itself become a traumatic experience with self-perpetuating uncontrolled anxiety as a result.

It was unavoidable that these children should have failed to develop such crucial ego functions as neutralization of aggression, impulse control, frustration tolerance, and the ability to limit anxiety to "signal anxiety." All of which, in turn, contributed to a lessened attention span, to mention only one function essential to the acquisition of skills and information.

I previously quoted Freud to the effect that externalization is one of the chief elements in hallucinations. Externalization as a pathological phenomenon goes hand in hand with the failure of the process of internalization. Successful internalization, which leads to the formation of autonomous ego structures, to realistic self representation, and to the development of the superego, is impossible in the absence of stable object relationships and of models for identification. Successful internalization is also necessary for individuation-separation, for differentiation of self- and object representation, and for a stable differentiation between inside and outside.

It may be stated that many, if not most, of these ego disturbances can be found in children who develop severe phobias, behavior disorders, severe inhibitions, etc., but had never hallucinated. *However, in all of my case material—and this holds true for case histories published in the literature as well—I found traumatic situations or a single trauma had either precipitated the hallucination or served as an "organizing" element.* (See the discussions of the consequences of infantile trauma by Greenacre, 1952, 1964; Lipin, 1963; and others.)

The result of any trauma depends on the nature of the traumatic stimulus and the state of the responding organism. In the case of children, it depends on their age, the phase of their psychosexual development, and particularly on the stage of development of all the ego functions discussed above. This interplay between the underlying developmental pathology and the hallucinations can be clearly traced in the cases of Jane and Richie.

With Jane, the organizing element for the auditory hallucination was the violent death of her father, and specifically the fact that she was the last to hear his voice, along with her gnawing doubt about whether the lie she had told him at her mother's insistence was in some way responsible for his death. In the language of the primary process, both she and her mother had murdered the father. She was helplessly torn between her contempt and hatred for the psychotic, alcoholic, nonsupporting father and her wish for identification with his maleness and some of his other physical attributes.

Freud (1917c) has convincingly described how normally the lost object is given up through partial identification with it. The disturbance of Jane's capacity for internalization made it impossible for her to deal with her conflict through the normal mourning process, or to develop a reactive depression. She had to resort to the primitive defense of undoing and denial. By externalization she could, by means of her hallucinations, hold on to the distorted idealized father image. She was afraid of verbalizing whose voice she was hearing because of her dread of having to give up the fantasy and expose it to reality testing. She would also have had to admit to herself that her father was dead. The threat of the tonsillectomy, which was being insisted upon by her mother, had precipitated a crisis. She was torn by conflicting impulses and fears. The operation and the general anesthesia represented both violence and complete passivity which increased her sexual fantasies, clearly represented in her dreams at this period.

On her own, she could cope neither with external danger nor with her instinctual demands. She therefore had to turn in her hallucinations to her idealized protective father. On the one hand she turned for help to her transference object, who represented reality to her;

on the other hand she dreaded losing the externalized fantasy object by exposing it to reality testing. She therefore resorted to an even more encompassing fantasy, including father and a father substitute, which permitted her to wish for a bisexual oedipal child.

What I have called the organizing trauma had resulted, in Richie's case, not only in the derailment of his ego development, but in hallucinations, visual in character. There were two sets of traumatic experiences. One was the constant exposure to primal scenes, with the added factor that Richie could predict, expect, dream, and fantasize these scenes because they occurred regularly when father came home for the weekend. The second set was traumatic in the most real sense of the word trauma. He had suffered three head injuries, two of them directly connected with his father. The boy could not integrate the primal-scene observation with anything approaching a normal psychosexual development. In these observations, both the father and the mother were equally overwhelming, threatening figures. Any meaningful identification was therefore impossible. The two screen memories—one of being caught in the folding bed and the other of a head injury which followed a nightmare—were symbolic representations of the two organizing traumata.

The monster was a condensation of father and mother. It appeared both in his nightmares and in his hallucination. Because the hallucination is a form of externalization, his statement that the monster was always with him is an illustration of his confusion between self- and object representation, between inside and outside.

I have indicated that the main purpose of this paper is to discuss such ego impairment as makes the hallucinations possible. I will therefore add only a note on the nosological aspect of hallucinations in childhood. From my material I was able to draw conclusions similar to those of Bender (1954), Despert (1948), Kanner (1935), Sachs (1962), etc., to the effect that hallucinations in childhood are, per se, not an indication of a psychosis, specifically not of schizophrenia. The age of the child and his position along the developmental line of various ego functions play an important role in the appraisal. Although visual hallucinations appear to be a more regressive symptom than auditory ones, neither of them is a diagnostic or prognostic sign as such. Each type must be evaluated within the context of all other functions.

CHAPTER 17

The Analysis of a Phobia in a Latency Child

Marjorie Harley, Ph.D.

To submit to this volume the following report of the analysis of a childhood phobia and the concomitant transference neurosis which emerged has seemed fitting on two counts. In the first place, there are features of this infantile neurosis which would appear to correspond with certain of Max Schur's findings with respect to the adult phobic: specifically his emphasis on (1) the contribution of pregenital and preoedipal factors to the final clinical picture; (2) the gratification obtained through the erotization of anticipatory anxiety; and (3) the ego's basic fear of helplessness in the face of the overwhelming anxiety within the traumatic situation, itself (see M. Schur, Chapter 4, This volume).

Second, for several years I have drawn relentlessly and persistently on Max Schur's knowledge in my attempts to justify my skepticism and questions concerning the usage of the term *transference neurosis*. It was largely under the impetus of these discussions that I arrived at what I thought was its original, historical meaning, that is, a neurotic symptom formation, arising from regressed conflicts activated by the analytic situation and centered on the analyst or his surroundings (Harley, 1968). It is in this limited sense that I shall utilize the term in the following account of the course and determinants of a dog

---

Dr. Harley is Supervising Child Analyst and Faculty Member, Baltimore-District of Columbia Psychoanalytic Institute.

Adapted from a paper read to The First Annual Meeting of The American Association for Child Analysis in Topeka, Kansas, April, 1966.

phobia which was dissolved in the third year of a child analysis, although the analysis, itself, extended over a five-year period.[1]

To start from the beginning: Anne was her mother's first child. The mother, herself a first-born, quite admittedly had been in an intensely competitive situation with her younger brother. When first she saw her infant girl, she experienced a sense of enormous disappointment which she was unable to explain even to herself. Later, she told how she had found herself weeping because her baby had seemed so ugly, an attitude in marked contrast to that she had experienced toward her younger child, Amelia, born when Anne was not quite two.

The mother described Anne as a restless and irritable infant. Not knowing how to ease the child, she found herself constantly "jamming bottles into her mouth." Anne was given no preparation for the advent of her sibling until the moment of the mother's departure for the hospital. Upon the mother's return home with her new infant, Anne welcomed her mother warmly and for a period was excessively clinging, utterly ignoring the baby's existence for some weeks. When Amelia was two months old, her nurse left, and the two children were placed in the same room. From then until she was past three, Anne paid almost nightly visits to the parents' bedroom. This behavior ceased when the mother moved Anne to her own room. She had never been able to defend herself against her sister or other children. When they took her toys or hit her, she dissolved helplessly into tears.

Although Anne's weaning was certainly not early, it would seem to have been abrupt. In short, she "weaned herself" not long after Amelia's birth. The circumstances were as follows: The mother had been reading a story book which contained a picture of a little boy holding a Teddy bear. Anne asked where his bottle was, and the mother said that, like her, he was too old for a bottle and had thrown it away. Anne's response was to ask the mother to throw her bottle away, which the mother promptly did. Immediately after-

[1] In a previous publication (Harley, 1967), I presented excerpts from the first nine months of this child's analysis. In the earlier report, my aim was to point up some of the initial transference manifestations through which defense analysis was mediated and which then led to the establishment of a therapeutic alliance and to the uncovering of certain aspects of the child's masturbation conflict, particularly as the latter pertained to her struggles with the preoedipal mother. I mention this first report by way of an apology to those who may have read it, and whom I now must ask to endure the monotony of some repetition.

ward, Anne began to cry, protesting she wanted her bottle back, but her mother explained repeatedly that it was too late; that is, Anne had asked her to throw it away, and she had done so. Henceforth the child never again requested the bottle.

Around the time of Anne's weaning, the mother reinstituted toilet training which she had first attempted in the early stages of her pregnancy with Amelia. She had abandoned this previous attempt after five or six weeks because of the child's strenuous opposition. Now, again, and in contrast to her compliance in the oral sphere, Anne put up a fierce resistance. There soon followed a period of such severe withholding that suppositories were resorted to. When these yielded no result, and upon the pediatrician's advice, an enema was administered one morning by the father, while the mother held the frantic child forcibly on the bathroom floor. That same afternoon, urged by the pediatrician to take a firmer stand with respect to training, the mother insisted that Anne remain on the toilet seat for almost two hours, alternately pleading and screaming at her in angry frustration and threatening her with another enema. The forced movement which Anne finally produced resulted in an anal fissure. From that day on, she was bowel- and bladder-trained, but became ever more submissive, and, up to the time of her analysis, displayed a lingering, albeit slight, tendency toward constipation when under stress.

Anne first evinced some discomfort in the presence of dogs shortly after Amelia's birth. Her maternal uncle, in an endeavor to avoid a future problem, and in the mother's presence, walked the child up to a large dog who snapped, but did not actually bite her. It was following this incident that the child began to show some "real fear" of dogs. After the events of the enema and the forced movement, this fear increased, and for several months thereafter Anne was afraid that a zebra in the toilet would bite her. It was not until she had passed her fourth birthday that her fear of dogs reached phobic proportions.

The mother was intelligent and sensitive, quick-tempered and controlling and genuinely eager to be a good mother. The father, also highly intelligent and sensitive, had a special affinity for Anne, empathizing, if not identifying, with her inability to express aggression and with her tendency to withdraw into the background in the face of competition with her sister. As he put it, she had not yet lost her spirit, but he was afraid she might. Although at the time of referral the mother seemed to be more highly cathected by Anne than was the father, on the surface the child's relationship with her father appeared to be smooth, and, for the most part, she showed him friendliness. This friendliness, however, struck me as possibly being tinged with an overcasualness which might well have served a defensive function.

In my two initial evaluation hours with Anne, she revealed her severe castration complex by depicting herself, through play, as a little boy. This little boy, however, was a sorry little boy, unable to hit back and unable to control and direct the splashing of his many tears. She also revealed her enormous aggression against her mother which at one point broke through the protective barriers of play and overwhelmed her with anxiety. And, in a direct communication, she conveyed her masturbation conflict in a derivative form, but nonetheless with manifest anxiety. There were times in these first two hours when she showed a happy exuberance, and when I could see that her father's observation had been correct: she had not yet lost her spirit. But there were other times when I sensed that her apparent inner freedom and spontaneity were not always quite real; rather they seemed almost measured or learned. Finally, there were times when I was especially impressed with what I can best describe as an aura of resignation, as something akin to a depressive quality and even hopelessness. A major factor in my decision to recommend treatment rested on my feeling that the child was complying too readily to her mother's demands, and that this factor, along with the related conflict around her aggression, might well result in the erection of constricting defenses in latency which would further impede the growth and expansion of her own individuality and her own self-forces. Eventually the mother herself expressed her awareness of Anne's overconformity when she volunteered her conviction that in some way, unknown to herself, she had forced the child to become too resigned and submissive to her.

Anne was told she was coming to see me because I would help her with her fear of dogs. She was also told that I had a dog, but had promised to keep him locked up—a promise which she was able to accept on faith. She introduced her symptom in our first hour together. With my help, she was able to say that she was not afraid a dog would bite her or jump on her; it was just that a great big frightened feeling swept over her, and she did not know why. She was eager to be rid of her symptom, and so, with this advantage, we began.

A major portion of the first year of Anne's analysis revolved around her conflict with the preoedipal mother. In the early weeks of treatment, as in a dream condensation, she reflected herself through the boy, girl, and baby dolls. At other times, the boy and baby were her little sister whom she saw as more loved and more adequate than herself. These children were exaggeratedly good. When I remarked on this, I was met with an adamant denial. As I began to interpret her denials, two themes appeared in her play. The first followed my interpretation of her denial of painful affects, evoked by her jealousy of other child patients, and appeared to relate to Amelia's birth. In this play, the mother went to the hospital, but upon her return was replaced by a dog who took over the maternal role. The other theme involved a baby who was forced to be good by "a bad person." But the baby revolted and killed the bad person. Now Anne expressed, through two dreams, the dangerous aspects of her mother who was "dressed up like a wolf," and who bit and hurt her child. She showed her equation of tears with urine and she also revealed her fantasy that she had been hurt in her vagina by "the bad mommy," but that "a good doctor" (that is, the analyst) had effected a cure. She pretended the stuffed dog was dangerous because a "bad mommy" was inside him, and attempted to attribute a benign character to my dog by asserting he was good since he had a "good mommy" inside him. It was at this point that Anne removed her underpants upon going to bed at night.

For several weeks thereafter, the analysis was characterized by Anne's state of exuberance in which she made clear her high hopes that I would endow her with the phallus which in numerous ways she indicated her mother had both denied her and robbed her of, but which she had bestowed on Amelia. When she began to assimilate that neither was it my function nor had I the power to grant such a wish, her negative feelings came to the fore. Simultaneously she could no longer maintain her assertion that my dog had a "good mommy" in him. Extremely anxious one day when she accidentally broke the toy dog's leg, she accepted my comment that when she destroyed something that belonged to me she felt almost as though she had hurt me. She then implored me not to go to the back of my apartment. I remarked she was especially afraid my dog would be angry today. Admitting this, she added with a defensive laugh, "I got you and your dog confused." Very seriously, I said I thought she really had.

Soon after that, Anne gradually introduced her masturbation conflict. First she climbed up on the high shelves, thus showing me she was tempted to do dangerous things. Then, as I related the dangerous fires she had so often mentioned to the little fires of excitement in herself, she proceeded to show me how she could make magic with her hand by turning on the light of my electric heater. She asked if the eraser would come off the pencil, should she rub it hard, adding, "If I were here at night would you lock your dog up?" and then answered herself by declaring, "No, you wouldn't." Here, it seemed, she was indicating the possibility, not only that my dog would punish her for her masturbation, but that he also reflected her own dangerous sexual excitement against which she feared I would not protect her.

Finally, she arrived for her hour with a little stuffed rabbit which she put into bed under a blanket. When I suggested that being under the blanket might give the bunny a safer, more private feeling, she showed me a big hole on his bottom, explaining his winding machine was gone. Before I could respond, she said, "*I* really broke it long, long ago. I pulled it out while I was rubbing him 'down there.' He felt so soft and furry." I recalled how she had been telling me of the wonderful fires of excitement she could make with her hand, and how she had wondered if the eraser would break if she rubbed too hard, and how she had broken the bunny's winding machine when she rubbed him "down there." I told her I knew, and I thought she knew too, that she was worried because she felt she had done something bad by rubbing herself "down there." It felt so good, yet seemed so bad. Maybe she was afraid she had been broken or would be broken "down there." "You're very, very wrong," she insisted.

Next day, however, she wore a tiger mask to her hour and impersonated the bad lady inside the tiger who would bite me for my naughtiness. I feigned fear lest the tiger-lady bite off my hand because I was naughty, adding I was just a little child and she seemed so big and powerful; and I expressed the wish that I had a tiger mask to make the scary tiger-lady into the one to be scared. At this, Anne removed the mask and insisted, "If you think I wore the mask because of yesterday you're wrong—and if you think the tiger has anything to do with dogs you're more wrong." In essence, I merely said that I might be all wrong, but that she was a very clever child to have such an idea.

Anne's ultimate understanding that behind her identification with the aggressor lay her fear of the consequences of her masturbation resulted in her enactment of her Peter Pan play, which occupied many weeks, and through which she conveyed her aggressive masturbation fantasies in relation to the phallic mother. Briefly, I was Captain Hook—though several times she slipped and called me "Mommy Hook"—and she was Peter Pan who hated all mothers. Repeatedly she stole my sword, emphasizing my helplessness in the face of her invulnerability. My missing hand was a condensation of both the missing genital and the instrument through which the forbidden act of masturbation was implemented. Occasionally she would shift my role to that of Cruella, who had caught and skinned the Hundred and One Dalmations, reiterating this was a terrible, terrible lady, more scary than a dog; for, she admitted, she would be "scareder" of a really bad lady than of a dog.

After I had linked her aggressive masturbation fantasies with the act, and on the day before Amelia's birthday, Anne demonstrated her masturbation and concomitant anxiety by pulling at the crotch of her tights and tearing them, apprehensively awaiting my response. As we discussed her feelings about what she had done, she admitted she did not know which worried her more: the worry of doing something she felt was naughty or the worry that I would be angry and hurt her for her naughtiness. In her next appointment, which immediately followed her sister's birthday, Anne came with her stuffed dog, Jamie. Jamie, as she had told me in past hours, was her ally in her nighttime struggles with the bad witch. Obviously she had brought Jamie both as a representation of her masturbation and as a source of protection. There soon ensued in this hour a tirade because I had not given her a consolation present on Amelia's birthday, reaching such a peak of anger that she put on her hat and coat and started out my front door. In the following session, after referring to the "awful yesterday," she volunteered she had shown "a secret to Dr. Harley," thus providing me with the opportunity to interpret that she felt I had not given her a consolation present because I did not like her after she had shown me her secret.

For some time thereafter, Anne referred to her secret as marking herself as a dirty, messy child, and said repeatedly, "Let's pretend I'm two—no, I don't want to." Simultaneously, she expressed the fantasy that I might have a baby and go to the hospital. Finally she volunteered that she recalled one happening when she was two, namely, her sister's birth. When we had discussed what sad days those must have been for her, she indicated quite explicitly her wish to exclude all other children from my office and thus to be my only child. She further expressed her hope of achieving this status by being the opposite of messy and dirty.

It was also in this context of "let's pretend I'm two" that there were three new developments in the treatment. The first of these was that Anne now became Wendy in the Peter Pan game, while I was cast as Wendy's mother. Like Peter Pan, she flew away to Never Never Land because I was such a bad mother; and once, like Peter Pan, she flew home, only to find the windows barred because I had had another baby. Several times she had me place beside my chair an imaginary dog who would try to chase and bite her for being such a bad child and hating her mother. Throughout this game she exclaimed with full affect, "I hate you; I hate mothers." Her stated reasons for her hatred were that I regarded her as a messy child, that I had replaced her with another child, and that I was a bad witch who had taken away her red balloon.

The second development occurred during the same hour in which she had first assigned me the role of the depriving and dangerous mother. Anne became afraid to flush my toilet and admitted her fear that my dog would jump out of the toilet and bite her. This symptom, which was confined to the analytic situation, that is, which referred only to my toilet, and which lasted many weeks, seemed to be a repetition of her earlier fear that a zebra in the toilet would bite her.

The third development was that Anne related the following anecdote. She had gone to the zoo with her mother when she was two, and an elephant had grabbed her long, red balloon. This part of her anecdote was, in fact, true. But she went on to say that the elephant had squirted water into the balloon until it had burst. I sympathized with how awful it must feel to be filled up with water, fearing one might burst and being helpless to do anything about it. She agreed and admitted it was awful for her, too, because it was her own balloon and "it was mommy's fault." Then, reflectively she said she thought the elephant had been a boy elephant and asked if my dog were a boy, informing me for the first time that her mother had let her uncle walk her up to a dog who had tried to bite her. I suggested she must have thought her mother was like Wendy's mother and like me, who sent that dog after her instead of protecting her from danger. To this comment, she replied with surprise, "You know, I'll bet I did." Now it seemed that in addition to serving as a representation of the mother, the dog might also be assuming the role of the dangerous father to whom the mother had exposed her. But for some weeks to come, the mother and the mother-dog were to occupy the forefront.

A short time after Anne had narrated her elephant fantasy, she overheard a three-year-old, whom I had seen in consultation, repeat to her mother, "I was angry at you and I thought you were angry at me." No sooner had we entered the office, than Anne remarked that this other child seemed around two and asked how I could help two-year-olds, since it must be hard for them to tell me things. I replied that sometimes it was easier for a two-year-old to tell things than for a child who was almost six, whereupon Anne interrupted me to say, "I know why. A two-year-old doesn't know it's wrong to be angry at her mommy but a six-year-old does." In ensuing hours we discussed how a child who was almost six would worry if she were angry at her mother, and slowly Anne was able to tell me that sometimes she did not like her mother; that sometimes she felt her mother had had Amelia "because she was mean and thought I was ugly and dirty"; and that sometimes she, that is, Anne, thought Amelia was a boy. "Not really," she hastened to say, "that part is a dream[!]." Ultimately, we got back to how it could also be a big worry for a two-year-old to be angry at her mother and how the feelings Anne now experienced, when she was almost six, had originated when she was little.

After the emergence of some of the genetic material relating to her sister's birth, her resentment against her mother, and her anal trauma, Anne was able to approach my dog, albeit gingerly, for her dog phobia was by no means dissolved. This step, I felt, was in part the result of the child's unconscious obedience to her mother's hope that she overcome her phobia before the summer, as well as a reflection of her wish to please me, both of which determinants I tried to show her. It seemed, however, also ascribable to the events within the analysis with which we had partially dealt. Significantly, on the day Anne first told me of her wish for a direct encounter with my dog, she became quite aggressive in the transference, threatening to make "pee-pee and b.m." on my floor. She also asked if my dog were toilet trained, if I would punish a child if she hurt my dog, and if the dog himself would bite the child in retaliation. In this hour, she made it quite clear that the dog reflected her own oral and anal destructive impulses against her sister and mother, and that he also represented the mother-analyst who would retaliate and punish her for these impulsive strivings. Before she had me bring the dog to her, she took care to clean all the paint brushes and to wipe up the paint from the floor, making the room, as she put it, "nice and clean" for him.

For some time thereafter, at the outset of each session, Anne requested my dog. Reversing passivity into activity, she accused him of being messy and dirty, declared she hated dog smell, and threatened to give him a "shot" which would cause all his "pee-pee and b.m." to come out. She was also furiously jealous of him, which we could relate to her jealousy of Amelia. In this connection, we were also able to discuss how babies and even little children bit when they were angry and jealous, and Anne seriously explained that they had not yet learned to hit; that was why they bit. When the dog yawned, Anne exclaimed with real feeling, "That was terrible when he opened his mouth—worse than Cruella and Captain Hook." Eventually she could see how both her projections of her own oral-aggressive impulses and her need for punishment contributed to her fear of being bitten by the dog. I would inject at this point that all this occurred while Anne was still afraid to flush my toilet.

Later, when Anne had obtained some relief from her preoedipal aggressive conflicts with her mother and when she had been able to express some of her feelings of sadness in connection with what she had felt to be the loss of her mother, oedipal material assumed a more paramount position in the analysis. She introduced this trend by asking if my dog were a father-dog, that is, did he have a wife and puppies. Before I could answer, she strode to the bathroom, for the first time in weeks flushed my toilet, but ran swiftly back, obviously manifesting erotized anxiety while shouting, "He almost got me!" "That animal?" I asked, and she replied, "Of course." She now told how sometimes after her appointments she thought "privately" to herself, and lately seemed to remember that when she was little she had been afraid an animal in the toilet would bite her. She was not sure; maybe it was a dream. She knew it had not been a dog, or a tiger, and then suddenly exclaimed, "It was a horse with stripes; I think he was in the cage with the elephant in the zoo." The hour was up, and, as she left, she announced excitedly, "The telephone wires are crossed."

Next day Anne arrived again with Jamie. She did not ask for my dog, but volunteered that she was planning to get married when she was 16; or, she said, she might do what I did and live with a dog instead. She decided that when she was 16, she would not be afraid of dogs, adding that when telephone wires were crossed people heard what they were not supposed to hear. She asked if people could dream at night when they were awake. I replied they could, in that they could imagine with their thoughts when awake just as when asleep. In a way, I said, that kind of dreaming seemed just as real as a sleep dream; but then next morning, when people were up and dressed, it could seem as unreal as a sleep dream. She listened so attentively, I dared to continue with the idea that sometimes, even when something really had happened in the nighttime that had seemed very scary, in the daytime, when one was dressed and doing everyday things, it might seem as though it never had happened, that it had been just a dream. Anne said thoughtfully, "I think that happened to me," and told how once she had hidden beneath the sideboard in the dining room in the middle of the night, had watched her parents eating, and they had had a "terrible fight," not with words, but a "real fight, hurting each other." Out of this communication emerged her wish to go into her parents' room at night and her fear of what she might see; she would shut her eyes tight and hold her ears tight, she said with a shudder. At the end of the hour, she earnestly told me that while I was with my dog at night, she had her own secret with Jamie. Hugging him close to her, she leaned over the side of the chair so that she was almost horizontal, lightly brushing her genital region against the edge of the chair. At that moment, I felt certain that the child had witnessed intercourse.

The end of the first analytic year was approaching, and much of the remaining hours was taken up with Anne's expression of fears in relation to the oedipal father. I should say here that Anne had occasionally alluded fleetingly to the father in the earlier months of treatment. Her initial reference was one in which the mother was banished and she lived alone with the father. At that time, however, he had appeared to serve more the function of a benign maternal figure who fed, dressed, and in other ways mothered his child. Further, there had been a session with primal-scene innuendos in which he had appeared as the victim and the mother as the castrating victimizer. Finally, Anne had made a few references to the father as being subjugated to the mother and unable to do other than what she wished. In scrutinizing my notes, I also began to wonder if there were not times when the oedipal father was disguised by the Captain Hook phallic mother. By and large, however, these earlier references to the father had been peripheral to the central theme of the mother and had seemed not yet usable in the analysis. Among other things, it was the mother who had been the prime "shot"- giver.

Now, rather than being the mother's agent, the father became the shot-giver in his own right. Having emphasized repeatedly how she could not wait to be 16 and married. Anne's denials crumpled, and she admitted she wanted to remain a child forever and never get married. The content of the sessions was replete with fantasies of the terrible things a husband could do to his wife with his sword and especially with his shot-giving equipment, which would not only cause all the "pee-pee and b.m." to come out, but which also would result in a terrible "boo-boo" (that is, injury) to the vagina. In fact, she said, a shot in the vagina would be much worse than being pierced with a sword, for if a husband tried to kill his wife with a sword he would be put in jail. On the other hand, if he gave her a shot, the police would not even know it. Her wish to be a boy and have the dangerous penis for herself asserted itself defensively against these oedipal fears in numerous ways and could be interpreted as she spoke directly of her anxieties about penetration and childbirth. In the transference I now became the oedipal father who would castrate her with my sewing needle. At this point in the analysis, I felt Anne had made explicit that not only had she organized pregenital and phallic conflicts in relation to the preoedipal mother around her anal trauma, but that this earlier experience had taken on the meaning of an oedipal sexual attack. I was later to learn that there was more to it than this. I would also add that Anne's fear of my toilet flush, which had initially made its appearance within the context of oral, anal, and phallic conflicts primarily in relation to the preoedipal mother, faded away as the primal scene and oedipal material moved into the foreground. And as my dog became the father-husband, once more she could not tolerate his presence.

After the summer vacation, to all intents and purposes this oedipal material had gone underground, and preoedipal and pregenital conflicts once more dominated the analysis. I attributed this in part to a renewed regressive defense in the face of her developing latency, but I also knew that these earlier problems had by no means been sufficiently worked with. Although the mother reported that the phobia had decreased in intensity, I believed this might be, at least to some degree, a reflection of the child's efforts to please her, or else of the mother's proneness toward denial. I also noted that, with me, Anne avoided any mention of dogs in general, and of my dog in particular.

In any event, once again material related to her anal trauma entered the sessions, indeed flooded them. Many of the hours were held in the bathroom where she placed the baby doll on the floor and, again reversing passivity into activity, repeatedly and relentlessly gave it "shots in the vagina." On the one hand, of course, the doll reflected herself; on the other hand, it represented Amelia to whom she would do what had been done to her.

During the next five and a half months, Anne and I covered considerable ground. In short, some of the events around her toilet training, especially the experiences of the forced enema, were reconstructed for her and the accompanying affects gradually restored. We went over her anger at her mother for trying to force her to make "b.m.," as though she were taking something of her own from her, and her wish to get back at her mother by making even more of a mess; the hurt she felt at Amelia's birth, and the oral aggressive strivings thus evoked; her fear that her mother did not love her because of her naughty feelings; her anal-vaginal confusion and castration fantasies which were related to the enema and the anal fissure; and, last but not least, the well nigh unendurable feeling of helplessness which must have overwhelmed her. We worked together on the externalization of her conflict over her aggressive impulses associated with her masturbation, by way of her image of the bad punishing mother, and she began to see more clearly her reasons for displacing this mother image onto the dog: that is, she would rather think he, not her mother whom she also loved, was the bad one. At this stage she could see the dog as representing the bad punishing mother and Amelia more clearly than as the reflection of her own impulses which she feared she could not control.

As we talked more about the various ramifications of her hostile jealousy of Amelia, Anne said repeatedly, "The dog is Amelia; that's very important." It was at this juncture that she reinstituted her play with the baby doll. The doll was patently Amelia, while the Yogi Bear who, as she equally frankly explained, represented herself, performed flagrantly sadistic acts on the helpless baby: administering shots, "pulling and biting off the baby's penis," and beating it mercilessly. I would add that during this play Anne bade me sit in the consulting room while she remained alone in the play room, with the door between open, so that I had a clear view of her activities. Mistakenly, at first I saw this seemingly endless repetitious play as a resistance and interpreted it as such, although without success. Actually, it was to lead to the uncovering of an earlier event and one which Anne evidently had experienced as another state of helplessness.

The monotony of this play was finally broken when Anne began to manifest more concomitant affects, both of mounting excitement and anxiety, as she made Yogi Bear enact his aggressive sadistic behavior. I remarked on how uncomfortable it would make not only Yogi Bear, but also a child, to feel swept away by such excited, angry, hurting feelings. She responded by saying she knew I would keep my dog locked up until she was over her fear. I replied that perhaps my keeping my dog locked up meant to her my keeping her excitement locked up for her. To this, she responded by putting Yogi Bear in her drawer and locking it herself. I remarked she was showing me that she felt she had to take care of her own excitement; maybe she felt I had not helped her enough to control that angry excitement toward Amelia; maybe she felt I should not have stayed in the other room as though I were leaving her alone with her excitement. Anne did not reply, but I felt she had assimilated what I had said.

At this time, a younger child, who generally preceded Anne, had to remain alone in the waiting room because her mother was invariably and unavoidably late in calling for her. As a result of this arrangement, Anne was frequently in the waiting room alone with this younger child for a few minutes between the two sessions. As might be expected, the other child had come up in the past in connection with Anne's jealousy of my other child patients.

In her next hour, no sooner had Anne entered the office, than she expressed criticism of the other child's mother for making her wait alone. Anne's criticism soon spread to include me for allowing this to happen. After all, I was supposed to understand children. When I suggested that Anne's reaction to being alone in the room with the smaller child might have something to do with her anger against Amelia and her fear of this, she produced a "very, very scary" dream—actually a dream within a dream.

> I dreamed I was telling you about a terrible dream. There was a cage with lots of wild animals and the keeper of the cage forgot to lock it and left the house. It was awful. I thought the wild animals would get out.

For some hours to come I used this dream to help Anne see these wild animals, as well as my dog, as her own pregenital aggressive impulses against her mother and sister. She was now able to assimilate these interpretations. We also discussed how I might be the keeper of the cage who left her alone with this other child, without having helped her to lock up her excitement. Finally, I linked up this present anxiety with the days when she was little, alone in the room at night with Amelia, and afraid then of her uncontrollable anger. She might have feared she would hurt Amelia, even though she did not want to and might well have feared, too, that her mommy would not love her for this. Perhaps that was one reason why, as her mommy had told me, she had kept going into mommy's room, looking for protection against her anger and making sure mommy still loved her. But in response to all these interpretations, Anne would inevitably confront me with: "I can understand that, but you wouldn't go out of the house and leave me alone; you're always in the next room." Or again, "But mommy never went out of the house; she was always in the next room." She kept reverting to that aspect of the dream in which "the keeper of the cage *had gone out of the house*," at the same time maintaining her assertions that "mommy never left me alone in the house." Ultimately, however, she began to waiver in these assertions, asking me to fortify them, as it were, by protesting, "*You* don't think she did leave me alone in the house, do you?" When I told her that maybe she herself was wondering this, she denied the possibility on the basis that the house in the dream was a little house with "no upstairs," while her home was in a big apartment house and so "the dream had nothing to do with mommy leaving me alone!" But when I pursued the meaning of the "little house," she came up with the association to the family's summer cottage. With the aid of information volunteered by the mother, I could now ascertain that Anne had indeed been left alone in the summer cottage when she was three. One night, eager to talk with a neighbor's wife, the mother had slipped next door, leaving the two children asleep in their room, certain she would hear their sounds through the open windows should they awaken. When she returned home, Amelia was sleeping soundly, but Anne was sitting up in her bed, crouched against the wall, white and trembling, obviously in a state of near or actual panic.

After Anne and I had gone over the meaning of this event, both from the aspect of being left alone at the mercy of her own "uncaged" animal impulses, which she feared would hurt Amelia, as well as from the aspect of her painful fear that her mother had abandoned her because of all her bad feelings, Anne apparently gave up her dog phobia in the outside world, that is, the outside world as distinct from the analytic situation.

This news came to me as a surprise, although the parents obviously assumed I would have been the first to be aware of it. In addition, the parents reported that Anne was much freer, had given up her excessively conforming behavior toward her mother, and now stood up to Amelia and her peers. While I felt this glowing report of Anne's behavior might be somewhat exaggerated, I was convinced that some change of this nature had taken place. And the description of Anne's casual attitude toward dogs on the street, her ability to play at her friend's house with their dogs, her new relationship with the superintendent's big dog, left me with no doubt that the phobia was not operating outside the analytic situation.

As for Anne, vis-à-vis myself, I was aware that she was becoming increasingly conforming and eager to please. In addition, and what was most striking, she had in no way revealed to me she was not afraid of dogs on the outside. If anything, she was even more afraid of my dog, taking care to ask the maid each day if he were surely locked up and making no mention of him in the sessions. I had several guesses about all this. One was that she feared I would disapprove. In the first year of treatment when she had first expressed a desire to approach my dog, I had told her that she might be trying to force herself to overcome her symptom prematurely to please me. She had construed this suggestion in such a way that when, a few weeks later she requested a cat (at the height of her phobia she had also expressed a fear of cats), she concealed this event from me lest I disapprove. In addition, the thought naturally occurred to me that she might have the fantasy that were she to give up her phobia she would have to terminate the analysis. This concern, in fact, had also expressed itself in the past. There was the possibility, too, that her preoedipal hostility for me in the transference had not been sufficiently worked with, and that rather than tolerate her ambivalence toward me, she had transferred the negative aspects to my dog, with all the implications that this had for the externalization of her conflict. Finally, I should underscore that I was keenly aware of the still existing oedipal problem with which we had done relatively little work. This last turned out to be the most valid of my explanations.

At any rate, during the next 15 months, Anne's analysis moved slowly and laboriously and, throughout this period, her dog phobia remained centered exclusively on the analytic situation. What constituted the most overwhelming resistance was her need to please me. I had been alerted to this potential danger from the outset but, so far as I could ascertain, it had entered into the analysis far less than I would have anticipated in the first year and a half of treatment. On the few occasions we discussed this problem, it had been mainly in relation to the mother rather than to myself, and Anne had made quite clear that one of its ingredients was her fear of her own aggression. Therefore, in my attempt to handle this powerful resistance, I employed the tack of approaching her fear of my not liking her lest she have angry feelings toward me, and then again, her fear lest her angry feelings emerge unless she do only what she felt I wanted her to. But my attempts were to no avail.

It was not so much that Anne produced no material during this period. On the contrary, she dramatized a renewed version of her Peter and Wendy play and brought up a number of dreams. This material, however, had so empty, even sterile, a quality, and her productions seemed so predominantly aimed at proving herself a good patient, that I felt the content hardly usable. Nonetheless, I became aware that this content had an unmistakable oedipal flavor. In her Peter Pan play she was Wendy going off to marry Peter. The theme of her dreams and daydreams was primarily that of the bad robber who would carry her off; and once, when the robber began shooting, the mother-figure who was with her fled, and she was left alone at the robber's mercy. In conjunction with this robber theme, she introduced the subject of my dog, first saying with joking defensiveness that he was the robber, then referring to him, as she had in the first year of treatment, as my dog-husband, and finally revealing her fantasy that I had an actual husband who resided in the rear of my apartment. Again, as in the first year of analysis, she asked if I would lock up my dog were she to come to me at night, adding I would be too busy with my husband to think about her. But this time she introduced another thought. Her real fear, she said, was that my dog would pin her down with his four paws so that she would not be able to get up, and then he could do terrible things to her. He was so jumpy, always jumping on her when he had come into the room when she was five. Did I not remember? I would here inject that my dog was extremely old and lethargic, with hind legs so weak he would have been incapable of jumping on anyone.

These fantasies of being "held down" by my dog-husband, and more occasionally by my "real" husband, became increasingly prevalent, as did Anne's accompanying erotized anxiety when she narrated them. Also, I noted that her desire to please me seemed to be lessening as I interpreted that possibly she felt a little jealous, even angry, at the idea of my having a husband or a dog-husband. I added that for her I thought these two, that is, my dog and husband, were very much one and the same. Now Anne introduced the idea that when she was held down she would get a shot and volunteered that "maybe I have these fears because of the enema mummy and daddy gave me." While I went along with this notion in part, and tried in various ways to interpret the sadomasochistic gratification she experienced in such fantasies of daddy doing such exciting things to her, and mummy letting him, I was beginning to realize the likelihood that once more the child was using this earlier trauma as a screen. Probably because I was influenced by the fact that her repetitious play with the baby-Amelia had led to the uncovering of another disturbing event, I pondered the possibility that "being held down" might relate to a further reality happening other than her anal trauma. When I mentioned this thought to Anne, she declared I "sure was getting cuckoo ideas." Nonetheless, she began to introduce a new trend of behavior which consisted of removing the shoe and sock from her right foot, first drawing attention to her exposed foot and then, excitedly feigning fear, attempting to conceal it under her dress. At the same time, she began to talk facetiously of being held down by me while my dog-husband gave her a shot in the foot and, more accusingly than facetiously, of my allowing him to do this, just as I would not keep him locked up if she came to my house at night.

At this juncture Anne produced a series of dreams involving brilliantly lit rooms (an obvious reversal but also possibly related to the "blinding" effects of a traumatic shock) in which "terrible things" were going to be done to her by a man, or men, and invariably with "mommy" or "some lady I don't know" (but with some identifying features of the analyst) present. In the final dream of this series the "terrible things" assumed more specificity, that is, she was going to have her toe cut off, a fantasy possibly deriving some of its raw material from an actual event when a little friend's toe had been amputated as a result of having been caught in the spoke of a bicycle wheel. It was in this context that I remarked perhaps something had once actually happened to her foot which had frightened her, whereupon she produced a distorted memory of having been given a "shot in my foot" by "a man I never saw before" in a dark room with "mommy holding me down and letting him hurt me." The actual event was corroborated by her mother and had to do directly with her right foot. In brief, her foot had turned slightly (something I had neither noticed nor initially been told of). Both parents had been loath to institute any therapy for this, but had agreed to an X ray. Anne, accompanied by her mother, had put up a fierce resistance, screaming in terror when the doctor had attempted to take the X ray. As in the case of the enema, she had been forcibly held down by the mother. In terms of the timing of this event, it had occurred when Anne was undoubtedly well in the oedipal period, that is, when she was four years old and, significantly, just prior to when her fear of dogs had developed into a full-blown phobia.

The analytic efforts were now bent toward helping Anne see the links between this event, when again she must have felt so helpless; the events of her enema and forced movement when she actually had got her "boo-boo"; and her frightening, yet exciting, primal-scene fantasies of hurting (castrating) and being hurt (castrated). I further showed her how her image of the X-ray doctor had fused with her image of her daddy and with that of my husband. Thirdly, I based a number of interpretations on her underlying wish that I expose her to this kind of excitement from my imaginary husband, yet her enormous fear of this too; and on the fact that my dog represented the husband-daddy. As she had done in the case of her mother, I said, probably she had substituted the dog for her daddy, since then she would not need to be afraid of the daddy she loved. Lastly, I underscored how she wanted me to protect her from her wishes to have this uncontrollable excitement with my dog-husband-daddy by keeping him locked up.

Although I worked for some time, and in various ways, toward loosening the pregenital sadomasochistic elements in her oedipal relationship, she clung to these with an almost desperate intensity. It was not until I had interpreted her desire to maintain these fearsome fantasies, not only as a defense against closeness to the oedipal father, but also as a means of keeping me allied with her in this struggle and thus avoiding the arousal of her hostile oedipal jealousy toward me, that she gave up her fear of my dog. On the day she requested him in the office, and after she had casually petted him and shown us both that she was unmistakably over her fear, she asked truly wistfully: "Do you suppose that if a really big dog came along, bigger than Gerome (Gerome was my dog's name, and he was an extremely large dog)—do you think then I might be afraid of dogs again?" We exchanged knowing looks after I had asked: "Do you mean a dog as big as daddy?"

It seems somewhat superfluous to elaborate on the various determinants of Anne's phobia, as these pertain to conflictual contents, for in this respect I believe the material of this presentation has spoken for itself and has shown the four meanings which the dog served: (1) the fearsome preoedipal mother; (2) the threatening oedipal mother; (3) the dangerous oedipal father; and (4) the projection of the child's own forbidden pregenital and genital aggressive and libidinal strivings. Throughout, her erotization of anxiety and her ego's fear of helplessness (numbered by Schur among the features of phobias) were conspicuous, as was the contribution of pregenital and preoedipal conflicts to the development of her phobia, which then reached its final edition in the oedipal phase.

Although there are many gaps in our knowledge of genetic factors until well into Anne's second year, certain data are known to us. First, there is the factor of the mother's need to control almost every facet of the child's activities—a need which became clearly elaborated both through the work of reconstruction and by the mother herself during the course of the child's treatment, but which I did not detail in this necessarily sketchy and incomplete account of the analysis of the phobia. As a result of the mother's attitude, the child's developing sense of her own ego autonomy was undoubtedly impeded.

More specific interferences with the development of this sense of her own inner controls may be traceable to the nature of her weaning and toilet training which occurred during, and again immediately following, that vulnerable second year of life when the child ordinarily is deeply involved with the task of individuation and separation

(Mahler, 1965). With respect to her maturational timetable, these events were certainly not premature, but they were indeed sudden and abrupt, robbing her as it were of a growing awareness of her own capacities, emphasizing her helplessness, and allowing little leeway for a gradual and thus soundly based mastery of her instinctual strivings. They further occurred when she was in a state of narcissistic hurt immediately following the birth of her sibling whose advent she also had been given little opportunity to assimilate. It would seem almost inevitable that massive amounts of oral and anal aggression, rooted in her earlier oral-anal experiences, but compounded by these recent traumatic events which she was ill-equipped to contain, were now mobilized and further contributed to her need to comply with her mother's over-readiness to assume the role of auxiliary ego. The result was a kind of dovetailing of the mother's excessive need to control and the child's possibly equally excessive need to seek this control. In this connection, Anne gave a significant response to a comment I made in the first year of her analysis. She had made clear in several ways that she repeatedly asked herself when faced with a question of "right and wrong"—and I would add parenthetically that much of her behavior was structured in these terms—"What would mommy want me to do?" Finally, I commented that I thought she hardly ever dared wonder what she, herself, might want to do. She replied by flexing her elbow to show me her muscle and stressing how strong she was, so strong that were she to get angry she might really hurt someone badly.

Much later (when she was nine) Anne went to a "sleep-away" camp for the first time. She had a wretched summer, was detached, relatively affectless, somewhat immobilized, and unable to function adequately in areas in which she had already proven her proficiency. On her return to analysis, we could understand this reaction in the light of the anxiety she had experienced while so far away from her mother, upon whose presence, or near-presence, she relied to prevent her from losing control over her aggressive impulses and to assuage her attendant and intense anxiety. In fact, most of the last two years of her analysis was spent on this ego problem. But so subtle was the interplay between mother and child, that at the termination of the treatment I could not be certain whether Anne's apparent freedom and independence were based on true structural changes, or whether this behavior was essentially another reflection of a continuing over-adaptiveness to her mother's demands, now designed to meet the mother's (and analyst's) standards for mental health.

One more word concerning Anne's insufficiencies in her sense of ego control: after the analysis of her phobia, she and I began to note minor acts of delinquency which pointed to certain superego lacunae. Wangh (1959) in particular has noted such superego deficiencies in the phobias. In his patient, Wangh attributed this state of affairs to an initial environmental lack of opportunity for sound ego-superego identifications. In Anne's case I have seen this ego-superego problem from a somewhat different angle. Specifically, it would seem that the sense of a separate, relatively autonomous self was not sufficiently established to allow for that process of internalization of *partial* identifications which in turn lead to the furtherance of ego and superego development. Instead, the tendency to rely on the mother as an auxiliary ego, and later as a superego figure, was exaggerated and prolonged. As a corollary, her proneness toward externalization was likewise exaggerated and prolonged, as was her inability to draw a demarcation line between potential danger and a traumatic situation (M. Schur, Chapter 4, This Volume).

As for the question of the transference neurosis in this child's analysis, twice a transference neurosis would seem to have manifested itself: first, in limited and circumscribed form, when she was afraid to flush only my toilet; and second, in a less limited and more extensive way, when she transferred her dog phobia exclusively to my dog. In the first instance, the transference neurosis appeared within the context of repressed pregenital and preoedipal conflicts which, as these became uncovered, were directed toward the analyst; and it faded away as primal scene and related oedipal material emerged. In the case of the transfer of the phobia to my dog, the transference neurosis came to a termination when the repressed pregenital destructive components of the oedipal conflict which were linked to traumatic events had been analyzed around the person of the analyst and the transference neurosis did not recur when *undistorted* oedipal longings, less contaminated by pregenital factors, were now able to achieve expression (quite possibly for the first time) in relation to the original objects.

In view of the foregoing, the following postscript is pertinent. Following the analysis of her dog phobia, Anne's tender affectionate feelings for her father began to unfold markedly, as did her hostile jealousy toward her oedipal mother. One weekend, when she and her father had taken a walk alone together, she had noticed a poster soliciting funds for a T.B. drive, and her father had explained that T.B. was a sickness of the chest. That evening Anne expressed the fear that she had T.B. and vomited. After overcoming her reluctance to tell me this lest I be angry, she was able to describe her fear in some detail. As she told how each time she thought of contracting T.B. she gagged and vomited, she promptly proceeded to vomit in my bathroom. This symptom was finally analyzed when, after speaking of other children's confused birth theories, Anne confessed that when she was a little girl she had thought the baby grew in the mommy's chest. The heart was in the chest, she explained, and she had thought that by lying in the chest the baby "would get its life" from the heart. It then also became clear that her fear of my anger had resulted from the externalization of her intersystemic conflict over her forbidden wishes for the oedipal baby. But despite recurring transference manifestations within the analysis, the original objects were the primary targets for the libidinal and aggressive strivings she was now experiencing within the context of her oedipal constellation. And concomitantly, her defensive need to please was again expressed toward her mother and others, and no longer exclusively centered on me. In other words, the transference neurosis, although a useful therapeutic tool during a particular phase of the treatment, by no means dominated the whole of the analysis. But I would nonetheless add that the occurrence of so relatively extensive a transference neurosis as this has been unique in my practice of child analysis to date.

CHAPTER 18

The Use of the Developmental Profile for the Prelatency Child

Martin A. Silverman, M.D. and Peter B. Neubauer, M.D.

APPLICATION OF THE PROFILE—PETER B. NEUBAUER, M.D.

During the past two years we have been applying Anna Freud's Developmental Profile as a tool for organizing information in a long-term study of eight preschool children. Our eventual purpose is to try to construct an outline of the child's functioning at this period of life. The use of the profile enables us to pinpoint the areas of development for which appropriate data are already available, while at the same time exposing the areas that are as yet uncharted or require further exploration. Thus we consider the profile to be more than a mere instrument for data organization. We expect it to lead us to see important new correlations between psychic structure and functioning which will clarify our basic understanding and assumptions. This, in turn, should suggest new questions to help us test metapsychology and review clinical findings within the framework of psychoanalytic theory.

Anna Freud's profile in *Normality and Pathology in Childhood* (1965) provides an over-all system of organization, but leaves the future detailing to be determined according to the particular develop-

Dr. Silverman is Research Psychiatrist, Child Development Center, New York City.

Dr. Neubauer is Chairman, Section of Child Analysis, Division of Psychoanalytic Education, Department of Psychiatry, State University of New York, Downstate Medical Center, Brooklyn, New York; and Director of the Child Development Center, New York City.

ment period that is assessed. Over the years, the profile has been applied to various age groups, and appropriate modifications have been proposed to take account of the specific aspects of each developmental phase. In the case of the preschool child, however, because development proceeds in a series of small but significant steps of ever increasing complexity, many more than the usual number of details will have to be added if the profile is to carry the requisite information to allow us to draw the "developmental line" for this period.

Perhaps the most fruitful effect of our use of the profile so far has been the search for a new ordering of data that in the past has been subsumed under clinical considerations or in the discussion of the dynamic processes. A closer look, demanded by the outline, gave focus to new areas of exploration. Even at this comparatively early stage in our project, the material we have gathered has already suggested a number of topics for a fuller profile; for example, the area of individual variation in developmental progression, or differential reaction to different environmental stimulation, and fantasy-action balance. We needed to add the topic of affect because we have found it to be a major factor in the clinical diagnostic summary; the mood swing, elation or affective restriction, the depressive quality, and the level of anxiety appear to be significant orientation points for the statement of normality and pathology.

One topic which seems to be fundamental to the success of the entire project is the evaluation of the information sources. The younger the child, the more we are dependent on information from other than clinical sources, i.e., parents and teachers, etc., to give us the developmental history and the child's relationship to the environment in which he grows. The clinical interview and direct observation of the child, no matter how carefully undertaken and even when conducted over long periods of time, by themselves cannot give us enough data for a developmental assessment. Nor is the information available to us from therapy sufficient for the purpose, since at this age analytic treatment of the child has usually only just begun. Even when therapy can reveal the major constellations of conflicts, it cannot supply data on other aspects of development. The question, "What kind of information can be provided by which source?" therefore becomes a central issue, and a systematic appraisal of the data that each of the various sources of information could be expected to contribute to the development profile is essential.

In the course of our studies, we have found the developmental differences between boys and girls during the preschool period to be much greater than suspected. We therefore evaluated the available information indicating these differences in order to determine how they contribute to later phallic and oedipal formation. Significant differences were discovered in symptom clustering and rates of development. Variation of ego function and preferences in channelization were so revealing that we decided to make an assessment of sex characteristics before the phallic phase. The existence of significant sex differences during the preschool period obviously has important implications affecting the evaluation of criteria for the respective developmental expectations of boys and girls.

In the present paper, however, we will deal with these topics only insofar as they relate to that area we have selected for preliminary discussion here: namely, the progression-regression balance.

The very aim of the profile, to assess pathology and normality against a yardstick of development, constitutes a direct challenge to our ability to understand the process of regression, fixation, and progression. For our inherent difficulties in diagnosing the preschool age group stem precisely from the fluidity of the child's psychic organization during this period and from our consequent inability to make predictions. Certainly, where disorders are severe, diagnostic statements can be made, but when these statements are checked against the child's developmental capacity, new questions immediately arise for which at present no diagnostic category exists. A fuller knowledge of the progression-regression balance is thus a prerequisite for valid developmental assessment.

Just as it was the application of the profile that originally pointed up the need for further studies in many areas, so the results of our exploration have, in their turn, indicated a need for the profile's enlargement to accommodate the new information. It is not our intention, however, to formulate specific recommendations at this stage of our project. The notes which follow are therefore in the nature of preliminary formulations and require further testing, not only by the study of more children but, more important, by the continued assessments of the same children throughout each succeeding phase of their development. Only when we are sure of what constitutes significant data in each phase of development, only when we know the range of individual variations, will we be in a position to make recommendations for the expansion of the profile.

EVALUATION OF DEVELOPMENTAL PROGRESSION AND REGRESSION—MARTIN A. SILVERMAN, M.D.

Anna Freud (1945) has demonstrated that diagnostic assessment of children is most meaningful when carried out according to developmental rather than symptomatic considerations. The hallmark of psychological health in the child is not freedom from symptoms, but optimal progression toward mature drive- and ego organization. Our longitudinal study at the Child Development Center of eight children between three and four-and-a-half years of age, in which we have been using Anna Freud's Diagnostic Profile (A. Freud, 1962, 1963, 1965; and Nagera, 1963), has led us to consider some of the difficulties in applying this developmental approach to the very young child. The following discussion will be limited to consideration of some general questions concerning the use of the Diagnostic Profile with this age group and is divided into two parts: (1) discussion of the issues involved in identifying the pattern of over-all developmental progression in the very young child, and (2) examination of the specific problems involved in assessing fixation and regression at this age. It is our belief that the developmental fluidity characteristic of these children is responsible for most of the diagnostic difficulties and uncertainties. Methodological capacity to map out these fluid patterns facilitates the more specific tasks of identifying and evaluating the significance of fixations and regressions.

THE PROBLEM OF ASSESSING DEVELOPMENTAL PROGRESSION

Development in the three- to four-and-a-half-year-old child is characterized by rapid, fluctuating changes in an evolving and as yet incompletely formed psychic apparatus. There is wide individual variation in drive and autonomous ego endowment and in rates of maturation and development. Patterns of drive and ego organization are characterized by shifting reorganization so that new configurations are observable at the same time as derivatives of previous drive- and ego-configurations are still in evidence. Development does not proceed in a smooth progression but in a series of irregular and overlapping progressive and regressive movements. Some investigators suggest that the pattern of expression of the various zonal consolidations is not only highly specific to each individual child, but is predetermined at birth. As Greenacre (1954a) has pointed out:

> We are used to speaking of the oral, anal, phallic and genital phases as though they were a series of fairly discrete stages in a regular time table of successive development. It is certainly recognized, however, that there is a great overlap in these phases of development, and that a certain flexibility of the schedule increases the adaptability of the organism.
>
> It may be, however, that this overlap is even greater than we have customarily thought: that in fact all lines of activity are present in some degree at birth or soon thereafter, but rise to a peak of maturational activity at different rates of speed. It is the maturational peak and its relative prominence in the total activity of the individual organism which marks the *phase*; and the succession of the maturational peaks which creates the appearance of a succession of phases [p. 20].

The observer of the three- or four-year-old is confronted by a fuzzy picture of overlapping and oscillating organizational patterns, in contrast to the relatively clearer picture available at a later stage of development, when time has smoothed out the peaks and troughs of the various developmental curves. The younger the child at the time of observation, the less available (as a rule) are data on the forthcoming changes and crystallizations of the oedipal phase, and the more multipotential are the evolving organizational patterns. Autonomous ego endowments have not in all cases reached a stage of sufficient expression for their adequate appraisal. Stimulus-response patterns, preferred receptive and expressive channels, and *Anlagen* of later defensive modes are not always clearly definable. Developmental assessment bearing reasonable predictive value can nevertheless be carried out with a method combining historical, cross-sectional, and longitudinal approaches.

HISTORICAL DATA REQUIRED FROM THE PARENTS

Paradoxically, information on the first three years after birth is even more essential at three-and-a-half than it is at a later age, when greater crystallization has taken place and investigators can reconstruct earlier trends from their later effects. Hence, inferences drawn from direct observation and from data supplied by parents and teachers of necessity play a larger role in assessment than might be the case at a later time. Moreover, although psychoanalytic investigation has been carried out with a number of very young children, providing important data about early fantasies, object relations, defenses, etc., there are limitations to the investigator's ability to draw reconstructive conclusions from therapeutic work with very young children, so that it is worthwhile and necessary to supplement knowledge derived from analytic investigation with that derived from direct observation (Kestenberg, 1956).

From the parents, we need information on constitutional factors, the environmental circumstances within which the *Anlagen* have developed, and the modifications that have evolved. If we have these data, we can draw inferences from certain quantitative or qualitative variations which might present themselves in different areas. For example, evidence of a significant intensification or shift in certain patterns in response to specific maturational or environmental influences will alert us to possible points of fixation which threaten to impede progress or to persist as potential attraction points for future regressive movements. The following clinical example illustrates how early variations can serve as danger signals of later disorders.

F., a three-and-a-half-year-old boy, had been a subject in an infant study, the report of which included an isolated reference to low frustration tolerance, motor perseveration, and toeing outward in the earliest months. F.'s parents also disclosed that, between the ages of 10 and 24 months, he had sporadically become very interested in opening and closing doors, and that between two and two-and-a-half years he had a tendency, when tired or irritable, to bump into walls and trip over his feet. These data, extracted from a profusion of historical information, alerted us to the possibility of an organic disturbance, despite the absence of any clinical evidence of organicity at three-and-a-half years. Careful observation and study over the next six months revealed a neurologically very mild but *developmentally* highly significant aphasic disorder. Painstaking identification of the specific components of this disorder not only clarified certain puzzling aspects of F.'s development, but led to specific remedial intervention in the educational process.

After early historical data have been gathered, the next step is to compile a cross-sectional profile of current patterns of functioning. Inasmuch as this can be done with the combination of observation, interview, and psychological testing ordinarily used in child-study today, no detailed discussion of the process is required here.

STUDY OF THE MUTUAL INFLUENCES IN THE PARENT-CHILD INTERACTION

Because of the preschool child's special vulnerability to influence from his objects, we have to pay particular attention to his environment and to his object relationships. The ego's attitude to the id, while derived from multiple sources, is still significantly related to the need to comply with parental standards of behavior and performance in order to ensure the love of the primary objects. It is necessary, therefore, to scrutinize the interaction between the child and his objects so as to elucidate all the factors which influence the balance between progressive and regressive forces. We need, for instance, to determine the way in which parents ally themselves with their children's progressive and regressive trends. Parents do not react the same way to different lines of activity in their children. They encourage advancement in some areas and exert an infantilizing effect in others. They also have varying reactions to the *same* lines of development during different phases in the child's development (M. Kris, 1957). The following case illustrates how information on the psychological state of the parents during different phases of their child's development assisted us in pinpointing developmental interferences influencing the child's later structural configurations.

C., a three-year-old girl, presented a pattern of marked ego restriction, overcontrol, unusually intense visual activity, and eating disturbances which persisted (with some modification) over the next

18 months. Intense phallic envy was also observed. History revealed that during the year after C.'s birth, her parents had had serious marital difficulties and that her mother had been depressed and extremely erratic in the feeding situation. At times she failed to respond to her daughter's needs; at other times she intervened inappropriately, so that C.'s level of oral, tactile, and kinesthetic stimulation varied widely. Moreover, during this period, the doctors had performed several painful probings of the child's lachrymal ducts, from which her mother had recoiled in horror.

The effect of the early intrusions and traumatic situations partially explains the precocious structuralization, oral-sadistic fixation, and unusual cathexis of the visual sphere observable at three years. The last phenomenon appears to be related in part to the direct traumatization of the eyes, and in part to a splitting of the oral and visual aspects of the disturbed nursing experience, a splitting which contributed to the development of acute vigilance in reaction to the mother's unpredictability.[1] To some extent the intensity of C.'s phallic envy was understandable in terms of the vicissitudes of her early relationship with her mother. Her intense yearning for the lost breast must be related to mother's intermittent unavailability during the first year, and to her having been weaned abruptly from the breast to a cup after 10 months of repeated prolonged (30-45 minute) feedings. Then too, C. had always been acutely jealous of her only sibling, an older brother who was his mother's undisguised favorite.

Whereas the child is subject to the influence of parental pressures, his role in the parent-child interaction is not a purely passive one. The child possesses, at each successive phase of his development, a significant capacity to influence environmental responses to him (M. Kris, 1957). If he is able to provoke environmental responses that provide a high degree of preoedipal satisfaction, for example, his impetus to seek more advanced kinds of gratification will be correspondingly reduced. In this context, it is especially important to be able to distinguish children who can consistently satisfy the expectations of their parents while simultaneously experimenting with new ways of reacting to other objects, from those who have developed rigid patterns of interaction which they must follow in their relations

[1] This follows a formulation of Ernst Kris (1956a).

with all objects. The capacity to appraise objects and respond differentially is an indication, at this age, of the ego's flexibility and freedom of action. A child who can act so as to ensure a minimum of tension in its relations with both the primary objects and later objects is obviously in a much more fortunate position for coping with developmental pressures than one who must react to all objects uniformly (Nagera, 1964).

THE NEED FOR SERIAL PROFILES

It is not sufficient, particularly where the very young child is concerned, merely to compile a detailed history of the earliest developmental trends and construct a cross-sectional profile of current functioning. Hartmann (1954), referring to the "phase-adequate neurotic reactions of the child," states that "what appears as pathological in a cross-section of development, may, viewed in the longitudinal dimension of development, represent the best possible solution of a given childhood conflict" (p. 34). We have found that a single cross-sectional profile of a child in this period of life can be misleading—usually in the direction of underestimating the ego's resilience, or failing to take proper account of variations in developmental rates, which in turn naturally leads to a more ominous prediction than the facts warrant. On the other hand, a series of cross-sectional profiles, each one covering consecutive periods of several months, provides useful data concerning the direction, magnitude, oscillatory range (progression is not linear), and mutual influences of the different areas of the unfolding personality. Serial observation, in helping to elucidate trends, is the most effective procedure for investigating this complex period. Our longitudinal study has only been in progress for a year and a half, but we have already been able to see how even a second profile can greatly clarify a situation.

An investigator, in his first profile on J., a boy of almost four, was impressed by apparent excessive physical inactivity or passivity which suggested strong pathological regressive tendencies. A second profile, drawn six months later, revealed strong activity in the mental sphere, in the form of unusually good powers of observation, reasoning, and problem solving, which had not been previously observable.

The early impression of inactivity resulting from not enough information and lack of appreciation of the style of ego functioning was thus rectified on the basis of additional information gathered during the second investigative period.

A final comment on the interpretation of the data is required. It is clear that the conclusions we can draw during this stage of the child's life are in the nature of inferences about certain trends within the over-all developmental timetable. Awareness of these trends guides the investigator in determining the areas in which additional or more specific data are required before more specific diagnostic conclusions bearing predictive value can be reached. Assessment, for this age group in particular, is not a static process, but is always a dynamic and open one, in which each new clarification points the way toward the gathering of additional information which will illuminate still another aspect of the child's development.

THE PROBLEM OF ASSESSING FIXATION AND REGRESSION

As has been stated, manifestations of early drive- and ego-configurations coexist in this age group with those reflecting higher levels of organization. Delays in development, persistence of early forms, and regression to earlier levels signify pathological trends only when they interfere with the development of the total personality, or of some of its components, so as to impede adaptational processes. It should be emphasized that the individual timetable of development needs to be mapped out before meaning can be ascribed to any cross-sectional data. For children in the three- to four-and-a-half-year age group, general norms of progression exist only in very broad terms, and the range of individual variation is so wide that each child must, to a large extent, serve as his own control.

Examination of the correspondence among the different rates of progression of the various lines of development (A. Freud, 1963), allowing for each child's individual range of progressive/regressive fluctuation, provides us with a picture of the degree of evenness or unevenness of developmental progression. Significant developmental unevenness alerts us to the possibility of defects in ego equipment, which are not necessarily congenital, as "equipment is not a static but a dynamic force" (E. Kris, quoted by M. Kris, 1957), maturational imbalances, environmental interferences which partially inhibit development, and fixation of regression. Uniform lag in progression of all modalities indicates an unusually slow, although not necessarily foreboding, rate of over-all progression.

Fixation points need to be identified, as Nagera (1964) has pointed out, not only in terms of the developmental level involved, but with regard to the specific form that the fixation takes:

> We speak of fixation to a given component instinct, to a phase of libidinal and aggressive development, to a type of object choice, to a type of object relationship, and to a traumatic experience. We further know that all these different forms of fixations are expressions of similar and somewhat equivalent phenomena. . . . Nevertheless, our clinical experience shows that there are differences among our cases with respect to where it is that the emphasis is placed in terms of fixation [p. 225].

Arrest of or disturbance in the development of particular ego functions is particularly important to identify because the clinical significance of a fixation depends in large measure upon the degree to which critical ego processes are implicated or affected.

The situation is similar with regard to the assessment of regressive movements. Again, we must concern ourselves with the specific form the regression takes. Regressive shifts involve specific component instincts, drives, forms, aspects of object relations, and ego functions. Identification of the specific aspects involved is necessary for an adequate understanding of the impact of the regression upon over-all functioning and progressive development. As with fixation, the structural aspects of the regressive process are most crucial. Regression in critical ego functions seems to exert the most deleterious effect upon over-all progression and are less well tolerated by the organism than regressive shifts primarily involving drive forms.

THE PROBLEM OF EVALUATING THE SIGNIFICANCE OF FIXATIONS

Adequate over-all progression does not require complete advance from earlier levels of organization to higher ones, nor is such total reorganization necessary (perhaps it is not even desirable). There is always partial adherence of drive energies to earlier forms as the bulk of the available cathectic quantity moves on to new levels of organization. Anna Freud (1965) mentions "a specific characteristic of drive development, namely . . . that while libido and aggression move forward from one level to the next and cathect the objects which serve satisfaction on each stage *no station on the way is ever fully outgrown*" (p. 95; italics added). Fixation to early levels of organization can be considered pathological only when the economic effect is so great as to impede the general progressive movement of drive- and ego organization. Viewed in developmental terms, the pathological effect of fixations resides in the fact that "they have the function of binding and retaining drive energies and . . . thereby impoverish later drive functioning and object relations" (p. 96).

Not all fixations, however, exert such a depleting effect upon drive and ego development. Drive energy can persist in part at early stages of organization without necessarily preventing the child from functioning generally at age- and phase-adequate levels. Miss Freud (1954b) describes

> well-developed children of four or five, who are clean, intelligent, responsive, humorous, in excellent contact with their environment, with more than the beginnings of character and personality development. Their whole demeanor leaves no doubt that they have reached the phallic phase, or even entered the prelatency period. Yet, their favorite indulgence before going to sleep, when relaxing in tiredness, or under emotional strain, remains thumb sucking. They may be solving a difficult intellectual or emotional problem at one moment, and be found the next with their finger in their mouth, soothing and lulling themselves in repetitive sucking activity. That part of their libido has been left behind at the oral stage is obvious. Yet this fixation seems to interfere remarkably little with the progress of libido development [p. 27].

In other words, fixation to early levels can exist without significantly influencing over-all progression. It is not enough, therefore, to diagnose the presence of a fixation in the very young child. We have to determine how and to what extent it interferes with adaptation and over-all development before we can determine whether or not a fixation can be considered pathological.

We would tend to agree, in fact, with Nagera's (1963) interesting speculation that, although in general the existence of strong fixation points is a potentially dangerous situation, there can be instances in which the attractive pull exerted by such strongly cathected points serves the forces of progression. Where massive regression involving the ego as well as the drives has led to disorganization of the whole personality, fixation points in stages of development higher than those to which the regressive movement has led may exert a forward pull on the libido and thus promote recovery. The fixations would thus prove to have been highly advantageous to the ultimate development of the personality.

THE PROBLEM OF EVALUATING THE SIGNIFICANCE OF REGRESSION

The problem of assessing the significance of regressive movements, i.e., return to earlier forms and modes, is an even more complicated one. First, it is often difficult to distinguish between persistence of earlier patterns into subsequent phases and regression to a previous phase. Then too, current conflicts and behavior can sometimes spread over from a dominant area to a related one so as to produce a spurious picture of apparent regression. An excellent example of this situation is provided by Frijling-Schreuder (1966):

> A child negotiating with his mother about bowel control may be obstinate in regard to eating as well. In that case, we need not think that it has regressed to the oral level. We only diagnose regression to the oral level if the process of eating has the same libidinal cathexis as it had in the oral phase [p. 365].

Backsliding of a function or modality from a higher to a lower level of organization does not necessarily indicate that pathological forces are at work. To a greater or lesser extent, regression is a mechanism which is regularly employed by the ego in the service of mastery (E.

Kris, 1952). There is, of course, great variation from one child to another in the range of progressive/regressive swing consistent with healthy over-all progression. Some children progress relatively smoothly, with little *apparent* regression, even in fantasy, while other children regularly respond to maturational or environmental stress with wide regressive swings, from which they rebound to new heights. There are instances in which failure (i.e., inability) to regress in appropriate fashion portends difficulty later on. The following is an example of a child who regressed in response to stress, only to rebound to new ego achievements.

R., the youngest child in her family, learned at age three that her mother was pregnant. There was no immediate behavioral effect discernible, but during the final trimester of her mother's pregnancy, she became increasingly whiny, clinging, and babyish, and lost some of her capacity for independent functioning. She grew more and more interested in the idea of a baby in "mommy's tummy" and began to wonder about babies in general. After the birth of her brother (when she was three and a half), her anxiety about separation disappeared, she became active as mother's helper in caring for the baby, and succeeded in recovering her ability to function independently. Not only did she regain the ground she had lost in the previous three months; the investigator was impressed with her improved social adaptation, newly acquired ability to draw representational human figures, and significantly increased intellectual curiosity and interest. Psychological testing revealed a striking cognitive advance and an increase of 11 I.Q. points over the score obtained before the pregnancy. Presumably, identification with the feeding, caring mother and a widening and sharpening of the body image (Schilder, 1950), the result of her thoughtful observation of her mother's progressive body changes and production of a baby from her insides, facilitated not only recovery from the libidinal and ego regression that had taken place, but advance to even higher levels of ego functioning.

THE ADAPTIVE FUNCTION OF REGRESSION

In some children, it would seem that a period of regression regularly precedes any new advance, a pattern which can be viewed as one developmental variation among many. Fraiberg (1952) reported such a case. Many children regress temporarily when confronted with an unfamiliar situation without showing any later untoward effects, so that this period of temporary reversion to old forms can be viewed as a harmless and, perhaps, beneficial preamble to mastery of new situations:

> Children in new situations may study the situation for a while without active participation. In this period many regressive autoerotic activities can be observed, thumbsucking, genital play, etc. At the same time, the child is busy exploring what is going on. Other children may throw themselves actively into new situations, but this active participation does not always lead to the best ultimate adaptation. In young children it often means identification with the aggressor and the underlying anxiety may lead to failure [Frijling-Schreuder, 1966, p. 365].

The children in our study at the Child Development Center showed various responses to entering nursery school for the first time. The vignette which follows illustrates the adaptive function of regression in a new and unfamiliar situation.

J., a boy of nearly four, during his first three months in the nursery school appeared to be lethargic, passive, and withdrawn. He declined to take part in group activities, spent a considerable amount of time lying down "resting," and altogether gave the appearance of a passive observer. As time wore on, he became increasingly active and assertive, began to woo one of the girls in a masculine, phallic-assertive way, and proved to possess unusually fine capacities for reasoning and problem-solving. At the end of the year, he was the only one of the group to be advanced beyond the next level to the oldest group, where he was observed to be the early leader in constructive and intellectual projects.

ASSESSMENT OF THE EFFECT OF A REGRESSIVE MOVEMENT

We must follow the course of a regressive movement over a reasonable period of time before concluding that it has exerted a deleterious effect on the child's over-all development. Reversion to old modes of drive- or ego organization may represent temporary retreat from insoluble conflict followed by resumption of forward movement at a more propitious time. It may represent mobilization by the ego of old tools to assist in attempts to solve current conflicts. A newly strengthened ego may reach back in order to deal anew with earlier conflicts whose resolution had previously been beyond its power. This new attempt, which can be conceived of as a spontaneous effort at self-healing, may lead to the ego's further enrichment. The child who is unable to regress because of restriction of the ego's freedom of mobility suffers as much from ego weakness as the child who automatically swings into a deep regressive movement in response to stress. In either case, we are observing an ego lacking in resiliency, one bound to respond automatically, an ego which is passive, hence, weak (Rapaport, 1951a).

L., a three-and-a-half-year-old girl entering the nursery school, moved immediately into active participation in the program and seemed lively and competent. It gradually became apparent, however, that her display of competence and forthright independence was largely defensive in nature, serving to vigorously suppress an intense yearning for an exclusive, dependent relationship with the teacher, which conflicted with the role she was required to play within her family. Her inability to depart from the stylized behavioral pattern that fulfilled her neurotic requirements for inner tranquility and supported her ideal self-image prevented her from forming close relationships with her teachers and peers. She remained somewhat on the fringe of the group, except when she could assume the role of a competent, matronly, caring figure, and consistently impressed all observers as inappropriately old beyond her years.

Identification of these various patterns of regression, each with its own diagnostic implications, depends upon observation of their effect upon the movement of other lines during and following the regressive period. Speaking of childhood development, Anna Freud (1965) says:

> In our clinical appraisal of regressions as ongoing processes, it is almost impossible to determine whether in a given child's case the dangerous step from temporary to permanent regression has already been taken or whether spontaneous reinstatement of former-

> ly reached levels is still to be expected. Thus far, I know of no criteria for this, even though the entire decision about the child's abnormality may depend on this distinction [p. 106].

The significance of regressive movements can be judged according to three criteria: (1) reversibility of the regression; (2) the extent to which the various aspects of the personality are involved in the regression; and (3) the degree to which adaptation is affected by the regression (Frijling-Schreuder, 1966). Again, as with fixation, the significant issues revolve about economic (quantitative) and adaptive factors. The question of whether a regressive movement exerts a pathological effect on development depends upon the extent to which essential functions are implicated, the quantity of energies mobilized in the movement, and the degree to which the movement reverses itself. Hence, we can speak, in this regard, of "the economy of regression."[2]

Precocious development of certain functions to higher levels can also lead to pathological development (Hartmann, 1954). The role of premature activation of ego defenses against instinctual forces in disposing the child to later obsessional illness is well known (Freud, 1913b). The case of L., quoted above, illustrates the disturbing effect that precocious independence can exert upon object relations.

Progression in the three- to five-year-old child is fluid and highly individual. It is therefore difficult to distinguish in this period between interference in over-all development and transient manifestations of patterns of response to stress characteristics of the psychic apparatus at particular points in the individual's developmental timetable. Applying the Developmental Profile to prelatency children, therefore, is an exceedingly complex task. The difficulty is highlighted by Anna Freud's (1965) remarks on progression and regression:

> An individual child's capacity to function on a comparatively high level is no guarantee that the performance will be stable and continuous. On the contrary: occasional returns to more infantile behavior have to be taken as a normal sign. . . . In fact, what we regard

[2] An apt term suggested by Miss Annie Hermann in a personal communication.

as surprising are not the relapses but occasional sudden achievements and advances. . . . convenient as such transformations may be for the child's environment, the diagnostician views them with suspicion and ascribes them not to the ordinary flow of progressive development but to traumatic influences and anxieties which unduly hasten its normal course. According to experience, the slow method of trial and error, progression and temporary reversal is more appropriate to healthy psychic growth [p. 99].

Part V

Special Problems of Transference and Transference Neurosis

CHAPTER 19

Introduction

Peter B. Neubauer, M.D.

In line with the program of the Psychoanalytic Association of New York of setting up study groups among its members, the child analysts formed such a group and have met over a period of two years in order to exchange clinical experience and discuss subjects of mutual theoretical interest. A description of our method of work will explain the nature of the reports to follow and may also be helpful to colleagues wishing to engage in similar projects.

Most psychoanalytic study groups center their discussion on the available clinical data and slowly formulate a topic as a focus for further exploration. In our case, we felt it would be more profitable to select a theme that was fundamental to the work of all members which then could serve as the basis for a centered discussion of the various questions and problems that arise in our daily practice. The subject of transference in childhood appeared to us to provide such a sufficiently broad context.

Having chosen our project, we had to decide on the procedure we should follow. Should we begin by outlining a theoretical formulation to be subsequently tested by the clinical data, or should we look first at the transference phenomena as they became available during analysis and then formulate appropriate theoretical propositions? The study group was divided on this matter. Some members felt that a theoretical formulation which was not grounded in prior clinical exploration might be too ambiguous. Others, however, considered an initial hypothesis necessary in order to help organize the clinical material into a comprehensive, metapsychological format covering the dynamic, genetic, economic, structural, and adaptive perspectives. In the end, we agreed to adopt the theoretical approach.

The study group started out by defining transference as a repetition of past conflicts relating to the primary objects which results in the transferral of these experiences to the analyst as a new object. Yet, when we came to apply the various criteria for the occurrence of transference phenomena according to this definition, we found that the clinical material often enough provided incontrovertible evidence of transference but none of transference neurosis. Hence, in order to make the clinical assertion that transference neurosis does indeed occur in child analysis, we realized we would have to look for clinical evidence of transference rather than for material which only conformed to theoretical formulae.

Although disquieting, this discovery of the gap between the theory and our subsequent findings served a constructive purpose in exposing the general lack of clarity on the whole subject of transference. Moreover, it has stimulated us to search for new refined formulations which can more adequately express the available clinical data. It is our belief that the search for a fuller understanding of transference manifestations in childhood will require a thorough exploration of the developmental genetic processes.

Clearly, an informal group such as ours does not proceed by trying to reach a consensus of views. At this comparatively early stage of our work, clarification of problems rather than final agreement on formulation is our immediate goal. Divergence of opinion is in itself a powerful spur to the posing of new questions, which in turn leads to a renewed investigation of both theory and clinical data. Another factor which discouraged any attempt to proceed by consensus was the desire of individual members to present studies on special aspects of our subject. While some of these studies followed the general trend of the group discussion, others—inspired in part by a member's previous interests—remained on the periphery of our deliberations. All the studies, however, were regarded as valuable contributions to our efforts at clarifying the basic issues.

For these reasons, the reader should not expect to find here a coordinated or systematic exploration of transference in childhood. The report essentially comprises a number of separate papers which, when taken together, have the effect of highlighting certain aspects of the topic at the expense of others. There is, for example, no paper devoted to the issues of technique, or to describing different transference manifestations which may be characteristic for special clinical entities such as the delinquent or the psychotic or borderline patients. Similarly, the paper on "Transference Phenomena in Adolescent Analysis" is not complemented by equivalent studies of other developmental phases. Naturally, we hope it will be possible in the future to explore systematically the transference expressions at each level of development.

Owing to the highly individual nature of the different papers, there is no consistency of presentation. That is to say, while certain authors explore their chosen subject in considerable detail, others have confined themselves to a preliminary formulation. For instance, in the paper on "Dreams and Transference" a brief statement of the theoretical point of view which emphasizes the difference in mental processes between fantasy and action and between fantasied and real expression is followed by an outline for the future organization and review of data. Because of the clinical significance of transference expression in dreams, we hope it will eventually be possible to undertake a much more elaborate presentation of this topic. Similarly, although developmental considerations continuously imposed themselves on our discussion, we have included here only a short summary of the developmental perspective. While we felt that the developmental viewpoint deserves its own heading and should not be subsumed under the genetic approach, we were unable to marshal our data clearly enough for a detailed presentation at this time. Nevertheless, we are convinced that a better knowledge of developmental factors will help to fill the gaps in our present understanding of transference phenomena in child analysis and expect that the use of the development profile will assist us to expand this topic in our future work.

All these and other shortcomings of presentation (which include some overlapping of material, the result in part of the dynamic interaction of the various processes involved in transference) are an unavoidable consequence of an interim report representing a composite effort. Our justification for presenting this statement on a study still uncompleted is our belief that we have achieved a useful clarification of certain aspects of a subject which is under continuous review in the field.

CHAPTER 20

A Survey of Recent Contributions on Transference and Transference Neurosis in Child Analysis

Paul Kay, M.D.

This survey relies heavily on the contents of three panels of the American Psychoanalytic Association held in 1960 (Harley, 1961), 1963 (Abbate, 1964), and 1965 (Van Dam, 1966), and reflects current thought regarding the subject of transference and transference neurosis in child analysis.

Ambiguity, uncertainty, and change have, from the outset, marked the evolution of the concepts of transference phenomena (henceforth I shall use the term "transference phenomena" when referring to both "transference" and "transference neurosis") in both child and adult analysis. Freud himself rarely used the term, "transference neurosis." In his final papers, such as "Analysis Terminable and Interminable" (1937a) he did not use it at all, and in the *Introductory Lectures* (1916-17) he applied the term, transference, to what most contemporary analysts would regard as transference neurosis.

Most analysts today, whether they work with adults or children, would probably agree with the definition of transference offered by Ritvo (Van Dam, 1966), as a "tendency to repeat in the psychoanalytic situation with the analyst the relationships with the original objects of childhood," and transference neurosis as "the repetition of neurotic conflicts of earlier times in the psychoanalytic situation and in relationship to the analyst" (p. 528).

Dr. Kay is Assistant Clinical Professor, Division of Psychoanalytic Education, Department of Psychiatry, State University of New York, Downstate Medical Center, Brooklyn, New York.

The concept expressed in the latter definition includes several important features generally accepted since Freud (1914d, 1916-17). In contrast to transference, which may be regarded as spontaneous and ubiquitous, transference neurosis is viewed as a clinical creation arising out of the analytic process in which repressed infantile conflicts are reactivated around the analyst so as to reproduce the symptoms which had brought the patient to treatment. This clinical neurosis is worked through in the analytic situation, accompanied by the disappearance of the old neurosis and its symptomatology outside the analysis. In neither adult nor child analysis does the transference neurosis completely dominate the analytic experience. In child analysis, however, its intensity may be greater than the original pathogenic experiences with the parents.

The traditional concept of transference neurosis, derived from adult analysis, continues to be accepted by many child analysts, even though it has long been known that, in fact, transference neurosis as thus defined rarely occurs with children. Indeed, Anna Freud (1926) originally asserted that transference neurosis is not possible in child analysis. Among several important reasons in support of her assertion, she cited the fact that the child is still dependent on the original objects and has no need to replace them with new ones. Twenty years later (1946), however, she restated her position to admit the possibility of transference neurosis in a modified form: ". . . one part of the child's neurosis is transformed into a transference neurosis as it happens in adult neurosis . . . another part of the child's neurotic behavior remains grouped round the parents" (p. 70).

The continued availability of, and the child's reliance upon, the original objects have generally been regarded as the greatest obstacles to the development of a transference neurosis in children. Nevertheless, most analysts have accepted Fraiberg's (Van Dam, 1966) hypothesis that a transference neurosis can develop in the presence of the original objects if total repression has occurred, i.e., if the connection between drive derivatives and original object has been severed. An important part of Fraiberg's thesis was her qualifying assertion that the first revival of oedipal wishes in the analysis of a child occurs at home.

Kut, in 1953, offered some interesting observations of transference developments (some of which approached transference-neurosis proportions) which relate to Fraiberg's hypothesis of "total repression."

Kut's 10-year-old patient had to work through the conflicts with her original love objects in the transference (and, in fact, in whatever situation they appeared) as well as with the original objects at home before she could progress. Kut explained this process as a shift in libidinal cathexis from the original objects to the new object, the analyst.

To date, there are only four recorded instances of transference neurosis in child analysis. In none of these, however, did the transference neurosis ever dominate the analysis to the extent that it normally does in adult analytic situations. On the contrary, the evidence seemed to suggest that the transference neurosis tended to be overshadowed in the child's mind by the new objects and experiences that occur in his real world. This hypothesis would appear to support Anna Freud's recent assertion (1965) that transference neurosis in child analysis does occur, but not at all to the same degree of intensity as is normal with adults.

Such findings, coupled with the rarity of reported instances of transference neurosis, invite the question of whether the traditional definition and concept of transference phenomena can be applied to the analyses of children. The 1965 Panel generally endorsed the view that transference neurosis occurs when the preoedipal or oedipal wishes which have been reanimated by the analysis have already undergone total repression. Harley (Van Dam, 1966) also referred to repressed strivings in connection with transference. How does one distinguish total from subtotal repression? How does one determine both the degree to which a conflict has been repressed and then the extent to which it reappears in relation to the analyst?

Transference phenomena may be viewed in terms of content and mode of expression. Anna Freud (1936) referred to the transference of id impulses, defenses, and acting out. Later (1965) she stressed the repetition of all levels of object relationships, especially preoedipal ones. The prominence of preoedipal relationships often gives the transference a hostile, active coloring which constitutes a formidable resistance. She also referred at this time to the transfer of primitive needs, i.e., symbiotic attitudes. Lastly, she distinguished a "subspecies" of transference, "externalization," by which she meant the projection of the child's personality structure onto the analyst. Settlage (Van Dam, 1966), in his review of transference phenomena, referred to externalization, noting that it could be a form of repetition in the transference of some previous experience with the original object. He also observed that transference may be regarded as a resistance as well as a defense and that the "core" of transference is a libidinal drive. He stressed the mastery of earlier traumatic experiences and conflicts through transference reactions in which the patient shifts from passive to active roles. The concept of mastery through the transference is now firmly established and might well supersede the earlier (though still accepted) concept of the repetition compulsion as the driving force behind the transference phenomena.

Of the four recorded examples of transference neurosis in child analysis already mentioned, two were reported by Fraiberg, one by Harley, and one by Brody. An abstract of their content merits consideration. The original repressed conflicts in both of Fraiberg's cases were activated and worked through in the analysis. In neither case were the liberated impulses redirected toward the original object.

Fraiberg's (1962) first example occurred with Roger who was brought for analysis at the age of four because of violent, destructive behavior. During the fourth year of his treatment, there was a recurrence of his uncontrolled behavior in the analysis. At home, he showed no symptoms. Fraiberg analyzed his behavior as transference resistance representing his fear of losing his feces and penis. His castration fear was associated with anal masturbation, with the fantasy of having a hole like a girl, and with passive homosexual wishes. The analysis of his castration fear uncovered the archaic fear of losing his identity by surrendering to the preoedipal mother. It was this fear which had manifested itself in the wild behavior that had originally caused his parents to bring him for treatment and which had now recurred as a resistance. Maenchen (Van Dam, 1966), asserting that oedipal material is not repeated in transference phenomena of children, thought that the central conflict in Roger's transference neurosis was preoedipal.

In 1966, Fraiberg reported a transference neurosis in an older child. Nancy, at the age of eight, was brought for analysis because of epileptic seizures accompanied by "deterioration in all areas of ego functioning." She developed a transference neurosis in the third and fourth years of her analysis. The recovery of primal-scene memories was achieved almost exclusively from the analysis of the transference neurosis. These memories, in contrast to those recovered in the analysis of earlier transference reactions, had been completely repressed. The analysis of another instance of Nancy's transference neurotic manifestations uncovered a memory of her mother bathing and washing her genitals. This recollection, however, did not, as it usually does in transference behavior, lead to attempts at gratification of the repressed impulse with the original object, who was still available. The impulse remained instead within the transference neurosis.

Harley (1967) described a transference neurosis in the case of a five-year-old girl who was then in the second year of her analysis.* Based on the fantasy that the analyst's dog would jump out of the toilet and bite her, Anne had developed a fear of the analyst's toilet flush. This fear occurred at a time when she had been producing clinical material relating to her traumatic toilet training. It was a repetition of her earlier fear of a zebra in her toilet at home. The fear was now "confined exclusively to the analytic situation . . . and seemed to fulfill the criteria for a transference neurosis." Through the transference, Anne was able to see how the dog represented her own oral and anal destructive impulses against her sibling and mother.

Brody (1961) described transference resistance in the analysis of a prepubertal girl. Sara had been brought for treatment chiefly because of irresponsibility, sulking, quarrelsomeness, and fears at night. The transference resistance made its initial appearance in the form of a commonly observed positive transference. Sara's "overt obliging manner, her conscious determination to change her behavior by intellectual mastery of it, and her attempt to associate freely" were analyzed as resistance representing defenses against aggressive and libidinal impulses directed toward preoedipal and oedipal images of her mother. Sara re-experienced with the analyst the defenses and impulses of her early conflicts with the original object. This reliving was paralleled by the abatement of her symptoms outside of the analysis and a considerable improvement in her relationship with her mother.

DEVELOPMENTAL CONSIDERATIONS

Although Ritvo (Van Dam, 1966), Fraiberg (Harley, 1961), and Harley (Geleerd, 1967) have asserted the possibility of transference

*See also M. Harley, Chapter 17, This Volume.

neurosis in preschool children, the earliest age recorded was in Harley's analysis of Anne who was apparently seven years old when the transference neurosis developed. The rarity of transference neurosis in prelatency children and the fact that it begins to appear more frequently during latency invite a study of developmental factors.

The following ego achievements are considered necessary for the establishment of a therapeutic alliance: object constancy,[1] insight, self-observation, self-reflection, and secondary-process functioning. These achievements, or rather their beginnings, accompany the emergence and resolution of the oedipus complex. The therapeutic alliance is vital for the development of the transference neurosis although "long stretches" (A. Freud, 1965, p. 36) without this alliance occur in child analysis.

Settlage (Van Dam, 1966) noted that by means of object constancy, past experiences could be represented "intrapsychically" and that an enduring relationship with the analyst became possible. Object constancy starts somewhere between 24 and 36 months. Settlage also stressed the importance of ego and superego autonomy for the development of the therapeutic alliance and transference neurosis. Ego autonomy permitted the child to tolerate painful deprivations, decreased his fear of drives and affects, and heightened his control of motility. Superego autonomy promoted independence of the parents and, therefore, the ability to transfer parental attachments to the analyst.

Fraiberg (Abbate, 1964) described the changes in Roger's thinking and other ego functions which occurred between the ages of five and six and a half in the course of his analysis. During that time, he had made remarkable progress. He could communicate verbally rather than through play. He could accept responsibility for his thoughts, feelings, dreams, and actions. His need to project and deny lessened. Internalization of conflict had increased. He could think causally, look for motives, and appreciate the unconscious. He had become self-observant, reflective, capable of reporting and associating to dreams. These "achievements," of course, like the others referred to in this paper with regard to the development of psychic structure,

[1] Greenson (1967), speaking about transference phenomena in adult analysis, stressed the importance of achieving constancy of the self-representation as well.

represented beginnings. With Roger, his innate intellectual ability[2] and his "education" as an analysand must also be taken into account. He was certainly no average six-and-a-half-year-old.

With respect to the ego development necessary for the attainment of a therapeutic alliance and transference neurosis, Brody (1961; Harley, 1961) has, in addition, noted the importance of the patient's ability to identify with the analyst and his aims; to be realistic about his parents and to value other objects; to not only give up childhood play for abstract, verbal forms of thinking and communicating but to be able to enjoy thinking; and to be able to replace identification with object love. These changes tend to occur between latency and prepuberty. Around prepuberty, the child can speak of the past and accept repeated, painful interpretations if he can move about freely. Just as play is a "primary, phase-specific mode of expressive discharge" for the prelatency child (as speech is for the adult), so the "biologically determined" motor activity is a phase-specific mode of discharge and resistance of the prepuberty child. This resistance is designed to avoid or minimize the experience of passive aims and affects toward the analyst.

The overwhelming importance of the new object and the real world in the child's experience has long since been recognized. Anna Freud (1965) observed that the child analyst has the difficult task of not disappointing the child's natural "hunger" for a new object, but must, at the same time, also make himself available for repetition. The prelatency child, as Fraiberg (1951) and others have pointed out, is struggling to distinguish between fantasy and reality. He has difficulty in perceiving his transferred feelings as unreal. Brody (1961) has indicated that it is generally around prepuberty that the child begins to perceive as well as to react to the new object as being largely or wholly new.

The concept of the new object might be scrutinized more closely because it is deceptively simple. Aside from the child's naturally strong tendency to repeat, his elementary stage of individuation, his difficulty in discriminating between objects, and his tendencies to

[2]Ritvo (Van Dam, 1966), Rochlin (Harley, 1961), and others, noting the impressive intellectual endowment of Fraiberg's patient, Roger, and Brody's patient, Sara, have stressed the importance of cognition in the development of a therapeutic alliance.

project and displace might easily make his experience of the new object largely that of himself and his introjects, i.e., the past (including the immediate past), especially where conflict is involved. But, one factor, identification with the original object, has an enormous influence on the child's very ability to perceive, approach, and learn about the new object. The past, then, is not only repeated in the new object and the new experience but to a large extent makes it possible, subject to the limitations imposed by endowment, maturation, and the characteristics of the current developmental phase.

The crucial factor determining the child's ability to replace his parents with new objects, to allow oedipal and preoedipal conflicts to reappear in the form of transference neurotic manifestations is the degree to which he has achieved superego autonomy. This, in turn, is dependent upon the degree to which the oedipal conflicts have been resolved or repressed. I have already referred to Fraiberg's hypothesis of "total repression" as a means of solving the problem of transference-neurosis developments in the presence of the original object. Van Dam (1966) prefers, instead, Katan's concept of "object removal." This process, he believes, begins in latency and gains momentum in adolescence. Most child analysts agree that this is not achieved until late or postadolescence.

The rare published instances of limited transference neuroses in latency and prepuberty as traditionally defined and described in this paper testify to the need of a definition more appropriate to childhood in which development, mastery, and adaptation, rather than repetition, are accorded a central position.

TECHNICAL CONSIDERATIONS

It is inescapably clear that development, technique, and the analyst's personal and professional stance are inseparably and reciprocally interwoven with the occurrence of transference neurosis in the analysis of children. The technical factor, already referred to, warrants a more elaborate statement.

Like Anthony and other child analysts, Brody (1961) has stressed the analyst's readiness to perceive or deny transference-neurosis manifestations. She cautioned child analysts against being too impressed with the child's resistance to transference, clearly implying that the resistance could be transference resistance.

In 1926, Anna Freud stressed the necessity for an educative and what today might be regarded as a manipulative, seductive approach to the child, especially in the introductory phases of the analysis. By interesting and pleasing the child, the analyst might help him become aware of his difficulties and experience the need for treatment. Unfortunately, as became apparent over the years, this approach made the development of a transference neurosis most difficult if not impossible. In 1946, she referred explicitly to the interpretation of the child's defenses as in adult analysis (pp. 70-71). In 1965, she stressed the importance of verbalizing those strivings which the child can not verbalize because of developmental arrests or defects (pp. 32-33).

In her preface to Roger's analysis, Fraiberg (1962) noted that education and intervention had now been replaced by interpretation, i.e., defense analysis. Participants at the three Panels unanimously endorsed the value of an orderly defense analysis as a means of facilitating the development of a therapeutic alliance which then made possible the subsequent analysis of the hostile, pregenital transference followed by the development of a transference neurosis.

Geleerd (Abbate, 1964) stressed the importance of the real attributes of the analyst in establishing a therapeutic alliance. Harley (Abbate, 1964) elaborated on the significance of the therapeutic alliance which enhances the child's ability to perceive the analyst as a real object, to endure the negative transference, and to make use of the interpretation of the positive transference resistances. At the same time, the therapeutic alliance is, to some degree, based upon a positive transference, which most child analysts tend to maintain at a higher level than is necessary in adult analysis in order to continue the analysis because of the child's limited ability to tolerate frustration and anger. The traditional "abstinence" is relative (Brody, 1961) (as it is in adult analysis).

Anthony (Van Dam, 1966), on the other hand, was concerned about "de-realizing" the child analytic situation, particularly by means of the analyst's assuming a fixed position in the room in order to be less "exciting" to the child and to function only as "commentator, clarifier, and interpreter." The analyst should be a real object only for externalization and transference reactions and should offer a "non-gratifying environment."

With regard to interpretations, several points have been made. Brody (1961) noted that the interpretation of defense may arouse a child's intellectual curiosity and facilitate the analytic process, while other types of interpretation may be threatening. Brody (Harley, 1961) stressed the importance of educating the younger child about the unconscious so that interpretations, especially transference ones, would not be confusing. (She was not explicit about the meaning of "younger child," but implied one who had not reached prepuberty.) Lustman (Abbate, 1964) as well as most of the participants affirmed the value of educating the child in the meaning of transference and other aspects of analysis in order to achieve a transference neurosis.

Fraiberg (Abbate, 1964) stressed the importance of making an initial "contract" with the child so that his play can be used effectively as a vehicle for communication. Brody (Harley, 1961) had observed earlier that up to late latency, play offered the equivalent of transference to the child with regard to "immediacy" and "objectification." Lustman (Abbate, 1964) observed that with the help of the analyst's verbalization of ideas and affects, play could be used to develop the child's ability to function on the secondary process level strengthening, therefore, his ability to express his problems in the analysis.

Helping the child to recognize and understand his feelings has been emphasized by several child analysts (Daunton, Rochlin, Fraiberg's presentation of Roger's analysis: Harley, 1961). Haug (Harley, 1961), in accordance with her specific concept of transference neurosis, has underlined the importance of dealing with the child's denial of internal conflict through externalization.

Interpretation of defense has not proved to be a simple technique to apply. Fraiberg (1962) related how Roger, her wild, four-year-old patient, could not at first be reached by the analytic method. It was only after she had induced the parents to abandon their spankings (which had gratified Roger's masochistic demands and reinforced his provocative behavior) that he became accessible (with the help of "education") to the interpretation of his defenses.

The issues in Roger's analysis raised the question of the role of the parents in relation to the analysis. Rochlin (Harley, 1961) asserted that proper management of the parents definitely facilitated the development of a transference neurosis in Roger's case. His view is in contrast to the common, older one held by Anna Freud and others that the analyst's contact with the parents is vital to the maintenance of the analysis, even though it hinders the development of a transference neurosis. There has been general agreement on the necessity for contact with the parents to conduct the analysis until such time as the child's development permitted him to be an adequate reporter and to have the capacity to sustain the analytic work on his own. Anthony (Abbate, 1964; Van Dam, 1966) asserted the necessity of de-realizing the analytic situation by avoiding contact with the parents.

As a result of developmental changes, Anthony (Abbate, 1964) has suggested the following approach to the analysis of a latency child: a "mock-serious" attitude; anticipation of future insights; use of conscious communications to prepare for interpretation of the unconscious; "screen games" to approach the basic conflict; and finally, discovering and analyzing the nuclear fantasy wherever it is found.

The profound effect of developmental factors on technique has been most clearly elucidated by Fraiberg (Abbate, 1964) who noted, for example, that as a result of the changes which occurred in Roger between the ages of five and six and a half, she could become less of a participant in the child's productions and more of a neutral observer. She was then more capable of "free floating attention" and could, therefore, more effectively assess transference reactions, i.e., help to bring about a transference neurosis.

POSSIBLE FUTURE TREND

Stone's (1967) paper, "The Psychoanalytic Situation and Transference," seems to have particular relevance to the evolution of concepts dealing with transference phenomena. He introduces a radical hypothesis which seems wide enough to encompass transference phenomena in both child and adult analysis and which therefore deserves special comment.

Stone distinguishes three levels of transference. The first is that of the "primordial transference" (p. 8), which he defines as a "parasymbiotic transference drive . . . an original organismic drive" (p. 21) toward a "symbolic bodily reunion with mother" (p. 9). It is derived from the effort to master the various separations since birth. ". . . erotic and aggressive strivings . . . express, facilitate or subserve the primordial transference" (p. 9). "The oedipus complex . . . provides a link between this climactic experience of childhood separation and the most primitive psychophysiological separation" (p. 11).

The second level of transference is defined as the "mature transference," a "nonrational," largely "nonsensual" urge consisting of "the wish to understand and to be understood; the wish to be given understanding. . ."; the wish to be helped to adapt and sublimate; and "the wish . . . to be seen in terms of one's developmental potentialities" (p. 24). In contrast to the primordial transference, the mature transference seeks individuation and reality.

The third level of transference is called the "transitional object transference" (p. 52) in which the analyst and the analytic situation represent a transitional object to the patient.

Stone's hypothesis, although perhaps not immediately clinically useful, is heuristically important. It helps to express both the artificiality and the reality of the analytic experience. The concepts of "primordial" and "mature" transference not only stress the developmental aspects of child and adult analysis, but they also draw attention to their biological roots. By means of his concepts, specific ego functions and drive derivatives important in the analysis as well as in the real life of the patient may be more easily viewed in the larger context of their relationship to the original object, new object, reality, conflict, and development.

The primordial transference concept, in underlining the basic and inextinguishable striving for the mother, compels the analyst to realize that a powerful, natural regressive force is constantly in operation affecting the patient's numerous cognitive and emotional bonds with him. This realization may give the analyst a more authentic, richer, and, therefore, more useful understanding of the patient's total reaction to the analysis. Conversely, the concept of the "mature transference," with its emphasis on progression, the present, and the future, enhances the analyst's understanding of the patient's adaptive potential.

It is tempting to dismiss these concepts, especially that of the "mature transference," since, by definition, transference refers to repetition and regression. In addition, to refer to transference as a "drive" is to use both terms in an unusual way. I suggest that this concept be appreciated from the point of view of the child's actual developmental experiences. These must occur within a relationship to a mothering or fathering person which is saturated with drive energy during the symbiotic, postsymbiotic, and subsequent phases until, at least, the end of adolescence. Conflict, along with regressive and progressive trends, remains from the start a permanent part of this dynamic, child-parent bond. The development of the functions which subserve curiosity, perception, control of feeling and movement, thinking, the wish and ability to solve problems through understanding, and the ability to neutralize drive energy takes place within this primarily affective, conative tie to the parent. Certain aspects of this complex, developmental experience may even be appreciated as potential precursors of vital elements in the analytic process. The child-parent dual-unity, for example, resembles a primitive therapeutic alliance in that the parent to some extent helps the more or less eager child to perceive, master problems through understanding, control impulses, and tolerate frustrations. Communication is both verbal and nonverbal. The child identifies with the parent's ability to replace disruptive feelings and impulses with understanding and control. Also, the child has an opportunity to experience and identify with the parent who can be introspective. Finally, the child's ability to split itself into experiencing, observing, and reflective selves probably also originates in identification with the observing, reflecting mother attempting to understand and to transmit that understanding to itself, the as yet nonobservant, nonreflective, experiencing child. Both aspects of the process would be a part of the child's developing self-representation.

These considerations would seem to point inescapably to the fact that both the therapeutic alliance and transference phenomena are intertwined with, dependent upon, and arise from developmental processes and conflictual experiences which normally consist of progressive and regressive elements. One can even view the child's transference phenomena, for example, as inevitably including a repetition of the proto-therapeutic alliance which the child has been experiencing and, very likely, is still experiencing with one or both parents.

Stone's hypothesis of different levels of transference makes greater allowance for major progressive and regressive shifts in the patient and, therefore, offers more room for understanding variations in structuralization, psychopathology, and adaptation. Ordinarily, it is psychopathology which speaks with a loud, clear voice in the analytic situation, while developmental processes are apt to be silent. The utilization of Stone's hypothesis might lead to a clearer, much bolder appreciation of developmental processes in the transference. The classical concepts of transference phenomena, in contrast, are expressed almost entirely in the narrower terms of drive, defense, conflict, repetition, and regression. They tend to minimize, if not repudiate, that which is so special in the life and analysis of a child: his reality and his development. (These same factors are also more important in the adult, Stone indicates, than is generally appreciated. Anna Freud [1965], Lustman [Abbate, 1964], and others have underlined the adult's perception of the analyst as a "new" and "real" object.)

No satisfactory, integrating global concepts exist which can do justice to these complex, contradictory (in terms of logic but not in terms of the actual growth experience) progressive and regressive processes in the child, adolescent, and adult. Stone's concept of the "mature transference" is valuable if viewed as an evocative concept to be ultimately replaced by one that is scientifically rigorous and definitive. I hope that Stone's ideas signal the beginning of an attempt to conceptualize transference (as well as other analytic) phenomena in a comprehensive formulation capable of being verified by observation and providing a natural bridge between the two worlds of child and adult analysis.

Analysts may, in the future, seek increasingly to understand the child's reactions to analysis in the unique terms of his experiences within the developmental progression and, at the same time, to be able to translate them into the realms of adolescent and adult analysis. Rangell (Casuso, 1965) has anticipated these views: "Psychoanalysis is indivisible. Both child and adult analysis, and I hope that eventually geriatric analysis as well, will one day be part of one continuous mainstream of understanding."

CHAPTER 21

Transference and Transference Neurosis in Child Analysis

Roy K. Lilleskov, M.D.

TRANSFERENCE

After discovering the phenomenon of transference in analytic work, Freud not only elaborated upon the concept in clinical terms, he characterized it as a universal aspect of human relationships. At times he used the term loosely, equating transference with the patient's relationship to the analyst. Subsequent writers have continued all of these usages. Although the study group accepted the general formulation of transference as an aspect of all object relationships, we decided to limit our discussion of transference in children to the analytic situation. It is no accident that transference was discovered in clinical work. The conditions in analytic treatment are, after all, ideal for its production, enhancement, and isolation as an observable phenomenon.

A DEFINITION OF TRANSFERENCE IN THE CLINICAL SITUATION

Transferences were defined by Freud (1901) as "a special class of mental structures, for the most part unconscious. . . . They are new editions or facsimiles of the impulses and phantasies which are aroused and made conscious during the progress of the analysis; but

Dr. Lilleskov is Clinical Assistant Professor, Division of Psychoanalytic Education, Department of Psychiatry, State University of New York, Downstate Medical Center, Brooklyn, New York.

they have this peculiarity, which is characteristic for their species, that they replace some earlier person by the person of the physician" (p. 116). (Subsequent definitions made it clear that Freud thought the "earlier person" is usually a parent.) Translating this definition into modern terminology and elaborating upon it slightly, we arrive at the following formulation: transference is a process in which instinctual drives originally directed toward a primary object, and still attached to repressed representations of that primary object, are now directed toward the analyst as if he had become that original object. These drives and their object representations are organized into unconscious fantasies, which, although related to earlier experiences, are not necessarily exact replicas thereof. In the development of these fantasies, phasic representations of the objects are formed, which may either be condensed into a single representation or else registered sequentially. Simultaneous phasic ego development contributes various defensive and adaptive aspects to the expression of the transference.

VARIATIONS IN THE EXPRESSION OF TRANSFERENCE

Even in adult analysis, transference varies widely in its texture and referents (Greenacre, 1959), but in child analysis the variability is compounded by developmental factors and by the necessary modifications in analytic technique (A. Freud, 1965). This may account for the difficulty encountered by most writers, as well as by our study group, in defining an unequivocal transference manifestation in the clinical situation. One way of arriving at greater clarity is to specify the variations in the instinctual drives, object representations, and ego functions which are expressed in transference phenomena.

1. *Modulations of original wishes.* The original instinctual wish may reappear in the transference almost undisguised. An example of this might be a borderline patient or patient long in analysis who experiences an undisguised wish to defecate on the analyst's rug or to touch the analyst's penis. More frequently the wish is expressed in a sublimated form or modified by other defensive distortions. We might in the first instance then see a child making piles of toys on the floor or throwing paper scraps out of the window; or, in the second, he might arrange "accidently" to be physically close to the

analyst, without even realizing the significance of his action. These modifications of the original wish may have been present in the primary object relationship and thus be "transferred" from that experience, or else the modification may take place at the time of the revival of the wish in analysis.

2. *Role reversals.* It is not uncommon for a trauma which was passively experienced in the primary object relationship to be revived in analysis in an active form, or vice versa. For instance, a child who has been force-fed might repeat that event by trying to force the analyst to swallow something, thereby placing the analyst in the role he himself had originally experienced. If the child's wish to retaliate against the primary object was present in the original relationship, this is clearly transference. But if the active form of the wish developed later, or only at the time of its revival in analysis, it would have to be considered a defense against the transferred passive wish.

3. *Phasic condensations of representations.* Overdetermination affects transference phenomena in many ways. For example there are some patients who feel threatened or assaulted by interpretations and act as if the analyst's words had to be kept out, shut out, or not swallowed, etc. Analysis may reveal that these reactions simultaneously or successively represent an unconscious memory or fantasy of being force-fed, or receiving an enema, or of being raped. There is, thus, a layering and condensation of instinctual drives from several libidinal phases.

4. *Object condensations and distortions.* The primary object of the wish may either be represented in the transference in relatively undisguised form or it may be distorted beyond recognition through defensive elaboration in fantasy. Just as several instinctual levels may be found in one fantasy, so multiple representations of the object may be condensed into a single representation. In the reaction mentioned under number 3 above, the object representation transferred is a fusion of preoedipal mother representations and father representations from the oedipal period which have been condensed in the unconscious fantasies. Although some degree of condensation is probably always present, it assumes particular importance in those children whose mothering was provided by more than one person. Neubauer (1965) has observed that children raised by a series of nurses in kibbutzim fuse the several object representations into a

single mother image. This process is related to, but not identical with, another phenomenon found in many, if not all, children and which is of special significance when a parent is missing. We are referring here to the formation of an idealized or degraded parent representation around which oedipal fantasies are worked out (Neubauer, 1960). With idealizations, the primary object representation is condensed with heroic or godlike representations, whereas with degradations, the condensation is with castrated, demonic, or witchlike representations. It is clear that when we say the analyst is perceived as if he were a past object, we do not always mean a literal or exact reproduction of a primary object.

THE TRANSFERENCE PROCESS AS DISTINGUISHED FROM OTHER RELATIONSHIP PROCESSES

The actual quality of the patient's relationship to the analyst at any given time is determined by the interweaving of the transference process with other relationship processes. Some of these have often been confused with transference, but they should be distinguished from it if metapsychological clarity is to be achieved. Below are examples of relationship processes that resemble transference, but which result from defects of ego development, current conflicts, or character formation.

1. *The analyst as undifferentiated from the primary object.* If a child is too young to have achieved object constancy, or if he has failed to develop this function, he may not be able to differentiate between objects at all. The analyst would then be perceived as a parent, because no new object is distinguished from any old object (nor in such cases are the primary objects distinguished from each other). Stone (1967) calls the phenomenon "pure transference," but this is to stretch the definition of transference, inasmuch as the elements of repression, unconscious primary-object representation, and repetition are lacking.

2. *The analyst as object undifferentiated from the self.* If the experience reproduced in the analytic situation is narcissistic, containing representation of the drive and its activity but little or no reference to an external object, the analyst may then be seen as a part of

the self or as a "part-object." This is not a true transference, but a form of externalization, and is another instance of a defect in ego development. It has been referred to as a "narcissistic transference."

3. *Displacement of a current conflict on to the person of the analyst.* There are many displacements which lack the elements of repression and repetition and are therefore not, strictly speaking, transferences. Examples abound in every analysis, as, for instance, on those occasions when the child is angry at parent, sibling, teacher, or school monitor and displaces it on to the analyst.

4. *Generalized reactions expressed toward the analyst.* Under this heading we must place a large number of the attitudes and feelings expressed toward the analyst which are also expressed in all other aspects of the child's life. These include age-adequate behavior patterns derived from phasic conflicts and/or developmental achievements (e.g., defiance in the anal phase, secrecy in latency, or showing off to express heroic fantasies in prepuberty). Also included are generalized regressions in response to developmental or situational stress—an example of this type of regression might be a child who customarily reacts with temper tantrums to frustrations, whether or not he is with the analyst.

5. *Expression of character traits in the analysis.* Character traits are relatively stable psychic configurations which are compromise formations consisting of instinctual drive gratifications and defenses against them. They are formed in relation to objects and so are often expressed. Even though one of these objects may happen to be the analyst, it would be stretching the term to call this behavior transference, especially after the trait has achieved secondary autonomy. It is a different matter, however, when remnants of a repressed infantile character are revived in the analytic situation and directed exclusively toward the analyst. Then transference is often clearly involved. There is probably a continuum between such instinctualized character traits and those which have become autonomous.

6. *The "real relationship" with the analyst.* To the extent that the analyst is cathected as analyst and not as substitute parent, he is a "real" object in his own right. Although this new object representation is contaminated by transference of past relationships, there is usually some element of reality in the patient's perception of the analyst. The therapeutic alliance, or working relationship, is related

to this "real relationship," but is not identical with it. When the primary objects are absent or deficient, the real relationship becomes especially important, because the analyst may serve as the primary object while the child passes through the developmental phases. In these circumstances particularly, new levels of fantasies and wishes originating around the person of the analyst may occur. Reactions, such as those to separations, may be partly current and genuinely concern the analyst in his own right and not merely as a transference object. The child may also form structure-building identifications with the analyst. Although we stress the case of the absent or deficient parent, all these phenomena are found to some extent in most if not all child analyses—and may also be an important part of adult analyses (Loewald, 1960).

TRANSFERENCE NEUROSIS

The literature concerning the existence and nature of the transference neurosis in child analysis is largely in agreement with Anna Freud's (1965) view that the transference neurosis in children "does not equal the adult variety in every respect." Some stress the immature state of the child's ego and his continuing relationships with the primary objects as major factors of difference between child and adult analysis. Others argue that these differences can be reduced if a rigorous analytic approach is maintained. These opinions are advanced with strong emotional overtones, which reflect the great importance attributed to the attainment of a transference neurosis. Indeed, for some, analysis is equated with the production and resolution of a transference neurosis.

A DEFINITION OF TRANSFERENCE NEUROSIS

The transference neurosis is a new version of the clinical neurosis which develops in the course of an analysis when the original conflicts are displaced on to the person of the analyst. It involves the repetition compulsion and is a re-enactment of the essentials of the infantile neurosis. One point implicit in the concept, but often ignored, concerns the definition of neurosis. The term transference *neurosis*, is applicable only when the central conflict and the defenses against it are organized as a psychoneurosis. In other words, the conflict must involve oedipal wishes and defenses against them.

CLINICAL CRITERIA FOR THE PRESENCE OF A TRANSFERENCE NEUROSIS

It is usually held that a neurotic patient properly handled in the analytic situation will develop a transference neurosis. Free association, combined with analysis of resistances and avoidance of extra-interpretive interventions, leads to the regressive processes essential for its development. Freud (1914d), in presenting the concept of transference neurosis, described the clinical situation as one where the symptoms (in hysteria and obsessive-compulsive neurosis) diminish outside of the analysis and become concentrated on the analyst and the analytic situation; old symptoms take on a new meaning and new symptoms arise in relation to the analyst.

Different aspects of Freud's description of the clinical situation have since been emphasized as criteria for determining the presence of a transference neurosis. Most of those interested in the problem apply the criterion of centrality and maintain that a transference neurosis exists when the analyst and the analytic situation become a central concern in the patient's emotional life. Others apply various criteria, such as restriction of symptoms to the analytic situation, the formation of new symptoms during the analytic hour, or even the appearance of the analyst in dreams. Some appear to use the concepts of transference and transference neurosis interchangeably, so that any sign of transference is viewed as a sign of transference neurosis.

No doubt each of these clinical phenomena can occur separately and may sometimes represent the re-enactment of an infantile neurosis, oedipal in content, around the person of the analyst. In such instances we are justified in using the term, transference neurosis. However, if we consider any one aspect of the clinical constellation described by Freud as equivalent to the whole, we run the risk of obscuring the true nature of the process involved.

APPLICATION OF CLINICAL CRITERIA TO CHILD ANALYSIS

Reviewing cases of children in analysis, the study group found that convincing evidence for the presence of a transference neurosis in the full sense outlined above was rare. Although we found instances where the analyst became a central figure in the child's life, this seldom occurred as part of the development of transference neurosis. The analyst, for example, can become a person of central importance in children who have not reached the oedipal period. In fact, some of the most intense relationships are found in borderline and affect-starved children whose main conflicts and defenses are prephallic. Similarly, new symptoms can develop in the analytic situation in cases where the central conflict is preoedipal and the disorder is therefore not a neurosis. Nor was restriction of symptoms to the analytic situation a frequent finding. Regressive and progressive movements, affective displays, and symptom formation usually occurred concurrently in the child's home or school life. When oedipal conflicts were being uncovered, simultaneous involvement of analyst and parents was the rule.

Although transference neurosis has been a valuable concept both clinically and theoretically, its uncritical use in the past may have delayed our progress in understanding the full range of relationship processes in the analytic situation. (We felt this to be true in adult analysis as well as child analysis.) Nor would it clarify matters much to add such terms as "transference developmental fixation," "transference character disorder," or "transference psychosomatic disorder" to the already established "transference psychosis." Rather, we suggest that just as single word diagnoses have given way to diagnostic profiles, so the term, transference neurosis, should be replaced by a paragraph describing phenomenologically and metapsychologically the actual nature of the different relationship processes involved in a given analytic situation—which would, of course, include the transference process. If used at all, the term, transference neurosis, should be restricted to those phenomena which meet all the clinical and theoretical criteria.

These considerations are offered not only for the purpose of achieving better theoretical conceptualization, but for technical reasons as well. An accurate assessment of the processes involved in the analytic situation will facilitate correct interpretations. Correct interpretations not only advance the analytic process, they also cement the "real" relationship with the analyst by gratifying the patient's need to be understood.

CHAPTER 22

A Metapsychology of Transference

Samuel Abrams, M.D.

A metapsychological view of transference provides concepts which serve several purposes. Its postulates offer frames of reference within which transference may be clinically differentiated from allied states, facilitate the formulation of such research questions as the relationship between transference potential and the phase achievement of different developmental moments, and enable the phenomenon of transference to be placed within a systematic psychoanalytic psychology.

No broad consensus exists as to which group of postulates best fulfills such ends. Rapaport and Gill (1959), however, have suggested that the dynamic, economic, structural, genetic, and adaptive perspectives provide the most useful frames of reference. (The reasoning for this selection appears in a highly condensed form in Rapaport and Gill, and somewhat more elaborately in Rapaport, 1960.) This paper will examine both the value and the intrinsic limitations of each of these five perspectives.

THE DYNAMIC POINT OF VIEW

Viewed dynamically, transferences reflect infantile psychological forces whose energic sources originate primarily in instinctual drives. Characteristically, these forces present themselves along certain func-

Dr. Abrams is Assistant Clinical Professor, Division of Psychoanalytic Education, Department of Psychiatry, State University of New York, Downstate Medical Center, Brooklyn, New York.

tional routes, e.g., infantile sexuality, affect states, defensive modalities; and they can act either in cooperation or in conflict with each other.

The dynamic perspective permits the use of the central infantile sexual conflict as the nosologic point of departure for classifying the various types of transferences. Transference neurosis, for example, may be viewed as involving transference forces in which instinctual drives are represented functionally in phallic wishes with incestuous aims, and/or in which the affect forces are castration anxiety and guilt. Transferences based on oral or anal constellations designate dynamic clusterings about prephallic infantile sexual derivatives; fear of loss of the object and of loss of love are the usual concomitant inhibitory affect forces. Defensive styles vary, although preferred mechanisms of defense, e.g., repression in the phallic phase, are often seen to coexist along with infantile sexual fixation-points.

By itself, the dynamic postulate does not permit a differentiation of transference from the emergence of "new" aims toward the analyst, a phenomenon often observed in the analysis of young children or in severely fixated prephallic character disorders. Nor does it permit a distinction between transference on the one hand and a "real" relationship on the other. In a "real" relationship, the analyst actually *is* an on-going object of infantile gratifications, as distinct from merely being *desired* as one. (See Glenn et al., Chapter 26, This Volume for specific clinical distinctions between transference, "new," and "real" relationships; and Lilleskov, Chapter 21, This Volume for further theoretical exposition of the distinctions between transference and transference neurosis.)

THE ECONOMIC POINT OF VIEW

A consideration of economic issues permits an exploration of the energies available for the transference forces according to the cathectic distribution, i.e., narcissistic as contrasted with object-directed; the extent of fusion and defusion; and degrees of energy neutralization. Moreover, energies are regarded as being subject to certain regulatory principles. For example, the pleasure principle, the unpleasure principle, and the repetition-compulsion principle have been offered by various authors as alternative or as complementary conceptions of the underlying economic "laws" which govern transference wishes (for specific details, see Schur, 1966a).

The economic perspective is useful, firstly, in differentiating externalizations from transferences. By definition, transference mirrors a relationship with some *other* person. Hence, the displacement of narcissistic cathexes on to the analyst is, strictly speaking, not a transference but an externalization, although, of course, it may be a stage in the development of transference if the narcissistically cathected image reflects a defensive shift from a primary object-tie.

Secondly, the economic postulate is useful in cataloguing differing transferences from the standpoint of fusion-defusion. For example, the phallic function is said to reflect a greater fusion of libido and aggression in the hysterical character than in the obsessional, for whom the sadistic aspects of the phallic phase are conceptualized economically as a regressive defusion.

Thirdly, energies available for the affect forces are ordinarily viewed as in a continuum of degrees of neutralization. However, when the functions of guilt or anxiety themselves become sexualized or instinctualized, this is manifested in the transference representation, and the clinical picture is complicated proportionately.

Finally, certain qualitative distinctions between transference and therapeutic alliance lend themselves to economic configurations. For instance, the protracted instinctualization of the alliance relationship, which cathectically characterizes the so-called erotized transference, can be usefully contrasted with the far briefer erotization and reinstinctualization usual in a good therapeutic situation. Two case histories will illustrate the difference between these relationships.

For years, a young man was unable to view interventions or interpretations as other than advice, criticism, berating, seductions, etc. He would complain that the analyst's silences or words stood for abuse or admiration, depending upon his prevailing state of mind. At the same time, he regarded the analytic situation as a magical talisman that protected him from all potential dangers, which tied him definitively and resolutely to it. Contrasted with this protracted "instinctualized" relationship was the situation of another young man who, in the course of his treatment, began to experience interpretations as "pinpricks" or "stabs in the back." A period of difficulty in comprehending interpretative remarks lifted when he perceived that the process of understanding had itself become sexualized, i.e., had come to represent his wish for impregnation through the analyst's words. (Also see Nunberg, 1951.)

THE STRUCTURAL POINT OF VIEW

Transferences must also be studied from a structural perspective, specifically by reference to the capacities of those mental functions which act as the main channels for the discharge of the forces which appear in the form of transference representation.

A partial listing of the relevant ego functions would include the capacity for laying-down a memory trace of an experience, for object relations and object constancy; functions relating to reality testing and to issues of reality; identificatory modes and capacities; the function of differentiation; the capacity to symbolize, to form fantasies; "removal," and especially its role in adolescence (see also Scharfman, Chapter 24, This Volume); the availability and use of different defense mechanisms; and the development of affect expressions. Relevant superego contributions include inhibiting and prohibiting functions, the nature of the ego ideal, and the stability of earlier identifications and of internalization processes. Delineating id functions beyond the mental representations of infantile sexuality entails special conceptual problems (see, for example, Schur, 1966a), and is outside the scope of this paper.

The structural point of view assists in clarifying varying aspects of the analyst-analysand relationship. Obviously it is not possible to conceptualize a transference state before memory traces are laid down, or before the capacities for displacement and symbolization and for differentiation and object constancy emerge. The attainment of object constancy and postoedipal object relationships are minimal requirements for a therapeutic alliance.

Once all these different functions are surveyed, the structural hypothesis serves several conceptual purposes. The patient's preferred level of object relationship offers one approach to the classification of transferences as, for example, those which are variously characterized by the wished-for magically omniscient mother, or by the controlling and dominating image, or by the incestuously desirable parents. Structural considerations are also valuable in helping to differentiate narcissistic and object-directed configurations, and to distinguish transference from character style and other simpler displacements. In addition, they broaden the concept of the differences between a "new" and a "real" relationship, when the states in dispute are appraised in terms of the functions of object relationships, object constancy, reality testing, and differentiation. Idealization, as it appears clinically in adolescence, is often erroneously labeled transference, a confusion which is less likely to occur within the structural perspective.

THE GENETIC POINT OF VIEW

The mere fact that transference is an attempt to repeat a past relationship in itself invokes the need to take genetic considerations into account. The repeated relationship may have originally been either real or fantasied, conscious or unconscious. And there are other conceptual complications too: infantile object relationships emerge from an undifferentiated self-object matrix and are regularly misperceived through narcissistic distortions. Furthermore, these and other distortions shape the character of subsequent phase development. It is this synthesis of earlier constellations into later ones which so often makes precise clinical assessment of the presenting conflict difficult. (See Silverman, Chapter 23, This Volume, for a summary of the developmental aspects of transference.)

The genetic viewpoint implies a certain sequential unfolding of psychological functions. With regard to the sequence of the function relating to object ties, if the earlier childhood interactions have proceeded within average expectable limits, a resultant regularity in the development of that function may be anticipated. In such circumstances, the initial relationships of childhood may come to be represented in the analytic situation as the basic matrix of trust within which the analysis proceeds, or periodically, as a necessary but transient regression in the service of some on-going developmental achievement. On the other hand, the progression of object relationships may have been halted or disrupted at some critical point in the developmental process. Under these circumstances, the repetition, when it appears in analysis, may come to occupy a central position as "resistance," i.e., as both an obstacle to and a vehicle of the work of therapy.

Hence the genetic perspective, with its developmental frame of reference, affords a point of view which assists in differentiating transference in the service of the analytic task ("basic" transference) from transference as a resistance. Similarly, it also permits a distinction between a genuine repetition of an old relationship from the emergence of a new one. Often this distinction between the new relationship and transference is difficult to discern clinically, and premature judgement may impede analytic work. The following case will illustrate this difficulty.

A boy of six-and-a-half entered analysis with an obvious impairment of various psychological functions. His parents had seen no evidence of his having entered a period of jealousy, competition, phallic masturbation, or sexual curiosity. They remarked that this was very different from the development of his older brother. After some months of analysis the boy recalled an anxiety dream which he dated—accurately, as it turned out—from the age of three or four. In this dream, bubbles were coming through the grate of his bedroom air conditioner. Three years later at the age of nine, when he had quite obviously entered the oedipal phase, he recalled the dream again. But this time it came back in a context which led him to remember noises he had heard emerging from his parents' bedroom through the air conditioner grate which apparently joined his room acoustically to theirs. It seems that the boy had unconsciously attributed these noises to the sound of his father urinating into his mother, thereby evoking the thought of "bubbles" somewhat like those he himself produced while urinating into the toilet bowl. This piece of clinical data supported the view that the oedipal phase had been attained earlier after all—unconsciously, to be sure, but to a sufficient degree to suggest that castration anxiety and regression had contributed to the presenting pathological picture.

THE ADAPTIVE POINT OF VIEW

Although the factors of force, energy, structure, and evolutionary sequence collectively lend depth to the transference concept, an adaptive viewpoint is necessary to highlight the specific influences of external reality on psychological manifestations. These influences must be studied at all points in time. Concerning the past, the study must include the specific familial and societal settings for the emerging psychological functions, themselves phylogenetically derived guarantees of adaptation. Concerning the present, it must determine whether the behavior and technique of the analyst impede or foster transference presentations.

Transference, in fact, reflects past states of adaptedness to earlier environmental conditions, including specific attitudes and behavioral modes of the parents. Although in average expectable conditions infantile sexuality and castration anxiety are universal in childhood, often the specific nature of the transference mirrors the degree to which the parents were genuinely seductive or menacing. For example:

One boy in analysis regularly approached a transference expectation of love or special attentiveness with a dogged determination that seemed to know no bounds. Sensitive to the least distraction on the part of the analyst, he would set about furiously "figuring out" either how to evoke praise or how to use the office so as to evoke controls or rebuke. Central to his view of child-rearing was a "beach-ball" image; that is, the image of children being tossed about from one parent to another, much like a beach-ball, without regard for the youngsters' feelings, but only for the pleasure of the activity itself. Yet, as it happens, this was indeed an accurate description of the real attitude of his parents, a divorced couple who regularly tossed him to and fro between them, more as an expression of their own "playfulness" toward each other than as a reflection of a true regard for him.

The adaptive perspective also focuses attention on the role of therapeutic technique in the development of transference. Naturally, transference may occur with only minimal activity on the part of the analyst; in fact it may even develop prior to the establishment of any formal analytic setting. Nevertheless, the technical procedures of analysis are specifically designed to foster a crystallization and resolution of certain potential transference states (it is precisely these procedures which distinguish analysis from all other psychotherapies). In child analysis, however, the attitudes and behavior of the analyst necessarily have to be influenced by the varying phase requirements of the patient; by the proclivity for identification during latency, for instance, and for idealizations during adolescence. These changing requirements undoubtedly complicate the analyst's task of establishing a situation in which transferences can crystallize. Although the problem of how to cope with the different phase requirements has been frequently discussed in the psychoanalytic literature, the necessary variations in analytic technique remain to be delineated.

In addition, the adaptive viewpoint facilitates the distinction between the so-called basic transference and the transference that develops as a specific adaptation to the special environmental circumstances of a given analytic situation—that is, between transference as a regression in the service of the on-going task of analysis and transference as a resistance.

Finally, because the adaptive view emphasizes the role of the analyst and his technical procedures, it also helps to isolate the part played by the analyst's technical mismanagement in producing an infiltration of a "real" relationship either into the alliance or into the transference.

CHAPTER 23

Transference and Development

Jerome S. Silverman, M.D.

The interaction of developmental processes and transference phenomena raises clinical and theoretical complexities, requiring that the analyst go beyond the relatively simple question of determining whether a relationship is "real" or "new" or "repeated." Development implies the existence of a thrust forward, perhaps of an order comparable to the "wish" for pleasure or the "need to repeat." Within that thrust, each new developmental step necessarily draws upon earlier object-ties, organizational modes, states of adaptedness, and so forth. This postulate suggests that in a treatment situation the child's relationship to the analyst may become the essential focal point of a newly evolving phase-adequate organization which is assimilating past modalities and relationships. Thus the "real," "new," and "repeated" relationships come together in a unique synthesis, producing a situation that in some respects lies outside the conventional psychoanalytic classification of therapeutic interactions. Such a synthesis must be distinguished not only from transient transference states, i.e., regressions in the service of developmental progress, but also from those unrelenting repetitions expressed as typical transference resistances which, if they are allowed to go unexamined, act as impediments to the analysis.

A study of the interaction of the developmental process and transference phenomena entails consideration of the following aspects: (1) the concept of the developmental thrust; (2) the hypothesis that

---

Dr. Silverman is Assistant Clinical Professor, Division of Psychoanalytic Education, Department of Psychiatry, State University of New York, Downstate Medical Center, Brooklyn, New York.

a new developmental step is based on new psychic organizations which have assimilated past phases; (3) the clinical effects of the interaction of development and transference phenomena; and (4) the different manifestations of transferences at different developmental periods.

The concept of the developmental thrust is inherent in any ontogenetic framework. It is implicit, for example, in Freud's (1905) theory of infantile sexuality which postulated libidinal phase organization. Variously described as "maturational processes," or a "manifestation of biology or of Eros," the developmental thrust has also been psychologically conceptualized as a new principle of mental functioning (Lipin, 1963). Anna Freud (1965) characterized it more simply as "the inner urge toward maturation, i.e., toward progressive development," and again as an "urge to complete development."

The urge to repeat can be distinguished from the child's hunger for "new experiences" (A. Freud, 1965) which is a more specific developmental factor in children. The maturational point of view makes it easier to distinguish those situations in which the analyst is a "new" object, from others in which the object-tie to the analyst is a "repetition" of an earlier relationship. This raises some meaningful questions: Is it possible to regard an apparent repetition as being oriented toward mastery—or does the repetition have to be detached from problems of mastery? Should the hunger for new experiences and for these "new object" attitudes, more central in the child than in the adult, be regarded as transference, or be distinguished from it? Does not the significance of these observed phenomena recommend a concept of transference more specific to the child?

The hypothesis that a new developmental step is based on new psychic organizations which have assimilated past phases is illustrated in the following vignette:

A boy of eight described an elaborate fantasy in which he skillfully murdered his analyst, skinned him, donned the skin, and successfully replaced him. The fantasy coincided with the beginning of an increasing tolerance of certain intense feelings, the development of a curiosity about scientific matters, and enhanced verbal skills. The boy's description of his replacement of the analyst, however, stopped abruptly with his contemplation of simultaneously possessing the analyst's wife. For a short period he became agitated, upset, and lost interest in treatment.

An interpretation of this fantasy which merely stressed the re-experiencing of the oedipal situation, would not do justice to the young patient's current need for identifications in the service of structure-building, a phase-adequate requirement of latency. The model chosen by the patient for the purpose of identification was derived from an oedipal father, utilizing perceived traits in the analyst, a current important figure in his life. The process of identification, however, became temporarily disrupted when it involved castration anxiety appropriate to the oedipal identification. At that moment a transference intruded, obstructing the coordination of the inner developmental thrust with the past and present "real" strivings toward new achievements. A correct interpretation would therefore emphasize the boy's interest in learning from others, and would seek to remove the inhibitions by demonstrating the confusion between present and past relationships. It would not single out the oedipal motives as providing the only impetus to the patient's need for identification with the analyst.

The developmental thrust thus incorporates progressively each newly achieved phase-specific level of instinctual and structural organization with the corresponding affects, object relations, and adaptational modes, all exerting their influence on the clinical transference phenomena.

The analyst as a "new object" may help the child to achieve a new organizational state which must be differentiated from regression in the service of the ego, from other transient regressions, and from fixations such as occur in atypical ego development. A six-year-old girl, troubled by curse words she heard at home, listed them for the analyst and slipped as she remarked, in offering them to him, "Here Daddy . . . I mean Dr.–." (Her father was also a physician.) The capacity to distinguish between the analyst as a real object (doctor) and as a fantasied object was easily visible here. Phase-specific vicissitudes in the genetic development of object relations are also illustrated by this parapraxis. Correspondingly, our therapeutic technique must reflect our recognition of developmental factors. To say: "You do here what you do at home," is quite different from the interpretation: "You behave to me as if I am your parent."

In another case, when receiving a gift that she and the analyst had agreed would be given her at a particular time, the patient's irrational reactions–crying bitterly and suddenly afraid something had happened to her mother who was outside parking the car—were understood by the analyst as a transference reaction and perhaps even as indicating a transference neurosis. Thus, the behavior was not regarded merely as a "new" experience, but as evidence of a newly achieved phase-specific organization that centered about the positive oedipal wish for the analyst as father.

A young patient, as the first summer separation approached, gave her analyst a going-away present (a pipe) which he did not accept. This patient then had a temper tantrum, which was regarded as a transference-neurosis manifestation, since it centered about the person of the analyst, and since such tantrums had been disappearing at home. The patient clearly had the ego development to tolerate the affect generated and could also distinguish between the analyst and the parent, thus making it possible to retain the therapeutic alliance. The appearance of new feelings involving the analyst occurring developmentally would not be regarded as transference. In this case, progressive and regressive aspects of the developmental line of organization of affect appeared, especially with respect to an object. The child's ability to make a distinction between parent and analyst, and the primary object from other objects, including the same object both as current and past object, was a prerequisite for the transference development.

A child may relive castration anxiety on a new hierarchical level of organization with the analyst as the father figure. With regression there is, therefore, more than merely repetition. Moreover, repetitive elements may arise principally out of schemata that are involved in conflict. The existence of a benign progressive transference makes possible the development to the next phase, with progressive integration, as well as "working through" of the regressive transferences.

Transferences need to be considered on the basis of their clinical effects on development as well as for their therapeutic value. In order to highlight the progressive and regressive aspects of transferences, an attempt should be made to formulate distinctions between transferences which occur in the service of development and transferences which impede development. During the course of an analytic situation, a certain basic relationship of trust, which mirrors part of the original mother-child unit, must be evoked. On the other hand, repetitions of past relationships in the service of regression or as a defense against analysis are, by definition, antithetical to developmental progress, at least until they have been effectively interpreted. In addition, the patient's interaction with the analyst is continuously being altered by the developmental movement, which in turn complicates the transference presentation. (One instance of the possible clinical use and misuse of the altering interaction between patient and analyst was illustrated in the first two cases described above.) The urge to complete development implies a developmental movement serially incorporating the past in its progression to newly achieved phase-specific hierarchical levels of organization. The latter, in phase-appropriate manners, variously color and modify the transference picture.

The interaction of development and transference must be explored further. The normal ontogenetic unfolding process may be either supported or disrupted in the course of an analysis. Conversely, transferences are complicated by developmental factors. The developmental aspect of the analyst-patient interaction can best be studied in the treatment of children and adolescents.

CHAPTER 24

Transference Phenomena in Adolescent Analysis

M. A. Scharfman, M.D.

Adolescence, like earlier periods of childhood, is a developmental phase characterized by major changes in structure and function. It is the view expressed in this paper that the complexity of transference phenomena in adolescent analysis is in effect a reflection of the complexity of developmental progression during this phase. A survey of the literature on adolescence reveals the existence of comparatively little direct reference to transference phenomena and even less to transference neurosis. Many of the clinical observations and data, however, as well as the theoretical formulations concerning adolescence as a developmental phase, have important implications for our conceptualizations of transference and transference neurosis and their role in the analysis of adolescents.

Freud (1905) pointed out that adolescence is characterized by a revival of infantile sexuality and stressed its relationship to two of the goals of that period—namely, the attainment of genital primacy and the finding of a new love object. With regard to the second goal, he emphasized the importance of the incest barrier as causing the search for a new love object. Jones, writing in 1922, also stressed the revival of the oedipal feelings, and described in detail the recapitulation of earlier development during adolescence.

Dr. Scharfman is Assistant Professor of Psychiatry, Division of Psychoanalytic Education, Department of Psychiatry, State University of New York, Downstate Medical Center, Brooklyn, New York.

During the 1930's, several analysts, notably Bernfeld (1938) and Aichhorn (1925), contributed to a fuller understanding of adolescence, but Anna Freud's (1936) *The Ego and the Mechanisms of Defense* was the first serious attempt to formulate a systematic psychoanalytic psychology of this critical developmental phase. Miss Freud spoke of the increase in the amount of libido available during this period and the consequent possibility of emergence into consciousness, because of the heightened cathexis, of wishes, fantasies, and instinctual processes which in other periods remain unconscious. Emergence of these fantasies can constitute a threat to the integrity of the ego, in spite of the fact that the ego's organization is by now comparatively advanced. Moreover, although the ego responds with the same defensive measures it previously employed, these now take on a much more exaggerated form. To illustrate the point, Anna Freud cited two peculiarities typical of this period, asceticism and intellectualization. She also suggested that the massive forms of defense utilized by the ego during adolescence represent a repudiation of drive, which is different from the usual process of repression in that it stems from the fear of the intensity of drive (quantitative factor) rather than from a fear of any particular kind of drive (qualitative factor). This dread of the intensity of drive refers to that earlier period when differentiation of ego and id first occurred; the massive defensive measures represent the ego's attempt to maintain differentiation and ensure the constancy of its organization.

Anna Freud emphasized the withdrawal of cathexis from the childhood love objects as well as from their internalized representations in the form of the superego, and showed how this decathexis of the superego increases the intensity of the drive. She described the adolescent's search for new objects, pointing out that while the relationships formed at this time may be passionate and exclusive, they are characterized by their short duration and the ready substitution of a new object. In these relationships the adolescent does not aim at possessing the object, but rather attempts to identify himself with it.

Anna Freud's book undoubtedly stimulated other analysts to take a greater interest in the problems of adolescence. Katan (1951) described how a 14-year-old girl broke off her analysis when she found a new boy friend, feeling she could not talk about this relationship.

Katan thought the break occurred at a time when she and her patient were on "good terms" and without any antagonism. Indeed, she viewed the disruption as a normal developmental phenomenon, more important than continued analysis, because it symbolized the adolescent's need to renounce the incestuous object once and for all by "removal" from that object prior to forming a new relationship. She felt that this "removal" process ought to be distinguished from the usual displacement, because it is an "irreversible process in a specific direction." Inasmuch as the nature of transference requires as exact a reproduction of the past as possible, it is therefore diametrically opposed to the developmental need in adolescence to remove oneself from that past. Analytic interpretation of transference, which is aimed against the displacement of feelings from the incestuous objects to the analyst, would also run counter to the normal developmental thrust.

Katan's point here seems not quite clear. If one assumes that what she described was indeed transference, at least part of the difficulty would appear to be that her patient could not recognize the transference for what it was and perceived the analyst as an actual earlier infantile object instead of merely representing one. It must therefore be supposed that the disruption of the analysis was the result of either Katan's failure to interpret the transference adequately, or, as this author would assume, the patient's inability to discriminate the transference because of ego regression occurring during this phase.

Gitelson (1948) suggested that the treatment of the adolescent cannot be directed toward providing a benign re-experiencing of his past, but must provide him with a new emotional experience. He said that the therapeutic situation needs to be dependable rather than dependent, and saw the therapist as simultaneously fulfilling the roles of catalyst, synergist, and model. Asserting that departures from classical analytic technique are unavoidable in the treatment of adolescents, he cautioned against the analysis of defense and also the interpretation of the transference.

Spiegel (1951) noted earlier warnings against analyzing adolescents and suggested that psychoanalysis should perhaps be adapted to the adolescent's particular situation, and that use might be made of an introductory phase as with the analysis of children and delinquents.

He observed, as did Reich (1950) and Fraiberg (1955), that adolescents frequently withheld transference fantasies right through to termination of the analysis. Reich (1950) believed that full-blown transference can never really develop in the adolescent, and, as a consequence, the analysis necessarily remains incomplete.

Fraiberg (1955) suggested that the fantasies withheld are negative transference fantasies which represent the psychiatrist as the omnipotent parent, all-seeing and all-knowing. She warned that too early an interpretation merely tends to re-enforce the fantasies and so threatens the adolescent with a loss of autonomy through submission to a powerful being. Because she viewed the fear of loss of autonomy as the greatest threat to the adolescent, Fraiberg stressed the need for supporting the ego in the early stages of treatment by replacing the basic rule of free association by the more permissive one of "you don't need to tell me anything you don't wish to." She disagreed, however, with Spiegel's (1951) suggestion for an introductory phase. She thought the analysis of resistance and defense should be applied to the adolescent as it is to the adult, using interpretation to counter the resistances produced by fear of the strength of the drives; that there are certain factors in the maturational push of puberty conducive to analysis which can be used to support the analysis once the initial difficulties are overcome. She made no mention, though, of the development of the transference neurosis or of its analysis.

In 1956 a panel of the American Psychoanalytic Association on "The Psychology of Adolescents" (Buxbaum, 1958) produced several contributions relevant to our subject. Geleerd referred specifically to both transference and transference neurosis. She divided adolescence into phases with early and preadolescence characterized by the rejection of parental figures and analyst alike. This rejection tendency, combined with a paucity of material about fantasy life, imposes natural limitations upon the amount of analytic work that can be achieved. The situation in mid-adolescence, which she defined as extending roughly from age 14 to 16, is quite different. Unconscious fantasies are then more readily available in the analysis than at almost any other time in life and can be more easily interpreted as a consequence; also, the analysis seems to move faster because of the fluidity of material. On the other hand, chaotic situations can be created, because continuous changes in imbalance of id, ego, and superego do not allow for the relative stability essential for working through. Moreover, the recathexis of oedipal fantasies must be warded off with increased vigor at this age because the genital nature of the relationship with the analyst makes the incestuous threat more real as it becomes more capable of fulfillment.

Writing about the occurrence of transference neurosis during mid-adolescence, Geleerd (1957) made the following observations:

> It is self-evident that the adolescent does not develop a transference neurosis like the adult patient. Like the younger child, he develops transference reactions which coexist with the relationship to the analyst as a need-satisfying object. To interpret this latter part of the relationship to the adolescent would undo the treatment aim of the analysis. However, as in all analytic work, negative feelings should be interpreted and if possible analyzed dynamically and genetically. Transference reactions proper should of course be handled as in all analyses [pp. 168-169].

Geleerd thought that during the final period of adolescence, the analysis increasingly resembles that of adults. She pointed out that the handling of transference, however, is necessarily quite different with adolescents. Working through can be achieved only to a limited extent, and systematic analysis of old defense mechanisms is not possible. The analyst must also fulfill the need of a parent substitute, although in a restrained and neutral way. He has to make a greater effort to increase the tolerance of the ego to pathogenic conflict and help the patient test reality.

The panel agreed to the usefulness of dividing adolescence into three phases. It also agreed that technique with the adolescent must often be modified according to the individual balance of the psychic forces, and that the handling of transference likewise requires modification. It was generally considered that transference neurosis is unlikely to develop except in late adolescence. Some believed, however, that analysis was contraindicated during adolescence, that psychotherapy was more effective.

Erikson (1956) saw transference affected by the adolescent's need to retain at least a basic core of identity, when he is still seeking his own identity. Full development of the transference threatens the adolescent with the loss of his identity in that of the analyst, particularly during what Erikson called an "identity crisis." This threat precludes the development of what we usually know as transference, or else it diffuses it. Implicit in Erikson's theory is the idea that the regression inherent in the classical analytic situation in itself constitutes a threat to the emerging ego identity.

Anna Freud (1958) described analysis of adolescents as a "hazardous venture," in part because of the rapidly shifting constellations of psychic forces and shifting patterns of resistance. She noted that certain reactions in adolescence bear a similarity to states of mourning and unhappy love in that the libido is fully engaged by a real love object of the present or of the recent past. There is thus insufficient libido available to cathect the person of the analyst, or to flow back regressively and reinvest former objects and positions. Consequently, neither the transference events nor past events are meaningful enough to yield material for interpretation. Where the analyst is libidinally invested, it tends to be as a new love object, which creates a specific difficulty because of the adolescent's urgency of need and his intolerance for frustration.

When defense against infantile object ties, Anna Freud suggested, is by displacement of the libido, the adolescent has decisively turned away from the infantile objects, and attempts to analyze him at this time are doomed to failure. Where the major defense against infantile objects is a reversal of affect, however, treatment may be more easily initiated, but as soon as true transference develops and infantile fantasies emerge into consciousness the reversal of affect is repeated in the analytic situation and treatment has to be broken off. Where the libido has largely withdrawn into the self, severity of the illness as a sign of possible psychosis demands analysis, but the treatment has to be limited to effecting a return from narcissistic withdrawal to object cathexis. Any deeper involvement in the transference may cause a return of the symptoms and termination of the analysis. Where the patient has an even greater anxiety about the infantile object ties, defense may be by regression to the state of "primary identification" and may lead to a fear of emotional surrender, with the accompanying fear of loss of identity. The type of regression fostered in the classical analytic situation would here be perceived as a threat of overwhelming proportions. In general, Miss Freud was cautious about the possibilities of successful analysis during adolescence and emphasized the need for modifications in techniques and goals.

Eissler (1958a) dealt at length with the question of techniques in the analysis of adolescents. He suggested that because of the psychic disequilibrium characteristic of the phase, the analyst may be forced to deal with neurotic symptoms (inhibitions), delinquency, perversion, and what resembles an acute schizophrenic reaction, all in the same patient, and possibly even all within any given hour or group of hours. He is thus presented with an ever changing clinical picture in which, at one moment, transference reactions may be analyzable, at another, they press for immediate gratification, and at still another, have to be actively induced. In other words, what appears as a workable transference relationship one moment may have to be dealt with entirely differently the next because of the unpredictability of the adolescent's response.

Geleerd (1961) suggested that a partial regression to the undifferentiated phase of an object relationship is responsible for the adolescent's increased need for a love object and for union with this love object. She thought this is always accompanied by the fear that the regression may go too far and result in the dissolution of the self. Rebelliousness, both in the analytic situation and at home, represents a defense against the fear of dissolution in this partial regression. It seems clear that at such times, analysis, particularly with regard to the regressive aspects of the transference, can intensify this threat. Although regression may thus lead to pathological reactions, it appears to be a necessary vicissitude of the ego for full growth and maturation. When such ego regressions occur, the analyst can be a source of stability to the adolescent rather than a mere transference figure.

Lampl-de Groot (1962) examined the problems of the role of the superego and ego ideal in adolescence. She advanced the theory that the patient simultaneously maintains what seems to be diametrically opposing views of the parents, which are repeated in the transference. The adolescent needs to maintain, often unconsciously, an ideal image of omnipotent parents and analyst in order to sustain a degree of narcissistic cathexis and also to diminish guilt aroused by his own hostile and aggressive feelings toward these objects. Precisely because the parents and analyst are seen as omnipotent and therefore invulnerable, the patient feels less guilty about expressing aggression toward them. This thesis has important implications, not only for the form of the transference, but also for the degree to which specific aspects of the transference may be analyzed during adolescence.

Laufer (1964) spoke of the important function of the ego ideal during that period in adolescence when "superego regression" is apt to occur. Ego ideal facilitates possible compromises between the psychic structures by enabling new adaptations to evolve. It also assists in maintaining a degree of narcissistic cathexis when excessive disequilibrium threatens. The analyst has a particularly important role to play in this context. In offering himself as an ego ideal, the analyst gives the adolescent a degree of narcissistic satisfaction which may be essential in effecting a therapeutic alliance so that analysis may proceed. At times he must not only offer himself as an object for identification, but actively encourage the identification process by serving as auxiliary ego, ego ideal, or auxiliary conscience. Only in later stages can he adopt a more classically aloof position. Indeed, it is incumbent on him to make this modification when he is required to deal with regressions in id, ego, and superego, which sometimes occur simultaneously.

DEVELOPMENTAL FACTORS AFFECTING TRANSFERENCE PHENOMENA IN ADOLESCENCE AND THEIR IMPLICATIONS FOR ANALYTIC TECHNIQUE

There is general agreement that the requisite degree of differentiation of psychic structure for the development of transference, as defined by the study group, occurs prior to the onset of adolescence. Nevertheless, from preadolescence until late adolescence partial and temporary regressions frequently take place in each of the psychic structures, with resultant fluctuations and disequilibria in the level of psychic organization and functioning. These affect the transference process. Transference as an operational and functional concept requires a relatively stable psychic organization if it is to be at all effectively utilized as the vehicle for the therapeutic revival and re-experiencing of earlier infantile object relationships, and for the working through of pathogenic conflicts therein.

In the classical analytic situation, the development of a transference neurosis (which should evolve consequent to analysis of defense and be fostered by the specific analytic setting)—and its subsequent analysis—is one of the most effective indicators of the probability of therapeutic success. Although none of the reports I have cited described an actual transference neurosis in an adolescent analysis, several observers—Anna Freud (1958), Geleerd (1961), Katan (1951), and Erikson (1956)—suggested, either directly or by implication, that its emergence could be disruptive. Various reasons were advanced to support this belief. Firstly, transference, involving as it does an enormously increased dependence upon the analyst as a central figure, can threaten the adolescent with loss of his tenuous ego autonomy or ego identity. Second, as a vehicle for the revival and re-experiencing of earlier infantile relationships, the transference process runs directly counter to the developmental task of achieving some degree of "removal" or freedom from those ties. Third, to the extent that it may focus the emerging genital impulses and the earlier infantile object representations onto the person of the analyst, transference may create a markedly intensified incestuous threat or erotize the earlier relationships at a different level. Any of these eventualities could interfere with the developmental task of turning toward nonincestuous heterosexual love objects. Finally, considerations of possible ego regressions suggest that even if a transference neurosis developed, the degree of ego distance or the "splitting of the ego" required for the analysis of the revived experiences would not necessarily be achieved.

Implicit in these views of the disruptive nature of transference phenomena in adolescent analysis is the recognition that transference neurosis may indeed develop, and one must wonder at the absence of reported cases. Clinical material has in fact been described which would appear to meet one or another of the accepted criteria for transference neurosis (for example, analytic situations in which the analyst serves as the object of re-experienced infantile wishes and/or a repetition of symptoms occurs). Yet even in these instances, the term "transference neurosis" has not been used. Perhaps one reason the term has been avoided is because transference manifestations in adolescents and adults are not identical. There is hence an obvious need to describe the phenomena in terms specifically applicable to adolescent analysis. This need becomes even more evident in view of the fact that the concepts of transference-neurosis phenomena applied to adult analysis (supposedly our norms for other types of analysis) are themselves not very clearly defined.[1]

The absence of reported cases of adolescent transference neurosis may be the result of the inherent difficulty of recognizing the manifestations of transference phenomena at this phase of development. In adolescent analysis, the clinical transference picture can very often be obscured by the fact that the phase-specific libidinal push and the defensive attempts to deal with it involve the analyst in additional roles. The analyst, for example, may be involved in displacement of libido from the parental figures as defense against the infantile object tie (Anna Freud, 1936). Or the defense by reversal of affect may manifest itself in the analysis. Or more narcissistic modes of relationship and primitive identifications may appear. The analyst may be not only transference object, or object of displacement, he may also be a "new" object. New and previously undeveloped levels of object relationship and adaptation can and do appear, in addition to the repetition of earlier relationships with the original objects or their representations in fantasy. Because of the multiple and rapidly shifting uses the adolescent makes of the analyst, what specifically constitutes transference is not as well defined or as clearly presented as in adult analysis.

As has been shown, most of those interested in transference phenomena in adolescent analysis emphasized the complications deriving from its occurrence. Some even went so far as to caution against the desirability of analysis. Others, however, proposed various "modifications" of technique which in effect are attempts either to minimize the development of the transference neurosis or to limit the threat from the transference. Although such proposals resemble the various parameters used in specific adult analytic situations, it would be misleading to look upon them as modifications of technique merely because they represent a departure from classical adult analytic practice. (Actually, since the introduction of the structural theory and the many changes consequent thereupon, adult analysis itself has changed considerably.) Classical analytic techniques are not necessar-

[1] For a discussion of this point, see Lilleskov, Chapter 21, This Volume.

ily the appropriate norms for the analysis of children and adolescents. And, in fact, methods for reducing the disruptive effects of transference on adolescent analysis may constitute the basic technique appropriate and necessary to this developmental phase.

A major problem for most of those studying adolescents is the difficulty of forming and maintaining a therapeutic alliance during those periods when the transference (or transference neurosis) may represent a threat to the analysis. Hence the central issue may be to determine how transference can be kept within useful limits—a challenge which also arises, though to a lesser degree, in some adult analyses. I herewith offer some tentative ideas for utilizing developmental factors to direct analytic technique toward this end.

A consideration of developmental factors above all suggests the need to exercise restraint in interpreting transference. For to the extent that interpretation with an adolescent is concentrated predominantly on transference repetitions of earlier relationships, it may hinder and ultimately prevent the evolution of new levels of phase-adequate reactions that occur with the analyst as their chief focus. The developmental push for a new object outside the family, be it romantic heterosexual love-object, ego ideal, object of a "crush," or whatever, may fix upon the analyst as its object at a given period. To interpret at this time the analyst's role as simply heir to earlier feelings for the father would therefore exclude the additional role in which he is being experienced and which may be the result of a constructive developmental step.

Multiple representations of the analyst obviously coexist, and the correct representation selected for interpretation has to be determined according to the balance of the psychic economy at a given time. At certain periods, an interpretation of the transference experience may be both appropriate and valuable. It should be remembered, however, that the very intensity of affect during adolescence creates special technical problems in the analysis, constituting additional reasons to curb the transference interpretation. These intense affects in relation to their oedipal origins while the ego and superego are still in flux may make it impossible to continue the analysis.

A clinical excerpt may illustrate how developmental considerations can guide the analyst in choosing when to make a transference interpretation:

A 16-year-old girl entered analysis because of a severe sleep disturbance, fear that someone would break into her house and harm her, periods of marked depression, frequent difficulty in getting along with her parents, and masochistic involvements with young men. After some months in analysis, she became anxious and almost phobic about lying down on the couch, something she had done easily enough before the transference developed intensity. Clearly she was afraid of, and unconsciously wished for, a sexual approach from the analyst. Although it was obvious that she was repeating earlier experiences with her father and older brother, I chose to confine my interpretation to her anxiety and how it occurred in connection with men.

Further, I pointed out again, as I had earlier, that when she was anxious she confused fantasy thoughts and reality (transient ego regression). Following this she could discuss the sexual fantasy which was the basis of her fear. Somewhat later she could see that she was afraid she might accept such an approach (as she had indeed done prior to analysis). This limited confrontation, directed at her present anxiety, seemed to relieve it without acting out. She began to develop a more typical, less sexualized adolescent crush on the analyst, describing him as the first man she really liked—the first who could understand her. During this phase a workable transference existed, combining aspects of the analyst as a new object with repressed positive oedipal wishes. She began to deal with her father in analysis, proceeding from her conscious feelings, antagonism and disgust, to fragments of pleasurable experiences in her early childhood. She was able to analyze them, in part because of the present attachment to the analyst as a new heterosexual object. During this time, her detachment from her father, which was tenuous and easily reversible, was aided by the attachment to the analyst. Transference interpretations would have been untimely. The working through of her feelings toward her father were long and complicated. Eventually, a memory returned, and was documented, of occasions during preadolescence when her father had "jokingly" teased her sexually, touching her, and making fun of her lack of development. She had felt helpless and terrified, but also excited. She was overwhelmed and disorganized, and then not sure it had really happened. This episode and others similar to it had distorted reality testing in this area. When these feelings were revived in the transference, she felt helpless and anxious and repeated her regression. The transient ego regression when she was anxious would have made it difficult for her to differentiate the analyst from his transference representation. Transference interpretation could not be experienced or utilized as such. As indicated earlier, such transient ego regressions are quite common during this phase of adolescence, and require interpretation be limited at those times. Ego regression may occur in response to anxiety, and can then, itself, become a source of anxiety. Interpretation on this level should precede or accompany transference interpretations where this occurs.[2]

Only after the preadolescent material had been worked through could she see her responses to the analyst as a repetition of her feeling for her father; only then could she begin to deal with her own wishes. This occurred at a time of much greater psychic equilibrium, probably the result of analysis, together with several years of maturation (although it seems unlikely that psychic maturation would have proceeded as smoothly without analysis). She also had a relationship with a more stable young man at the time. Earlier relationships had been sadomasochistic, repeating her experiences with her father and brother. All of these factors contributed to allow the analysis of the transference.

It would seem that a crucial element in keeping adolescent transference phenomena within useful limits is the timing of the transference interpretation. Appropriately timed interpretations may aid the ego in synthesis and re-enforce the therapeutic alliance. It may not be too far-fetched to postulate that the extent to which the patient may develop the full transference experience (i.e., transference neurosis) depends largely on whether the analyst has chosen the right moment to interpret the transference representation.[3] In view of its importance, it is perhaps unfortunate that the capacity for correct timing appears to be a function of what has been termed, somewhat unsatisfactorily, "psychoanalytic intuition."[4]

[2]Schur has described this and also its technical implications (see Chapter 4, This Volume).

[3]It would require much more detail than can be presented here to document the above case as transference neurosis, but it was certainly intense, repetitive, included symptoms, and yet remained within workable limits.

[4]Adolescent analysis may also involve to a greater degree what Loewenstein (1951) has called "reconstruction upwards."

These formulations have emphasized the adaptive aspects of the transference—the patient uses the analyst as a new real object in order to achieve a new level of relationship, drawing upon the libidinal ties of the regressive aspects of the transference but also adding to them. If sensitively handled, transference in adolescent analysis may serve as a vehicle for furthering some of the developments of the phase, facilitating their differentiation and synthesis. This point of view would seem to fit in with our study group's thoughts about the need to evaluate and define transference in relation to developmental factors. The role of developmental phase can be applied to other aspects of technique in both child and adolescent analysis. Consideration of developmental factors may, for example, suggest that the sex of the analyst is an important element in determining whether or not analysis of a child or an adolescent will be possible in a given case at a given stage.

Adolescence is a period in which the search for new objects and new levels of relationship is central as a developmental goal. We should therefore be surprised if this search did not manifest itself in the analytic situation and affect the extent to which transference develops in its purest form, i.e., as a repetition of the earlier relationships. The intensity and depth of the transference phenomena in adolescent analysis show great variation; and whether or not transference neurosis occurs will depend upon whether we use a definition of transference neurosis which is derived solely from adult models or—as is here advocated—one that is specifically applicable to the requirements of the adolescent phase.

CHAPTER 25

Dreams and Transference

Charles A. Sarnoff, M.D.

The study group examined children's dreams which contained representations of the analyst to discover whether they could be used as indicators of the existence of transference. As a result of our exploration, we were able to adduce a number of conditions which have to be met before a dream involving the analyst can be taken as evidence that a transference relationship has actually been established.

The first requirement, of course, is to determine whether the child has yet developed the capacity for "symbol formation"—for representing the primary object (i.e., the parent) by another object (i.e., transference to the analyst). It is important here to distinguish the process of symbol formation which participates in transference formation, from the psychically simpler process of direct object representation. Object representation merely entails the displacement of an idea, concept, wish, or fantasy from one object to another; in other words, the patient is usually aware that he is representing the primary object by a new object. The essence of symbol formation, on the other hand, consists precisely in a repression of the link between that which represents and that which is represented. Hence, symbol formation is the more restricted process: all symbols are object representations, but not all object representations are symbols.

In clinical terms, the development of the capacity for symbol formation, as distinct from object representation, implies that the child

Dr. Sarnoff is Director of Child Psychiatry, Director of the Outpatient Department, and Director of Residency Training, Brookdale Hospital Center, Brooklyn, New York.

had passed from the stage of consciously displacing concepts and fantasies from old objects to new objects—known as "symbolic play"—to the stage of performing this process unconsciously. Only when the child has reached the stage of repressing the link between the primary object and the object that represents it—which has been observed during the third year of life—can he cast the analyst unconsciously into the role of (i.e., symbol of) the parent; only then can a transference relationship be established.

The appearance of fantasies involving the analyst cannot by itself, however, be viewed as *prima facie* evidence of the existence of transference. The fantasies may represent a currently real situation, not a transference situation. Moreover, the influence of the past on the contents of the present fantasy and relationship with the analyst must also be taken into account. It is possible, for instance, that the appearance of the analyst in the child's dreams may indicate a failure in psychic development, signifying that the patient has not progressed beyond the level of part-object relations. That is to say, the analyst may appear, not as a new entity which has now become the object of displacement for an earlier fantasy, experience, or wish (transference), but merely as a "part-object," undifferentiated from parents or any other individuals. In the latter case, dreams involving the analyst cannot be taken as indicators of transference; they are evidence, rather, of externalization of a narcissistic representation of object relations. Hence, in addition to the capacity for symbol formation, the child must also have developed a capacity for differentiation between self and object to the extent that he can perceive the analyst as a discrete entity and a new object existing in its own right. Clearly a normal child over three has the potential for the formation of transference. Clinical proof of the existence of transference is, however, another matter. Through the study of children's dreams containing the analyst, we may be able to demonstrate its existence.

Using a broad definition of the term, we can say that transference occurs when internalized conflicts are manifested in the relationship with the analyst. In terms of dreams reported in the course of child analysis, we can refine this definition further by saying that a transference is indicated when the dream involves the analyst as the object of wishes or activities which represent repressed early experiences, fantasies, or instinctual wishes, and the defenses against them.

In order to exclude deceptive clinical phenomena which resemble transference, it is necessary to extend the definition of transference to include additional factors:

The manifest content of the transference material must be a representation of latent unconscious material from early life, consisting of specific contexts for specific objects. Early life experiences in which narcissistic libidinal distribution determines the objects do not form the basis for transference in child analysis.

The link between that which represents and that which is represented must be unavailable to consciousness, but must have the potential for being brought into consciousness.

That which is represented, i.e., the latent content, must be a repressed element consisting of instinctual discharge related to the primary object.

There must be constancy of psychic representation of the primary object.

The patient must be able to differentiate the latent objects and the manifest transference object—e.g., as it presents itself in the dream.

This extended definition forms the basis for questions to test whether a given piece of clinical data, such as a dream involving the analyst, can be regarded as evidence of transference having taken place.

Of course, to be able to ask and answer all of these questions represents the ideal. In actual practice this would be too cumbersome. We have to be satisfied if we can posit, much less answer, just a few of them. These questions are presented only as tentative guides. Greater weight should be applied to their heuristic value than to their possible use as everyday clinical tools.

a. *Does it repeat a recent experience?* If yes, the phenomenon is not transference.

b. *Does it repeat an earlier experience?* If yes, the phenomenon could be transference and any of the following questions should be asked, all of which require an affirmative response if the phenomenon is to be called transference.

c. *Did the experience involve primary objects? Is the object represented a primary object?*

d. *Is the clinical manifestation a re-creation of an infantile wish of the child toward the primary object?*

e. *Is the link between that which represents and that which is represented unavailable to the system consciousness?* If yes, is it potentially available to consciousness?

f. *Is object constancy present?*

g. *Can the subject differentiate the latent objects and the manifest transference object?*

On the other hand, affirmative answers to any of the following questions would rule out the presence of transference.

h. *Did the earlier experience contain a narcissistically cathected object such as the thumb or anus?*

i. *Did the earlier experience occur before the subject was capable of differentiating objects?*

j. *Is the clinical manifestation a re-creation of the child's recollection of his own representation of an attitude of the primary object?*

The following dream and its subsequent discussion by the study group is presented as an example of how these questions may be used to determine through the medium of a dream containing the analyst whether a transference has occurred.

A seven-year-old girl reported a dream in which she was frightened by a spooky figure whom she designated as the analyst. It was one of a series of anxiety dreams that occurred just before her parents were to go on a short trip; the patient was to sleep away from home for the first time. The patient's anxiety dreams not only awakened her, but left her frightened; she wanted her mother to be with her all the time and was unable even to dress alone. She illustrated the dream of the analyst by making clay objects. First she made a long thick snake-like object, which, she explained, was the spook and the analyst. She hollowed out a large stomach, leaving the snake a shell from stem to stern; a large mouth, two eyes, and a control box completed the figure. Next, the patient set little pieces of clay on the table, saying: "Watch him eat houses and people and junk. I'll make his mouth bigger. Watch him kill and eat people." After she put the clay houses and objects into his stomach, she reported that her recent periods of silence during analysis had been associated with thoughts about her dreams. Then she became afraid of the analyst, didn't talk, and wanted to telephone home.

The group reviewed this dream from the standpoint of the 10 questions. No recent experiences in reality could be posited as day residues for the manifest content of the dream (question a). The child's inability to associate freely to the dream elements precluded the uncovering of repressed infantile memories (b). Insofar as there was no evidence for the repetition of a specific early or recent experience, the representation of the analyst as a devouring snake was posited as a projection of a current wish of the patient toward the analyst. This, too, had to remain a conjecture in view of the absence of corroboratory material. Taking a lead from question j, it was suggested that the analyst as devouring snake was a projected re-creation of her own representation of her mother's attitude toward her. Some clinical corroboration existed for this. There was no evidence that the representation of the analyst as a devouring snake was a projection of an earlier experience related to the narcissistic cathexis of a thumb (h). The patient was a thumb sucker, but her fantasy while sucking had to do with katabasis (the doing and undoing of the death—i.e., the concept of someone going away).

Up to this point, transference had been neither proven nor disproven. Then question d was put in the following form: "Could the analyst as devouring snake be a projection and re-creation of an earlier wish of the child toward the primary object?" This could be answered in the affirmative and specifically corroborated. When the child first came to treatment, she had had repeated bad dreams which invaded her daytime thinking and interfered with her ability to work in school. The specific content of the earlier repetitive dream was, "A bloody-headed ghost leading thousands of snakes comes toward me. It goes by me and goes to my mommy. They wind themselves around her and crush her to death."

The subsequent dream image of the analyst as devouring monster was thus clearly a clinical manifestation of a re-creation of an earlier wish of the child toward the primary object, and could therefore be called a transference on the basis of the criteria currently used by the group.

We suggest that these questions may be applied to any clinical phenomena to test whether they are indicators of a transference relationship with the analyst. Application of the questions will also enlarge our understanding of transference phenomena generally. It is hoped that the suggested questions will compensate for the uncertainties resulting from the absence of free associations in child analysis.

The group studied several children's dreams in which the analyst was directly involved and noted that, interestingly enough, many of them occurred at times when the child experienced a separation from the primary object in reality. This suggests a possible area for fruitful exploration in the future.

CHAPTER 26

Clinical Illustrations of Transference Phenomena

Jules Glenn, M.D., Paul Kay, M.D., and Henry Rosner, M.D.

Members of the study group presented material from the analysis of several children in order to discuss the criteria for the occurrence of transference phenomena in a given analytic situation. This paper consists of extracts from the clinical data on three patients at different stages of development, and includes a brief account of the questions raised by the study group in considering each case.

CASE 1

The youngest patient in the survey was Betty, who was in analysis for approximately 12 months, from the age of three and a half. When she was almost three years old, while her mother was in the seventh month of her pregnancy, she started a prolonged period of fecal retention which terminated near the end of her analysis. The disorder was found to result from her identification with her pregnant mother: she conceived of her bowel movement as a beloved and hated baby, her little brother.

Betty looked upon the analyst as a real person who could help her become, as she put it, "like other people," if she told him her

Drs. Glenn, Kay, and Rosner are Assistant Clinical Professors, Division of Psychoanalytic Education, Department of Psychiatry, State University of New York, Downstate Medical Center, Brooklyn, New York.

thoughts and feelings. She communicated largely by play, directing the analyst to participate in games with her. He was told to act specific roles and do certain things in response to the roles she herself assumed. For instance, Betty would play a game in which she fed the analyst who was the baby. She would withhold food, and the analyst-baby brother would cry. Once in the course of this game, Betty forgot she was playing. Her rage at the infant got out of hand, as she threw clay and broke a dish. This behavior was much like that of an adult patient who free-associates and loses control. The analyst was first pictured as he really is, a helper. But during the course of the play-communication, the child's equivalent of free association, it became evident that Betty had displaced feelings toward her brother on to the analyst; and when she lost control, the displacement became even clearer.

Betty also displaced on to the analyst feelings toward her mother. Once she remained with the analyst after her mother left the office with her brother. Throughout the session she asked for her mother. She wanted to play at painting the wall and the analyst. The fact that she wanted to smear the analyst was an obvious indication of her anger, and the interpretation was made that she wished her mother were there so that she would not have to be angry with her for leaving with her brother. When Betty's mother returned, Betty crawled on the floor like her brother. She did not want to leave the analyst at the end of the session.

Although the displacements so far noted may well have been transferences—displacements of feelings from past experiences with the mother and brother to the analyst—all that could be conclusively demonstrated was that Betty's *present* angry feelings and defensive, clinging behavior had been displaced to the analyst. Later in the analysis, however, it could be conclusively demonstrated that the feelings and defenses displaced were those originally experienced at the time of the birth of her brother.

During one session Betty expressed irritation toward her brother and then became angry at a baby doll. As part of a cooperative attempt to find out why she felt this way, she played several scenes with dolls. In one sequence, the mother went to the doctor while the baby, played by the analyst, remained with her father. The analyst-baby was angry and emptied a Tinkertoy box, the equivalent of having a bowel movement. The significance of the material became clear when it was learned that Betty's aunt had just given birth. This event reactivated memories of the birth of Betty's brother, her anger at him and her mother, and her desires to injure them. In the next session, anger burst forth toward the analyst. Talking of her aunt's new baby, Betty wanted to put a baby and a mother out. She then played being a baby fed by the analyst-mother. The analyst said it felt nice to be a baby. Betty replied that her brother hit her mother. Then she hit the analyst's genitals. She said boys have penises and girls have vaginas. Her penis envy became clearer as she broke the penis of a clay figure of a boy.

It will be noted that during the first of these two sessions, Betty assigned to the analyst the role which she herself had played in the original experience. During the second session, the analyst was perceived as the mother and brother in the memory of that original experience, and she repeated her earlier anger with her mother, her penis envy, and her desire to attack and castrate her brother—which was much more clearly a transference phenomenon.

There was good reason to believe, from data presented by Betty's mother, that the little girl had achieved a stage in which oedipal longings appeared fleetingly early in, and probably prior to, the analysis. In the third month of the analysis, Betty said to the analyst, "I'm not going to talk to daddy . . . . unless he does something for me." Although she behaved antagonistically to her father at that time and usually would not kiss him, she kissed him when her mother was away. She said that she liked to be with her father except when her mother was present. Openly affectionate oedipal thrusts apparently conflicted with Betty's love for her mother and her fear of her mother's disapproval. Positive oedipal feelings were obscured by a sadomasochistic relationship with her father. Quite possibly, the patient's symptomatology resulted in part from a repression following anxiety resulting from oedipal wishes.

In the course of the analysis, sustained, openly affectionate feelings for her analyst and her father appeared. This paralleled a shift in cathexis from the anal zone to the genitals. Betty stopped retaining bowel movements and started to masturbate genitally. Once, in the course of playing a game, Betty asked the analyst to tickle her. Although he did not comply, Betty said she experienced a tickling sensation in her genitals. In a session soon after that, she asked the analyst to remove bowel movements from her anus and then to deliver babies from her genitals. It was known from previous material that Betty identified the deliverer of babies with the impregnator. At the next session it became apparent that she was also developing oedipal fantasies. Betty said that she disliked her mother and liked her father. Shortly thereafter, her desire to take the analyst's penis inside her became clear as she lunged for his penis which she wished to bite and incorporate orally.

This last episode stimulated several questions in the study group. Were the oedipal longings expressed toward the analyst repetitions of the early fleeting affectionate oedipal feelings toward her father and now released from repression? In this case, they would fit our definition of transference. However, if the attainment of sustained positive oedipal representations of her father and the analyst indicated the attainment of a new developmental level, the emergence of oedipal longings would not be repetitions. Those directed toward the analyst would then be either displacements of current feelings toward her father or else new feelings which originated around the person of the analyst. In the latter instance, we would have to consider the analyst a primary object of these wishes. It was the analyst's impression that both sets of feelings had occurred concurrently.

CASE 2

Phyllis was six years and three months old, when she began treatment for a severe problem of penis envy. She had been accustomed to going to the bathroom with her younger brother and holding his penis when he urinated. When he had begun to retain his urine, his parents had consulted an analyst, who had advised that Phyllis not be allowed to continue her bathroom activities with her brother. Whereupon Phyllis responded by stealing money, and by retaining her own urine and feces in plastic bags, hiding them behind the dresser in her room. It was then decided that Phyllis should have analysis.

The material described here is taken from sessions six months after the analysis began. It was just prior to the Christmas and Hannukah holidays. During one session, it was clear she was asking for a present. I discussed this with her, and it was agreed that I would give her some sticks of tempora paint which she had seen in a store near my office. (We had decided that the present was to be given in the next session, two days later.) At the end of the session, she inquired whether I was married and whether I was called "mister" or "doctor." When I asked why this was of interest to her, she said, "Because it seems easier for me to know if you are married and if you have a family, because when I do my homework I think about it and it is boring just to think of one person, so if you could tell me if you are married, I can make quite a story about you and your wife and children."

At the beginning of the next session, I found her crying hysterically. She was so upset she could not even hang up her coat. I asked what had happened. She said that while she had gone into a store to buy some candy, her mother had gone to park her car. She added, crying hysterically, "I'll never see her again. She doesn't know where I am, she'll never find me." When she finally came into my office after I helped her hang up her coat, she asked if I had the present. I explained that I had gone to the store, but they had said they would not have the particular paints she wanted until the following day; so I would give them to her at her next session. Phyllis then said, "I won't give you this card that I made for you until you give me the paints." Then she sat down on the couch and continued to cry hysterically, repeating that her mommy would never see her again, she was lost, she would never see her mommy again.

In the past, Phyllis had often come into the office by herself, while her mother looked for a place to park the car. Moreover, she had several times gone to the store to purchase things before the session, and if her mother had still not returned from parking the car she would enter the office and hang up her coat. I reminded Phyllis of these instances and asked her what was different about the present occasion. Instead of replying, she repeated, "She won't know where to look for me, she won't know where I am." Then she went over to the window and looked out. "I don't see her, I'll never see her again," she cried. "Maybe I'll call home. No, I don't want to call home." At this point she heard a noise in the waiting room and wondered, "Is it my mother coming? Maybe that's my mother." But she did not get up to look.

Then she turned to me and said, "Here, you can have this card." After reading the card which was filled with expressions of her love for me, I said, "Oh, you have so much feeling for me." She turned to me and replied, "You can't keep it. I may ask for it back sometime." She continued to cry. Then she again heard a noise from the outer office and said, "That must by my mommy. Should I go or shouldn't I go?"

Phyllis seemed to be experiencing positive oedipal feelings toward me as a stand-in for her father. At the same time, the aggressive death wishes toward the mother were reflected in her statement, "I will never see her again." When confronted with the possibility of seeing her mother in the waiting room, she could not decide whether she wanted to face reality or cling to her fantasy that her mother was dead and she would take her place. I tried to point this ambivalence out to her by saying, "It seems hard for you to decide if you want to go and see if your mother is there or not." She then went to the double doors of my office; she opened the inner door but not the outer one which led to the waiting room. Instead, she tried to peek under it, but could not decide if her mother was back or not. Then she came back into the room, although still listening intently to the noises from the waiting room (she had left the inner door open). When she heard sounds that told her her mother was there, she stopped crying and began to play with a rubber stamp. She would not discuss her crying or fears about not seeing her mother any more. Nor would she analyze this incident in the next session. She came in with her doll, Thumbelina, and told me that her mother had found a parking place and had come up to the office. She then asked for the paints and played with the present during the remainder of the session. At the end she forgot the doll.

At the very beginning of the next session, she rushed in and asked, "Where is my doll? Did she suffocate in the closet?" When she had Thumbelina in her hands, she smiled happily and would not accept that her forgetting the doll has any significance in terms of her relationship with me. At the end of the session, she again forgot to take the doll with her.

Next session she sheepishly asked for Thumbelina. It seemed clear that the doll was meant for me. But since Phyllis could not explore the analysis of these instances of forgetting, it could not be ascertained whether the doll (baby) was in exchange for the sticks of paint (the penis) or merely a way of saying thank you for the present. In any case, she appeared to be expressing a phallic-oedipal fantasy of getting a baby from her father through a transference of feelings to the analyst. In a later session, she continued her oedipal fantasy by symbolically presenting me with a baby.

This material was presented to the study group as an example of transference of positive oedipal love displaced onto the analyst. During the study group's discussion, several doubts were raised about the evidence for this interpretation. In order to describe Phyllis' behavior as transference, would we not have to demonstrate conclusively that her fantasy represented past feelings for her father which had been repressed, but which were now revived in analysis? And in fact might not her behavior represent current oedipal longings for the father? How should we evaluate the role of the analyst's gift in stimulating her fantasy? Might not the fantasy represent a new experience, with the analyst as primary object of the oedipal wishes? In the end, it was felt that the evidence of death wishes toward the mother convincingly indicated that the fantasy reaction was really a displacement from the concurrent primary oedipal situation.

CASE 3

Bob, at 10-and-a-half years, started analysis because he stuttered, had temper tantrums, could not get along with either adults or peers, and was unable to do his school work. His mother, with whom he had had an intensely close relationship in which mutual affection and sadomasochistic trends were prominent, had been killed in an automobile accident two years before he entered analysis. Prior to her death, he had already lost her several times: at the age of two, when his brother was born; and after he was four, when his father began to spend more time at home. His father subsequently remarried. In the analysis, Bob reported fantasies of joining his mother in heaven where she was still alive and of being filled with an infinite number of babies.

During one phase of the analysis, Bob brought his school work to the session. He pressed me to help him, protesting that he did not know what to do. In refusing, I encouraged him to question his need for help and to talk about it. He described how his brother feigned helplessness in order to get attention from his step-mother and father. This led to the admission that he himself did the same thing, so as to get away from the "lonely" feeling that overcame him when he was in his room. This, in turn, led to memories of being helped with his school work by his mother. He wished she were still helping him. Bob seemed to be able to grasp the idea that he was reacting to me as if I represented his dead mother, by making himself helpless and stupid. He responded to my interpretation by doing his homework cheerfully and without difficulty.

Bob's apparent helplessness was interpreted as a repetition based on a perception of the analyst as mother, that is, as a transference. But although it was clear that he was repeating behavior with the analyst which had also occurred with the mother, the group did not think the evidence proved that he actually perceived the analyst as mother. It seemed rather to point to characteristic and nonspecific behavior, insofar as he also attempted to secure his father's and step-mother's attention by the same device of helplessness. If this was indeed the case, a more accurate interpretation would have been that he was using helplessness in order to get the attention of the analyst, his father, and his step-mother, because it had proved successful with his mother.

Later on, more conclusive evidence of transference phenomena occurred. With the approach of the summer vacation at the end of the first year of the analysis, Bob wished to give me a gift. However, he agreed to talk about his wish to give me a pipe instead of giving it to me. If this became too painful for him, I was to take the pipe and smoke it as he wished. Superficially, the gift, coming as it did soon after he had given his father a gift on Father's Day, represented a transference of the father image. Although it was a current displacement, he reacted to me as if I were his father, even though he could clearly distinguish me as his doctor.

The frustration and rage Bob experienced and expressed in the analysis as a result of my not accepting the gift amounted to a modified temper tantrum, a symptom which had practically disappeared outside of the analysis. The temper tantrums had originally developed in connection with forcing his mother to give him his way. In effect, this had amounted to keeping her close to him and making her give him things. The urge to control his mother reached its height after his brother was born. In the context of revealing how the pipe would keep us united through the impending separation, he now brought out the similarity between his rage at me for not permitting him to give me the pipe and his rage at his mother in the past when she failed to let him have his way.

Thus, what was specifically transferred was the wish to control the loss of the needed object and the means by which that control was to be achieved—the temper tantrum. He had in several ways feared and experienced the loss of his mother earlier in life; her changed attitude toward him when his brother was born, her interest in the latter and diminished interest in him, and, finally, her actual death in an automobile accident two years before the analysis. Because the pipe was found, on further analysis, to represent a baby, positive and negative oedipal wishes were also involved in the transference. As became evident, both in his fantasy and in his careful treatment of his stepmother's new baby, Bob simultaneously identified with the mother who gives birth to and rears a child and with the proud father.

This episode was offered to the study group as an example of a complicated transference phenomenon which, because of the intensity of the symptomatology and its restriction to the analytic situation, could also be considered an example of transference neurosis. The giving of the gift represented manifest expression of a latent wish to receive one which Bob actually expressed. This latent wish was interpreted as representing a series of condensed repressed previous wishes toward the parents. On the one hand, it represented negative oedipal longings for the father's penis and, possibly, a wish to castrate him. On the other hand, and this was felt to be more crucial, it also represented earlier longings for the mother, or a part of her, to ward off fears of loss and separation. Because the tantrums had originated in connection with the mother, their occurence in analysis was seen as evidence that the analyst was perceived as the mother.

The group, however, raised several questions. Should not the gift-giving wish and the tantrums be regarded as characteristic behavior toward people whom Bob felt to be of particular importance to him? Although the analyst was clearly an object of importance, how could we be sure his importance was due to repetition of earlier feelings and not an aspect of a new object relationship? As with the episode of the helplessness over his school work, Bob's current behavior clearly resembled his previous behavior with the mother, but this alone was not convincing evidence that he actually experienced the analyst as if he were the mother. With regard to the interpretation of the pipe episode as an example of transference neurosis, the group felt that more evidence was needed to resolve the following ambiguities: whether Bob's behavior developed specifically out of the analytic situation (the mere restriction of the tantrums to the analytic situation was not considered sufficient proof of transference neurosis), whether the conflict involved in the behavior was an oedipal one, and whether the transference itself was actually a repetition of an infantile neurosis.

CHAPTER 27

Transference in Childhood: Review of Special Issues

Peter B. Neubauer, M.D.

Inasmuch as this report has consisted of individual contributions on different aspects of the problem of transference in childhood, it may be valuable to indicate the status of the study group's thinking on certain underlying issues. As I explained in the Introduction, the group began by defining transference as a repetition of past experiences that involves the transferral of those experiences from the primary object to the analyst as a new object. The issues that have most engaged our attention to date, and which will continue to do so in the future, crystallize around two of the basic concepts contained in this definition. Namely, the concept of repetition and the concept of the analyst as a new object.

THE PROBLEM OF DEFINING THE NATURE OF REPETITION

The search for clinical evidence of transference phenomena compelled us to try to clarify our understanding of what we meant by the term "repetition of past experiences." To this end, we have asked the following questions: Does the experience which is repeated during the analysis have to be an exact replica of an early life experience, or can a partial repetition fulfill the requirements of transference? Can transference be achieved through a repetition of past fan-

Dr. Neubauer is Chairman, Section of Child Analysis, Division of Psychoanalytic Education, Department of Psychiatry, State University of New York, Downstate Medical Center, Brooklyn, New York; and Director of the Child Development Center, New York City.

tasies or only of actual events? Which part of the past experience is in fact observable, and how should we assess those repetitions which are an elaboration of an original experience but which may nevertheless have a significant dynamic meaning as transference phenomena? Does the analyst need to reconstruct the whole or only a part of the early experience? What is the significance of the child's secondary objects with respect to the development of transference?

For some analysts, the concept of repetition applies only to a repeated experience of an actual event, while for others it may include repetitions of past fantasies which, though related to the primary object, were never directly expressed. This divergence of view naturally brings us back to Freud's differentiation of external and psychic reality as he explored it with reference to the trauma of seduction. Freud pointed out that what is injurious to a child is seldom a real event but the significance which the child attaches to particular experiences because of his own drive expressions and wishes. The economic point of view then is of particular importance in understanding the concept of repetition and therefore, by extension, of transference.

The problem of partial repetition also arises when there is only the transference of affects and special mood qualities rather than those events to which they were originally attached. Similarly, in those cases where certain sensory modalities, such as touch or smell, were highly cathected in the original experience, only this part of the past is relived and the image of the primary objects remains comparatively unclear.

From early infancy on, most children are involved in meaningful relationships with a number of secondary objects (e.g., relatives, nurses, teachers, and sometimes even inanimate objects as well). Representations of these objects may later be condensed into a single parental image or several separate parental images; or there might be a cathexis of some of the secondary objects as if they were the parents. In either case, a variety of constellations results, which again blurs the quest for a clear repetition of the primary object. Moreover, the fact that the child frequently reproduces in the analytic situation experiences which have been displaced from the primary object to a secondary object, raises the question of whether such repetitions ought not to be included as clinical proof of transference.

Thus it is clear, even after this briefest of reviews, that there is a wide range in content and form of what constitutes "repeated experiences" occurring in the analysis of children. Hence, what constitutes clinical evidence of transference phenomena, as the concept has been defined by different analysts, varies so greatly. For this reason, the study group found it necessary to expand the definition of transference so as to encompass the complexity of repetition phenomena.

THE PROBLEM OF THE ANALYST'S FUNCTION AS A NEW OBJECT

Because the child has meaningful relationships with several secondary objects, it is conceivable that at the beginning of the analysis he may perceive the therapist as being merely another new object in his immediate environment. This means that at the initial stage of the analysis the transferral of experiences with the primary object onto the analyst may be essentially no different in kind from other instances of displacement. That is to say, the displacement will not result from the work of analysis or from the child's response to the unique posture adopted by the analyst—his attitude of understanding, his avoidance of criticism, his nonparticipation in the patient's direct need-satisfaction, his sympathetic assistance in attempts to achieve gratification in future life, and so forth. To put the point at issue in the form of a question: Should we continue to insist on the criterion that the therapeutic alliance must always precede the development of a transference, or should we include in our concept of transference those repetitions of the past which occur at the beginning of the analysis? This is a matter under review in the study group; the answer will depend on the understanding of the differences in the relationship to the analyst, its implication for technique of treatment, and other considerations.

Moreover, when assessing the role of the analyst as a new object we see his continuously changing meaning for the child during treatment. The child will perceive the analyst differently at different times, depending on the stage of the analysis, the developmental phase he has reached, and the nature of his conflicts; and these varying representations of the analyst will also be blended with past images. This blurring of vision is, of course, characteristic of all transference phenomena, but in the child it has a particular reference to his developmental process. In order to assess the balance between present psychic organization and the re-experience of the past at a given period in the child's life, we need to know how much ego organization and regression to previous experiences can be expected at each developmental stage. Do we include all forms of regression to points of fixation leading to repetition?

During the early stages of the analysis, the child does not fully re-experience the past as it really was, but only to the degree that his still-developing ego capacities permit him to do so by establishing a relationship with his newly acquired object, the analyst. As the treatment proceeds and regression and fixation are gradually eliminated, the analyst becomes a new person for the child, endowed with features appropriate to the particular developmental phase which has just been attained. Eventually, by helping to reorganize the primary experiences and modify them as appropriate to the newly acquired phase, the analyst, for instance, may become the first oedipal person for the child. This new relationship to the analyst may be transferred back to the parents, to the primary object-relation which may also become oedipal. This may serve the therapeutic aim—it addresses itself to the new experiences which the child may have with the analyst. If, on the other hand, this experience with a new object is transferred to past experiences with the parents, to which it did not belong, for which it is unreal, and if it distorts past memories, one could speak of a *reverse transference.*

Such considerations of the analyst's role should be explored in the context of the developmental progression, with particular reference to the concept of the continuous assimilation of the old into new forms of structural organization. The implications of the developmental perspective on the technique of treatment are apparent. For it appears that in addition to the traditional view of the analyst as a vehicle for old object ties, equal stress should be given to his function as a new model for organizing development. Some aspects of this dual role have already been examined in the paper on adolescent analysis, but the whole subject needs to be investigated and related to the requirements of analysis at earlier developmental phases. Indeed, a clearer understanding of the problems of technique may well help us to resolve the many questions of theory that remain to be answered before a satisfactory concept of transference phenomena in child analysis can be formulated.

Part VI

Applied Psychoanalysis

CHAPTER 28

The Naming of America

William G. Niederland, M.D.

History—according to Webster's (1947) definition, "the branch of knowledge that records and explains past events . . . the study of the character and significance of events"—has certain features (and problems) in common with analysis. Perhaps more than others, historians and analysts alike are aware of the fundamental fact that the past survives in the present. Indeed, inasmuch as the word history means *inquiry*, thus pointing itself to the genetic approach so vital in psychoanalysis, it is surprising that the investigation of historical phenomena or events plays a comparatively small role in analytic discussions today. In spite of Freud's pioneering work in *Civilization and its Discontents*, (1930) and *Moses and Monotheism*, (1939) followed by a limited number of more recent contributions (Eissler, 1965; Kris, 1952; Waelder, 1967; Wangh, 1964; etc.), psychoanalysts engaged in the field of applied research have for the most part continued to focus their attention on the psychobiographical study of historical personalities. To be sure, analysis is primarily a method of clinical investigation. Every individual analysis represents at the same time a biographical effort. Insofar as psychobiographical reconstruction is an inherent part of the psychoanalytic process, analysis is a

Dr. Niederland is Associate Clinical Professor, Division of Psychoanalytic Education, Department of Psychiatry, State University of New York, Downstate Medical Center, Brooklyn, New York.

biographical science par excellence.[1] Thus, topics dealing with biographical studies, so far as the domain of applied psychoanalysis is concerned, have traditionally been regarded as the most fertile areas for investigation.

The present course of historical events, nevertheless makes it, in my view, imperative for analysts (and nonanalytic scholars as well) to gain a fuller understanding of the historical process per se or, at least, to sharpen our knowledge of the unconscious forces involved in the course of those past events, the effects of which demonstrably survive in the present. In this paper I propose to examine a specific historical incident of the past,—the naming of America—from an analytic point of view. Because the study of the episode, aside from the intrinsic and lasting significance of the event as such, offers an instructive example of the fecundity of combined research in the two disciplines, psychoanalysis and history, it seems to me that an investigation of this kind is both relevant and timely.

It may not be superfluous to mention that contemporary geographers (Wright, personal communication; Goldstein, 1964), in speaking of the evolution of geographic thought as a significant element in the history of science, have recently called for "pioneering efforts designed to throw light on (this) crucial, but still essentially dark area of knowledge." Thus, I think it becomes the task of psychoanalysis, confronted with the influence of such notions, to make its methods and insights available in this hitherto neglected area and to trace the vicissitudes of the *Imago Mundi*, the mental representation of the world or, more precisely, that of the earth, to its unconscious sources. In the present study, this attempt will be focused exclusively on the historical incident under scrutiny.

Every schoolchild knows that the name *America* is derived from the name of Amerigo Vespucci, the man who first called the newly discovered western continent *Mundus Novus*, or New World. Known

[1] Few physicians realize that medicine too, is in some respects a biographical science. Medical practice draws heavily from biographical data such as anamnestic findings, history of the disease, development and duration of the symptomatology. When Hippocrates recommended that a sick individual should be studied as a whole in the setting in which his condition developed, he was teaching "biographical" medicine and he indeed gave us the "biographical configuration" of certain clinical entities. Freud, of course, taught us how to delve methodically into the early life-history of a patient and how to correlate the past with the present in the analysis of each individual. He thus transformed descriptive psychiatry into a science of biography.

equally well is the fact that the name is the result of a historical error. Quite apart from causing a permanent and grievous injustice to the discoverer of America, it is an error that has given rise to a centuries-old controversy among historians, geographers, students of the humanities and other scholars interested in the clarification of historical phenomena. It is noteworthy—or perhaps indicative of the reluctance to use psychoanalysis as a tool in historicopsychological research—that such a momentous error, probably the most firmly established erratum in recorded history, has been left unattended by us analysts in whose work the study of parapraxes and mistakes in general is thought to play no minor part. Be that as it may, in the present communication an attempt is made to correct this omission.

As I have shown in a previous paper (Niederland, 1957), the history of geographic exploration is permeated by a multitude of fantasies, myths, superstitious beliefs, and other subjective elements of great interest to the analyst. The study of this period is facilitated by the availability of masses of records, vast collections of data and primary source material, especially cartographic documents, the latter providing a sort of "documentary backdrop against which the history of geographical discovery unfolds almost like a dream on a dark or foggy dream screen" (p. 50). It is indeed the key verb *discover*, with its obvious analytic implications, that links the search for unknown lands and the mysterious routes that lead to them with the colorful lore of adventure and exploration down the ages. The unconscious meaning of the ancient Mappae Mundi, with their rich pictorializations of the sea, the ships, the hidden lands and passages, is obvious too. They may mark, as demonstrated by Kanzer (1951) in an illuminating example from the literature, "the haunting lineaments of the feminine form" (p. 435). It is well to remember, in this connection, that geography is the study of Gaea, *the Ur-Mutter*, and that the great problems of geographical research, i.e., the relentless investigation and exploration of the earth, imply and, in a sense, repeat the universally held Ur-fantasies. It will be seen that the geographical lore of the past bears a striking resemblance to Robert Louis Stevenson's treasure-map cartography which Kanzer analyzed.

To return to the erroneous name-giving, the historical facts as such are known: In 1507, a young cartographer, Martin Waldseemueller, who resided and worked in the town of St. Dié in the erstwhile dukedom of Lorraine was, with his friend Mathias Ringmann, in the process of revising and preparing a new edition of Claudius Ptolemy's old "Cosmographia"—the standard work on geography during the Middle Ages. Waldseemueller had been given a copy of Amerigo Vespucci's account of his voyages to the west. The account had been transmitted from Florence to René II, Duke of Anjou and Lorraine whose secretary saw to it that a copy reached the young cartographer in St. Dié. It was on Waldseemueller's map of 1507 that the name AMERICA appeared for the first time, the word firmly marking an island-shaped western region in the area of today's Brazil.

With this single act a young, obscure map maker in a remote and even more obscure mountain town, in the Vosges mountains, created history. For the name conferred upon the new world by the geographer of St. Dié became so promptly and generally popular throughout the old one that its originator was later unable to undo his error. When in 1516, after having apparently become aware of his mistake, he issued another world map and therein omitted the word America, leaving the island nameless, he met with no success as far as his original misnomer was concerned. The new name was accepted almost everywhere. It captured the fantasies and thoughts of countless people, was soon to be applied to the entire western continent and to become irreversibly ingrained in the minds of men. How did this come about? And what were the circumstances and motivating forces which led the cartographer in St. Dié to commit his momentous error?[2] When one visits St. Dié today, one finds a small provincial town, hardly more than an oversized village, with many modern buildings and a newly-built cathedral. The whole old town had been destroyed by the Germans during their 1944-retreat in World War II. To the question, "What is St. Dié famous for?", most inhabitants still answer with a certain pride: *"St. Dié è la marraine de l'Amérique"*— St. Dié is the *godmother of America.* But few of those who give this reply know why.

Fortunately, the geographer Waldseemueller himself, a lifelong bachelor who lived together with his young friend Mathias Ringmann, a poet and likewise a lifelong bachelor, supplies us with the

[2]My findings are based on documents from archives and libraries in Portugal, Spain, and other places. I especially thank Albert Ronsin, Bibliothécaire de la Ville Saint-Dié, for making available to me some of the primary source material.

first-hand evidence which an analytic investigation requires. In his "Cosmographiae Inductio" (Waldseemueller, 1507) which forms the accompanying text to his geographic chart, Waldseemueller explains his naming of the newly discovered transatlantic land AMERICA thus:

> Now that these parts are largely explored and another fourth part has been discovered by Americus Vesputius, I do not see why it should not rightfully be called by the name of the ingeniously wise discoverer Amerigo the land of Americus or America; *since the names of both Europe and Asia are derived from women.** [Literally: *from wives—a mulieribus*; italics added.]

As the text indicates, the young map maker, then in his mid-twenties or thirties (available sources do not clearly state his age, some speaking of his birth in Radolfzell near the Lake of Constance in 1470, others in 1480), was no great admirer of the female sex. The bisexual connotations of the transformations of the name Amer*igo* and its Latinized version A*mericus* into the word A*merica* are obvious. I need not go into further detail regarding the choice of the name by a young and single man who lived in close friendship with a young poet, the latter having assumed as the Hellenized version of his own name the designation *Philesius*, the *male friend*, while Waldseemueller himself, in the spirit of the times, had changed his name to *Hylacomylus* or *Ylacomylus.* In fact, Waldseemueller and Ringmann belonged to a circle of young, able scientists (mathematicians, engineers, geographers, writers) whom the Duke of Lorraine, René II, had brought together in that solitary mountain region in order to use their services in preparation for a projected campaign of his own, namely the reconquest of Naples, capital of the kingdom of Anjou which once had been ruled by the duke's ancestors. Waldseemueller and his friend lived within the enclosed precinct of the cathedral of St. Dié or in special quarters adjoining the precinct. With the help of the duke's aide, they had set up their own printing press there. Waldseemueller had come to St. Dié from Strasbourg, at that

*NUNC VERO ET HAEC PARTES SUNT LATIUS LUSTRATAE ET ALIA QUARTA PARS PER AMERICUM VESPUTIUM INVENTA EST, QUAM NON VIDEO CUR QUIS IURE VETET AB AMERIGO INVENTORE SAGACIS INGENIO VIRO AMERIGEM QUASI AMERICI SIVE AMERICAM DICENDAM; *CUM ET EUROPA ET ASIA A MULIERIBUS SUA SORTITA SINT NOMINA* (italics added; p. 50).

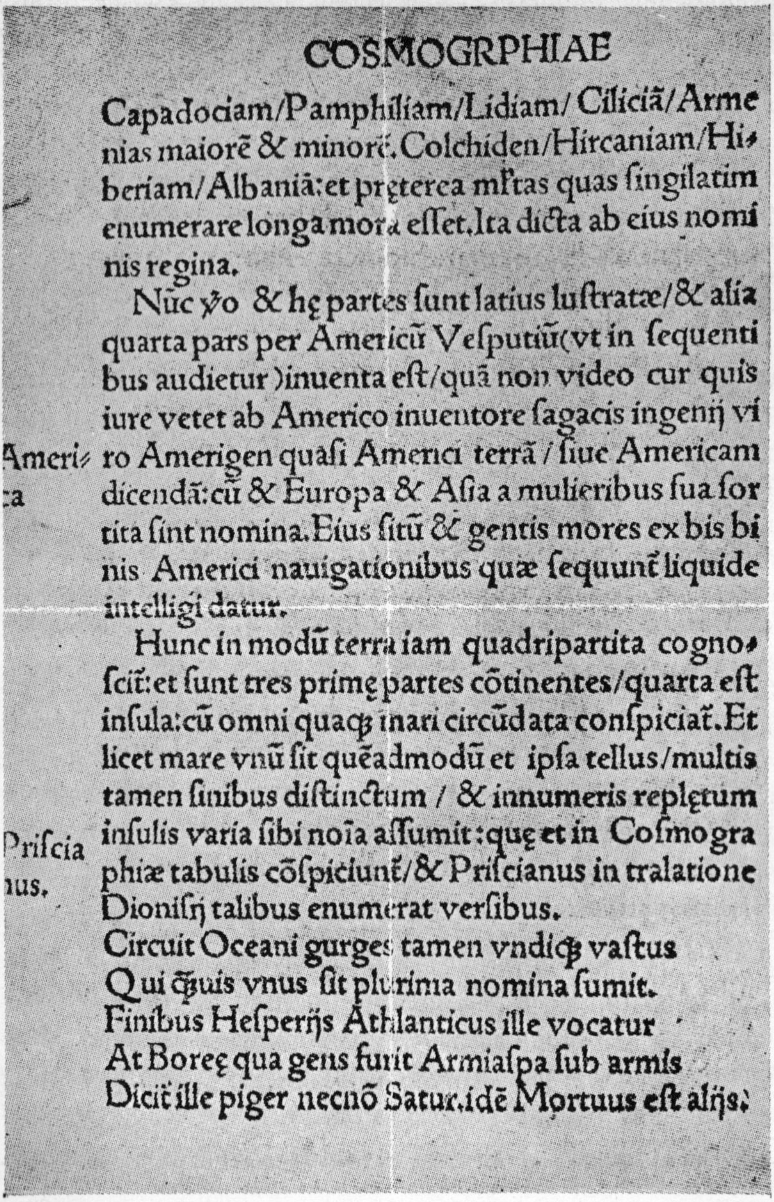

COSMOGRPHIAE

Capadociam/Pamphiliam/Lidiam/ Ciliciã/Arme nias maiorẽ & minorẽ. Colchiden/Hircaniam/Hi- beriam/Albaniã: et preterea mltas quas singilatim enumerare longa mora esset. Ita dicta ab eius nomi nis regina.

Nũc vero & hę partes sunt latius lustratae/& alia quarta pars per Americũ Vesputiũ (vt in sequenti bus audietur) inuenta est/quã non video cur quis iure vetet ab Americo inuentore sagacis ingenij vi ro Amerigen quasi Americi terrã / siue Americam dicendã: cũ & Europa & Asia a mulieribus sua sor tita sint nomina. Eius sitũ & gentis mores ex bis bi nis Americi nauigationibus quae sequunt liquide intelligi datur.

Ameri- ca

Hunc in modũ terra iam quadripartita cogno- scit: et sunt tres primę partes cõtinentes/quarta est insula: cũ omni quaqз mari circũdata conspiciat. Et licet mare vnũ sit quẽadmodũ et ipsa tellus/multis tamen sinibus distinctum / & innumeris replętum insulis varia sibi noĩa assumit: quę et in Cosmogra phiae tabulis cõspiciunt/& Priscianus in tralatione Dionisij talibus enumerat versibus.

Priscia nus.

Circuit Oceani gurges tamen vndiqз vastus
Qui q̃uis vnus sit plurima nomina sumit.
Finibus Hesperijs Athlanticus ille vocatur
At Borec qua gens furit Armiaspa sub armis
Dicit ille piger necnõ Satur. idẽ Mortuus est alijs.

time a leading intellectual center in Central Europe where Johannes Gutenberg had resided half a century before. The above text was printed on their own press, a circumstance which adds to its authenticity as well as to its subjective significance. Old reports have it that the two friends were also members of the local clergy, *chanoins*, i.e., canons. If so, it appears likely that they were made canons at the request of the duke who prudently planned to avail himself of their knowledge and technical skills in preparation for his military project.[3]

At any rate, Waldseemueller's unequivocal statement and the fact that he had received Vespucci's *Mundus Novus* account while still unaware of Columbus's voyages of discovery, seem to settle the matter of the erroneous name choice in one swoop, as it were. But there is more to it. As we have seen, within a short time the name *America* became so popular that the attempt to recall it proved fruitless. Even the kingdom of Portugal, the one country which presumably, for reasons of maritime policy and national prestige, refrained from using the new name for a period of time, persisting in calling the new world by other names (Indias Occidentales, Terra dos Papagaios, Brazzil, Isla de Santa Cruz, etc.), ultimately had to accept it. How is this rapid spread, with its irreversible course, explainable?

To find an answer to this question, we have to go back to the emotional climate and temper prevalent during the Age of Discovery. The first point to note is that, in addition to the personal factor involved in Waldseemueller's name choice, there must also have been a historical factor at work, no doubt a highly effective one that made the cartographer's error "stick." Throughout the history of geography, "erroneous notions have exerted a powerful fascination over men's minds and mistaken concepts have been hardly less influential than those to be found correct" (Wright, 1925).

What, then, was the historical factor that, in the wake of Waldseemueller's naming of America, lent such an extraordinary "staying power" to the error committed in 1507? Here we must turn to some of the oldest and most cherished illusions of mankind, the fantasy of the lost continent Atlantis of which Plato spoke, and the fantasy of the *Insulae Fortunatae*, the islands of bliss and happiness. These

[3] The project came to naught because of the duke's death in 1508.

islands can be found on most ancient maps, usually in pairs or multiples of pairs. For centuries the presumed existence of these legendary islands excited much interest, and by the time of Columbus's voyages, the oceans were replete with imagined islands. (In speaking of them as "legendary," "imagined," etc., it is well to bear in mind that according to common belief throughout millenia of geographic imagery their existence was a factual, not a presumed one). The "Isles of the Blessed," sometimes also called *Insulae San Brandani*, were supposed to have been visited by an Irish monk named Brendan (also Brandon or Brandan) who in the sixth century undertook a long sea voyage in search of Paradise and to whom the island group he had reached, *was* Paradise. St. Brendan's Island, a stock subject of romance through centuries, is usually associated with *Madeira.* On the famous Behaim Globe of 1492—whose original name, *Erdapfel* with its oral and maternal connotations, is worth noting—St. Brendan's isles appear at the site of the Canary group where a merman and mermaid are shown sporting. On later maps their site is moved to an area west of Ireland. There were two more phantom islands located off the Irish coast, named *Daculi* (from the Italian *culla*, cradle) and *Bra*, appearing on the Pareto map of 1455 and, according to the inscription on that map, helpful in situations of difficulties with pregnancy and childbirth. The map of the brothers Pizigani or Pizzigani of 1367 likewise shows a group of such islands and connects them with slumber, sleep, and the presence of females (*puellam* or *puellarum*) at the site. There is a group of six *Fortunatae Insulae* on the Hereford *Mappa Mundi—Fortunatae Insulae sex sunt*, the legend reads—whereas the earlier *Beatus* maps, stemming from the tenth and eleventh centuries, usually depict Paradise as an island which is referred to as *Garden of Eden* or *Garden of Delights.* Likewise, the controversial *Vinland Map* depicts Vinland as a distinct island in the Atlantic.

In an interesting passage from Petrus Apianus' *Cosmographia*, (referred to in Miller, 1896-1898) published less than 20 years after Waldseemueller's work, America is presented as a typical example of an *island* in contrast to continental lands such as Bohemia or Saxony. One of the most important cartographic documents of the sixteenth century is the worldmap of Sebastian Muenster, issued in Basle ca. 1540. Under the heading *NOVAE INSULAE*, it shows the new world in the form of two connected, fantastically shaped islands; the one located in the south is marked: *nova insula Atlantica quam vocant Brasil & Americam.* The long-continued search for an insular *Quarta Pars Mundi*, for the legendary *Illea das Sete Cidades (the Isle of the Seven Cities*) and the "Fountain of Youth" in Florida (believed to be the island of Bimini) was a matter of consuming interest throughout the sixteenth and seventeenth centuries. A century after Columbus, Brazil was still being called an island. One of the most celebrated books of all times, Thomas More's "Utopia" (published in 1516) describes the life and mores on such an isle of fortune. The author characteristically attributes its discovery to a Portuguese seaman who sailed as a crew member in Amerigo Vespucci's alleged 1504 expedition.

The fact that some of these mythical islands appear on nautical charts as late as 1759 indicates the strength of the belief in them. Since the earlier charts often showed them in locations where no islands were later found, on succeeding maps their sites were simply moved to other areas for instance to the West Indies, or to the estuary of the Delaware River. For more than two centuries after Columbus, Portuguese expeditions were still searching for them, until finally their mythical character was established and it was found that shifting them from one imaginary position to another on successive charts was no effective remedy for their nonexistence.

The extraordinary persistence of such beliefs, however, demands an explanation. In our assessment of the unconscious factors at work in the creation and "staying power" of these myths with their implications of ever-lasting happiness, bliss, paradise, it is not difficult to recognize the underlying infantile concept of a utopian life without pain, restriction, or frustration; a kind of eternal infancy lived out in happy lands where the narcissistic, oral-regressive wishes can be gratified and where the existence of death itself can ultimately be denied, that is, be put out of existence. With Jones (1951) I am inclined to believe that the various beliefs and legends associated with the idea of an island Paradise express "our deepest feelings about birth, death, and mother," and that "the geographical fact of insularity" attaches itself in the unconscious to fantasies of "woman, virgin, mother, and womb" (p. 98) ultimately to fantasies about birth and rebirth. In those insular lands, according to widespread belief, men lived without restraint or laws, in natural beauty and ease, and the infantile fantasies of returning to the early nursing situation of a "blissful" state of plenty, is common to all such beliefs.

If now we consider once more the prompt acceptance of the name AMERICA, with the equally prompt emergence of its familiar utopian connotations (land of happiness, land where "milk and honey" flow, and the like), it becomes apparent that the attributes of happiness originally ascribed to the *Insulae Fortunatae* readily attached themselves to the newly-discovered land in the west which, on the first map naming it, appears as an island-shaped area in the region where the islands of fortune were thought to exist. It is likely, furthermore, that the phonetic and onomatopoetic qualities of the name given to the area may have contributed to its rapid acceptance and spread. The point to note here is the word AMERICA, especially its first half. The phonemic forms, A*M*, A*M*E (in German: A*MM*E–wet nurse; A*MM*A–in infantile linguistic pattern, *MAMMA*, Mutter) and *MER*, *MÈR*E (in French, sea and mother, respectively), are apt to evoke orally- and maternally-tinged images or ideas.[4] The linguistic equivalents of the same roots, AM, AME, MER, can be found in many other languages. We have only to remember what Freud (1916-1917) wrote about the above-mentioned names, *MADEIRA-MATER*, and Greenson (1954) about the oral meaning of the sound, *M.* In my own clinical work with orally-fixated or regressed patients, I have come across similar connections between such sound patterns and markedly strong oral strivings.

On the basis of our inquiry into the sources and history of the name AMERICA, it would seem, then, that its originator–in calling the new world after its presumed discoverer Amerigo, and consciously doing so because of his personal misogyny–unconsciously chose a name with phonetically and onomatopoetically feminine connotations. If so, we have here a typical case of "the return of the repressed."

We can now attempt to formulate the essential characteristics of the historical process under scrutiny in psychoanalytic terms: owing to a combination of special circumstances and under the impact of the excitement aroused by the new discoveries and the momentous

[4]Franz Kafka (1962) observed that "The first days of a European in America can certainly be compared with a birth" (p. 39).

changes resulting therefrom (with their accompanying potentialities for expansion, wealth, mastery, freedom), the mental representation of the transatlantic world named America was charged with prevalently narcissistic and pregenital cathexis. The mental representation of these areas thus became overcathected and remained so for centuries. Within a short time after the discovery of America, a movement of people set in which never stopped and which at times reached the proportions of a new and veritable migration of peoples. From the very beginning, European immigrants settled in America, with the utopian image of a huge *Isle of Fortune* and its unconscious concomitants, that is, of sharing in the mother's magic powers and bounty. (A good many years ago I analyzed a newcomer from Europe who expressed his amazement at the presence of railroads and railroad stations in this country; their existence simply did not fit into what he called his "nebulous image of America." The writer H. Natonek [1943] describes how, on his day of arrival in a New Jersey port, he set out to *walk* from there to Manhattan; neither Natonek nor my patient were psychotic or illiterate.)

Looking at the historical process in this light and viewing its course with particular emphasis on the unconscious factors involved therein, one may feel inclined to speculate that certain typically American phenomena such as the Monroe Doctrine, the history of isolationism, the traditional resistance to social change, the utopian faith in universal progressivism, perhaps even the deep-seated maternalism, are rooted in the unconscious "Island"[5] imagery of the population groups that settled in the new world. Conversely, one may wonder whether certain disturbing phenomena which characterize the present social actuality have the same unconscious origin: the frustration, the feeling of deprivation, the widespread impression of having been "let down," of not having received "a proper share"—all this may well have evolved against the backdrop of experiences at variance with the expectations originally linked to the mental image of a land of bounty and bliss, that is, the bountiful, all-giving mother. (This is not to minimize the relevant and legitimate demands with respect to social,

[5] A contemporary "island-dwelling" author, J. R. Ullman (1968), astutely remarks: "With islands, rather more than with other terrain, most of us are conservatives. We bewail change —as did Captain Cook when he returned to Tahiti a few years after his first visit to observe sadly that it was not what it used to be." (p. 48)

economic, and racial inequities; the clarification of pertinent psychological connections in the historical process, as attempted in the present study, does not exclude the equally important investigation of causal factors operative in other areas.) It is, however, with mankind's timeless illusions, as Eissler (1965) has pointed out, that "history deals . . . with terrible cruelty" (p. 235).

Returning once more to the naming of America in 1507, two more aspects require our attention. As for the homosexuality implied in the above quoted statement from the "Cosmographiae Inductio," Fumagalli (1952), in a different context, has indicated that it was not infrequently practiced among members of the cultural elite at that time; apparently it was not uncommon among literati, humanists, scholars, members of the nobility and clergy. More recently, German historians such as Laubenberger (1959) and Konetzke (1963)[6] have expressed the view that the authorship of the Latin text in the "Cosmographiae Inductio"—and thus the coining of the word *America*—should not be attributed to Waldseemueller, but to his friend Mathias Ringmann, the poet, who had travelled to Italy a year or two before the publication of the work. If we accept this opinion, it confirms even more pointedly the close friendship and collaboration between Waldseemueller and Ringmann; for no one questions the former's placing the new name on the epoch-making world map. In other words, according to the views expressed by these authors, the name *America* was not conceived by Waldseemueller alone, but was a joint creation of both men. Psychoanalytic experience speaks in favor of such a thesis. My own research from source material on this community of scholars—mostly young men living and working together closely, has led me to believe that the entire group of young scholars and scientists assembled in St. Dié at that time was animated by an intense *esprit de corps* on the nature of which Freud commented (1911b).

Be that as it may, of greater importance is the frankness of the St. Dié-team in describing the reasons for the particular name choice. A careful study of the pertinent documents and their analytic evaluation make it clear that not only the naming by Waldseemueller (or, Waldseemueller and Ringmann), but also the frank statement for so

[6] Konetzke (1963) also holds that the sound of the word *America* must have had "some attracting, perhaps exotically alluring element ... to arouse so much interest" (p. 67). However, he does not elaborate on the nature of this "attracting element" or its relation to infantile sound patterns.

doing are linked with Amerigo Vespucci's *Mundus Novus* report. We know that Amerigo's account was the only one available in St. Dié at that time, little if any information having leaked from Spain because of the secretiveness which the Spanish authorities attempted to maintain with regard to Columbus' discoveries. What is striking about the Amerigo account, on the other hand, is the likelihood that parts of its contents may have played directly into the fantasies (and anxieties) of the men in St. Dié. For, aside from the still unresolved problem of its veracity (which, however, was not doubted in St. Dié), the account is an intriguing and explicit document. Its text contains a number of passages which would be apt to give expression to precisely those fantasies and fears which, as analysts, we so often observe in the psychology of manifest or latent homosexuality. To be sure, the period of transition from the Middle Ages to the Renaissance during which the great discoveries took place, was not a squeamish time, and Vespucci's most frequently quoted comment about the inhabitants of the new lands—"*vanno nudi .. come dal ventre de la matre sono usciti*" ("they walk nude . . . in the same way as they came out of the mother's belly")—reads like a model of moderation and verbal restraint. Turning to the *vita sexualis* of the inhabitants, the account then continues:

> . . . I learned from them about another custom, rather an enormous one and beyond any human credibility: Inasmuch as their wives are voluptuous, they make the penises of their husbands swell to such a size that they appear deformed and monstrous and this [is done] with a certain skill and the biting of certain poisonous plants or herbs [?]; and for this reason many of them lose it and remain eunuchs . . . they take as many wives as they desire; and the son copulates with the mother and the brother with the sister . . . and everybody with everybody[7] . . . there is no law . . . they live according to nature. . . .*

[7]The translation is somewhat freer than the original text which reads "lo scontrato con quello che se scotra," i.e., "the one encountered with the one whom one encounters."

*. . . UN ALTRO COSTUME APPRESSO DE QUELLI ASSAI ENORME E SOPRA DE OGNI HUMANA CREDULITA: INSCOCHE LE MOGLIER LORO ESSENDO LIBIDINOSE FANNO SGIOFARE LE MEBRI DE ILOR MARITI IN TANTA GROSEZZA CHE DEFORME PARENO ET BRUTI ET QUESTO CON UNO CERTO ARTIFICIO ET MORDICAZIONE DI CERTI AIALI VENENOSI; E PER QUESTA COSA MOLTI DI LORO LO PERDONO ET RESTAO EUNICHI . . . TANTE MOGLIER MENANO QUANTE VOGLIANO: ET EL FIGLIO SE MISIDA CON LA MADRE ET EL FRATELLO CON LA SORELLA . . . E LO SCONTRATO CON QUELLO CHE SE SCOTRA . . . NISSUNA LEGGE TENGONO . . . VIVONO SECODO LA NATURA . . .

If indeed this text corresponds to Vespucci's original account, it must be regarded as a revealing statement of considerable import. In the first part of the quoted passage we have a description of the haunting castration fears which we not infrequently encounter in our clinical work with respect to fantasies about the female genital, especially in patients with bisexual conflicts, cases of manifest or latent homosexuality, etc. The dangers for the penis entering the vagina are depicted as concrete events and attributed to the voluptuousness and seductive powers of "le *moglier* loro"—their *wives.* It is interesting to note that the Latinized version of the same word, *moglier*, appears in the misogynous statement about the names of Europe and Asia which "are derived . . . from wives." Not unexpectedly, the young men in St. Dié must have felt the need to turn to the name of the ingeniously wise *man Amerigo, sagacis ingenio viro Amerigo*, whose very account was proof not merely of his personal sagacity, but also of his masculine capacity to master the dangers to which men are exposed—*a mulieribus.* Withal, the *Mundus Novus* account cites most of the ingredients of the archaic-regressive imagery already mentioned: the life without restraint or law, the lack of the incest taboo, the freedom from any frustration or want. Amerigo's narrative culminates in the characteristic statement: "If there is an Earthly Paradise in this world, it cannot be far from these . . . lands."

With this, we have returned full circle to the fantasies about Paradise and *Insulae Fortunatae*. As we have seen, in the evolution of the historical process which started with the discoveries in the west, and in the wake of the naming of the new continent, those age-old fantasies began to converge on the mental representations of the areas thus named. The fact that the New World *actually* provided more space, more food, and often a better living than the old one served but to reinforce and concretize these fantasies in the manner familiar to psychoanalysts—*the nucleus of truth* as the organizer and concretizer of such notions and fantasies. It would be wrong to assume, on the basis of these findings alone, that the evidence presented solves all the problems connected with the naming of America. As psychoanalysts, we are well aware of the complexity of interrelated processes, their overdetermined aspects and other implications. I am inclined to believe, however, that an analytic approach to a specific historical incident of the past demonstrates the extent to which historical events are linked to unconscious conflicts and infantile strivings.

CHAPTER 29

Freud and Joseph

Leonard Shengold, M.D.

After reading Thomas Mann's *Joseph in Egypt* (1938), Freud wrote the author: "I keep wondering if there isn't a figure in history for whom the life of Joseph was a mythical prototype, allowing us to detect the phantasy of Joseph as the secret daemonic motor behind the scenes of his complex life. I am thinking of Napoleon I" (E. Freud, 1960, p. 432). What Freud goes on to say of Napoleon as Joseph, and of Napoleon's relation to his older brother, Joseph, provides a fascinating way of looking at the Emperor. In this paper, I try to show Freud, too, living out a Joseph fantasy, in the hope of adding dimension to our view of a great and complex man.

Mann (1936), in his essay on Freud, agrees with and quotes "a Viennese scholar of the Freudian school"[1] who spells out Mann's "fundamental motif" in the Joseph novels (1938, 1948) of an individual living out the life of a mythical character type—"precisely this idea of the 'lived life,' life as succession, as a moving in other's steps, as identification" (pp. 24-25) with figures from the past. This concept implies the importance of great men—spiritual fathers and brothers from myth and history—for the formation of the ego ideal. How passionately Freud identified himself with some of the great leaders and heroes of the actual and mythical past: Moses, Oedipus,

Dr. Shengold is Assistant Clinical Professor, Division of Psychoanalytic Education, Department of Psychiatry, State University of New York, Downstate Medical Center, Brooklyn, New York.

I thank Drs. Max Schur and Mark Kanzer for their advice and encouragement which contributed so much to the writing of this paper.

[1] I am indebted to Dr. Samuel Abrams for the information that this analyst was none other than Ernst Kris.

Hannibal, Julius Caesar, Napoleon, we know from his writings, especially from *The Interpretation of Dreams.* There, Freud (1900) presents himself as Joseph for the first time and documents his involvement with the Biblical Joseph and other people of that name: "It will be noticed that the name Josef plays a great part in my dreams (cf. the dream about my uncle [Josef]). My own ego finds it very easy to hide itself behind people of that name, since Joseph was the name of a man famous in the Bible as an interpreter of dreams (p. 484n)." But Freud's interest in Biblical heroes had started much earlier, and in his *Autobiographical Study* (1925a) he mentions this as a determinant of his curiosity about human beings and his ultimate choice of a life's work: "My deep engrossment in the Bible story (almost as soon as I had learnt the art of reading) had, as I recognized much later, an enduring effect upon the direction of my interest" (p. 8). Even earlier, his Catholic nurse, whom he called the "primary originator" of his neurosis, had deeply impressed him with her stories "about God and Hell" (Freud, 1887-1902).

As a child, Freud's specific interest in the Biblical tale of Joseph must have been very great because it reflected his own family situation (see Eissler, 1963, p. 1104). Similarity and identity of names always impressed Freud. His own father's name was also Jacob; this Jacob, too, had had two wives; Sigmund, like Joseph, was the eldest child of the beloved younger wife. Jacob Freud was born in 1815 and married when he was 17. His first son, Emmanuel (father of Freud's childhood companion, John), was born in 1832 or 1833. His second son, Phillip, was born in 1836 and was therefore 20 years older than Sigmund. Jacob Freud married again when he was 40. He and Amalie Nathanson (*his* Rachel) had eight children. Sigmund was the eldest; then a little less than a year later, came Julius—he died at eight-months. Ten years after Sigmund, the youngest child, Alexander, was born. In between were five girls.

Jones (1953) has described how Freud's unusual family constellation gave spur to his curiosity and facilitated his later discovery of the universality of the Oedipus complex. The relations between father and brothers (with concomitant relations to mothers and sisters) in the Joseph story parallel those of Freud. Joseph was the favorite son, not only of the doting Rachel, but also of Jacob who had eleven others. Sigmund was Jacob's pride and joy and was, of course, the first born and lifelong favorite of his mother. Freud (1917a) says of Goethe what is equally applicable to Joseph and to himself: "... if a man has been his mother's undisputable darling, he retains throughout life the triumphant feeling [Freud uses the German word *Eroberergefühl*: literally, feeling of a *conqueror*], the confidence in success, which not seldom brings actual success with it" (p. 156).

Freud was ambitious; when already dedicated to scientific and medical study, he wrote to his friend, Wilhelm Fliess: "I am not really a man of science ... nothing but by temperament a *conquistadore*" (Jones, 1953, p. 348). As a child, he identified with many great heroes. Ambition, the natural heritage of a gifted "indisputable" family favorite (young Joseph's strength as well as the sin that led him to the pit), is attested to by Joseph's dreams. He dreams first that his sheaf stands up and remains upright, while those of his brothers gather around and bow low to it; then he dreams that the sun, the moon, and eleven stars bow down to him. The first dream is of phallic ascendancy over his brothers—to be first in the eyes of the parents.[2]

Joseph's second dream has him also ruling over his parents. Jacob reproaches him, "Are we to come, I and your mother and your brothers, and bow low to you to the ground." (Genesis, 37:10) Joseph's brothers are infuriated by his dreams.

Freud (1900) writes of his own fraternal rivalries. We learn most about his relations with his much older half-brother, Phillip; his younger brother, Julius, who lived such a short time; his nephew, John (Emmanuel's son), who was a year older than Sigmund. Phillip was old enough to be—and was confused with—a father; Julius was a younger brother; John's role was that of an older brother. We read of warm and loving feelings toward the 10-year-younger Alexander (Sigmund's *Benjamin*).

[2]Zeligs (1955) interprets these dreams of ambition as defensive—the greatness compensatory to the feelings of the weaker younger brother vis-à-vis his hostile stronger older brothers.

FRATRICIDE AS A DISPLACEMENT OF PARRICIDE

If, as Freud hypothesized, and work with patients suggests, the primal crime (as "felt" by the superego) is parricide,[3] the biblical myth portrays a displacement in the murder of Abel by Cain. The father is defied in the eating of the forbidden fruit, but the first murder is that of brother by brother, out of jealousy for the father's love: "The Lord paid heed to Abel and his offering, but to Cain and his offering he paid no heed" (Genesis, 4:45). Here is the parallel in the Joseph story: "Now Israel [Jacob] loved Joseph best of all his sons, for he was the child of his old age, and he had made him a coat of many colors. And when his brothers saw that their father loved him more than any of his brothers, they hated him . . ." (Genesis, 37:3,4).

Genesis is full of stories of hatred and rivalry between brothers: Cain and Abel; Isaac and Ishmael; Esau and Jacob. In every instance the father is spared, and rage is turned against the brother. Jacob, with the connivance of his mother, Rebekah, steals by trickery his older brother's birthright and his blessing. The paternal blessing not only passes on the goods and power of the father, it also confers the privilege of carrying on the Covenant with God—that special relationship with God the Father (the primal parent) which led to Cain's murder of Abel. It is largely the not unwarranted expectation that Joseph will be the recipient of Jacob's blessing that rouses the older brothers' hatred and fear of the young boy. Reuben, the eldest and the natural heir (like Esau), had offended against his father by seducing his father's concubine Bilhah. Mann portrays Reuben as partly motivated toward the incest by his jealous rage at the prospect of the young Joseph (then seven) being preferred over him. It is when Joseph is 17, following the telling of his overweening dreams, that the brothers attempt to kill him, thereby venting their fury against

[3]"If the Son of God was obliged to sacrifice his life to redeem mankind from original sin, then by the law of talion, . . . that sin must have been a killing, a murder. . . . And [if] the original sin was an offense against God the Father, [then] the primal crime of mankind must have been a parricide, the killing of the primal father of the primitive human horde, whose mnemic image was later transfigured into a deity" (Freud, 1915c, pp. 292-293).

their father. Joseph is first cast down into the pit and then, Reuben having managed to dissuade the more zealous from murder, is sold into slavery. He again descends—to Egypt, called by Mann, Hell or the Lower World. He rises by becoming the steward of Potiphar, again is cast down—this time into prison—because of the accusation of Potiphar's wife. His power of dream interpretation enables him to rise again. He gains Pharaoh's trust and becomes his overseer. He is the highest in all the land, save Pharaoh himself. (The descents and ascents, from the lower regions to the upper world, are reminiscent of Freud's imagery in his masterpiece, *The Interpretation of Dreams*[4] (see Shengold, 1966). Joseph, through his ability to leave his father and transcend his dependency on him, finally attains a position from which he can become the father to his father and his brothers.

The displacement from father-murder to brother-murder is also seen in Hamlet, where Claudius (Act III Scene iii) says of his crime:

> O, my offense is rank, it smells to heaven.
> It hath the primal eldest curse upon't,
> A brother's murder.

The play, though, is about the paralysis that murderous wishes toward the father brings out. Freud comments on this in the momentous letter to Fliess announcing his discovery of the Oedipus complex, and in so doing, he provides, by way of a slip, the counterpart of his own father-to-brother displacement. It is the letter of 10/15/1897, written a year after his father's death had launched the great task of his self-analysis. Hamlet, Freud (1892-1899) says, hesitates to avenge his father by killing his uncle because of his unconscious feeling of guilt, for he himself "had meditated the same deed against his father from passion for his mother" (p. 266). It is not characteristic of Hamlet, Freud adds, to avoid aggressive action, considering that "he is the same man, who sends his courtiers to their deaths without a scruple, and who is positively precipitate in killing

[4]The motto of which is "Flectere si nequeo superos, Acheronta movebo" (p. ix) (If I cannot bend the higher powers, I shall move the lower regions), the motto of a conquistador.

Laertes" (p. 266, italics added). Hamlet, of course, is not "precipitate" in killing Laertes; he does it unwittingly, having no knowledge of the poison that makes his slight scratching of Laertes fatal. But he does precipitately kill Polonius, Laertes' father, whom he hears behind the arras in his mother's bedchamber. That Freud made a slip is confirmed by the parallel passage in *The Interpretation of Dreams* (1900): " . . . Hamlet is far from being represented as a person incapable of taking any action. We see him doing so on two occasions: first in a sudden outburst of temper, when he runs his sword through the eavesdropper behind the arras, and secondly in a premeditated and even crafty fashion, when, with all the callousness of a Renaissance prince, he sends the two courtiers to the death that had been planned for himself" (p. 265). In both passages he couples the killing of Rosencrantz and Guildenstern with that of Polonius, and his writing *Laertes* (also see Freud, 1887-1902, p. 224) represents a slip of the pen, the dispensable brother figure (Phillip, Julius, John) replacing the needed and beloved Jacob whose loss he was mourning at that time. Polonius is especially important in the play as the father-figure that Hamlet can kill freely (Claudius is dispatched only when Hamlet is already dying). Polonius can evoke the murdered father. Freud even refrains from naming him in the above quoted passages.[5]

FREUD AND HIS "BROTHER" JOHN

Jones (1953) considers John "the most important person in Freud's early childhood . . . next to his parents" (p. 8). In trying to account for the aggressive ambition which colored his boyhood pre-

[5] James Joyce in *Ulysses*, that novel of fathers and sons in which the hero searches for and finds a maternal father (as Mann characterizes Jacob), also shifts the focus of hatred away from the father onto the mother and the brothers. Joyce's theory, stated by Stephen Daedalus in the Scylla and Charybdis episode of *Ulysses*, is that the play, *Hamlet*, represents Shakespeare's reaction to his having been cuckolded by his brothers Edmund and Richard, Shakespeare portraying himself in the play as both old Hamlet, the murdered father, and young Hamlet, the dispossessed son (paralleling Joyce who represents himself as both Stephen and Bloom in his novel). Joyce also states that Shakespeare wrote Hamlet immediately after his father's death. This may not be true, but it parallels the timing of Freud's writing about Hamlet after *his* father's death. Joyce emphasizes *Hamlet* as evidence of Shakespeare's obsession with the theme of the "false, or usurping, or adulterous *brother*." (Blamires 1966, p. 90; italics added.)

occupation with the military heroes, Hannibal and (Napoleon's) Marshal Masséna,[6] Freud (1900) says, "[Perhaps] the development of this martial ideal is traceable still farther back into my childhood: to the times when, at the age of three, I was in a close relation, sometimes friendly but sometimes warlike, with a boy a year older than myself [John], and to the wishes which that relation must have stirred up in the weaker of us" (p. 198). The relationship was intense and ambivalent:

> Until the end of my third year we had been inseparable. We had loved each other and fought each other; and this childhood relationship, as I have already hinted, had a determining influence on all my subsequent relations with contemporaries. Since that time my nephew John has had many re-incarnations. . . . [p. 424] . . . my warm friendships as well as my enmities with contemporaries [go] back to my relations [with John]. . . . My emotional life has always insisted that I should have an intimate friend and a hated enemy. I have always been able to provide myself afresh with both, and it has not infrequently happened that the ideal situation of childhood has been so completely reproduced that friend and enemy have come together in a single individual. . .[p. 483].

Freud wrote this at a time when he had, at least in large part (Schur, *Freud: Living and Dying*, in press), come to terms in his mind with the then current revenant of John, Wilhelm Fliess. Fliess was a kind of analyst for Freud and, as in most important relationships in life, including the one to the analyst, was kaleidoscopically invested with transferences of all Freud's important early love-objects, including brothers and father.

[6]One of Napoleon's generals who was, Freud believed, like Hannibal, of semitic origin. That Masséna was born a hundred years to the day earlier than Freud furthered the boy's sense of identification with him. Freud thought that Masséna was a variant of the Jewish name Manasseh. The first Manasseh was the eldest son of Joseph. In Jewish lore, stemming from the times of the Roman occupation of Palestine, it is written that the first Messiah would be a warrior, preparing the way for the spiritual Messiah-ben-David who would rule forever; this military hero Messiah was expected to come from the seed of Joseph. This eventual "conquistadore" was alternatively called Messiah-ben-Joseph, or, from Joseph's sons, Messiah-ben Ephraim or Messiah-ben-Manasseh (Bakan 1958). Here was material for young Sigmund's fantasies of military glory.

FREUD AND PHILLIP

Freud had another important ambivalent, although perhaps more consistently hostile, relationship with his much older half-brother, Phillip, who was the same age as Freud's mother. In his oedipal fantasies, Freud spared the beloved, feared, and respected Jacob, focusing instead on Phillip as his rival. When Freud was two and a half and just after his sister, Anna, was born, his nurse was dismissed for stealing. Freud asked Phillip where she had gone. He took literally Phillip's joking answer, "Sie ist eingekastelt" (she has been put into a chest), and confused it with his pregnancy fantasies. According to Jones (1953), Freud had the fantasy that "his half-brother and his mother, who were of the same age, had cooperated in producing the usurping Anna" (p. 10). This made Phillip the hated rival, bypassing Jacob. The attribution of the paternal role to Phillip is at least unconsciously implicit in relation to an incident following the birth of Freud's youngest sibling, Alexander, when Sigmund was 10. Jacob had asked the boy to choose a name, and he had suggested calling the infant Alexander after one of his conqueror heroes, Alexander the Great, son of *Philip* of Macedon (Jones, 1953).

Freud's Philippic fantasies are evident in one of his dreams which is only dimly interpreted in *The Interpretation of Dreams* (1900). He calls it an anxiety dream from his seventh or eighth year in which "I saw *my beloved mother, with a peculiarly peaceful, sleeping expression on her features, being carried into the room by two (or three) people with birds' beaks and laid upon the bed*" (p. 583). Freud associates to illustrations of Egyptian gods in *Phillippson's* Bible. He does not mention brother Phillip, but tells of a namesake who also had supplied sexual information—the son of a concierge named Philipp who told him the vulgar word for intercourse—*Vögeln*, derived from *vögel* (bird). Freud had awakened from the dream screaming and had awakened his parents. He traces the anxiety back "to an obscure and evidently sexual craving that had found appropriate expression in the visual content of the dream" (p. 584). The dream links incest, Phillip (not Jacob) as the rival, and Egypt—here connoting, as for Mann's Joseph, the underworld, the sexual world, the land of the dead.

FREUD AND JULIUS; THE SIN OF CAIN

His younger brother Julius figured large in Freud's personal mythology. Freud was 19 months old when the eight-month-old Julius died. He tells Fliess (Freud, 1887-1902), "I welcomed my one-year-younger brother (who died within a few months) with ill-wishes and real infantile jealousy, and . . . his death left the germ of guilt in me" (p. 219). The theme of self reproach, founded not only on guilt for oedipal wishes, but on the fulfilled wish to get rid of Julius, is dealt with in terms of the many Joseph-meanings (as well as in relation to many Josephs) in another famous dream of Freud's: the *non vixit* dream (Freud, 1900).[7]

The dream is full of Josephs; it deals mainly with death wishes and reproaches for death wishes. The main contemporary object of the hostile wishes was Fliess,[8] who can be seen as a current incarnation of Julius. Fliess had for many years been Freud's closest friend and the "only audience" for his ideas. It is in connection with the *non vixit* dream that Freud writes of the series of "revenants" of John in whom "friend and enemy have come together in a single individual" (1900, p. 198). As had happened before with others, the close relationship with Fliess was heading for a break-up (still several years away), partly because Freud's self-analysis rid him of his dependency needs, partly because of Fliess' intolerance of dissent.

"The central feature of the dream" [which is too long to be reproduced here] was, Freud says, "a scene in which I annihilated [Josef Paneth] with a look" (p. 422). Josef Paneth, younger than Freud, had been his successor at Brücke's Physiological Institute. One of the reasons Freud had left Brücke's laboratory was because he had little chance of advancement there; both the capable Sigmund Exner and the gifted, tragic Ernst Fleischl being senior to him. Freud reproached himself for contributing to Fleischl's death by his well-meant attempt to cure the older man's morphine addiction with cocaine.

[7] I am indebted to Max Schur for pointing out to me the importance of Julius for this dream.

[8] Freud to Fliess: "In my *non vixit* dream I find I am delighted to have survived you" (Freud 1887-1902, p. 299).

Freud had been shocked at Josef Paneth's open wish to have the seriously-ill Fleischl out of the way, but was honest enough to realize that he himself had had the same wish when he was a demonstrator in Brücke's laboratory, "but, as was to be expected, the dream punished my friend [Josef P.] and not me, for the callous wish" (p. 484). At the time of the dream, both Josef Paneth and Fleischl (who had also appeared in the dream) were dead, as was the Emperor Josef II from whose monument the dream had borrowed the words *non* and *vixit.*

The dream is full of ghosts who return, and Freud had felt while dreaming that "*people of that kind only existed as long as one liked and could be got rid of if someone else* [!] *wished it*" (p. 421). Freud's death wishes gave him the lethal power of the basilisk,[9] to be able to kill with a look, reversing the scene from the past in which the father-figure Brücke had crushed him with an unforgettable piercing look of reproach from "his terrible blue eyes" (p. 422).

The dream occurred during a time when Fliess was about to undergo an operation. Freud was worried about him, and "the dream thoughts now informed me that I feared for my friend's life" (p. 481). Freud recognized the hostile wish toward Fliess and connected it with desires to get rid of a series of "revenants," especially John and Fleischl, older-brother figures: "I had replaced one Josef by another in the dream and found it impossible to suppress the similarity between the opening letters of the name 'Fleischl' and ('Fliess') (p. 486).

The dream is a demonstration of the hostility toward the father (Brücke, Emperor Josef) being displaced onto brother figures. Another Josef in the dream was Josef Breuer who had been like a father to Freud, helping him with advice and money. With their joint work on hysteria, Breuer became more of an older brother. As Freud began to outstrip Breuer in the sweep of his imagination, increasing hostility arose between the two, especially on Freud's part (Jones, 1953). "Freud's intellect is soaring at its highest. I gaze after him as a hen at a hawk" (p. 242), Breuer had written to Fliess. There came a

[9] After his own father's death, Freud had dreamt of a sign that read: "You are requested to close the eyes" (Freud 1887-1902, p. 171) which obviously involves Oedipus' symbolic talion punishment of blindness.

time when the hawk began to attack the hen; Jones feels that Freud was chiefly at fault. This Joseph, Breuer, had become a revenant of John as the enemy, and the closeness between the two men became "violent antipathy" (Jones, 1953, p. 255) on Freud's side, during the last years of the friendship with Fliess.

But the dream also alludes to brother Julius. Freud associates to Brutus' speech of self-justification in Shakespeare's *Julius Caesar* (Act III, Scene ii): "as he was ambitious, I slew him". (This was the brother's response to Joseph's dreams of ambition.) Sigmund had acted the part of *Brutus* to John's *Caesar* as a child. The dream also said, 'My friend [Fliess] came to Vienna in July' (p. 421), and Freud associates to July's being named after Julius Caesar. Fliess, to whom Freud had looked up as a leader for so many years, was actually younger than Freud, about as much younger as Julius had been. There can be no doubt of the tremendous effect of the death wish toward that first Julius which actually had coincided with his having been "got rid of." (Schur, *Freud: Living and Dying*, in press).

The Fliess family had asked Freud not to mention Fliess' illness to anyone. The implication that his discretion was not taken for granted annoyed him, for it implied he could not keep a secret.

> I was very disagreeably affected by the veiled reproach because it was—not wholly without justification. . . . [At an earlier time] I caused trouble between two friends . . . by quite unnecessarily telling one of them, in the course of conversation, what the other had said about him. At that time, too, reproaches had been levelled at me, and they were still in my memory. One of the two friends concerned was Professor Fleischl; I may describe the other by his first name of 'Josef' [Breuer]—which was also that of P. [Josef Paneth], my friend and opponent in the dream" (1900, pp. 481-482).

This reproach for being a tattle-tale foreshadows the final quarrel between Fliess and Freud about Freud's unauthorized talking of Fliess's ideas of bisexuality to an analysand. It also connects Freud with Joseph, who was reproached by his brothers for being a talebearer: "And Joseph brought bad reports of them [his brothers, the sons of Bilhah and Zilpah] to their father" (Genesis 37:2).

It is in connection with the *non vixit* dream that Freud makes the statement about his own ego "hiding behind" people named Joseph. Freud has taught us that any figure in a dream can stand for not only the dreamer himself, but also for any of the important people in his life. Parents, siblings, mate, children, friends–all can be Joseph. If Fliess, in dream or in life, was a "revenant", he could represent for Freud at various times Julius, John, Phillip, or Jacob. The combinations and complications made by trying to delineate object relations and identifications with each of the above (not to mention the possible representation of mother and sisters by a male figure) show the constantly changing complexity of human identity. *To be* Joseph, then, means being many other people at the same time. To see clarity amidst these complications is the analyst's daily task.[10] This is done in large part by the awareness of the predominant role the patient is transferring onto the analyst at any given time. It is to be remembered that Freud made use of Fliess as a kind of analyst during the years of his heroic self-analysis.

UNCLE JOSEF

Hostility to brothers is also evident in Freud's "Uncle Dream" (1900). The hostility is disguised by being transferred to his father's generation. This also allows for the expression of ill-will toward his father who had suffered from the misconduct of his ne'er-do-well brother Josef. The dream took place at a time when Freud had been recommended for appointment as Professor, so again ambition is involved. The dream led to thoughts disparaging two colleagues who had not been appointed to professorship, supposedly for reasons that would leave Freud's hopes untouched. Freud dreamed: ". . My friend R. was my uncle–I had a great feeling of affection for him." And here are his associations:

[10]One can see the oversimplification involved in the (nonetheless breathtaking) insight contained in Freud's comment to Fliess, "And I am accustoming myself to the idea of regarding every sexual act as a process in which four persons are involved." (Freud 1887-1902, p. 289).

> '*R. was my uncle.*' What could that mean? I never had more than one uncle—Uncle Josef. [Freud adds a footnote here: "... my memory ... was narrowed at this point .... Actually I have known five of my uncles, and loved and honoured one of them ..."]. There was an unhappy story attached to him. Once—more than thirty years ago,—in his eagerness to make money, he allowed himself to be involved in a transaction of a kind that is severely punished by the law, and he was in fact punished for it. My father whose hair turned grey from grief in a few days, used always to say that Uncle Josef was not a bad man but only a simpleton ... [pp. 137-138].

Freud goes on to show that the feeling of affection in the dream was really hypocritical; his dream had contained a slander against R. and "in order that I might not notice this, what appeared in the dream was the opposite, a feeling of affection for him" (p. 141). The "Uncle Dream" expresses hatred in a competition for the lordly position (in Vienna) of Professor. And is it too fanciful to speculate that here Freud is himself the uncle Josef (he *was* an uncle to the beloved enemy, John), not only putting himself in a position to turn his father's hair grey again, but also reducing the five brothers to the one Josef? Could not the missing four brothers be Emmanuel, Phillip, Alexander, and Julius, leaving Freud "standing erect" as in the Biblical Joseph's first dream of ambition?

JOSEPH AS FATHER: THE EMPERORS JOSEF II AND NAPOLEON

Kings and emperors symbolize the father, illustrating the power and majesty of the head of the household as seen from the cradle. Freud (1936) tells an anecdote about Napoleon when that ruler invoked *his* original ruler: "Napoleon, during his coronation as Emperor in Notre Dame, turned to one of his brothers—it must no doubt have been the eldest one, Joseph—and remarked: 'What would *Monsieur notre Père* have said to this, if he could have been here today?' " (p. 247).

Freud wrote this in the course of describing to Romain Rolland a peculiar feeling of unreality he had when, in fulfillment of his infantile wish to travel, he climbed the hill of the Acropolis accompanied by his brother, Alexander. He described the symptom as the result of his feeling guilty for having gone further (and seen more!) than his father. Implicit is the conquest of the mother, symbolized by climbing the hill. Joseph's climbing to the pinnacle of power in Egypt also meant the fulfillment of the forbidden wish of ruling over his father and family; he was able to take care of them, showing *his* father how far *he* had come.

Wittels (1924) speaks of the influence the name Joseph had for Freud and stresses the effect of the Freud family's many years of residence in the Kaiser Josef Strasse when Sigmund was growing up. The 19th century regarded Emperor Josef II (1741-1790) of the Holy Roman Empire as a kind of philosopher-king, contrasting his attempt to fulfill the ideals of liberty and equality of the enlightenment philosophers by benevolent despotism with the repressive regime of the Hapsburg Kaisers. The attitude was expressed by Austria's greatest poet, Grillparzer, who in his poems would periodically trot out Josef II to give paternally reproachful lectures to his successors (Barea, 1966). Josef II had abolished serfdom; curtailed the feudal privileges of the nobles; clashed openly and rudely with the Pope; built many hospitals, preparing Vienna for her role as center of medical education; and published an Edict of Toleration for Protestants and Jews.

We know that Freud was influenced by Emperor Josef II. He appears in the *non vixit* dream, and Freud in his writings often expresses the wish for the therapeutic power of Emperor Josef: "the benevolent interference of a powerful personage before whose will people bow and difficulties vanish" in order to fight neurosis by alleviating the misery imposed by the realities of poverty and oppression (Freud 1916/17, p. 432; see also 1919a, p. 167).

The childhood wish to be emperor appears in an anecdote told by Jones (1953). Once, when Freud (having attained the rank of Professor Extraordinarius) was giving a lecture at the University, "Abraham, Ferenczi, Rank, Sachs, and myself [Jones] were seated in the front row, he made a graceful little bow, waved his hand towards us, and murmured [as Napoleon had in the theater at Erfurt]: 'Un parterre de rois' " (p. 342). (Also see Grotjahn, 1967, p. 15.)

That Josef II had not only granted equal civil rights to the Jews but also equal duties—he was the first monarch in Europe to make Jews liable for service in the Army (Palmer and Colton, 1965)—must have been particularly important to young Sigmund, whose alter egos were military heroes of semitic origin. Freud (1900) wrote: "I can still remember sticking labels on the flat backs of my wooden soldiers with the names of Napoleon's marshals written on them. And at that time my declared favorite was already Masséna (or, to give it its Jewish form, Manasseh)" (p. 197). To be son of an emperor is to be Manasseh, son of the powerful vizier of Egypt. Freud had bitterly contrasted his father who had allowed a Christian to force him into the gutter and knock his hat off, with "Hamilcar Barca, [who] made his boy swear . . . to take vengeance on the Romans" (Freud, 1900, p. 197). Hannibal, a "semitic general," was the favorite hero of Freud's later schooldays. To be the emperor Josef himself would mean that no antisemite would dare to force *his* father, Jacob, into the gutter again; he too could be Joseph, savior of Jacob. Napoleon was the son (not the oldest) who became the savior of his entire family—lifting them all up to partake of his power.

HOSTILITY DISPLACED ONTO THE BROTHERS

Mann makes obvious what is implicit in the Bible: that for all his hostility, the young Joseph loves his brothers. He is easily able to suppress his hatred because he has had the experience of successful narcissism. He assumes the superiority conferred both by his great natural gifts of beauty and intelligence and by the favoritism of his parents. But when his pre-eminence is threatened, his hatred shows. He wants his brothers out of the way if there is any hint that one of them might obtain the blessing of the parent-god. His hatred is evident in his telling his dreams and of the gift of the coat of many colors to his brothers. It is evident in his tale-bearing, a fault allied to his curiosity. The defensive nature of his assertions of supremacy is obvious: the smaller brother must suppress the murderous hostility that pits him against the frightening superior strength of the older brothers. Freud says of Napoleon,

> His eldest brother was called Joseph . . . the elder brother is the natural rival; the younger one feels for him an elemental, unfathomable deep hostility for which in later life the expressions 'death-wish' and 'murderous intent' may be found appropriate. To eliminate Joseph, to become Joseph himself, must have been Napoleon's strongest emotion as a young child. It is strange no doubt and yet it has been correctly observed that just these excessive, infantile impulses tend to turn into their opposites—the hated rival becomes the loved one. This was the case with Napoleon. We assume that he started out with an ardent hatred of Joseph, but we learn later on he loved him more than any other human being and could hardly find a fault with this worthless, unreliable man. Thus the original hatred had been overcompensated, but the early aggression released was only waiting to be transferred to other objects. Hundreds of thousands of unknown individuals had to atone for the fact that the little tyrant had spared his first enemy [E. Freud, 1960, p. 432].

We are reminded of Freud's own excessive admiration and love for Fliess in the years before the publication of *The Interpretation of Dreams*; the man looked up to as a kind of "Messiah" in the early letters (Freud, 1887-1902) is finally broken with—"a brutal personality," as Freud wrote of him in 1906.

Hatred for the usurping younger brother is also suppressed. Benjamin had taken Joseph's place as *the* son of Rachel, and worse, his birth had caused her death. Yet Joseph truly loved Benjamin, as Freud was apparently truly fond of Alexander. Freud's hatred for Julius was especially pathogenic because he had actually died at a time when no working over of the original impulses was possible. But siblings are relatively dispensable; hatred of the vitally-needed parents is much more frightening. In his explanation of Napoleon's career of conquest and slaughter, Freud, the discoverer of what he for so long called the "father complex," strangely leaves the great man's hatred of his father out of account, although Napoleon was 16 when his father died.

A child's primal hatred must first of all be directed outward to the mother (or the mothering figure[11]) who is at the same time gradually being distinguished from the self. The caretaking mother earns

[11] Anna Freud (1965) says infants at the beginning of life choose their objects on the basis of function, not of sex.

hostility as what Anna Freud (1965) calls "the first external legislator" (p. 168). Hostility is displaced from the mother onto others: the father and siblings. The father is cathected early as "a symbol of power, protectiveness, ownership of the mother" (p. 186). Sexual differentiation of the object becomes important in the phallic phase, and the "oedipus complex itself . . . is based on the recognition of sex difference" (p. 187). It is during the phallic phase, under the impact of the castration complex, that the boy most fully and frighteningly feels hostility for the father. His power to protect and his presence as a focus for masculine identification make him appear indispensable to the young boy.

The son, like Joseph or Sigmund, turns this access of oedipal hatred toward the unwelcome brothers who have already been resented as rivals for the parent's care and love. The stories of Cain and Abel (with God preferring Abel) and Joseph show that the hostility to the sibling exists chiefly in relation to the parent. A parent with small children can observe daily that the previously peaceful siblings begin to quarrel *after* the parent enters on the scene.

A man, involved professionally in treating psychologically disturbed patients, had a brother who was several years his senior (as was his analyst, whose age he had looked up in a medical directory). At the beginning, the hostility expressed in the analysis was that of a sibling rival for the love of a parent; this parent was Fortune or Fate as with Oedipus.[12] God had smiled on the analyst who must have been lucky enough to have the right contacts and who earned more, lived better, and was happy. The hatred was intense and genuinely rooted in the relationship to his brother. His parents had always played one child off against the other, training them, as it were, to become Cain and Abel. This level of hatred was rather easily voiced. In contrast, appearing later in the analysis was a terrifying and paralyzing hatred for the analyst as parent: the preoedipal "bad" mother merging into the oedipal father. In dealing with the analyst as father, castration anxiety brought out the full terror of the fury that he expressed with relative freedom in life in his rather successful competition with

[12]It is Oedipus' last heroic, ironically pathetic attempt at denial. As he is about to be crushed by Fate, he claims Fate as a loving parent. Why should he care who his parents are, he says, when "I am Fortunes child, not man's; her mother face hath ever smiled above me." (Sophocles, 1943).

brother figures. He could always beat a brother, but in any competition with fathers he had to lose.

For Freud, it was terrible to want to get rid of John, but at least John could fight back. It is the power of the older brother that makes hating him dangerous, evoking fear of retaliation and punishment. To want to get rid of Julius was worse; it is the vulnerability of the younger brother, the fear of one's own aggression, that makes hating him more dangerous. But to want to get rid of Jacob was unthinkable and yet it is man's fate to think of it; the full force of the guilt associated with the Oedipus complex is involved with fear of both the power of, and the punishment for, one's own aggressive wishes. Freud always emphasized the phylogenetic impact of the phallic phase and of the castration complex. Clinically it would seem that, whatever the explanation, the intensity of hostile feeling for the father is more than can be accounted for by ontogenetic experience. The necessary search for substitutes to hate instead of the father begins with the rival brothers. This was the essence of the story of Joseph for Freud.

THE SUBLIMATION OF THE DRIVE FOR POWER

In his middle seventies, Freud again became involved with the Bible stories, no doubt partly as a reaction to the Nazi persecution of the Jews. In 1934 he began to write his last book—on Moses. Moses had long been (like Joseph) an engrossing mythopoeic figure for Freud, appearing often in his writings (1900, 1914b, 1939), now as a "formidable father-image" (Jones, 1957), now as Freud himself. Moses, like Joseph, was associated with Egypt, had a messianic role in relation to the Jewish people, a covenant with God. But his story lacked the element of conflict with the brothers.[13]

By 1934 Freud had come a "long way from the child who devoured Thiers' story of Napoleon's power and who identified himself with the Marshal Masséna" (Bernfeld, 1946, p. 163). Joseph was 17 when, after expressing his overweening ambition to his brothers, he

[13] Aaron appears only once in *Moses and Monotheism*; Freud even casts doubt on the fraternal relationship by describing him as "Aaron, *called* (Moses') brother" (italics added).

was cast into the pit to begin his struggle for greatness. Greatness came only after he had left his father Jacob. The dreams of glory and worship were fulfilled in Egypt; conquest was achieved not by killing, but by Joseph's charm and especially his wisdom, specifically his ability to interpret dreams. Seventeen marked an important turning point for Freud too. Adolescence meant a reawakening of hostility for the father, and a renewed need to turn the oedipal wishes away from the parents onto contemporaries—brothers; but here too naked aggression is sublimated. Both Bernfeld and Jones set Freud's renunciation of military and political ambition at 17, "shortly after his graduation from high school, Freud suddenly retreats from his search for power over men" (Bernfeld, 1949, p. 169). Freud, like Joseph, "perceived that the ultimate secret of power was not force, but understanding" (Jones, 1953, p. 53). In his forties, and only after *he* had lost *his* father Jacob, Freud began his self-analysis, accomplished largely through *his* ability to interpret dreams. The exploration of his own past led to mastery, to the attempt at conquest of that "unexplored region of the mind in which I have been the first mortal to set forth" (Freud, 1887-1902). He emerged as the successful "conquistadore," not by blood and killing, but by understanding. It was the discovery of the Oedipus complex and his acknowledgement of his own murderous and incestuous wishes that made it possible for him to come to terms with Jacob and with his brothers, by way of altered identifications and object relationships. Fratricide and parricide had been transmuted to psychic analysis; incest and the sexual probing of his mother's body to the exploration of the human mind.

EGYPT: THE JOURNEY WEST

I have remarked on the Egyptian setting of Freud's dream about his mother. Egypt had always fascinated Freud, as it had Napoleon, of whose Egyptian campaign Freud wrote, asking "where else could one go but Egypt if one were Joseph and wanted to loom large in the brothers' eyes" (E. Freud, 1960, p. 433)? He loved to collect antiquities; his consulting room was filled with Egyptian statuettes. This collection was "his only extravagance" (Jones, 1957 p. 297). Freud, like Oedipus, was the solver of the riddle of the sphinx, that fabulous monster of Egyptian origin. During his last five years, the heroic, cancer-ridden man had Egypt in the background of his still active and creative mind—Egypt as a kind of ground bass against which the themes of Joseph and Moses could play in counterpoint. Freud was writing and revising his Moses book in the years 1934-1938. Moses, according to Freud's idea, was—like Joseph, like Freud himself—a Jew and yet not a Jew. Freud had him an Egyptian, as Joseph had become an Egyptian. In the family romance fantasy, the child tries to evade his impulses toward his own parents by claiming another, usually a royal or divine, parentage. Moses was "found" by Pharaoh's daughter. Thus Pharaoh, and not Jacob, is the father to be reckoned with. The ambivalence inherent in the father-son confrontation, deflectable onto the struggle between siblings, figures in the Hebrew myths as the struggle between Egyptians and Jews. When Freud's book appeared in 1939, it was resented by many Jews because it attributed to an Egyptian the lineage and ideas of the greatest of Jewish cultural heroes. Moses, the godlike father-figure, was presented as the spiritual son of the Pharaoh Ihknaton![14]

Egypt had another ambivalent meaning for Freud during these years. It was both the place of refuge and plenty, and the land of exile and persecution. The Nazi invasion of Austria finally forced the old "conquistadore," who in his life and in the imagery of his books[15] was so often indulging his "earliest passion" (Freud 1887-1902) for travelling, to take his penultimate great journey to England. We know from his letters that he was thinking of earlier flights west[16]—from Israel into Egypt. His forebears had been forced to flee from Palestine to Bessarabia to Cologne to Bohemia; and when he was two, his father, Jacob, had chosen, because of anti-

[14]Like Joseph, Freud had even had an Abraham who preceded him to Egypt. In his study of Amenhotep IV (Ihknaton), Abraham (1912) anticipated some of the things Freud was to say in *Moses and Monotheism*. It is so absolutely uncharacteristic of Freud not to mention Abraham's study (which Freud surely had read) in the Moses book, that one can only assume this represented a slip, and the forgetting was based on the hostility unconsciously associated with rivalry brought out by things Egyptian. Abraham was 20 years younger than Freud—the age difference that separated Freud from his older brother, Phillip. Abraham had died (in 1925) and therefore could also be a "revenant" of dead younger brother Julius.

[15]The central image of his masterpiece, *The Interpretation of Dreams*, is that of a journey (Shengold 1966).

[16]According to Altman (1959) *west* symbolizes death; so, Freud (1900) says, does a *journey*.

semitic outbursts, to leave Sigmund's birthplace, Freiburg, for Leipzig and finally for Vienna. Now the escape to England could be seen as both a journey into, and a journey out of, Egypt. Egypt had been a haven offering sustenance—for Joseph fleeing from his persecuting brothers, for Jacob and his sons fleeing from famine. Up to the time of Moses, Egypt is represented in the Bible as a place for the Jews to go and live in freedom, thanks to Joseph and his providing for them the land of Goshen. But Egypt was also a land of exile and persecution. Moses led his people out of Egyptian bondage into the promised land of Canaan. And when he did so, the Bible says (Exodus 13:19), "Moses took with him the bones of Joseph who had exacted an oath from the children of Israel, that they would take his body back to the land of Jacob." For Freud, England had long been a promised land, but it was also a land of exile away from the city of Vienna, so often described in his letters to Fliess as detested and destestable,[17] but now become a "beloved prison." His feelings were most ambivalent; for all his threats of leaving, mutterings of hatred, he finally had to be forced to leave the city by his children, friends, and pupils, even after the Nazi takeover had made the hatred eminently justifiable. Not only was he leaving behind the many, many years of his past, he was also separating himself from the bones of his parents. The grave evokes the womb. For Joseph, this meant the cave of Machpelah where he could lie at peace with the bones of his ancestors. But Joseph never was buried with either Rachel or Jacob. His tomb lies apart, as does Freud's; and that of Oedipus who was not permitted burial in Athens but only at nearby Colonus. The city is a symbol for the mother, and to finally come to terms with that first object of hostility and love is to return to earth in a hallowed spot. It was perhaps in this sense that Freud longed for Vienna.

Freud was very ill, very aware of his old age and of his identity as father and patriarch. He was no longer Joseph going in to Egypt to triumph over his brothers. He had come to terms with, and now again identified with, a greater and older rival, Jacob. The Biblical Jacob had gone to Egypt to be reunited with his lost son, Joseph, and was to die there in exile. It is as Jacob that Freud, awaiting

[17]"I hate Vienna with a positively personal hatred, and, just the contrary of the giant Antaeus I draw fresh strength whenever I remove my feet from the soil of the city which is my home" (letter of 3/11/1900, 1887-1902, p. 311).

emigration in Vienna, writes to his son, Ernst, in England: the role of Jacob that can coalesce himself as father, his own father, Jacob, the Biblical Patriarch, Jacob, and the Wandering Jew: "Two prospects keep me going in these grim times: to rejoin you all and—*to die in freedom* [last four words in English]. I sometimes compare myself with the old Jacob who, when a very old man, was taken by his children to Egypt, as Thomas Mann is to describe in his next novel. Let us hope it won't be also followed by an exodus from Egypt. It is high time that Ahasuerus[18] came to rest somewhere" (E. Freud, 1960, p. 442). He was going to England to die:

> To go back to the earth in London
> An Important Jew who died in exile [Auden, 1945, p. 163].

The great road from childhood to paternity had been completely traversed, the drive for power over father and brothers had been transcended. He had himself become a patriarch, the undisputed leader of a new school of thinking about, and helping, human beings:

> To us he is no more a person
> Now but a whole climate of opinion [Auden, 1945, p. 167].

And just before crossing the channel into England, the ambition of Joseph shows itself again. The old man dreams of himself as William the Conqueror! The wish to be the "conquistadore," Messiah-ben-Joseph conquering the promised land, still stirred as he was about to embark on the last journey.

[18] The Wandering Jew—forced, like Oedipus, to travel for his sins.

CHAPTER 30

Narcissistic Fusion States and Creativity

Gilbert J. Rose, M.D.

The term, narcissism, is used in this paper to refer to primary narcissism or the initial blurring between mother and child from which the sense of self begins to evolve. This is admittedly but one facet of an enormously complex concept. I will refer to it as a narcissistic fusion state, although the word "fusion" somewhat overdraws the case.

Psychological growth begins with the development of the sense of self as the infant separates from its primary unity with the mother. At first the boundaries between mother and child are hazy, with constant remerging taking place. From the latter half of the first year through the third, the child gradually develops a conception of himself as separate from the mother and other external objects. Satiation, as well as deprivation, may predispose him to return to a psychic state similar to the earlier unity with the mother, and to a relative refusion of the representations of self and objects within the ego. Even into adult life, the boundaries between self-and object representations may remain somewhat fluid and interchangeable. We have learned from psychoanalytic studies of early ego development, as well as from quantum theory in physics (Heisenberg, 1958), that reality consists of shifting rather than rigid boundaries between self and world.

In the actuality of experience, stability is a dynamic tension rather than a static state, a workable equilibrium subject to continuing negotiation and redjustment. We do not "overcome" orality and pri-

Dr. Rose is Associate Clinical Professor, Department of Psychiatry, Yale University Medical School.

mary narcissism, and "achieve" genitality and complete object relationships. We keep fashioning new syntheses between ourselves and the outside, creating areas of relative constancy and temporary balance in the midst of the continuously flowing regressive and progressive tides within the mind. In the fluid processes which make up our workable equilibria, projection and introjection oscillate; activities and objects are invested with varying amounts of narcissistic libido; and multiple microscopic acts of narcissistic fusion might be said to occur. Earlier modes of functioning become orchestrated within later ones and continue to play a part.

Effecting multiple fusions and separations is one early technique by which the ego seeks to simplify, shape, and control its world. Attempting thus to master something by fusing with it, obliterating the boundaries between self-and object representations, recalls the primary narcissism of the infant and the acutely psychotic. But to merge, in order to re-emerge, may remain part of the fundamental process of psychological growth on all developmental levels, dominating the most primitive ones, but contributing richness to the others. It was Freud (1933) who wrote, "We cannot do justice to the characteristics of the mind by linear outlines like those in a drawing or in primitive painting, but rather by areas of colour melting into one another as they are presented by modern artists. After making the separation we must allow what we have separated to merge together once more" (p. 79).

The fluid boundaries which originate in narcissistic fusion states contribute to a wide range of mental phenomena, from psychotic episodes and identity problems, through normal development and the achievements of creative imagination. In this paper we will sketch some of these, with special reference to creativity in both its unusual and its everyday forms.

Following an LSD-induced psychotic episode, a patient felt reborn. The world appeared luminous with fresh color, and it was as if she were experiencing it for the first time with immense wonder and intense pleasure. For months thereafter she had recurrent nocturnal episodes in which her vision underwent massive instinctualization after masturbation. She had vivid illusions and hallucinations of gigantic genitalia of both sexes, sometimes condensed into a bisexual symbol like a crocodile. While she knew she was experiencing a kind of waking dream, perceiving all orifices as vaginal and all projections as phallic, the real and solid things around her seemed imbued with variable and shifting qualities. Size, shape, and distance had no constancy. The elements of a visual gestalt would disintegrate, and the fragments would then appear to fuse and copulate with each other. To protect herself from the terror of these experiences, she developed intense fantasies of fusing with her surroundings. She imagined she was part of the walls and hallucinated this. She explained that if everything became part of herself through fusion, she had control and need not fear either attacking others or being attacked. Real meant separate, and this meant no control over it. Therefore, she had to obliterate any distance or separation from herself by making everything a part of herself. In the process, her sense of self became so thinned out and "selfless" that it approached the boundarylessness of primary narcissism.

In another context (Rose, 1966), I have described individuals whose sense of identity depends on the persistence of unconscious fantasies of fusion with objects as suffering from a narcissistic identity disorder. They are preoedipally fixated and have hazy boundaries between self-and object representations within the ego. They may conceive of themselves as phallic extensions, anal products, breasts, or mouths; their view of the world may bear corresponding part-object imprints. Sense of self and of reality may be proportionately impaired.

Individuals with a narcissistic identity disorder are engaged in a process of self-creation, attempting to set and stabilize their ego boundaries as they emerge and re-emerge from narcissistic fusion states. As psychological growth continues, ego boundaries continue to expand and constrict as the reality of the self becomes more firmly established. It may then reaffirm itself more freely in work and love. It uses itself as a sensitive and stable instrument to make further determinations and corrections, explore wider realities, and lose and refind itself in higher degrees of differentiation. This may be the extent of self-creation that most individuals can perform as maturation proceeds.

Implicit in this is the idea that the need to create is basic to the working of the mind. Growth is a form of self-creation. If we think of the creative impulse as the need to construct viable forms of reality for oneself, then it is clear that this need is as basic as growth. More specifically, the ego's integrative function, among others, is always involved in normal, garden-variety creativity. The data of ego psychology can show that perception and memory are minor "creative" events. Likewise, a case could be made for the "creativity" of identity formation as well as for some dream imagery. Identity formation, for example, is a continuing process of progressive integration which relates continuity to change. To the extent that identity shapes reality, orients one within it, and imparts direction, it is a "creative" form, part of the creativity of everyday life. Such ordinary creativity has been rendered more recognizable by the evolution of psychoanalysis from a theory of the abnormal toward a general psychology of behavior.

This highlighting of the ordinary finds a parallel on the contemporary art scene. For example, the "happenings" of the recent art scene force a hypervigilant attention to the ordinary processes of perception. Pop art compels an observation of the banalities which we, unseeing, are immersed in; if it is fixed, repetitive, big, and sufficiently common, it must be Real. Then, within the static space thus constructed, optical art can turn a mirrored lens back upon the eye, repeat old visual experiments in applied physics and physiology, and rediscover and celebrate the pulsations Within. Psychedelic art, on the other hand, seems to point the way to refuge in narcissistic fusion states, and the nostalgia of earlier, wondrous self-stimulations and masturbatory self-discoveries.

A distinction should be made between progressively and regressively integrative aspects of the creative process. The dream and paranoid fantasies, perhaps like some of the art forms just mentioned, are examples of regressive integration. The dream is a painting, by a temporarily psychotic artist, of an elaborate, narcissistic projection. It is not art in that it may not show the unique organization and variation of material which characterize art. It is certainly imaginative and involves primary-process manipulation of time and space, and bears panoramic individual significance. Though there may be a sense of expansion, there is an actual reduction of ego boundaries and a saving of energy as part of the ego becomes dedifferentiated and drawn closer to the original ego-id matrix. Some dream imagery may be "creative" in the sense of being uniquely formative and integrative. Although all dream images are orchestrated with primarily latent personal meanings, some may leap over conventional boundaries to illuminate hidden connections which are not purely private. (Space does not permit examples.)

Normal psychological growth and identity formation are examples of progressive integration from narcissism. As growth is self-creation, identity-formation is the creation of self from the fusions of narcissism. In contrast to the regressive integration of dreams or psychotic fusions, this progressive integration leads to an enhanced sense of self and perspective on the world.

Analytic treatment offers an opportunity for further growth. Growth in analysis is often accompanied by unconscious birth fantasies. It is not uncommon in my experience, having collected more than twenty examples, often retrospectively, for these birth fantasies to follow an "unconscious calendar" and concentrate at the end of the ninth month of treatment (Rose, 1962 and 1969). Although a curious finding, it seems typical of the concreteness of the unconscious. Of the many meanings of birth fantasies in analysis, one is pertinent to the present context: in individuals with fragile ego boundaries, unconscious birth fantasies often represent a defense against narcissistic fusion. Sometimes the defense against this fear of fusion takes the form of acting out—the patient temporarily leaves treatment. The separation is a symbolic act of birth. Like other manifestations of birth fantasies, these interruptions of treatment for a week or more tend also to occur more frequently near the end of the ninth month. Whether the birth fantasy is acted out in an interruption of treatment or takes more analytically acceptable forms, it often accompanies the progressive integration of psychological growth and identity formation, and presages improvement.[1]

While maturation makes use of the ordinary creativity of the ego's coordinated functioning, a mature personality is hardly a work of art. Philosophers of culture tell us that a real work of art results from the discovery of a new aspect or an intensification of reality which

[1] In one published case (Milner, 1950), five years of clinically unfruitful analysis were succeeded by significant changes only after termination, the termination being experienced as a kind of rebirth. Likewise, the massive dedifferentiations which Peto (1967) has observed, often preceding therapeutic gains, may have a similar significance. Such dedifferentiations may possibly be perceived as deaths of the self and are then followed by fantasies of rebirth from narcissistic fusion states, accompanied by clinical improvement.

has never before been seen in this shape. In contrast to play, which deals with illusive images, the new forms disclosed by real art continue to be seen. They construct reality by reshaping it into something which it had not been before and teach us how to see. Like art, language, science, myth, and religion all suppress and pass over certain parts of the immediate factuality to construct reality from a unique direction. Each one provides the building stones of "reality" (Cassirer, 1953). Language, for example, is an arrangement of the stream of sensory experience which results in a certain picture of the universe; it determines what our reality will be (Whorf, 1956).

Van Gogh wrote to his brother, " 'I am an artist' . . . means 'I am seeking' . . ." Seeking what? Seeking an increased apprehension of the nature of reality, I would suggest. "The artist," according to Focillon (1948), "must live all the primitive experiments over again . . . He starts from the beginning. Is it not more or less the same with the child? Adult man . . . loses this attitude of trial and error, and because he has grown up, he stops growing. The artist prolongs the child's curiosity far beyond the limits of childhood. He touches, he feels, he reckons weight, he measures space, he molds the fluidity of atmosphere, to prefigure form in it, he caresses the skin of all things . . ." (p. 47).

What features of narcissistic fusion states might contribute to the creative imagination of the artist? If creative imagination is a search for new solutions to the nature of reality, then the beginnings of reality from narcissistic fusion states contribute in at least two ways to the impulse to create these new solutions: (1) the potential for trauma inherent in the emergence from narcissistic states may stimulate the creative impulse to efforts at mastery, and (2) the fluidity of early ego boundaries encourages the development of imaginative forms.

The infant, emerging from the fusions of primary narcissism, is in danger of being flooded with stimulation. This is more likely to be traumatic if it is endowed with special sensitivity and responsiveness, such as that postulated for the artist (Greenacre, 1957). The likelihood is increased if the infant does not receive optimal amounts of instinctual gratification and deprivation graded to his strengths and needs. In an effort to master the threat of overstimulation, the ego returns repeatedly to narcissistic fusion states with a partial dissolution of ego boundaries. In addition, repetitiveness is inherent in all physiological and psychological growth patterns (Schur, 1966a). For this reason, and because of the threat of trauma, the initial formation of ego boundaries stimulates repeated returns towards partial dissolution of them. Having been partially dissolved, they are then re-formed, often to the accompaniment of unconscious birth fantasies. The birth fantasies signify the re-establishment (rebirth) of ego boundaries from the fusions of primary narcissism. The re-emergence from narcissistic fusion and the re-establishment of ego boundaries carry the possibility of a somewhat fresh arrangement of the building blocks of reality.

Such new arrangements are potentially at hand in the fluidity of early ego boundaries. Here there are rapid interchanges between thought and microscopic actions (Rose, 1963), and there are loose arrangements of time, space, and sense of self. Self and other, thought and action, time and causality have not yet imposed order on things to build reality. Because of the mobility of all these elements, and because none of the categories have become frozen, imagination is unrestricted. Imagination can form representations of things not present to the senses, it can elaborate memories and combine them playfully with new ingredients as they are observed. Ambiguities, contradictions, and absurdities nurture the imaginative play rather than foreclose possibilities and opportunities for new combinations.

Just as any number of non-Euclidean geometries can give equally perfect accounts of space configurations, any particular language is an equally logical, but provisional abstraction from an infinite variety of possibilities. Every culture provides some ground-plan of language, as well as a pattern of emphasis for sight, hearing, and smell. Within this linguistic and perceptual milieu, an individual creates a personal reality, that of his own historical identity. If he comes from a poly-cultural background, a situation not uncommon for a creative individual, multiple frames of reference may more easily arise and co-exist. They can further stimulate the search for new solutions for reality, or new constructions of it, but only if reality, itself, is treated as a question which is still somewhat open for negotiation.

Such is the climate that prevails with the early ego boundaries which emerge and re-emerge from the narcissistic fusion states on which the artist draws. Questions have not been stilled by too-conclusive answers. At the interfaces of the shifting boundaries of reality, new equilibria may appear with unique dimensions and nascent meanings. They comprise both the private identity forms with which we create our *Umwelt*, and the major forms of creative imagination which transcend the private.

The artist, like the psychotic and the individual with a narcissistic identity disorder, is seeking an increased apprehension of the nature of reality by repeatedly dissolving ego boundaries and re-emerging from narcissistic fusion states. Like an individual with a traumatic neurosis, he attempts to master reality by returning repeatedly to its beginnings to reshape it. Unlike the psychotic, his reality testing is sufficiently moored in healthy early object relations to permit the reactivation of the early narcissistic traumata, yet withstand being overwhelmed by them. As Weissman (1967) has suggested, the ego in creativity may operate in a coordinated process of desynthesis and resynthesis, not unlike Peto's (1961) fragmentizing function of the ego. It disrupts established solutions and temporarily suspends self- and object representations to resample narcissistic fusion states before synthesizing a new equilibrium between self and reality. In this new equilibrium there is a kind of amalgamation of body imagery with outer forms and a mutual permeability or sense of fusion with the world (Greenacre, 1957).

Unlike the individual with a narcissistic identity disorder, or a psychotic criminal, the artist is not wholly engaged in re-creating himself from his own narcissism, or in perpetrating a death and rebirth through some victim. His own work becomes his fetish, or his transitional object (Eissler, 1962; Kohut, 1966). It is invested with narcissistic libido and takes on the intensity of an addiction. By making his own work serve as his proxy, the artist can safely relive the primitive experiments of testing reality by repeated fusions and separations. He builds it up and melts it down again and again, repeating vicariously through the work the building up and melting down of psychic structure in its emergence from narcissism.

The artist gives himself up to his object and impresses himself upon it in repeated alternations of active mastery and passive surrender, of controlled fusion, letting go, and reimposing control to rediscover depths and limits. He resamples the earliest body imageries, perhaps in an unconscious fantasy of fusion and rebirth, to return to the real and universal with an expanded awareness of both the inner and outer worlds. Body-image clusters of the various psychosexual stages of development may play a part in guiding and enriching the rapid oscillating interchanges between thought and microscopic action (Rose, 1963). Archaic bodily senses may impart a sense of physical investment from the center, as awareness of time and space are expanded at the periphery (Rose, 1964).

The model of center and periphery, or of ego "core" and its oscillating cathexis with ego boundaries may have heuristic value in studying creative imagination. A cross-section of the self from an ego point of view can discern a number of elements which contribute to stability in the midst of the ebb and flow of differentiation. Early ego identifications, bodily self representations, reality testing, and integrative functions of the ego represent a cluster of forces which might be conceptualized as ego core (Rose, 1964).

The patterning of the forces within the ego core may help to describe what happens when the ego makes a reparative attempt to master the birth of ego boundaries by returning to a narcissistic fusion state and the beginnings of reality. The integrative function of the ego acts to unite and organize the various drives and tendencies within the personality, amalgamating them into the most nearly adaptive compromise that is possible for the individual at that particular time. If reality testing is not based on healthy early ego identifications and bodily self representations, the integrating function of the ego may be unable to harmonize the reactivated narcissistic state in the light of a correct appraisal of the external world and its generally accepted meanings. The result is regressive integration.

If reality testing is based on healthy early ego identifications and bodily self representations, the return toward narcissistic fusion is subjected to continuing exploration and testing. Through a process of work and energy expenditure, there is an alternating constriction and expansion of ego boundaries, corresponding to regressive and progressive integration. The relatively fluid boundaries between self- and object representations within the ego are subjected to the force of the integrative function and corrected by the reality-testing function of the ego. This interaction between ego core and boundaries may effect an over-all expansion of ego boundaries: a higher degree of self- and object differentiation and an enhanced sense of self and of the world. This is the progressive integration of normal maturation. It is uniquely formative for the individual and constitutes the private task of continuing self-creation from narcissism.

The rare major forms of creative imagination transcend the private and restructure reality itself. A real work of art simplifies, but also expands and deepens the view of the world and of the self. In doing this, the artist, through his work, recapitulates progressively as well as regressively the struggle each of us has to continually test reality and master it by relating inner and outer, in repeated fusions and separations.

It may be only at this point that the artist is able to relax his preoccupation with his work and go on to other things. The work of art remains behind as the cast of a mind "reborn," and objectified in the process of thought, feeling, and action. The mind itself, having finished this particular labor of reality testing and re-emergence from narcissism, is free to loosen its hold and go elsewhere—to test reality again, surrender to it and perhaps master it and even leave an imprint upon it, by another process of fusion and separation.

In view of my emphasis on the ego's use of the early boundaries which emerge from narcissistic fusion states, it is relevant to ask if this is a form of regression in the service of the ego. Because early modes of functioning are normally available to the ego alongside more advanced forms of ego functioning, the use of primitive mechanisms such as projection or introjection does not, per se, indicate that ego regression has taken place. More pertinent is the question: Is the integrative function able to harmonize the primitive modes in the light of sound reality testing, based on healthy early ego identifications and bodily self-representations? If it is, ego regression has not taken place.

An analogy with vision may be pertinent. The rod cells of the retina are located primarily at the periphery. In contrast to the cone cells of the central retina, they are particularly sensitive to light of low illumination at the blue end of the spectrum. When we utilize the periphery of the retina to perceive this kind of light, vision has not regressed from central cone cell type to peripheral rod cell type. Nor is it a lapse from truth to illusion. The change of focus from ego core to boundaries is a similar shift from one order of factuality to another. It is made possible by an attention which roves from the daily, high-noon awareness of the unities of time, space, and sense of self, to the discernment, one might say at twilight, that these boundaries are somewhat fluid.

This low illumination, peripheral insight ultimately has to do with birth and death. An unconscious reminiscence of early narcissistic fusion portends an intimation of future death. The creative impulse may well be related to this intution of the tragic: birth and death on either side of the self, enhancing the sense of self and of the world, and adding richness to the moment.

CHAPTER 31

To "Lick" a Problem

Sandor S. Feldman, M.D.

Metaphors frequently expose the primary, concrete, bodily meaning of human communication. The bodily signal is selectively and symbolically expressed in language. At times, a word or expression can be translated literally, in the same idiom, from one language to another, with no loss of meaning. The very same expression may be used to indicate opposite meanings. The symbols (words) convey love, aggression, and ambivalence between the two in oral- and anal-erotic terms.

The phrase "to lick a problem" fuses the action of the mouth, lips, and tongue in a verbal form; the tongue becomes identical with language (indeed, "tongue" is a synonym for language). All are "oral" and, as such, the source of strong ambivalence: love-hatred, kindness-aggression, unification-separation. The verb, to lick, aside from its literal meaning, has certain special meanings in at least five different languages: English, German, French, Russian, and Hungarian, e.g., to lick the boots or feet of a superior in order to gain his favor (English, French, Russian), to be a "bottom-licker" (Hungarian) or "ass-kisser" (English, Russian). With regard to the last, I believe that ass and bottom actually mean anus. The aggressive invitation, as seen in the expression, "you can lick my ass," represents a struggle between friendship and hostility (oral and anal erotism). It is impossible actually to lick someon'e anus or permit one's anus to be licked and to remain hostile. If hostile warriors would lick each

Dr. Feldman is Clinical Professor of Psychiatry, Department of Psychiatry, University of Rochester School of Medicine and Dentistry.

other's anuses, fighting would either not occur or would cease, whatever the cause of the conflict. The British professor of psychology, John Cohen (1961), writes: "if the disposition to swear is as deeply ingrained in human life as it appears to be, we could put it to good use in international affairs as a substitute for war at any temperature. We might envisage the Security Council advising its members to adopt a swearing technique for settling disputes such as has long been traditional among the Eskimos" (pp. 280-281).

The newborn infant is already able to lick, according to the observations of Preyer and Stirnimann (Peiper, 1963, pp. 463-464); ". . . the infant does not suck but presses out the nipple like the milkmaid milks the cow" (Hoffer, 1950, p. 158). Probably the first problem one has to "lick," i.e., to solve or to conquer, is finding the nipple (breast or bottle), licking it, sucking it, and obtaining digestible fluid, or liquid. The term "liquidation" is related to this. Evans (1964) writes: "As 'animistic misunderstanding' sees all pain as coming from 'outside,' it is possible to understand that which first mediates the external world. The breast or body of the mother, should be imagined as the source of danger" (p. 69).

The gullible "sucker" is orally fixated and easily believes in whatever is offered. To him, every offering is the breast; every acceptance and rejection is an oral act. Like a baby, he incorporates the good food and spits out the bad. In fantasy, the sucker is always at the breast. When frustrated or facing a problem, children will resort to sucking their thumb, and adults will often turn to smoking, as though in an effort to provide for themselves, by the original means, the same satisfaction which they found at the breast.

Slang brings language close to the primary bodily signals and points up the ambivalent meaning of words. "Licker" is used to denote a person who is decisive. "Licking"also means superiority, excellence, or goodness. To be "licked" may mean liquidation or imminent death. To lick also means to beat or to thrash, and "to lick the pants off" someone expresses an anal-sadistic, ambivalent intention (Barry and van Den Bark, 1942). Licking can connote healing, "to lick one's wounds"; hostility, "to lick the dust" (*Holy Bible*, Micah 7:17, Psalms 72:9); cure, "licking an illness"; mastery, "licking fear."

Ambivalence is also present in the contemptuous phrase, "I spit upon you," or, "I wouldn't even spit on you." Spitting on someone is a form of oral contact and *could* have friendly implications. In my book on mannerisms (Feldman, 1959, p. 281), I traced the finger-snapping gesture used when one prompts oneself or someone else to action (especially to remember something, which is often connected with a motion of the lips and with a sound), to the two lips finding the nipple and taking possession of it. It appears to me that this life-preserving action (second only to breathing) has a mighty imprint on us, and that every remembering is prompted by the desire to recapture the first joy. This jubilant feeling is reflected in the experience of overcoming the resistance and restoring the forgotten to consciousness. In another paper (Feldman, 1953), I presented a collection of very common symptoms found in our everyday life showing specifically the aggressive orality in eating.

We never quite relinquish the breast. As Lewin (1946) has shown, even when we dream in visual images, we are resting on the "dream screen," on the breast upon which we have fallen asleep after being sated. Advertisements, especially when the product is food, drink (milk), cigars, or cigarettes, often show a young, attractive woman with prominent breasts. Topless waitresses whet the patrons' appetites. The maternal breast (or bottle) being the first "restaurant" may provide the basis for certain kinds of subsequent restaurant behavior. Examples of this are expressions such as, "You can now bring me *my* coffee," or the bitter complaint of many people when they cannot get their first choice on the menu, or when the waiter is not sufficiently attentive to them. This also helps explain the custom of tipping, by means of which the waiter and waitress are transformed into mother. In Hungary, the tip is called *borravalo* (for wine); in French, *pourboire* (for drink); in russian, *na tchai* (for tea); German, *Trinkgeld* (drink money). Arlen (1964) quotes an official of the waiters' union as saying that the tip "gives the customer a sense of personal contact" (p. 38).

A little girl, hardly two-and-a-half-years-old, was walking along one hot summer day holding her mother's hand. The little girl said, "Mommy, I want an ice cream cone." The mother said, "No, you just had one a little while ago." The little girl replied, "I don't love you anymore," and they walked off without saying anything further. Ice cream cones are licked. Oral gratification in humans and animals creates love and friendship; oral frustration elicits withdrawal of love, separation, and hostile feelings and behavior.

At the age of three, my grandson (for the first time) tried to master the descent of a cement slope, several yards long, which stood in front of a building. The slope was on both sides of a set of steps and had a very smooth, slippery surface. First he got on all fours to size up the situation. He looked down. His face showed concern, for he did not yet know how he would accomplish the task. Then, while still on the platform, he put his left leg on the slope and realized that he would not succeed. His third attempt was to stand erect on the platform and put his left foot a short way out on the slope, as if to walk down. He smiled, realizing the impossibility. Finally, on the fourth attempt, he got on all fours, stretched out his two arms, tested the slope with his hands, felt that he had enough friction with his two palms, and jubilantly crawled down, with his mouth open and his tongue sticking out. He had "licked" the problem.

One can often observe the following in both children and adults: a soft, slimy creature, say a caterpillar or a strange-looking fish, is held up with a self-encouraging smile mixed with fear. The person struggles with himself whether to keep holding it or to throw it away. He holds the creature gingerly, away from his body, and grimaces, opening his mouth and sticking out his tongue. It is common to stick out one's tongue as a sign of rejection. A recalcitrant child may stick out his tongue in a teasing manner as a gesture of defiance. The gesture serves to express his aggression as well as to maintain some friendly contact.

The human wish to be cared for "from the cradle to the grave," from mother-breast to mother-earth, derives, structurally speaking, from the id. It remains cathected with instinctual energy from birth until death. In the course of development, it pervades and finds expression in a host of increasingly complex activites.

References

References

Abbate, G. (1964), Panel Report: Child Analysis at Different Developmental Stages. *J. Amer. Psychoanal. Assn.*, 12:135-150.

Abraham, K. (1909), *Dreams and Myths*. Monograph 15; New York: Nervous and Mental Disease Publishing Co., 1913.

______(1912), Amenhotop IV: Psycho-analytic Contributions towards the Understanding of His Personality and of the Monotheistic Cult of Aton. In: *Clinical Papers and Essays on Psycho-Analysis*. London: Hogarth Press, 1955, pp. 262-290.

______(1918), Observations on Ferenczi's Paper on "Sunday Neuroses." In: *The Psycho-Analytic Reader*, ed. R. Fliess. New York: International Universities Press, 1948, pp. 312-315.

______(1924), A Short Study of the Development of the Libido, Viewed in the Light of Mental Disorders. In: *Selected Papers of Karl Abraham*. New York: Basic Books, 1953, pp. 418-501.

Aichhorn, A. (1925), *Wayward Youth*, New York: Viking Press, 1948.

Albee, E. (1959), The Zoo Story. In: *The American Dream and The Zoo Story. Two Plays*. New York: New American Library.

Aldrich, J. W. (1964), The Gooney Birds of Midway. *National Geographic*, 125, 6:838-851.

Alexander, F. (1950), *Psychosomatic Medicine: Its Principles and Application*. New York: W. W. Norton.

______(1954), Some Quantitative Aspects of Psychoanalytic Technique. *J. Amer. Psychoanal. Assn.*, 2:685-701.

Altman, L. (1959), "West" as a Symbol of Death. *Psychoanal. Quart.*, 28:236-241.

Ames, L. B. (1946), The Development of the Sense of Time in the Young Child. *J. Genet. Psychol.*, 68:97-125.

Arlen, M. J. (1964), Tips on Tipping and Tipees. *The New York Times Magazine*, May 31, p. 38.

Arlow, J. A. (1953), Masturbation and Symptom Formation. *J. Amer. Psychoanal. Assn.*, 1:45-58.

______(1961), Ego Psychology and the Study of Mythology. *J. Amer. Psychoanal. Assn.*, 9:371-393.

______(1963), Conflict, Regression and Symptom Formation. *Internat. J. Psycho-Anal.*, 44:12-22.

______(1964), The Madonna's Conception Through The Eyes. *The Psychoanalytic Study of Society*, 3:13-25. New York: International Universities Press.

______ & Brenner, C. (1964), *Psychoanalytic Concepts and the Structural Theory*. New York: International Universities Press.

Auden, W. H. (1945), In Memory of Sigmund Freud. *The Collected Poetry of W. H. Auden*. New York: Knopf.

Bak, R. C. (1953), Fetishism. *J. Amer. Psychoanal. Assn.*, 1:285-298.

Bakan, D. (1958), *Sigmund Freud and the Mystical Tradition.* Princeton: Van Nostrand.

Barea, I. (1966), *Vienna.* New York: Knopf.

Barry, L. U. & van Den Bark, M. (1942), *The American Thesaurus of Slang.* New York: Crowell.

de Beauvoir, S. (1951-1952), Must We Burn Sade? In: *The Marquis de Sade*, ed. P. Dinnage. New York: Grove Press, 1953, pp. 9-82.

Bender, L. (1954), *A Dynamic Psychopathology of Childhood.* Springfield, Ill.: Charles C Thomas.

Benedek, T. (1956), Toward the Biology of the Depressive Constellation. *J. Amer. Psychoanal. Assn.*, 4:389-427.

Beres, D. (1962), The Unconscious Fantasy. *Psychoanal. Quart.* 31:309-328.

Bergler, E. (1947), Differential Diagnosis between Spurious Homosexuality and Perversion Homosexuality. *Psychiat. Quart.*, 21:399-410.

——(1951), *Neurotic Counterfeit Sex.* New York: Grune and Stratton.

——and Eidelberg, L. (1933), The "Mama" Complex in the Male. *Internat. Zeitschrift für Psychoanalyse*, 19:547-583.

—— & Róheim, G. (1946), Psychology of Time Perception. *Psychoanal. Quart.*, 15:190-206.

Bernfeld, S. (1938), Types of Adolescence. *Psychoanal. Quart.*, 7:243-253.

——(1946), An Unknown Autobiographical Fragment by Freud. *Amer. Imago*, 4:3-19.

——(1949), Freud's Scientific Beginnings. *Amer. Imago*, 6:163-196.

Best, E. (1924), *The Maori as He Was.* Wellington, New Zealand: H. E. Owen, 1952.

Bettelheim, B. (1963), *The Empty Fortress.* Glencoe, Illinois: Free *Press.*

Bibring, E. (1953), The Mechanism of Depression. In: *Affective Disorders*, ed. P. Greenacre. New York: International Universities Press, pp. 13-48.

Bibring, G. L., Dwyer, T. F., Huntington, D. S. & Valenstein, A. F. (1961), A Study of the Psychological Processes in Pregnancy and of the Earliest Mother-Child Relationship. *The Psychoanalytic Study* of the Child, 16:62-71. New York: International Universities Press.

Bieber, I., ed. (1962), *Homosexuality.* New York: Basic Books.

Blamires, H. (1966), *The Bloomsday Book.* London: Methuen.

Bonaparte, M. (1928), L'Identification d'une Fille à sa Mère Morte. *Rev. Franc. Psychanal.* 2:541-565. In: Hilgard, J. R. & Fisk, F. Disruption of Adult Ego Identity as Related to Childhood Loss of Mother Through Hospitalization for Psychosis. *J. Nerv. & Ment. Dis.*, 131:47-57, 1960.

——(1940), Time and the Unconscious. *Internat. J. Psycho-Anal.* 21:427-468.

Boring, E. G. (1936), Temporal Perception and Operationism. *Amer. J. Psychol.*, 48:519-522.

Bornstein, B. (1935), Phobia in a Two-and-a-Half-Year-Old Child. *Psychoanal. Quart.*, 4:93-119.

——(1949), The Analysis of a Phobic Child. Some Problems of Theory and Technique in Child Analysis. *The Psychoanalytic Study of the Child*, 3/4:181-226. New York: International Universities Press.

Bouvet, M. (1958), Technical Variation and the Concept of Distance. *Internat. J. Psycho-Anal.*, 39:211-221.

Bowlby, J. (1958), The Nature of the Child's Tie to the Mother. *Internat. J. Psycho-Anal.*, 39:350-373.

—— (1959), Psychoanalysis and Ethology. Paper given at the Symposium on Ethology and Psychoanalysis at the 21st International Psychoanalytic Congress, Copenhagen, July.

—— (1960), Grief and Mourning in Infancy and Early Childhood. *The Psychoanalytic Study of the Child*, 15:9-52. New York: International Universities Press.

Bradley, N. D. (1948), The Growth of Knowledge of Time in Children of School Age. *Brit. J. Psychol.*, 38:67-78.

Brenner, C. (1951), A Case of Childhood Hallucinosis. *The Psychoanalytic Study of the Child* 6:235-243. New York: International Universities Press.

Breuer, J. & Freud, S. (1893-1895), Studies on Hysteria. *Standard Edition*, 2:1-335. London: Hogarth Press, 1955.

Brodey, W. M. (1965), On the Dynamics of Narcissism. *The Psychoanalytic Study of the Child*, 20:165-193. New York: International Universities Press.

Brody, S. (1961), Some Aspects of Transference Resistance in Prepuberty. *The Psychoanalytic Study of the Child*, 16:251-275. New York: International Universities Press.

Bromberg, W. (1938), The Meaning of Time for Children. *Amer. J. Orthopsychiat.*, 8:142-147.

Brown, N. O. (1959), Life Against Death. New York: Vintage Books, p. 366.

Browne, W. A. F. (1874), The Perception of Time as a Feature in Mental Disease. *J. Ment. Sci.*, 19:519-532.

Bruner, J. et al. (1966), *Studies in Cognitive Growth.* New York: Wiley & Sons (2nd ed., 1967).

Brunswick, D. (1954), A Revision of the Classification of Instincts or Drives. *Internat. J. Psycho-Anal.*, 35:224-228.

Buck, P. (1950), *The Coming of the Maori.* Wellington, New Zealand: Whitcombe and Tombs.

Bunker, H. A. (1943), Body as Phallus: A Clinico-etymological Note. *Psychoanal. Quart.* 12:476-480.

_____ (1951), Psychoanalysis and the Study of Religion. *Psychoanalysis and the Social Sciences*, 3. New York: International Universities Press.

Buxbaum, E. (1958), Panel Report. The Psychology of Adolescence. *J. Amer. Psychoanal. Assn.*, 6:111-120.

Bychowski, G. (1945), The Ego of Homosexuals. *Internat. J. Psycho-Anal.*, 26:114-127.

Cannon, W. B. (1920), *Bodily Changes in Pain, Hunger, Fear and Rage.* New York: Harper, 1936.

Cassirer, E. (1953), *The Philosophy of Symbolic Forms.* New Haven: Yale University Press.

Casuso, G. (1965), Panel Report; The Relationship Between Child Analysis and the Theory and Practice of Adult Psychoanalysis. *J. Amer. Psychoanal. Assn.*, 113:159-172.

Chambers, J. (1961), Maternal Deprivation and the Concept of Time in Children. *Amer. J. Orthopsychiat.*, 31:406-416.

Chapman, A. H. (1959), The Concept of Nemesis in Psychoneurosis. *J. Nerv. Ment. Dis.*, 129:29-34.

Cohen, John (1961), The Natural History of Swearing. *Etc.: A Review of General Semantics*, 18:275-281.

Cohen, J. (1967), *Psychological Time in Health and Disease.* Springfield, Ill.: Charles C Thomas.

Cohn, F. S. (1957), Time and the Ego. *Psychoanal. Quart.*, 26:168-189.

Coren, H. Z. & Saldinger, J. S. (1967), Visual Hallucinations in Children. *The Psychoanalytic Study of the Child*, 22:331-356. New York: International Universities Press.

Despert, J. L. (1948), Delusional and Hallucinatory Experiences in Children. *Amer. J. Psychiat.*, 104:528-537.

Deutsch, H. (1925), The Psychology of Woman in Relation to the Functions of Reproduction. In: *The Psychoanalytic Reader*, ed. R. Fliess. New York: International Universities Press, 1948, pp. 192-207.

_____(1929), The Genesis of Agoraphobia. *Internat. J. Psycho-Anal.*, 10:51-69.

_____(1942), Some Forms of Emotional Disturbance and Their Relationship to Schizophrenia. In: *Neuroses and Character Types.* New York: International Universities Press, 1965.

_____(1966), Post-traumatic Amnesias and Their Adaptive Function. In: *Psychoanalysis—A General Psychology*, ed. R. M. Loewenstein, L. M. Newman, M. Schur, & A. J. Solnit. New York: International Universities Press, pp. 437-455.

Dickes, R. (1963), Fetishistic Behavior: A Contribution to its Complex Development and Significance. *J. Amer. Psychoanal. Assn.*, 11:303-330.

——— (1965), The Defensive Function of an Altered State of Consciousness: A Hypnoid State. *J. Amer. Psychoanal. Assn.*, 13:356-403.

Dinnage, P., ed. (1953), *The Marquis de Sade.* New York: Grove Press.

Dollard, J., Miller, N. E., Doob, L. W., Mowrer, D. H. & Sears, R. R. (1939), *Frustration and Aggression.* New Haven: Yale University Press.

Dooley, L. (1941), The Concept of Time in Defense of Ego Integrity. *Psychiat.*, 4:13-23.

DuBois, F. S. (1954), The Sense of Time and Its Relation to Psychiatric Illness. *Amer. J. Psychiat.*, 111:46-51.

Dubos, R. (1969), Biological Individuality. *Columbia Forum* (Spring), pp. 5-9.

Eidelberg, L. (1957), An Introduction to the Study of the Narcissistic Mortification. *Psychiat. Quart.*, 31:657-668.

———(1962), On Narcissistic Mortification. *J. Amer. Psychoanal. Assn.*, 10:593-605.

Eisenbud, J. (1956), Time and the Oedipus. *Psychoanal. Quart.*, 25:363-384.

Eissler, K. R. (1952), Time Experience and the Mechanism of Isolation. *Psychoanal. Rev.*, 39:1-22.

——— (1953), The Effect of the Structure of the Ego on Psychoanalytic Technique. *J. Amer. Psychoanal. Assn.*, 1:104-143.

———(1958a), Notes on Problems of Technique in the Psychoanalytic Treatment of Adolescents. With Some Remarks on Perversions. *The Psychoanalytic Study of the Child*, 13:223-254. New York: International Universities Press.

———(1958b), Remarks on Some Variations in Psycho-Analytical Technique. *Internat. J. Psycho-Anal.*, 39:222-229.

——— (1962), On the Metapsychology of the Preconscious: A Tentative Contribution to Psychoanalytic Morphology. *The Psychoanalytic Study of the Child*, 17:9-41. New York: International Universities Press.

———(1963), *Goethe: A Psychoanalytic Study.* Detroit: Wayne State University Press.

———(1965), *Medical Orthodoxy and the Future of Psychoanalysis.* New York: International Universities Press.

Engel, G. L. & Reichsman, F. (1956), Spontaneous and Experimentally Induced Depressions in an Infant with a Gastric Fistula. A Contribution to the Problem of Depression. *J. Amer. Psychoanal. Assn.*, 4:428-452.

———(1962), Anxiety and Depression-Withdrawal. *Internat. J. Psycho-Anal.*, 13:89-97.

——— (1965), Some Considerations of the Psychoanalytic Theory of Somatic Symptoms. Panel presentation: American Psychoanalytic Association on Psychoanalytic Theory of Somatic Symptoms.

Erikson, E. H. (1950), *Childhood and Society.* New York: Norton.

———(1956), The Problem of Ego Identity. *J. Amer. Psychoanal. Assn.*, 4:56-121.

———(1962), Reality and Actuality. *J. Amer. Psychoanal. Assn.*, 3:451-474.

Esman, A. H. (1962), Visual Hallucinoses in Young Children. *The Psychoanalytic Study of the Child*, 17:334-343. New York: International Universities Press.

Evans, W. N. (1964), The Fear of Being Smothered. *Psychoanal. Quart.*, 33:53-76.

Fairbairn, W. R. D. (1957), Freud, the Psychoanalytic Method and Mental Health. *Brit. J. Med. Psychol.*, 30:53-62.

———(1958), On the Nature and Aims of Psychoanalytical Treatment. *Internat. J. Psycho-Anal.*, 7:374-385.

Fanon, F. (1963), *Wretched of the Earth.* New York: Grove Press, 1966.

Federn, P. (1952), *Ego Psychology and the Psychoses.* New York: Basic Books.

Feldman, S. S. (1953), A Syndrome Indicative of Repressed Oral Aggression. In: *The Yearbook of Psychoanalysis*, 10, ed. S. Lorand. New York: International Universities Press, 1955, pp. 96-100.

——— (1959), *Mannerisms of Speech and Gestures in Everyday Life.* New York: International Universities Press, pp. 276-281.

Fenichel, O. (1936), The Symbolic Equation: Girl = Phallus. *The Collected Papers of Otto Fenichel*, Second Series. New York: Norton, 1954, pp. 3-18.

______ (1940), The Study of Defense Mechanisms and Its Importance for Psychoanalytic Technique. *The Collected Papers of Otto Fenichel*, Second Series. New York: Norton, 1954, pp. 183-197.

______ (1941a), *Problems of Psychoanalytic Technique.* Albany: The Psychoanalytic Quarterly.

______ (1941b), The Ego and the Affects. *Psychoanal. Rev.*, 28:49-60.

Ferenczi, S. (1916-1917), Disease or Patho-Neuroses. *Further Contributions to the Theory and Technique of Psycho-Analysis.* New York: Basic Books, 1926, pp. 78-88.

______ (1919), Sunday Neurosis. *Further Contributions to the Theory and Technique of Psycho-Analysis.* New York: Basic Books, 1926, pp. 174-177.

______ (1926) Gulliver Phantasies. *Final Contributions to the Problems and Methods of Psychoanalysis.* New York: Basic Books, 1955, pp. 41-60.

Fisher, C. (1954), Dreams and Perception. *J. Amer. Psychoanal. Assn.*, 2:389-445.

______ (1956), Dreams, Images and Perception. *J. Amer. Psychoanal. Assn.*, 4:5-48.

______ (1965), Psychoanalytic Implications of Recent Research on Sleep and Dreaming. *J. Amer. Psychoanal. Assn.*, 13:197-303.

Flavell, J. H. (1963), *The Developmental Psychology of Jean Piaget.* Princeton: Van Nostrand.

Focillon, H. (1948), *The Life of Forms in Art.* New York: Wittenborn, Schultz.

Ford, C. F. & Beach, F. A. (1951), *Patterns of Sexual Behavior.* New York: Harper.

Fraiberg, S. (1951), Clinical Notes on the Nature of Transference in Child Analysis. *The Psychoanalytic Study of the Child*, 6:286-306. New York: International Universities Press.

______ (1952), A Critical Neurosis in a Two-and-a-Half-Year-Old Girl. *The Psychoanalytic Study of the Child*, 7:173-219. New York: International Universities Press.

______ (1955), Some Considerations in the Introduction to Therapy in Puberty. *The Psychoanalytic Study of the Child*, 10:264-286. New York: International Universities Press.

______ (1962), Technical Aspects of the Analysis of a Child with a Severe Behavior Disorder. *J. Amer. Psychoanal. Assn.*, 10:338-368. New York: International Universities Press.

______ (1966), Transference in Latency. *The Psychoanalytic Study of the Child*, 21:213-237. New York: International Universities Press.

Freud, A. (1926), Introduction to the Technique of Child Analysis. *The Psychoanalytical Treatment of Children.* New York: International Universities Press, 1946, pp. 3-53.

______ (1936), The Ego and the Mechanisms of Defense, *The Writings of Anna Freud*, 2. New York: International Universities Press, 1966.

______ (1945), Indications for Child Analysis. *The Psychoanalytic Study of the Child*, 1:127-140. New York: International Universities Press.

______ (1946), *The Psychoanalytical Treatment of Children.* New York: International Universities Press.

______ (1952), The Mutual Influences in the Development of the Ego and the Id. *The Psychoanalytic Study of the Child*, 7:42-51. New York: International Universities Press.

______ (1954a), The Widening Scope of Indications for Psychoanalysis: Discussion. *J. Amer. Psychoanal. Assn.*, 2:607-620.

______ (1954b), In: Problems of Infantile Neurosis: A Discussion. *The Psychoanalytic Study of the Child*, 9:16-74. New York: International Universities Press.

______ (1958), Adolescence. *The Psychoanalytic Study of the Child*, 13:255-278. New York: International Universities Press.

______ (1962), Assessment of Childhood Disturbances. *The Psychoanalytic Study of the Child*, 17:149-158. New York: International Universities Press.

______ (1963), The Concept of Developmental Lines. *The Psychoanalytic Study of the Child*, 18:245-265. New York: International Universities Press.

______ (1965), Normality and Pathology in Childhood. New York: International Universities Press.

Freud, E. L., ed. (1960), *The Letters of Sigmund Freud.* New York: Basic Books.

Freud, S. (1887-1902), *The Origins of Psychoanalysis: Letters, Drafts and Notes to Wilhelm Fliess.* New York: Basic Books, 1954.

——— (1892-1899), Extracts from the Fliess Papers. *Standard Edition*, 1:175-289. London: Hogarth Press, 1966.

——— (1894), The Neuro-Psychoses of Defence. *Standard Edition*, 3:43-61. London: Hogarth Press, 1962.

——— (1895), Project for a Scientific Psychology. *Standard Edition*, 1:283-397. London: Hogarth Press, 1966.

——— (1896), Further Remarks on the Neuro-Psychoses of Defence. *Standard Edition*, 3:159-185. London: Hogarth Press, 1962.

——— (1900), The Interpretation of Dreams. *Standard Edition*, 4 & 5. London: Hogarth Press, 1953.

——— (1901), Fragment of an Analysis of a case of Hysteria. *Standard Edition*, 7:3-122. London: Hogarth Press, 1953.

——— (1904), Freud's Psycho-Analytic Procedure. *Standard Edition*, 7:248-254. London: Hogarth Press, 1953.

——— (1905), Three Essays on the Theory of Sexuality. *Standard Edition*, 7:125-243. London: Hogarth Press, 1953.

——— (1907), Delusions and Dreams in Jensen's *Gradiva. Standard Edition*, 9:3-95. London: Hogarth Press, 1959.

——— (1908), Creative Writers and Day Dreaming. *Standard Edition*, 9:142-153. London: Hogarth Press, 1959.

——— (1909a), Analysis of a Phobia in a Five-Year-Old-Boy. *Standard Edition*, 10:3-147. London: Hogarth Press, 1955.

——— (1909b), Notes Upon a Case of Obsessional Neurosis. *Standard Edition*, 10:153-249. London: Hogarth Press, 1955.

——— (1910a), Leonardo Da Vinci and a Memory of His Childhood. *Standard Edition*, 11:59-137. London: Hogarth Press, 1957.

——— (1910b), The Psychoanalytic View of Psychogenic Disturbance of Vision. *Standard Edition*, 11:209-218. London: Hogarth Press.

——— (1911a), Formulations on the Two Principles of Mental Functioning. *Standard Edition*, 12:215-226. London: Hogarth Press, 1958.

——— (1911b), Psychoanalytic Notes on an Autobiographical Account of a Case of Paranoia (Dementia Paranoides). *Standard Edition*, 12:3-82. London: Hogarth Press, 1958.

——— (1912a), The Dynamics of Transference. *Standard Edition*, 12:99-108. London: Hogarth Press, 1958.

——— (1912b), A Note on the Unconscious in Psycho-Analysis. *Standard Edition*, 12:257-266. London: Hogarth Press, 1958.

——— (1913a), On Beginning the Treatment. *Standard Edition*, 12:122-144. London: Hogarth Press, 1958.

——— (1913b), The Disposition to Obsessional Neurosis. *Standard Edition*, 12:313-326. London: Hogarth Press, 1958.

——— (1913c), Observations and Examples from Analytic Practice. *Standard Edition*, 13:191-198. London: Hogarth Press, 1955.

——— (1913d), The Theme of Three Caskets. *Standard Edition*, 12:290-301. London: Hogarth Press, 1958.

——— (1913e), Totem and Taboo. *Standard Edition*, 13:1-161. London: Hogarth Press, 1955.

——— (1914a), On the History of the Psycho-Analytic Movement. *Standard Edition*, 14:3-66. London: Hogarth Press, 1957.

——— (1914b), The Moses of Michelangelo. *Standard Edition*, 13:211-236. London: Hogarth Press, 1957.

——— (1914c), On Narcissism: An Introduction. *Standard Edition*, 14:67-102. London: Hogarth Press, 1957.

——— (1914d), Remembering, Repeating and Working-Through. *Standard Edition*, 12:146-156. London: Hogarth Press, 1958.

——— (1915a), Instincts and Their Vicissitudes. *Standard Edition*, 14:111-140. London: Hogarth Press, 1957.

______ (1915b), Repression. *Standard Edition*, 14:143-158. London: Hogarth Press, 1957.

______ (1915c), Thoughts for the Times on War and Death. *Standard Edition*, 14:274-300. London: Hogarth Press, 1957.

______ (1915d), The Unconscious. *Standard Edition*, 14:159-215. London: Hogarth Press, 1957.

______ (1916-1917), Introductory Lectures on Psychoanalysis. *Standard Edition*, 15 & 16. London: Hogarth Press, 1963.

______ (1917a), A Childhood Recollection from *Dichtung und Wahrheit*. Standard Edition, 17:146-156. London: Hogarth Press, 1955.

______ (1917b), A Metapsychological Supplement to the Theory of Dreams. *Standard Edition*, 14:219-235. London: Hogarth Press, 1957.

______ (1917c), Mourning and Melancholia. *Standard Edition*, 14:237-258. London: Hogarth Press, 1957.

______ (1918), From the History of an Infantile Neurosis. *Standard Edition*, 17:3-122. London: Hogarth Press, 1955.

______ (1919a), Lines of Advance in Psycho-Analytic Therapy. *Standard Edition*, 17:158-168. London: Hogarth Press, 1955.

______ (1919b), A Child Is Being Beaten: A Contribution to the Study of the Origin of Sexual Perversions. *Standard Edition*, 17:177-204. London: Hogarth Press, 1955.

______ (1919c), The Uncanny. *Standard Edition*, 17:218-252. London: Hogarth Press, 1957.

______ (1920), Beyond the Pleasure Principle. *Standard Edition*, 18:1-64. London: Hogarth Press, 1955.

______ (1923a), The Ego and The Id. *Standard Edition*, 19:3-66. London: Hogarth Press, 1961.

______ (1923b), Two Encyclopedia Articles. *Standard Edition*, 18:235-259. London: Hogarth Press, 1955.

______ (1924), The Economic Problem of Masochism. *Standard Edition*, 19:157-170. London: Hogarth Press, 1961.

______ (1925a), An Autobiographical Study. *Standard Edition*, 20:3-74. London: Hogarth Press, 1959.

______ (1925b), Negation. *Standard Edition*, 19:234-239. London: Hogarth Press, 1961.

______ (1925c), A Note Upon The 'Mystic Writing Pad.' *Standard Edition*, 19:225-232. London: Hogarth Press, 1961.

______ (1926), Inhibitions, Symptoms and Anxiety. *Standard Edition*, 20:77-174. London: Hogarth Press, 1959.

______ (1927), The Future of an Illusion. *Standard Edition*, 21:3-56. London: Hogarth Press, 1961.

______ (1930), Civilization and Its Discontents. *Standard Edition*, 21:59-145. London: Hogarth Press, 1961.

______ (1933), New Introductory Lectures on Psycho-Analysis. *Standard Edition*, 22:1-182. London: Hogarth Press, 1964.

______ (1936), A Disturbance of Memory on the Acropolis. *Standard Edition*, 22:239-248. London: Hogarth Press, 1964.

______ (1937a), Analysis Terminable and Interminable. *Standard Edition*, 23:211-253. London: Hogarth Press, 1964.

______ (1937b), Construction in Analysis. *Standard Edition*, 23:256-269. London: Hogarth Press, 1964.

______ (1939), Moses and Monotheism. *Standard Edition*, 23:3-137. London: Hogarth Press, 1964.

______ (1940a), An Outline of Psycho-analysis. *Standard Edition*, 23:141-207. London: Hogarth Press, 1964.

______ (1940b), Some Elementary Lessons in Psycho-Analysis. *Standard Edition*, 23:281-286. London: Hogarth Press, 1964.

Frijling-Schreuder, E. (1966), The Adaptive Uses of Regression. *Internat. J. Psycho-Anal.*, 47:364-369.

Frosch, J. (1966), A Note on Reality Constancy. In: *Psychoanalysis: A General Psychology*, ed. R. M. Loewenstein, L. M. Newman, M. Schur, A. Solnit. New York: International Universities Press, pp. 349-376.

_____ (1967), Severe Regressive States During Psychoanalysis. *J. Amer. Psychoanal. Assn.*, 15:606-625.

Fumagalli, G. (1952), *Eros Die Leonardo.* Milano: Garzanti.

Gabe, S. (1965), Panel Report: The Genetic Determinants of Obsessive-Compulsive Phenomena in Character Formation. *J. Amer. Psychoanal. Assn.*, 13:591-605.

Galambos, R. (1956), Suppression of Auditory Nerve Activity by Stimulation of Efferent Fibres to Cochlea. *J. Neurophysiol.*, 19:424-437.

Geleerd, E. R. (1946), A Contribution to the Problem of Psychoses in Childhood. *The Psychoanalytic Study of the Child*, 2:271-291. New York: International Universities Press.

_____ (1957), Some Aspects of Psychoanalytic Technique in Adolescence. *The Psychoanalytic Study of the Child*, 12:263-283. New York: International Universities Press.

_____ (1961), Some Aspects of Ego Vicissitudes in Adolescence. *J. Amer. Psychoanal. Assn.*, 9:394-404.

_____ (1967), *The Child Analyst at Work.* New York: International Universities Press, pp. 115-141.

Gero, G. (1951), The Concept of Defense. *Psychoanal. Quart.*, 20:565-578.

Gifford, S. (1960), Sleep, Time and the Early Ego. *J. Amer. Psychoanal. Assn.*, 8:5-42.

Gill, M. (1963), Topography and Systems in Psychoanalytic Theory. [*Psychological Issues*, Monogr. 18] New York: International Universities Press.

_____ & Brenman, M. (1959), *Hypnosis and Related States.* New York: International Universities Press.

Gillespie, W. H. (1956), The General Theory of Sexual Perversion. *Internat. J. Psycho-Anal.*, 37:396-403.

_____ (1964), Symposium on Homosexuality. *Internat. J. Psycho-Anal.*, 45:203-209.

Gitelson, M. (1948), Character Synthesis—The Psychotherapeutic Problem of Adolescence. *Amer. J. Orthopsychiat.*, 18:422-431.

_____ (1952), The Emotional Position of the Analyst in the Psychoanalytic Situation. Internat. J. Psycho-Anal., 33:1-10.

Glover, E. (1948), The Future Development of Psychoanalysis. In: *On The Early Development of Mind.* New York: International Universities Press, 1956, pp. 333-351.

_____ (1955), The Technique of Psycho-Analysis. New York: International Universities Press.

Goethe, J. W. von (1923), *Goethe's Collected Works.* Leipzig: Inselverlag.

Goldstein, T. (1964), Fifteenth-Century Geography Against the Background of Medieval Science. Unpublished lecture, Minneapolis.

Goldstone, S. & Goldfarb, J. L. (1966), The Perception of Time by Children. In: *Perceptual Development in Children*, ed. A. H. Kidd & J. L. Rivoire. New York: International Universities Press, pp. 445-486.

Granit, R. (1955), *Receptors and Sensory Perception. The Aims, Means and Results of Electrophysiological Research on the Process of Reception.* New Haven: Yale University Press.

Greenacre, P. (1952), *Trauma, Growth and Personality.* New York: International Universities Press, 1969.

_____ (1954a), In: Problems of Infantile Neurosis: A Discussion. *The Psychoanalytic Study of the Child*, 9:16-74. New York: International Universities Press.

_____ (1954b), The Role of Transference. *J. Amer. Psychoanal. Assn.*, 2:671-684.

_____ (1957), The Childhood of the Artist. *The Psychoanalytic Study of the Child*, 12:47-72. New York: International Universities Press.

______(1958a), Early Physical Determinants and the Developments of the Signs of Identity. *J. Amer. Psychoanal. Assn.*, 6:612-628.

______(1958b), Toward An Understanding of the Physical Nucleus of Some Defence Reactions. *Internat. J. Psycho-Anal.*, 39:69-76.

______(1959), Certain Technical Problems in the Transference Relationship. *J. Amer. Psychoanal. Assn.*, 7:484-502.

______(1964), The Influence of Infantile Trauma on Genetic Patterns. In: *Psychic Trauma*, ed. S. Furst. New York: Basic Books, 1967, pp. 108-152.

Greenson, R. (1954), About the Sound "M. . ." *Psychoanal. Quart.*, 23:234-239.

______(1965), The Working Alliance and the Transference Neurosis. *Psychoanal. Quart.*, 34:155-181.

______(1967), *The Technique and Practice of Psychoanalysis*, 1. New York: International Universities Press.

Gross, A. (1949), Sense of Time in Dreams. *Psychoanal. Quart.*, 18:466-470.

Grotjahn, M. (1967), Sigmund Freud and the Art of Letter Writing. *J. Amer. Med. Assn.*, 200:13-18.

Harley, M. (1961), Panel Report: Resistance in Child Analysis. *J. Amer. Psychoanal. Assn.*, 9:548-562.

______(1967), Transference Developments in a Five-Year-Old Child. In: *The Child Analyst at Work*, ed. E. Geleerd. New York: International Universities Press, pp. 115-141.

______(1968), The Current Status of the Transference Neurosis in Child Analysis. Paper read at Panel on the Current Status of the Transference Neurosis, Annual Meeting of the American Psychoanalytic Association, Boston, May.

Harnik, J. (1924), The Various Developments Undergone by Narcissism in Men and Women. *Internat. J. Psycho-Anal.*, 5:66-83.

Hartmann, H. (1939) *Ego Psychology and the Problem of Adaptation.* New York: International Universities Press, 1958.

______(1948), Comments on the Psychoanalytic Theory of Instinctual Drives. In: *Essays on Ego Psychology*. New York: International Universities Press, 1964, pp. 69-89.

______(1950a), Comments on the Psychoanalytic Theory of the Ego. In: *Essays on Ego Psychology*. New York: International Universities Press, 1964, pp. 113-141.

______(1950b), Psychoanalysis and Developmental Psychology. *The Psychoanalytic Study of the Child*, 5:7-17. New York: International Universities Press.

______(1951), Technical Implications of Ego Psychology. *Psychoanal. Quart.*, 20:31-43.

______(1953), Contribution to the Metapsychology of Schizophrenia. In: *Essays on Ego Psychology*. New York: International Universities Press, 1964, pp. 182-206.

______(1954), In: Problems of Infantile Neurosis: A Discussion. *The Psychoanalytic Study of the Child*, 9:16-74. New York: International Universities Press.

______(1956), The Development of the Ego Concept in Freud's Work. In: *Essays on Ego Psychology*. New York: International Universities Press, 1964, pp. 268-296.

______Kris, E. & Loewenstein, R. M. (1946), Comments on the Formation of the Psychic Structure. *The Psychoanalytic Study of the Child*, 2:11-38. New York: International Universities Press.

______ ______ ______(1949), Notes on the Theory of Aggression. *The Psychoanalytic Study of the Child*, 3/4:9-36. New York: International Universities Press.

Heisenberg, W. (1958), *Physics and Philosophy*. New York: Harper.

Hilgard, J. R. & Fisk, F. (1960), Disruption of Adult Ego Identity as Related to Childhood Loss of a Mother through Hospitalization for Psychosis. *J. Nerv. Ment. Dis.*, 131:47-57.

Hoffer, W. (1950), Oral Aggression and Ego Development. *Int. J. Psycho-Anal.*, 31:156-160.

______(1954), Defensive Process and Defensive Organization: Their Place in Psychoanalytic Technique. *Internat. J. Psycho-Anal.*, 35:194-198.

Isakower, O. (1938), A Contribution to the Psychopathology of Phenomena Associated with Falling Asleep. *Internat. J. Psycho-Anal.*, 19:331-345.

______(1939), The Exceptional Position of the Auditory Sphere. *Internat. J. Psycho-Anal.*, 20:340-348.

Jacobson, E. (1954), Contributions to the Metapsychology of Psychotic Identification. *J. Amer. Psychoanal. Assn.*, 2:239-262.

______(1961), Adolescent Moods and the Remodeling of the Psychic Structures in Adolescence. *The Psychoanalytic Study of the Child*, 16:164-184. New York: International Universities Press.

______(1964), *The Self and the Object World.* New York: International Universities Press.

Jaques, E. (1965), Death and the Mid-Life Crisis. *Internat. J. Psycho-Anal.*, 46:502-514.

Jones, E. (1922), Some Problems of Adolescence. *Brit. J. Psychol.*, 13:31-47.

______(1927), The Early Development of Female Sexuality. In: *Papers on Psycho-Analysis.* London: Bailliere, Tindall and Cox, 1948.

______(1931), *Nightmares, Witches and Devils.* New York: Norton.

______(1951), *Essays in Applied Psycho-Analysis*, 1. London: Hogarth Press.

______(1953), *Sigmund Freud, Life and Work*, 1. New York: Basic Books.

______(1957), *Sigmund Freud, Life and Work* 3. New York: Basic Books.

Joyce, J. (1934), *Ulysses.* New York: Random House.

Kafka, F. (1962), *Amerika.* New York: New Directions.

Kanner, L. (1935), *Child Psychiatry.* Springfield, Ill.: Charles C Thomas, 1960.

Kanzer, M. (1951), The Self-Analytic Literature of Robert L. Stevenson. In: *Psychoanalysis and Culture*, ed. E. Wilbur & W. Muensterberger. New York: International Universities Press, pp. 425-435.

______(1953), Past and Present in the Transference. *J. Amer. Psychoanal. Assn.*, 1:144-154.

______(1964), On Interpreting the Oedipus Plays. *The Psycho-analytic Study of Society*, 3:26-38.

Katan, A. (1951), The Role of Displacement in Agoraphobia. *Int. J. Psycho-Anal.*, 32:41-50.

______(1952), Further Remarks about Schreber's Hallucinations. *Internat. J. Psycho-Anal.*, 33:429-432.

Kaufman, I. (1958), Panel Report: Superego Development and Pathology in Childhood. *J. Amer. Psychoanal. Assn.*, 6:540-551.

Kaufman, M. R. & Heiman, M. (1964), *Evolution of Psychosomatic Concepts. Anorexia Nervosa: A Paradigm.* New York: International Universities Press, pp. 198-201.

Keiser, S. (1947), On the Psychopathology of Orgasm. *Psychoanal. Quart.*, 16:378-390.

______(1952), Body Ego During Orgasm. *Psychoanal. Quart.*, 21:155-166.

Keniston, K. (1965), *The Uncommitted. Alienated Youth in American Society.* New York: Harcourt, Brace & World.

Kestenberg, J. (1956), Vicissitudes of Female Sexuality. *J. Amer. Psychoanal. Assn.*, 4:453-476.

Kidd, A. H. & Rivoire, J. L. (1966), Social Aspects of Perception. In: *Perceptual Development in Children*, ed. A. H. Kidd & J. L. Rivoire. New York: International Universities Press, pp. 191-192.

Klein, G. S. (1959), Consciousness in Psychoanalytic Theory: Some Implications for Current Research in Perception. *J. Amer. Psychoanal. Assn.*, 7:5-34.

Kluever, H. (1933), Eidetic Imagery. In: *A Handbook of Child Psychology*, ed. C. Murchison. Worcester, Mass.: Clark University Press, pp. 699-722.

Knight, R. P. (1953), Borderline States. In: *Psychoanalytic Psychiatry and Psychology*, ed. R. P. Knight & C. R. Friedman. New York: International Universities Press, pp. 97-109.

Kohut, H. (1966), Forms and Transformations of Narcissism. *J. Amer. Psychoanal. Assn.*, 14:243-272.

Kolb, L. C. & Johnson, A. M. (1955), Etiology and Therapy of Overt Homosexuality. *Psychoanal. Quart.*, 24:506-515.

Konetzke, R. (1963), *Entdecker und Eroberer Amerikas.* Hamburg: Fischer-Buecherei.

Kris, E. (1934), The Psychology of Caricature. In: *Psychoanalytic Explorations in Art.* New York: International Universities Press, 1952, pp. 173-188.

——— (1950), On Preconscious Mental Processes. In: *Psychoanalytic Explorations in Art.* New York: International Universities Press, 1952, pp. 303-320.

———(1951), The Development of Ego Psychology. *Samiksa*, 5:153-163.

——— (1952), *Psychoanalytic Explorations in Art.* New York: International Universities Press.

——— (1956a), The Recovery of Childhood Memories in Psychoanalysis. *The Psychoanalytic Study of the Child*, 11:54-88. New York: International Universities Press.

——— (1956b), On Some Vicissitudes of Insight in Psychoanalysis. *Internat. J. Psycho-Anal.*, 37:445-455.

Kris, M. (1957), The Use of Prediction in a Longitudinal Study. *The Psychoanalytic Study of the Child*, 12:175-189. New York: International Universities Press.

Kubie, L. S. (1963), The Central Affective Potential and Its Trigger Mechanisms. In: *Counterpoint: Libidinal Object and Subject*, ed. H. S. Gaskill. New York: International Universities Press.

Kut, S. (1953), Changing Patterns of Transference. *The Psychoanalytic Study of the Child*, 8:355-381. New York: International Universities Press.

Lacan, J. (1953), Some Reflections on the Ego. *Internat. J. Psycho-Anal.*, 34:11-17.

Lampl-De Groot, J. (1956), On Defenses and Development: Normal and Pathological. *The Psychoanalytic Study of the Child*, 12:114-126. New York: International Universities Press.

——— (1960), On Adolescence. *The Psychoanalytic Study of the Child*, 15:95-103. New York: International Universities Press.

———(1962), Ego Ideal and Superego. *The Psychoanalytic Study of the Child*, 17:94-106. New York: International Universities Press.

Laubenberger, F. (1959), *Ringmann oder Waldseemueller?* Berlin: Erdkunde.

Laufer, M. (1964), Ego Ideal and Pseudo Ego Ideal in Adolescence. *The Psychoanalytic Study of the Child*, 19:196-221. New York: International Universities Press.

Levin, M. (1932), Auditory Hallucinations in Nonpsychotic Children. *Amer. J. Psychiat.*, 11:1119-1152.

Lewin, B. D. (1933), The Body as Phallus. *Psychoanal. Quart.*, 2:24-47.

———(1935), Claustrophobia. *Psychoanal. Quart.*, 4:227-233.

———(1946), Sleep, the Mouth and the Dream Screen. *Psychoanal. Quart.*, 15:419-434.

———(1950), *The Psychoanalysis of Elation.* New York: Norton.

——— (1952), Phobic Symptoms and Dream Interpretations. *Psychoanal. Quart.*, 21:295-322.

Lichtenstein, H. (1961), Identity and Sexuality: A Study of Their Interrelationship in Man. *J. Amer. Psychoanal. Assn.*, 9:179-261.

———(1964), The Role of Narcissism in the Emergence of a Primary Identity. *Internat. J. Psycho-Anal.*, 45:49-56.

——— (1970), Changing Implications of the Concept of Psychosexual Development: An Inquiry Concerning the Validity of Classical Psychoanalytic Assumptions concerning Sexuality. *J. Amer. Psychoanal. Assn.*, 18:300-318.

Liddell, H. S. (1949), The Role of Vigilance in the Development of Animal Neuroses. In: *Anxiety*, ed. P. H. Hoch & J. Zubin. New York: Grune and Stratton.

Lipin, T. (1963), The Repetition Compulsion and "Maturational" Drive Representatives. *Internat. J. Psycho-Anal.*, 44:389-406.

Litten, E. M., Griffin, M. E. & Johnson, A. M. (1956), Parental Influence in Unusual Sexual Behavior in Children. *Psychoanal. Quart.*, 25:1-15.

Loewald, H. (1955), Hypnoid State, Repression, Abreaction and Recollection. *J. Amer. Psychoanal. Assn.*, 3:201-210.

———(1960), On the Therapeutic Action of Psycho-Analysis. *Internat. J. Psycho-Anal.*, 41:16-33.

______(1966), Book Review: *Psychoanalytic Concepts and the Structural Theory. Psychoanal. Quart.*, 35:430-436.

Loewenstein, R. M. (1935), Phallic Passivity in Men. *Internat. J. Psycho-Anal.*, 16:334-340.

______(1951), The Problem of Interpretation. *Psychoanal. Quart.*, 20:1-14.

______(1958), Remarks on Some Variations in Psycho-Analytic Technique. *Internat. J. Psycho-Anal.*, 39:202-210.

Löfgren, L. B., (1968) Panel Report: Psychoanalytic Theory of Affects. *J. Amer. Psychoanal. Assn.*, 16:638-650.

Lorenz, K. (1937), The Nature of Instincts. In: *Instinctive Behavior*, ed. C. Schiller, New York: International Universities Press, 1957, pp. 129-175.

______(1950), The Comparative Method in Studying Innate Behavior Patterns. *Symposium of the Society for Experimental Biology*, 4. Cambridge: Cambridge University Press, 1950.

______(1952a), *King Solomon's Ring*. London: Methuen.

______(1952b), The Past Twelve Years in the Comparative Study of Behavior. In: *Instinctive Behavior*, ed. C. Schiller. New York: International Universities Press, 1957, pp. 288-310.

______(1963), *On Aggression*. New York: Harcourt, Brace & World.

Lovell, K. (1966), The Development of Scientific Concepts. In: *Perceptual Development of Children*, ed. A. H. Kidd & J. L. Rivoire. New York: International Universities Press, pp. 407-444.

Macalpine, I. (1950), The Development of Transference. *Psychoanal. Quart.*, 19:501-539.

Mahler, M. S. (1952), On Child Psychosis and Schizophrenia: Autistic and Symbiotic Infantile Psychoses. *The Psychoanalytic Study of the Child*, 7:286-305. New York: International Universities Press.

______(1958), Autism and Symbiosis: Two Extreme Disturbances of Identity. *Internat. J. Psycho-Anal.*, 39:77-83.

______(1963), Thoughts About Development and Individuation. *The Psychoanalytic Study of the Child*, 18:307-324. New York: International Universities Press.

______(1965), On the Significance of the Normal Separation-Individuation Phase. In: *Drives, Affects, Behavior*, ed. M. Schur, New York: International Universities Press, pp. 161-169.

______(1968), *On Human Symbiosis and the Vicissitudes of Individuation*. New York: International Universities Press.

______& Gosliner, B. (1955), On Symbiotic Child Psychosis. *The Psychoanalytic Study of the Child*, 10:195-212. New York: International Universities Press.

______& McDevitt, J. (1968), Observations on Adaptation and Defense in Statu Nascendi: Developmental Precursors in the First Two Years of Life. *Psychoanal. Quart.*, 37:1-21.

Mann, T. (1936), Freud and the Future. In: *Freud, Goethe, Wagner*. New York: Knopf, 1937, pp. 3-45.

______(1948), *Joseph and His Brothers*. New York: Knopf.

Marcovitz, E. (1963), Panel Report: The Concept of the Id. *J. Amer. Psychoanal. Assn.* 11:151-160.

Masters, W. H. & Johnson, V. E. (1966), *Human Sexual Response*. Boston: Little, Brown.

Meerloo, J. A. M. (1948), Father Time. *Psychiat. Quart.*, 22:587-608.

______(1950), Father Time II. *Psychiat. Quart.*, 24:657-671.

Menaker, E. (1942), The Masochistic Factor in the Psychoanalytic Situation. *Psychoanal. Quart.*, 6:171-186.

Michaels, J. J. (1944), A Psychiatric Adventure in Comparative Pathophysiology of the Infant and Adult with Some Theoretical Suggestions in Regard to Regression in Somatic Visceral Functions. *J. Nerv. Ment. Dis.*, 100:49-63.

Miller, K. (1896-1898), *Mappae Mundi*. Stuttgart: J. Roth Verlag.

Milner, M. (1950), A Note on the Ending of an Analysis. *Internat. J. Psycho-Anal.*, 31:191-193.
Mintz, I. L., The Anniversary Reaction: A Manifestation of the Unconscious Sense of Time (in press).
Mitscherlich, A. (1965), Auf dem Wege zur Vaterlosen Gesellschaft. In: *Ideen zur Sozialpsychologie.* Munich: Piper.
Moore, B. E. & Fine, B. D. (1967), *Glossary of Psychoanalytic Terms and Concepts.* New York: American Psychoanalytic Association.
More, T. (1516), *Utopia.* New York: Oxford University Press, 1904.
Nacht, S. (1958), Variations in Technique. *Internat. J. Psycho-Anal.*, 39:235-237.
Nagera, H. (1963), The Developmental Profile: Notes on Some Practical Considerations Regarding Its Use. *The Psychoanalytic Study of the Child*, 18:511-540. New York: International Universities Press.
_____ (1964), On Arrest in Development, Fixation and Regression. *The Psychoanalytic Study of the Child*, 19:222-239. New York: International Universities Press.
Natonek, H. (1943), *In Search of Myself.* New York: Putnam.
Nelson, M. C. (1967), On the Therapeutic Redirection of Energy and Affect. *Internat. J. Psycho-Anal.*, 48:1-15.
Neubauer, P. (1960), The One-Parent Child and His Oedipal Development. *The Psychoanalytic Study of the Child*, 15:286-309. New York: International Universities Press.
_____ (1965), Children in Collectives. Springfield, Ill.: Charles C Thomas.
Niederland, W. (1957), River Symbolism. *Psychoanal. Quart.*, 2:50-75.
_____ (1959), The "Miracled-up" World of Schreber's Childhood. *The Psychoanalytic Study of the Child*, 14:383-413. New York: International Universities Press.
_____ (1960), Schreber's Father. *J. Amer. Psychoanal. Assn.*, 8:492-499.
_____ (1968), Clinical Observations on the Survivor Syndrome. *Internat. J. Psycho-Anal*, 49:313-315.
Nunberg, H. (1938), Homosexuality, Magic and Aggression. *Internat. J. Psycho-Anal.*, 19:1-16.
_____ (1947), Circumcision and Problems of Bisexuality. *Internat. J. Psycho-Anal.*, 28:145-179.
_____ (1951), Transference and Reality. *Internat. J. Psycho-Anal.*, 32:1-9.
Oberndorf, C. P. (1941), Time—Its Relation to Reality and Purpose. *Psychoanal. Rev.*, 28:139-155.
Orgel, S. (1965), On Time and Timelessness. *J. Amer. Psychoanal. Assn.*, 13:102-121.
Ostow, M. (1960), Panel Report: Psychoanalysis and Ethology. *J. Amer. Psychoanal. Assn.*, 8:526-534.
Palmer, R. & Colton, J. (1965), *A History of the Modern World.* New York: Knopf.
Panel: Mythology and Ego Psychology. *The Psychoanalytic Study of Society*, 3:9-93. New York: International Universities Press, 1964.
Peiper, A. (1963), *Cerebral Functions in Infancy and Childhood.* New York: Consultant Bureau, pp. 463-464.
Peto, A. (1961), The Fragmentizing Function of the Ego in the Transference Neurosis. *Internat. J. Psycho-Anal.*, 42:238-245.
_____ (1967), Dedifferentiations and Fragmentations During Analysis. *J. Amer. Psychoanal. Assn.*, 15:534-550.
Piaget, J. (1936), *The Origins of Intelligence in Children.* New York: International Universities Press, 1952.
_____ (1951), *Play, Dreams and Imitation in Childhood.* New York: W. W. Norton.
_____ (1955), The Development of Time Concepts in the Child. In: *Psychopathology of Childhood*, ed. P. M. Hoch and J. Zubin. New York: Grune and Stratton, pp. 34-44.
_____ (1967), *Six Psychological Studies.* New York: Random House.

Pollock, G. (1968), The Possible Significance of Childhood Object Loss in the Josef Breuer - Bertha Pappenheim (Anna O.) - Sigmund Freud Relationship: I. Josef Breuer. *J. Amer. Psychoanal. Assn.*, 16:711-739.

Rapaport, D. (1951a) The Autonomy of the Ego. *Bull. Menninger Clin.*, 15:113-123.

——— (1951b), The Conceptual Model of Psychoanalysis. In: *Psychoanalytic Psychiatry and Psychology*, ed. R. P. Knight & C. R. Friedman. New York: International Universities Press, 1954, pp. 221-247.

——— (1951c), *Organization and Pathology of Thought.* New York: Columbia University Press.

——— (1953a), On the Psychoanalytic Theory of Affects. *Internat. J. Psycho-Anal.*, 34:177-198.

——— (1953b), Some Metapsychological Considerations Concerning Activity and Passivity. *Collected Papers.* New York: Basic Books, 1967, pp. 530-568.

——— (1955), *Seminars on Psychoanalytic Ego Psychology.* ed. S. C. Miller. Western New England Institute for Psychoanalysis (mimeographed).

——— (1960), *The Structure of Psychoanalytic Theory.* [Psychological Issues, Monogr. 6] New York: International Universities Press.

——— & Gill, M. M. (1959), The Points of View and Assumptions of Metapsychology. *Internat. J. Psycho-Anal.*, 40:153-162.

Rappaport, E. (1959), The First Dream in an Erotized Transference. *Internat. J. Psycho-Anal.*, 40:240-245.

Reed, A. W. (1963), *An Illustrated Encyclopedia of Maori Life.* Wellington & Aukland, New Zealand: A. H. & A. W. Reed.

Reich, A. (1950), On Termination of Analysis. *Internat. J. Psycho-Anal.*, 31:179-183.

——— (1953), Narcissistic Object Choice of Women. *J. Amer. Psychoanal. Assn.*, 1:22-44.

——— (1954), Early Identifications as Archaic Elements in the Superego. *J. Amer. Psychoanal. Assn.*, 2:218-238.

——— (1958), A Special Variation of Technique. *Internat. J. Psycho-Anal.*, 39:230-234.

Reik, T. (1962), Ritual. New York: Grove Press, Inc.

Ritvo, S. (1962), Panel Report: Object Relations. *J. Amer. Psychoanal. Assn.*, 10:102-117.

——— (1966), Correlation of a Childhood and Adult Neurosis. *Internat. J. Psycho-Anal.*, 47:130-133.

Róheim, G. (1942), Transition Rites. *Psychoanal. Quart.*, 11:336-374.

Roland, A. (1967), The Reality of the Psycho-Analytic Relationship and Situation in Handling of Transference-Resistance. *Internat. J. Psycho-Anal.*, 48:504-510.

Rose, G. J. (1962), Unconscious Birth Fantasies in the Ninth Month of Treatment. *J. Amer. Psychoanal. Assn.*, 10:677-688.

——— (1969), Transference Birth Fantasies and Narcissism. *J. Amer. Psychoanal. Assn.*, 17:1015-1029.

——— (1964), Creative Imagination in Terms of Ego "Core" and Boundaries. *Internat. J. Psycho-Anal.*, 45:75-84.

——— (1966), Body Ego and Reality. *Internat. J. Psycho-Anal.*, 47:502-509.

——— (1969), Transference Birth Fantasies and Narcissism. *J. Amer. Psychoanal. Assn.*, 17:1015-1029.

Rosenfeld, H. A. (1965), *Psychotic States: A Psychoanalytic Approach.* New York: International Universities Press.

Rubinstein, B. (1967), Explanation and Mere Description: A Metascientific Examination of Certain Aspects of the Psychoanalytic Theory of Motivation. In: *Motives and Thought, Psychoanalytic Essays in Honor of David Rapaport.* [*Psychological Issues*, Monogr. 18-19] pp. 18-77. New York: International Universities Press.

Rubinfine, D. L. (1959), Panel Report: Some Theoretical Aspects of Early Psychic Functioning. *J. Amer. Psychoanal. Assn.*, 7:561-576.

Sachs, L. J. (1962), Emotional Acrescentism. *J. Amer. Acad. Child Psychiat.* 1:637-655.
Sandler, J. (1959), The Body as Phallus: A Patient's Fear of Erection. *Internat. J. Psycho-Anal.* 40:191-198.
_____ (1960), On the Concept of the Superego. *The Psychoanalytic Study of the Child*, 15:128-162. New York: International Universities Press.
Schafer, R. (1960), The Loving and Beloved Superego in Freud's Structural Theory. *The Psychoanalytic Study of the Child*, 15:163-190. New York: International Universities Press.
_____ (1965), Panel Report. Contributions of Longitudinal Studies to Psychoanalytic Theory. *J. Amer. Psychoanal. Assn.*, 13:605-618.
Schecter, D. E., Symonds, N. & Bernstein, I. (1955), Development of the Concept of Time in Children. *J. Nerv. Ment. Dis.*, 121:301-310.
Schilder, P. (1936), Psychology and Psychopathology of Time. *J. Nerv. Ment. Dis.*, 83:531-546.
_____ (1950), *The Image and Appearance of the Human Body*. New York: International Universities Press.
Schmale, A. H., Jr. (1964), A Genetic View of Affects: With Special Reference to the Genesis of Helplessness and Hopelessnes. *The Psychoanalytic Study of the Child*, 19:287-313. New York: International Universities Press.
Schneirla, T. C. (1959), An Evolutionary and Developmental Theory of Biphasic Processes Underlying Approach and Withdrawal. In: *Nebraska Symposium on Motivation*, ed. M. R. Jones. Lincoln: University of Nebraska Press, pp. 1-41.
Schnurman, A. (1949), Observation of a Phobia. *The Psychoanalytic Study of the Child*, 3/4:253-270.
Schur, M. (1950a), Basic Problems of Psychosomatic Medicine. In: *Elements of Psychoanalysis*, ed. H. Herma & G. M. Kurth. Cleveland & New York: World, pp. 237-266.
_____ (1950b), Case Analyses of Chronic, Exudative, Discoid and Lichenoid Dermatitis (Sulzberger-Garbe's Syndrome). *Internat. J. Psycho-Anal.*, 31:73-77.
_____ (1950c), Psychosomatic Aspects of Respiration and Respiratory Diseases. Paper read at the Schilder Society, New York.
_____ (1953a), Case Presentation of a Pheochromocytoma and Implications for the Problems of Anxiety and essential Hypertension. *Psychosomatic Forum*, New York: March 11.
_____ (1953b), The Ego in Anxiety. In: *Drives, Affects and Behavior*, ed. R. M. Loewenstein. New York: International Universities Press, pp. 67-103.
_____ (1955), Comments on the Metapsychology of Somatization. *The Psychoanalytic Study of the Child*, 10:119-164. New York: International Universities Press.
_____ (1958), The Ego and the Id in Anxiety. *The Psychoanalytic Study of the Child*, 13:190-220. New York: International Universities Press.
_____ (1960a), Discussion of Dr. John Bowlby paper. *The Psychoanalytic Study of the Child*, 15:63-85. New York: International Universities Press.
_____ (1960b), Phylogenesis and Ontogenesis of Affect and Structure Formation and the Phenomenon of Repetition Compulsion. *Internat. J. Psycho-Anal.*, 41:275-287.
_____ (1962), The Theory of the Parent-Infant Relationship. *Internat. J. Psycho-Anal.*, 43:243-245.
_____ (1964a), The Problem of Death in Freud's Writings and Life. The Fourteenth Freud Anniversary Lecture. New York Psychoanalytic Society, May 19.
_____ (1964b), Symptom Formation and Character Formation. *Internat. J. Psycho-Anal.*, 45:147-150.
_____ (1966a), *The Id and the Regulatory Principles of Mental Functioning*. New York: International Universities Press.
_____ (1966b), Some Additional "Day Residues" of the Specimen Dream of Psychoanalysis. In: *Psychoanalysis—A General Psychology*, ed. R. M. Loewenstein, L. Newman, M. Schur & A. Solnit. New York: International Universities Press, pp. 45-85.
_____ (1969), The Background of Freud's Disturbance on the Acropolis. *Amer. Imago*, 26:303-323.

_____ & Medvei, C. V. (1937), Hypophysenvorderlappeninsuffizienz. *Wiener Arch. Inn. Med.*, 31.

Scott, W. C. M. (1948), Some Psychodynamic Aspects of Disturbed Perception of Time. *Brit. J. Med. Psychol.*, 21:111-120.

Searles, H. F. (1965), Collected Papers on Schizophrenia and Related Subjects. New York: International Universities Press.

Shengold, L. (1966), The Metaphor of the Journey in *The Interpretation of Dreams. Amer. Imago*, 23:316-331.

Sherman, M. & Beverly, B. L. (1924), Hallucinations in Children. *J. Abnorm. Soc. Psychol.*, 19:165-170.

Shevin, F. F. (1963), Countertransference and Identity Phenomena Manifested in the Analysis of a Case of "Phallus Girl" Identity. *J. Amer. Psychoanal. Assn.*, 11:331-344.

Silberer, H. (1909), Report on a Method of Eliciting and Observing Certain Symbolic Hallucination Phenomena. In: *Organization and Pathology of Thought*, ed. D. Rapaport. New York: Columbia University Press, 1951, pp. 195-207.

Socarides, C. (1968), A Provisional Theory of the Etiology in Male Homosexuality: A Case of Preoedipal Origin. *Internat. J. Psycho-Anal.*, 49:27-38.

Sontag, S. (1966), *Against Interpretation.* New York: Farrar, Straus & Giroux.

Sophocles, Oedipus King (tr. Murray.) *Ten Greek Plays.* New York: Oxford Press, 1943.

Sperling, O. (1965), Classification and Definition of the Phenomena Associated with Transference. Unpublished.

Spiegel, L. A. (1951), A Review of Contributions to a Psychoanalytic Theory of Adolescence: Individual Aspects. *The Psychoanalytic Study of the Child*, 6:375-393. New York: International Universities Press.

_____ (1966), Superego and the Function of Anticipation with Comments on "Anticipatory Anxiety." In: *Psychoanalysis–A General Psychology*, ed. R. M. Loewenstein, L. M. Newman, M. Schur & A. J. Solnit. New York: International Universities Press, pp. 315-337.

Spitz, R. A. (1945), Hospitalism. *The Psychoanalytic Study of the Child*, 1:53-74. New York: International Universities Press.

_____ (1956a), Some Observations on Psychiatric Stress in Infancy. In: *Fifth Annual Report on Stress, 1955-1956*, ed. H. Selye & G. Heuser. New York: M. D. Publications, pp. 193-204.

_____ (1956b), Transference: The Analytic Setting and Its Prototype. *Internat. J. Psycho-Anal.*, 37:380-385.

_____ (1957), *No and Yes.* New York: International Universities Press.

_____ (1961), Some Early Prototypes of Ego Defenses. *J. Amer. Psychoanal. Assn.*, 9:626-651.

_____ (1963), Life and the Dialogue. In: *Counterpoint: Libidinal Object and Subject*, ed. H. S. Gaskill. New York: International Universities Press.

_____ (1964), The Derailment of Dialogue. Stimulus Overload, Action Cycles, and the Completion Gradient. *J. Amer. Psychoanal. Assn.*, 12:752-775.

_____ (1965), The Evolution of Dialogue. In *Drives, Affects, Behavior*, 2, ed. M. Schur. New York: International Universities Press, pp. 170-190.

_____ (1966), Metapsychology and Direct Infant Observation. In: *Psychoanalysis: A General Psychology*, Eds. R. M. Loewenstein, M. Schur, A. Solnit. New York: International Universities Press, pp. 123-151.

Springer, D. (1952), Development in Young Children of an Understanding of Time and the Clock. *J. Genet. Psychol.*, 80:83-96.

Stein, M. H. (1953), Premonition as a Defense. *Psychoanal. Quart.* 22:69-74.

_____ (1965), States of Consciousness in the Analytic Situation Including a Note on the Traumatic Dream. In: *Drives, Affects, Behavior*, 2, ed. M. Schur. New York: International Universities Press, pp. 60-86.

Steiner, G. (1965), Night Words. In: *Language and Silence. Essays on Language, Literature and the Inhuman.* New York: Athenaeum, 1967, pp. 68-77.

Stekel, W. (1912), Time in Its Relationship to the Neurotic. *Amer. J. Urol.*, 14:437-447.

Stern, M. (1951), Pavor Nocturnus. *Internat. J. Psycho-Anal.*, 32:302-309.
______(1957), The Ego Aspect of Transference. *Internat. J. Psycho-Anal.*, 38:1-12.
______(1964), Ego Psychology, Myth and Rite. *The Psychoanalytic Study of Society*, 3:71-93. New York: International Universities Press.
Stoller, R. J. (1964), A Contribution to the Study of Gender Identity. *Internat. J. Psycho-Anal.*, 45:220-227.
______(1965), The Sense of Maleness. *Psychoanal. Quart.*, 34:207-219.
______(1968), The Sense of Femaleness. *Psychoanal. Quart.*, 37:42-56.
Stone, L. (1954), The Widening Scope of Indications for Psychoanalysis. *J. Amer. Psychoanal. Assn.*, 2:567-594.
______(1961), *The Psychoanalytic Situation.* New York: International Universities Press.
______(1967), The Psychoanalytic Situation and Transference: Postscript to an Earlier Communication. *J. Amer. Psychoanal. Assn.*, 15:3-58.
Straus, E. (1947), Disorders of Personal Time in Depressive States. *South. Med. J.*, 40:254-259.
Strauss, A. (1959), *Mirrors and Masks. The Search for Identity.* Glencoe, Ill.: Free Press.
Sullivan, H. S. (1953), *The Interpersonal Theory of Psychiatry.* New York: Norton.
Szasz, T. S. (1963), The Concept of Transference. *Internat. J. Psycho-Anal.*, 44:432-443.
Tarachow, S. (1962), Interpretation and Reality in Psychotherapy. *Internat. J. Psycho-Anal.*, 43:377-387.
______(1964), Mythology and Ego Psychology. *The Psychoanalytic Study of Society*, 3:9-12. New York: International Universities Press.
Tausk, V. (1919), On the Origin of the "Influencing Machine" in Schizophrenia. In: The Psychoanalytic Reader, ed. R. Fliess, New York: International Universities Press, 1948, pp. 52-85.
Thompson, H. S. (1966), *Hell's Angels. A Strange and Terrible Saga.* New York: Random House.
Thorpe, W. H. (1956), *Learning and Instincts in Animals.* Cambridge: Harvard University Press.
______(1956), *Learning and Instincts in Animals*. Cambridge: Harvard University Press.
Tinbergen, N. (1951), *A Study of Instinct.* Oxford: University Press.
______(1952), "Derived" Activities. Their Causatism, Biological Significance, Origin and Emancipation During Evolution. *Quart. Rev. Biol.*, 27:1-32.
Torah, *The Five Books of Moses*, Philadelphia: Jewish Publication Society of America, 1962.
Ullman, J. R. (1968), An Abundance of Islands. *Sat. Rev.*, Sept. 14, p. 48.
Unamuno y Jugo, M. de (1954), *Tragic Sense of Life.* New York: Dover.
Valenstein, A. F. (1965), Introduction, Panel: The Genetic Determinants of Obsessive-Compulsive Phenomena in Character Formation. *J. Amer. Psychoanal. Assn.*, 13:591-604.
Van Dam, H. (1966), Panel Report: Problems of Transference in Child Analysis. *J. Amer. Psychoanal. Assn.*, 14:528-537.
Varendock, J. (1921), *The Psychology of Day-Dreams*, New York: Macmillan.
Von Uexkull, J. (1934), A Stroll Through the World of Animals and Men. In: *Instinctive Behavior*, ed. & tr. C. H. Schiller. New York: International Universities Press, 1957, pp. 5-80.
Waelder, R. (1956), Introduction to the Discussion on Problems of Transference. *Internat. J. Psycho-Anal.*, 37:367-368.
______(1962), Psychoanalysis, Scientific Method, Philosophy. *J. Amer. Psychoanal. Assn.*, 10:617-637.
______(1967), *Progress and Revolution.* New York: International Universities Press.
Waldseemueller, M. (1507), *Cosmographiae Inductio.* Herausgegeben von R. V. Wieser. Strassburg: J. H. Heitz Verlag, 1907.
Wangh, M. (1959), Structural Determinants of Phobia: A Clinical Study. *J. Amer. Psychoanal. Assn.*, 7:675-695.
______(1964), National Socialism and the Genocide of the Jews. A Psycho-Analytic Study of a Historical Event. *Internat. J. Psycho-Anal.*, 45:386-395.

Webster, (1947), *New International Dictionary*, 2nd ed., Springfield, Mass.: Merriam.
Weiner, M. F. (1961), Hallucinations in Children. *Arch. Gen. Psychiat.*, 5:544-553.
Weisman, A. D. (1965), *The Existential Core of Psychoanalysis.* Boston: Little, Brown.
Weissman, P. (1967), Theoretical Considerations of Ego Regression and Ego Functions in Creativity. *Psychoanal. Quart.*, 36:37-50.
Werner, H. (1957), *Comparative Psychology of Mental Development.* New York: International Universities Press.
Wexler, M. (1951), The Structural Problem in Schizophrenia. *Internat. J. Psycho-Anal.*, 32:157-166.
——— (1952), The Structural Problem in Schizophrenia: The Role of the Internal Object. In: *Psychotherapy with Schizophrenics*, ed. E. B. Brody & F. C. Redlich. New York: International Universities Press.
——— (1960), Hypotheses Concerning Ego Deficiency in Schizophrenia. In: *The Out-Patient Treatment of Schizophrenia*, ed. S. S. Scher & H. R. Davis. New York: Grune and Stratton, pp. 33-45.
Whorf, B. L. (1956), Language, Thought and Reality, Cambridge, Mass.: M. I. T. Press.
Wilking, N. & Paoli, C. (1966), The Hallucinatory Experience. *J. Amer. Acad. Child Psychiat.*, 5:431-440.
Winnicott, D. W. (1953), Transitional Objects and Transitional Phenomena. *Internat. J. Psycho-Anal.*, 34:89-97.
——— (1955), Metapsychological and Clinical Aspects of Regression within the Psychoanalytical Set-up. *Collected Papers.* New York: Basic Books, pp. 278-294.
——— (1965a), *The Maturational Processes and the Facilitating Environment.* New York: International Universities Press.
——— (1965b), A Clinical Study of the Effect of a Failure of the Average Expectable Environment on a Child's Mental Functioning. *Internat. J. Psycho-Anal.*, 46:81-87.
Wittels, F. (1924), *Sigmund Freud. His Personality, His Teaching and His School.* London: Allen & Unwin.
Wright, J. K. (1925), The Geographical Lore of the Time of the Crusades. *American Geograph. Research Series*, 15.
——— (1966), *Human Nature in Geography.* New York: Dover Press.
Yates, S. (1935), Some Aspects of Time Difficulties and Their Relation to Music. *Internat. J. Psycho-Anal.*, 16:341-354.
Yazmajian, R. V. (1964), First Dreams Directly Representing the Analyst. Psychoanal. Quart., 33:536-551.
Zeligs, D. F. (1955), The Personality of Joseph. *Amer. Imago*, 12:47-67.
Zetzel, E. R. (1949), Anxiety and the Capacity to Bear It. *Internat. J. Psycho-Anal.*, 30:1-12.
——— (1956), Current Concepts of Transference. *Internat. J. Psycho-Anal.*, 37:369-376.
——— (1964), Symptom Formation and Character Formation. *Internat. J. Psycho-Anal.*, 45:151-154.
——— (1965), Depression and the Incapacity to Bear It. In: *Drives, Affects, Behavior*, 2, ed. M. Schur. New York: International Universities Press.

SUPPLEMENTARY REFERENCES FOR MAX SCHUR

(1955), Constitutional Aspects of Psychosomatic Disorders. *Samiksa*, 9:104-115.
(1959), Panel: Phobias and Their Vicissitudes, rep. L. Ferber. *J. Amer. Psychoanal. Assn.*, 7:184,191.
(1960a), Panel: An Examination of Nosology According to Psychoanalytic Concepts. rep. N. Ross. *J. Amer. Psychoanal. Assn.*, 8:550, 551.
(1960b), Animal Research Panel, 1960: A Psychoanalyst's Comments. *Amer. J. Orthopsychiat.*, 31:276-291.

(1961), Panel: Aggression and Symptom Formation, rep. E. L. Lipton. *J. Amer. Psychoanal. Assn.*, 9:588, 591.
(1962), Panel: Narcissism, rep. J. F. Bing and R. O. Marburg. *J. Amer. Psychoanal. Assn.*, 10:602.
(1963a), Marie Bonaparte (1882-1962) *Psychoanal. Quart.*, 32:98-100.
(1963b), Panel: The Significance of Intrapsychic Conflict, rep. J. C. Nemiah. *J. Amer. Psychoanal. Assn.*, 11:623.
(1964), Panel: Repetition Compulsion, rep. S. Gifford. *J. Amer. Psychoanal. Assn.*, 12:648.
(1965), Editor's Introduction: Marie Bonaparte, 1882-1962. In: *Drives, Affects, Behavior*, 2. New York: International Universities Press, pp. 9-20.
(1967), Panel: Instinctual Drives in Relation to Recent Developments. rep. H. Dahl. Mid-Winter Meeting of American Psychoanalytic Association, December 15.
(1968a), Affect and Cognition: Interdisciplinary Colloquia of the American Psychoanalytic Association, May 9.
(1968b), Panel: Psychoanalytic Theory of the Instincual Drives, rep. H. Dahl. *J. Amer. Psychoanal. Assn.*, 16:619-623, 630-633.
Schur, M., Loewenstein, R. M., Newman, L. M. & Solnit, A. J. (1966), *Psychoanalysis—A General Psychology*. New York: International Universities Press.
——— & Ritvo, L. B. (1966), The Concept of Development and Evolution in Psychoanalysis. In: *Development and Evolution of Behavior*, ed. L. R. Aronson et al. San Francisco: W. H. Freeman, 1970.
——— ———(1967), A Principle of Evolutionary Biology for Psychoanalysis: Schneirla's Evolutionary and Developmental Theory of Biphasic Processes Underlying Approach and Withdrawal and Freud's Unpleasure and Pleasure Principle. Paper delivered at the 25th International Psychoanalytic Congress, Copenhagen, July.

Indices

Author Index

Subject Index